DATE DUE

DE 20 '96			
AP 23 '98			
OC 24 '02			

DEMCO 38-296

TEACHING PSYCHOLOGY IN AMERICA: A HISTORY

/3

TEACHING PSYCHOLOGY IN AMERICA: A HISTORY

Edited by
Antonio E. Puente, Janet R. Matthews,
and Charles L. Brewer

American Psychological Association
Washington, DC

Published by the
American Psychological Association
750 First Street, NE
Washington, DC 20002

Copies may be ordered from
APA Order Department
P.O. Box 2710
Hyattsville, MD 20784

Typeset in Goudy by Easton Publishing Services, Inc., Easton, MD

Printer: BookCrafters, Chelsea, MI
Cover and jacket designer: GrafikCommunications Ltd., Alexandria, VA
Production coordinator: Peggy Schlegel
Copyeditors: Peggy Schlegel and Christine P. Landry

Cover photograph of a Harvard University psychology laboratory taught by Hugo Münsterberg (circa 1892) is courtesy of the Harvard University Archives.

Library of Congress Cataloging-in-Publication Data

Teaching psychology in America: a history / edited by Antonio E.
    Puente, Janet R. Matthews, & Charles L. Brewer.
        p.   cm.
    Includes bibliographical references and index.
    ISBN 1-55798-181-7 (acid-free paper). —ISBN 1-55798-183-3 (pbk.:
acid-free paper)
    1. Psychology—Study and teaching (Higher)—United States—
History.   2. Psychology—Training of—United States—History.
I. Puente, Antonio E.   II. Matthews, Janet R.   III. Brewer, Charles L.
BF80.7.U6T43   1992
150'.71'173—dc20   92-32027
                                                                CIP

Printed in the United States of America
First edition

*This book is dedicated to
the students and professors of psychology's next 100 years.*

CONTENTS

CONTRIBUTORS

Bernard C. Beins, Department of Psychology, Ithaca College, Ithaca, New York

Cynthia Belar, Department of Clinical Psychology, University of Florida, Gainesville, Florida

Charles L. Brewer, Department of Psychology, Furman University, Greenville, South Carolina

Helio Carpintero, Departamento de Psicologia Basica, Universidad Complutensa de Madrid, Spain

Ruth Hubbard Cousins (retired), Psi Chi, Chattanooga, Tennessee

Robert S. Daniel, Professor Emeritus, Department of Psychology, University of Missouri, Columbia, Missouri

Stephen F. Davis, Department of Psychology, Emporia State University, Emporia, Kansas

Florence L. Denmark, Department of Psychology, Pace University, New York, New York

Donald A. Dewsbury, Department of Psychology, University of Florida, Gainesville, Florida

Linda C. Fernandez, Department of Psychology, Pace University, New York, New York

John J. Furedy, Department of Psychology, University of Toronto, Toronto, Ontario, Canada

Peter J. Giordano, Department of Psychology, Belmont University, Nashville, Tennessee

C. James Goodwin, Department of Psychology, Wheeling Jesuit College, Wheeling, West Virginia

L. Philip Guzman, American Psychological Association, Washington, DC

Jane S. Halonen, Department of Psychology, Alverno College, Milwaukee, Wisconsin

Margaret A. Lloyd, Department of Psychology, Georgia Southern University, Statesboro, Georgia

Janet R. Matthews, Department of Psychology, Loyola University, New Orleans, Louisiana

Thomas V. McGovern, Administration, Arizona State University West, Phoenix, Arizona

Paul D. Nelson, American Psychological Association, Washington, DC

James L. Pate, Department of Psychology, Georgia State University, Atlanta, Georgia

Wade E. Pickren, Department of Psychology, University of Florida, Gainesville, Florida

David J. Pittenger, Department of Psychology, Marietta College, Marietta, Ohio

Antonio E. Puente, Department of Psychology, University of North Carolina at Wilmington, Wilmington, North Carolina

Stephen Schiavo, Department of Psychology, Wellesley College, Wellesley, Massachusetts

Charles D. Spielberger, Department of Psychology, University of South Florida, Tampa, Florida

Randolph A. Smith, Department of Psychology, Ouachita Baptist University, Arkadelphia, Arkansas

George Stricker, Derner Institute, Adelphi University, Garden City, New York

Carol Tracy, Psi Beta, Chattanooga, Tennessee

Mark E. Ware, Department of Psychology, Creighton University, Omaha, Nebraska

Wayne Weiten, Department of Psychology, Santa Clara University, Santa Clara, California

Randall D. Wight, Department of Psychology, Ouachita Baptist University, Arkadelphia, Arkansas

FOREWORD

Since the founding of the American Psychological Association (APA) in 1892, the teaching of psychology has represented a major commitment of nearly everyone trained in our discipline. Teaching is not only a paramount activity of those who provide instruction in formal courses at colleges and universities; it is also a part of the everyday responsibility of industrial/organizational, counseling, school, and clinical psychologists in working with their clients and patients and in supervising the professional training of their students.

Although the history of psychology is well documented in numerous books and articles, relatively little attention has been directed to examining the history of *teaching* of psychology. In providing a comprehensive and definitive account of the evolution and current status of this discipline, this unique volume meets an important need. It examines critical issues and significant events in the history of the teaching of psychology and highlights the contributions of key individuals and institutions to this history.

The preparation of this volume was endorsed at the outset by the Board of Directors of the APA Division of the Teaching of Psychology. Contributions of organized psychology and, in particular, the APA and its division devoted to teaching are placed in historical perspective. In addition, the outcomes of the major conferences on undergraduate instruction in psychology, on education and training at the graduate level, and on internship and postdoctoral training are reviewed.

The editors of this volume are exceptionally well qualified to undertake an examination of the history of the teaching of psychology. As senior faculty at universities with excellent undergraduate programs, they have each contributed to high quality teaching of psychology for a number of years. As dedicated and caring instructors who have worked closely with their students, the editors' perspective encompasses an understanding of the needs of the learner as well as a mastery of the subject matter of psychology. As long-serving leaders of the APA Division of the Teaching of Psychology, they have exceptional knowledge of the contributions of organized psychology to teaching. Moreover, through their collective personal experience, the editors have firsthand knowledge of issues relating to gender and ethnicity in psychology's pedagogy.

The authors of each chapter in this volume were carefully selected by the editors on the basis of their knowledge and expertise in relation to the assigned subject matter. They represent a broad spectrum of the discipline, teach in diverse institutional settings, and reside in different geographical regions. Thus, the teaching of psychology is examined from many different perspectives, including those of women and ethnic minorities, and the personal views of distinguished teachers are shared. Information is also supplied on numerous publications that pertain to the teaching of psychology, ranging from textbooks and specialty volumes to key journal articles. Histories of the two major undergraduate honor societies in psychology, Psi Chi and Psi Beta, are also provided.

The preparation of this volume has benefited from the continuous and frequent interaction between the editors and chapter authors and from the openness of all concerned in taking into account many different perspectives. The editors also managed to obtain substantial program time at the 1992 APA Centennial Convention for four symposia in which 16 contributors to this volume participated. The book has also profited from the critical reactions of students enrolled in Antonio Puente's senior-level undergraduate course, History and Systems of Psychology.

Students and teachers of psychology at all levels will find this volume interesting and informative and will benefit from the comprehensive understanding that is provided on many different facets of the history of teaching psychology in America. Perusing its contents demonstrates that the editors' intent to facilitate learning about the discipline has been clearly realized. They have admirably succeeded in achieving their goal of providing a strong foundation for understanding the historical development and status of the field today.

CHARLES D. SPIELBERGER
President, 1991–1992
American Psychological Association

PREFACE

Ebbinghaus (1850–1909) stated that "psychology has a long past but a short history." This year (1992) the American Psychological Association celebrates its 100th anniversary. Thus, even the "short" history of psychology in America has become quite substantial. With it comes the responsibility to document and integrate the past and provide a direction for the future.

The history of psychology as a science has been and is being well documented relative to such general issues as theories and systems. What is critically missing, however, and the unmet need that led to the writing of this book, is the documentation and analysis of psychology's foundation — its pedagogy. To date, no book or series of journal articles has presented the history of the teaching of psychology in the United States. Although a few articles have addressed teaching the history of psychology, the history of teaching all facets of psychology has been neglected. With the ever-increasing importance being placed on education, it is surprising that a history of education in psychology has yet to be published.

The present volume is an attempt to fill this gap. Thirty-one authors from the United States, Canada, and Spain have written articles that together provide an archival analysis of the past 100 years of teaching psychology in America. We offer this volume in celebration of a century of quality teaching in psychology and in anticipation of the changes in such teaching the next century will bring.

This contribution has been a composite effort involving many individuals and institutions in addition to the 3 editors and 31 contributors. The Board of Directors of the American Psychological Association (APA)

Division of the Teaching of Psychology provided initial endorsement of the project. Gary VandenBos, Director of APA's Publication Office, and his staff have been extremely supportive from the inception to the publication of this volume. VandenBos carefully reviewed the draft manuscript and assisted in revising its organization. Mary Lynn Skutley and Peggy Schlegel significantly contributed to the ensuing development and production process. For helping us select and locate the cover photograph, a special thanks goes to John Popplestone, director of the Archives of the History of American Psychology at the University of Akron in Ohio.

Each chapter of this book was reviewed by one or more of the section editors, at least one other contributor from the volume (in most cases, they were from the respective section), and an APA Publication Office staff member. Internal departmental and external reviews were also secured. In addition, a majority of the chapters were critiqued by students in Antonio E. Puente's senior-level History and Systems of Psychology course in the fall of 1991 and the spring of 1992.

Finally, most of the chapters were presented in abbreviated form at APA's Centennial Convention in Washington, DC, in August 1992. Randolph A. Smith, Division 2 program chairperson, helped to orchestrate the four separate 1-hour symposia. In addition, Candy Won at APA's Convention Office provided guidance in scheduling these sessions, which were jointly sponsored by Divisions 2 (Teaching of Psychology) and 26 (History of Psychology) of the APA.

Our respective departmental chairs provided the necessary support and endorsement to complete this project.

To all of those who have been involved, we are greatly indebted.

The royalties of the editors of and contributors to this volume will be donated to the Fund for Excellence of the APA Division of the Teaching of Psychology.

ANTONIO E. PUENTE
JANET R. MATTHEWS
CHARLES L. BREWER

INTRODUCTION

ANTONIO E. PUENTE, JANET R. MATTHEWS, AND CHARLES L. BREWER

In the first sentence of the second edition of *The Structure of Scientific Revolutions* (1970), Kuhn states that history should be more than a repository of anecdotes and chronology. It should be a byproduct of science for the purposes of teaching, generating knowledge, and passing on tradition. History formulated from the work of pioneers in a field, Kuhn contends, should serve as foundation for a transformation of or revolution from a particular way of thinking—paradigm—to another approach. Moreover, these shifting paradigms serve as tools for building an intellectual framework for professional activities. However, Kuhn's theory presupposes two conditions. First, anecdotes and chronology must already be available and accessible (presumably in a published format). Second, a paradigm must already exist from which to revolt, although it may be so widely accepted as to seem immune from questioning or change.

Another philosopher of science, Lakatos (1978), contends that a program of inquiry is only as viable as the questions the program poses. Such programs build on and revise previously accepted notions. Presumably, the history of a discipline contributes to this viability by identifying and critiquing these programs and the issues that they raise.

HISTORY AND THE TEACHING OF PSYCHOLOGY

The question arises as to whether the ideas of Kuhn (1970) and Lakatos (1978) can be applied to psychology and to the discipline of teaching psychology. Is psychology a valid scientific enterprise, with identifiable paradigms and programs of inquiry? Gholson and Barker (1985), among others, suggest that there are viable paradigms and research programs in the field of psychology. Therefore, psychology's empirical and theoretical history and progress can be viewed from the perspective of these philosophies of science. However, like others, these authors completely avoid the question of how paradigms and programs of inquiry in psychology address one of the science's most basic activities—the teaching of psychology.

The history and enterprise of psychology has been well documented through the general history and systems approach. For example, in his classic textbook. *A History of Experimental Psychology* (1950), Boring presented a scholarly analysis of major trends and people in psychology. In numerous more recent texts, Leahey (1987) and Robinson (1981), among others, have updated, expanded, or revised these earlier efforts. However, an examination of these and other history books fails to reveal specific references to the pedagogy of psychology.

Furthermore, a review of the primary journals in the teaching of psychology (e.g., *Teaching of Psychology*) and the history of psychology (e.g., *Journal of the History of the Behavioral Sciences*) reveals a paucity of articles on the history of the teaching of psychology. The articles that are available are directed toward teaching in general but not toward the teaching of psychology in particular. Some interest in strategies and possibly even paradigms regarding teaching the *history* of psychology has been shown during the past decade, a hopeful sign (Brooks, 1985; Cole, 1983; Hart, 1986; Raphelson, 1982; Tobacyk, 1987).

Today, an ever-growing segment of the college population enrolls in one or more psychology courses or majors in the discipline. However, the paucity of information on the history of the teaching of psychology makes it difficult to discern whether the teaching of psychology is part of the problem in higher education discussed in the national report by the Carnegie Foundation (1977) or in such books as *The Closing of the American Mind* (Bloom, 1987) and *Illiberal Education* (D'Souza, 1991), or, more important still, whether it can be part of the solution. Such questions can hardly be answered when the facts and chronology of the discipline have not been consolidated or, in some cases, even documented. Fortunately, these limitations may be more reflective of how psychologists have recorded their history than of a genuine lack of progress in the teaching of psychology.

ORIENTATION OF THE PRESENT BOOK

As contributors to the current volume attest, the teaching of psychology in America has been quietly active over the past 100 years. Organizations have been formed, conferences have been held, books and journals devoted to the subject have been published, and individuals have devoted their life's work to the facilitation of teaching in psychology. The documentation and analysis of these important activities is a central aim of this book.

In selecting chapters, we have relied for direction on two seminal articles—one by Young (1966) and the other by Leahey (1986). Their analyses suggest ways the history of psychology (and its subdisciplines) should shift in order to be historically accurate as well as heuristically valuable. Although their analyses focused on the history of science, they are clearly applicable to the history of a discipline such as the teaching of psychology.

First, Young (1966) and Leahey (1986) contend that present-mindedness must be replaced by past-mindedness. History was made in a particular context and should be considered in that context rather than created retrospectively (and in a possibly biased manner) in the present (Young, 1966). As Leahey (1986) stated, historical contributions must be more than a "Whig" history of "inevitable progressive steps," in which "the past is best seen as a series of 'anticipations' of the present" (p. 648). The past must live in the way the history is told, rather than being excluded from it (Leahey, 1986). In the present case, we must recover the way active teachers perceived themselves and their discipline as the century progressed.

Second, ceremonial history must give way to critical analysis (Young, 1966). While Kuhn (1970) stated that history should be more than a repository of anecdotes and chronology, such historical data must first be documented before critical analyses can occur. In the present case, only then can we begin to examine the serious attempts psychology teachers have made to solve persistent problems in pedagogy.

Third, "great men" approaches to history should give way to zeitgeist approaches because "the logic of problems can't conform to a 'great man' approach" (Young, 1966, p. 3). According to Leahy (1986), such zeitgeist approaches should take into account the largest scientific, professional, and social context as far back and as deeply enough to establish a link to the larger history of humankind. Historians of science must weave into the history of a discipline "other strands of the history of the world" (Leahey, p. 648). Such an approach should also not fail to consider all of the behind-the-scenes players, as well as the events and organizations that support this cast of characters.

Finally, in documenting the history of a discipline, primary sources or archival material rather than secondary sources should be used whenever possible. Primary sources help ensure the accuracy of accounts, help to avoid present-mindedness, and provide valuable clues as to the nuances of a given event in the context of the surrounding culture.

As much as possible, these four recommendations were followed by the authors of this book. Although the content of their work is briefly summarized in the introductions to each of the five sections of the book, here we would like to point out some ways Young's (1966) and Leahey's (1986) ideas governed the perspective taken by the authors.

Present- Versus Past-Mindedness

One of the sometimes unpleasant results of past-mindedness, is the reminder that things in the past were not always what we would have liked them to have been. Consider, for example, Goodwin's chapter on the contributions of the American Psychological Association (APA) to the teaching of psychology before 1945. He characterizes the APA's involvement then as "sporadic at best" and "minimal." Whereas more present-minded accounts might link the APA's later involvement in teaching to such happenings as the 1899 APA meeting devoted to the teaching of psychology. Goodwin's past-minded approach shows that this meeting was an anomaly and that prior to 1945, the APA was too preoccupied with establishing itself as a professional organization and psychology as a specialized discipline to make pedagogy a high priority.

In a similar fashion, in their chapter on the influence and impact of women on the teaching of psychology, Denmark and Fernandez document that women's contributions were in large part overlooked during most of the past 100 years, a fact that some present-minded psychologists might prefer to forget. Their critical analysis includes a scrutiny of social norms proscribing higher education for women in the 19th century and an examination of the influence of Darwin and Spencer on these norms. In a separate chapter, Guzman, Schiavo, and Puente provide information on the role of ethnic minorities. Unfortunately and yet not surprisingly, little is known about this part of psychology's pedagogy. In large part, this paucity of data is due to the sheer lack of minorities involved in psychology, at least until the mid-1970s.

In an entirely different way, past-mindedness permeates Halonen's interview with master teacher Wilbert McKeachie. As the only person to have participated in all formal curriculum projects undertaken by the APA, McKeachie can take a long view of the developments in the field. More informally, in this interview he relates the challenges psychology teachers faced when their students greeted their scientific enthusiasm with hostility and suspicion in the radical 1960s. He contrasts these students' quest for social relevance with the less idealistic bottom-line results demanded by today's highly career-conscious students.

Ceremonial History Versus Critical Analysis

Rather than a chronological review, in his chapter on collegiate advising, Ware applies a life-cycle perspective to the evolution of the activity as he differentiates academic versus career advising and vocational guidance versus career guidance and career education. His analysis yields a view of contemporary advising that emphasizes and integrates career decision making, information about one's self, and knowledge of the world of work.

In her two chapters on training conferences (graduate, internship, and postdoctorate), Belar not only documents their history but applies Altman's (1990) analysis of centrifugal and centripetal trends in higher education. These conferences are further viewed in the context of the social, political, and educational issues of the times.

Even such concrete instruments of teaching as textbooks and handbooks benefit from a more abstract critical analysis. Chronicling the use of introductory psychology texts in America from 1880 to the present, Weiten and White show how these books "defined the boundaries of an emerging science of psychology and mobilized students, psychologists, and ideas in ways that transformed the discipline." The authors' empirical comparative analyses of these books adds another valuable dimension to their critique.

Pate provides a parallel analysis of the functions and types of psychology handbooks available over time. He shows how empirical analyses of the number of editions of a handbook over a specified period of time reflect the amount and nature of change in particular subdisciplines. His content analysis of general handbooks is enlightening as well, when, for example, one notes that cognitive psychology was not even mentioned in a 1929 handbook but accounted for a full five chapters in a similar handbook in 1988.

Perhaps the most philosophical analysis in this book is Furedy's chapter on the Socratic-sophistic continuum in teaching. He compares the American system of teaching psychology with that of Canada and Europe, highlighting the student–discipline distinction in graduate education, differences in discipline- versus person-centered education, and the role of "disinterestedness" vis à vis the pressures of social opinion and financial backing of research. His warnings regarding the "binding of the discipline with the tenets of sophistic instrumentalism" should be heeded by all who teach psychology or are responsible for administration.

Great Men Versus Zeitgeist Approaches

Many of the chapters in this book provide zeitgeist interpretations of the history of the teaching of psychology in America. Briefly, McGovern traces the evolution of undergraduate curricula in psychology from 1892 to 1992 in the context of the institutional parameters of religious versus secular goals in education, the rise of science in the baccalaureate curriculum, and student demands for applied and specialized education. He shows how these all lead to the current "academic shopping center era" (Carnegie Foundation, 1977) in liberal arts education in general and psychology education in particular.

In a broader geographical context, Carpintero's historical synopsis of ideas, institutions, personalities, curricula, and texts in psychology around the world illustrates the development of psychology from a "little science" to a "big science" (Price, 1965). His account provides important background for understanding the development of psychology in America.

With an emphasis on "behind-the-scenes" players, Dewsbury and Pickren note that "a critical problem confronting the student of the history of the teaching of psychology is that many of the best teachers are the least visible to the historian." In their sketches, they provide a fresh perspective on a number of psychologists through their students' impressions of them. They illustrate that there are many ways to be a good teacher and that the key is for psychologists to discover a style that is exactly right for them. In a similar fashion, Pittenger's analysis of 34 winners of the American Psychological Foundation's Distinguished Teaching Awards also shows that a diversity of means can achieve the same goals in teaching: "[to] attract new students to the discipline, [to] imbue their students with the values and goals of psychology, and [to] help their students mature intellectually, and thus [to] assure the vitality and longevity of the science." He shows that many individuals accomplish these goals despite the fact that the "contingencies of the academic milieu" do not always reinforce teaching excellence.

Organizations also play an essential behind-the-scences role, as illustrated by Davis in his account of teacher and student regional conferences, Lloyd and Brewer in their historical review of undergraduate teaching conferences in psychology, and Smith in his description of the founding, purposes, development, and impact of four councils supporting the teaching of psychology in America. Such organizations contribute to excitement about teaching, reinforce research activities, provide opportunities for communication among those who might otherwise be isolated, and aid in the professional development of students and teachers alike.

Primary Versus Secondary Sources

A majority of the authors in this book rely to some degree on primary sources. However, several chapters stand out as repositories of archival data. Beins, for example, relies on primary journal articles to document the role of students, teachers, classroom activities, and subject matter in the "quest for relevance" in the teaching of psychology. Nelson and Stricker provide an insider's view of the APA after World War II as they trace the role of the APA governance as the field of psychology "expanded exponentially as an applied scientific discipline and profession." Similarly, Wight and Davis trace the five stages of development of APA's Division 2 (Teaching of Psychology) from 1944 to the present, using the Division's public records. Their account traces teachers' evolving perception of their status in the context of Division 2's struggles to attain a sense of identity.

As the journal's first editor, Daniel chronicles the evolution of *Teaching of Psychology* from a 4-page mimeographed newsletter in 1950 to its birth as a professional journal in 1974. Focusing on psychology's students (i.e., through psychology's honor societies), Cousins, Tracy, and Giordano use Psi Chi's and Psi Beta's able historians' accounts and archival records to document the birth and development of the two organizations.

CONCLUSION

A discipline that is separated from its history lacks direction and promises a future of uncertain importance (Murchison, 1961). As noted earlier, the history of the teaching of psychology in America suffers from a dearth of documented information. This book represents an initial and partial solution to that problem. However, these chapters are much more than a repository of facts and anecdotes or a chronology of the field. They represent a careful analysis of such data in the context of the larger professional, social, political, and scientific spirit of the times. Although not meant to be the final word, this collection is reasonably exhaustive and thought provoking, raising questions that provide an impetus for further analyses in the field and a baseline from which to trace developments into the 21st century.

Like all psychologists, teachers of psychology have a responsibility to document and integrate their past and provide a direction for the future. To again paraphrase Kuhn (1970), history should be a byproduct of science, meant for the purposes of facilitating teaching, generating knowledge, and passing on tradition. Toward those ends, we trust that this book brings psychology one step closer to excellence in teaching psychology in America.

REFERENCES

Altman, I. (1990). Centripetal and centrifugal trends in psychology. In L. Bickman & H. Ellis (Eds.), *Preparing psychologists for the 21st century; Proceedings of the National Conference on Graduate Education in Psychology* (pp. 39–61). Hillsdale, NJ: Erlbaum.

Bloom, A. D. (1987). *The closing of the American mind.* New York: Simon & Schuster.

Boring, E. B. (1950). *A history of experimental psychology* (2nd ed.). New York: Appleton-Century-Crofts.

Brooks, C. I. (1985). A role playing exercise for the history of psychology course. *Teaching of Psychology, 12,* 84–85.

Carnegie Foundation for the Advancement of Teaching. (1977). *Missions of the college curriculum.* San Fancisco: Jossey-Bass.

Cole, D. L. (1983). The way we were: Teaching history of psychology through mock APA conventions. *Teaching of Psychology, 10,* 234–236.

D'Souza, D. (1991). *Illiberal education.* New York: Free Press.

Gholson, B., & Barker, P. (1985). Applications in the history of physics and psychology. *American Psychologist, 40,* 755–769.

Hart, J. J. (1986). A strategy for teaching the history and systems of psychology. *Teaching of Psychology, 13,* 67–69.

Hilgard, E. R. (1987). *Psychology in America: A historical survey.* San Diego, CA: Harcourt Brace Jovanovich.

Kuhn, T. S. (1970). *The structure of scientific revolutions* (2nd ed.). Chicago: University of Chicago Press.

Lakatos, I. (1978). *The methodology of scientific research programmes.* Cambridge, England: Cambridge University Press.

Leahey, T. H. (1986). History without the past. *Contemporary Psychology, 31,* 648–650.

Leahey, T. H. (1987). *A history of psychology: Main currents in psychological thought* (2nd ed.). Englewood Cliffs, NJ: Prentice-Hall.

Murchison, C. (Ed.). (1961). *A history of psychology in autobiography* (Vol. 1). New York: Russell & Russell.

Price, D. J. S. (1965). *Little science, big science.* New York: Columbia University Press.

Raphelson, A. C. (1982). The history course as the capstone of the psychology curriculum. *Journal of the History of the Behavioral Sciences, 18,* 279–285.

Robinson, D. N. (1981). *An intellectual history of psychology* (rev. ed.). New York: Macmillan.

Tobacyk, J. J. (1987). Using personal construct theory in teaching history and systems of psychology. *Teaching of Psychology, 14,* 111–112.

Young, R. M. (1966). Scholarship and the history of the behavioural sciences. *History of Science, 5,* 1–51.

I

GENERAL ISSUES IN THE TEACHING OF PSYCHOLOGY

INTRODUCTION

GENERAL ISSUES IN THE
TEACHING OF PSYCHOLOGY

ANTONIO E. PUENTE

Part I focuses on a variety of topics that not only serve as a foundation for other issues but also afford different perspectives on basic assumptions about the teaching of psychology.

Thomas McGovern provides a comprehensive assessment of curricular issues in undergraduate psychology. Although the primary emphasis is on more recent developments, that is, those occurring during the past decade, the historical roots of current practices are also established.

Mark Ware presents the history and background of advising in psychology, with special emphasis on the undergraduate experience. The current practice of advising in psychology is reviewed against the backdrop of college advising in general.

John Furedy addresses the basic issue of how psychology is taught. The concept of critical thinking is examined in the context of classroom as well as laboratory learning. The Socratic method, which uses questions and discussion as primary methods of learning, is viewed as more desirable in most cases than the currently used sophistic approach. The perspectives of the British and Australian systems of teaching psychology are also reviewed.

Psychology germinated in Western Europe during the late 19th century and flowered in North America during the 20th century. This expansion of knowledge, in turn, eventually affected psychology's later development in Europe. In the final chapter of Part I, Helio Carpintero provides a synopsis of these developments that lays the groundwork for understanding the teaching of psychology in America.

1

EVOLUTION OF UNDERGRADUATE CURRICULA IN PSYCHOLOGY, 1892–1992

THOMAS V. McGOVERN

Webster (1983) defined curriculum as the courses offered by an educational institution. This simple description does not capture why departmental faculty can ascend to heights of eloquence or descend to crass demagoguery when discussing changes in existing requirements. Nor does it explain why administrators tout their curricula, both traditional and avant-garde variations, as symbols of a unique approach to higher education. Finally, the definition does not explain what motivates many larger universities to follow Ezra Cornell's pledge made over 100 years ago—to ensure that any individual could find instruction in any course of study. Rudolph (1977), however, gave a richer insight into why the American course of study is such an important part of faculty and public life:

I want to thank several people for their assistance in preparing this chapter. Without Priscilla Van Dam's work on the development of the bibliography, this review would have been much less comprehensive. Mark Ware reviewed an earlier draft and offered excellent suggestions for revisions. Finally, three undergraduate students of the history of psychology reviewed the chapter for their class with Antonio Puente at the University of North Carolina at Wilmington. Their substantive comments stimulated an entirely fresh look at the concluding section of the chapter.

The curriculum began as an import, arriving in the intellectual baggage of the settlers of Massachusetts Bay. Over three hundred years of change have given it a thoroughly American character, reflecting the diversity and flexibility of the culture around it, lending itself to society's major purposes. . . . Curricular history is American history and therefore carries the burden of revealing the central purposes and driving directions of American society. As the curriculum has moved across time from being wholly prescribed to greatly elective, the loss of philosophic purpose and neatness has been repeatedly but unsuccessfully countered by structural devices designed to support some coherent, defensible general education. (pp. 23–24)

Scholars from the Carnegie Foundation for the Advancement of Teaching (1977) divided curricular history into three eras. They characterized the first era (1636–1870) as having a relatively standard course of study. The heritage of Western civilization was the curriculum's content; its goal was "to identify the members of the class of educated persons" (p. 3). The university as a public service institution in which new knowledge was utilitarian in purpose exemplified the second era (1870–1960); with the creation of new technologies, there was a need to train new populations of students for future employment and professional life. The label for the third era (post-1960) was the "academic shopping center" (p. 5); faculty created specialized programs in response to increasingly complex social expectations and an almost universal access to higher education.

During the second era, G. Stanley Hall founded the American Psychological Association (APA) in 1892. The APA was one of seven learned societies founded at the turn of the 20th century (Modern Language Association in 1883; American Historical Association in 1884; American Economics Association in 1885; American Philosophical Association in 1901; American Political Science Association in 1904; and American Sociological Society in 1905). The professional identities that coalesced with the forming of these primarily social science groups reflected major changes taking place in American higher education. The Morrill Act of 1862 expanded the legitimate course of study beyond the traditional baccalaureate program; new students responded to the availability of new and especially more applied programs. Universities struggled to implement the 1855 observation by Francis Wayland of Brown University that "the American people expected the colleges to educate a democracy of talents and a democracy of vocations" (Rudolph, 1977, p. 111). During the entire second era, requirements in the major field were the dominant force in curriculum development.

Psychology, as an undergraduate program of study, prospered during the third era when a "shift from elite to mass education and to universal access to higher education" (Carnegie Foundation for the Advancement of Teaching, 1977, p. 5) took place. In the decades after World War II, first veterans, then women, and then people of color helped postsecondary educational institutions (community colleges, 4-year colleges, and universities) achieve a level of accessibility that is uniquely American. In 1988, institutions awarded more than 48,000 baccalaureates in psychology, including 70% to women, making it the most popular single major among traditional arts and sciences disciplines in academe ("Almanac," 1991).

The thesis of this chapter is that the undergraduate psychology curriculum reflects (a) the evolution of the body of knowledge and practice of the discipline and (b) changes in American higher education institutions from 1892 to 1992. An evolution of thinking about institutional mission, general education, major field specialization, and cocurricular programs and an increased understanding of how the undergraduate experience differentially affects students shaped the curriculum.

This brief history of the psychology curriculum is presented in three parts. In the first section, I describe three factors (religion, science, and applied and specialized knowledge) that influenced all curricula and illustrate these factors by using selective departmental case studies. In the second section, I describe curricular developments in the third era, emphasizing developments from the early 1950s until 1991. Some of the material in this section is also covered by Lloyd and Brewer's chapter on national conferences in psychology (see chapter 10 of this book); the chapter by Beins on teaching as depicted in psychology journals (see chapter 22) highlights similar topics as well. In the third section, I conclude by identifying future directions stemming from this 100-year history.

THREE INSTITUTIONAL PARAMETERS AFFECTING THE UNDERGRADUATE CURRICULUM

Three institutional parameters significantly affected the American curriculum: (a) the conflict between religious and secular goals for institutions in general and course objectives in particular; (b) the integration of new knowledge, especially science, into the curriculum and the consequent transformation of institutional cultures and courses; and (c) the continual modification of departmental majors, motivated by student and social demand for more applied and specialized education. Before describing those institutional parameters and their case study illustrations, I describe how it was sometimes possible for past curricula to reflect just one person's influence.

An undergraduate curriculum begins with faculty. Their perspectives emerge from their graduate training experiences, mentors, areas of specialization, and capacity to integrate new knowledge. Faculty develop individual courses and, over time, a collection of courses aggregate into a program of study. Benjamin and Bertelson's (1975) report on the University of Nebraska and Furchtgott's (1990) history of the University of South Carolina provide illustrative cases of how one faculty member's unique vision can shape curricula.

Harry Kirk Wolfe joined the faculty of the University of Nebraska in 1889, where he had also received his baccalaureate degree. He had been one of the first two Americans to receive a PhD under Wundt at Leipzig. From 1889 to 1897, Wolfe taught the new science of psychology to undergraduates at the University of Nebraska. He built a library and one of the earliest psychology laboratories (see Garvey, 1929), despite minimal support from his administration. Wolfe (1895) wrote,

> It ought to be unnecessary to describe the effect on the student, of a laboratory course in psychology, and yet, like chemistry and physics and botany and zoology, this new science will have to fight for every inch of ground. (p. 385)

Wolfe's singular influence established the groundwork for that department's emphasis on training undergraduates in scientific psychology. By 1975, years after his departure, the University of Nebraska would list among its undergraduate alumni no less than six presidents of the APA (Benjamin & Bertelson, 1975).

The early curriculum at the University of South Carolina (USC) was the product of another idiosyncratic perspective. From 1911 to 1918, four courses (elementary psychology, psychology of religion, psychology of crime, and a unique course titled "race problems") formed the USC curriculum. This array of offerings was taught by Josiah Morse, the first and only psychologist at USC until 1926. Morse studied under G. Stanley Hall and received his PhD from Clark University. He was Jewish, a staunch and vocal advocate of improved race relations in the South, and was elected president of the Southern Society of Philosophy and Psychology in 1929. Furchtgott (1990) portrayed the context in which Morse's curriculum was developed as one in which the governor forced the university president to resign in 1913 and described him as the "nigger lover who took money from white girls in South Carolina for the education of free Negroes." (Hollis, 1955, pp. 259–260; cited in Furchtgott, 1990, pp. 1161–1162)

Despite the significant effect that individuals can have, several factors more typically influence curricular change. Institutional cultures, not individual passions, more often determine what types of faculty are recruited, what types of programs are fostered, and how a particular curriculum is assimilated into the broader mission of the college or university. The specific institutional parameters on curriculum development in psychology in the late 19th and early 20th century included (a) how faculty resolved the religious versus secular aspirations of the institution, (b) how new knowledge in the sciences transformed a classical baccalaureate curriculum, and (c) how the applied and specialized goals of the professions and the disciplines challenged the liberal arts curriculum. Trapp's (1984, p. 4) list of forwarding addresses for psychologists at the University of Arkansas symbolizes all three parameters:

1884	Department of Psychology, Ethics, Sociology, and Evidence of Christianity
1886	Department of Psychology, Ethics, and Political Economy
1889	Department of Psychology of Ethics
1898	Department of Philosophy and Pedagogy
1912	Department of Philosophy
1913	Department of Education
1918	Department of Philosophy and Psychology
1950	Department of Psychology

In the following pages, I describe the three institutional parameters of religion, science, and specialization for higher education in general and for psychology departments in particular.

Religious Versus Secular Goals

Harvard's first president, Henry Dunster, taught all 12 subjects in the undergraduate curriculum of 1642. In the first year, Dunster taught logic, Greek, Hebrew, rhetoric, divinity catechetical, history, and the nature of plants. In the second year, Dunster taught ethics and politics, Greek, rhetoric, Aramaic, and divinity catechetical. In the third year and final year, he taught arithmetic, astronomy, Greek, rhetoric, Syriac, and divinity catechetical. The goal of educating a learned clergy was evident.

The emerging American character had a secularizing influence. Knowledge of biblical languages was replaced by an emphasis on reading English texts. By the beginning of the 18th century, the course on moral philosophy, a capstone experience taught by the university president, became a practical homily that blended Christian teachings with philosophical ethics and scientific inquiry. At graduation, new baccalaureates demonstrated their learning to their parents and to an inquisitive public by debating one another on contemporary political issues. At many institutions, the capstone moral philosophy and ethics course evolved naturally into the beginnings of a psychology course. In some institutions, however, psychology seemed to be always in conflict with dominant religious goals. Two Mormon-inspired institutions, Weber State College and Brigham Young University, illustrated that tension.

May (1988) reported that a faculty member trained in German and drawing first taught psychology at Weber Academy in 1892. From 1892 to 1924, an elementary psychology course was offered solely as an "aid to those planning to teach" (p. 28). In 1924, psychology was deemed important enough to be listed as a utilitarian general education requirement for business, nursing, and education students. In contrast, Spilka (1988) reported that another Rocky Mountain school, University of Denver, was offering as early as 1900 a seven-course scientific curriculum (introductory, experimental, systematic, comparative, physiological, and abnormal and pathological psychology, and an applied course titled "psychology in relationship to sociology, ethics, and sciences"). Not until 1969, with what May described as the "secularization of the department" (p. 29) did the first non-Mormon, non-Utah PhD get hired at Weber State.

Conflicts at Brigham Young University (BYU) went beyond restricting the type of courses in the curriculum. During a period that Brown and Allen (1988) labeled as "auspicious beginnings" (p. 34), BYU hired as its president a Mormon who had studied psychology and mathematics at the University of Michigan. He instituted a summer seminar series and recruited G. Stanley Hall in 1897, John Dewey in 1901, and others to deliver lectures. Four outstanding Mormon faculty were recruited from 1907 to 1909; one of them was Joseph Peterson, a University of Chicago PhD who had studied with James Rowland Angell and was John B. Watson's assistant. Peterson increased offerings in psychology to nine courses and developed the library and its journal holdings. But in 1909, the zeal for science communicated by the new faculty during the Darwin centennial came into direct conflict with Mormon leaders. Peterson was summoned to Salt Lake City in 1911 for a hearing with the General Church Board. After refusing to recant, he resigned from BYU and joined the faculty at the University of Utah, where he became 1 of 15 faculty at that institution who were forced to resign in 1915. Peterson became chair of psychology at the University of Minnesota and was elected president of the APA in 1934. Brown and Allen's commentary on this episode was that

> it was many years, perhaps well into the 1960's, before the Psychology Department attained an academic level comparable to what Peterson had established in his few short years at Brigham Young University at the beginning of the century. (p. 37)

New Knowledge and Scientific Transformation

By the founding of Yale at the beginning of the 18th century, what Rudolph (1977) labeled the "new learning" (p. 27) from Europe began to influence the solely theological emphases of the classical curriculum. The scientific writings of Copernicus, Descartes, and Newton found their way into the Yale Library and into the Yale tutors' lessons. The College of William and Mary established the first professorship in natural philosophy (physics) and mathematics in 1711. By 1788, all eight colonial colleges had established similar positions, and by the end of the century, there were professorships in chemistry at Princeton and botany and natural history at

Philadelphia. As Rudolph noted, "The sciences had not only found their way into the curriculum—they were also speaking a new language, rearranging old priorities, and changing the definition of a college education" (p. 36).

Transforming any curriculum has never been easy. Despite student and public dissatisfaction with their classical curriculum, "the Yale faculty issued a spirited defense in the form of the Yale Report of 1828. It was the first formal statement of educational philosophy in the history of American higher education" (Levine, 1978, p. 544). The defense was an acknowledgment of the new knowledge of European science for which the Yale faculty had become a principal American advocate, but it was also a staunch message that the quality of an educational experience was based on a thorough understanding of traditional, classical subjects.

A careful reading of the Yale document reveals an enduring concern for higher education. For those authors, the goal of a baccalaureate education was what has become the hallmark of the liberal arts and sciences, a capacity to learn for a lifetime. Although their understanding of human learning was based on the "discipline and the furniture of the mind" (Levine, 1978, p. 545), their emphasis on mastering content as a means of building the skills of inquiry, analysis, and presentation remains a contemporary concern for many disciplines (McGovern, Furumoto, Halpern, Kimble, & McKeachie, 1991). However, the Yale faculty chose not to embrace the practical and empirical knowledge that sprang from human experience. Rudolph (1977) summarized it this way:

> The authors of the Yale Report confronted the college course of study within a psychological framework that allowed them little room for imagination. Their respect for quality, for standards, for certain enduring definitions of human worth, was class bound. They were blinded to much that was insistent and already out of control in American life. (p. 75)

But Yale faculty challenged the concept of a commonly required university curriculum determined by the central administration rather than by departmental faculty. George Ticknor, a graduate of the German university system, was an influential member of the Harvard foreign languages faculty during this period. In response to vociferous student unrest and increasingly negative public reaction in Cambridge, he proposed broad reforms, including elective studies. One of Ticknor's reforms, which was not adopted, was the creation of university departments whose purpose was to focus the course of study on specialized knowledge, to hire faculty trained to accomplish that end, and thereby to transfer curricular and personnel responsibility away from a centrally administered model.

The Johns Hopkins University was established in 1876 as the first research university in America. Modeled after the German university, the primary emphasis at Johns Hopkins was on postbaccalaureate study. However, the institutional value on advanced study had its influence at the undergraduate level. Levine (1978) traced the first use of the terms *major* and *minor* to the Johns Hopkins 1877–1878 catalog. Thus, Ticknor's 1825 prototype of the academic department was created in its current form at Johns Hopkins 50 years later.

Many departmental histories demonstrate how an institutional emphasis on science significantly affected the development of the psychology curriculum. University of Colorado administrators supported hiring psychology faculty who were trained in research-oriented universities in Germany and the United States (Chiszar & Wertheimer, 1988). Administrators supported developing laboratory facilities for faculty and student research at the University of Nevada at Reno (McReynolds, 1988) and understood psychology's place among other sciences at the University of New Mexico (Norman, 1988) and at Indiana University (Capshew & Hearst, 1980; Hearst & Capshew, 1988). All of the authors cited saw the shaping of a scientifically based psychology curriculum as affected by the institutional culture.

Another institution, the University of Michigan, further illustrates this environmental influence. Raphelson (1968) began his description of the history of psychology at Michigan with a period of the philosophers, 1852–1896. A succession of Protestant minister–university presidents, who taught philosophy, set the stage for hiring John Dewey to the faculty in 1884. Dewey taught three courses: empirical psychology; a special topics offering in physiological, comparative, and morbid psychology; and a psychology and philosophy course. From 1887 to 1897, Dewey's *Psychology* (1887) became the standard text. James Tufts initiated experimental activity with the establishment of a laboratory at the University of Michigan in 1890.

In 1901, when an elective system replaced a required curriculum at Michigan, Walter Pillsbury introduced two year-long courses in psychology. The first was a general elective introductory course, and the second was for students seeking more technical work in psychological and experimental psychology. Despite being housed in a philosophy department, psychology under Pillsbury forged its ties with the biological sciences. In 1911, undergraduates were able to take courses in apperception, history of modern psychology, and memory from Pillsbury, and advanced experimental psychology, systematic psychology, psychophysical methods, genetic psychology, and comparative psychology from John Shepard. Undergraduates participated fully in laboratory work in comparative psychology. By 1925, faculty taught additional courses in physiological psychology and sensory–perceptual psychology, as well as applied offerings such as advertising and salesmanship, management, applied and vocational psychology, mental measurement, biometric methods, and individual and race differences. Special topics courses reflecting a growing faculty's interests included the psychology of language, of religion, of music, of aesthetics, and of social service, and criminal and legal psychology.

In 1929, psychology achieved administrative autonomy from philosophy at the University of Michigan. In 1936, another experimental psychology course was introduced as a supplement to the nonmajor introductory offering. The strong emphasis on the physiological and experimental aspects of psychology was not without its trade-offs, especially in emerging areas of clinical psychology. Raphelson (1968) reported a frosty relationship between departmental faculty and the newly established Psychological Clinic in 1937. It was only at the request of nursing students who were working in a psychopathic hospital that a course in personality was first offered in 1935, over objectives by some.

The Michigan curriculum illustrates a scientifically based model that had the capacity to offer students an array of more applied topics. This balancing of experimental and applied courses in the curriculum became an important issue for faculty at other universities in the post-World War II period, especially during the "academic shopping center" era described in the second section of this chapter, Psychology in the Academic Shopping Center.

Applied and Specialized Knowledge Goals

With Jefferson's founding of the University of Virginia in 1824, a distinct American undergraduate curriculum was created. The University of Virginia represented a profound change in American education; as knowledge expanded, specialized knowledge became more valued. With the establishment of eight unique professorships, students could choose a course of study in ancient languages, modern languages, mathematics, natural philosophy, natural history, anatomy and medicine, moral philosophy, or law. If funds were available, Jefferson's blueprint also recommended applied chairs in commerce, manufacture, and diplomacy. He saw that education for the professions and the new knowledge of science would replace the classically prescribed course of study. Vocational outcomes and scientific inquiry were intellectually synthesized by Jefferson's experimental university in Charlottesville.

The establishment of the United States Military Academy at West Point in 1802 and the founding of Rensselaer Polytechnic Institute in 1824 institutionalized technical education that was scientific in concept and vocational in purpose. Jefferson's notions of science and its applications were taken another step by the utilitarian climate in the latter half of the 19th century. The Morrill Act, signed by Abraham Lincoln in 1862, expanded higher education by setting aside federal land for institutions with a breadth of programs and an emphasis on accessibility to new types of students. State universities and, in particular, higher education in the West, became major beneficiaries. Through the sale of public lands, states became able to endow, support, and maintain

> at least one college where the leading object shall be, without excluding other scientific and classical studies, and the military tactics, to teach such branches of learning as are related to agriculture and the mechanical arts . . . in order to promote the liberal and practical education of the industrial classes in the several pursuits and professions in life. (Levine, 1978, pp. 557–558)

New knowledge and a utilitarian vision combined to shape this important piece of legislation. Created in 1868, Cornell University exemplified the land-grant university. Its multiple curricula were designed to provide "better means for the culture of all men of every calling, of every aim" (Levine, 1978, p. 561).

Viney and Punches (1988) summarized their history of the psychology department at Colorado State University (CSU) in the land-grant context as follows:

> Colorado State University, an institution steeped in the land grant tradition, has been guided largely by practical concerns. Cast in this pragmatic mold, the Psychology Department has developed programs relevant to industry, education, and human adjustment. (p. 64)

Psychology was first offered at CSU in 1881 as a required senior-year course, taught by the president, a Professor of Moral and Mental Science. Viney and Punches (1988) suggest that the course was the traditional presidential homily, especially important in a frontier town known for its opportunities for immoral behavior. From 1890 to 1915, psychology had different demons to exorcise. There were four majors: "Agriculture, Mechanical Engineering, Irrigation Engineering, and the 'Ladies Course' . . . renamed [in 1901] General and Domestic Science" (Viney & Punches, 1988, p. 65). The applied emphasis of the land-grant school relegated all subjects in the humanities, social sciences, and sciences to programs for women, not farmers. Psychology thus was taught from the English and History Department in 1911 and from the Rural and Industrial Education Department in 1917. With the appointment in 1918 of the first psychology PhD (from Stanford) came courses in experimental, general educational, and experimental educational psychology. However, for the next 25 years, the department remained a service provider to vocational educators, extension workers, and teachers. Only in 1961 was a separate Department of Psychology approved.

The development of psychology at Purdue University occurred in a similar applied environment. In 1908, the Department of Education listed General Psychology and Educational Psychology among their offerings.

These were general education courses designed for students in agriculture, sciences, and engineering, as well as for teachers in training. The University's first psychologist, George Brandenburg, a Wisconsin PhD, joined the faculty in 1916 and added General and Applied Psychology. Naylor (1971) characterized this course as "one of the earliest courses in industrial psychology offered by any university" (p. 4). Over the next decade, faculty added many other courses. By the 1929–1930 academic year, courses in the following areas formed the psychology curriculum: elementary, educational, general (two courses designed for different majors), childhood, leadership, applied, mental measurements and employment, adolescence, experimental applied, personality, standardized tests in educational measurements, and a course titled Learning and Teaching Applied to College Work. The last course was described by Naylor as "one of the earliest courses designed to increase the competence of graduate students" (p. 6). In the 1930s, the emphasis on applied offerings continued with the addition of new courses in social psychology, industrial psychology, attitudes, and psychology of public opinion. Experimental laboratory courses were taught at Purdue for the first time in 1938.

In summary, institutional parameters significantly affected the early development of psychology curricula in American universities. Religious values, support for science and its demand for rethinking of the traditional baccalaureate, and the advent of specialized and applied programs affected the ways in which psychologists understood and shaped their curricula.

In the next section, I describe how faculty from increasingly diverse institutions sought to create psychology curricula for the post-World War II era. It wasn't an easy task. The discipline was "splintering" (McGovern et al., 1991). Higher education was moving into what the Carnegie Foundation for the Advancement of Teaching (1977) labeled the *academic shopping center era* and led them to conclude that: "disciplines are better at analysis than synthesis; compartmentalizing than bridge-building; dividing events, people, and knowledge, than integrating them" (p. 12).

PSYCHOLOGY IN THE ACADEMIC SHOPPING CENTER

In this section, I describe psychology curricula after World War II. Whereas in the previous section I drew heavily on individual departmental histories, in this section I rely primarily on published reports that were the results of (a) questionnaire surveys or catalog studies of departments or (b) study groups, task forces, or panels of "experts" who recommended model curricula. The former mapped the actual landscape of undergraduate psychology from the 1930s to the 1980s; the latter described what ought to be for psychology curricula after 1950. The interested reader should also review the early studies completed on the introductory course as taught in "colleges with no laboratory" (Calkins, 1910), "colleges and universities with laboratories" (E. C. Sanford, 1910), and "normal schools" (Whipple, 1910), as well as a set of overall recommendations (Seashore, 1910).

Archival and Empirical Studies of Undergraduate Curricula

Henry (1938)

This study described introductory and advanced courses found in the catalogs of 157 "colleges of liberal arts scattered throughout the country" (p. 430). Virtually all of these schools offered one or more elementary courses in psychology; only 26 (16.6%) required laboratory instruction with the course. Thirty-six (27.1%) schools offered advanced laboratory instruction, with 17 (11.5%) offering more than one such course. The 10 most frequently offered advanced undergraduate courses in order were social (72%), abnormal (69.4%), educational (43.3%), applied (42.7%), tests and measurements (42%), systematic (38.2%), comparative (34.4%), personality (30.6%), physiological (29.3%), and research (28%).

F. H. Sanford and Fleishman (1950)

These authors repeated Henry's (1938) earlier catalog study, expanding it by using a stratified random sample of representative institutions prepared by the Research and Statistical Service of the U.S. Office of Education (USOE). The 1947 USOE sample of 330 from a population of 1,778 institutions nationwide included complex universities, technical schools, theological seminaries, professional schools, colleges of arts and sciences, teachers colleges and normal schools, junior colleges, and Black institutions. The authors found that introductory psychology was taught at 78.2% of the institutions, almost always as a one-semester course. That percentage was somewhat lower than one might expect because less than 40% of the seminaries and professional schools in the sample offered the course, compared with 94% of the universities and colleges of arts and sciences. The 10 most frequent courses taught in all types of institutions after the first course were educational (43%), social (38.5%), child (37.9%), abnormal (28.5%), applied (27.6%), adolescent (26.1%), educational tests and measurements (22.7%), experimental (21.2%), mental hygiene (20.9%), statistics (18.8%), personality (18.2%), and tests and measurements (18.2%).

Daniel, Dunham, and Morris (1965)

The authors designed this study as a replication of F. H. Sanford and Fleishman's (1950) study, examining which changes had occurred in the 15-year interval and whether the recommendations made in the early 1950s by the Wolfle committee (described in Task Force and Committee Reports on the Undergraduate Curriculum, later in this chapter) had had any influence on curricular practice. They limited their sample ($N = 207$) to catalogs from universities, liberal arts colleges, teachers colleges, and junior colleges in which a psychology department was the unit offering the course. Course titles showing the largest gain in percentage of institutions offering them were (in order of magnitude) Tests and Measures, Personality, Developmental, Abnormal, Learning, Child, and Adjustment. On the basis of their data, the authors concluded that there was limited movement in the direction of the Wolfle recommendations; they noted in particular the lack of response to the recommended integrative, senior-year course, such as History and Systems.

Kulik (1973)

This APA-sponsored and National Science Foundation-funded study sought "to describe undergraduate education in psychology nationwide and report on innovative approaches that may point the way to the future" (p. 3). The author combined a catalog study, a mailed questionnaire returned by 463 four-year schools and 99 two-year schools, and 17 site visits to campuses exemplifying the diversity and innovativeness in undergraduate psychology of the early 1970s. Kulik reported that "99% of all universities, 98% of liberal arts colleges, 100% of state colleges, and 98% of two-year colleges offered an introductory psychology course" (p. 23).

Comparisons of the F. H. Sanford and Fleishman (1950) data with Kulik's (1973) results revealed several trends. Curricular emphases on courses in applied areas (e.g., industrial and educational psychology) declined, but those in natural science processes (e.g., learning, sensation and perception, and physiological) increased. Courses in social science processes (e.g., personality, social, developmental, and child) had become the dominant content areas, accounting for approximately one third of all psychology courses offered in the curriculum, compared with one fifth in natural science processes. A course in statistics and a course in experimental methods had become required in a majority of the institutions that Kulik studied.

The descriptive information from the survey responses and from the catalog study were supplemented by rich case studies from the site visits. In the report, chapters that were based on these visits described innovative programs at a large university, small liberal arts colleges, community colleges, and British universities. Kulik (1973) described curricula that were based on behavioral principles, on a laboratory-centered approach, on a student-centered approach, and on social commitment by its undergraduates.

The Kulik (1973) report effectively captured the conflicts experienced by department faculty trying to respond to the diversity of study goals in the academic shopping center era: "The diverse goals of students in psychology courses suggest that pluralism may be a valuable concept in the design of programs in psychology" (p. 203). This empirical study broadened the definition of liberal arts education espoused by Buxton et al. (1952) and McKeachie and Milholland (1961).

Lux and Daniel (1978)

The authors replicated the Daniel et al. (1965) study, finding over 1,356 different psychology course titles offered by faculty in psychology departments. This 1975 catalog study demonstrated a 519% increase in course titles since the F. H. Sanford and Fleishman (1950) study of 1947 course offerings. Lux and Daniel identified six factors to account for the proliferation of courses: "new areas of interest . . . fragmentation of subject matter . . . combinations appeared to be more popular . . . highly specialized courses . . . [courses offer] practical experience to the student . . . [institutions] make the courses sound more lively and provocative" (pp. 14–15).

Lux and Daniel (1978) concluded that their data were consistent with Kulik's (1973) results, demonstrating the increasing emphasis on natural science offerings in both university and liberal arts college curricula and on social science and applied course offerings in 2-year college curricula.

Scheirer and Rogers (1985)

These two APA staff members completed a mail survey of 400 randomly selected 4-year and 2-year institutions. There were responses from 165 four-year and 122 two-year colleges. Virtually all schools reported offering an introductory course and having a substantial number of total enrollments. One institution reported an annual enrollment of 5,500 students. The authors concluded that "about 27% of all full-time students . . . take introductory psychology in any given year" (p. 13). Using approximate numbers from the F. H. Sanford and Fleishman (1950) and the Kulik (1973) studies, Scheirer and Rogers found that both natural science and social science course emphases continued to increase at the expense of applied courses, which continued to decline as a percentage of total offerings.

These five studies described the nature of curricular offerings in undergraduate psychology over the approximately 50-year period from 1938 to 1985. There were five major reports that were not empirical but that recommended what ought to be in the psychology curriculum and the overall undergraduate program: Gregg et al. (1947/1970), Buxton et al. (1952), McKeachie and Milholland (1961), Morris (1982), and McGovern et al. (1991). A summary of those reports appears in the next section.

Gregg et al. (1947/1970)

The president of Harvard University commissioned this study to inform that institution about psychology's potential contributions to undergraduate and graduate education. Wolfle (1948) evaluated the commission's report thus: "By all means read this book. . . . The first university to follow all the Commission's suggestions will have the best department of psychology in the country" (p. 61).

The six psychologist and six nonpsychologist authors defined the nature of the discipline at that time, emphasizing psychology's methods of experimentation, observation, and interpretation. Recognizing psychology's increasing popularity among students and the general public, the authors described in detail the goals and effective pedagogy for an ideal introductory course. Their support of a concentration in psychology at the baccalaureate level was contingent on including courses in mathematics, natural and life sciences, and social sciences as essential corequisites. "Psychology has an important role to play as a link between the biological and the social sciences" (p. 403). Although the report was not specific on the content of an undergraduate curriculum for majors, it was very specific in listing psychology courses that would be appropriate for preprofessional study of medicine, business, engineering, teaching, ministry, sociology, and government.

Two decades later, in a special issue of the *American Psychologist* initiated by the APA's Education and Training Board, Appley (1970) revisited the Gregg et al. (1947/1970) report. Five of the original authors evaluated their document in light of their subsequent experience as scholars and teachers. Commenting on the Harvard commission's work, Appley emphasized the roles that both intellectual tradition and administrative organization had in shaping the curriculum. "The centrifugal forces acting on such subareas of psychology are as strong or stronger than centripetal factors holding the psychological disciplines together" (Appley, 1970, p. 388). It is interesting to note that a broad definition of a psychology department was espoused, including faculty to be cross-appointed in multiple professional schools. In the midst of writing this report, however, the Harvard faculty voted to divide the then-existing unit into the Department of Psychology and the Department of Social Relations.

Buxton et al. (1952)

For 8 weeks in the summer of 1951, six psychologists from Cornell, Maryland, Michigan, Vanderbilt, and Yale met to accomplish, in the words of their chair Dael Wolfle, "an audit to determine the objectives, examine the content, and appraise the results of the instruction we have been giving"

(p. v). Their report described the objectives of undergraduate instruction in psychology and recommended a curriculum to achieve those objectives. They identified four possible objectives:

> (1) Intellectual development and a liberal education; (2) a knowledge of psychology, its research findings, its major problems, its theoretical integrations, and its contributions; (3) personal growth and an increased ability to meet personal and social adjustment problems adequately; (4) desirable attitudes and habits of thought, such as the stimulation of intellectual curiosity, respect for others, and a feeling of social responsibility. (pp. 2–3)

The authors, however, preferred to emphasize only three, including knowledge (e.g., problems, facts, and principles of psychology; psychology as science; and structure and functioning of science), habits of thought (e.g., observation, quantitative thinking, and multiple causation), and values and attitudes (e.g., knowledge as a value and caution and responsibility as attitudes).

Buxton et al. (1952) recommended that a curriculum include five elements: introductory course, elementary special-interest courses, core courses, specialized advanced courses, and integrative courses. They viewed the first course as an overview of behavior and experience, with an emphasis on scientific content and not on practical applications. Special-interest courses could be relabeled as electives in psychology primarily for nonmajors. Those courses included such titles as Educational Psychology and Industrial Psychology. Five intermediate core courses formed the "heart of the program" (p. 27): perception, motivation, thinking and language, ability, and statistical reasoning. The authors did not recommend a separate course in experimental methods because they believed that *all* of the core courses should accomplish that learning. Moreover, they saw previously taught versions of the experimental methods course as covering areas of psychology which were *not* scientific, satisfying a need that they felt no longer existed because "basic methodology and scientific attitudes seem to be essentially the same throughout all psychology" (p. 27). Finally, this study group recommended a set of advanced courses that could be integrative in purpose (e.g., history and systems, personality) or specialized (e.g., learning, comparative, or physiological). Interdisciplinary courses were other examples of advanced specialized courses.

McKeachie and Milholland (1961)

When McKeachie and Milholland from the University of Michigan, along with Cole (Oberlin), Hunt (Northwestern), Leeper (Oregon), and Ray (Bethany) met in 1960 to develop *Undergraduate Curricula in Psychology*, the academic shopping center had arrived! The authors introduced their text with an analysis of projected student enrollments and a discussion of emerging conflicts between expectations for faculty members to be scholars and to be teachers, with the former function seen as increasingly more important. They recalled that the Wolfle (1948) group, 10 years earlier, recommended its particular curricular model because psychology undergraduates were doing too much shopping. The Wolfle remedy was a sequence of required courses to reduce overlap and to foster increasing sophistication in scientific thinking. However, McKeachie, Milholland, and their colleagues were confronted with both an increasing number of students entering higher education and an increasingly diverse student body whose needs were increasingly vocational. They wrote,

> In the college with a heterogeneous student body, how can one teach all levels effectively? We suggested earlier that one of the functions of required sequences was to guarantee homogeneity of background in the advanced courses, but normally it has the added function of increasing homogeneity in ability as well. If one thus eliminates the less intensely motivated, less able students from some courses, does one have the responsibility to offer other courses suited to their abilities and interests? (p. 27)

Ultimately, McKeachie, Milholland, and their colleagues resolved this dilemma of matching curricula to student need and ability level by reaffirming psychology as a liberal arts discipline, preparing students to be citizens and lifelong learners, not just vocationally trained individuals. "Let the student study test theory rather than test administration, personality theory rather than personnel practice" (pp. 37–38), they concluded.

In contrast to the Buxton et al. (1952) group's recommended curriculum, the McKeachie and Milholland (1961) group proposed three different models that they labeled the *inverted pyramid*, the *hourglass*, and the *flexible curriculum*. The labels reflected different structures that would enable different types of students in different types of institutions to satisfy their needs and yet accomplish similar objectives for the curriculum that Buxton et al. (1952) espoused 10 years earlier. About content, the McKeachie and Milholland group reached some consensus on requiring introductory psychology, statistics, experimental methods, followed by core courses, integrative courses (e.g., history and systems), vocationally oriented courses, and elective courses representing special interests of the faculty. Core courses could be defined differently by each department, as "those which are regarded by psychologists as the most important areas of theoretical and research development" (p. 92). For example, courses in learning, social psychology, personality, and principles of psychological testing seemed central to these six psychologists.

Morris (1982)

In a special issue of *Teaching of Psychology*, several authors addressed the topic of "undergraduate psychology education in the next decade." In particular, Candland (1982), Cole (1982), Furedy and Furedy (1982), and Mann (1982) wrote on the curriculum as a whole. Those essays indicated that psychologists were struggling to fashion responses to the demands of new populations of students in the academic shopping center. Furedy and Furedy conceptualized curricular responses along a "Socratic versus sophistic" continuum; Candland used a metaphor of "the fox and the hedgehog"; Cole described psychology as a "liberating art." The message from each of the authors was that psychology faculty must reconcile their traditional objectives of lifelong learning (e.g., education and general skills) with student expectations for career employability (e.g., training and specific skills).

Mann (1982) wrote that "a curriculum that can address the developmental needs of conformist, cynical, autonomous, mature, and all remaining sorts of students could seem almost beyond the realm of possibility unless one looked again at the great teachers of the field" (p. 14). He proposed a curricular model with six orientations: psychology as a science, applied field, and helping profession, and as a facilitator of self-development, as human wisdom, and as paradigm.

Mann's (1982) vision for undergraduate psychology was based on a complex view of the field and an understanding of the developmental patterns of a more and more heterogeneous student body. His work was influenced by his collaboration on an earlier work (Chickering & Associates, 1981) that stressed that developmental stages and issues should be integrated with curricular design across the disciplines. Although Mann's essay lacked recommendations for specific course content or curricular requirements, it amply compensated with a breadth and depth of recommended responses to student and faculty goals. McGovern and Hawks (1986, 1988) based their curricular development and evaluation work primarily on Mann's model.

McGovern et al. (1991)

The Association of American Colleges invited representatives from 12 learned societies to work together as the Project on Liberal Learning, Study-in-Depth, and the Arts and Sciences Major (1991). The APA sponsored the McGovern et al. (1991) task force, and their report identified eight common goals for the undergraduate curriculum that were adaptable to a variety of institutional settings. The goals included a knowledge base, thinking skills, language skills, information gathering and synthesis skills, research methods and statistical skills, interpersonal skills, history of psychology, and ethics and values. Recognizing that institutional cultures, resources, and faculty differ, the authors described four hypothetical curricular models to accomplish these goals. The models were not meant to be prescriptive but were offered as stimuli for departmental faculty discussion and modification.

The McGovern et al. (1991) report acknowledged that conflicts existed among psychologists because of their different views of science (Cronbach, 1957), values (Kimble, 1984), and the appropriate forum to study topics of gender, ethnicity, culture, and class (Bronstein & Quina, 1988). How departments resolved those conflicts (if they chose to address them at all!) would affect the shape of the curriculum. Moreover, what Appley (1970) described in his earlier commentary as splintering the knowledge base of the discipline was now of considerable concern to many faculty. The principle of "less is more," therefore, became an underlying theme of the McGovern et al. report. To accomplish the skills goals *and* to ensure an appropriate coverage of the knowledge base, the authors' curricular models had five common elements with some variation in content: (a) introductory psychology; (b) methods courses (statistics, research methods, psychometrics, and individual differences); (c) two survey courses followed by two matched, specialized courses with laboratory instruction; (d) integrating senior-year project or seminar; and (e) interpersonal skills and group process laboratory.

CONCLUSION

The thesis of this chapter is that undergraduate psychology curricula reflect the changing base of knowledge and practice in the discipline and were influenced by larger forces in American higher education from 1892 to the present. In the first section, I described three institutional parameters that affected the American curriculum in general—religion, science, and applied and specialized knowledge. The stories of individual departments of psychology illustrated how psychology was also being shaped by those three forces. In the second section, I described how psychology continued its development, flourishing during the era of the academic shopping center. In this third and concluding section, I project future directions in the evolution of the undergraduate curricula that are based on changes in the field of psychology in particular and emerging forces in higher education in general.

Responding to the Splintering of the Discipline

In a recent article, Scott (1991) predicted that

just as psychology left the care of the established disciplines that gave it birth in the 19th century, so the maturing subareas of psychology will realize separate identities in the next 50 years. The administrative unit that currently houses an integrated department of psychology will be viewed from the 21st century as having been a necessary phase in the *bildungsroman* of the behavioral sciences. (p. 975)

Although Scott's personal view is about graduate education and training, developments at that level significantly affect the content and structure of the undergraduate curriculum, especially in universities in which so many psychology undergraduates pursue their baccalaureates.

In his response to a proposal for the preparation of professional psychologists by Fox, Kovacs, and Graham (1985), Prokasy (1986) framed the debate over breadth versus specialization at the undergraduate level.

I oppose professionalization of the undergraduate curriculum. The overdetermination of undergraduate curricula for ostensibly professional ends represents one of the most serious problems in higher education . . . heavily structured undergraduate curricula provide training rather than education; and leaders in professional fields are calling for broader education of those who join their professions. (p. 1176)

It is important to remember, however, that this is not a new debate and that espousing liberal arts breadth in undergraduate curricula is not a new response. Buxton et al. (1952), McKeachie and Milholland (1961), Cole (1982), and McGovern et al. (1991) were well aware of students' demands for increased specialization to satisfy their perceived career needs. All of these authors advocated the continuing emphasis on psychology as part of a liberal arts education.

A new perspective is taking shape in contemporary psychology curricula and should continue to evolve into the 21st century. Whereas Scott (1991) predicted that changes in the knowledge base of the field would stimulate curricular adaptation, this new perspective is stimulated by broader forces in American higher education. In particular, the definition of a liberal arts education is changing.

Redefining Liberal Arts

There are signs that the curricular free-for-all of the academic shopping center era may be waning. Blue ribbon reports challenging this state of affairs have been sponsored by the National Endowment for the Humanities (Bennett, 1984), Carnegie Foundation for the Advancement of Teaching (Boyer, 1987, 1990), Association of American Colleges (Project on Redefining the Meaning and Purpose of Baccalaureate Degrees, 1985; Project on Liberal Learning, Study-in-Depth, and the Arts and Sciences Major, 1991; Zemsky, 1989), and the National Institute of Education (Study Group on the Conditions of Excellence in American Higher Education, 1984). What the effects of these reports will be on psychologists remains an open question. Fretz's (1982) observation about the influence of national conferences and their reports remains relevant.

> A major challenge for undergraduate psychology education in the next decade is to involve a greater proportion of leading psychologists in discussion of the issues in developing and maintaining effective undergraduate education in a rapidly changing educational environment. (p. 55)

In 1991, the APA sponsored its own National Conference on Enhancing the Quality of Undergraduate Education in Psychology at St. Mary's College in Maryland. Unlike past groups assembled to study the curriculum, psychologists at the St. Mary's conference were charged with developing a scholarly review and practical resources and recommendations for advising, minority student recruitment and retention, faculty development, faculty networking, active learning, assessment, and the curriculum. Lloyd and Brewer's chapter in this book (see Chapter 10) provides detailed coverage of this conference's contributions.

The St. Mary's conference participants had a more expanded charge than previous APA groups because the steering committee that organized the agenda recognized the importance of three broader forces in contemporary higher education. I believe that (a) the assessment movement, (b) curricular reform that is based on cognitive and developmental research, and (c) interdisciplinary scholarship in such areas as feminist studies and multicultural studies will challenge liberal arts curricula in general and psychology curricula in particular into the 21st century.

First, state legislatures and regional accreditation groups have demanded that institutions become accountable for the quality of student learning. Early responses to this politicized demand were appropriately negative by campus faculties, but by the late 1980s, the assessment movement had established academic legitimacy as a catalyst for change in the curriculum. Teachers must be able to identify measurable outcomes of their undergraduate instruction; faculty must be able to demonstrate what their students learn. In psychology, the assessment movement significantly shaped recommendations in the McGovern et al. (1991) report and recommendations from the St. Mary's conference.

Second, faculty and curriculum development projects, applying cognitive and developmental psychology research, have sharpened our focus on effective means for accomplishing student learning. Writing-across-the-curriculum, critical thinking, and active learning activities are some examples of how faculty are rethinking individual courses objectives and teaching strategies. Whole departments have initiated changes in their programs on the basis of new understandings of how students learn most effectively. For example, faculty at the University of Richmond collected data from students, graduate school admissions officers, and employers.

Then, they structured the curriculum by using student development levels and a sequence of courses designed to achieve sophisticated cognitive outcomes (Walker, Newcomb, & Hopkins, 1987). The Project on Liberal Learning, Study-in-Depth, and the Arts and Sciences Major (1991) final report emphasized that liberal arts curricula must enable students to make connections between disparate ideas and different methods of studying problems. Psychology faculty could benefit from reviewing this report, especially in light of the splintering of our own discipline.

Third, interdisciplinary research and curricula in areas such as feminist studies and multicultural studies are transforming the curriculum in higher education and have the potential to do so in psychology. Walsh (1985) described how the psychology of women course has been a catalyst for changing faculty conceptions of the knowledge base in the discipline since the mid-1970s. Furumoto's (1985) and Scarborough and Furumoto's (1987) historical investigations of women in the history of psychology provide a wealth of material for broadening the content of courses. Bronstein and Quina's (1988) text, published by the APA, extends faculty's models for gender balancing the curriculum by treating cultural diversity strategies in a similar fashion. The inclusion of such topics, courses, and programmatic emphasis is not without conflict. Many of the comments on an early version of the McGovern et al. (1991) paper were in reaction to this topic, leading the authors to conclude that

> gender, ethnicity, culture, and class are seen by some teachers as issues that challenge the contemporary curricula. Such a challenge also questions traditional research methodologies that are empirical, quantitative, and positivist, and may advocate alternative psychological methods that are contextual, interpretive, and more qualitative. Other psychologists believe that, although these topics and the new knowledge generated by research have legitimacy in the discipline, they should be subtopics best left to treatments determined by an instructor's sensitivities and commitments. (p. 600)

The St. Mary's conference group who focused on ethnic minority recruitment and retention captured the importance of this issue by using the metaphor of teaching a "psychology of variance," suggesting that this should be an essential outcome of every curriculum.

Psychology was, is, and will continue to be a conflicted field. There are conflicts in the content of the discipline and in the values of the psychologists who teach it. Although the story of the undergraduate curriculum from 1892 to 1992 may be fraught with conflict, there is a wonderfully integrating sentiment suggested over 80 years ago. Designers of future curricula can draw their inspiration from Seashore's (1910) conclusions:

> Psychology is perhaps unequalled by other college subjects in its power to influence the life of the student. . . . Psychology perhaps

suggests more unsolved problems than any other science; there is, therefore, a special demand upon practical ingenuity and philosophical insight. . . . "The teacher is everything." (p. 91)

REFERENCES

Almanac: Earned degrees conferred, 1988–89. (1991, August 28). *Chronicle of Higher Education*, p. 28.

Appley, M. H. (1970). The place of psychology in the university. *American Psychologist, 25*, 387–390.

Benjamin, Jr., L. T., & Bertelson, A. D. (1975). The early Nebraska psychology laboratory, 1889–1930: Nursery for presidents of the American Psychological Association. *Journal of the History of the Behavioral Sciences, 11*, 142–148.

Bennett, W. J. (1984). *To reclaim a legacy: A report on the humanities in higher education*. Washington, DC: National Endowment for the Humanities.

Boyer, E. L. (1987). *College: The undergraduate experience in America*. New York: Harper & Row.

Boyer, E. L. (1990). *Scholarship reconsidered: Priorities of the professoriate*. Princeton, NJ: Princeton University Press.

Bronstein, P. A., & Quina, K. (Eds.). (1988). *Teaching a psychology of people: Resources for gender and sociocultural awareness*. Washington, DC: American Psychological Association.

Brown, D. L., & Allen, M. K. (1988). Psychology among the saints: The development of behavioral science at Brigham Young University. *Journal of the History of the Behavioral Sciences, 24*, 33–40.

Buxton, C. E., Cofer, C. N., Gustad, J. W., MacLeod, R. B., McKeachie, W. J., & Wolfle, D. (1952). *Improving undergraduate instruction in psychology*. New York: Macmillan.

Calkins, M. W. (1910). The teaching of elementary psychology in colleges supposed to have no laboratory. *Psychological Monographs, 12*(4, Whole No. 51), 41–53.

Candland, D. K. (1982). Selective pressure and the teaching of psychology: The fox and the hedgehog. *Teaching of Psychology, 9*, 20–23.

Capshew, J. H., & Hearst, E. (1980). Psychology at Indiana University: From Bryan to Skinner. *Psychological Record, 30*, 319–342.

Carnegie Foundation for the Advancement of Teaching. (1977). *Missions of the college curriculum*. San Francisco: Jossey-Bass.

Chickering, A. W. & Associates. (1981). *The modern American college: Responding to the new realities of diverse students and a changing society*. San Francisco: Jossey-Bass.

Chiszar, D., & Wertheimer, M. (1988). The Boulder model: A history of psychology at the University of Colorado. *Journal of the History of the Behavioral Sciences, 24,* 102–106.

Cole, D. L. (1982). Psychology as a liberating art. *Teaching of Psychology, 9,* 23–26.

Cronbach, L. J. (1957). The two disciplines of scientific psychology. *American Psychologist, 12,* 671–684.

Daniel, R. S., Dunham, P. J., & Morris, C. J. (1965). Undergraduate courses in psychology: 14 years later. *Psychological Record, 15,* 25–31.

Dewey, J. (1897). *Psychology.* New York: Harper.

Fox, R. E., Kovacs, A. L., & Graham, S. R. (1985). Proposals for a revolution in the preparation and regulation of professional psychologists. *American Psychologist, 40,* 1042–1050.

Fretz, B. R. (1982). Aftermath of the renaissance in undergraduate psychology: Enlightenment or Machiavellian? *Teaching of Psychology, 9,* 55–59.

Furchtgott, E. (1990). Contributions to the history of psychology: LXXIII. The history of psychology at the University of South Carolina. *Psychological Reports, 67,* 1155–1170.

Furedy, J. J., & Furedy, C. (1982). Socratic versus sophistic strains in the teaching of undergraduate psychology: Implicit conflicts made explicit. *Teaching of Psychology, 9,* 14–20.

Furumoto, L. (1985). Placing women in the history of psychology course. *Teaching of Psychology, 12,* 203–206.

Garvey, C. R. (1929). List of American psychology laboratories. *Psychological Bulletin, 26,* 652–660.

Gregg, A., Barnard, C. I., Bronk, D. W., Carmichael, L., Dollard, J., French, T. M., Hilgard, E. R., Hunter, W. S., Thorndike, E. L., Thurstone, L. L., Whitehorn, J. C., & Yerkes, R. M. (1970). The place of psychology in an ideal university: The report of the university commission to advise on the future of psychology at Harvard. *American Psychologist, 25,* 391–410. (Original work published 1947)

Hearst, E., & Capshew, J. H. (1988). *Psychology at Indiana University: A centennial review and compendium.* Unpublished manuscript, Department of Psychology, Indiana University, Bloomington.

Henry, E. R. (1938). A survey of courses in psychology offered by undergraduate colleges of liberal arts. *Psychological Bulletin, 35,* 430–435.

Kimble, G. A. (1984). Psychology's two cultures. *American Psychologist, 39,* 833–839.

Kulik, J. (1973). *Undergraduate education in psychology.* Washington, DC: American Psychological Association.

Levine, A. (1978). *Handbook on undergraduate curriculum: Prepared for the Carnegie Council on Policy Studies in Higher Education.* San Francisco: Jossey-Bass.

Lux, D. F., & Daniel, R. S. (1978). Which courses are most frequently listed by psychology departments? *Teaching of Psychology, 5,* 13–16.

Mann, R. D. (1982). The curriculum and context of psychology. *Teaching of Psychology, 9,* 9–14.

May, M. J. (1988). From Mormon Academy to four-year state college: Psychology at Weber State College. *Journal of the History of the Behavioral Sciences, 24,* 25–32.

McGovern, T. V., Furumoto, L., Halpern, D. F., Kimble, G. A., & McKeachie, W. J. (1991). Liberal education, study in depth, and the arts and sciences major—psychology. *American Psychologist, 46,* 598–605.

McGovern, T. V., & Hawks, B. K. (1986). The varieties of undergraduate experience. *Teaching of Psychology, 13,* 174–181.

McGovern, T. V., & Hawks, B. K. (1988). The liberating science and art of undergraduate psychology. *American Psychologist, 43,* 108–114.

McKeachie, W. J., & Milholland, J. E. (1961). *Undergraduate curricula in psychology.* Glenview, IL: Scott, Foresman.

McReynolds, P. (1988). Psychology at the University of Nevada at Reno: A restrospective account. *Journal of the History of the Behavioral Sciences, 24,* 74–80.

Morris, C. G. (Ed.). (1982). Undergraduate psychology education in the next decade [Special Issue]. *Teaching of Psychology, 9*(1).

Naylor, J. C. (1971). *Psychology at Purdue.* Unpublished manuscript, Purdue University, West Lafayette, IN.

Norman, R. D. (1988). Natural science, functionalism, and psychology at the University of New Mexico, 1889–1960. *Journal of the History of the Behavioral Sciences, 24,* 69–73.

Project on Liberal Learning, Study-in-Depth, and the Arts and Sciences Major. (1991). *The challenge of connecting learning.* Washington, DC: Association of American Colleges.

Project on Redefining the Meaning and Purpose of Baccalaureate Degrees. (1985). *Integrity in the college curriculum: A report to the academic community.* Washington, DC: Association of American Colleges.

Prokasy, W. F. (1986). Preparation and regulation of professional psychologists. *American Psychologist, 41,* 1176–1177.

Raphelson, A. C. (1968). *Psychology at the University of Michigan: 1852–1950.* Unpublished manuscript, University of Michigan, Flint College, Ann Arbor.

Rudolph, F. (1977). *Curriculum: A history of the American undergraduate course of study since 1636.* San Francisco: Jossey-Bass.

Sanford, E. C. (1910). The teaching of elementary psychology in colleges and universities with laboratories. *Psychological Monographs, 12*(4, Whole No. 51), 54–71.

Sanford, F. H., & Fleishman, E. A. (1950). A survey of undergraduate psychology courses in American colleges and universities. *American Psychologist, 5,* 33–37.

Scarborough, E., & Furumoto, L. (1987). *Untold lives: The first generation of American women psychologists.* New York: Columbia University Press.

Scheirer, C. J., & Rogers, A. M. (1985). *The undergraduate psychology curriculum: 1984.* Washington, DC: American Psychological Association.

Scott, T. R. (1991). A personal view of the future of psychology departments. *American Psychologist, 46,* 975–976.

Seashore, C. E. (1910). General report on the teaching of the elementary course in psychology: Recommendations. *Psychological Monographs, 12*(4, Whole No. 51), 80–91.

Spilka, B. (1988). From soul to psyche and frontier to mainstream: A history of psychology at the University of Denver to 1960. *Journal of the History of the Behavioral Sciences, 24,* 51–55.

Study Group on the Conditions of Excellence in American Higher Education. (1984). *Involvement in learning: Realizing the potential of American higher education.* Washington, DC: U.S. Department of Education.

Trapp, E. P. (1984). *A century of psychology at the University of Arkansas.* Paper presented at the 25th anniversary of the doctoral programs in psychology, Fayetteville, AK.

Viney, W., & Punches, A. (1988). Nature and necessity in the land grant context: History of psychology at Colorado State University. *Journal of the History of the Behavioral Sciences, 24,* 64–68.

Walker, W. E., Newcomb, A. F., & Hopkins, W. P. (1987). A model for curriculum evaluation and revision in undergraduate psychology programs. *Teaching of Psychology, 14,* 198–202.

Webster's ninth new collegiate dictionary. (1983). Springfield, MA: Merriam-Webster.

Walsh, M. R. (1985). The psychology of women course: A continuing catalyst for change. *Teaching of Psychology, 12,* 198–203.

Whipple, G. M. (1910). The teaching of psychology in normal schools. *Psychological Monographs, 12*(4, Whole No. 51), 2–40.

Wolfe, H. K. (1895). The new psychology in undergraduate work. *Psychological Review, 2,* 382–387.

Wolfle, D. (1948). The place of psychology in an ideal university [Book review]. *American Psychologist, 3,* 61–64.

Zemsky, R. (1989). *Structure and coherence: Measuring the undergraduate curriculum.* Washington, DC: Association of American Colleges.

2

COLLEGIATE CAREER ADVISING: STATUS, ANTECEDENTS, AND STRATEGIES

MARK E. WARE

A book about the history of teaching psychology recognizes and celebrates the importance of effective pedagogy. For some individuals, a chapter on advising in such a book may seem out of place. However, experienced teachers can testify to the daily challenge they face as advisers, responding to many undergraduates who want to know what they can do with psychology after graduation. Examination of the higher education, student services, career guidance, and teaching of psychology literature in the 1980s reveals extensive attention to undergraduate career advising. Why has so much attention been devoted to advising? What are the historical roots that contribute to collegiate career advising? What strategies exist for teachers of psychology to assist students in evaluating this important component of their collegiate experience? The goal of the present chapter is to answer these questions.

STATUS

Views About Advising

Ender, Winston, and Miller (1984) summarized the results of several studies of students' views about their college experience. The authors noted growing evidence of students' disillusionment about promises for challenge and stimulation in college. DeCoster and Mable's (1981) remarks captured students' frustration with academia: "Students frequently described the idea of approaching one of their instructors as scary, threatening or demeaning. At the same time, the very mention of academic advisers would invariably be met with a roar of laughter" (pp. 43–44). Advising has not only failed to support and encourage most students' development, but, as one author wrote, "Faculty advising of students . . . is at most large institutions . . . at best an embarrassment, at worst a disgrace" (Riesman, 1981, p. 258). Moreover, as Trombley and Holmes (1981) pointed out, as recently as the late 1970s, "advising has remained an unexamined function" (p. 3).

One explanation for students' dissatisfaction with college and advising may be the discrepancy between students' needs and expectations and actual advising practices. Swanson and Tokar (1991) documented that students perceived lack of information and lack of capability as the greatest barriers to choosing a career. Moreover, studies at larger and smaller universities (Lunneborg, 1986; Ware, 1986) identified students' interest in acquiring more job-related information and skills. To what extent have advising practices addressed students' needs and expectations? Answers to that question are found in Crockett and Levitz's (1984) description of the results of the survey of academic advising by the National Academic Advising Association (NACADA).

Advising Practices: The NACADA Survey

Background

The emergence of NACADA in the late 1970s and early 1980s (Beatty, 1991) brought a renewed advocacy for advising. More important, NACADA encouraged and supported the American College Testing (ACT) Program in the first National Survey of Academic Advising in 1979. The ACT Program repeated the survey in 1982. The survey included advising goals that NACADA developed. Table 1, adapted from Crockett and Levitz (1984), contains the range of advising goals and the mean ratings of each, as explained in the Method section below.

Method

Surveys were sent to a random sample of 1,095 two- and four-year public and private higher education institutions. There was a 69% return. The director/coordinator of academic advising at each institution received the survey. At institutions in which individual departments handled advising, the person overseeing advising services received the survey. Because more than 75% of the respondents reported that their institutions had no systematic evaluation of the advising program and because of the tendency

TABLE 1
Mean Ratings of NACADA Goals for Advising Programs

Goals	Mean rating
Provide accurate information about institutional policies, procedures, resources, and programs	3.99
Assist students in developing an educational plan consistent with life goals and objectives (alternative course of action, alternative career consideration, and selection of courses)	3.35
Assist students in evaluation or reevaluation of progress toward established goals and educational plans	3.33
Make referrals to other institutional or community support services	3.30
Provide information about students to the institution, colleges, and/or academic departments	3.25
Assist students in their consideration of life goals by relating interests, skills, abilities, and values to careers, the world of work, and the nature and purpose of higher education	3.01
Assist students in self-understanding and self-acceptance (values clarification and understanding abilities, interests, and limitations)	2.73
Assist students in developing decision-making skills	2.55

Note: Ratings are based on a scale from 1 to 5, in which 1 = *does not apply, no services have been implemented to address this goal*; 2 = *achievement not very satisfactory*; 3 = *achievement somewhat satisfactory*; 4 = *achievement satisfactory*; and 5 = *achievement very satisfactory*. NACADA = National Academic Advising Association. The data in Table 1 are from "Current Advising Practice in Colleges and Universities," in H. B. Winston, Jr., T. K. Miller, & S. C. Ender (Eds.), *Developmental Academic Advising: Addressing Students' Educational, Career, and Personal Needs.* Copyright 1984 by Jossey-Bass. Adapted by permission.

to overestimate self-evaluations (i.e., social desirability), the findings reported in the 1982 survey should be treated with caution; the figures may be inflated.

Respondents rated the extent to which advising services met each of the NACADA goals listed in Table 1. Ratings were on a 5-point scale that ranged from *no services* (1) to *achievement very satisfactory* (5). The intermediate values of *achievement somewhat satisfactory* (3) and *achievement satisfactory* (4) were important to the present description of findings.

Results and Discussion

The mean ratings in Table 1 are in rank order from highest to lowest. At least three of the NACADA goals related uniquely to career advising. The goals included "assisting students in developing an educational plan consistent with life goals and objectives," "assisting students in their consideration of life goals by relating interests, skills, abilities, and values to careers, the world of work, and the nature and purpose of higher education," and "assisting students in developing decision-making skills." Advising directors/coordinators reported that, at best, career-related advising goals were being met somewhat satisfactorily.

The NACADA data also indicated that almost two thirds of the institutions selected faculty for advising by virtue of their employment contract, and virtually no institutions used competency criteria to select faculty advisers. Almost 75% of the institutions reported offering little or no training in advising. When training was provided, more than 75% gave advisers information about regulations, policies, and procedures or about campus referral sources. Information about careers and employment or about decision-making skills was least common in training programs. When asked about the needs of advising programs, respondents identified greater administrative recognition of the importance of advising (particularly at 4-year public institutions) and expanded adviser training programs.

In summary, the NACADA study indicated that even though institutions have expected faculty to advise students they have provided little training or recognition for such responsibilities. When institutions have provided training, it usually has consisted of information on institutional procedures and only infrequently on advising students about how to make decisions about life after graduation. The NACADA findings support the contention that students' advising needs and expectations have not been met by advising practices.

How have professionals in higher education responded to the dissatisfaction with advising? The advising and student services literature of the 1980s evaluated advising's place in higher education. The following section summarizes contemporary views on this topic.

Advising Conceptualizations

Kramer and Gardner (1983) contributed to the collegiate advising literature with unambiguous statements defining academic and career advising. They described the two as follows:

1. Academic advising refers to specific academic matters, such as course selection, programming, dropping and adding courses, and advice rendered to your students concerning academic programs and careers.

2. Career advising is that form of academic advising that you do to translate career choices into educational goals and programs and to related academic curricula to career opportunities. (Kramer & Gardner, 1983, p. 35)

Kramer and Gardner (1983) further distinguished between informational and developmental advising. Informational advising consisted of "knowledge about the requirements, policies, and procedures of the institution, and very likely . . . about courses, resources, and various student services or helping agencies on campus" (p. 38). Developmental advising consisted of helping students to process feelings of uncertainty about "self, goals, and abilities or . . . the nature, rationale, and consequences of academic requirements" (pp. 24–25).

Although it might be convenient to think about advising in such dichotomous terms, there is evidence to the contrary. Trombley (1984) conducted a factor analysis of students' perceptions about the importance of 13 advising tasks. The author labeled the two resulting factors as Information (or informational advising) and Counseling (or developmental advising) roles, with the former including clerical and the latter involving more professional kinds of responsibilities. However, Trombley also pointed out that several tasks were common to both factors, suggesting that, in practice, advising can require complex skills "to balance information giving with helpful confrontation" (p. 238). Thus, although Kramer and Gardner's (1983) distinctions between informational and developmental advising may be instructive, effective advising probably requires a more subtle combination of the two. Ender et al. (1984), for example, described such an integrated developmental advising model, "intended to aid students in achieving educational, career, and personal goals" (p. 19). Those authors also argued that advisors could model self-directed behavior, in part, by sharing with students their decision-making strategies.

These contemporary advising views provide a framework for addressing students' career needs and expectations. A prominent theme is that of encouraging students to acquire and use career decision-making skills along with information about their selves and the world of work to identify, clarify, and progress toward career goals. In the next section, I describe several historical forces that contributed to a contemporary conceptualization of collegiate career advising.

ANTECEDENTS

Early Years

Higher Education

An examination of the history of higher education and counseling during the last decade of the 19th and first decade of the 20th century (Williamson, 1965) reveals an emerging emphasis on the development of the individual versus individuals *en masse*. William Rainey Harper (1905), president of the University of Chicago, characterized the latter perspective when he said, "Institutions of higher learning are accustomed to accord a common treatment to all the students within their walls . . . no matter how different their temperaments, how varied their tastes, or how peculiar their physical conditions. They are treated in mass" (pp. 93–94).

As an alternative to this mass education, Harper (1905) advocated that educators should assess "each student, in order to discover his capacities, his tastes, his tendencies, his weaknesses and his defects; and upon the basis of such a diagnosis his course of study should be arranged" (p. 94). Although Harper acknowledged that such an approach would be costly, he pointed out that "the waste avoided would more than counterbalance the cost" (p. 94).

Harper translated his vision for individualizing higher education into a close personal relationship between faculty and students directed at personal, social, and academic advising (Engle, 1954), designed to provide "assistance so essential to [the student's] highest success" (Harper, 1905, p. 321). Although Harper's goal of individualizing and personalizing student advising was innovative, he lacked a comprehensive model and an effective and widespread delivery system. Moreover, the time was not right. As Engle noted, the broader student personnel movement did not become widespread until the 1920s.

Maverick (1926) reported evidence for academicians' interest in and concern about formal advising involving vocational guidance. Beginning in 1911, several Stanford University faculty committees participated in the study and evaluation of vocational guidance at that institution. Reports included the results of guidance offered by individual departments (e.g., botany, mechanical engineering, and history). In its final report to the Stanford Academic Council, the Committee on Individual Training and Vocational Guidance recognized the wide variety of employment opportunities available to liberal arts graduates. However, the Committee noted that students' limited knowledge about occupations failed to prepare them to make wise choices. They further noted that departments were not providing students with effective vocational advising. The report stated that relying on departments for advising "insures that a large number of students shall not receive effective guidance" (Maverick, 1926, p. 26). To remedy these problems, the Committee recommended establishing an administrator to identify students' occupational information needs and to disseminate that information to them.

The Stanford Academic Council established a Committee on Vocational Guidance. The charge to this latter committee included "studying the vocations which are open to graduates of the university and the kinds of training needed by those who enter these vocations; and in disseminating among students the information necessary to make an intelligent choice of a vocation" (Maverick, 1926, p. 28). The new committee conducted an alumni survey of the occupational pursuits of its graduates and reported the results. By the end of 1914, the Committee completed its work, but the proposed administrator for vocational guidance was not appointed.

Apparently the Committee continued to perform quietly until recommending in a report to the president in 1923–1924 that the Committee add a vocational psychologist to its membership. The Committee also recommended offering a course in vocations, observing that

> students do not appreciate that they need vocational information, and therefore do not seek it. Some of them come to a realization of their need in the senior year and appeal for eleventh-hour advice, but others do not learn of their need until after graduation. (Maverick, 1926, p. 63)

A national survey of institutions offering vocational courses during the early 1920s revealed that all but three were in engineering and secondary schools. When offered, vocational courses emphasized characteristics of the occupation, including number of workers in the field, indicators of public interest in the occupation, information about salary, and education and training required for a position in that field. Maverick (1926) characterized the progress of such courses as "marked by failure and discontinuance" (p. 126).

To summarize, during the first quarter of the 20th century, advising for liberal arts students was limited, and vocational guidance was almost nonexistent. William Harper at the University of Chicago was one advocate for advising students, but his effectiveness was rather limited. In the long run, studies of and recommendations for vocational guidance, particularly by Stanford University faculty, were largely unsuccessful. Maverick (1926) identified at least one of the reasons for the lack of success. He said that when "vocational is applied to guidance, the phrase [vocational guidance] appears . . . to threaten the foundations of liberal education" (p. v). Judging from the limited extent of vocational guidance in colleges and universities during the first quarter of this century, I would have to conclude that most faculty and administrators agreed with Maverick's observation.

When and where then does one find evidence for the beginning of the practice and formal conceptualization of vocation advising or guidance? A wave of social and political reforms swept over many segments of the United States during the first two decades of the 20th century. Illustrative events included the massive migrations from Europe, the fight for women's suffrage, the founding of the National Association for the Advancement of Colored People, the beginning of the child study movement, and the emergence of the profession of social work. Vocational guidance constituted one of these reforms directed at improving the welfare of citizens by helping them to choose a vocation rather than simply to take a job.

Vocational Guidance

Most authorities identify Frank Parsons as the founder of vocational guidance in the United States. Although his bachelor's degree was in engineering and he was trained to practice law (Brewer, 1942), Parsons's vocation was that of a social reformer. He advocated such radical ideas as annual minimum wage, proper education, equal division of wealth, recalls, direct primaries, proportional representation, and women's suffrage (Mann, 1950).

Parsons's primary work was to develop an organization, known as the Vocation Bureau of Boston, to help youth choose a vocation. In a yearly report to the Executive Committee, Parsons stated that the Bureau had consulted with "over 80 young men and women from 15 to 39 years of age" (Brewer, 1942, p. 303) and concluded with his vision for the profession of vocational guidance. This instance was the first recorded use of the term (Brewer, 1942). He advocated that the profession "should become a part of the public school system in every community with experts trained as carefully in the art of vocational guidance as [those] trained today for medicine" (Brewer, 1942, p. 308).

Probably Parsons's most important legacy was not his recognition of the need for vocational guidance but rather his conceptualization of an integrated set of component elements for the profession. In his book, *Choosing a Vocation*, Parsons (1909) described the components:

> (1) A clear understanding of yourself, aptitudes, abilities, interests, ambitions, resources, limitations, and their causes; (2) a knowledge of the requirements and conditions of success, advantages and disadvantages, compensation, opportunities, and prospects in different lines of work; (3) true reasoning on the relations of these two groups of facts. (p. 5)

I would summarize those components as *who, what,* and *how.* "Who am I?" emphasizes a thorough knowledge of one's self. "What do occupations entail?" emphasizes a thorough knowledge of the world of work. "How do I evaluate the match between the self and work?" emphasizes a process of career decision making. I return to these three conditions later in the chapter.

Advocates for a thorough study of the self or person component in Parsons's model included well-known figures in the history of psychology. In 1911, Helen T. Woolley, president of Mount Holyoke College and trustee of the Vocation Bureau, initiated some of the earliest recorded research comparing the results of psychological testing of school children with peers who had left school for work. She reported that school children outperformed working children in logical thinking and language skills (Brewer, 1942, p. 204). In 1912, at the second meeting of the fledgling vocational guidance organization (subsequently called the National Vocational Guidance Association), Woolley recommended that schools develop psychology laboratories in conjunction with their vocation bureaus (i.e., guidance services; Brewer, 1942). Woolley made her recommendations despite concern about the limitations of experimental psychology in measuring subtle and complex phenomena of children, education, and work.

Industrial and Clinical Psychology

Hugo Münsterberg, a contemporary of Woolley's and an industrial psychologist, conducted selection studies on motormen, telephone operators, and ship officers (Münsterberg, 1913/1973). He identified advantages in using information from experimental psychology for vocational guidance saying,

> More important than the naked commercial profit on both sides, is the cultural gain which will come to the total economic life of the nation, as soon as every one can be brought to the place where his best energies may be unfolded and his greatest personal satisfaction secured. (p. 309)

In short, Münsterberg realized that, with information about the personal qualities of successful persons in different occupations, counselors could help young people choose vocational pursuits in which they would more likely be successful. However, a closer reading of Münsterberg (1913/1973) reveals his doubts and reservations regarding the short-term success in realizing the first component in Parsons's model, a thorough knowledge of one's self. Münsterberg said that "this work [assessment] of the experimental psychologist is the next step necessary" (p. 48). He also pointed out that counselors could "take up the results of such work . . . as soon as the experimental psychologist has developed the significant methods" (p. 48).

The scope of the present chapter precludes doing justice to the contributions of many other industrial psychologists to vocational guidance. I should mention, however, at least in passing, the work of Scott and Bingham, who developed ways to measure vocationally relevant mental traits, of Paterson and Elliott, who initiated the measurement of mechanical abilities that produced standardized tests of mechanical aptitudes for different occupations, of Strong, who measured vocational interests and used criterion groups, of the United States Employment Service, which produced a dictionary of occupational titles resulting from comprehensive job analyses, and of Thurstone, who developed techniques of factor analysis to identify an internal organization of psychological capabilities.

Industrial psychologists were not the only psychologists to appreciate the value of psychological testing for increasing an understanding of the person. Most readers are probably familiar with Litner Witmer, whom authorities credit with founding the first psychological clinic at the University of Pennsylvania in 1896. However, few individuals know about the work of Morris Viteles who, in 1921, founded a unit within Witmer's clinic and called it the Vocational Guidance Clinic. The Guidance Clinic conducted extensive individual assessments of "individuals of minimum working-age level and over" (Viteles, 1925, p. 78) and addressed educational problems to the extent that they were pertinent to vocational adjustment. The emphasis in the Clinic was on the administration and use of psychological tests, that is, the assessment of the individual.

Despite the acknowledged advantages of assessment, during the first 20 years of the 20th century, psychological science was not sufficiently developed to assist Parsons and others with individual assessment instruments. To quote Paterson (1938), "Parsons knew what was needed, but when he went to the psychological laboratories for techniques he found that the cupboard was bare" (p. 37).

Decline in Emphasis on Assessing Individuals

In addition to the limitations of relevant vocational instruments for individual assessment, the successful application of the first part of Parsons's model was dealt a death blow from at least two sources. Meyer Bloomfield, Parsons's successor at the Vocation Bureau, wrote in 1911 that "it is very doubtful whether psychological tests can be used to advantage by the counselor. . . . Laboratory psychology, however, is not far enough advanced to enable one to fathom bent and aptitude" (Bloomfield, 1911, p. 94). Bloomfield further recommended and emphasized the value of using community resources to learn more about the demands of occupations, that is, he emphasized Parsons's second step, knowledge of the world of work.

A second source that contributed to a reduction in the perceived importance of individual assessment was school administrators' decision to place teachers, not psychologists, in charge of vocational guidance (Williamson, 1965). Such a decision was unfortunate, according to Williamson, because "Münsterberg, and later industrial psychologists, understood Parsons' reasoning and strategy better than did vocational educators" (p. 98) even though, according to Brewer (1942), the early psychologists "were more interested in selection than in guidance" (p. 202). It is ironic that the same task (assessment) that could be used to advise students about selecting positions was developed in large measure through the influence of those who needed similar tools to select employees.

The failure of educators to consider fully Parsons's first step, to adopt Woolley's recommendation of psychology laboratories in schools, to recognize Münsterberg's approach for identifying personal characteristics of successful workers in different occupations, or to implement Viteles' model of extensive individual assessment was not limited to vocational guidance at the high school level. As I pointed out earlier in describing the Stanford University study, there was no evidence that the first step in Parsons's model was a significant factor in faculty advising during at least the first 25 years of the 20th century.

Separating vocational guidance from psychological laboratories with assessment instruments produced a wide gap between high school counselors and industrial psychologists. This split later caused Paterson (1938) to refer to vocational counselors "as being arrested in their professional development on the level of occupational information" (p. 38). Paterson further admonished counselors (advisers and teachers) by asserting, "Mere knowledge of industry and of vocational information is not enough" (p. 42). However, the practice of assessing personal attributes and traits in the fields of vocational guidance and counseling would occur only after World War II.

From the 1920s to the 1940s, there was an evolution in vocational guidance theories. The matching of "people and machines" emphasized the job, whereas the trait-factor approach emphasized the individual. Moreover, according to Crites (1969), the trait-factor approach to counseling contended "that vocational choice is largely a conscious, cognitive problem-solving process" (p. 119). The problem-solving facet of the trait-factor view constituted the seeds for the emergence of Parsons's third component, a decision-making process, for matching characteristics of workers and attributes of work. An emphasis on decision making also emerged after World War II.

Coming of Age: Parsons Revisited

If the changes during the 1920s to the 1940s constituted an evolution in vocational guidance, then changes during the 1950s constituted a revolution (Aubrey, 1977). Forces that undermined the trait-factor approach to vocational guidance grew out of the experiences of the Great Depression and World War II and their aftermath, including such developments as the benefits of the GI Bill and increased economic prosperity. A mood in the population favoring increased freedom and autonomy contributed to a breakthrough in thinking about people and work, as well as in professional theory and practice.

In his 1950 National Vocational Guidance Association (NVGA) presidential address, Hoppock stated that the traditional view of vocational guidance was crumbling. In his 1951 NVGA presidential address, Super recommended a new definition for vocational guidance that included the concepts of self and satisfaction. After almost 40 years, NVGA expanded its objectives from emphasis on occupational information to include "mental health," that is, individuals and their well being (Williamson, 1965). In 1952, NVGA and several other groups, including the Guidance Supervisors and Counselors Trainers (now called the Association for Counselor Education and Supervision) and the American College Personnel Association, formed a federation of organizations known as the American Personnel and Guidance Association (now called the American Association for Counseling and Development), "giving more adequate expression to the current interest in general adjustment" (Super, 1955, p. 6).

Not coincidentally, in 1951, a group of 60 prominent leaders in vocational guidance and counseling held the Northwestern Conference. Those leaders met and gave formal definition to the term *counseling psychologist*; they also established standards for training doctoral-level psychologists. The NVGA and the Division of Counseling and Guidance (DCG) had areas of overlap and distinctiveness regarding personnel and mission. Many individuals belonged to both organizations, and members of both organizations were interested in problems associated with work. They differed in that the membership of NVGA was considerably more heterogeneous, including individuals from "education, community service, psychology, and business" (Super, 1955, p. 6), whereas membership in the DCG consisted primarily of psychologists. In addition, members of the NVGA focused on vocational choice and adjustment, whereas members of the DCG were interested in problems of life adjustment that included but were not limited to a person's vocation.

Formal recognition of counseling psychology occurred in 1952 when the Veterans Administration revised job specifications and replaced vocational counselors with counseling psychologists. Subsequently, the American Psychological Association's (APA) Division 17 changed its name from the Division of Counseling and Guidance to the Division of Counseling Psychology (DCP; Super, 1955).

In the 1950s, investigators in vocational guidance and counseling psychology revised their perspectives about people and work. The emphasis on self-concept and satisfaction recognized the importance of identifying one's interests, values, preferences, and aptitudes and using those personal characteristics in selecting employment that could lead to greater satisfaction with and success in one's chosen field. As a parenthetical note, the emphasis on satisfaction was not without its critics. Brayfield (1961) argued that vocational counseling was "putting a premium on *satisfaction* and de-emphasizing *performance*" (italics in the original; p. 40). Brayfield further concluded that "vocational counseling conducted with a self-realization or happiness orientation *may* induce job expectancies which cannot be realized" (italics in the original; p. 42).

Not only was the emphasis on self and satisfaction revolutionary, the emphasis on choosing (i.e., decision making) and development was novel as well. In 1951, Ginzberg, Ginzberg, Axelrad, and Herma published a book that presented an explicit theory of career decision making, and they conceptualized the choice of a vocation as a developmental process spanning several years from late childhood to early adulthood. From a guidance perspective, viewing individuals as choosing a vocation focused attention on skills and the process of decision making and away from the needs of the market place. By the end of the 1960s, advocates of a decision-making perspective argued that counseling should be a learning experience in decision making (Herr & Cramer, 1979). Krumboltz's (1979) social learning theory of career decision making illustrates one of the most elaborate decision-making perspectives. His model identified a wide range of environmental conditions, learning experiences, and personal variables that can influence career choices.

Concomitant with the conceptual changes in guidance and counseling was a name change. As Herr and Cramer (1979) pointed out, "By the late 1960s and early 1970s, the term career guidance was appearing in the professional literature almost as frequently as the term vocational guidance" (p. 9). However, changes in the names of journals and organizations did not take place until the 1980s. For example, the *Personnel and Guidance Journal* became the *Journal of Counseling and Development* in 1984. The *Vocational Guidance Quarterly* became the *Career Development Quarterly* in 1987; and the *Journal of College Student Personnel* became the *Journal of College Student Development* in 1988.

In summary, factors that contributed to contemporary career advising for college students involved professional and social–economic developments. Professional developments included evolutions in the fields of vocational guidance, industrial and clinical psychology, counseling psychology, and career guidance, as well as the emergence of life-cycle perspectives. Market place conditions during the Great Depression and World Wars I and II placed a premium on survival needs and industrial production. After World War II, with increased sophistication in test construction and job analysis and greater emphasis on the autonomy and welfare of workers, the modern framework of career guidance incorporated Parsons's three-fold vision but in ways that Parsons could not have imagined. Organizing themes for guidance included not only self-understanding and decision making, but also self-concept, satisfaction, alternatives, and contingency planning to cope with rapidly changing conditions. How this history of career guidance contributed to collegiate career advising is clarified in the next section.

Career Guidance and Career Education

The field of career education emerged after career guidance and counseling psychology in the 1950s and 1960s. Career education possessed many of the same themes as career guidance and achieved objectives in classrooms that were similar to ones that career guidance achieved in counselors' offices.

Identifying the similarities and differences between career development, career education, and career guidance might help in understanding how career guidance contributed to collegiate career advising. The observations and distinctions that follow draw extensively from Hoyt (1978).

Most experts view career development as part of a broader process of human development, but with an emphasis on career awareness, career planning and preparation, career initiation and maintenance, and so forth. Although both career guidance and career education use this career development perspective, they differ in two fundamental ways. Career guidance emphasizes services to increase self-understanding, knowledge of education and employment opportunities, career decision making, and job-entry skills, whereas career education emphasizes teaching and learning processes. Participants in career guidance are usually limited to professional counselors. By contrast, participants in career education include classroom teachers, parents and other members of the family, members of the work force, and professional counselors.

What are the goals of career education? Preparation for work is one of the basic goals of education, including career education, at all educational levels. Authorities view the attainment of this goal as the responsibility of both teaching faculty and student personnel officials. The requisite knowledge associated with career education includes knowledge about self and about educational and occupational opportunities. The requisite skills include decision making; job-entry skills such as job seeking, resumé preparation, and interviewing; and job-holding skills. Career education also seeks to promote positive job-related attitudes and behaviors. Such transferable attitudes and behaviors include showing up on time, completing assigned tasks on time, and performing as a team member by cooperating with fellow students.

Hoyt (1978) observed that the implementation of career education has been limited to elementary and secondary schools. Colleges and universities have been very resistant to career education. Recall Maverick's comments (1926) quoted earlier in the chapter about the perceived threat to liberal education. I examine this criticism later when describing the advantages of a life-cycle perspective.

Although career guidance and career advising commentators of the 1980s offered comprehensive and integrated approaches to advising, they failed, by themselves, to identify and articulate pertinent developmental stages and tasks for higher education or collegiate advising. In the following section, I describe salient features of Chickering and Havighurst's (1981) life-cycle perspective, which included developmental stages and tasks, and identify the advantages of their perspective.

Life-Cycle Perspective for Higher Education

Life-cycle investigators looked for an orderly, age-related sequence of behavioral changes called *life stages*. The results of three studies reported in the 1970s (Gould, 1972; Levinson, Darrow, Klein, Levinson, & McKee, 1978; Sheehy, 1976) described a general pattern of development beginning with a transition from adolescence to young adulthood (in the late teens and early 20s) and then to late adulthood. The identification of life stages during the adult years stimulated research that contributed landmark insights into an understanding of adult behavior.

Although the identification of age-related adult life stages was noteworthy, the significance of findings about gender differences was profound.

The variability among students is not only age related but gender related as well. A concise summary is that most men and women have experienced adulthood differently. A traditional role expectation has been for young women to maintain diffuse ego boundaries until marriage, so that ego development could conform to spouse and family. Moreover, in the traditional roles, young men left the family to explore and develop a career, but young women transferred commitments from their parents' family to their own. For women, developing autonomy and a career had been inconsistent with traditional expectations for starting a family. Events in the 1980s and 1990s have modified this simplified view of traditional role expectations for women and men. But with increased opportunities for women, such as day care facilities, parental leave policies, and prospects for pursuing both family and career, the young adult stage for women has become even more demanding and complicated. One implication of the findings about these differences is the necessity to understand and use knowledge about developmental gender differences to increase the quality and effectiveness of advising.

Identification of relevant developmental tasks provides another opportunity for enhancing the quality of advising all undergraduates. Chickering and Havighurst (1981) described the following developmental tasks for traditional college-age students: achieving emotional independence, preparing for marriage (or a committed relationship) and family, choosing and preparing for a career, and developing an ethical system. I elaborate on two of these tasks for illustrative purposes. Achieving emotional independence consists of becoming less dependent on family and other supports and becoming more reliant on one's self. Accomplishing this task can be more complicated for those women who conform to a traditional role that dictates a diffuse ego that adapts to the demands of spouse and family and avoids autonomy and career pursuits. Astin (1984) clarified the career-related issues facing women in her sociopsychological model of career choice. She asserted that women and men have similar work motivations but different work expectations. The differences in work expectations come about as a consequence of difference in sex-role socialization.

Choosing and preparing for a career constitutes "the organizing center for the lives of most men and women" (Chickering & Havighurst, 1981, p. 32). Since at least the 1950s, most individuals in the United States have not been employed primarily for satisfying the survival needs for food, clothing, and shelter. For many people, employment represents an expression of the individual's self, serving to challenge and satisfy more than survival needs. Moreover, because of the complexity of the marketplace and because of changes over time in personal (interests, abilities, etc.) and situational (economic, technological, etc.) variables, there is little likelihood that colleges or graduate and professional schools can prepare individuals for work that can extend to 70 years of age and beyond.

An additional implication of mastering developmental tasks is that career preparation and liberal education perspectives need not be antagonistic. If one views the former as having a greater emphasis on instrumental tasks and the latter on expressive tasks, the combination of both perspectives offers more than either does alone. Later in the chapter, I return to and elaborate on an integrated perspective for career preparation and liberal education.

Chickering and Havighurst (1981) also identified developmental tasks and educational implications for life stages at 23 to 35, 35 to 45, 45 to 57, 57 to 65, and 65 years of age and over. Limiting my description of developmental tasks to the traditional college-age population serves to illustrate the value of identifying stage-specific developmental tasks. Readers should note, however, that adjustments to and revisions in one's work and career constitute important tasks at each of the developmental stages.

A life-cycle perspective consisting of developmental stages and tasks offers advantages that include a framework to (a) emphasize vocational development during and after college, (b) incorporate decision-making skills among the many skills that students acquire and highlight the inextricable importance of knowledge about self and the world of work in career decision making, and (c) integrate seemingly disparate views about career preparation and liberal education. I examine each of these advantages in turn.

Career Development During and After College

The life-cycle perspective offers an understanding of a range of problems that students can experience during and after college. Some problems seem inherent in being a student. Other problems appear related to the contemporary environment or culture.

An examination of vocational development during and after college reveals a consistent pattern. Blocher and Rapoza (1981) summarized the research findings for students entering college by reporting "that most students enter . . . with pat, superficial 'pseudo-plans' heavily influenced by the expectations of significant others, and that these 'plans' are quickly abandoned" (p. 215). For many students, college experiences contribute to an identification of or a change in their perceptions of themselves, others, and the world around them and to planning and decision making for work and career. Many students accomplish the developmental task of making a commitment to pursue a career after college. However, many other students, including so-called adult learners who have started college later in life or who have returned to college after several years, find themselves grappling with a reevaluation of career alternatives.

The circumstances facing female students have unique facets. The evidence indicates that "powerful negative influences inhibit the career development of women in the college years" (Blocher & Rapoza, 1981,

p. 219). Additional problems include a lack of experiences (a) promoting an awareness of the range of career alternatives available to women, (b) development career planning and decision-making skills, and (c) facilitating the acquisition of strategies for resolving conflicts involving career, marriage (or a committed relationship), and family.

Finally, educators must recognize the realities of employment for the foreseeable future. Career investigators have reported that undergraduate school, graduate school, or professional training cannot completely prepare students for work. The data indicate that traditional college-age students "will change jobs seven times and careers three times" (Shipton & Steltenpohl, 1981, p. 690) during a lifetime. A life-cycle perspective helps one to realize that changes in marketplace conditions contribute to changes in careers after graduation from college.

Career Decision-Making Skills

Given what is known about factors contributing to success and failure in accomplishing the developmental task of choosing, as well as changing and preparing for, a career, what skills can advisers and teachers foster to facilitate students' development toward career maturity? Career decision-making skills, emphasizing knowledge of both the self and the world of work, seem to constitute a core requirement.

Shipton and Steltenpohl (1981) described an educational advising and career counseling decision-making model that includes defining the task, gathering information, establishing a values hierarchy, making a choice, and taking action. The authors pointed out that in the second stage of decision making, the ideal approach is to gather information about one's self and the external world. Relevant information about one's self includes interests, skills, values, and life-style preferences. In my review of vocational advising before World War II (Ware, 1991) and from my experiences with faculty advisers, I have found a chronic omission of the importance of obtaining and using information about one's self in career decision making. Historically, the emphasis has been on providing students with information about the world of work; there has been a failure to encourage students to examine their personal attributes. In the context of this chapter, the advantages to emphasizing self-exploration include

> gaining an understanding of tasks already accomplished and those yet to be achieved, realizing that one's interests and preferences change over time, understanding the crises and strains of transition periods, and visualizing what is yet to come give students of *all ages* [italics added] a broader perspective on future possibilities as well as deeper insight into present needs. (Shipton & Steltenpohl, 1981, p. 695)

Fostering the acquisition of career decision-making skills, in general, equips students with transferable skills and prepares them for changing and adjusting to subsequent career choices. In brief, teaching students career decision-making skills has both short- and long-term benefits.

Teaching students these transferable skills cannot be limited to advisers because of faculty's heavily committed schedules and students' inability to learn career development principles in a vacuum (i.e., without observing the struggles and successes of their peers). In planning strategies and materials for advising, we cannot rule out the classroom as a suitable environment, at least for some students. Crites (1974) distinguished between students experiencing indecision and students experiencing indecisiveness. With indecision, anxiety is more transient and is a consequence of a career choice. With indecisiveness, anxiety is chronic and precedes a career choice. The classroom may be better suited for the students with the former type of condition and the counselor's office with the latter.

Critics abound who testify to the contradiction between career preparation and liberal education. Although this chapter will not likely resolve that contentious debate, examining the overlap between career preparation and liberal education might foster collaboration rather than dispute among advocates for each.

Career Preparation and Liberal Education

There are several themes that point to a convergence between career preparation and liberal education. As I pointed out earlier in this chapter, one need not view career preparation and liberal education as dichotomous but rather as approaches to learning that vary in emphasis on instrumental and expressive tasks. Recall that instrumental tasks involve goals beyond the tasks themselves and expressive tasks goals as ends in themselves. Because both career preparation and liberal education require instrumental and expressive tasks and because most life activities require both kinds of tasks, career preparation and liberal education have much in common.

Career development specialists view career development as part of the general development of individuals that includes asking and answering questions about self, interests, values, and ways of thinking about the world of work. Such views are not inconsistent and even overlap with views about the goals of higher education, including "(a) knowledge, skills, and attitudes, (b) self-determination, and (c) an ability to control one's environment" (Ender et al., 1984, p. 10).

Advocates for psychology in the liberal education tradition (McGovern, Furumoto, Halpern, Kimble, & McKeachie, 1991; see also the chapter by McGovern in this book) have pointed out that, historically, psychology educators have emphasized "breadth, content, scientific methodology, and intellectual sophistication. The aim was to teach students to ask questions about behavior and to understand the ingredients of good answers" (McGovern et al., 1991, p. 599). Most of the psychology major's common goals (McGovern et al., 1991), including acquiring a knowledge base, thinking skills, language skills, information-gathering and synthesis skills, interpersonal skills, and a historical perspective are also among the goals and strategies of at least one career development course (Ware, 1988). Thus, there is no necessary contradiction between career preparation and the liberal arts tradition for the undergraduate psychology major.

Unless a person holds a dogmatic position that dichotomizes career preparation and liberal education, Hogan's (1991) suggestion for a "liberal skills model" (p. 152) provides additional common ground. The model "focuses attention on the many competencies that have broad applicability to work and nonwork situations" (Hogan, 1991, p. 152). Hogan's proposal resonates with comments from McGovern et al. (1991), who said that liberal arts education and the study of psychology constituted "a preparation for lifelong learning, thinking, and action . . . [emphasizing] specialized and general knowledge and skills" (p. 600). The authors also acknowledged that "definitions of liberal education may need some rethinking" (p. 600). This latter assertion about reevaluating the meaning of a liberal arts education seems sympathetic to a career preparation view (Ware, 1982).

Hogan (1991) proposed that strategies should "include improved career education and . . . that career preparation should be enhanced across the psychology curriculum" (p. 152). Hogan's proposal may sound radical to individuals who identify career preparation with the historical tradition of vocational education. Distinguishing the two, using Hoyt's (1978) conceptualization, can be useful in this regard.

The thrust of career education is on acquiring skills, including basic academic skills as well as decision-making skills, job-acquisition and retention skills, and personally meaningful work values. By contrast, the focus of vocational education is on a substantive knowledge designed for specific job entry. In addition, career education is targeted at students at all educational levels, including the college or university level, whereas vocational education is targeted at students at the secondary or prebaccalaureate levels only. On the other hand, all educators can participate in career education; on the other hand, vocational educators are usually the only ones who participate in vocational education programs. Finally, career education consists of developing students' skills in several areas, such as communication, critical thinking, logical reasoning, and competition, but vocational education concentrates on specific vocational skills. In contrast to vocational education with its short-term goals, career education advocates long-term goals and emphasizes transferable skills for employment, family, and leisure time activities, consistent with the goals of liberal education.

This examination of the roots of collegiate advising leads to an inquiry regarding specific advising strategies or practices in the field of psychology. In the section that follows, I describe a case study, with historical details, of the career advising program at one institution, Creighton University.

The purpose of the case study is to identify the several components and benefits of such career-advising programs. In this case, the components include academic courses, conversation hours, videotapes, a colloquium series, printed materials, a skill-identification project, and faculty advising, each of which are discussed below.

STRATEGIES: A CASE STUDY

By the mid-1970s, one survey (Haney & Howland, 1978) revealed that 63% of those 2- and 4-year colleges that responded to a survey offered career courses for credit. A literature review I conducted in the spring of 1991 identified 27 published studies describing or evaluating credit-earning career courses. (I will provide a copy of those references to individuals requesting it.) Although comprehensive career education programs at the collegiate level are rare, courses and strategies emphasizing career development are quite common. Examples include courses in career choice and field placement, and programs in career guidance and college placement services (Ware & Millard, 1987).

Using the three-component career guidance model, in the following section I describe a career development course (Ware, 1981; Ware, 1985; Ware & Beischel, 1979), including the results of evaluative research (Ware, 1991) and other components of the career advising program.

Career Development Course

Logistics

The class meets for 50 minutes, three times a week for 14 weeks. I use a traditional lecture format, small group discussion, written assignments, locally and commercially produced videotape programs and booklets, career inventories, and out-of-class skill development tasks. This multidimensional approach to the course engages students in as many ways as possible and illustrates what some refer to as *active learning*. Printed materials include books by Figler (1988) and Super and Super (1982) and two booklets about career development and graduate school (Ware, 1987; Ware, 1990a). I have also compiled several published articles in a booklet (Ware, 1990b). These articles are listed in Appendix 1.

Content

The content of the course involves three components: increasing students' knowledge about themselves, increasing their awareness of postgraduate educational and occupational opportunities, and enhancing their job-entry skills. (Interested readers may obtain a more detailed description of the course by writing to me.)

Evaluation

Ware (1988) summarized the results from four studies conducted from 1979 to 1985 that evaluated the effectiveness of the career development course. All four studies included junior and senior psychology majors who either took or did not take the course. Students taking the course reported significantly greater increases in (a) knowledge about themselves, the world of work, and job-entry skills, (b) information-seeking thoughts and behaviors, (c) career maturity, and (d) identity; students also reported decreases in (e) occupational information seeking and (f) occupational barriers.

What conclusions follow from the findings? Quoting from the chapter,

> The finding of this research program demonstrate that students entering the course needed more than information about the world of work and job search skills. Restricting one's efforts to providing information about work and job skills may limit students' career development by failing to establish a foundation in interest, value, and ability exploration and clarification. (Ware, 1988, p. 72)

Although those comments are still appropriate in the context of Parsons' model for vocational guidance, I am now particularly aware of a significant limitation in teaching and evaluating the career development course. As a consequence of teaching the course, observing students' career-related behaviors outside of the classroom, and preparing this chapter, I have concluded that we need to give significantly greater attention to developing career decision-making skills. I believe that developing such skills in students is one of the most productive endeavors we can pursue.

Other Components of the Program

With its many advantages, the career development course only reaches from 10 to 20% of psychology majors. What are some other ways to promote career awareness, exploration, and decision making? Additional components of the program include a field placement course, conversation hours, videotapes, a colloquium series, printed materials, a skill-identification project, and faculty advising. In general, all of the components transmit information about the world of work or graduate school and information that is specifically work related; some components of the program also emphasize the importance of understanding one's self in the career selection process.

Field Placement Course

A second career-related course is a field placement course called Externship in Psychology. Each semester, this course has a maximum enrollment of 15 junior and senior psychology majors in each of two sections. One section of the course concentrates on placements in human services settings and the other on placements in business or governmental settings. Primary goals include exposing students to a range of psychological or business-related work environments. Placement activities vary depending on the setting and the student's skills. Professionals at the agency and the instructor provide supervision.

Ware, Millard, and Matthews (1984) described the course and an evaluation of its effectiveness. Students enrolled in the course and a similar group of students not enrolled in the course were pre- and posttested, using quantitative measures of inter- and intrapersonal characteristics. The results of analysis of difference scores revealed no significant differences between the groups on any of the 22 measures. Because personality measures appeared resistant to change, we developed an activities checklist and used it in a subsequent study (Ware, Pusanik, & Matthews, 1990) evaluating field placement and comparison groups from different universities. Analysis revealed more differences between placement and comparison groups than between placement groups from different universities. The activities checklist appeared more sensitive than personality measures and offered a first step in assessing the impact of placement experiences. Preliminary findings indicated that field placement experiences contributed to enlightening students about some facets of the world of work and developing occupationally relevant skills.

Conversation Hours

Each semester, I conduct two conversation hours. Topical presentations about graduate school and occupational opportunities for bachelor's-level psychology graduates allow contact with students who might be missed in the career development and field placement courses. In each conversation hour, I emphasize that an integral part of deciding about employment or graduate school is identifying one's career goals. I also point out that because one's values, interests, and abilities contribute directly or indirectly to the identification of those goals, increasing knowledge about one's self can assist in identifying one's goals. As measured by student attendance and follow-up contacts, the conversation hours are moderately successful.

Colloquium Series

Ware and Matthews (1980) designed a colloquium series to stimulate career exploration and research among undergraduate students. Speakers included individuals both within and outside the department. Students gave presentations at the last meeting of the spring semester. The results from a formal student evaluation supported the value of the series for increasing student awareness regarding career alternatives. Moreover, the number of students participating in research increased at least 10-fold since initiation of the series.

Printed Materials

The print medium provides another way to communicate to students. Printed materials have the advantage of being widely disseminated and available to students during their leisure time. I have developed brochures designed to answer three questions students commonly ask: "What can I do with a major in psychology?" "What can I do now that I'm a psychology major?" and "What if I want to go to graduate school in psychology?" All brochures are available from the department, and new majors automatically receive copies of the first two brochures in the mail. Another valuable resource, published by the APA, that may be recommended is the book *Is Psychology the Major for You?* (Woods & Wilkinson, 1987).

In response to many students' request about what courses they should take, I have developed five curricular guides. There is one guide each for students wanting to pursue (a) employment in business following graduation, (b) employment in human/social services following graduation, (c) graduate education at the doctoral level in psychology, (d) professional education in medicine or dentistry, and (e) professional education in law. The guides identify specific courses in the major, supporting areas, and skill areas. Students can acquire these materials at no cost from the department.

I have also produced two booklets for psychology majors; one is *Career Development and Opportunities for Psychology Majors* (Ware, 1987). This booklet contains sections describing a career development model, self-assessment, the world of work and occupations that psychology majors pursue, strategies for developing one's credentials, and information about developing the job search skills, such as establishing personal contacts, writing a resumé, and preparing for job interviews.

A second booklet, *Pursuing Graduate Study in Psychology* (Ware, 1990a), describes approaches for preparing and learning about graduate schools, as well as for taking standardized tests, selecting and applying to graduate school, surveying graduate pursuits of Creighton psychology alumni, deciding on which school to attend, setting a timetable for preparing for graduate school, and discussing salient issues about the Graduate Record Exam and the Miller Analogy Test. Another valuable resource that is currently being revised is *Preparing for Graduate Study in Psychology: NOT for Seniors Only!* (Fretz & Stang, 1980). For selecting specific graduate schools, APA's biannual *Graduate Study in Psychology and Associated Fields* is recommended. Students who are definitely planning on graduate school might find the book *How to Manage Your Career in Psychology*, published by the APA, useful for long-term planning (Kilburg, 1991).

TABLE 2
Grouping of Skills That Students Can Acquire From Psychology Courses

Type of skill	Description
Communication	Speak in a clear, concise, and persuasive manner
	Write coherent and well-organized essays
Team member	Develop rapport at group level and stimulate enthusiasm
	Adapt readily to organizational rules and procedures
Human relations	Tolerant of values and attitudes different from mine
	Identify and understand emotional disorders in children, adolescents, or adults
Data collection, analysis, and retrieval	Collect, record, organize, analyze, or interpret empirical data
	Use computers to retrieve information from library sources
Laboratory research	Formulate hypotheses
	Design and conduct an experimental or quasi-experimental study
Cognitive	Assimilate large amounts of information
	Think logically, critically, and creatively

Videotapes

Videotape programs are a supplement and sometimes an alternative to the conversation hours. I have developed two videotapes, *Career Development and Opportunities for Psychology Majors* (Ware & Sroufe, 1984a) and *Pursuing Graduate Study in Psychology* (Ware & Sroufe, 1984b). Student, faculty, and administrative evaluations of the tapes have been favorable (Ware, 1984). The APA also has available a videotape, *Career Encounters in Psychology*, which many undergraduates have found useful. Advantages of the videotapes include gaining and maintaining students' attention and providing an easily accessible medium in the university's library.

Skill-Identification Project

By adapting a strategy that McGovern (1979) reported, I initiated a skill-identification project. In helping students prepare resumés and applications for work and graduate or professional school, I have observed that many students experience great difficulty in identifying the skills they have acquired from psychology and other courses. When applying for a job or to graduate or professional school, a salient description of one's skills can increase the odds of being selected.

To assist students in identifying such skills, psychology faculty selected skills that they thought students could acquire from their classes. Table 2 contains a partial listing of those skills. (Interested readers may obtain a detailed description of the skills by writing to me.) Publishing this list of skills for each course has assisted students in identifying and communicating about those skills they have acquired. Because I only recently undertook this project, there has been insufficient time to evaluate its effectiveness.

Faculty Advising

The department maintains a long-standing academic advising program. However, the broader career-advising perspective has varied with the skill and interest level of individual faculty members (Ware, 1986). One effort at improving advising consisted of raising the consciousness level of faculty, sensitizing them to students' career needs and providing them with referral sources when they did not feel comfortable or competent in handling students' inquiries. Another book published by the APA, *Is Psychology for Them?* provides a good overview of the departmental advising process for new faculty (Woods, 1988).

Students' Perspectives

Components of the career development program emerged primarily from faculty's perceptions about students' needs. To assess career concerns from the students' perspective, I constructed a two-page questionnaire and distributed it to a random sample of psychology majors (Ware, 1986). Students rated the types and sources of career information that were available in the department and at the university. Students gave higher ratings to information about courses, careers, and job-entry skills than to information about career aptitudes and interests. From the students' perspective, the comprehensive program described in this chapter appeared successful in meeting their priorities for career information. However, the results also suggested that faculty must continue (a) to educate students about the importance of acquiring information about themselves as a part of their career development and (b) to produce a variety of sources and types of career information and services.

One thing some students failed to recognize and what the career advising program failed to address was the importance and role of career decision making. In the context of the history of vocational guidance and now career guidance, I urge teachers to help student develop career decision-making skills. Teaching decision-making skills is wholly compatible with a liberal arts tradition that promotes critical thinking and problem solving. Career decision making simply directs those skills to a particular task.

CONCLUSION

In the first part of this chapter, I examined collegiate career advising by documenting the status quo, that is, by describing students' negative views toward advising during the last decade. Evidence from the NACADA survey indicated that one of the reasons for students' dissatisfaction was the discrepancy between what they wanted and what they were getting. I concluded the first part of the chapter with a brief description of a contemporary advising conceptualization that emphasized career decision making, information about one's self, and knowledge about the world of work.

Drawing from literature about higher education, vocational guidance, industrial and clinical psychology, counseling psychology, career guidance, and the life-cycle perspective, in the bulk of the chapter I examined the antecedents for career advising that emerged during the 20th century. Documented themes consisted of assessment of the individual (who), knowledge of the world of work (what), and career decision-making skills (how), all in a life-cycle or developmental perspective. A few academicians were sympathetic to vocational guidance, but the impetus for vocational guidance came from the contexts of settlement houses and precollege education. Early leaders in industrial and clinical psychology were advocates for developing techniques for individual assessment and job analysis. By midcentury, professional organizations of counselors and psychologists placed a renewed emphasis on the importance of personality variables. The benefits of a life-cycle perspective applied to higher education included (a) emphasizing vocational development during and after college, (b) incorporating decision-making skills among the many skills that students acquire, and (c) integrating seemingly disparate views about career preparation and liberal education. Significant historical and social events that contributed to the evolution in perspectives about advising and work constituted another dimension in this section of the chapter.

The final section of the chapter presented a case study and historical account describing strategies developed for one career advising program. The program illustrated ways to address the salient themes (who, what, and how) and issues that have characterized the history of collegiate career advising in America.

REFERENCES

American Psychological Association. (1990). *Graduate study in psychology and associated fields*. Washington, DC: Author.

Astin, H. S. (1984). The meaning of work in women's lives: A sociopsychological model of career choice and work behavior. *Counseling Psychologist, 12*, 117–126.

Aubrey, R. F. (1977). Historical development of guidance and counseling and implications for the future. *Personnel and Guidance Journal, 55*, 288–295.

Beatty, J. D. (1991). The National Academic Advising Association: A brief narrative history. *NACADA Journal, 11*, 5–25.

Blocher, D. H., & Rapoza, R. S. (1981). Professional and vocational preparation. In A. W. Chickering (Ed.), *The modern American college: Responding to the new realities of diverse students and a changing society* (pp. 212–231). San Francisco: Jossey-Bass.

Bloomfield, M. (1911). *The vocational guidance of youth*. Boston: Houghton Mifflin.

Brayfield, A. H. (1961). Vocational counseling today. In M. S. Viteles, A. H. Brayfield, & L. E. Tyler, *Vocational counseling: A reappraisal in honor of Donald G. Paterson*. Minneapolis: University of Minnesota Press.

Brewer, J. M. (1942). *History of vocational guidance: Origins and early development*. New York: Harper.

Career encounters in psychology [Videotape]. (1991). Washington, DC: American Psychological Association.

Chickering, A. W., & Havighurst, R. J. (1981). The life cycle. In A. W. Chickering (Ed.), *The modern American college: Responding to the new realities of diverse students and a changing society* (pp. 16–50). San Francisco: Jossey-Bass.

Crites, J. O. (1969). *Vocational psychology: The study of vocational behavior and development*. New York: McGraw-Hill.

Crites, J. O. (1974). Career counseling: A review of major approaches. *Counseling Psychologist, 4*(3), 3–23.

Crockett, D. S., & Levitz, R. S. (1984). Current advising practices in colleges and universities. In R. B. Winston, Jr., T. K. Miller, & S. C. Ender (Eds.), *Developmental academic advising: Addressing students' educational, career, and personal needs* (pp. 35–63). San Francisco: Jossey-Bass.

DeCoster, D. A., & Mable, P. (1981). Interpersonal relationships. In D. A. DeCoster & P. Mable (Eds.), *Understanding today's students* (pp. 35–47). San Francisco: Jossey-Bass.

Ender, S. C., Winston, R. B., Jr., & Miller, T. K. (1984). Academic advising reconsidered. In R. B. Winston, Jr., T. K. Miller, & S. C. Ender (Eds.), *Developmental academic advising: Addressing students' educational, career, and personal needs* (pp. 3–34). San Francisco: Jossey-Bass.

Engle, G. W. (1954). William Rainey Harper's conceptions of the structuring of the functions performed by educational institutions (Doctoral dissertation, University of Michigan, Ann Arbor; University Microfilms, No. 369, pp. 109–111, 147–148).

Figler, H. (1988). *The complete job-search handbook: All the skills you need to get any job and have a good time doing it* (rev. ed.). New York: Henry Holt.

Fretz, B. R., & Stang, D. J. (1980). *Preparing for graduate study: NOT for seniors only*. Washington, DC: American Psychological Association.

Ginzberg, E., Ginzberg, S. W., Axelrad, S., & Herma, J. L. (1951). *Occupational choice*. New York: Columbia University Press.

Gould, R. L. (1972). The phases of adult life: A study in developmental psychology. *American Journal of Psychiatry, 129*, 521–531.

Haney, T., & Howland, P. A. (1978). Career courses for credit: Necessity or luxury? *Journal of College Placement, 38*, 75–79.

Harper, W. R. (1905). *The trend in higher education.* Chicago: University of Chicago Press.

Herr, E. L., & Cramer, S. H. (1979). *Career guidance through the life span.* Boston: Little, Brown.

Hogan, P. M. (1991). Vocational preparation within a liberal arts framework: Suggested directions for undergraduate psychology programs. *Teaching of Psychology, 18,* 148–153.

Hoyt, K. B. (1978). *A primer for career education.* Washington, DC: Office of Career Education, U.S. Office of Education.

Kilburg, R. R. (Ed.). (1991). *How to manage your career in psychology.* Washington, DC: Author.

Kramer, H. C., & Gardner, R. E. (1983). *Advising by faculty.* Washington, DC: National Education Association.

Krumboltz, J. D. (1979). A social learning theory of career decision making. In A. M. Mitchell, G. B. Jones, & J. D. Krumboltz (Eds.), *Social learning and career decision making* (pp. 19–49). Cranston, RI: Carroll Press.

Levinson, D. J., Darrow, C. N., Klein, E. B., Levinson, M. H., & McKee, B. (1978). *The seasons of a man's life.* New York: Knopf.

Lunneborg, P. W. (1986). Assessing students' career needs at a large state university. *Teaching of Psychology, 13,* 189–192.

Mann, A. (1950). Frank Parsons: The professor as crusader. *Mississippi Valley Historical Review, 37,* 471–490.

Maverick, L. A. (1926). *Vocational guidance of college students.* Cambridge, MA: Harvard University Press.

McGovern, T. V. (1979). The development of a career planning program for undergraduate psychology majors. *Teaching of Psychology, 6,* 183–184.

McGovern, T. V., Furumoto, L., Halpern, D. F., Kimble, G. A., & McKeachie, W. J. (1991). Liberal education, study in depth, and the arts and sciences major—Psychology. *American Psychologist, 46,* 598–605.

Münsterberg, H. (1973). *Psychology and industrial efficiency.* Boston: Houghton Mifflin. (Original work published 1913)

Parsons, F. (1909). *Choosing a vocation.* Boston: Houghton Mifflin.

Paterson, D. G. (1938). The genesis of modern guidance. *Educational Record, 19,* 36–46.

Riesman, D. (1981). *On higher education: The academic enterprise in an era of rising student consumerism.* San Francisco: Jossey-Bass.

Sheehy, G. (1976). *Passages: Predictable crises in adult life.* New York: Dutton.

Shipton, J., & Steltenpohl, E. H. (1981). Educational advising and career planning: A life-cycle perspective. In A. W. Chickering (Ed.), *The modern Amer-*

ican college: *Responding to the new realities of diverse students and a changing society* (pp. 689–705). San Francisco: Jossey-Bass.

Super, D. E. (1955). Transition: From vocational guidance to counseling psychology. *Journal of Counseling Psychology, 2,* 3–9.

Super, D., & Super, C. (1982). *Opportunities in psychology.* Skokie, IL: VGM Career Horizons.

Swanson, J. L., & Tokar, D. M. (1991). College students' perceptions of barriers to career development. *Journal of Vocational Behavior, 38,* 92–106.

Trombley, T. B. (1984). An analysis of the complexity of academic advising tasks. *Journal of College Student Personnel, 25,* 234–239.

Trombley, T. B., & Holmes, D. (1981). Defining the role of academic advising in the institutional setting: The next phase. *NACADA Journal, 1,* 1–8.

Viteles, M. S. (1925). A psychological clinic for vocational guidance. *Vocational Guidance Magazine, 4,* 78–79.

Ware, M. E. (1981). Evaluating a career development course: A two year study. *Teaching of Psychology, 8,* 67–71.

Ware, M. E. (1982). Acknowledging the preparation of students for post graduate life. *Teaching of Psychology, 9,* 40–42.

Ware, M. E. (1984, September). *Teaching life choices through videotape.* Paper presented at the meeting of the International Congress of Psychology, Acapulco, Mexico.

Ware, M. E. (1985). Assessing a career development course for upper-level college students. *Journal of College Student Personnel, 26,* 152–155.

Ware, M. E. (1986). Assessing students' career needs at a small private university. *Teaching of Psychology, 13,* 185–188.

Ware, M. E. (1987). *Career development and opportunities for psychology majors* (2nd ed.). Omaha, NE: Creighton University Press.

Ware, M. E. (1988). Teaching and evaluating a career development course for psychology majors. In P. J. Woods (Ed.), *Is psychology for them? A guide for undergraduate advising* (pp. 64–74). Washington, DC: American Psychological Association.

Ware, M. E. (1990a). *Pursuing graduate studying in psychology* (3rd ed.). Omaha, NE: Creighton University Press.

Ware, M. E. (1990b). *Readings for Psy 330: Career Development in Psychology.* Omaha, NE: Kinkos.

Ware, M. E. (1991, August). *"You are majoring in what? What can you do with psychology?!"* Paper presented at the G. Stanley Hall Lecture Series, 99th Annual Convention of the American Psychological Association, San Francisco, CA.

Ware, M. E., & Beischel, M. L. (1979). Career development: Evaluating a new frontier for teaching and research. *Teaching of Psychology, 6,* 210–213.

Ware, M. E., & Matthews, J. R. (1980). Stimulating career exploration and research among undergraduates: A colloquium series. *Teaching of Psychology, 7*, 36–38.

Ware, M. E., & Millard, R. J. (1987). *Handbook on student development: Advising, career development, and field placement.* Hillsdale, NJ: Erlbaum.

Ware, M. E., Millard, R. J., & Matthews, J. R. (1984). Strategies for evaluating field placement programs. *Psychological Reports, 55*, 571–578.

Ware, M. E., Pusanik, R. P., & Matthews, J. R. (1990). *Activities in field placement programs at different universities.* Omaha, NE: Creighton University, Department of Psychology. (ERIC Document Reproduction Service No. ED 309330)

Ware, M. E. (Producer), & Sroufe, P. (Producer-Director). (1984a). *Career development and opportunities for psychology majors* [Videotape]. Omaha, NE: Creighton University.

Ware, M. E. (Producer), & Sroufe, P. (Producer-Director). (1984b). *Pursuing graduate study in psychology* [Videotape]. Omaha, NE: Creighton University.

Williamson, E. G. (1965). *Vocational counseling: Some historical, philosophical and theoretical perspectives.* New York: McGraw-Hill.

Woods, P. J. (Ed.). (1988). *Is psychology for them? A guide to undergraduate advising.* Washington, DC: American Psychological Association.

Woods, P. J. & Wilkinson, C. S. (Eds.). (1987). *Is psychology the major for you? Planning for your undergraduate years.* Washington, DC: American Psychological Association.

APPENDIX

SELECTED READINGS FOR CAREER DEVELOPMENT IN PSYCHOLOGY

Bloom, L. J., & Bell, P. A. (1979). Making it in graduate school: Some reflections about the superstars. *Teaching of Psychology, 6*, 231–232.

Donald, K. M., & Carlisle, J. M. (1983). The "diverse decision makers": Helping students with career decisions. *Vocational Guidance Quarterly, 31*, 270–275.

Eddy, B., Lloyd, P. J., & Lubin, B. (1987). Enhancing the application to doctoral professional programs: Suggestions from a national survey. *Teaching of Psychology, 14*, 160–163.

Foley, J. M. (1979). Gaining experience by volunteering. In P. J. Woods (Ed.), *The psychology major: Training and employment strategies* (pp. 19–26). Washington, DC: American Psychological Association.

Halgin, R. P. (1986). Advising undergraduates who wish to become clinicians. *Teaching of Psychology, 13*, 7–12.

Hatcher, L., & Crook, J. C. (1988). First-job surprises for college graduates: An exploratory investigation. *Journal of College Student Development, 29*, 441–448.

Lunneborg, P. W., & Wilson, V. M. (1982). Job satisfaction correlates for college graduates in psychology. *Teaching of Psychology, 9*, 199–201.

McGovern, T. V., & Carr, K. F. (1989). Carving out the niche: A review of alumni surveys on undergraduate psychology majors. *Teaching of Psychology, 16*, 52–57.

McGovern, T. V., & Tinsley, H. E. A. (1978). Interviewer evaluations of interviewee nonverbal behavior. *Journal of Vocational Behavior, 13*, 163–171.

Ware, M. E. (1987). *Career development and opportunities for psychology majors* (2nd ed.). (Available from Mark E. Ware, Department of Psychology, Creighton University, Omaha, NE.)

Ware, M. E. (1990). *Pursuing graduate study in psychology* (3rd ed.). (Available from Mark E. Ware, Department of Psychology, Creighton University, Omaha, NE.)

Ware, M. E., & Meyer, A. E. (1981). Career versatility of the psychology major: A survey of graduates. *Teaching of Psychology, 8*, 12–15.

Wilson, V. M., & Lunneborg, P. W. (1979). Beyond the bachelor's degree. In P. J. Woods (Ed.), *The psychology major: Training and employment strategies* (pp. 319–331). Washington, DC: American Psychological Association.

3

THE SOCRATIC–SOPHISTIC CONTINUUM IN TEACHING PSYCHOLOGY AND PSYCHOLOGICAL RESEARCH IN AMERICA

JOHN J. FUREDY

There is an old story that reflects most of the basic themes of higher education. It is about the passion for inquiry that Socrates showed during the last few hours before his death some 24 centuries ago. The first to tell this story was his most famous student, Plato, in the dialogue called *Phaedo* (Plato, 1952). I shall retell the tale, emphasizing those aspects that are relevant to the themes to be elaborated in this chapter.

Socrates has been condemned to die, having been found guilty of "corrupting the youth," but the Athenian democrats would like nothing better than to avoid an actual execution. The strength of the penalty was

The preparation of this chapter was aided by funds from the National Science and Engineering Council of Canada. A preliminary draft was commented on by Jane Halonen, Antonio Puente, and students in one of Puente's undergraduate classes, and I am indebted to all these sources for their advice. A later version was also read by Christine Furedy, to whom I am indebted not only for editorial help but also—as the references indicate—for conceptual collaboration in thinking and writing about the Socratic strain in higher education.

forced on them by Socrates's refusal to propose a more reasonable penalty (instead he proposed that the state support him for life to go on with his teaching—an early version of tenure?), and now they are faced with the embarrassing prospect of killing, for a crime that is clearly not a capital one, a 70-year old citizen with a good record of military service (in the Spartan wars of the mid-5th century BC). So during the days leading up to his execution (which, for Athenian citizens, was forced suicide by hemlock), Socrates has been lightly guarded, a fact that has been noted by his friends who have come to visit him on the last day and who urge him to escape and thereby save both his life and the Athenians from further embarrassment.

However, Socrates refuses the offer and elects to spend his last hours engaged in the activity that is his primary passion: discussion. The topic of discussion, moreover, is one that held considerable general interest as well as having immediate relevance for Socrates—whether the soul was immortal. Perhaps not surprisingly, Socrates argues for the affirmative, but his two favorite followers, Simmias and Cebes, argue strongly for the negative. On their part, this is the height of tactlessness at this time, but Simmias and Cebes are Socrates's intellectual students and not his indoctrinated disciples. The purpose of the discussion is to consider the issues in terms of a conflict of ideas rather than to be concerned with the propriety of the particular doctrinal conclusion that will be reached, no matter how tactless or unpleasant that conclusion may seem for the man whom they love and respect and who has chosen to die. So even at this 11th hour, his companions—being students rather than disciples—are ready critically examine Socrates's view that the soul is immortal.

In this chapter I hope to present an account of, and some justification for, the Socratic method of teaching. My presentation is interpretative and even polemical, rather than explicative and balanced. Still, the basic terms and distinctions need elaboration, and I do this in the first section. In the second, I apply the interpretation to some of the major events of American psychological college and university teaching in the past 100 years.

INTERPRETATION: BASIC DISTINCTIONS AND TERMS

It may be that in an unambiguously scientific field, such as physics or chemistry, the frontiers of knowledge are so advanced that, especially at the level of undergraduate teaching, instruction can be mostly informational rather than reflective or interpretational. That is, in these "harder" sciences, there is a relatively uncontroversial body of knowledge that must be transmitted to the neophyte before he or she can begin to grapple with the frontier issues that are, in any science, controversial. However, I suggest that in a "softer" science, such as psychology, there is little by way of such basic knowledge, so that even the neophyte is at the frontier and has, therefore, to engage in critical, reflective thought about the subject. Hence, in my view, the main task of the *teacher* of psychology is to facilitate that sort of reflective thought in the student. In this endeavor, there are some important distinctions and terms of relevance, and in the rest of this section I examine these.

The Socratic-Sophistic Distinction

Like all binary distinctions, the one between Socratic and sophistic approaches to education should be considered as a continuum, the poles of which represent extremes that are never actualized. Nevertheless, the distinction does refer to an important difference in directions taken by teachers of psychology. A decade ago we suggested (Furedy & Furedy, 1982) that the distinction was relevant to resolving conflicts in the teaching of psychology (see also Kimble, 1984). One of the points we emphasized was that the distinction applied to approaches rather than to individual teachers, so that all individual teachers had elements of both aspects in their approach to teaching. Nevertheless, to clarify the nature of the distinction, it is useful to refer to individuals who best exemplify each extreme of the Socratic–sophistic continuum, and Socrates is the clearest example of the essence of higher education: a passion for discussion, an attitude of disinterestedness, and an emphasis on the conflict of ideas. It is these aspects that distinguish higher education from indoctrinational or merely informational education.

As I have detailed elsewhere (Furedy, 1988, pp. 42–43), the Socratic (or "Greek-way-of-thinking-about-the-world") tradition is not all there is to higher education. Nor is it necessary for the occurrence of highly complex civilizations. The cognitive complexity of an education concerned only with the passing on of culture, ritual, and the skills of living can be enormous, but what is missing in this sort of indoctrinational–informational education is a "disposition for disciplined inquiry based on a readiness to question all assumptions and an ability to recognize when it is necessy so to question" (Furedy & Furedy, 1986, p. 41)—namely, the capacity for genuine *critical thinking*.

The Student–Disciple Distinction

For critical thinking in this sense to occur, the learner must function as a student rather than as a disciple of the teacher. I ended my tale of Socrates's last few hours with this student–disciple distinction, and it is one that is of contemporary relevance.

There are elements, albeit implicit, of the disciple approach in American higher education. At the graduate level, the term *X-PhD* is an expression that is uniquely meaningful in North America and denotes that the person so described had X as her or his doctoral-thesis supervisor. There is also the connotation that, as regards major general issues in psychology, that person and X have congruent views, which is a disciplelike rather than a studentlike connotation.[1] So also is the expression *worked under* rather than *worked with* to describe a doctoral supervisory relationship. Again, the term *training* is commonly used to describe graduate education as regards to the teaching of research both by the doctoral supervisor and by the department or program in which the student (or is it disciple?) works. Moreover, the evaluation of the PhD thesis is essentially left to the supervisor, because even when there is a thesis committee, the other members, who are in the department and have generally been involved in the planning of the research, are apt to follow the supervisor's opinion. There is, in other words, no *external* evaluation of the thesis work. Finally, in financial terms, the typical PhD candidate is almost completely dependent on the supervisor.

Consider, in contrast, the graduate system in the British–Australian tradition, which is different in certain subtle but important respects. For illustration I cite my own experience at the University of Sydney from 1963 to 1965. I learned the meaning of the expression *Champion-PhD* only on my arrival at Indiana University, and the connotation of the expression applied not at all to this particular supervisor–student relationship. R. A. Champion, who did his graduate work "under" K. Spence at the University of Iowa, was and is a radical stimulus-response (S-R) theorist who eschews any reference to cognitive and mental events. In contrast, my undergraduate thesis that Champion supervised showed, I thought, that rats learned cognitions à la Tolman and contrary to Spence (Furedy & Champion, 1963). Despite our joint publication, Champion did not agree with me, and his defense of Spence's S–R interpretation occupies most of the (small-print) part of the discussion section of the Furedy and Champion (1963) article. Similarly, an article that was based on my PhD ends by referring to "certain *thoughtful* subjects whose temporal discriminations are sufficiently acute for them to turn *thought* into action" (Furedy, 1966, p. 261; emphases mine) and includes a footnote in which I thank Champion for his advice on the write-up but "hasten to add that he is unlikely to approve of the final version." I still recall the many sessions we had regarding our differing interpretations of these results and our clear conclusion that, on the interpretation of these reaction-time results, as on the interpretation of the rat-learning results (Furedy & Champion, 1963), we would have to remain in disagreement, although we were in close agreement with the S-R interpretation of human classical-conditioning experiments (e.g., Champion &

---

[1]It is relevant to note that surface manifestations such as the use of Christian names are not necessarily related to the degree to which the student is in a disciplelike intellectual role. German doctoral students may be more formal in their modes of addressing their supervisors than American doctoral students, but the uniquely North-American *X-PhD* expression suggests a disciplelike role for the student even if the "master" is addressed by her or his first name.

Jones, 1961; Furedy, 1965, 1967a, 1967b). All this suggests that I worked *with* rather than *under* Champion and that both he and the department *educated* me in the Socratic, conflict-of-ideas sense rather than *trained* me in the sophistic, informational–indoctrinational sense. When the PhD thesis was written, it was sent to external (overseas) examiners for evaluation, so again, in this respect, I benefited only from my supervisor's knowledge rather than from his judgmental power. Finally, my financial support came from a scholarship granted by the government rather than from my supervisor, although, of course, the equipment to carry out the research was provided by his laboratory.

I suggest that a different picture emerges in the undergraduate teaching of psychology in North America. There may be a diversity of views among faculty, but each professor is the sole judge of his or her own course, and contrasting positions of different faculty members on fundamental issues in psychology are seldom brought to the attention of undergraduate students. Similarly, the system at the University of Toronto, whereby the written versions of senior undergraduate research theses are evaluated externally by other faculty members rather than by the supervisor (Furedy & Furedy, 1977), appears to be unique in North America. In contrast, external evaluation of undergraduate work is routine in most Australian and British universities. And at least my own experience as an undergraduate included having a "mentalist staff member lead our Wednesday 3rd year honours seminar, a behaviorist staff member lead our Thursday seminar," and we would test "the positions of each by bringing up the criticisms we had heard in the previous class," because "I took it as a matter of course that there were conflicting views about the discipline of psychology, and that the process of education was one of presenting us with these conflicting views" (Furedy, 1991, p. 14). As the then head of the department stated (and it should be noted that as the sole professor, he enjoyed much greater power than any American departmental chair does) regarding educating undergraduates,

> I have never had any doubt about the unacceptability of what Mc-Dougall called extrinsic teleology, but I always thought that epistemological idealism and extrinsic teleology were worth a historical exposition before rejection. Let them see what the circus is capable of before arguing on the basis of both logical and observational evidence about which horse to ride. *You may prefer the bay and I may prefer the grey, but if we are serious scholars we must justify our preferences.* (O'Neil, May, 16, 1987, personal communication; emphasis mine)

Discipline- Versus Person-Centered Education

This distinction is related to the Socratic–sophistic continuum. An example of the discipline-centered approach is the Oxford-Cambridge tutorial system of the past. This was a one-on-one discussion, but the tutor was meant to focus solely on the discipline and not at all on the person of the student who was working in the discipline. So the typical tutor could quite safely say that he or she was not at all concerned with the personal life or development of the student but only with the student's understanding of the subject being studied. Similarly, as an undergraduate at Sydney I used to take strong criticisms of my written work without offense but was offended when a marker stated that she thought that I should apply her comments on the paper "to my life as well." In the discipline-oriented context of my undergraduate education, I and my fellow students considered that remark to be inappropriate and impertinent. However, in the smaller American colleges, especially, the "counseling"[2] function of faculty is considered to be an important one. The undergraduate education is a much more person-centered one, and advice from a professor about how to live one's life would be considered to be completely appropriate.

In fact, of course, all actual teaching of both the content of, and research in, psychology includes both the discipline-centered Socratic and the person-centered sophistic strains, but there are differences in the degree to which each strain is emphasized. There are also social influences that tend to weaken the Socratic, discipline-oriented approach. I nevertheless hold that an educational system that does not include the Socratic component fails to provide a genuinely *higher* education over and above an indoctrinational or informational one.

The Role of Disinterestedness

The essence of a Socratic education is disinterestedness, which is not to be confused with uninterestedness. Disinterestedness as a concept is clearly part of our current intellectual, and even political, heritage. In addition to being expert in the issues under discussion, a board of inquiry has, in principle, to be independent or detached, namely, without a specific ax to grind. The fact that this idea is understood by the population at large rather than by intellectuals alone and that attacks on such a board's independence are politically as well as logically effective indicates that the concept of disinterestedness is woven into our culture.

---

[2]The term is in quotes in recognition of the fact that the person- or student-centered approach is not the same as professional counseling, not only because the former may be done by teachers who are not qualified as counselors but also because, as detailed by McKeachie (1982), the student-centered approach involves many more academic components than does counseling. Nevertheless, an element of counseling enters into the student-centered approach in a way that it does not, as indicated in the text, in the discipline-centered approach. To put it another way, in terms of the Socratic–sophistic continuum we proposed (Furedy & Furedy, 1982) and of a later article in which we elaborated on strengthening the Socratic strain in higher education (Furedy & Furedy, 1986), the notion that it is part of the Socratic strain for the student to become part of the teacher and vice-versa (McKeachie, 1982) was one that I would oppose. That notion, rather, is part of a sophistic, person-centered strain that has an element of counseling in it.

Nevertheless, disinterestedness is a relative newcomer to civilization and is constantly opposed by other influences. The notion of disinterested inquiry, or "considering X for its own sake," first arose among a group of Ionian philosophers who are generally known as pre-Socratics. They were the first to demonstrate "thinking about the world in the Greek way" (Burnet, 1930, p. *vi*) and laid the foundation for a problem- rather than a person-oriented approach to both scientific and literary fields of inquiry.

It is just this phenomenon-centered aspect that was missing from an otherwise technically advanced civilization, such as that of Babylon, which had a well-developed system of nonscientific astrology but no genuine science of astronomy. To look at the heavens in the "Babylonian way" is to engage in observation and quantified data-gathering activities, but these observations are made from an "interested" perspective, namely, from the assumption that these movements are related to and influence human affairs. The Greeks, who amassed far less information about those heavenly body movements, nevertheless developed astronomy, because they treated those movements as a problem to be considered for its own sake rather than in relation to individual or societal concerns.

Similarly, for teaching in the Socratic mode, the "uncritical acceptance of tradition . . . is no education at all" because any tradition "requires the most careful scrutiny and until this process of examination has begun, education has not begun" (Anderson, 1962b, p. 207). Nor does it affect the Socratic scrutiny that an overwhelming majority of one's peers may hold the view being criticized with complete conviction, because "as Socrates says in the *Crito*, though the 'many can kill us,' that is no reason for setting their opinions on a level with the opinions of the wise, for believing, though they have a certain power over life and death, that they have any power over truth" (Anderson, 1962a, p. 199).

Disinterestedness is not only a relatively new concept; it is also a frail one that can be destroyed by opposing forces. Sometimes the opposition between inquiry and ideology is explicit and obvious, as was the case with Galileo's heliocentric position (denying that a stationary earth was the center of the universe) and the Church's opposition to it. Clearly, the Church (and society) had an interested attitude regarding the issue of whether the sun rather than the earth was a stationary body, the interest being not in the truth of Galileo's heliocentric assertion but in the *relation* of this assertion to Church (and hence societal) doctrine or tradition. Galileo's public recantation constitutes the bowing to this interested (or sophistic) approach when faced with the threat of torture. On the other hand, his private (and probably apocryphal) *sotto voce* remark of *eppur si muove* (and yet it moves) denied the public recantation. The content of the remark encapsulates the disinterested approach; that the remark was made, if at all, under his breath, illustrates the frailty of the approach when threatened by force.

In modern higher education, especially in democratic countries, there are no strictures on disinterested inquiry of the severity that Galileo faced. Still, teachers can be subjected to pressure, and this pressure is not only related to the facts of the case but also to the *relation* that the questions bear on certain received social opinions. In the teaching of psychology, questions concerned with intelligence testing in general, and the role of genetic components in group differences in intelligence in particular, are of this socially loaded variety. Even if no outright physical violence is perpetrated, to the extent that criticisms of certain positions are *ad hominem* (subjective) rather than *ad res* (to the thing itself, i.e., objective), to that extent the approach is sophistic and the education of students is indoctrinational rather than issue based.

The Teaching of Psychology Versus the Teaching of Psychological Research

This distinction is far less controversial than those discussed above and refers simply to the difference between course work and research work. The distinction is important if only because it has to be recognized that the vast majority of undergraduate students and a significant proportion of graduate students (i.e., those intending to embark on a professional rather than a research or academic career) are not interested in learning how to do research. Still, because of psychology's ambiguous status as a science when compared with say, physics, chemistry, and astronomy, there is a need for reflective, critical inquiry concerning fundamental assumptions made not only about the teaching of psychological research but also about the teaching of psychology. Chemistry, at the introductory level, can be taught in an almost fully informational mode, because there are established introductory facts in that discipline that can be accepted without question. Psychology, in this respect, is quite different, as there are few, if any, such introductory psychological facts.

Another relevant dimension is the degree of specialization, which clearly increases from the 100-level introductory undergraduate course through to postdoctoral research in the discipline. Nevertheless, it is a mistake to assume that there is a one-to-one relationship between degree of specialization and the Socratic, discipline-centered, critical-thinking-oriented approach. Especially in the teaching of research, I have detailed arguments elsewhere (Furedy, 1988) that the undergraduate final thesis presents a better and "more golden" opportunity than later graduate and postdoctoral work, by which time the student is beginning to feel the pressures that beset the modern researcher who, to survive financially, has to forego exercising her or his critical skills and act more like a salesperson than a scientist.

APPLICATION OF THE INTERPRETATION TO THE HISTORY OF TEACHING PSYCHOLOGY IN AMERICA

There is little question that at the end of the 19th century it was the German rather than the British influence that was predominant on American academic psychology, and it is only to exaggerate slightly to say that American academics of the period learned how to do experimental psychology in German laboratories.

Wilhelm Wundt (1832–1920) was the undisputed father figure of this movement, and his influence was spread through such "disciples" as Edward Titchener (1867–1927). From the perspective of the teaching rather than of the content of psychology, however, it is not the structuralism of Wundt and Titchener that is critical but rather the model of graduate education that was adopted by American academics, many of whom at that time obtained doctoral degrees at German universities. That model had all the hierarchical and authoritarian characteristics of German universities of the time. While the *content* of structural psychology was subjected to continuing criticism, the *pedagogical method* used to promulgate that particular school of psychology was left largely unexamined. This may seem strange in the light of the self-professed democratic nature of the American psyche, but recall that democracy and intellectual freedom are not necessarily coterminous, as illustrated most dramatically by the case of Socrates.

Wundt's structuralism itself was challenged, not only by American functionalists such as William James (1842–1910) and John Dewey (1859–1952) but also by the later behaviorist movement spearheaded by John Watson (e.g., Watson, 1913). However, in these famous schools-of-psychology battles, there was little tolerance of intellectual dissent *within* a particular camp, and students were expected to function in a disciple- or even soldierlike mode in relation both to their supervisors and to other members of their "school." In terms of the Socratic-sophistic distinction discussed earlier, this mode of academic operation is clearly toward the sophistic end of the continuum.

It is also relevant to recall that the late 19th and early 20th century was a period during which, in the universities, psychology was seeking to emancipate itself as a separate discipline from philosophy. At a politico-administrative level, this emancipation occurred relatively earlier in the New World; the University of Pennsylvania and the University of Wisconsin established independent departments of psychology in 1887 and 1888, respectively. British, Canadian, and Australian departments of psychology emerged as separate institutions only after the 1920s, and some, such as Oxford (1947), were later still in recognizing psychology as a separate discipline.[3] By that stage there was such a significant body of psychological

---

[3]For an account of the young experimental psychologist, D. E. Berlyne, chafing under the philosophic yoke as late as 1949 at the University of St. Andrews, see Furedy and Furedy (1981).

research that psychology's claim to be a separate discipline was almost self-evident. That was not the case during the first half of psychology's first century in America, and it is generally true that during periods of political emancipation there is little tolerance for dissent within the group that is engaged in the struggle for recognition.

I suggest that American psychological academia adopted this sort of group orthodoxy for the relatively new science of psychology. In this respect, one might contrast the sophistic-oriented American style with the Socratic-oriented British model, as exemplified, in philosophy, say, by the many arguments that G. E. Moore had with his Cambridge colleague Bertrand Russell about philosophy. One is hard put to think of examples of faculty disagreements *within* the same department in American universities of the same period. Perhaps, especially after the Watsonian behaviorist revolution, there was also the view that such disagreements belonged to psychology's "prescientific," "philosophical" era and had no place in the new science of behavior, for which reflective, armchair-philosophy methods had to be eschewed.

Although I have not seen this explicitly stated as a principle, practice suggests that the place of philosophy in the current teaching of experimental psychology is quite minimal. It is true that some cognitive scientists consider themselves to be engaged in active interdisciplinary inquiry that includes the disciplines of experimental psychology, computer science, and philosophy (see, e.g., Slezak, 1989), but for the actual teaching of psychology at the graduate level, most American institutions no longer require courses in what used to be called History and Systems.[4] This does not mean, of course, that students and teachers do not have a philosophy (and often conflicting and internally inconsistent philosophies), but that one's philosophy of psychology is regarded, essentially, like one's religion, as a matter of individual preference rather than as a position to be subjected to critical examination through open discussion.

This may seem to be a jaundiced and even unsubstantiated view of the matter, but consider also the fact that a *theoretical* doctoral dissertation in psychology is not acceptable in American graduate institutions, in contrast to the situation in physics. As to the place of history and theory in

---

[4]At the undergraduate level, courses in the history of psychology are common, but those dealing with the philosophy of psychology (i.e., "systems") are less so. And both history and systems courses are generally regarded as a desirable luxury but not as a necessary part of undergraduate psychology education. This distinction between desirability and necessity was dramatically illustrated to me when, some years ago, I proposed in a faculty meeting in my department that for a "specialist" undergraduate degree in psychology (akin to a 4-year honors degree in psychology at most other universities), a student be required to take *one* of three one-term (half-year) courses (two in history and one in theory or systems). This proposal was overwhelmingly voted down on the grounds that undergraduate physics and chemistry students do not need to take such "reflective" or "navel-gazing" courses, so neither should psychology students be required to do so. It should be noted that the University of Toronto department is very much an "academic," "experimental" one and does not even have a graduate clinical or any other applied program.

undergraduate education, the latter aspect, in particular, is seldom taught in a systematic manner as a subject in its own right although, of course, each instructor provides her or his individual (and unexamined) philosophy of psychology to undergraduates. Because these undergraduates are not exposed to faculty challenging each others' philosophies and because each instructor is essentially in total charge of grading students in her or his course, the message that undergraduates receive may be that theoretical issues are more a matter of dogma than of critical examination. Consider also that the only theoretical psychology center in North America, at the University of Alberta, has recently been closed down. Gone are the days when, at graduate-training powerhouses such as the University of Iowa in the 1940s and 1950s, every student had to take Gustav Bergmann's systems course and when the examination of theoretical issues was considered to be an important part of the education of students.

Actually, from a Socratic, conflict-of-ideas perspective, these systems courses of that period were far from ideal. In contrast to O'Neil's approach (cited earlier) or letting the student decide, the Iowa educational experience was almost doctrinal as far as the tenets of logical positivism (Bergmann) or S-R behaviorism (Spence) were concerned. In many respects, Spence was arguably experimental psychology's most outstanding graduate educator. During some two decades, he supervised 79 PhD students, of whom most went on to be active and influential researchers themselves. This feat of graduate supervision is stupendous and is unlikely ever to be duplicated. But Spence's teaching style was clearly authoritarian, and even faculty had to submit the designs of their experiments for his approval before those experiments could be run in his department. And Bergmann, although an eminent academic philosopher in his own right, served in a doctrinal teaching role in the "training" of Iowa PhDs. Moreover, as I have noted elsewhere (Furedy, 1989, footnote 1), he used to tell his "boys" at the end of the course that, having learned it all, they could now "forget it" as far as their future empirical research was concerned. Here we see the view that, for the empirical research psychologist, philosophy was something to be learned and then forgotten rather than to be the subject of continuous examination in the light of opposing views and evidence.

From a Socratic perspective, psychology's cognitive revolution or "paradigm shift" (Segal & Lachman, 1972) is also much less a liberating event than a further binding of the discipline with the tenets of sophistic instrumentalism. In the 1930s and 1940s, the main issue of contention between the Hull–Spence S-R group and the Tolman sign-significate (S-S) group was that of "what is learned." This question was mainly examined through the aid of the "little white test-tube" (Osgood, 1953), namely, in experiments using the albino, laboratory-bred rat as the subject. The S-R theorists of the Hull–Spence school contended that only S-R connections or responses were learned, whereas the S-S theorists led by Tolman argued, on the basis of evidence such as from latent-learning experiments, that sign-significate expectancies or "cognitive maps" were also learned. The modern cognitive position is much more in line with the Tolmanian S-S position, but the changeover occurred in a sophistic rather than in a Socratic way. That is, as Segal and Lachman (1972) also argue, the shift to cognitivism was made not on the basis of the evidence but on the basis of a scientific opinion change or "paradigm shift," with the criterion being "man as the measure" rather than truth.

This instrumentalist way of looking at the matter was evident in the (then) S-R theorist Kendler's (1952) article titled "What Is Learned?—A Theoretical Blind Alley." Kendler, a former student of Spence, argued in his widely cited article that the problem of what is learned was not a genuine empirical issue but merely a pseudoproblem or a matter of semantic pref-erence. In the Socratic–sophistic terminology, he was suggesting that "man was the measure" for determining the central bone of contention between the Hull–Spence and Tolman groups rather than truth. And in those days, if it was the relative scientific prestige of the two camps that was to decide the matter, there was little doubt that the Hull–Spence S-R group would prevail. This sophistic recommendation was caricatured in a *reductio ad absurdum* reply by one of Tolman's students, Ritchie (1953), in what is essentially a Socratic refutation of the sophistic man-as-measure position.

In logical terms, there is little question that Ritchie's (1953) position is the stronger one. His refutation drew no reply from Kendler or any of the other S-R theorists of the time. However, the hard-science status of the Hull–Spence school was undeniably higher than that of Tolman and his students, the latter being regarded by many as Californian dilettantes.[5] Indeed, the fact that Ritchie used humor in his article (this is perhaps the only deliberately humorous paper in the prestigious *Psychological Review*) may well have weakened his case on the grounds that no serious scientist would ever joke about such matters, no matter how strong the logic of his arguments.[6] Admittedly, however, the above discussion involves specula-tions about peoples' motives. On a more factual note, and as detailed elsewhere (Furedy & Furedy, 1982, pp. 15–16), Ritchie's article was in-cluded in a text by Goldstein, Krantz, and Rains (1965), which was ex-

---

[5]Yale's Hull had produced the axiomatic and formalized *Principles of Behavior* (1943) and several years later Iowa's Spence published his *Behavior Theory and Conditioning* (1956), which was based on the prestigious Silliman Lectures, given for the first time that year by a non-hard-science lecturer. In addition, the research and "PhDs produced" output of the Hull–Spence group was much greater during this period than that of the Berkeley-based Tolman. Because much of graduate education (and some of undergraduate education) is a process of modeling (i.e., the implicit transmission of information rather than its explicit transmission), the importance of these factors for the teaching of psychology and research in psychology is considerable.
[6]In an interview with R. C. Bolles (1978), who was, with Ritchie, a student of Tolman, Bolles suggested that this humorous style was primarily responsible for the scientific community's ignoring of Ritchie's (1953) article, although on Ritchie's own account (personal communication, 1977), the journal's editor was well pleased to publish it.

plicitly designed to present controversies to undergraduates. The book not only included Kendler's (1952) article but also referred students to other papers for "replies" to Kendler. These papers were less logically relevant to Kendler's article than to Ritchie's (1953) omitted reply, but the authors of these papers were more eminent or "visible" than Ritchie.

The Sophistic Shift From a Socratic Perspective

Graduate students of the Hull–Tolman era were misled when they thought that their experiments would produce certain resolutions to their disputes. Much of the debate was colored by emotion. Still, the debates were centered on rival explanations of psychological phenomena rather than on competing political predilections. In modern psychology, the most recent example of the man-is-the-measure approach is constructivism. An eminent exponent of this "wave-of-the-future" position states that "we do not discover facts; we invent them" (Scarr, 1985, p. 499). This, I suggest, is a sophistic prescription for following fads rather than investigating phenomena.

The sophistic shift in the American teaching of psychology has occurred partly because, at the graduate level, as noted earlier, the supervisor came to assume total and almost sole financial and academic control over her or his students. In this connection, it is interesting to note that the term "research *assistant*ship" describing a graduate student's duties towards her or his supervisor is a North American expression, in contrast with the English and Australian term "research *student*ship."[7] As faculty research funding became increasingly difficult to obtain following the halcyon days of the 1960s, the supervisor's financial control came to have even more importance. As this occurred, graduate students could be increasingly expected to function as assistants carrying out their supervisor's orders rather than as apprentices who were oriented toward the discipline and whose main purpose was to learn how do independent research.

Another effect of the difficulty of obtaining funds was the increased emphasis on grantsmanship skills for each faculty member's laboratory (see also Furedy, 1987b). Over the past decade, even journals devoted to obtaining funding have appeared. It is a common complaint on the part of

---

[7]In fact, the distinction between the North American (i.e., Canada included) terms "graduate student" and the English and Australian term "research student" is also of significance. Implicit in the North American designation is someone whose status is that of a student and one who can be *employed* both as a research assistant (to her or his faculty advisor) and as a teaching assistant (to her or his faculty-level instructor). A research student, on the other hand, is someone who is learning how to do research under the supervision of a faculty-level researcher, who neither pays nor employs the research student. The supervisor's only responsibility is to provide adequate supervision of research and guidance for the thesis write-up, which itself, however, is examined *externally*. It is clear that the supervisor–student relationship in England and Australia is quite different from the North American one.

faculty that they spend a major amount of their time not only preparing grant applications but also arranging those all-important site visits. It is likely that these activities will involve a shift in emphasis from science-oriented, epistemic attitudes to advertising-oriented, promotional ones, although individual faculty researchers will probably deny indignantly that this has occurred. But even if faculty are able to distinguish between scientific and advertising concerns, can their graduate students do the same? I suggest that this is quite unlikely, especially as these troublesome issues are seldom discussed in the hurly-burly of trying to keep the laboratory financially afloat. The learning going on here is of the modeling sort: Students acquire ways of behaving from their supervisors without reflection. And those ways are increasingly those of the promoter rather than those of the scientist.

Another important source of graduate education is the specialist conference, during which research presentations are made before one's peers. The stated purpose of these conferences is the scientific interchange of information, and an important element of that interchange is debate between the speakers and the audience about differing interpretations of the phenomena. Such conflicts of ideas, however, can lead to conflict between persons, and the dangers from such personal conflict have dramatically increased over the past two decades of scarce funding. Consider the typical North American faculty researcher, whose research is almost completely reliant on external funding and whose institution (in search of the important overhead funding) provides additional subtle and not-so-subtle pressures to increase levels of research funding.[8] Now, evaluators or grant applications include not only senior scientists who are on committees and who attend site visits but also many more peers who serve as referees of applications. For a grant application to be unfunded, it is not necessary that gross methodological errors be present but only that one or two evaluators be relatively "cool" about the application or the applicant. At a specialist conference, then, each participant is surrounded by former and future grant evaluators who have the power to cut off funding.

It is not surprising that, as we have indicated elsewhere in connection with one American-based specialist conference (Furedy & Scher, 1985), discussion and the conflict of ideas have come to play a lesser part in conferences. We suggested in that article that there had been "an increasing tendency over the past few years toward the reduction of critical discussion from the floor at SPR [Society for Psychophysiological Research] sessions,"

---

[8]It has become common practice in departments like my own to factor the amount of research funds obtained into faculty members' annual merit increases, and it is also not unusual to see departments put out booklets of annual performance that list the amount of funding obtained by each faculty member. Such measures, which have only been explicitly introduced during the past two decades, carry the clear implicit message that a faculty member's academic worth can be characterized by the amount of money that she or he obtains.

and that, "for those younger members [i.e., graduate students] who have not experienced the days when SPR sessions included active audience participation," there was the "implicit message" that it "is an appropriate way for a scientific, research-oriented body to 'discuss' its findings, where 'discussion' consists only of the communication of findings rather than also including the critical questioning of those findings" (Furedy & Scher, 1985, p. 368).

But perhaps the most important factor that has led to a shift in the sophistic direction is the fragmentation, and even the disappearance, of psychology as a uniquely identifiable discipline. In a recent symposium on this issue at the meeting of the Canadian Psychological Association (Furedy, 1991), the majority of the academic participants concluded that there was no "intellectually definable discipline of psychology," which "has now become merely a political and socially convenient label to designate departments in the Universities" (Furedy, 1991, p. 462). A publication by a former APA president (Fowler, 1990) also noted those "who foresee a grim future for psychology: exodus of our best scientists to other disciplines and the gradual withering away of our science" (p. 6). It is important to recognize that this problem is not the older, academic-versus-professional conflict with which American psychology has had to contend from its inception. It is only during the past decade or so that academic psychologists can not agree on what they have in common as a discipline. It is not surprising that, under these conditions, arguments over the structures of graduate programs are based more and more on subjective predilections than on psychological disciplinary considerations. With this change, each graduate student's supervisor increasingly becomes the only "measure" of truth in the sophistic sense of that term.

There is also the broader context of higher education to consider. Especially from the perspective of undergraduate teaching, there has been a shift from a discipline-oriented approach according to which both faculty and students were seen as "serving" whatever discipline or disciplines they were engaged in studying, although that "service" was recognized to be at different levels of expertise. Most learning was expected to be by students from faculty, but faculty also sometimes learned from students, especially those whose work "challenged"[9] the ideas held by faculty. In the current view, faculty are viewed as having two functions. The first is the *production* of knowledge, so that, in exercising this function, faculty *do* research and are rated in this function by their peers. The second is the *teaching* of students, which is evaluated both by their peers and by students via ratings.

---

[9]An example of this discipline-oriented approach was when, as a tutor at Sydney University in the early 1960s, I received instructions from the professor that, in marking written work of undergraduates, I should discriminate among first-class, second-class, and third-class work, respectively, by whether the paper provided continuous, occasional, or no challenge to my own ideas about psychology.

These two functions are not only viewed as separate but may often be seen as conflicting. Students (especially undergraduates) are consumers in this scheme of things, rather than devotees of the discipline, and the university or college is viewed as just another sort of industrial plant. The "products" of such tertiary-education plants come from the (noncomplementary) activities of research and teaching. The former is evaluated not in terms of its logical relevance to the discipline but in terms of its perceived relevance to current technology. The latter is also evaluated in terms of discipline-extrinsic criteria. Faculty teaching is judged in terms of the perceived success of "communicating" to students, as measured by student ratings and degree of student personal development. "Man" indeed is the "measure" of truth in this sophistic, modern view of tertiary education.

SOME CAVEATS AND AN ENVOI

The interpretations I have offered in this chapter are not beyond criticism. The brush I have used is broad. In particular, the contrasts I have drawn between American and other systems are, at best, statistical rather than universal ones. For example, external examining is used in many American colleges, so that this contrast between American and other systems is not an all-or-none affair. Still, there do seem to be clear differences of degree of the sort I have discussed, and there even seem to be quasi-universal differences when it comes to whether the PhD thesis is subjected to genuine external examination or whether, in fact, it is basically the supervisor who is effectively the only evaluator.

It is also important to stress that although, in this chapter, I have obviously favored the Socratic approach, I do not hold that the sophistic approach is irrelevant in higher education. Although the original sophist, Protagoras, mostly wears the black hat in the Socratic dialogues, Protagoras's important contributions to philosophy were and are recognized. In contemporary higher education, all teachers display elements of both approaches in their teaching, and both approaches have an important contribution to make. Nevertheless, as we first suggested a decade ago (Furedy & Furedy, 1982), the two approaches embody not only real differences but also potential conflicts. And if I am correct in my claim that American psychological teaching and research has shifted in a sophistic direction during the past century, then the consequences of this bear explicit consideration.

REFERENCES

Anderson, J. (1962a). Classicism. In J. Anderson, *Studies in empirical philosophy* (pp. 189–202). Sydney, Australia: Angus & Robertson.

Anderson, J. (1962b). Socrates as an educator. In J. Anderson, *Studies in empirical philosophy* (pp. 203–213). Sydney, Australia: Angus & Robertson.

Burnet, J. (1930). *Early Greek philosophy*, London: A & C Black.

Champion, R. A., & Jones, J. E. (1961). Forward, backward, and pseudoconditioning of the GSR. *Journal of Experimental Psychology, 62*, 58–61.

Fowler, R. D. (1990). Psychology: The core discipline. *American Psychologist, 45*. 1–6.

Furedy, J. J. (1965). Reinforcement through UCS offset in classical aversive conditioning. *Australian Journal of Psychology, 17*, 205–212.

Furedy, J. J. (1966). Reaction time as an index of masking, and the effect of check trials on thoughtful subjects. *Australian Journal of Psychology, 18*, 266–270.

Furedy, J. J. (1967a). Aspects of reinforcement through UCS offset in classical aversive conditioning. *Australian Journal of Psychology, 19*, 159–168.

Furedy, J. J. (1967b). Classical appetitive conditioning of the GSR with cool air as UCS, and the roles of UCS onset and offset as reinforcers of the CR. *Journal of Experimental Psychology, 75*, 73–80.

Furedy, J. J. (1987a). Specific versus placebo effects in biofeedback training: A critical lay perspective. *Biofeedback and Self-Regulation, 12*, 169–182.

Furedy, J. J. (1987b). Why peer-reviewed research funding may negate the critical benefits of open journal review: It is not the show, but the dough. *American Psychologist, 42*, 267.

Furedy, J. J. (1988). On the relevance of philosophy for psychological research: A preliminary analysis of some influences of Andersonian realism. *Australian Journal of Psychology, 40*, 71–77.

Furedy, J. J. (1989). On the relevance of philosophy for psychological research: Some autobiographical speculations concerning the influence of Andersonian realism. *Australian Psychologist, 24*, 93–100.

Furedy, J. J. (1991). W(h)ither the discipline? *Canadian Psychology, 32*, 439.

Furedy, J. J., & Champion, R.A. (1963). Cognitive and S-R interpretations of incentive-motivational phenomena. *American Journal of Psychology, 76*, 616–623.

Furedy, J. J., & Furedy, C. P (1977). Modeling the realities of research experience: Collaboration against common and merciless foes. *Teaching of Psychology, 4*, 107–110.

Furedy, J. J., & Furedy, C. P. (1981). "My first interest is interest": Berlyne as an exemplar of the curiosity drive. In H. Day (Ed.), *Advances in intrinsic motivation & aesthetics* (pp. 1–17). New York: Plenum Press.

Furedy, J. J. & Furedy, C. P. (1982). Socratic and Sophistic strains in the teaching of undergraduate psychology: Some implicit conflicts made explicit. *Teaching of Psychology, 9*, 14–20.

Furedy, J. J., & Furedy, C. P. (1986). On strengthening the Socratic strain in higher education. *Australian Journal of Education, 30*, 241–256.

Furedy, J. J., & Scher, H. (1985). On the decline of audience participation at

SPR: The unexamined session is not worth attending. *Psychophysiology, 22,* 368–369.

Goldstein, H., Krantz, D. L., & Rains, J. D. (1965). *Controversial issues in learning.* New York: Appleton-Century-Crofts.

Hull, C. L. (1943). *Principles of behavior: An introduction to behavior theory.* New York: Appleton-Century-Crofts.

Kendler, H. H. (1952). What is learned?—A theoretical blind alley. *Psychological Review, 59,* 269–277.

Kimble, W. (1984). Psychology's two cultures. *American Psychologist, 38,* 833–839.

McKeachie, W. J. (1982). Undergraduate education in the next decade: Discussion. *Teaching of Psychology, 9,* 62–63.

Osgood, C. E. (1953). *Method and theory in experimental psychology.* New York: Oxford University Press.

Plato. (1952). *Phaedo* (R. Hackforth, Trans.). New York: Liberal Arts Press.

Ritchie, L. (1953). Circumnavigation of cognition. *Psychological Review, 60,* 206–211.

Scarr, S. (1985). Constructing psychology: Making facts and fables for our times. *American Psychologist, 40,* 499–512.

Segal, E. M., & Lachman, R. (1972). Complex behavior or higher mental process: Is there a paradigm shift? *American Psychologist, 27,* 46–55.

Slezak, P. (1989). The relevance of philosophy to psychology: Response to J. Furedy. *Australian Journal of Psychology, 4,* 123–130.

Spence, K. W. (1956). *Behavior theory and conditioning.* New Haven, CT: Yale University Press.

Watson, J. B. (1913). Psychology as the behaviorist views it. *Psychological Review, 20,* 158–177.

4

INTERNATIONAL DEVELOPMENT OF PSYCHOLOGY AS AN ACADEMIC DISCIPLINE

HELIO CARPINTERO

A book on the history of teaching psychology in America would be incomplete without a discussion of the birth and growth of academic psychology in Europe and a survey of related developments in other countries. This genealogy pertains not only to the content of what is taught in America but also to the institutional framework of the academic discipline in American universities.

The Western tradition of thought since the Renaissance period paved the way for the emergence of psychology as a "new" science. Psychophysical dualism, as Descartes conceived of it, had failed to solve the question of man's essential unity and the nature of the body–mind relationship. In search of a scientific view of the world that would coherently explain whole phenomena, philosophers and scientists since Descartes have given priority to questioning the grounds of valid knowledge. In the rationalist view, man's mind has appeared as the priori factor for all knowledge. But for others, inasmuch as such a mind developed in a physical body as as result of evolution, the body structures have been considered the true a priori factors for all human knowledge and action.

This debate may in part explain the changing ways psychology has been classified since its beginnings. For some, psychology has been mainly viewed as a science attempting to generate a great deal of empirically based knowledge. For others, psychology has been considered in its related context, and its philosophical implications have been emphasized. Psychology's proper place in the world of knowledge was thus an open question during the early decades. As a result, its place in the academic world has frequently changed from a natural to a moral science (*Naturwissenschaft* or *Geistwissenschaft*) and vice versa, according to the interests of the dominant groups in each case. However, in the long run, with some significant exceptions, the pervasive goal in the early years was to establish an independent scientific psychology without the constrictions of a philosophical outlook. For this purpose, only a positivistic *weltanschauung* was acceptable.

Despite such an approach, psychology has never had a strong theoretical unity. Instead, a series of problems and questions have been addressed as they arose, using both data and ideas. Moreover, theoretical concerns have never pervaded the entire field of psychology. Practical applications became increasingly significant in the light of pressing social problems. The value of psychological concepts was then seen as highly dependent on their practical utility. For this reason, the technical value of knowledge in this science has greatly influenced theoretical developments. Indeed, modern psychology has developed as an experimental field as opposed to an "armchair" discipline. It has profited from laboratory research and technological development in gathering data for theory construction.

Interest in the new science arose unevenly, and its development took place in the context of various cultural influences. As will be shown, the dominant views in a given country regarding philosophical and ideological questions and the various levels of technical development, religious beliefs, and social needs have undoubtedly influenced that development. Whereas some countries have become deeply involved in promoting research and profiting from its applications over time, other less developed countries have paid little or no attention to this scientific enterprise. A comparison of contributions to international congresses between 1889 and 1960 may be taken as a rough indicator of such a differential involvement: United States, 32.04%; United Kingdom, 12.19%; France, 11.44%, Germany, 10.70%; and Italy, 8.57% (Montoro et al., 1984).

In each of these countries, academic settings have played a significant role in supporting the new discipline. Universities have offered faculty the possibility of developing a theoretical and empirical science with a unique identity, clearly differentiated from the other sciences. In addition to prescribing applications, the academic world has demanded from the new science an epistemological demarcation of the field to be maintained by professors and departments. Theoretical independence in Europe has been seen as only attainable through conceptual differentiation among the sciences.

Likewise, in America, scientific progress in teaching and research hinged on effective university support. Although important resources were required from governments and industries to develop specific "technical" knowledge and practical training (Titchener, 1898), universities appear to have been the most suitable centers for developing the new science. This trend continued until about 1945 (Misiak & Sexton, 1966).

In conclusion, modern psychology, conceived of as scientific knowledge regarding mental phenomena and behavior, was founded in Europe a century ago. In Western countries, psychology has grown as both a science and a profession at the same time that questions regarding its identity, unity, and methodological assumptions have repeatedly been raised. In this context, psychology has continued to be cultivated in Europe and in other countries, while undergoing its greatest development in the United States. In the remainder of this chapter, these forerunners to and companions in the development of psychology in America are considered.

THE GROWTH OF EUROPEAN PSYCHOLOGY

Psychology in Germany

The foundation of the new, scientific psychology was laid in Germany. It has been suggested that the organizational regime of German universities and the very unusual situation in which physiologists applied for vacant philosophy chairs resulted in a "role-hybridization" (Ben-David & Collins, 1966) that may have influenced the new discipline. Psychology heretofore had been well-rooted in physiology and philosophy. The positivist mentality, the involvement of physiologists deeply interested in the study of sensory knowledge, and the flexible organization of university studies are some of the factors that may explain the birth of psychology in Germany.

In Germany, the universities were the center of science (Viqueira, 1915), although they were more oriented toward theory construction than toward applied research (Ben-David, 1974). Two specific liberties characterized German universities at the time: the freedom to teach and the freedom to learn (Dobson & Bruce, 1972; Behrens, 1984). Teachers could choose their topics and ways of presenting them, and students could organize their curricula according to their own interests. "Taken together, the twenty-one universities on the territory of the German Empire might well be called the social system of German science. . . [whose] primary function, however, was the training of Germany's educated elite" (Ash, 1982, pp. 3–4). Professors with tenure were appointed under strict scrutiny, with both academic and political criteria in mind.

The prestige of scientific research extended across cultural fields, from chemistry to philology. "In that atmosphere the scientific study of the human mind by men like Wundt and Fechner may be regarded as an inevitable consequence" (Dobson & Bruce, 1972, p. 206).

In 1914, there were many German universities offering courses in psychology (Ash, 1982; Bonaventura, 1914), but they were held under very difficult conditions. Notwithstanding this, they attracted large numbers of students from all over the world wishing to profit from the German scientific spirit.

Of utmost significance in this regard was the Leipzig group headed by W. Wundt, the so-called "father of modern psychology." W. Wirth and E. Spranger, among others, also worked at the University of Leipzig. Wundt, whose Institute of Experimental Psychology was known the world over, had arrived in 1875 after special invitation to be "a specialist on the relationship between the natural sciences and philosophy" (Bringmann, Bringmann, & Ungerer, 1980, p. 130). Wundt occupied a chair of philosophy, and he began lecturing on the psychology of language, anthropology, logic, and methodology. A list of his courses in the first years at Leipzig shows his commitment to both psychology and philosophy.

Almost all historians of psychology agree that the foundation of the first laboratory at Leipzig in 1879 is the starting point of scientific psychology. Such a psychological laboratory not only made a certain type of research possible, it also implied an epistemological change in psychology from philosophy to natural science (Cattell, 1888; Danziger, 1990; Titchener, 1898).

The founding of laboratory psychology has to be seen as a fact among others of a similar nature that can be explained by the zeitgeist of the day. In 1875, W. James assembled various instruments at Harvard University to perform psychological experiments. In 1877, J. Ward tried to establish a laboratory at Cambridge (United Kingdom), only to find strong political opposition. However, in a few years, many laboratories were created in Western countries according to the Leipzig model.

Year after year, students came from all over the world to attend Wundt's lectures, many of them staying to complete their doctoral dissertations at his laboratory. G. S. Hall wrote a very interesting academic portrait of Wundt:

> Wundt is a superb academic lecturer and to this he owes much. He was the first professor in the philosophic field to experiment before his classes, as he used to do when the laboratory was a small private venture of his own. He always had a talent for making philosophical and psychological topics interesting and popular for students of medicine, theology and even law and his service in stemming the tide of specialization by attracting attention to the most humanistic of all fields has been very great. . . . Some have thought he simplified too much before his

large academic audiences and made topics too easy by passing lightly over difficulties. . . . Outside his own class-room, Wundt has never been a popular lecturer. . . . So far as he has attempted to make propaganda of his own views, it has been within academic walls by elementarizing what he has written in greater detail. (Hall, 1912, p. 313)

Lectures, small weekly seminars, and long stays at the laboratory working and writing filled most of the time of this exceptional teacher, who directed 186 theses from 1875 to 1919 (Tinker, 1980).

Berlin was to become another center of utmost importance for psychology. There were two philosophy chairs; E. Zeller held one of them, and W. Dilthey, the other. H. Ebbinghaus (1850–1909) began lecturing there on psychological and aesthetic topics as an assistant professor (1886–1894) and at that time also founded a psychological laboratory. He lectured on such topics as elements of psychophysics, psychology of sensations and sense representations, color perception, and the philosophy of Schopenhauer. When a third philosophy chair was created in 1894, C. Stumpf (1848–1936) was appointed to the newest chair and also became head of the laboratory. Zeller and Dilthey supported his application for this position, as they wanted a person "who, familiar with the natural sciences and with mathematics, is able to cover subjects which depend on them" (See Sprung & Sprung, 1985). Ebbinghaus left Berlin for a chair at Breslau in 1894. Around 1914, Stumpf, G. Störring, and Wentzel were offering courses in psychology, with practical exercises done under the supervision of H. Rupp (1880–1954). In 1900, Stumpf founded a Psychological Institute and "made out of the Berlin Institute one of the world's biggest and most efficient psychological centres of research and teaching" (Sprung, Sprung, & Kernchen, 1984, p. 352). The Institute had an important collection of acoustic records on primitive languages and folklore. Stumpf was succeeded as the head of the Institute in 1922 by W. Köhler. With Köhler came the new Gestalt psychology that eventually began to dominate psychology.

Various other universities were offering courses in psychology with an emphasis on experimentation. According to one carefully written report of that period (Bonaventura, 1914), there was a Psychological Institute at Würzburg, directed by K. Marbe, who had succeeded his master, O. Külpe (1862–1915), the founder of the laboratory (in 1896) and organizer of the Würzburg School. This group was oriented toward the investigation of thought processes using experimental introspection, which represented great progress with regard to the Wundtian approach to the topic. As Humphrey wrote, "Until the advent of the Würzburg group, experimental psychology had not come to grips with the problem of the higher mental processes" (Humphrey, 1951, p. 31). In addition to Marbe, A. Mayer, J. Orth, N. Ach, A. Messer, and K. Bühler worked under Külpe's direction, forming one of the most important groups in modern scientific psychology.

Külpe himself, after staying some years at Würzburg, went to the University of Munich (1913–1915), where he succeeded T. Lipps (1851–1914), who is best known for his aesthetic theories about empathy. Soon after Külpe's departure, the Würzburg group dispersed.

There was another important group at Göttingen, headed by G. E. Müller (1850–1934), whose studies on memory are well known. He founded a laboratory there in 1881 that was second only to that of the one in Leipzig. There, well-known experiments on color and space perception were carried out by D. Katz and E. Jaensch, among others (Viqueira, 1915).

According to Bonaventura's (1914) report, there were also psychological courses at Bonn (under Störring), Freiburg (under H. Rickert and J. Cohn), Kiel (under C. Martius), and Strasburg (under E. Schneider). These Institutes and laboratories had limited resources, and most of them had only two or three researchers. Although the University of Berlin had 3,000 DM, and the University of Leipzig, 2,600 DM, some other universities had no budget at all or at least suffered from great economic difficulties (Bonaventura, 1914). The combined budgets of the five most important institutes (Leipzig, Berlin, Munich, Würzburg, and Göttingen) for that year rose to slightly over 13,000 DM, less than one fifth of the resources for the physiological institute at the University of Berlin in the same year (Ash, 1982).

The teaching of psychology at these Centers would normally include an introductory course for a general audience, with some demonstrative experiments. Another introductory course in laboratory experimentation provided practical training in the use of apparatus. A course for advanced students, to help them prepare a personal paper, was also required. Specialized psychology talks (*Psychologisches Colloquium*) on current topics and literature were held once a week, and special courses on various topics were offered regularly. Finally, a few students who had first been "experimental subjects" (*Versuchspersonen*) were accepted as research collaborators, charged with completing some parts of a research project. Proper training in experimental psychology required always working with a subject using a well-defined methodology (Viqueira, 1915). Basic knowledge of mathematics and natural science were normally prerequisites.

It is not an easy task to select those textbooks that best represent the various approaches dominating the German academic world at that time. Wundt's *Grundzüge der Physiologischen Psychologie* (1872) is a masterpiece that influenced the historical evolution of the discipline. "The text (ed. 1874) is divided into six subdivisions: Introduction (20 pages, 2.32% of text) . . . Physiological characteristics of the nervous system (252 pages, 29.20% of text) . . . On sensations (191 pages, 22.13% of text) . . . On the nature of images (243 pages, 28.16% of text) . . . Consciousness and its influence on ideas (113 pages, 13.09% of text) . . . and . . . On movement (44 pages, 5.10% of text)" (Bringmann & Hope, 1983).

Soon there was a need for a shorter and easier text to introduce students to the complexities of the new science. A highly praised work addressing that issue was Ebbinghaus's *Abriss der Psychologie* (Outline of Psychology, 1908). This book was divided into five parts (Introduction, General Psychology, Special Facts of Consciousness, Complications of Mental Life, and Highest Accomplishments of Consciousness), and was written from a broad functionalist point of view (Caparrós, 1986).

Written several years later, Jesuit Father J. Fröbes's *Lehrbuch der Experimentellen Psychologie* (1923) has been considered the best work, second only to Wundt's classic textbook (Spearman, 1961). In this volume, many topics were covered: sensation, perception (including thought), psychophysics, associative processes, brain localizations, cognitive complex processes (including attention, self, memory, imagery, and language), emotions, will (including personality and social psychology), abnormal conscious processes, and psychopathology.

Throughout the first decades of the 20th century, German hegemony over the field of psychology was disrupted by the growing influence of American thought. American psychologists outnumbered their German colleagues not only in their total output but also in their impact in the psychological community, as measured by references in psychology texts and periodicals. For example, in the *Psychological Review*, one of the best exponents of theoretical evolution in psychology, references to German literature in the early years occupied a third of the total number, while they occupied less than 10% after World War I (Calatayud, 1984, p. 308). Similar data can be found in American psychological textbooks (Ben-David & Collins, 1966). Careful review of citations during this period suggests that the change took place in the early 1930s (Maller, 1934).

With the death of Wundt in 1920, the University of Berlin's psychology department undeniably occupied the primary position among the German psychological centers. There, Köhler maintained a vast research program in Gestalt topics. Closely related to it were other groups, such as those of K. Goldstein at Frankfurt University (1916–1930), and K. Koffka at Giesen University (until 1927). Bühler and his wife C. Buhler organized an important group at the newly founded Vienna Psychological Institute in 1922, which during its first decade became a leading center for developmental psychology in the world. P. Lazarsfeld, M. Jahoda, and others did important research there, but Hitler's occupation of Austria in 1938 terminated such efforts (Ash, 1987).

German psychology suffered a tremendous blow during the Nazi period. After the 1933 decree that dismissed all Jews from government and civil positions, many professors were forced to leave or to ask for retirement, and most of them emigrated (Geuter, 1987). The entire psychological field was thus dramatically changed. In a certain sense, an entire epoch of psychology was closed with the war, and a new era began.

Psychology in the United Kingdom

T. Ribot, in his classic study, *La Psychologie Anglaise Contemporaine* (1872), wrote, "Since Hobbes and Locke, England is perhaps the country that has done most for psychology" (Ribot, 1885). Although this may be arguable today, it is true that scientific psychology has, as Boring stated, one of its main roots in the British empiricist approach to the study of the human mind (Boring, 1950). The associationist movement appears strongly connected with empiricist philosophy, and associationism has provided psychologists with a broad theory for understanding how the mind works. (Darwin's works helped create an important tradition of comparative psychology but that is beyond the scope of this chapter.)

At the same time, the British academic world resisted including among its disciplines the new science of mind that had been conceived of in Germany as an experimental and quasi-physiological enterprise. It is noteworthy that when in 1887 J. Ward and J. Venn made the first move to establish experimental psychology as a discipline at Cambridge University, the academic senate rejected the idea of a psychophysical laboratory on the basis that it would "insult religion by putting the human soul in a pair of scales" (Hearnshaw, 1964, p. 171). This was one (among other) result of the conflict between science and religion that dominated the British academic and social world in the second half of the 19th century and that had been greatly stimulated by Darwin's scientific contributions.

For decades, British psychologists showed little enthusiasm for experimentalism and for physiological approaches, whereas, at the same time, the "educated British public came to regard psychology—as they mostly did till Freud and World War I changed the tune—as merely a rather odd sub-species of philosophy" (Hearnshaw, 1964, p. 136).

All of these factors clearly influenced the development of both psychological research and teaching, and the moral climate selected to some extent the people that were able to engage in these activities.

In the United Kingdom, a philosophical, nontechnical psychology preceded the creation of an institutional network supporting the new science. Independent scholars unrelated to any university greatly influenced the early stages of British scientific psychology, such as in the cases of H. Spencer, A. Bain, and Sir F. Galton.

Spencer (1820–1903), whose writings on philosophical evolutionism included a large and detailed analysis of psychology, biology, and sociology, remained all his life a private person nevertheless interested in offering to his readers the results of his personal reflections. After working as a schoolteacher and a civil railway engineer, he devoted his life to writing about psychology, without an academic position.

Galton (1822–1911), pioneer of the "new" psychology in Great Britain (Boring, 1950), became deeply involved in anthropological and psychological research. Although he never obtained a degree, his studies brought him great honors, including becoming a Fellow of the Royal Society in 1856. He succeeded in creating some institutional basis for his evolutionary studies on hereditary and abilities. Galton opened his Anthropometric Laboratory at the London International Exhibition in 1884 and then transferred the Laboratory to the South Kensington Museum, where it existed for six years. In addition, he founded the Eugenics Society in 1907 and was a chair of eugenics at the University College in London. Among his distinguished students were K. Pearson, J. M. Cattell, and C. Spearman. His efforts in the psychological field brought important results at the institutional level, laying the groundwork for later developments.

Quite similar to Galton's situation was the case of Bain, whose psychological works are well rooted in J. S. Mill's empiricist philosophy. After many years of efforts, Bain finally was appointed to a chair at Aberdeen University, where he became professor of logic and English in 1860. He remained there for the next 20 years, offering courses in mental philosophy and various other subjects. Bain also helped create a new climate in British psychology. His two-volume treatise, *The Senses and the Intellect* (1855) and *The Emotions and the Will* (1859), soon became the first widely used textbook, offering a broad coverage of the field and an empirical approach. In 1876, he also founded *Mind*, a philosophical and psychological journal whose contributors paid special attention to the new experimental approach. Bain's textbook and journal clearly influenced the beginnings of British psychology.

Thus, before the study of psychology had been formally in universities, some steps had been taken to institutionalize psychology by developing a textbook, a laboratory, and a specialized periodical. As already mentioned, it was far from easy for psychology to enter into universities and to be included in formal curricula. In 1891, Cambridge was the first university that had a chair of psychology with a laboratory but, as Hearnshaw wrote, "All that happened was that in 1891 James Ward had obtained £50 for psychological apparatus" (Hearnshaw, 1964, p. 3). Cattell, having trained with Wundt in Leipzig, gave some instructions (1886–1888) for the practical working of a laboratory. In the end, a physiologist, W. H. R. Rivers (1864–1922), took charge of the laboratory, orienting it toward the study of sensory physiology. In the years after, more facilities were obtained. In 1913, with C. S. Myers as its new director, a new building was dedicated to such studies.

All these changes took place as part of a broader reform of curricula by Cambridge University, where the study of classics, mathematics, and physics had previously been the central focus. Finally, the possibility to concentrate on mental philosophy without a previous qualification in mathematics was accepted, opening the way to psychological studies.

Acceptance by Cambridge University of the new psychology was clearly influenced by the efforts of Ward (1843–1925) (a former student of H. Lotze in Germany), who substituted the old British associationism with the new German act psychology. Experimentalism in psychology moved forward rapidly at Cambridge thanks to the efforts of Rivers (1864–1922) and Myers (1873–1946). The latter, after joining the Cambridge expedition to the Torres Straits directed by A. C. Haddon, exhibited an enduring interest in a human scientific psychology (Bartlett, 1961). Researchers in Myer's laboratory worked in close collaboration with researchers in the physiological laboratory. As Bartlett wrote, "All students reading moral science then did . . . four hours of experimental work weekly in the psychological laboratory" (Bartlett, 1961, p. 39). Myers and Sir C. Burt, then an assistant of Myers, were in charge of such courses. Myers's experimental bias clearly appears in his autobiography. He was deeply interested in psychophysical methods and maintained that the diversity of psychological schools was largely due to a "lack of training in these methods and to the undisciplined conduct of research, the rash generalizations, the prejudice and the influence of suggestion thus engendered" (Myers, 1961, p. 220). Hence, he promulgated a mental cure for psychology's ills through rigorous experimental methods. In 1912, a new laboratory was opened, where work on the psychology of music and individual differences was performed regularly.

Myers promoted applied courses of study, such as those leading to a Diploma in Psychological Medicine (1912), and through his influence courses in animal and educational psychology were offered, with varying degrees of success (Myers, 1961). In 1909, he was succeeded as head of the laboratory by F. C. Bartlett, who held the first chair of experimental psychology at Cambridge University in 1931.

At University College in London, a center of the liberal arts tradition, a laboratory was established by J. Sully (1843–1923) in 1897. Sully also lectured in mental philosophy and psychology, after succeeding G. C. Robertson, student of Bain and H. von Helmholtz, and editor of *Mind*. Sully wrote "the most scholarly, comprehensive and well-balanced factual textbook of psychology ever produced by a British psychologist," according to Hearnshaw (1964, p. 134). He was first succeeded by C. Read and then (in 1911) by Spearman (1863–1945). It is noteworthy that it was not until 1928 that the title of the Spearman chair was changed from "Grote Chair of Mind and Logic" to "Chair of Psychology," a symbol of the new climate permeating the British academic world.

While Spearman worked hard on differential psychology and on factors of the mind, W. McDougall joined University College at the turn of the century, bringing with him the spirit of Müller's exact methodology, which he learned working with him at Göttingen. McDougall helped Sully in laboratory work, with "a short course of lecture-demonstrations . . . at a nominal salary" (McDougall, 1961, p. 205). But as Sully recalled it, McDougall was interested in the psychophysics of vision and the functioning of the brain and wrote that "there were only two or three persons in Great Britain interested in the special problems with which I was busy" (McDougall, 1961, p. 206).

McDougall was appointed to the Wilde Readership in Mental Philosophy at Oxford University in 1904, and there he said, "The scientists suspected me of being a metaphysician; and the philosophers regarded me as representing an impossible and non-existent branch of science. Psychology had no recognized place in the curricula and examinations" (McDougall, 1961, p. 207). McDougall succeeded G. F. Stout (1860–1944), author of one of the best known textbooks on psychology, who had relocated to the University of St. Andrews in Scotland. McDougall wrote books on social psychology and papers on experimental problems, developing his hormic psychology on the basis of the concept of instinct. While at Oxford, McDougall had a small but highly qualified group of students, including W. Brown, Sir C. Burt, and G. F. Flügel, among others. Brown succeeded McDougall and was able to create the Oxford Institute for Experimental Psychology in 1936. After World War I, feeling himself not completely adapted to the Oxford academic climate, McDougall accepted an invitation to teach and work at Harvard University.

One after another, lectureships on psychology were created at various universities. At Manchester, T. H. Pear was first appointed lecturer in 1909 but later was named to Manchester's new chair of psychology, which was created in 1919. This chair was "the first full-time chair properly and exclusively psychological" in the United Kingdom (Hearnshaw, 1964, p. 179). There, a Diploma of Psychological Medicine was inaugurated in 1910 that included courses in psychology, and a course in experimental psychology was organized at the Faculty of Science in 1913 (Hearnshaw, 1964). At Liverpool, Sir C. Sherrington created a course on psychophysiology in 1899, and courses on psychology were offered to education and philosophy students in the first years of the 20th century. The teaching of psychology was conducted by W. Smith in 1905, H. Watt in 1906 and Burt from 1907 to 1912. All eventually left Liverpool for other positions; Smith went as a lecturer to Edinburgh, while Watt did the same at Glasgow. World War I postponed the growth of psychology in Liverpool for the next 25 years (Hearnshaw, 1964).

Just before World War II, the situation in British psychology was rather complex but the approach mainly centered on the study of human faculties through quantitative and experimental techniques. At Cambridge University, Bartlett performed his famous studies on thought and memory; Brown (1881–1951), at Oxford University, maintained his personal views on intelligence factors, in opposition to the Spearman tradition; Burt (1883–1971), after succeeding Spearman at London, did a vast amount of research on intelligence, education, and criminal behavior. Other significant researchers were also busy at work including Drever (at Edinburgh), Aveling (at King's College), and Vernon (at the Institute of Education), among others.

The British psychological tradition has appeared on many occasions as a coherent stream in which the study of organisms could be characterized by its empirical approach, strong evolutionist basis, and frequently used correlational methods. Faculties and abilities, including intelligence, were seen as the main tools that organisms have for adaptation. The analysis of adaptive responses paved the way for correlating outcomes to justify such hypothesized faculties.

Certain idiosyncratic traits of this tradition, however, may perhaps be inferred from some frequently cited textbooks, such as G. F. Stout's *Manual of Psychology* (1899), McDougall's *An Introduction to Social Psychology* (1908), and Myers's *Textbook of Experimental Psychology* (1909).

Stout's *Manual of Psychology* (1899) was divided into four "books" ("General Analysis," "Sensation," "Perception," and "Ideational and Conceptual Process"), with the largest number of pages (more than 40%) dedicated to sense perception. While James, Ward, and Weber were frequently cited in this book (24, 21, and 10 times respectively), no references to Pavlov, Wundt, Binet, or Freud could be found. Stout, "completely unempirical in his discussions" (Thomson, 1968, p. 176), rejected psychological atomism and psychophysical dualism and maintained that teleology served to characterize the specific psychological point of view. McDougall's book, *An Introduction to Social Psychology* (1908), was divided into two parts: "The Mental Characters of Man of Primary Importance for his Life in Society" and "The Operation of the Primary Tendencies of the Human Mind in the Life of Societies." It offered a dynamic and purpose-centered view of psychism that was based on a certain number of "inherited tendencies" or "instincts" determining the subject's perceptions, feelings, and actions. Finally, Myers's *Textbook of Experimental Psychology* (1909) has been viewed as one of the most significant works in its field. Accepting both introspection (as "retrospection") and the objective study of behavior, Myers presented "the methods and principles of psychological experiment" (1909, p. vi), chiefly focusing on sensation (eight chapters) and perception and attention. Other topics, such as memory, reaction time, mental work, feeling, and psychophysical and statistical methods, were also covered.

Concentrating mainly on human phenomena, the British empirical approach to the study of higher mental processes appeared deeply rooted in previous analyses of the faculties of the human mind. Factorialists, such as Spearman, Burt, Thomson, Brown, Stephenson, among others, broadened the views of man's cognitive abilities. More complex approaches followed, focusing on the whole field of personality, such as those of Cattell and H. Eysenck. When later influences of psychoanalysis or American behaviorism are found, they can be seen as rooted in the strong continuity of this tradition of British psychology.

Psychology in France

The development of French scientific psychology is related to the specific cultural context of that country. Early psychological debate in France was expressed in the philosophical terms of materialism versus spiritualism. On this ground, two different social and political views of the world were at odds. Among the former, enlightened writers such as P. H. d'Holbach, C. A. Helvetius, and P. G. Cabanis stressed the total dependence of mind on body. In contrast, P. Maine de Biran and V. Cousin rejected reductionism in accordance with their introspective analysis of experience. Positivist A. Comte rejected psychology as a science, dividing its subject matter between sociology and physiology, with the latter including phrenology as the organic study of mental faculties. At the same time, psychiatrists such as M. de Tours and B. Morel stressed the role of organic degenerative factors in causing mental diseases.

During the second French empire founded by Napoleon III in 1852, a brilliant critic and historian, H. Taine, performed an analysis of mental faculties in his *De l'Intelligence*. Meanwhile J. M. Charcot (1825–1893), a psychiatrist at the hospital in Salpêtriere, discovered hysteria as a functional nonorganic disease. Both men relied on associationism as a tool for understanding the mind, and both developed a pathological and biological approach to psychology as the study of mental faculties.

Then came the work of the so called "founder" of French scientific psychology, T. Ribot (1839–1916). For the first time, here was someone who provided a complete and personal picture of psychology; his contributions included *La Psychologie Anglaise Contemporaine* (1870) and *La Psychologie Allemande Contemporaine* (1879). The former stressed associationism, whereas the latter mainly focused on psychophysiological experimentalism. These works laid the foundation for actual research programs, mostly restricted to nonuniversity settings. Reuchlin wrote that the character of French psychology up to the Second World War was to be found in frameworks that were more flexible than the faculty paradigm. Whereas universities could be seen as oriented toward traditional and conservative teaching, some other organizations, the "grands établissements" (e.g., Collège de France, and École Pratique des Hautes Études) offered room for developing the new psychology (Reuchlin, 1965).

Under Renan's influence, the Collège de France, an independent institution for higher culture, created a chair of psychology. After teaching a course on experimental psychology at the Sorbonne between 1885 and 1889, Ribot was appointed to the chair at the College, which he held from 1888 to 1896. An empirical approach to the discipline began to emerge, following positivistic and evolutionistic guidelines. Younger researchers could be trained both in medicine and in philosophy, thereby contributing a perspective on psychopathology to the work performed during that period.

Ribot "instigated" the creation of a laboratory of physiological psychology "as a part of the section of the natural sciences within the School for Advanced Studies (L'École Pratique des Hautes Études) in the Sorbonne" (Wolf, 1973, p. 9). H. Beaunis was invited to direct this effort in 1889. Two years later, Binet succeeded Beaunis as head of the laboratory.

It was very important to the development of French psychology that A. Binet, with training in medicine but not in philosophy, was not appointed to succeed Ribot when the latter retired. Neither was Binet selected for a new chair of experimental psychology created in 1905 at the Sorbonne. Instead, P. Janet (1859–1947) was appointed chair at the Collège de France in 1901, and G. Dumas (1866–1946) was appointed chair at the Sorbonne (Trognon et al., 1987). As foreign students could not obtain degrees in the laboratory, Binet had neither students nor subjects, and he spent increasingly less time at the laboratory. When the opportunity arose to do research on elementary school children, his interests changed considerably (Wolf, 1973), resulting in the founding in 1905 of a new laboratory for experimental pedagogy in Paris. However, this reduced Binet's time for pure experimentation in psychology.

In those early days, students were allowed to enroll or audit courses in psychology but had to graduate either in philosophy or physiology (Bonaventura, 1914). At the Sorbonne, researchers at several laboratories began to do empirical studies at the beginning of the 20th century. They included a center for experimental psychology at the asylum in Villejuif (director, E. Toulouse, assisted first by H. Piéron (1901) and then by J. Lahy, who carried out important work on applied psychotechnics). Several other laboratories were established, including one for sensory physiology (director, C. Henri), another one for psychopathology at Villejuif (director, A. Marie, assisted by N. Kostyleff and Thoores), and a unit on comparative psychology at the Sciences Faculty (director, G. Bohn). Dumas headed the Sainte Anne Hospital for mental diseases.

Piéron (1881–1964), who, according to Fraisse (1981), became the "founder of psychology in France," took over the direction of the physiological psychology laboratory after Binet's death and expanded the research program there. When he was appointed to the chair of Physiology of Sensations at the Collège de France in 1924, the two related laboratories joined, forming a larger one ("Laboratoire de Psychologie Experimentale et de Physiologie des Sensations"). This successful union lasted from 1925 to 1951. Another step forward was taken with Piéron's creation of an "Institut de Psychologie" at the University of Paris in 1921. This institute focused on both theoretical and applied studies. Connected with the Laboratory of Experimental Psychology, it was organized by Piéron with I. Meyerson as secretary. H. Delacroix and Dumas, professors at the Faculté des Lettres, E. Rabaud, and Janet also supported the enterprise. There were three sections, General, Applied, and Educational Psychology, each offering its own diploma.

The Institut offered courses in general psychology (taught by Delacroix and then M. Pradines and P. Guillaume) and pathological psychology (taught by Janet and Dumas, and then by J. Delay). Piéron was in charge of physiological psychology, along with Meyerson, Francois, H. Durup, and P. Fraisse. Pedagogical psychology was organized by T. Simon and H. Wallon, who were able to create a new laboratory (directed by Ombredane and Gratiot-Alphandery, and then by R. Zazzo).

It is also noteworthy that in the first decades of the 20th century, three other private centers were founded in Paris: the "École de Psychologie" (directed by Berillon), the "Institut Catholique" (with a laboratory headed by Jeanjean), and the "Institut Géneral Psychologique" (directed by D'Arsonval).

Other universities—Rennes, Montpellier, and Dijon—created some facilities for laboratory work in connection with a philosophy chair oriented toward psychology. B. Bourdon, M. Foucault, and A. Rey were, respectively, in charge of these centers. In all cases, psychology was included in the philosophy curriculum.

Because of space limitations, many important contributions to this tradition cannot be summarized here. Only a few salient pieces of work, in order to provide a synthetic view of the development of psychology in France, can be discussed in this chapter. One significant textbook that offers a detailed picture of psychology in the French tradition is Dumas's *Traité de Psychologie*. This volume was partly written before World War I but was not printed until 1923–1924. The revised edition appeared in 1931 (*Nouveau Traité de Psychologie*). Dumas's projected volume on applications of psychology became Piéron's seven-volume *Traité de Psychologie Appliquée*). This work included several chapters on preliminary biological notions (8.1% of the text); the elements of mental life (sensation, feeling, imagery, and movement; 15.7%); sensory-motor associations (9.5%); general organizing structures (habit, association, and mental strength; 8.5%); systematic functions of mental life (perception, memory, intellectual processes, will, and creativity; 22.5%); mental syntheses (consciousness, personality, character, activity, and fatigue; 7.29%); and related disciplines (animal, genetic, and interpersonal psychology, and sociology; 24.6%). This work "reflects with enough precision the various orientations dominating French psychology between the two World Wars" (Foulquié & Deledalle, 1965, p. 42).

As has been frequently noted, French psychology was strongly determined by the sociocultural aspects of the times. "Laboratories have not played an important role in the development of French psychology. . . . Preoccupied with clinical problems, . . . [the French] preferred clinics, asylums, and hospitals, and even libraries as the places of research" (Misiak & Sexton, 1966, p. 239). In fact, the French were deeply interested in psychopathology and in applied questions, especially those dealing with children and education. Influences from both philosophy and medicine dominated the early scene. Theoretical and experimental psychology began to develop in France only after World War II. In 1947, a degree in psychology was created, and universities came to play a larger role in the development of the field, offering new avenues of research and reinforcing theory-building efforts.

The historical evolution of psychology in France clearly shows how the unusual aspects of its academic institutions have influenced the development of new psychology, whose destiny seems everywhere to be highly dependent on its institutional background and support.

Psychology in Italy

Italian psychology was also greatly influenced by various sociocultural factors. In Italy, the earliest approaches to psychology were formulated by philosophers and physicians interested in psychological questions.

Nineteenth century philosophy in Italy included a wide range of world views, from the spiritualism of "ontologists" A. Rosmini and F. Gioberti to the positivistic materialism of R. Ardigó. Their reflections on the human mind, consciousness, and human nature paved the way for other scientifically based views on these topics.

At the end of the century, a scientific fermentation was occurring in various parts of the country. Although spiritualism and idealism prevailed in large cultural areas, the growing influence of positivism, which was largely based on Spencer's ideas, renewed interest in empirical questions and research at certain universities. Closer contacts were created between scientists from Germany and Italy, and in this manner the ideas of the new psychology reached Italy.

One of these advanced centers was Turin, where some well-known professors completed interesting research projects. Such was the case of the criminal anthropologist C. Lombroso (1835–1909) in whose books, *L'Uomo Criminale*; *La Dona Delinquente*; *L'Uomo di Genio*, the idea of a genetic predisposition for delinquency as well as for the insanity of genius were developed. Also at the University of Torino, the physiologist A. Mosso, a former student of C. Ludwig, carried out an extensive program of research on emotions and their somatic phenomena. His "ergograph," which registered physiological changes due to fatigue, offered new possibilities for research. As a result, an interest in anthropological and physiological questions were stimulated throughout Italy.

At the same time, Ardigó (1828–1920), a former priest who gave up his position in the Catholic Church because of his scientific beliefs, tried to create a coherent philosophical system with the tenets of evolutionism and Darwinism. He maintained a consistent psychologism according to which all sciences should be based on psychology or sociology. Ardigó also tried to establish a psychological laboratory, first at a high school in Mantua and then at the University of Padua. His book, *La Psicologia come Scienza Positiva* (1870), has been considered as the "birth certificate of Italian scientific psychology" (Marhaba, 1981).

G. Buccola had a more empirical approach than Ardigó. As a "proto-psychologist" (Marhaba, 1984), he wrote a well-documented book on re-action time, *La Legge del Tempo nei Fenomeni del Pensiero* (1883). Working at the Psychiatric Institute of Turin, Buccola related reaction-time measures with various mental abnormalities, in search of criteria for a differential diagnostic system.

Slowly, psychology was developing resources as well as possibilities. G. Sergi (1841–1936), a professor of anthropology at the University of Rome, rejected animism as well as spiritualism on the basis of his reading of the works of Darwin and Spencer. Instead, he offered a biologically based view of psychism and its phenomena. He was also committed to the study of anthropology, his research approaching to some extent the Wundtian ethnological works, and he introduced some laboratory apparatus for psychological research. His *Principi di Psicologia* (1873) has been seen as one of the basic sources of Italian psychology (Misiak & Staudt, 1955).

At the beginning of the century, new changes took place. A journal, *Rivista di Psicologia*, was founded in 1905 by G. C. Ferrari (1869–1932). Ferrari had previously translated James's *Principles of Psychology* in 1901 and had organized a small laboratory at Reggio Emilia in 1896.

The Fifth International Congress of Psychology in Rome in 1905 was a great opportunity for Italian researchers. In 1906, psychology chairs were established at Rome, Turin, and Naples. S. de Sanctis (1862–1935), F. Kiesow (1858–1940), and C. Colucci were appointed to each of them, respectively. The institutionalization of psychology had thus completed its first significant stage.

Additional chairs—one at the University of Padua in 1919 and another at the private Universitá Cattolica del Sacre Cuore (in Milan) in 1921—were established. V. Benussi was appointed to the former; Father A. Gemelli held the latter. Between 1925 and 1941, under the fascist regime, the political and intellectual climate deteriorated and by the end of that period only two chairs remained, one at Rome and the other at the Sacre Cuore.

De Santis was a student of and later collaborator with Sergi. After completing his medical degree at Rome with a thesis on aphasia, de Santis became more involved in the study of feelings, emotions, psychopathology, and social applications. He taught forensic psychology at the School of Juridico-Criminal Application, founded by E. Ferri at the University of Rome, and organized a Neuropsychiatric Clinic, as he was also a specialist in child neuropsychiatry. As professor of experimental psychology at Rome from 1907 to 1930, he considered his discipline "the 'experimental' determination of what I call 'pure psychical energy,' " whose origins and nature are unknown to science (de Santis, in Murchison, p. 109). De Santis's two-volume *Psicologia Sperimentale* (1930) has been considered the first true Italian psychology handbook. In this text, he maintained that behavior is an integration of psychological and somatic dimensions in varying proportions. De Santis also indicated that according to his "law of the cycle," the existence of a certain kind of body–mind feedback link was maintained.

F. Kiesow (1859–1941), a German-born student of both Wundt and C. Ludwig at Leipzig, was appointed to the Turin chain. He came by invitation from A. Mosso and established a laboratory in 1895, carrying out research on taste sensibility. At Naples, Colucci worked on psychopathology and considered psychology as a specialty that should be based on medicine (Marhaba, 1981).

Benussi (1878–1927) was considered a great experimentalist by Boring (1950), who perceived him as an Austrian rather than an Italian psychologist. Born in Trieste, Benussi became an Italian citizen after World War I. After studying with A. Meinong at Gratz, Benussi organized an Italian Gestalt group that was centered in Padua. He did research on visual perception, forensic testimony, symbolic processes, and hypnosis.

Psychophysics, perception, child study, and characterology were the early dominant topics in Italian psychology (Misiak & Staudt, 1955). But, as psychology grew, strong opposition arose from Catholic schools and institutions that saw in the new science an outbreak of positivism.

Psychology's advances were also counteracted by an increasing resistance from the idealistic philosophy that dominated Italy from the 1910s to the 1930s. Idealism, as represented by G. Gentile and B. Croce, opposed all forms of positivism and was against all efforts to establish a naturalistic psychology. The fight for and against an independent psychology was maintained throughout the years by individuals such as de Sanctis and Mussati. Nonetheless, in 1935, psychology was made a requirement in certain academic curricula (Misiak & Sexton, 1966) especially for those wanting to become teachers. For decades, psychology had been considered an optional subject in philosophy and education departments (Zunini, 1965).

While proponents of this idealism opposed scientific psychology, some Catholic groups became involved in a process of cultural modernization and *aggiornamento*. Dominican friars at Angellicum and Jesuits at Universitá Gregoriana, among others, began to incorporate psychology into their curricula. In the latter case, Father J. Fröbes (1866–1947) was appointed to a chair of experimental psychology, which opened the way to the recognition of psychology as a discipline independent from philosophy in that institution.

Gemelli (1872–1959), a Franciscan monk, is largely responsible for the scientific development which took place in the years before and after

World War II. He suggested that the scholastic view that was based on Aristotelian and Thomistic concepts could solve most of the problems in the dispute between philosophy and psychology. Gemelli founded the *Rivista di Filosofia Neo-Scolastica* and also the *Archivio di Psicologia, Neurologia e Psichiatria* (1920–1921) with Kiesow. Around World War I, Gemelli created a psychophysiological laboratory for the Italian Army, and he organized a laboratory for psychology applied to education at Milan in 1919. In 1921, he succeeded in creating an entire university, the Universittá Cattolica del Sacre Cuore (at Milan), which soon became an important center of psychological research and teaching. A series of monographs, mainly on the topics of perception, personality, and language, titled the *Contributi del Laboratorio di Psicologia*, were widely read. Gemelli's *Introduzione alla Psicologia* (1964), written in collaboration with G. Zunini, offered his personal views on the subject. In 1964, these authors argued that the person should be the proper subject matter of psychology and that both the person's behavior and his or her internal experience should be taken into account (Gemelli & Zunini, 1964). According to this view, higher and lower functions cooperated in every human action. Although some positive aspects of behaviorism were acknowledged in this book, its perspective relies mainly on European schools, with Gemelli's debt towards his master, Külpe, clearly visible. A large part of Gemelli's research was devoted to applied topics (e.g., the psychology of the soldier and of the criminal personality, the study of pilots, educational guidance, etc.). His basic tenets are in accordance with scholastic philosophy as well as with his religious beliefs (Misiak & Staudt, 1955). Furthermore, he was very active and received much support from the fascist government. He also chaired the psychological meetings at a congress of Italian and German psychologists, organized in Rome in 1941 (Marhaba, 1981).

During the last years of fascism, studies in experimental psychology were again called *philosophy*. This renaming opened the way for philosophers to opt for academic posts in the field (Marhaba, 1981). At the same time, a School for Psychology (Scuola di Specializzazione in Psicologia) was created, offering a diploma to people who had a degree in medicine.

At the Consiglio Nazionale delle Ricerche (or CNR, the National Council for Research) an experimental center for applied psychology was created in 1940. Researchers at the center developed programs for intervention in various social fields. The center was inspired by Gemelli and headed by F. Banissoni (1888–1952). Some significant figures who agreed to collaborate there included M. Ponzo, C. Musatti, and A. Massuco Costa (Mecacci, 1989). A special German–Italian meeting of psychologists was organized by the center in 1941, at which time psychological interventions in the European crisis and war were discussed. After the war, the center became the Istituto Nazionale di Psicologia at the CNR, now headed by L. Canestrelli and still in existence in Rome. The fall of fascism and the reintegration of Italy into the Western world paved the way for a scientific recovery in the country. Psychology as a degreed program became available at three universities—Rome, Palermo, and Padua—and other psychology chairs were created at other universities.

Psychology in Russia

In Russia, the evolution of psychology was also strongly influenced by political and social changes, as its contents were viewed from a particular conception of man inseparable from the rest of the *Weltanschauung*.

Several important individuals addressed psychological questions in the last decades of the 19th century in Russia. These included V. G. Belinsky (b. 1811) and A. Herzen (b. 1812), who stressed a progressive and materialistic view of man. Their efforts found some continuity in the works of N. Chernishevski (1828–1889) and I. Sechenov (1829–1905). While Sechenov's *Reflexes of the Brain* is commonly understood as the intellectual foundation from which I. Pavlov's ideas were built, Chernishevski's psychophysical monism provided a philosophical materialistic basis for the emerging revolutionary view of man.

By that time, other empiricist and positivistic minded people—M. M. Troitskii and N. Grot (1852–1899)—had begun the process of institutionalizing psychology. The former wrote "the first Russian treatise on the new discipline," *Nemetskaia* (1867), and became professor at Moscow University. He was joined there by Grot, with whom he founded the Moscow Psychological Society in 1885. Only a few years later, they also launched the first journal of the discipline in Russia, *Voprosy Filosofii i Psikhologii* in 1889 (Joravsky, 1989).

Moscow and St. Petersburg were the two major centers of psychological research in Russia, but there were also laboratories in Kazan. The first laboratory was established in Russia in 1885 by Z. M. Bekhterev and focused on the study of behavioral pathology. Soon other laboratories were established at Kiev (founded by G. Chelpanov) and Odessa (founded by N. Lange; see Kozulin, 1984).

Several tensions dominated Russian psychology at an early stage—the relationship between philosophy and psychology, the controversy between an applied and a more theoretical point of view in psychology, and the battle between materialism and phenomenalism.

A reaction against 19th-century materialists, as exemplified by Sechenov, was promoted by Chelpanov and other idealist thinkers. Chelpanov succeeded Grot at Moscow University and taught courses in experimental and general psychology. He also wrote an *Introduction to Experimental Psychology* in 1915, an interesting textbook according to some (Kozulin, 1984). Chelpanov created a Psychological Institute in 1912, in which psychology was clearly separated but not completely cut off from philosophy. By 1914, the Institute was attended by 70 students—a large number at the time. Chelpanov invited promising young people to join the center, such as K. Kornilov, A. Smirnov, and P. Blonskii. When he was replaced by his former research assistant, Kornilov (1879–1957), as the head of the Institute in 1923, the separation between philosophy and psychology came to an end. Marxist philosophy became the ultimate basis of the new approach to psychology. While the Moscow Institute retained its committment to applied activities in educational areas, another center, the School for Experimental Psychology, was created by A. P. Nechaev in St. Petersburg. This school strongly promoted the use of tests and psychological assessment in schools. It was equipped with laboratory apparatus, and researchers carried out an experimental program from a materialistic point of view (Massucco Costa, 1977).

Educational psychology soon became a largely cultivated field, and two other centers were founded. These were the Institute of Neuropsychology at St. Petersburg, headed by Lazourski (who wrote *Classification of Personalities*) and whose institute was devoted to testing psychology), and the Moscow Institute of Neuropathology, directed by G. Rossolimo (who focused on personality profiles). Five congresses on educational psychology took place between 1906 and 1916, at which significant discussions occurred regarding the role of psychology in the schools.

In the 1930s, research was concentrated in several centers: (a) The Moscow Psychological Institute, directed by the "reactologist" Kornilov, included such well-known names as A. R. Luria, B. M. Teplov, and L. S. Vygotsky. It was eventually reorganized into various areas including psychotechnics, pedagogical psychology, pedology and defectology, general psychology, comparative psychology, and animal physiology. Creativity and psychotechnics were said to be the primary goals of investigation (Petrovsky, 1990); (b) The Institute for Studies of the Brain and Mental Activity (St. Petersburg) was founded by Bekhterev. Here Osipov, B. Ananiev, and others collaborated on reflexological research, as well as on education in the schools (Petrovsky, 1990); (c) The Psychoneurological Department at the Communist Academy in Moscow was organized in 1925. The Society of Psychoneurologists–Materialists staffed this center in which the work of Luria, Vygotsky, and Kornilov played a significant part. Luria and Vygotsky also worked in the N. K. Krupskaya Academy of Communist Education, where A. Leontiev and others also collaborated; (d) The Ukrainian Psychoneurological Institute, founded in Kharkov in 1921, was oriented toward personality research. The Institute hosted a variety of investigators including Protopopov, K. Platonov, and others. As Petrovsky has stated, "All this demonstrates that by 1933 Soviet Psychologists had a broad and smoothly functioning network of scientific research establishments at their disposal" (Petrovsky, 1990, p. 107).

By the mid-1930s, conflicts between political authorities and scientific groups became crystallized when the use of tests in psychological interventions were banned in 1936. New efforts to build a Marxist-based psychology came from S. Rubinstein and others who stressed the theoretical role of reflexes and consciousness. World War II brought forth new possibilities for neuropsychological studies, such as those carried out by Luria, Leontiev, P. K. Anokhin, and others. During the Stalin era, the dependence of scientific work on guidelines issued by the Communist Party was strongly reinforced. As Ananiev once said, "The real founders of Soviet psychology as a dialectical–materialist discipline are neither schools nor trends . . . but the founders of Marxism-Leninism" (see Kozulin, 1984, p. 21).

PSYCHOLOGY IN OTHER COUNTRIES

Psychology did not develop at the same pace in every country. Its growth may be better described as an undulatory movement with waves spreading out from Germany and from the Anglo-Saxon countries into the United States.

Around the German epicenter, various other nuclei began to form. In the Netherlands, a pioneer group was founded at the University of Gröningen by the philosopher and psychologist G. Heymans (1857–1930). After studying with Windelband in Freiburg, he established a laboratory at Gröningen (1893) and did research on differential psychology and temperaments (Eisenga, 1978).

In Belgium, two private centers for psychology had been established before World War I. One was in Brussels and was directed by Ioteyko, whose work on applied and industrial psychology is well known. The other, at the Faculty of Medicine of the Université Catholique de Louvain, was directed by A. Michotte (1881–1965).

Louvain, under the guidance of Cardinal D. Mercier, also a distinguished psychologist, gave a great impetus to the study of scientific psychology as part of a response to the call of Pope Leo XIII (*Aeterni Patris*, 1879). The Pope had asked for a revival of Thomistic philosophy as a basis for an understanding between Catholic religion and modern science. Mercier (1851–1926) invited one student of Wundt's, A. Thiéry, to organize a psychological laboratory in 1891. He finally succeeded in creating a School for Education and Applied Psychology (*École de Pédagogie et de Psychologie Appliquée à l'Education*) at the university. He wrote a textbook on psychology and various other works on psychological topics.

Michotte succeeded Thiéry as the head of the Institute in 1906. After studying with Wundt and Külpe, Michotte became interested in the study of the will, and he later did significant research on Gestalt topics, including the perception of movement and of phenomenal causality. He was also the founder of the Association Belge de Psychologie. Under his direction, the

Institut (which became *Institut de Psychologie Appliquée et de Pédagogie* in 1944) offered degrees in education and in applied psychology. Psychology was thought of as a natural science, and some basic scientific knowledge was required to follow such studies. Significant names in this group included A. Fauville (b. 1894), in educational psychology; Rev. J. Nuttin (b. 1909), in personality and motivation; G. de Montpellier (b. 1906), in comparative psychology; and R. Buyse (b. 1889), in experimental pedagogy. Current research at both Catholic universities has been affected by Michotte's efforts (Richelle, Janssen, & Brédart, in press).

Another interesting group, which mainly focused on educational psychology and therapeutic pedagogy, was headed by O. Decroly (1871–1932). After working in several private centers for exceptional children at Brussels, Decroly became professor at the Free University of Brussels. Here he performed significant research on abnormal child psychology (Segers, 1985). Psychology was closely related to education in this setting, and it took some time for psychology to be considered as a separate entity.

In more northern countries, scientific psychology became an independent discipline after breaking with a previous philosophical tradition, and it developed under the main influence of the German tradition. Danish philosopher H. Höffding (1843–1931), largely influenced by James's functionalism and Spinoza's monism, wrote a widely read textbook, *Psychology Based on Experience*. However, it was A. Lehmann (1858–1921), an engineer who studied at Leipzig with Wundt, who founded a laboratory in 1886 and became professor at the University of Copenhagen. One of his students, E. Rubin (1886–1951), a well-known Gestalt-oriented psychologist, succeeded him as the leading figure in the Copenhagen psychological school. Rubin did significant research in perception phenomena. In Norway, philosopher A. Aall (1867–1943) founded the first center for psychology at the University of Kristiania (1909), where some experimental research was performed by physiologists and medical doctors (e.g., Aas and Thorkelson). One of Aall's students, H. Schjelderup-Ebbe (1895–1974), was appointed to the first psychology chair at Oslo and wrote a *Textbook of Psychology* (1927), in which experimental and psychoanalytic approaches were combined. Twelve psychologists were graduated during the years 1928–1940 from the Oslo Psychological Institute (Jääskeläinen, 1985a).

In Sweden, some philosophers began to study empirical psychology in the last decades of the 19th century, such as C. J. Boström (1797–1866), K. Geijer, and H. Larsson (1862–1944), the latter an author of a widely used textbook, *Textbook of Psychology on Empirical Bases* (1899). However, it was not until the turn of the century that empirical research began to flourish there. S. Alrutz (1868–1925), at Uppsala University, founded a psychological center at the Institute of Physiology and did research on sensory phenomena and hypnosis. A. S. Herrlin (1870–1937), a former student of Müller, became professor at Lund University and worked on psychopathology. Some of his students, G. A. Jaederholm (1882–1936) and R. Anderberg (1892–1955), worked on differential psychology, and an important psychometric and applied tradition began to develop there (Jääskeläinen, 1985a).

Finally, Finnish psychology, at an early time influenced by Hegelian philosophy, became more empirically oriented after G. H. G. Neiglick's stay (1860–1889) at Wundt's laboratory in Leipzig, where he did research on psychophysics in 1887. But it was E. Kaila (1890–1958), the so called "father of Finnish psychology," who did most for the institutionalization of the new discipline in his country. Professor at Helsinki and Turku, Kaila founded a psychological laboratory at the University of Turku in 1922 and another one at Helsinki University in 1932. He wrote a PhD thesis in the Würzburg tradition and worked mainly on personality and applied problems (Jääskeläinen, 1985b).

In Switzerland, interest in psychology was greatly promoted by T. Flournoy (1854–1920), who did significant research in abnormal and paranormal psychology. He founded a psychological laboratory at Geneva University in 1892 that was open to all the students for both theoretical and practical purposes. E. Claparède (1873–1940), a student of Flournoy's succeeded him as head of the laboratory and did important research in educational psychology. Together with Flournoy, he founded *Archives de Psychologie* in 1901 and the Jean Jacques Rousseau Institute in 1912. The latter was a teacher training center at which the empirical study of the child was developed as a basis for all educational activities. P. Bovet was appointed as its director, but it was J. Piaget (1896–1980) who made the Geneva school of developmental and child psychology first rank among the centers working in these fields. After Piaget began working at the Rousseau Institute, he organized courses in psychology and epistemology at the Universities of Geneva and Lausanne and also founded the International Center of Genetic Epistemology at Geneva (1955–1980), in which interdisciplinary research was performed.

In Spain, the first chair of scientific psychology was created at the University of Madrid, where postgraduate optional courses for a degree in sciences were offered. L. Simarro (1851–1921), a psychiatrist who trained in Paris with Charcot, was appointed to this chair, and a Spanish version of Wundt's *Outlines of Psychology* was used as a textbook. In 1914, only three people enrolled for that course (Bonaventura, 1914). Seminars were then organized in the 1920s to offer a postgraduate diploma that enabled trained individuals to work in the few psychotechnics laboratories created for testing and assessment in educational guidance and personnel selection. In Barcelona these efforts were directed by E. Mira-López (1896–1964), and in Madrid they were organized by J. Germain. These two main centers worked on psychotechnics and applied psychology. The Spanish Civil War (1936–1939) destroyed the existing institutional network. Some groups from the academic world unsuccessfully tried to reestablish a philosophical (neoscholastic) psychology, while a small group headed by Germain slowly reorganized the field with a scientific approach (Carpintero, 1982; Peiró, 1984).

In Portugal, a reform of higher education in 1911 created the need for both a chair of experimental psychology and a laboratory. This provided a means of training psychologists and granting degrees in philosophy and education. At the University of Coimbra, the philosopher A. J. Alves do Santos (1866–1925), after being trained in Geneva, created the first laboratory in 1912. Some experimental work was performed in that laboratory by Alves do Santos and his colleagues. A similar laboratory was established at the University of Lisbon by J. Martos Romão in 1930. By that time, the works of A. da Costa Ferreira and M. Faria de Vasconcelos had also influenced the training of a group that was characterized by its reliance on the experimental method (Abreu, 1991).

Centuries of isolation in Japan ended in the last decades of the 19th century, with psychology entering the scientific culture as a part of the Western legacy to that country. As early as 1888, Y. Motora (1858–1912), a former student of Hall, began lecturing on psychophysics at Tokyo University. In M. Matsumoto (1865–1943), after studying with Wundt and E. Scripture, established a psychological laboratory at Tokyo University in 1903 and another at Kyoto University in 1907. Matsumoto is credited with the training of "almost all of the senior psychologists in Japan" (Zusne, 1984). Western psychology gained an even greater influence in the following decades. After Motora's functionalism, behaviorism seems to have enjoyed a short period of acceptance; but it was soon banned as a result of the influence of the Gestalt school introduced by K. Sakuma (1888–1970), which was dominant until the end of World War II (Sahakian, 1975). The new schools did not, however, hinder the attention paid to psychological prescientific interests which included the religious and cultural *weltanschauung* (Kodama, 1984).

In China, the psychological tradition was also influenced by Wundt. T. Yuan-Pei (1868–1940), an important figure in the Chinese academic world in the 1920s, attended the lectures of Wundt at Leipzig and, as a consequence, created a psychological laboratory at Beijing University in 1917 and founded a Research Institute of Psychology in 1928 at the National Central Academy in Beijing. Wundt's *Einleitung zur Psychologie* was translated into Chinese in 1923 by S. G. Wu. The first professor of psychology at Beijing University, C. Da-chi, wrote an introductory textbook, *Outlines of Psychology* in 1918, which eventually was widely used in colleges. By 1927, 10 departments of psychology in Chinese universities existed (Misiak & Sexton, 1966). At that time, American pragmatism and functionalism seem to have exerted the greatest influence on the development of the discipline (Chin & Chin, 1969). After the founding of the People's Republic of China, however, Soviet psychology dominated the Chinese discipline (Shu & Li, 1983).

The development of scientific psychology in India was again also influenced by the German tradition. In the early 19th century, Western education received increased support and attention in India, and at Calcutta University, Sir A. Mukherjee introduced a postgraduate course in psychology in 1905. A syllabus for the course on experimental psychology, largely influenced by Wundt and Titchener, was prepared by Sir B. N. Seal, but it was N. N. Sengupta, a former student of H. Münsterberg's at Harvard University, who took charge of the fledging discipline in 1915. Research projects were performed at India's first psychological laboratory at Calcutta University. Sengupta was also greatly influenced by E. B. Titchener's ideas; structuralism was dominant in his work and his lectures. When he went to Lucknow University in North India in 1929, he established another laboratory there. G. Bose took over the Calcutta department, and despite being a psychoanalyst, he maintained the Wundtian experimental approach. At Mysore, a former student of Spearman's, M. V. Gopalswami, created a laboratory and performed experiments there. However, as Sinha noted, "Calcutta became the focus of psychological studies in those days and scholars from all over India came for varying periods of time to learn the techniques of psychological experimentation. As a result, Wundtian and Titchenerian techniques became popular all over" (Sinha, 1983, p. 153).

Psychology in Latin America

Notwithstanding its great wealth of pre-Columbian cultures and complex social situations, Latin American countries (including Brazil) were strongly influenced in preindependence times by cultural events in Spain, Portugal, and other European countries, especially France and Germany, during the 19th century. Through these contacts, ideas about positivism and evolutionism were transported to Latin America, and an interest in psychology was born. Although it was not until the 1940s that professional programs on psychology were established in Latin American countries, some antecedents from what has been called the "pioneers period" (Ardila, 1989) are considered here.

Argentina had a laboratory for experimental psychology as early as 1898, which H. Piñero founded at the Colegio Nacional de Buenos Aires, and where research on perception was performed. By that time, J. Ingenieros (1877–1925), professor of experimental psychology of the Faculty of Philosophy at the University of Buenos Aires, extended positivistic ideas into such areas as criminology, education, and social studies. His efforts were continued by E. Mouchet (1886–1977), who directed the Instituto de

Psicologia at the University of Buenos Aires. Mouchet also founded a journal in which some of his own research was published (Vezzetti, 1988).

In México, E. A. Chavez (1868–1946) stimulated interest in educational psychology and translated into Spanish works by Titchener (Luna, 1981). An Institute of Psychology and Psychiatry was established at the Universidad Nacional de México in 1916, along with a laboratory that was founded by E. C. Aragón. A program in psychology was also established within the Department of Philosophy in 1937, through the efforts of Chavez (Dçaz-Guerrero, 1981).

Interest in psychology in Brazil was stimulated by the arrival of a Polish psychologist, W. Radecki (1887–1953), founder of a laboratory in 1923 and organizer of a Latin American Congress of Psychology in 1950. The Spanish emigré Mira-López (1896–1964) was also influential in developing Brazilian psychotechnics at the Getulio Vargas Foundation in Rio de Janeiro in the late 1940s (Gomes Penna, 1986–1987; Massimi, 1990).

After some tentative work in educational assessment by L. Miró-Quesada in Perú in the 1920s, the German emigré W. Blumenfeld (1882–1967), arriving in 1935, promoted experimental psychology there.

Some of these pioneer efforts had no continuity, although in a few cases some strong personalities influenced small groups for a time. In several countries, development of psychology was carried out according to this model: "First a laboratory based on the Leipzig lab, then an Institute of Psychology (. . . in the decade of the 1930s or 1940s approximately . . .), and then a Department of Psychology with training goals" (Ardila, 1982). Little by little, the potential of psychology to help solve social problems and the expansion of psychoanalytic ideas influenced the development of psychology in some of these countries. Eventually these movements paved the way for a true professional approach to the field in Latin America after World War II that was due in large part to increasing contacts with American culture.

CONCLUSION

Louttit (1932) stated that "the history of psychology shows that by far the greatest portion of the experimental work and theoretical discussion has come from men engaged in university work" (p. 44). It is true that in recent times private centers and professional societies have devoted enough resources to develop theories and research methodology, but basic research and theoretical progress have normally been a result of academic work that is essentially focused on such enterprises.

In many countries, the creation of an academic degree in psychology has been anteceded by the establishment of a professional diploma or certificate with an applied emphasis. Such diplomas could be obtained through special training of those who had a degree more or less closely related to psychology. In many countries, psychological training was seen as complementing other existing curricula. When psychology became totally independent of philosophy and other sciences, the related academic community tried to establish for itself a well-defined field of knowledge, with its own academic organization and institutional structure. Chairs, departments, journals, and laboratories can be seen not only as scientific instruments and media but also as social indicators of societal support for an idiosyncratic "paradigm" or "research program" in psychology.

As seen in this chapter, institutional support and acceptance of scientific psychology has progressed at a different pace in different countries, with national trends affecting such progress. Influences that were clearly visible in one country were perhaps not to be seen in another.

At the same time, psychology everywhere seems to have been influenced by a common root or model that is to be found in the Wundtian tradition. This tradition played a critical role at an early time by providing a scheme according to which institutionalization of the new science could be achieved. Many countries, such as the United States, Belgium, Japan, India, Finland, and Sweden, may claim an immediate connection with Wundt. In other cases, such a nexus, although not so easily perceived, has also been shown to exist.

Psychology, often situated between the social and natural sciences on epistemological grounds, became in the central decades of our century a unique and expanding discipline. In early times it focused on a theoretical understanding of man's knowledge and behavior largely dependent on scientific methods and concepts. However, the application of psychology to practical problems soon changed the whole outlook, and the pragmatic values of efficiency and applicability became more relevant in psychological work. Although lacking a theoretical unity, psychology's great capacity for originating social and individual interventive programs garnered both the attention of governmental agencies and the interest of large numbers of students. Singular social events, such as World War I and II, brought to the forefront the practical utility of psychological techniques for selection and therapeutic intervention in a time in which societies were experiencing dramatic changes and problems. It could be said that psychology moved from a "Little Science" stage to that of a "Big Science" (Price, 1965) during this time, with the resulting characteristics and related problems—exponential growth; differential impact of work, groups, and people; and complexities of organizational dimensions. In many cases, the world of psychology has grown immensely while resources have grown at a much slower rate. Each time that monetary resources for psychology centers have been compared with those for other "hard sciences" or technologies, a significant gap has been shown to exist.

The multiplicity of approaches and tendencies in contemporary academic psychology has endangered psychology's quest for an independent status among sciences. Other disciplines close to psychology have proved to be competing rivals in providing suggestions and solutions for many social problems. At times, the pressure for practical results has obscured the importance of building a basic and coherent theoretical system in psychology.

However, the unity of a science is today, as in the early days, both a problem and a goal (Mayor & Pérez Rços, 1989; Staats, 1983; Yela, 1989). Such unity will require a substantial body of scientific evidence and methodological rigor in support of basic tenets. This in turn will require more research funds and more efficient research strategies, with some degree of independence from funding sources. Private centers as well as university departments are now dependent for their resources from government agencies that act according to prioritized and often politicized goals. To obtain more independent support, psychology must gain widespread interest and broad social approval that will depend on the utility of its applications and the soundness of its conceptual construction. As its second century begins, psychology needs to cultivate its academic and pedagogical roots that support the scientific creativity needed to solve the demanding problems the world now faces.

REFERENCES

Abreu, M. V. (1991). A criacao do primeiro laboratorio de psicologia em Portugal: O laboratorio de psicologia experimental da Universidade de Coimbra (1912). Coimbra, II, 1–28.

Ardila, R. (1982). Psychology in Latin America today Annual Review of Psychology, 33, 103–122.

Ardila, R. (1989). La psicologia en Iberoamerica. In J. Arnau & H. Carpintero (Eds.), Historia, teoria y metodo. Madrid, Spain: Alhambra.

Ash, M. G. (1982). The emergence of gestalt theory: Experimental psychology in Germany 1890–1920. Unpublished doctoral dissertation, Harvard University, Cambridge, MA.

Ash, M. G. (1987). Psychology and politics in interwar Vienna: The Vienna Psychological Institute. In M. G. Ash & W. Woodward (Eds.), Psychology in 20th-century thought and society (pp. 143–164). Cambridge, England: Cambridge University Press.

Bartlett, F. C. (1961). Remembering: A study in experimental and social psychology. University Press: Cambridge, England.

Behrens, P. J. (1984). The first Ph.D. programs in experimental psychology at the Leipzig University, Germany, and the Johns Hopkins University, U.S.A. In S. Bem, H. Rappard, & W. Hoorn (Eds.), Studies in the history of psychology and the social sciences 2 (pp. 280–295). Leiden, South Holland, The Netherlands: Rijksuniversiteit Leiden.

Ben David, J. (1974). The universities and the growth of science in Germany and the United States. In S. P. Restivo & C. K. Vanderpool, (Eds.), *Comparative studies in science and society* (pp. 46–81). Columbus, OH: Charles E. Merrill. (Original work published 1968–1969)

Ben David, J., & Collins, R. (1966). Social factors in the origins of a new science: The case of psychology. *American Sociological Review, 31*, 451–465.

Bonaventura, E. (1914). L' insegnamento della psicologia all'estero. *Boillettino della Associazione di Studi Psicologici, I*(4), 69–100.

Boring, E. G. (1950). *A history of experimental psychology* (2nd ed.). New York: Appleton-Century-Crafts.

Bringmann, W., Bringmann, N., & Ungerer, G. (1980). The establishment of Wundt's laboratory: An archival and documentary study. In W. Bringmann & R. Tweney (Eds.), *Wundt studies* (pp. 123–157). Göttingen, Federal Republic of Germany: Hogrefe.

Bringmann, W., & Hope, S. A. (1983). A comparison of Wilhelm Wundt's "Principles" with modern textbooks on physiological psychology. *Revista de Historia de la Psicologia, 3*, 245–262.

Brozek, J., & Diamond, S. (1982). *Le origine della psicologia obiettiva*. Roma, Italy: Bulzoni.

Buccola, G. (1883). *La legge del tempo nei fenomeni del pensiero*. Milano, Italy: F. Dumolard.

Calatayud, C. (1984). *La psicologia Americana a traves del 'Psychological Review' (1894–1945)*. Unpublished doctoral dissertation, University of Valencia, Valencia, Spain.

Caparros, A. (1986). *H. Ebbinghaus. Un funcionalista investigador tipo dominio*. Barcelona, Spain: Edicions Universitat de Barcelona.

Carpintero, H. (1982). The introduction of scientific psychology in Spain. In W. Woodward & M. Ash (Eds.), *The problematic science: Psychology in nineteenth-century thought*. New York: Praeger.

Cattell, J. (1888). The psychological laboratory at Leipzig. *Mind, 13*, 37–51.

Chin, R., & Chin, A. L. (1969). *Psychological research in communist China: 1949–1966*. Cambridge, MA: MIT Press.

Danziger, K. (1990). *Constructing the subject. Historical origins of psychological research*. Cambridge, England: Cambridge University Press.

Dcaz-Guerrero, R. (1981). Momentos culminantes en la historia de la psicologia en México. *Revista de Historia de la Psicologia, 2*, 25–142.

Dobson, V., & Bruce, D. (1972). The German university and the development of experimental psychology, *Journal of the History of the Behavioral Sciences, 2*, 204–207.

Eisenga, L. K. A. (1978). *Geschiedenis van de Nederlandse psychologie*. Deventer, The Netherlands: Van Loghum Slat.

Foulquié, P., & Deledalle, G. (1965). *Psicologia contemporanea*. Barcelona, Spain: Labor.

Fraisse, P. (1981). The centennial celebration of Henri Piéron, founder of psychology in France. *French-Language Psychology, 2,* 211–222.

Gemelli, A., & Zunini, G. (1964). *Introduccion a la psicologia* (5th ed.). Barcelona, Spain: Miracle.

Geuter, U. (1987). German psychology during the Nazi period. In M. G. Ash & W. Woodward (Eds.), *Psychology in twentieth-century thought and society.* Cambridge, England: Cambridge University Press.

Gomes Penna, A. (1986–1987). *Historia da psicologia. Apontamentos sobre as fontes e sobre algumas das figuras mais expressivas da psicologia na cidade do Rio de Janeiro* (Vols. 1–4). Rio de Janeiro, Brazil: ISOP.

Hall, G. (1912). *Founders of modern psychology.* New York: Appleton-Century-Crofts.

Hearnshaw, L. S. (1964). *A short history of British psychology 1840–1940.* London: Methuen.

Humphrey, G. (1951). *Thinking.* London: Methuen.

Jaaskelainen, M. (1985a). The historical development of psychology in Scandinavia. A study on the history of science. *Revista de Historia de la Psicologia, 3,* 191–211.

Jaaskelainen, M. (1985b). The idea of development in the writings of Eino Kaila. In G. Eckardt, W. Bringmann, & L. Sprung (Eds.), *Contributions to a history of development psychology* (pp. 375–383). Berlin, Germany: Mouton.

Joravsky, D. (1989). *Russian psychology: A critical history.* Palo Alto, CA: Blackwell.

Kodama, S. (1984). Historiography of psychology in Japan. *Revista de Historia de la Psicologia, 1–2,* 187–192.

Kozulin, A. (1984). *Psychology in utopia.* Cambridge, MA: MIT Press.

Lombroso, C. (1988). *L'uomo di genio in rapporto alla psichiatria, alla storia ed all'estetica* (5th ed.). Torino, Italy: F. Bocca.

Louttit, C. M. (1932). *Handbook of psychological literature.* Bloomington, IN: Principia Press.

Maller, J. B. (1934). Forty years of psychology. A statistical analysis of American and European publications, 1894–1933. *Psychological Bulletin, 31,* 533–559.

Marhaba, S. (1981). *Lineamenti della psicologia italiana 1870–1945.* Firenze, Italy: Giunti Barbera.

Massimi, M. (1990). *Historia da psicologia brasileira. Da epoca colonial ate 1934.* Sao Paulo, Brazil: Pedagogica e Universitaria.

Massucco Costa, A. (1977). *Psychologie Sovietique.* Paris: Psyot.

Mayor, J., & Perez Rcos, J. (1989). Psicologca o psicologcas? Un problema de identidad. In J. Arnau, & H. Carpintero (Eds.), *Historia, teorca y metodo* (pp. 3–70). Madrid, Spain: Alhambra.

McDougall, W. (1961). Autobiography. In C. Murchison (Ed.), *A history of psychology in autobiography* (Vol. 1, pp. 191–224). New York: Russell & Russell. (Original work published 1936)

Mecacci, L. (1989). Dal Centro Sperimentale all'Istituto di Psicologia del Consiglio Nazionale delle Ricerche (1940–1968). *Storia della Psicologia, 1*, 61–68.

Misiak, H., & Sexton, V. (1966). *History of psychology: An overview.* New York: Grune & Stratton.

Misiak, E., & Staudt, V. M. (1955). *Los catolicos y la psicologia.* Barcelona, Spain: J. Flors.

Montoro, L., Tortosa, F., Carpintero, H., & Peiro, J. M. (1984). A short history of the International Congresses of Psychology (1889–1960). *Revista de Historia de la Psicologia, 5*, 245–252.

Myers, C. S. (1909). *A textbook of experimental psychology.* New York: Longmans, Green.

Myers, C. S. (1961). Charles Samuel Myers. In C. Murchison (Ed.), *A history of psychology in autobiography* (Vol. 1). New York: Russell & Russell. (Original work published 1936)

Peiro, J. M. (1984). Historical perspectives of work and organizational psychology in Spain. *Revista de Historia de la Psicologia, 1–2*, 267–282.

Petrovsky, A. (1990). *Psychology in the Soviet Union: A historical outline.* Moscow: Progress.

Price, D. J. S. (1965). *Little science, big science.* New York: Columbia University Press.

Reuchlin, M. (1965). The historical background for national trends in psychology: France. *Journal of the History of the Behavioral Sciences, 2*, 115–123.

Ribot, T. (1885). *La psychologie allemande contemporaine* (2nd ed.) Paris: Alcan. (Original work published 1879)

Ribot, T. (1914). *La psychologie anglaise contemporaine* (3rd ed.). Paris: Alcan. (Original work published 1870)

Richelle, M., Janssen, P., & Bredart, S. (in press). Psychology in Belgium. *Annual Review of Psychology.*

Sahakian, W. S. (1975). *History and systems of psychology.* New York: Wiley.

Santis, S. de (1930). *Psicologia sperimentale* (Vol. 1–2). Roma, Italy: A. Stock.

Segers, J. E. (1985). *En torno a Decroly (La psychologie de l'enfant normal et anormal d'aprés le Dr. Decroly).* Madrid, Spain: Minist. Educacion.

Shu, P., & Li, C. (1983). Wilhelm Wundt and the Chinese psychology. In G. Echardt & L. Sprung (Eds.), *Advances in historiography of psychology* (pp. 146–149). Berlin, Germany: Verlag der Wissenschaft.

Sinha, D. (1983). Wundtian tradition and the development of scientific psychology in India. In G. Echardt & L. Sprung (Eds.), *Advances in historiography of psychology* (pp. 150–155). Berlin, Germany: Verlag der Wissenschaft.

Spearman, C. (1961). Autobiography. In C. Murchison (Ed.), *A history of psychology in autobiography* (Vol. 1). New York: Russell & Russell. (Original work published 1930)

Sprung, L., & Sprung, H. (1985). Abriss der Geschichte der Psychologie an dcr

Berliner Universität (1809–1984). In L. Sprung & H. Sprung (Eds.), *Zur Geschichte der Psychologie an der Berliner Universität* (pp. 1–56). Berlin: Akad. der Wissenschaften der DDR.

Sprung, L., Sprung, H., & Kernchen, S. (1984). Carl Stumpf and the origin and development of psychology as a new science at the University of Berlin. *Revista de Historia de la Psicologia, 1–2*, 349–353.

Staats, A. W. (1983). Psychology's crisis of disunity: Philosophy and method for a unified science. New York: Praeger.

Stout, G. F. (1938). *A manual of psychology* (5th ed.). London: University Tutorial Press.

Thomson, R. (1968). *The pelican history of psychology*. Harmondsworth, Middlesex, England: Penguin Books.

Tinker, M. A. (1980). Wundt's doctorate students and their theses, 1875–1920. In W. Bringmann & R. Tweney (Eds.), *Wundt studies* (pp. 269–279). Göttingen, Federal Republic of Germany: Hogrefe.

Titchener, E. B. (1898). A psychological laboratory. *Mind, 23*, 311–331.

Trognon, A., Carroy, J., Chabert, M. A., Chiva, M., Hatwell, Y., Mendelsohn, P., Dorna, A., Jakolu, J. M., Matalon, B., Salhani, L., Leplat, J., Hurtig, M., Cauzinille-Marmeche, E., & Weil-Barais, A. (1987). France. In A. R. Gilgen & C. K. Gilgen (Eds.), *International handbook of psychology*. Westport, CT: Greenwood Press.

Vezzetti, H. (1988). *El nacimiento de la psicologia en la Argentina*. Buenos Aires, Argentina: Puntosur.

Viqueira, V. (1915). La ensenanza de la psicologia en las universidades alemanas. *Anales de la Junta para Ampliacion de Estudios e Investigaciones Cientificas, XVI*, 1–28.

Wolf, T. H. (1973). *Alfred Binet*. Chicago: University of Chicago Press.

Yela, M. (1989). Unidad y diversidad de la psicologia. In J. Arnau & H. Carpintero (Eds.), *Historia, teorca y metodo* (pp. 71–92). Madrid, Spain: Alhambra.

Zunini, G. (1965). *Psicologia*. Barcelona, Spain: Plaza & Janes.

Zusne, L. (1984). *Biographical dictionary of psychology*. Westport, CT: Greenwood Press.

II

KEY INDIVIDUALS IN THE TEACHING OF PSYCHOLOGY

INTRODUCTION

KEY INDIVIDUALS IN THE TEACHING OF PSYCHOLOGY

ANTONIO E. PUENTE

Part II provides information regarding the individuals and institutions that we consider to have played a major role in the teaching of psychology over the past 100 years. Most of this section focuses on people. However, whenever possible, the authors have discussed those individuals in the context of both the psychology of their day and the students whom they taught.

Donald Dewsbury and Wade Pickren discuss important teachers of psychology, with a special focus on individuals who are deceased. Teachers are presented in the context of their ideas as well as their particular teaching styles and interests. David Pittenger summarizes the work of contemporary individuals who have been acknowledged by the American Psychological Foundation as having made significant contributions to the teaching of psychology.

With ever changing trends in the demography of psychology, we were interested in addressing how women and ethnic minorities have played a role in the teaching of psychology. Florence Denmark and Linda Fernandez review the role of women and address the specific effects, both positive and negative, of having few women recognized in the early years of teaching psychology in America and a proliferation of women in the most recent decade of growth. Phillip Guzman, Stephen Schiavo, and Antonio Puente address the highly limited role of ethnic minorities in the field, both historically and currently. Because efforts to encourage and acknowledge minority contributions to psychology have been confined largely to the past 40 years, the 100-year period that is the focus of most of the chapters in this book has been truncated in this chapter. A more recent history—from the 1950s to the present—is examined. In this context, demographic information is provided, and specific suggestions are made for remedying the problem of the paucity of ethnic minorities in psychology.

Recollections of the first part of psychology's history become increasingly difficult to obtain using primary sources. Those sources are even more sparse when dealing with pedagogical issues. In the final chapter of Part II, Jane Halonen provides a glimpse of the early days through an interview with Wilbert McKeachie. Since McKeachie's career has evolved at the University of Michigan, this is a story not only of how one well-known teacher developed but also of how the University of Michigan's Department of Psychology grew in parallel fashion.

5

PSYCHOLOGISTS AS TEACHERS: SKETCHES TOWARD A HISTORY OF TEACHING DURING 100 YEARS OF AMERICAN PSYCHOLOGY

DONALD A. DEWSBURY AND WADE E. PICKREN

The history of psychology often is told as the story of "great men," "great dates," and "great ideas" (see Furumoto, 1989). The tendency to emphasize only dramatic events has been termed the *prodigious fallacy* (Fischer, 1970). The problem with such tales is that they neglect the multifaceted character of the subject under study and thus present one-dimensional pictures of multidimensional phenomena. There were other facets to the careers of the leading figures in the field. Furthermore, many others made important, though less publicized, contributions to psychology at the same time as the acknowledged leaders of psychology were developing the theories and perspectives that came to dominate the field. There were women and Blacks struggling to find a place; teachers in high schools, normal schools, small colleges, and community colleges; applied psychologists; and many

We thank the various psychologists who responded to our inquiries and thus provided help in assembling these materials.

others. A complete picture of the history of psychology should include all these perspectives. All are valid parts of the total discipline, even if their influence may be more circumscribed than that of the movers and shakers of the field. In this chapter, we consider an often-neglected dimension of the history of psychology—its college and university teachers (see also Boice, 1977). In accordance with the organization of this book, our coverage is limited to individuals who are deceased. Within that constraint, however, we feel free to move back and forth in time and approach with alacrity.

A critical problem confronting the student of the history of teaching in psychology is that many of the best teachers are the least visible to the historian. Often this is because they put so much of their effort into teaching that they produce little in the literature of psychology that makes them visible to the historian. The eyes of the students, however, often see psychologists very differently from those of historians of psychology; they are great levelers, admiring the well known and the unknown, depending on how they teach rather than on what they publish. One teacher of psychology in a liberal arts college put her position this way:

> We are little known to our university colleagues and more popular clinical associates, but at the same time the influence we may wield for the future of psychology is out of all proportion to our size. Not only do we represent the profession and the subject to large groups of students, but we are almost the sole source of knowledge about psychology to the many future citizens and future state legislators, as well as others who might some day help or hinder psychology as a profession. (E. O. Miller, 1953, p. 475).

A full-scale treatment of these relatively invisible teachers is much merited and long overdue. Here, in a limited chapter of a ceremonial history of the teaching of psychology, we can but point to the problem and discuss a few cases. Our treatment must be biased in favor of those who were outstanding teachers in addition to doing other things that made them visible. The chapter is dedicated to the many who were at least as good at teaching as the teachers we discuss, but who are less visible and thus are not included.

Our criteria for inclusion included considerations of judgment, availability of published information, and balance across criteria accepted as indicative of good teaching. We have tried to identify individuals meritorious of discussion for each of the accepted criteria of good teaching by searching the published literature to find some published documentation of merit. Many fine teachers were thus identified, and we chose among them on the bases of the strength of the relevant statements and balance for inclusion in relation to diverse criteria. Further work is needed to expand on this first effort.

A final caveat is in order; throughout we quote extensively from students' recollections of their teachers. Although we treat them at face value, it must be remembered that their authors are prone to hyperbole. We all remember our favorite teachers with fondness. Extended, critical study of these reminiscences seems overdue.

WHAT IS AN OUTSTANDING TEACHER?

Clearly, there are many views on what makes a teacher outstanding. Both the American Psychological Foundation (APF) and Division 2 of the American Psychological Association (APA) present awards to psychologists who are outstanding teachers. From the guidelines for these awards, one can distill nine criteria used by these bodies: (a) influence as a teacher of students who become psychologists; (b) performance as a classroom teacher; (c) development of innovative curricula or courses; (d) development of effective teaching methods or materials; (e) research on the teaching of psychology; (f) achievements in professional organizations related to the teaching of psychology; (g) training of teachers of psychology; (h) teaching of advanced research methods and practice in psychology; and (i) administrative facilitation of teaching. These provide the framework within which we discuss some outstanding teachers of psychology. We emphasize the first two criteria.

Teachers are multifaceted; most of these individuals merit recognition with respect to more than one criterion. To not become victims of our own device, we stray from these limits frequently. We emphasize that inclusion of psychologists in our discussion is a joint function of accomplishment and the visibility of that accomplishment.

Influence on Students Who Become Psychologists

One way to quantify the influence of teachers on students who become psychologists is to analyze the number of their students who become prominent in that field. M. D. Boring and E. G. Boring (1948) analyzed the master–pupil relationships of the 119 psychologists who received "stars" in the first seven editions of *American Men of Science*. The most influential teachers of each were determined by correspondence with living psychologists and by published or other sources for those 47 who were deceased. There were 84 individuals who came under the influence of one primary mentor and 22 who acknowledged two or three mentors. We have analyzed these data with respect to the number of students who named various influential teachers.

The data are presented in Table 1. A total of 49 individuals, all men, were listed. According to this analysis, the most influential teacher was G. Stanley Hall, who was listed as a mentor for 13 starred "men of science."

TABLE 1
The Number of Times Prominent Teachers Were Mentioned as Primary
Mentors by 119 Psychologists Receiving Stars in the First Seven Editions
of *American Men of Science*

Name	No. of entries
G. S. Hall	13
J. M. Cattell	11
W. Wundt	11
H. Münsterberg	9
J. R. Angell	8
R. S. Woodworth	8
E. L. Thorndike	7
E. B. Titchener	6
H. A. Carr	4
W. James	4
R. Dodge	3
K. Stumpf	3
H. K. Wolfe	3
E. G. Boring	2
E. B. Holt	2
O. Kulpe	2
K. S. Lashley	2
C. E. Seashore	2
L. M. Terman	2

Note: Minimum = 2 entries. Source: M. D. Boring and E. G. Boring (1948).

James McKeen Cattell and Wilhelm Wundt were close behind with 11. Other leaders were Hugo Münsterberg, James Rowland Angell, Robert S. Woodworth, and Edward L. Thorndike. Perhaps the most striking aspect of these data is the rather close match between the list of most influential teachers, as determined by this measure, and the attention given these individuals in textbook histories of psychology. The data suggest either that those psychologists emphasized in textbooks were also exceptional teachers or that these leaders controlled access to the corridors of power in psychology likely to bring recognition to their students and, thus, favored their students.

In this chapter we discuss many of the psychologists listed in Table 1. However, it would be a mistake to rely only on these data as a basis for selection. There are several sources of possible bias in the data in addition to the one just discussed. Consider, for example, the factors affecting the assignment of stars in *American Men of Science*. Furthermore, M. D. Boring and E. G. Boring's (1948) analysis covered only part of the past 100 years of American psychology. Therefore, we treat only some of these psychologists at this point and add several individuals who, in our judgment, merit inclusion despite their absence from Table 1.

The teachers we have chosen for discussion primarily on the basis of their influence on students who became psychologists are Harry K. Wolfe, Edward B. Titchener, William James, Hugo Münsterberg, Margaret Floy

Washburn, Clark Hull, Kenneth W. Spence, and Arthur W. Melton. These were very different kinds of psychologists and people, each of whom influenced many students, but each with his or her own style.

Perhaps a paradigmatic example of an influential teacher, and one whose influence is well documented, was Harry Kirke Wolfe (1858–1918; see Benjamin, 1991). His influence is indicated by the exceptional number of his undergraduate students who went on to graduate school in psychology. Three—Madison Bentley, Edwin R. Guthrie, and Walter B. Pillsbury— became APA presidents. Wolfe was a strong, early advocate of laboratory experience as an important part of undergraduate education (e.g., Wolfe, 1895). Although he maintained exceptionally heavy teaching loads, Wolfe spent much time with students, and his classes were extremely popular. As one student described them, his classes were "notoriously difficult; there was no room for the slacker there; but there was never an uninteresting lecture hour, and year after year the students filed in, willing to venture the work for the sake of the zest" (Benjamin, 1991, p. 132). Perhaps his approach to teaching was best revealed in a letter to Pillsbury concerning a possible faculty appointment, "Do you think he could give the same simple experiment separately to 100 students and make it just as interesting to the 101st?" (Benjamin, 1991, p. 83).

Edward Bradford Titchener (1867–1927) supervised the doctoral dissertations of 58 psychologists. In contrast to many psychologists discussed in this chapter, Titchener exercised tight supervision over his students' work, choosing their topics and doing much of the planning (Pillsbury, 1928). Titchener's laboratory manuals guided a generation of psychology students through their laboratory experience. E. G. Boring (1927) similarly described Titchener's lecture ritual, some details of which were remarkably like those of his mentor, Wilhelm Wundt:

> The demonstration was set out the hour before, and Titchener arrived shortly after ten to inspect it. Later the staff gradually gathered in his office. When the time of the lecture arrived, he donned his gown, the assistant brushed his coat for fear of ashes from the ever-present cigar, the staff went out the door for apparatus and took front seats, and Titchener then appeared on the platform from the office-door. . . . After the lecture the staff gathered in Titchener's office for an hour for talk and at one o'clock dispersed for lunch. (p. 500)

Among the many paradoxes of William James (1842–1910) are the facts that although he taught psychology regularly only between 1875 and 1892 and supervised few doctoral dissertations, he may have influenced more psychologists than any other (Thorndike, 1943). Much of the influence was effected through his books, especially *Principles of Psychology* (1890). It is remarkable to read psychologists' autobiographies and to note the number who record their reading of that work as a turning point. His *Talks to Teachers* (1899) spoke directly of the application of psychological knowledge to pedagogy and provided aid to many teachers.

Opinions were mixed about James as a classroom teacher. Dunlap (1930, p. 41), for example, regarded James as "a poor lecturer, passing hastily over the best points." By contrast, Baldwin (1911) regarded James as a good teacher, noting that "his strongest points as a teacher were that he made his students think because he was thinking and that he treated each topic with such richness, vividness and intensity that it became the most important and interesting topic of the year" (p. 372). All agreed on his effectiveness in discussion and in personal interaction with students. When sparring over debatable issues, "he would then become animated and fluent, with rising assertiveness, and throw off with apparent unconcern the verbal picturesqueness to which his writings have accustomed us. These clarifying interludes were our joy, and James' forte" (Angier, 1943, p. 132).

Although James's colleague, Hugo Münsterberg (1863–1916), ranks among the most influential teachers listed in Table 1, he is less well represented in the reminiscences of students than are others. Dunlap (1930) credits Münsterberg with great influence on both himself and psychology at large, although he viewed Münsterberg as "not a man to have disciples" (p. 42). For example, although Robert Yerkes (1956) gives Münsterberg great credit for attracting him to the field, Yerkes went in a very different direction from Münsterberg. Margaret Münsterberg (1922, p. 232) recalled the night of his birthday when Münsterberg celebrated the completion of 25 years of teaching and the "college boys" from his large lecture class came by to give him an ovation "by moonlight and the faint illumination of the street lantern."

During the early years of the growth of psychology in the United States, it was very difficult for women to obtain a doctorate, let alone sustain a career in psychology (see Scarborough & Furumoto, 1987). Because she spent most of her teaching career at Vassar College, which lacked a graduate program, Margaret Floy Washburn (1871–1939), the first woman PhD in psychology, worked primarily with undergraduates. She introduced students to research through collaborative studies, which resulted in a series of publications known as the "Studies From the Psychological Laboratory of Vassar College." A total of 69 studies, with 119 students as joint authors, were produced in this way (Goodman, 1980). Pillsbury (1940, p. 102) noted that "they constitute probably the longest series of studies from any of the American laboratories." Dallenbach (1940, p. 3) wrote, "That she was an inspiring teacher is evidenced by the growth of her department, by the many studies that were published by the girls [sic] from her laboratory, and by the number of her students who continued in psychology." One student recalled that

Miss Washburn's lectures . . . were brilliant, exact, clear, with such a wealth of references and citing of original sources as almost to overwhelm a student. . . . I recall wishing that the course in social psychology would never end, both because of the absorbing fascination of the material, and because of the consummate skill with which she unfolded and developed the theme. (quoted in Goodman, 1980)

Although the Hull–Spence approach to learning theory is no longer prominent in psychology, both Clark L. Hull (1884–1952) and Kenneth W. Spence (1907–1967) were very influential in attracting students to psychology and furthering their careers. According to Hovland (1952, pp. 348–349), Hull "had an unusual knack of getting his students so involved with their research problems that they continued related investigations when they took jobs at other institutions." Spence had 75 doctoral students. He influenced his students so that they "carry with them some of Spence's ideas and commitments and a desire to achieve a level of quality in their own work that would be acceptable to their Professor" (Kendler, 1967, p. 341).

Arthur W. Melton (1906–1978), the noted student of human learning, also possessed the ability to influence students.

By some means, which remain something of a mystery, he made a student feel that experimental psychology was the most important profession in the world. But at the same time, it was patent that to become a member of this profession the student must be prepared to sacrifice. . . . The master teacher views intellectual pursuits as tough and exacting challenges of the highest order and expects the students to view them in the same way. (Underwood, 1979, p. 1171)

Performance as a Classroom Teacher

Among the outstanding classroom teachers were some well-known psychologists, such as Donald Hebb, Gardner Murphy, Robert MacLeod, Samuel Fernberger, Edwin Boring, and Karl Dallenbach; and some lesser-known psychologists, such as Shammai Feldman, John Shepard, and Warner Brown. All possessed a classroom style that their students found memorable.

Some Well-Known Psychologists

It is remarkable that some distinguished research psychologists also retained long-term commitments to effective classroom teaching. Donald O. Hebb (1904–1985), who became both an APA President and a Fellow of the Royal Society, was a dedicated teacher. At one point the enrollment in his introductory psychology course exceeded 1,500, about three quarters of the intake of Arts and Science students at McGill University. Milner (1986) estimated that during the years he taught the course at least 25,000 students must have enrolled. Hebb (1958) wrote an unusual textbook, *A Textbook of Psychology*, which was remarkable for its brevity, unity of conceptual framework, and biological approach to mental phenomena. Divisions 2 and 6 of the APA recently have honored Hebb and his student James Olds by naming their lecture series on the teaching of psychobiology the "Hebb-Olds Lecture."

Few teachers were more beloved than Gardner Murphy (1895–1979; see L.B. Murphy, 1990). Although dry and even austere rather than dynamic, his lectures stimulated thought and had great impact on his students. One recalled that

> On the last day of the course the students applauded as usual, and Gardner left very quickly as usual, but they crowded after him following through the halls, out the door, all across the campus, up to the entrance of Townshend Harris Hall, where the psychology department was located. They applauded all the way. (Murphy, 1990, p. 13)

Murphy took an interest in individual students and helped them in many ways.

> The tone of Gardner's voice, his total manner, expressed personal concern, compassion with humanity and concern with you as part of humanity, going far beyond the academic routine. (p. 18)

The core of Gardner's message was that "the teacher has got to be the kind of person who can inculcate a spirit of freedom to explore, to enjoy, to face both tradition and challenge." (p. 27)

Few psychologists were more admired than Robert B. MacLeod (1907–1972; see Krech, 1973).

> To arouse interest in psychology and its history, to explore issues, to hone minds, to offer a model of serious, responsible, and passionate scholarship constituted MacLeod's conception of teaching, a conception as demanding in time and energy as it was productive of young psychologists." (Henle & Wertheimer, 1975)

MacLeod's wife reflected that

> In all of our years together, the MacLeod Homeplace has been open to students . . . conferring with students in a campus office was never quite the same as seeing them in his study. How many inspired ideas were conjured up through the smoke-rings of Robbie's ubiquitous pipe, how many confused thoughts set straight, how many challenges dared and accepted, only the silent book-lined walls can know. (MacLeod 1973, p. 25)

The University of Pennsylvania's Samuel Fernberger (1887–1956) was a similarly gifted teacher in both seminars and undergraduate lectures.

> For many years his Thursday afternoon graduate seminar on Problems

of Psychology was a principal focus of intellectual excitement in the department at Pennsylvania. On various memorable occasions, the roles of James, Wundt, McDougall, Titchener, Watson, Kohler, Freud, and others were dealt out to the members of the seminar, who were obliged to assume them in the discussion of a variety of questions. Fernberger used to claim with great glee that the students took on not only the theoretical attitudes of their noted exemplars but their personal traits as well. He was equally effective with undergraduates, and, to his last semester of teaching, students often infringed upon regulations by attending his lectures in elementary psychology instead of those to which they had been assigned. (Irwin, 1956, p. 679)

The multifaceted Edwin G. Boring (1886–1968) contributed to teaching in many ways. He helped establish the history of psychology as a course and produced an important introductory textbook. In addition, Boring's classroom performance, described by Stevens (1968), was remarkable.

The renowned indifference of the Harvard undergraduate disintegrated under the gay onslaught of a short, bear-shaped man bubbling with facts and ideas, the whole of it spiced by demonstration. The large lecture room, known as Emerson-D was usually full to overflowing, and the batting average was about .500 for a big burst of applause at the end of the hour. (p. 602)

The style that characterized Boring's writing was apparent in his teaching as well.

His lectures in systematic psychology were models of erudition, coverage, and depth as far as sensory psychology was concerned. The numerous references covered in each lecture required about half an hour merely to write on the board, and Boring would be found in the classroom working assiduously at this task before each lecture. (Helson, 1970, p. 626)

Karl Dallenbach (1887–1971) was effective with both undergraduate and graduate students. "He seemed to adopt his doctoral students, worrying after them as though they were his own children" (Evans, 1972, p. 475). A highlight of his courses was the end-of-semester social hour at the home of Dr. and Mrs. "Dall" featuring good food, good conversation, and home movies. McConnell (1978) paints Dallenbach as a great teller of anecdotes. They were what he thought his teaching assistants should remember from his course.

Don't be foolish. . . . The facts and data you can find in any stupid textbook. But the stories are priceless. They don't appear in print anywhere. If you want to capture the imaginations of young people, you have to tell them stories! Forget the facts, and copy down the anecdotes! (p. 160)

Dr. Dall believed that psychology was the scientific study of *people—*

not of behavior, or of concepts, or of the nervous system, or of personality. Rather, psychology was about real, live human beings. (p. 159)

Some Lesser Known Psychologists

Shammai Feldman (b. 1899), a 1925 PhD of E. B. Titchener at Cornell who stayed on at Cornell to teach, exemplifies the fate of many psychologists who put teaching above research. Ryan (1982) who took courses from many outstanding psychologists in an outstanding department, called him

> the best teacher I had in psychology. . . . Not only was he constantly presenting new material, but his theoretical interpretations were always fascinating and a little offbeat. . . . All of the students took their research problems to Feldman and received much valuable advice. (p. 360)
>
> It is one of the great tragedies of the modern system of promotion and tenure that Cornell psychology students were deprived of the services of a great teacher and mentor as well as a thorough scholar and original thinker. (p. 361)

The tragedy of the career of John F. Shepard (1881–1965) was that he rarely published his research (Raphelson, 1980). However, his students often acknowledged his influence. "Shepard taught well-organized courses with a great deal of confidence in what he said. He knew the literature so well that students felt in awe of his grasp of it" (Raphelson, 1980, p. 305). Students kept extensive notebooks that were comparable to the textbooks produced by some psychologists.

Although also an active, though generally unpublished, researcher, Warner Brown (1882–1956) filled an analogous role at the University of California at Berkeley. "He loved to teach and had a fine sense of pedagogical timing, encouraging the timid and deflating the pretentious. It can truly be said that he was more interested in making dedicated psychologists than in his own scientific achievements" (Gilhousen & Macfarlane, 1956).

Development of Innovative Curricula or Courses

Innovative curricula and courses of diverse types were developed by psychologists such as Thomas Upham, Edmund Sanford, Francis Sumner, Ethel Puffer Howes, Leta Hollingworth, Edna Heidbreder, Celestia Parrish, Theodore Newcomb, Robert Watson, and Goodwin Watson. They lived in very different times and worked in different ways, but each left a mark on curricula in psychology.

Perhaps the first major innovator in American psychology was Thomas C. Upham (1799–1872). His *Intellectual Philosophy*, published in 1827, was the first influential textbook in American psychology and defined the nature of psychology in this country for decades. His approach was to present the student with only "safe" ideas and to protect the student from new ideas, which might be confusing or lead him astray (Evans, 1984). An abridged version of Upham's 1831 *Elements of Mental Philosophy* was an influential textbook in the movement for the teaching of psychology in secondary schools.

Edmund Clark Sanford (1859–1924) is best remembered as the author of the first comprehensive laboratory manual in experimental psychology; it was published piecemeal (e.g., Sanford, 1891). Although later superceded, Sanford's manual, and the apparatus he devised, played a prominent role in establishing laboratory experience as an important part of undergraduate education in psychology. Mary Whiton Calkins (1930, p. 32) called Sanford "a teacher unrivalled for the richness and precision of his knowledge of experimental procedure and for the prodigality with which he lavished time and interest upon his students."

Francis C. Sumner (1895–1954) was the first Black psychology PhD in the United States, completing his degree at Clark University in 1920. As chair of the Department of Psychology at Howard University, along with Frederick P. Watts and Max Meenes, Sumner established a solid program that was critical in bringing psychology to Blacks and Blacks to psychology (see Guthrie, 1976). "His colleagues spoke of his deep interest in students and recalled 'the mimeographed newsletter he prepared and issued periodically, giving items of interest about graduates from his department' " (p. 187). The APA's first Black president, Kenneth B. Clark (1978, p. 80), wrote of Sumner,

> As I listened to this man I heard a wisdom, a comprehensive view of man in society, an attempt to deal rationally and systematically with human problems. . . . Dr. Sumner, without being aware of it, had made it clear to me that that was probably the most important area in which human intelligence should be involved.

One of the major trends in the history of psychology, and thus in its teaching, is the transformation of the field from male domination to its opening to women (see Scarborough & Furumoto, 1987). Most of the actors in the recent stages of this transformation are still alive and thus inappropriate for inclusion in this chapter. However, there were earlier pioneers as well. Ethel Puffer Howes (1872–1950) explored ways in which women could combine families and careers (see Scarborough & Furumoto, 1987). With her innovative approach to educating gifted children and her attack on the variability hypothesis concerning male–female differences, Leta Stetter Hollingworth (1886–1939) helped to open many doors (see Hollingworth, 1943/1990). Edna Heidbreder (1890–1985) not only contributed a major book on the history of psychology (Heidbreder, 1933) but also long served as a role model for students at Wellesley College. "She was intensely interested in the education of women and in the colleges that encouraged women to develop and enjoy their abilities, including intellectual abilities" (Henle, 1987, p. 95). Among the first laboratories in psychology was that founded by another talented early female teacher, Celestia Parrish (1853–1918), at the Randolph-Macon Woman's College in 1894 (Larew, 1942). Each in her own way played a role in opening the field to more women.

Innovative programs have been established at many universities. An example is the interdisciplinary social psychology program at the University of Michigan led by Theodore M. Newcomb (1903–1984). It provided a rare example of effective cooperation between departments of psychology and sociology and produced 226 doctorates in its 20 years of existence (Katz, 1986).

The only training program in the United States in the history of psychology was established by Robert I. Watson (1909–1980) at the University of New Hampshire. It has become a focus of the study of the history of psychology in this country.

> Bob Watson created an atmosphere of patient but firm fatherliness for his graduate students. . . . He could be stern and demanding of his students but behind it all was a softness and vulnerability that most of his students and associates were unable to recognize until they had left. (Evans, 1982, p. 321)

Such psychologists as Watson, Boring, Murphy, and Heidbreder contributed in establishing the field of the history of psychology that now is a legitimate and professionalized subdiscipline within psychology.

In addition to being an outstanding teacher, whose "classes were oversubscribed though reputedly demanding" (Newcomb, 1979), Columbia University educational psychologist Goodwin Watson (1899–1976) was an innovator along various lines. He developed the concept of the psychology guidance center, helped to found an experimental college, and developed the first overseas study course (Newcomb, 1979).

Development of Effective Teaching Methods or Materials

From among the many psychologists who developed new teaching methods and materials, we highlight James McConnell, Sidney Pressey, and B. F. Skinner. Surely the most important materials used in the teaching of psychology are its textbooks. (The development of introductory textbooks is covered by Weiten and Wight in chapter 20 of this book.) One innovator in the writing of textbooks was James V. McConnell (1925–1990). Influenced by Karl Dallenbach (McConnell, 1978), he set out to write a textbook that would be accessible to the student and to teach psychology in simple, clear language richly dotted with anecdotes. "My book aims to coax students into learning the rudimentary facts about scientific psychology; once they have the rudiments and realize they actually have learned difficult material easily, they typically want to learn more" (McConnell, personal communication, February 20, 1974). In 1976 he received the Distinguished Teaching Award from the APF and in 1979 he become president of Division 2 of APA.

Perhaps the most innovative, if controversial, method to emerge from psychology has been teaching machines. The history of teaching machines has been well documented (Benjamin, 1988; Buck, 1990). After some earlier attempts by others, serious teaching machines were developed by Sidney L. Pressey (1888–1979; see Pressey, 1967). Pressey published research on teaching machines in the 1920s and continued to explore their use, as in the teaching of psychology, after World War II. In its totality, Pressey's research encompassed a whole range of problems related to improved teaching and learning (see Hobbs, 1980). In 1970 he received the APF's Gold Medal for Distinguished Contributions to Education in Psychology. The development of teaching machines later became inextricably associated with B. F. Skinner (1904–1990). Skinner has told the story of the development of teaching machines both in specialized articles (e.g., Skinner, 1958) and in his autobiography (Skinner, 1984).

Research on the Teaching of Psychology

Carl Seashore, Herman Remmers, and Harold Guetzkow were notable for their contributions to research on the teaching of psychology. Among the important early studies of the teaching of psychology was the 1910 report of an APA committee on the teaching of psychology chaired by Carl E. Seashore (1866–1949). Others on the committee were James Rowland Angell, Mary Whiton Calkins, Edmund C. Sanford, and Guy M. Whipple; four committee members became APA Presidents. Seashore summarized the committee's work as follows:

> This committee regards it neither feasible nor desirable to recommend any one system of psychology, any fixed mode of treatment, or any exclusive set of aids to instruction. The content, the method, and the means of instruction must vary with the preparation of the teacher, the type of student, the place of the course in the curriculum, etc. (Seashore, 1910a, p. 80)

Among Seashore's innovative projects for higher education were placement examinations, independent project work in elementary psychology, and a proposal that APA develop a series of leaflets that would provide guidance for in-class experiments (Metfessel, 1950; Seashore, 1910b).

Another important individual in research on the teaching of psychology was Herman Remmers (1892–1969). He did early research on student rating of instructors. An example of his research can be found in his work on the effects of three different methods of instruction in psychology (Remmers, 1933). Among other results, learning achievement appeared generally maximized in classes with a lecture–recitation combination.

Perhaps the leading contemporary exponent of research on teaching, Wilbert J. McKeachie (1987), credits Harold Guetzkow (b. 1915), who coordinated the introductory psychology course at the University of Michigan, with stimulating his interest in the field. McKeachie recalled that "it was Harold's inspiration and support for effective teaching, as well as his persistent suggestion that we answer questions about teaching by empirical research, that were the major stimuli in directing me toward a career in this field" (p. 135).

Achievements in Professional Organizations Related to the Teaching of Psychology

Many professional organizations related to the teaching of psychology per se appear relatively new. Thus, psychologists associated with these organizations tend to be of recent vintage; most are still alive and thus are not eligible for inclusion in this chapter. We focus on Wilbert Ray, Marilyn Rigby, and Edwin Newman. Wilbert S. Ray (1901–1977) was an example of a multifaceted and dedicated teacher. Ray was a founding fellow of Division 2 and active in many of its functions, serving as editor from 1957 to 1960 and president from 1973 to 1974. On his election as Professor Emeritus, the laboratory at Bethany College was renamed the Wilbert S. Ray Laboratory of Psychology (Harper, 1978).

Marilyn K. Rigby (1927–1990) was a faculty member at Saint Louis University and Rockhurst College who was active in Division 2. Several students called her "the best teacher I ever had" (Korn, 1990). Rigby was especially helpful in advancing the careers of Black students. "She had an articulate lecture style and a kindly, helpful manner with students" (Korn & Richey, 1991).

The psychology honor society, Psi Chi (see chapter 18 in this book), was founded by Frederick H. Lewis and Edwin B. Newman in 1929 (Wertheimer, 1990). Psi Chi grew to include over 700 chapters with over 200,000 members inducted. Cofounder Edwin B. Newman (1908–1989) was best known as a long-term department chair at Harvard, mediating among Skinner, Boring, Stevens, Lashley, and others.

Training of Teachers of Psychology

It is one thing to influence students to become psychologists, but quite another to be effective in encouraging them to become outstanding teachers of psychology. Delos Wickens, Norman Triplett, Joseph Grosslight, and

Donald Marquis were especially notable for their contributions to the training of teachers of psychology. Delos D. Wickens (1909–1988), a researcher of such stature as to receive the Society of Experimental Psychologists' Warren Medal, also was an outstanding trainer of teachers. It is estimated that over 35 years he helped about 1,000 graduate students from all areas of psychology to become better teachers. His weekly tutorials instilled in teaching assistants a respect for the basic subject matter, the importance of good teaching, and the need for compassionate consideration of their students' needs (Cross & Miles, 1989, p. 1152). Wickens himself received the APF Distinguished Teaching Award.

Although Norman Triplett (1861–1934) is best known for his early research in social psychology, he spent most of his career as an undergraduate teacher and administrator at the Kansas State Normal School in Emporia (Davis & Becker, 1990). He was the classic undergraduate teacher with "a passionate interest in the intellectual growth of the students" (p. 9). His retirement brought letters from over 250 former students, 44 of whom were faculty members at colleges and universities, along with 12 public school principals and 19 public school superintendents.

Among Joseph H. Grosslight's (1921–1988) accomplishments was his establishment of the Junior College Teaching Program at Florida State University, providing an opportunity for graduate students to gain experience in teaching while offering service (Anker, 1989). He was a pioneer in recruiting minority students to psychology, cochaired the Morgantown Conference on Graduate Education in 1987, and received the APA's Distinguished Contributions to Education and Training in Psychology Award.

Donald G. Marquis (1908–1973) built the program at the University of Michigan into one of the best in the country. He was an outstanding developer of psychology teachers. McKeachie (1973, p. 236) recalled that "he supported graduate student training and supervision in college teaching. He arranged for us to participate in a national study of undergraduate curricula. He encouraged development of the first televised psychology course."

Teaching of Advanced Research Methods and Practice in Psychology

Important teaching takes place in the laboratory and in small seminars as well as in the lectures of the classroom. Of the many excellent mentors for advanced students in such settings, we focus on James McKeen Cattell, Robert Woodworth, Karl Lashley, Frank Beach, Harry Harlow, and S. S. Stevens.

James McKeen Cattell (1860–1944) ranked second only to Hall in the number of students listing him as their mentor (see Table 1). Woodworth (1930) recalled that the research activities of the students and staff centered on Cattell's seminar and that "Cattell's criticism could be keen as well as kindly" (p. 369). His style in arranging dissertation topics was the opposite of Wundt's—the student was to initiate the process. Although expressing great loyalty to Cattell, Wells (1944) was frank in acknowledging his limitations as a teacher. For Wells, the lack of direction was excessive, "Cattell pointed the way and said 'Go,' but the greatest teacher must be able to say 'Come' " (p. 271). Clearly, however, Cattell's system worked effectively for many students.

Robert S. Woodworth (1869–1962) also ranked high as an influence on psychologists entering the field (see Table 1). Like Cattell, his style was nondirective (Poffenberger, 1962). Dashiell (1967, p. 102) recalled that "his modest, almost hesitatingly delivered lectures in physiological and experimental psychology furnished solid ballast for the advanced students' programs." Murphy (1963) regarded his course from Woodworth as "the first great teaching I encountered in psychology" (p. 132). Murphy described his style:

> Entering the classroom in an unpressed, baggy old suit, and wearing army shoes, Woodworth would make his way to the blackboard, not quite sure how to begin. He would mumble; then stop dead; fail to find the phrase he wanted; turn and look at the class in a helpless sort of way; go back to the blackboard, and then utter some inimitable word of insight or whimsy, which would go into our notebooks to be remembered in the decades that followed. (p. 132)

According to Beach (1961), Karl S. Lashley's (1890–1958) professed philosophy was "those who need to be taught can't learn, and those who can learn don't need to be taught" (p. 182). Beach noted that "Lashley did a great deal of teaching, but this took place in small groups, the traditional coffee hour in his laboratory, or in individual conversations" (p. 183). Lashley generally was described as aloof, allowing his students to go it alone. Yet, this worked for Lashley, who always had a small coterie of devoted students and exerted enormous influence on the field through them. On the occasion of his 60th birthday, one student wrote to him,

> It seems to be true that the problem of education is one of selecting those who can learn and just putting them into places where there are things to learn and tools. You did more than that, though. You "stood by" and knew, almost occultly, I thought, when to offer a helping hand. You ever offered precepts on occasions so rare as to make them more memorable. (Ball, 1950, p. 2)

Frank A. Beach (1911–1988) was himself a remarkable teacher who shared some of Lashley's traits, as is revealed in a series of affectionate reminiscences from his students. He was a hard task master.

> When I complained and asked if all this rewriting was necessary, he responded with a quotation (I think from Fielding) to the effect that

if the dancing master tells you to dance in chains, you will do so—if only because when you remove the chains you will feel so free. (Adler, 1988, p. 427)

I counted 19 revisions, but I started counting only after I had thrown away many earlier drafts. I must say, however, that when my thesis was submitted for publication, it was accepted without a single change. (Clemens, 1988)

Yet, he was not close to his students and said that "I don't see how you can be a pal and a father figure at the same time" (Adler, 1988, p. 427).

He supported his students, but he neither coddled us nor allowed overly inflated egos. He would feed us the easy fastball when we needed a hit, but would often fool us with sharp curves and changes of pace when we got cocky. (Sachs, 1988, p. 439)

Although best known for his work with advanced students, Beach came to extensive undergraduate teaching late in life and was awarded the APF Distinguished Teaching in Psychology Award in 1985, when he was 75.

A total of 35 graduate students completed PhDs under Harry F. Harlow (1905–1981). The parallels to Lashley and Beach are notable. Rosenblum (1987) recalled that

Harlow was always there to bring you down to size when you were getting away from yourself, but his own early underdog struggles ever in mind, he was always there for you at his sturdiest, when things were looking bleak. (p. 487)

He helped guide students throughout their careers, establishing an "unofficial summer stipend program" in which he would bring back his recent PhDs to work in his laboratory and thus maintain bonds, build confidence, and ease the transition to independent faculty life (Gluck, 1984).

The teaching accomplishments of S. S. Stevens (1906–1973) were most notable at advanced levels. Indeed, he believed that the Harvard Psychology Department should abandon undergraduate instruction entirely (G. A. Miller, 1974). Miller (p. 282) quoted Stevens as writing that "two forms of teaching give me great joy: the joint endeavor of laboratory apprenticeship and editorial give and take." Although he really did not enjoy lecturing, "he was a master of clear, expository prose, marred only by a tendency, usually curbed, to become slightly more flowery than necessary" (G. A. Miller, 1974, p. 282).

Administrative Facilitation of Teaching

It is difficult to determine which psychologists were most effective in facilitating teaching through administration. Perhaps psychology's university presidents, such as William Bryan, James Rowland Angell, G. Stanley Hall, and Leonard Carmichael, were in the best position to do this. After chairing the department at Indiana, William Lowe Bryan (1860–1955) served as president from 1902 to 1937. During that time he, and his associates, established the Indiana program—always with a strong emphasis on service to students (Ellson, 1956; Hearst & Capshew, 1988). Terman (1930) regarded him as a brilliant and inspiring teacher.

James Rowland Angell (1867–1949) not only was central in the development of the functionalist school of psychology, but was an important administrator as well. As its chair, he developed the program at the University of Chicago. Later, he fostered the development of psychology as the president of Yale University. He established an Institute of Psychology and developed an outstanding faculty of psychologists at Yale (Angell, 1936).

Surely the most pivotal of the psychologist–university presidents was G. Stanley Hall (1844–1924). In 31 years as the founding president of Clark University, Hall shaped the University in his image, as he played an important role in shaping psychology at large (Ross, 1972). The Department of Psychology at Clark flourished and, in its prime, was among the very top departments in the world.

Hall was a teaching president. Averill (1982, p. 344) noted that "he never failed to hold his auditors in fascinated unbelief at his boundless psychological insight." Terman (1930) described Hall's seminars as "unique in character and about the most important single educational influence that ever entered their lives" (p. 335). They were long evening sessions with extensive discussion of two student presentations. "When the discussion had raged from thirty minutes to an hour, and was beginning to slacken, Hall would sum things up with an erudition and fertility of imagination" (p. 336).

Averill (1982, p. 343) saw Hall "permitting professors under him complete academic freedom to carry through their psychological research as they saw fit." According to Burnham (1925, p. 92), "Dr. Hall . . . gave freedom in large measure to his students and colleagues, and was not willing that they should be governed by artificial limitations and unnecessary inhibitions." Perhaps with the advantage of distance, his biographer, Ross (1972), noted that Hall could be considerably more dogmatic and arbitrary than is suggested in these reminiscences.

Leonard Carmichael (1898–1973), the fifth president of Division 2 of APA, continued the tradition of psychologist–presidents. As a psychology instructor at Brown University earlier in his career, "Carmichael was an excellent and popular lecturer. His elementary psychology lecture sections filled the largest hall on campus. . . . Leonard was voted the most popular teacher at the University a number of times by the students" (Pfaffmann, 1980, p. 29).

SOME IDIOSYNCRATIC APPROACHES TO TEACHING

Most of the teachers discussed in this chapter were models of dedication to teaching who, despite an array of personalities and approaches, followed relatively straight and narrow paths defining good teachers. Others, however, were effective with approaches that fell outside of this range and that would be disastrous in the hands of others. In addition to Karl Lashley (discussed earlier), Edward Tolman, James Olds, Edward Thorndike, John Dewey, and Abraham Maslow fit this pattern.

Paradoxically, students admired the style of Edward Chase Tolman (1886–1959), who was fired from his first teaching position, allegedly in part for poor teaching, precisely because he did not "overteach." Students wrote that "his lectures cannot be described as smoothly finished, carefully prepared expositions, but as galvanizers to creative thinking by his students" ("Foreword," 1961, p. *xiii*). His classes often evolved into loud free-for-alls in which student and teacher could not be differentiated. Students did not learn sets of static facts but rather shared in the act of creation. The result was not a group of disciples of the master but rather a group of independent thinkers, each stimulated "to carry on in their own ways with the open-minded and zestful spirit which he helped them discover and develop in themselves" ("Foreword," 1961, p. xiii). "Students did not leave his classes with tidy lecture notes, but they did carry away with them enlarged minds and a vision of scientific psychology as an exciting intellectual enterprise" (Crutchfield, 1961, p. 140).

In a similar vein, I (Dewsbury, 1992) found James Olds (1922–1976) to be at best an average lecturer when he prepared notes carefully. By contrast, on days when he let his remarkably rich intellect have free reign, we were witness to, and inspired by, the experience of a truly great mind at its creative best.

Edward Lee Thorndike (1874–1949) presents a problematical case. As can be seen in Table 1, he was one of the most influential teachers of psychology with respect to his effects on students. He spent most of his career in the Teachers College of Columbia University and devoted much effort to the study of issues in education. However, his influence on students occurred relatively early in his career; after 1921 he became more remote from students and exerted correspondingly less influence (Joncich, 1968). Thorndike favored the laboratory approach to teaching, writing "I am inclined to think that in many individuals certain things cannot be learned save by actual performance" (Joncich, p. 164). He was an effective, if unorthodox, lecturer. Dashiell (1967) noted, "What did it matter that Thorndike's talks were not tailored to a neat course organization: what he had to say was invariably pithy, arresting, and suggestive" (p. 103).

John Dewey (1859–1952) exerted an influence on American education matched by few others. Strangely, however, he seems to have been a rather poor classroom teacher. Leta Hollingworth recalled that "his considerable reputation notwithstanding, he was not an impressive speaker" (Shields & Mallory, 1987). Carr (1936) recalled Dewey's

> penchant for long and involved sentences—in the middle of which we would find ourselves in breathless suspense wondering how it would be possible for mere mortal to extricate himself from the bewildering maze of clauses with due conformity to the rules of syntax and grammar. (p. 75)

At the same time, however, students admired Dewey's keen and incisive intellect and, once they got to know him, "found him to be intensely human, stimulating, encouraging, and genuinely interested in our intellectual and scientific development" (p. 75).

Abraham Maslow (1908–1970) provides an example of the different effectiveness of teaching styles at different times and in different places (see Hoffman, 1988). Early in his career, at Brooklyn College, Maslow was known as a relaxed and effective lecturer, who was popular with students. He often invited students to his home for intense discussions of psychological issues. Later in his career, at Brandeis University, he felt less effective, as he tried to work with a generation of students who appeared lacking in drive and ambition—at least by Maslow's standards at the time. Hoffman (1988, p. 220) called Maslow's work with graduate students "perhaps the only real failure of his career." His laissez-faire, sink-or-swim approach provided too much freedom for most students. What worked in one context did not work in another.

CONCLUSION

What can we conclude from this brief and superficial survey of psychologists as teachers? First, it is clear that many psychologists were indeed excellent teachers, by all of the criteria used. Most important, however, the significance of individual differences is very apparent. There are many ways in which to be a good teacher; the psychologists discussed in this chapter worked within their particular abilities and temperaments to find a style that was right for them. On the other side of the teacher–student relationship, the best mentors understood the differences among their students and were sensitive to their changing needs. They adjusted their approaches to the situation. Probably no teacher is right for all students; individual differences among students and teachers interact. There are many ways in which to be a good teacher, and each must find the approach that works best for them and for their students. Eighty years later, the advice of the Seashore (1910a) committee rings true.

All of these psychologists would merit strong considerations for the

APF and the APA Division 2 Teaching Awards if they could be given posthumously. However, the citations would be very different for some very different, but effective, teachers of psychology.

REFERENCES

Adler, N. T. (1988). A memorial essay. *Hormones and Behavior, 22*, 427–428.

Angier, R. P. (1943). Another student's impressions of James at the turn of the century. *Psychological Review, 50*, 132–134.

Anker, J. M. (1989). Joseph H. Grosslight (1921–1988). *American Psychologist, 44*, 958.

Angell, J. R. (1936). James Rowland Angell. In C. Murchison (Ed.), *A history of psychology in autobiography* (Vol. 3; pp. 1–38). Worcester, MA: Clark University Press.

Averill, L. A. (1982). Recollections of Clark's G. Stanley Hall. *Journal of the History of the Behavioral Sciences, 18*, 341–346.

Baldwin, B. T. (1911). William James' contributions to education. *Journal of Educational Psychology, 2*, 369–382.

Ball, J. (1950, May 1). Letter to K. S. Lashley [Bound in volume presented to Lashley on the occasion of his 60th birthday]. Orange Park, FL: Author.

Beach, F. A. (1961). Karl Spencer Lashley 1890–1958. *Biographical Memoirs of the National Academy of Sciences of the United States of America, 35*, 163–204.

Benjamin, L. T., Jr. (1988). A history of teaching machines. *American Psychologist, 43*, 703–712.

Benjamin, L. T., Jr. (1991). *Harry Kirke Wolfe: Pioneer in psychology*. Lincoln: University of Nebraska Press.

Boice, R. (1977). Heroes and teachers. *Teaching of Psychology, 4*, 55–58.

Boring, E. G. (1927). Edward Bradford Titchener 1967–1927. *American Journal of Psychology, 38*, 489–506.

Boring, M. D., & Boring, E. G. (1948). Masters and pupils among the American psychologists. *American Journal of Psychology, 61*, 527–534.

Buck, G. H. (1990). A history of teaching machines [Comment]. *American Psychologist, 45*, 551–552.

Burnham, W. H. (1925). The man, G. Stanley Hall. *Psychological Review, 32*, 89–102.

Calkins, M. W. (1930). Mary Whiton Calkins. In C. Murchison (Ed.), *A history of psychology in autobiography.* (Vol. 1; pp. 31–62). Worcester, MA: Clark University Press.

Carr, H. A. (1936). Harvey A. Carr. In C. Murchison (Ed.), *A history of psychology in autobiography.* (Vol. 3; pp. 69–82). Worcester, MA: Clark University Press.

Clark, K. B. (1978). Kenneth B. Clark: Social psychologist. In T. C. Hunter (Ed.), *Beginnings* (pp. 76–84). New York: Crowell.

Clemens, L. G. (1988). Reflections. *Hormones and Behavior, 22,* 428–430.

Cross, H. A., & Miles, R. C. (1989). Delos D. Wickens (1909–1988). *American Psychologist, 44,* 1151–1152.

Crutchfield, R. S. (1961). Edward Chace Tolman: 1886–1959. *American Journal of Psychology, 74,* 135–141.

Dallenbach, K. M. (1940). Margaret Floy Washburn 1871–1939. *American Journal of Psychology, 53,* 1–5.

Dashiell, J. F. (1967). John Frederick Dashiell. In E. G. Boring & G. Lindzey (Eds.), *A history of psychology in autobiography* (Vol. 5; pp. 95–124). New York: Appleton-Century-Crofts.

Davis, S. F., & Becker, A. H. (1990, April). *Norman Triplett: Pioneer researcher and teacher.* Paper presented at the meeting of the Southern Society for Philosophy and Psychology, Louisville, KY.

Dewsbury, D. A. (1992). What comparative psychology is about. *Teaching of Psychology, 19,* 4–11.

Dunlap, K. (1930). Knight Dunlap. In C. Murchison (Ed.), *A history of psychology in autobiography* (Vol. 2; pp. 35–61). Worcester, MA: Clark University Press.

Ellson, D. G. (1956). William Lowe Bryan: 1860–1955. *American Journal of Psychology, 69,* 325–327.

Evans, R. B. (1972). Karl M Dallenbach: 1887–1971. *American Journal of Psychology, 85,* 463–476.

Evans, R. B. (1982). Robert I. Watson and the history of psychology program at the University of New Hampshire. *Journal of the History of the Behavioral Sciences, 18,* 320–321.

Evans, R. B. (1984). The origins of American academic psychology. In J. Brozek (Ed.), *Explorations in the history of psychology in the United States* (pp. 17–60). Lewisburg, PA: Bucknell University Press.

Fischer, D. H. (1970). *Historian's fallacies.* New York: Harper & Row.

Foreword. (1961). In E. C. Tolman, *Behavior and psychological man* (pp. *v–xiv*). Berkeley: University of California Press.

Furumoto, L. (1989). The new history of psychology. In I. S. Cohen (Ed.), *The G. Stanley Hall Lecture Series* (Vol. 9; pp. 9–34). Washington, DC: American Psychological Association.

Gilhousen, H. C., & Macfarlane, J. W. (1956). Warner Brown: 1882–1956. *American Journal of Psychology, 69,* 495–497.

Gluck, J. P. (1984). Harry Harlow: Lessons on explanations, ideas, and mentorship. *American Journal of Primatology, 7,* 139–146.

Goodman, E. S. (1980). Margaret F. Washburn (1871–1939): First woman Ph.D. in psychology. *Psychology of Women Quarterly, 5,* 69–80.

Guthrie, R. V. (1976). *Even the rat was white.* New York: Harper & Row.

Harper, R. S. (1978). Wilbert Scott Ray: 1901–1977. *Teaching of Psychology, 5*, 112.

Hearst, E., & Capshew, J. H. (1988). *Psychology at Indiana University*. Bloomington: Department of Psychology Indiana University.

Hebb, D. O. (1958). *A textbook of psychology*. Philadelphia: W. B. Saunders.

Heidbreder, E. (1933). *Seven psychologies*. Englewood Cliffs, NJ: Prentice-Hall.

Helson, H. (1970). E. G. B.: The early years and change of course. *American Psychologist, 25*, 625–629.

Henle, M. (1987). Edna Heidbreder (1890–1985). *American Psychologist, 42*, 94–95.

Henle, M., & Wertheimer, M. (1975). Preface. In R. B. MacLeod, *The persistent problems of psychology*. Pittsburgh, PA: Duquesne University Press.

Hobbs, N. (1980). Sidney Leavitt Pressey (1988–1979). *American Psychologist, 35*, 669–671.

Hoffman, E. (1988). *The right to be human: A biography of Abraham Maslow*. Los Angeles: Tarcher.

Hollingworth, H. L. (1990). *Leta Stetter Hollingworth. A biography*. Lincoln: University of Nebraska Press. (Original work published 1943)

Hovland, C. I. (1952). Clark Leonard Hull 1884–1952. *Psychological Review, 59*, 347–350.

Irwin, F. W. (1956). Samuel Weiller Fernberger: 1887–1956. *American Journal of Psychology, 69*, 676–680.

James, W. (1890). *Principles of psychology*. New York: Holt.

James, W. (1899). *Talks to teachers on psychology: And to students on some of life's ideals*. New York: Holt.

Joncich, G. (1968). *The sane positivist: A biography of Edward L. Thorndike*. Middletown, CT: Wesleyan University Press.

Katz, D. (1986). Theodore M. Newcomb: 1903–1984. *American Journal of Psychology, 99*, 293–298.

Kendler, H. H. (1967). Kenneth W. Spence 1907–1967. *Psychological Review, 74*, 335–341.

Korn, J. H. (1990). Marilyn K. Rigby (1927–1990). *Teaching of Psychology, 17*, 148.

Korn, J. H., & Richey, M. H. (1991). Marilyn K. Rigby (1927–1990). *American Psychologist, 46*, 533.

Krech, D. (Ed.). (1973). *The MacLeod Symposium*. Ithaca, NY: Department of Psychology, Cornell University.

Larew, G. A. (1942). Celestia Parrish. *Virginia Journal of Education, 35*, 342–346.

MacLeod, B. (1973). A word from Bea. In D. Krech (Ed.), *The MacLeod Symposium* (pp. 25–26). Ithaca, NY: Department of Psychology, Cornell University.

McConnell, J. V. (1978). Confessions of a textbook writer. *American Psychologist, 33*, 159–169.

McKeachie, W. J. (1973). Donald G. Marquis. *Behavioral Science, 18*, 236–238.

McKeachie, W. J. (1987). Teaching, teaching teaching, and research on teaching. *Teaching of Psychology, 14*, 135–139.

Metfessel, M. (1950). Carl Emil Seashore, 1866–1949. *Science, 111*, 713–717.

Miller, E. O. (1953). Teaching psychology in the small liberal arts college. *American Psychologist, 8*, 475–478.

Miller, G. A. (1974). Stanley Smith Stevens: 1906–1973. *American Journal of Psychology, 87*, 279–288.

Milner, P. M. (1986). Donald Olding Hebb (1904–1985). *Trends in Neurosciences, 9*, 347–351.

Münsterberg, M. (1922). *Hugo Münsterberg: His life and work.* New York: Appleton-Century-Crofts.

Murphy, G. (1963). Robert Sessions Woodworth 1869–1962. *American Psychologist, 18*, 131–133.

Murphy, L. B. (1990). *Gardner Murphy: Integrating, expanding and humanizing psychology.* Jefferson, NC: McFarland.

Newcomb, T. M. (1979). Goodwin Watson (1899–1976). *American Psychologist, 34*, 433–434.

Pfaffmann, C. (1980). Leonard Carmichael, November 9, 1898–September 16, 1973. *Biographical Memoirs of the National Academy of Sciences of the United States of America, 51*, 25–47.

Pillsbury, W. B. (1928). The psychology of Edward Bradford Titchener. *Philosophical Review, 37*, 95–108.

Pillsbury, W. B. (1940). Margaret Floy Washburn (1871–1939). *Psychological Review, 47*, 99–109.

Poffenberger, A. T. (1962). Robert Sessions Woodworth: 1869–1962. *American Journal of Psychology, 75*, 677–689.

Pressey, S. L. (1967). Sidney Leavitt Pressey. In E. G. Boring & G. Lindzey (Eds.), *A history of psychology in autobiography* (Vol. 5; pp. 313–339). New York: Appleton-Century-Crofts.

Raphelson, A. C. (1980). Psychology at Michigan: The Pillsbury years, 1897–1947. *Journal of the History of the Behavioral Sciences, 16*, 301–312.

Remmers, H. H. (1933). *Learning, effort, and attitudes as affected by three methods of instruction in elementary psychology.* Lafayette, IN: Purdue University.

Rosenblum, L. A. (1987). Harry F. Harlow: Remembrance of a pioneer in developmental pscyobiology. *Developmental Psychobiology, 20*, 485–488.

Ross, D. (1972). *G. Stanley Hall: The psychologist as prophet.* Chicago: University of Chicago Press.

Ryan, T. A. (1982). Psychology at Cornell after Titchener: Madison Bentley to Robert MacLeod, 1928–1948. *Journal of the History of the Behavioral Sciences, 18*, 347–369.

Sachs, B. D. (1988). Reminiscences. *Hormones and Behavior, 22*, 438–440.

Sanford, E. C. (1891). A laboratory course in physiological psychology. *American Journal of Psychology, 4*, 141–148.

Scarborough, E., & Furumoto, L. (1987). *Untold lives: The first generation of American women psychologists.* New York: Columbia University Press.

Seashore, C. E. (Ed.). (1910a). Report of the committee of the American Psychological Association on the teaching of psychology. *Psychological Monographs, 7*(51), 1–93.

Seashore, C. E. (1910b). The class experiment. *Journal of Educational Psychology, 1*, 25–30.

Shields, S. A., & Mallory, M. E. (1987). Leta Stetter Hollingworth speaks on "Columbia's legacy." *Psychology of Women Quarterly, 11*, 285–300.

Skinner, B. F. (1958). Teaching machines. *Science, 128*, 969–977.

Skinner, B. F. (1984). *A matter of consequences.* New York: New York University Press.

Stevens, S. S. (1968). Edwin Garrigues Boring: 1886–1968. *American Journal of Psychology, 81*, 589–606.

Terman, L. M. (1930). Lewis M. Terman. In C. Murchison (Ed.), *A history of psychology in autobiography.* (Vol. 2; pp. 297–331). Worcester, MA: Clark University Press.

Thorndike, E. L. (1943). James' influence on the psychology of perception and thought. *Psychological Review, 50*, 87–94.

Underwood, B. J. (1979). Arthur W. Melton (1906–1978). *American Psychologist, 34*, 1171–1173.

Wells, F. L. (1944). James McKeen Cattell: 1860–1944. *American Journal of Psychology, 57*, 270–275.

Wertheimer, M. (1990). Edwin B. Newman: In memorium. *History of Psychology, 22*(3), 50–54.

Wolfe, H. K. (1895). The new psychology in undergraduate work. *Psychological Review, 2*, 382–387.

Woodworth, R. S. (1930). Robert S. Woodworth. In C. Murchison (Ed.), *A history of psychology in autobiography* (Vol. 2; pp. 359–380). Worcester, MA: Clark University Press.

Yerkes, R. M. (1956). *The scientific way.* Unpublished autobiographical manuscript. Yerkes Papers, Yale University Library, New Haven, CT.

6

A BRIEF HISTORY OF THE AMERICAN PSYCHOLOGICAL FOUNDATION'S AWARD FOR DISTINGUISHED TEACHERS OF PSYCHOLOGY

DAVID J. PITTENGER

Although psychologists have long celebrated and rewarded those who have made monumental contributions to the advancement of psychology as a scientific discipline, the formal recognition of contributions made through exemplary teaching is a more recent phenomenon. As contemporary psychologists reflect on the history of psychology, they are most likely to recognize those individuals whose research and theoretical writings most influenced the trends and focus within their particular disciplines. Furthermore, individuals cited in the history of psychology are recognized more for their programs of research than for their accomplishments in teaching. Consequently, psychologists who have expressed their scholarship primarily through teaching and have attracted and molded a new generation of psychologists are largely ignored.

It is important to recognize the essential impact that teaching has had on the history of psychology as a scientific discipline. Gustav Fechner may arguably be considered the first experimental psychologist (e.g., Boring,

1950, 1966). His self-professed revelation on October 22, 1850, marks the point when the phenomena of behavioral and mental processes were first examined using systematic empiricism. Yet, Wilhelm Wundt is typically credited as being the founder of experimental psychology because he, unlike Fechner, began the systematic education of others in the science of psychology (e.g., Benjamin, 1988).

Although we honor Wundt for producing the first generation of psychologists, the efforts of one of his first American students have been largely ignored. After graduating from Wundt's doctoral program, Harry K. Wolfe chose to return to his native state, Nebraska, to establish a department of psychology. By the end of his career, Wolfe had developed one of the most productive undergraduate programs in psychology and had prepared a large number of students for graduate work. In spite of his accomplishments, Wolfe has only recently received recognition from contemporary psychologists (Benjamin, 1991; see Dewsbury and Pickren, chapter 5 of this book).

It should not be surprising that quality teaching and exemplary teachers are often ignored or given minimal attention. The contingencies of the academic milieu do little to reinforce teaching. At larger institutions, professional advancement is determined largely by research productivity; teaching quality, although evaluated, is of subsidiary value to the number of grants received and articles published in refereed journals. At smaller schools, where teaching is the primary service expected of faculty, teaching and advising loads compete with the time needed to pursue a comprehensive research program. As a consequence, these individuals do not have the opportunity to enhance their reputations beyond the confines of their institutions. Within the past 20 years, however, the teaching of psychology has begun to receive greater attention and recognition.

HISTORY OF THE AMERICAN PSYCHOLOGICAL FOUNDATION TEACHING AWARD

The American Psychological Foundation (APF) was the first national organization to initiate an awards program to recognize psychologists who have made extraordinary contributions to the teaching of psychology. The APF was incorporated in 1953 as a nonprofit organization that is independent of the American Psychological Association (APA). Broadly stated, the mission of the Foundation is to support the development of psychology. During its existence, the APF has used its funds to support an awards program, to provide grants to foreign students who want to pursue postdoctoral research in American and Canadian universities, and to assist scholars who are preparing textbooks for use in foreign countries.

The APF is probably best known for its establishment of the Gold Medal Award for lifetime contributions to psychology. The Gold Medals were first awarded in 1956 and have been given to psychologists who are 65 and older and who have distinguished themselves through their research and scholarly accomplishments. Thus, the initiation of the Gold Medals coincided with the retirement of psychologists who began their training in the early part of this century. In the same year, the APF established awards for journalists who have produced an outstanding popular presentation of psychology in the television, radio, magazine, and newspaper media.

The impetus for the creation of a teaching award came from Wilbert J. McKeachie. McKeachie argued that the award should be created as a complement to the Gold Medal Award to represent the importance that psychologists place on teaching and research. In addition, he used the royalties from his introductory textbook to help establish a fund for the award (personal communication, December 19, 1991). Thus, in 1970 the APF's Teaching Award program was begun, and the first recipients of the Distinguished Contributions to Education in Psychology Awards were announced at the Annual Convention of the APA.[1] Since then, this recognition has been given to 34 individuals for their accomplishments in the teaching of psychology (American Psychological Foundation Awards [APF], 1971–1990). Table 1 lists the names of the winners of the award and the years they received them.

Since 1987, the APA has also begun to recognize extraordinary contributions to the teaching of psychology. Their Education Programs Office has established two awards, the Distinguished Career Contribution Award and the Distinguished Contribution Award. In addition, Division 2 of the APA has an awards program for faculty who might not otherwise receive national recognition. These awards, first given in 1980, are made to faculty of 4-year institutions, community colleges, and high schools, as well as to graduate students for their early career achievements. This chapter focuses on the APF Teaching Awards. As will be apparent, however, many of those who have received the APF Teaching Award were similarly honored by the APA, Division 2, or both.

CATEGORIES OF AWARDS

On examining the work of these award winners, it is obvious that all are outstanding teachers who have attracted students to the study of psy-

---

[1] The original description of the award was broadly defined as a recognition of individuals who "have made unusual contributions to instruction in psychology either through their own teaching or through other instructional functions such as the development of new courses or execution of creative work in evaluation of research in the teaching of psychology" (APF, 1971). In 1980, the criteria for receipt of the award were reworded to include "(a) demonstrated influence as a teacher of students who become outstanding psychologists, (b) development of effective teaching methods and/or teaching materials, (c) engaging in significant research on teaching, (d) development of innovative curricula and courses, (e) outstanding performance as a classroom teacher, (f) being an especially effective trainer of teachers of psychology, and (g) being responsible for administrative facilitation of outstanding teaching" (APF, 1981).

TABLE 1

Recipients of the American Psychological Foundation Teaching Awards

Year	Name	Type of Award
1970	Freda Gould Rebelsky	Distinguished Contribution to Education in Psychology
	Fred S. Keller	Distinguished Contribution to Education in Psychology
1971	Theophile S. Krawiec	Distinguished Contribution to Education in Psychology
	Jack L. Michael	Distinguished Contribution to Education in Psychology
1972	James L. McCary	Distinguished Contribution to Education in Psychology
1973	James B. Maas	Distinguished Contribution to Education in Psychology
	Frank J. McGuigan	Distinguished Contribution to Education in Psychology
1974	Frank Geldard	Distinguished Contribution to Education in Psychology
	Ohmer Milton	Distinguished Contribution to Education in Psychology
1975	Bernice L. Neugarten	Distinguished Contribution to Education in Psychology
	Philip G. Zimbardo	Distinguished Contribution to Education in Psychology
1976	James V. McConnell	Distinguished Contribution to Education in Psychology
1977	Fred McKinney	Distinguished Contribution to Education in Psychology
1978	Douglas Candland	Distinguished Contribution to Education in Psychology
	Robert S. Daniel	Unique Contribution in the Teaching of Psychology
1979	Delos D. Wickens	Distinguished Contribution to Education in Psychology
1980	Elliott Aronson	Distinguished Teaching in Psychology
	Carlos Albizu-Miranda	Award for the Development of Psychology Education in Puerto Rico and the Caribbean
1981	James A. Bayton	Distinguished Teaching in Psychology
1982	Henry Gleitman	Distinguished Teaching in Psychology
	Carolyn Wood Sherif	Distinguished Contribution to Education in Psychology
1983	Michael Wertheimer[a]	Distinguished Teaching in Psychology
	Ben James Winer	Distinguished Teaching in Quantitative Methods in Psychology
1984	David L. Cole	Distinguished Teaching in Psychology
	Robert Freed Bales	Distinguished Teaching of Group Process
1985	Wilbert J. McKeachie[a]	Distinguished Teaching in Psychology
	Frank A. Beach	Distinguished Teaching in Biopsychology
1986	Ludy T. Benjamin, Jr.	Distinguished Teaching in Psychology
	Ellen P. Reese	Distinguished Contribution to Education in Psychology

TABLE 1
(Continued)

Year	Name	Type of Award
1987	Benton J. Underwood	Distinguished Teaching in Psychology
	Eileen Mavis Hetherington	Distinguished Teaching in Developmental Psychology
1988	Steven F. Davis[b]	Distinguished Teaching in Psychology
	Richard L. Solomon	Distinguished Teaching in Experimental Psychology
1989	Charles L. Brewer	Distinguished Teaching in Psychology

[a]This psychologist was also a winner of the American Psychological Association's (APA) Distinguished Career Contributions to Education and Training in Psychology Award.
[b]This psychologist was also a winner of the APA Division 2's Outstanding Faculty Teaching Award.

chology and have helped shape the perception of psychology among educated people. What is truly interesting is the diversity of means by which they have achieved this goal. To examine these contributions, I have used nine categories: (a) development of new teaching methods and materials, (b) development of new courses and curricula, (c) contributions to a discipline within psychology, (d) noteworthy leadership as chair of a department, (e) teaching of minority students and women, (f) extraordinary teaching and training of teachers, (g) teaching at smaller institutions, (h) provision of a forum for enhancement of teaching, and (i) authorship of noteworthy textbooks.

As with all systems of categorization, there are areas of overlap among the categories. These areas of ambiguity are due to two factors. First, no category system can adequately separate and distinguish among all behaviors. The second, and perhaps more telling influence, is the fact that each APF award winner has been active across all domains. For example, a teacher who creates a new and independent course will probably have to create new methods of teaching the material. Similarly, anyone who has the drive to create a new course or redesign a curriculum will surely express that enthusiasm in his or her teaching.

Development of New Teaching Methods and Materials

There is little doubt that Fred S. Keller introduced one of the most radical departures from conventional methods of teaching through the creation of the personalized system of instruction (PSI). Keller's worldview of psychology was much influenced by his graduate school classmate, B. F. Skinner. Indeed, Keller's coauthored introductory text, *Principles of Psychology* (1950), is an introduction and review of basic behavioral phenomena that is presented from the perspective of operant conditioning. It is not surprising, then, that Keller would apply the use of the operant paradigm to the teaching of a college-level course. According to Keller (1974), he conceived of the foundation of PSI while he was assisting in the development of the Department of Psychology at the then new University of Brasília. Within several years, the PSI approach to teaching psychology and other disciplines was practiced at many colleges in the United States.

Although the PSI has been criticized by others (e.g., Caldwell, 1985), it should be noted that Keller remained objective in his analysis of the utility of this method of instruction. As would any well-trained experimental psychologist, Keller relied on objective data to form his conclusions. Therefore, it is to his credit that Keller later recanted his own teaching method: "The system was unrealistic and involved too many people . . . and in the last analysis, it was unnecessary" (Keller, 1985, p. 8).

Others to be recognized for incorporating new technologies into the teaching of psychology include James B. Maas and Fred McKinney. During the late 1950s and early 1960s, college student enrollments increased rapidly and placed an excessive burden on the teaching resources of the institutions. In response, many faculty sought techniques to teach large-enrollment classes in an efficient and effective manner.

At the time that Maas received his award, he was credited with teaching 1,300 students each semester. His ability to introduce such a large number of students to psychology was made possible by using a multimedia program of slides and films. This multimedia program has since been used as a model for other institutions. In 1977, Fred McKinney was credited with pioneering the use of closed-circuit television in the teaching of psychology (see also Daniel, 1983). McKinney had received a Ford Foundation grant in 1962 to develop new techniques for teaching psychology. Shortly after receiving the grant, he began to provide closed-circuit course presentations of his classes and to produce videotapes of his lectures. Although Maas and McKinney taught large numbers of students in an environment that does not typically afford the development of reciprocal student–teacher relationships, both were seen as dedicated teachers who had a sincere interest in teaching psychology.

In 1986, Ellen P. Reese was cited for her development of many films, texts, workshops, and laboratory manuals. Like many APF award winners, Reese has devoted much of her attention to designing classes that allow students to understand the application of psychology in practical settings. Evidence of this orientation to teaching can be found in the characterization of her courses as "workshops," rather than lecture courses. Thus, her course design appears to precede current discussions of "active learning," "collaborative learning," and "critical thinking" by several decades.

Development of New Courses and Curricula

Of the many winners of the APF Teaching Award, several individuals stand out for their contributions to the development of new courses and curricula. In all cases, winners either created a unique perspective within psychology or built a new program of study where one had not existed before. For example, Freda G. Rebelsky, the 1970 award winner, developed the program in developmental psychology at Boston University. She is credited not only for creating the necessary course work, but also for creating a program of study that attended to the interests of students while retaining a strict orientation to the scientific foundations of the subject matter.

Several faculty have been credited with introducing new courses that addressed the need expressed by students to have "relevant" courses. In each case, the courses were designed to address the students' needs while retaining an emphasis on the empirical nature of psychology. For example, James L. McCary, a 1972 award winner, is noted for creating a course titled "Marriage, Family and Sex Education" at the University of Houston, one of the first college courses to address the study of human sexuality. Although such a course is not commonplace on college campuses, the introduction of the course in the 1960s was controversial, and it was met with considerable resistance from conservative forces in the community and on the campus. McCary also developed an introductory course that required students to examine the psychological aspects of contemporary social problems. Likewise, Jack L. Michael designed courses that allowed his students to learn techniques for applying operant conditioning techniques in various field settings.

In 1978, Douglas Candland received the Teaching Award for his development of several innovative programs. First, Candland developed at Bucknell one of the nation's first animal behavior programs for undergraduate students. Then, in 1975, he developed a program of study in gerontology that included course work and field settings that provide students the opportunity to work and live with retired citizens. He later introduced an environmental studies program to the Bucknell curriculum.

Contributions to a Discipline Within Psychology

Several APF Teaching Award winners are credited for their contributions to the development of a new field of study within psychology. In 1985, Frank A. Beach was recognized for his contributions to the teaching of biopsychology. Throughout his career, Beach was a persuasive advocate for the value of comparative psychology and was instrumental in introducing American psychologists to the theories and procedures of European ethologists. Furthermore, Beach was one of the first psychologists to define and establish behavioral endocrinology as an independent area of study (Glickman & Zucker, 1989).

Carolyn Wood Sherif and Robert F. Bales were recognized for their monumental contributions to the advancement of social psychology. In 1982, Sherif was cited for her contributions to the development and teaching of social psychology. During her career, Sherif published many books that have had a significant influence on the study of social psychology (Shaffer & Shields, 1984). Sherif was also considered to be a gifted teacher by her students and peers.[2] Bales received the APF Teaching Award in 1984 for his research on and teaching of group processes. More specifically, Bales was cited for his research on small group processes and for his development of some of the first computer software to simulate the behavior of small groups of people.

Eileen M. Hetherington was awarded a special citation for her work in the teaching of developmental psychology. She, like other recipients of the special Teaching Awards, is recognized both for making contributions to the discipline and for being an articulate spokesperson for the field. Students at the University of Virginia recognize Hetherington as one of the finest lecturers at the University, and students who have read her books on developmental psychology have profited from her clarity of expression.

The name Benton J. Underwood is well associated with experimental psychology. His books, *Experimental Psychology* (1966) and *Experimentation in Psychology* (1975), represent essential contributions to the advancement of experimental psychology. As with others in this section, one of his contributions was also sharing his passion for research and psychology with his students.

Noteworthy Leadership as Chair of a Department

Several APF award winners received recognition for providing leadership, introducing innovations to the curriculum, and improving the quality of teaching in their particular departments of psychology. Being a competent department chair is, at best, difficult. One is often required to resolve the conflict between the demands of the faculty and the restrictions of the administration. In addition, the department chair is responsible for setting the standard for teaching excellence in the department and assuring that the academic quality and the vitality of the program are maintained. Given these preconditions, it would appear that being an excellent department chair is nearly impossible. In spite of these odds, several individuals have ascended beyond conventional bounds.

For example, in 1973, Frank J. McGuigan was recognized for his development of a master's program at Hollins College that was later to prepare many students for a variety of PhD programs. Others who were cited for their work as department chairs include Theophile S. Krawiec, chair at Skidmore College; Frank Geldard, chair and then dean at the University of Virginia; William J. McKeachie, chair at the University of Michigan; and Charles L. Brewer, chair at Furman University.

---

[2] As an aside, it was noted in Sherif's citation that she had studied with Fred S. Keller while she was a graduate student at Columbia (APF, 1982). Keller received the first APF Teaching Award.

Teaching of Minority Students and Women

Psychology, as the other scientific disciplines, has had a long-standing commitment to increase the representation of ethnic minorities and women in the field. During the past 20 years, the number of minorities and women at both the baccalaureate and doctorate levels in psychology has increased (Howard et al., 1986). Although there is still much room for improvement, it is important to recognize that the current success is due in part to the efforts of faculty who encourage students from underrepresented groups to study and pursue psychology as a profession. Appropriately, several of the APF Teaching Award winners have been credited for their efforts to make psychology accessible to all interested students.

Carlos Albizu-Miranda, in 1980, and James A. Bayton, in 1981, received special recognition for developing new programs of study and for helping to make the study of psychology available to minority students. Albizu-Miranda received a special Teaching Award for working to establish the Instituto Psicologico de Puerto Rico and the Caribbean Center for Advanced Studies. Both institutions are responsible for training many of the psychologists now living and working in Puerto Rico.

In a similar fashion, Bayton is responsible for improving the quality of education for Black students in the United States. In most historically Black colleges, psychology has been taught as a subject within the school's department of education. Bayton helped establish psychology as a separate academic discipline at several Black colleges, including Virginia State College, Southern University, and Morgan State College. Bayton's greatest impact was on Howard University, where he taught from 1947 until his death in 1990 (Ross & Hicks, 1991). Many students under Bayton's supervision advanced to graduate programs where they received their doctorates in psychology.

Of the 34 APF Teaching Award winners, five were women: Freda G. Rebelsky, Bernice L. Neugarten, Carolyn W. Sherif, Ellen P. Reese, and Eileen M. Hetherington. Each of these women was rightfully recognized for her contribution to teaching as well as to the discipline of psychology. Each, however, has also served as an important role model for a new generation of women who sought to advance their education through the study of psychology. Lest we forget the barriers women faced in their attempt to receive graduate education, one should recall that Carolyn W. Sherif was not allowed to enter the graduate program at Princeton because of her gender (Shaffer & Shields, 1984) and that in 1972, 2 years after the APF Teaching Awards were initiated, only 26% of the doctorates in psychology were earned by women.

Extraordinary Teaching and Training of Teachers

The title of this subsection contains an apparent redundancy. It is obvious that all the recipients of the awards are recognized leaders in the teaching of psychology. Beyond this, it is instructive to examine the efforts these individuals have made that led to their recognition.

Those who have taught at large institutions are generally recognized for their programs of research as well as for their teaching and dedication to helping others become better teachers. For example, Delos D. Wickens made monumental contributions to the study of classical conditioning and human memory (see Cross & Miles, 1989). In addition to his research, he also oversaw the introductory psychology course at Ohio State University for 30 years. During that time, he is credited with preparing many graduate students for their first professional teaching responsibilities. William B. Pavlik, a student of Wickens during the early- to mid-1950s, remembers Wickens as a role model:

> But there was more to 'Wick,' the teacher, than just a mechanical deliverer of well-organized lectures. His courses were among the first hard-nosed, "scientific" psychology courses that most of us took in those days. . . . He personified the calm, objective, reasonable, bright, and always empirically-based scientist. . . . [Also], one's teacher–student relationship with Wick did not end when one graduated. . . . He managed to attend most of the conventions of interest to experimental psychologists, and he made a point to come to our papers or otherwise "look us up." We sought his advice on problems of managing our careers, and he always was helpful. . . . Wick now has been dead for a few years, but I find that I still try to evaluate my own performance by imagining what he would have thought of it. (personal communication, December 5, 1991)

Richard L. Solomon was awarded a special honor in 1988 for his distinction in the teaching of experimental psychology. Solomon's influence on psychology has been ubiquitous. As a researcher, he has had a long and distinguished career that includes discovering new phenomena, performing research that solved persistent riddles, and creating theories that helped to explain and predict complex behaviors. His students, both graduate and undergraduate, have become major contributors to the advancement of the science. Solomon received much recognition for his research. He was elected to both the American Academy of Arts and Sciences and the National Academy of Sciences, and he was a Guggenheim Fellow. In addition, he received awards for his research from the APA and Sigma XI. Solomon, as a teacher, was also gifted. In the citation for his Teaching Award, it was noted that "He trained an illustrious group of PhDs whose work dominates an important subfield within Experimental Psychology" (APF, 1989, p. 666).

Steven F. Davis was also recognized for teaching students by encouraging them to become active in research. In his citation, Davis was credited with many contributions, including an impressive array of administrative duties for regional and national associations. Davis's most prominent contribution may be, however, the extremely large number of publications he has coauthored with graduate and undergraduate students.

Teaching at Smaller Institutions

Most of the APF Teaching Award winners were teaching at large public universities when they received their awards. Almost all had the opportunity to train dozens of psychologists at the PhD level, teach a variety of courses in their areas of specialty, conduct original research, and write books that would be considered essential in the field. There are, however, several exceptions to this trend.

Several winners received awards for the work they had done while at smaller institutions. Included in this category are Frank J. McGuigan (Hollins College), David Cole (Occidental College), and Charles L. Brewer (Furman University). In each case, due recognition was given for developing a program of study that attracted quality students to psychology and prepared them for graduate work. In addition, these individuals assumed important leadership roles in promoting the teaching of psychology through work in Division 2 and through teaching activities sponsored by the APA.

Provision of a Forum for Enhancement of Teaching

Division 2 was created in the 1940s as part of the APA's reorganization (see chapter 16 of this book for a complete history of Division 2). Since then, it has been the only division that acts solely as an advocate and a forum for the teaching of psychology. Almost all the APF Teaching Award winners have had leadership roles in Division 2. Several winners have been president of the division: Robert S. Daniel, Fred McKinney, James Maas, Douglas Candland, Michael Wertheimer, David Cole, Charles L. Brewer, Ludy T Benjamin, Jr., and Stephen F. Davis.

The journal, *Teaching of Psychology*, is the publication of Division 2. The journal's mission is to provide information that improves the teaching of psychology across all domains of the discipline and at all levels of education. Although more complete reviews of the history of the journal can be found elsewhere (e.g., Cohen & Sechrest, 1976; Daniel, 1974, 1977; Daniel & Loveland, 1976; see also chapter 19 of this book), it is important to acknowledge those whose efforts made the creation of the journal possible. The 1971 APF Teaching Award winner, Theophile S. Krawiec, was the editor of the Division 2 newsletter that later evolved into an independent journal. During his tenure as editor, the newsletter is credited as becoming "an important clearinghouse for ideas on the teaching of psychology" (APF, 1972, p. 73). After Krawiec, Robert S. Daniel, the 1978 winner of a Unique Contribution Award, became editor of the newsletter and converted it into a refereed journal. Editorship of the journal was transferred in 1985 to Charles L. Brewer, the 1989 recipient of the APF Teaching Award. *Teaching of Psychology* was the first and remains the only periodical dedicated to improving the teaching of psychology. Given the efforts of those responsible for its development and perpetuation, it is no surprise that it remains an essential source of information for psychologists who value teaching.

The dissemination of information about the teaching of psychology has also been greatly influenced by several APF Teaching Award winners. One of the first to be recognized for excellence in teaching and for distribution of information on teaching was Ohmer Milton. Milton received particular attention for distributing a research-based pamphlet, *Teaching Learning Issues*. In addition, Milton is credited with advocating what is now known as active learning and for challenging myths that some faculty may have about teaching.

In 1983, Michael Wertheimer was recognized for both his classroom teaching and his research reports and books on the teaching of psychology. This work was done in conjunction with his many scholarly pursuits, teaching duties, and administrative roles in the various divisions of APA.

Wilbert J. McKeachie has also contributed much to the teaching of psychology. In his Teaching Award citation, McKeachie is credited for the continued growth of the University of Michigan's Department of Psychology as a premier program in psychology. He also served as the president of the APA (1975–1976). It may be argued, however, that he is most recognized for his many research articles on teaching effectiveness; his many book chapters on teaching; and his book, *Teaching Tips*, all of which have helped others become better teachers.

In 1986, Ludy T. Benjamin, Jr., was recognized for his many contributions to helping others become better teachers. After teaching at Nebraska Wesleyan University for several years, Benjamin joined the Educational Affairs Directorate of the APA. There, he initiated the G. Stanley Hall Lecture Series and the publication of the *Activities Handbook for the Teaching of Psychology* (1985) series. He has also published numerous books on the teaching of psychology and the history of psychology.

Authorship of Noteworthy Textbooks

Almost all of the APF Teaching Award winners have written at least one book. On several occasions, however, the contribution that a book has made has warranted special attention. Specifically, Ben J. Winer was recognized in 1984 for his "legendary" text on statistics and experimental design, *Statistical Principles in Experimental Design* (1971). It is telling that reviews of both editions of his book contain effusive praise. For example, Binder (1963) concludes of the first edition, "As a textbook for the graduate course . . . the book is outstanding, as a reference book for the practicing experimenter, it is superb" (p. 268). Likewise, Cotton (1973) concludes of the second edition, "Nothing else in the field of experimental design for psychologists even approaches Winer's text in quality and quantity of coverage" (p. 169).

Others have also been credited for their contributions to preparing textbooks that facilitate good teaching. For example, Philip G. Zimbardo is recognized for his text *Psychology and Life* (13th ed., 1992), and continuously attempts to improve on a variety of teaching methods and materials. Likewise, James V. McConnell received special praise in 1976 for his well-crafted textbook. In 1980, Elliot Aronson was recognized for several of his publications, including *The Social Animal* (1991), a book that is now in its sixth edition, and the five-volume *Handbook of Social Psychology* (3rd ed., 1985), which he coedited with Gardner Lindzey. Most recently, Henry Gleitman was recognized for his contributions to teaching with particular note being made of his textbook, *Psychology* (2nd ed., 1986), and the standard it established for the field.

A PROFILE OF STEPHEN F. DAVIS

Although each of the APF Teaching Award winners represents a model of teaching excellence, there are several reasons to single out Stephen F. Davis for a more considered examination. Like many of the other APF Teaching Award winners, Davis has an impressive program of research, which includes at least 158 publications on topics such as olfactory control of animal maze learning, conditioned taste aversion, behavioral effects of lead toxicity, death anxiety, and locus of control. What distinguishes Davis from other APF Teaching Award recipients is that the vast majority of Davis's publications were coauthored with one or more of his undergraduate students. As was noted in his citation, Davis believes that the only way a student can learn about psychology is to become involved in the research of psychologists. It should also be noted that Davis teaches at a state school that does not have a competitive admissions policy, a prestigious history, a national reputation, or a comfortable endowment, and that does not view itself as a research institution. Hence, Davis's level of activity appears to have been maintained by the reinforcing value of his continued interaction with his students.

Some tentative parallels can be drawn between Harry K. Wolfe and Stephen F. Davis. Both received advanced training in experimental psychology and were well qualified to become known for their research. Both, however, chose to return to smaller and less-known schools and, with enthusiasm and dedication to the science, to build departments of psychology. Both developed teaching styles that made students feel welcome in the laboratory and allowed students to take an active role in the process of conducting research. Sadly, Wolfe received little national recognition from his contemporaries for his work. Davis, however, has rightfully received national attention and accolade. Thus, the APF Teaching Award does appear to meet its goal: The Award gives recognition and affirmation to those who have contributed to psychology through teaching in the same way that the Gold Medal Award recognizes those who have contributed to psychology through research.

CONCLUSION

Although this chapter has been a review of the history of the APF Teaching Awards, it cannot be considered a complete history of those who have received the Award. Most of the recipients are still active in their academic pursuits and continue to make contributions to the teaching of psychology. Indeed, this chapter would have been much longer if I had chronicled the accomplishments of these people since the receipt of their awards. The information presented in this review can be used, however, to create a composite of the psychologist who is recognized by students and peers as an extraordinary teacher.

I attempted to divide the accomplishments of the APF Teaching Award winners into separate categories. Although this allowed me to identify the special contributions made by the individuals, it may suggest that teaching is made up of individual and mutually exclusive components. Such a conclusion is not, I believe, accurate. To reiterate a point made earlier, the enthusiasm and dedication that cause one to receive recognition for a singular contribution are a reflection of one's general attitude and behaviors that are applied to all teaching responsibilities. Thus, the APF Teaching Award winners represent psychologists whose dedication to the teaching of psychology is expressed in every facet of their work.

Several generalizations can be made about all of the APF Teaching Award winners. First, all of the award winners have been active writers. Some have focused their writings on their research or have written about speciality areas within psychology. Some have written textbooks that introduce students to psychology and its many aspects. Others have written material to help others become better teachers.

Second, good teaching and good writing are linked. To write well and to teach well, one must analyze, organize, and synthesize complex information and present it in a logical and systematic fashion. Good writers and teachers are able to anticipate potential areas of confusion and provide ample support for the reader or learner. Good writers and teachers are also able to hold the attention of their audience and effectively demonstrate the importance of the subject matter.

Third, psychology, as an academic discipline, places high value on the free and creative empirical study of behavior and mental processes. To this end, each of the APF Teaching Award winners has provided their students with a superior model to emulate. In other words, these individuals have demonstrated that psychology is more than the reading of textbooks, the transcription of lecture notes, and the learning of what is already known. These psychologists teach by having their students at all levels of education become involved in the process of inquiry. In each case, the teacher has been able to present psychology in such a way that its study becomes "relevant" from the perspective of the student.

Finally, each of these individuals has contributed to the improvement of the teaching of psychology. Some have helped teach their students to become good teachers. Some have introduced new methods of teaching and have conducted research on the effectiveness of these new techniques. Some have created and supported forums for the exchange of information on teaching. All have represented teaching as an essential component of contemporary scholarship and as one of the primary responsibilities of the profession.

As we begin the second century of psychology, it is essential to recognize that the existence and the future of psychology are dependent on the curiosity, inquiry, and original analysis of psychologists. Those teachers who attract new students to the discipline, who imbue their students with the values and goals of psychology, and who help their students mature intellectually assure the vitality and longevity of this science.

REFERENCES

American Psychological Foundation. (1971). Gold Medal Award and the Distinguished Contributions to Education in Psychology Awards: 1970. *American Psychologist, 26*, 91–95.

American Psychological Foundation. (1972). Gold Medal Award, Distinguished Contributions to Education in Psychology Awards, and the National Media Awards: 1971. *American Psychologist, 27*, 71–75.

American Psychological Foundation. (1973). Gold Medal Award, Distinguished Contributions to Education in Psychology Awards, and the National Media Awards for 1972. *American Psychologist, 28*, 75–81.

American Psychological Foundation Awards for 1973. (1974). Gold Medal, Distinguished Contributions to Education in Psychology, and the National Media. *American Psychologist, 29*, 48–53.

American Psychological Foundation Awards for 1974. (1975). Gold Medal, Distinguished Contributions to Education in Psychology, and the National Media. *American Psychologist, 30*, 79–83.

American Psychological Foundation Awards for 1975. (1976). Gold Medal, Distinguished Contributions to Education in Psychology, and the National Media. *American Psychologist, 31,* 83–86.

American Psychological Foundation Awards for 1976. (1977). Gold Medal, Distinguished Contributions to Education in Psychology, and the National Media. *American Psychologist, 32,* 98–101.

American Psychological Foundation Awards for 1977. (1978). Gold Medal, Distinguished Contribution to Education in Psychology, and the National Media. *American Psychologist, 33,* 84–87.

American Psychological Foundation Awards for 1978. (1979). Gold Medal, Distinguished Contribution to Education in Psychology, Unique Contribution in the Teaching of Psychology, and the National Media. *American Psychologist, 34,* 80–85.

American Psychological Foundation Awards for 1979. (1980). Gold Medal, Distinguished Contribution to Education in Psychology, and the National Media. *American Psychologist, 35,* 93–98.

American Psychological Foundation Awards for 1980. (1981). Gold Medal, Distinguished Teaching in Psychology, Development of Psychology Education in Puerto Rico and the Caribbean, and the National Media. *American Psychologist, 36,* 88–95.

American Psychological Foundation Awards for 1981. (1982). Gold Medal, Distinguished Teaching in Psychology, and the National Media. *American Psychologist, 37,* 86–90.

American Psychological Foundation Awards for 1982. (1983). Gold Medal, Distinguished Teaching in Psychology, Distinguished Contribution to Education in Psychology, and the National Media. *American Psychologist, 38,* 61–66.

American Psychological Foundation Awards for 1983. (1984). Gold Medal, Distinguished Teaching in Psychology, Distinguished Teaching of Quantitative Methods in Psychology, and the National Media. *American Psychologist, 39,* 310–314.

American Psychological Foundation Awards for 1984. (1985). Gold Medal, Distinguished Teaching in Psychology, Distinguished Teaching of Group Process, and the National Psychology Awards for Excellence in the Media. *American Psychologist, 40,* 340–345.

American Psychological Foundation Awards for 1985. (1986). Gold Medal Awards for Psychological Science, Psychological Professional, and Contribution by a Psychologist in the Public Interest; Distinguished Teaching in Psychology Award, Distinguished Teaching in Biopsychology Award, and the National Psychology Awards for Excellence in the Media. *American Psychologist, 41,* 409–417.

American Psychological Foundation Awards for 1986. (1987). Gold Medal Awards for Psychological Science, Psychological Professional, and Contribution by a Psychologist in the Public Interest; Distinguished Teaching in Psychology Award, Distinguished Contribution to Education in Psychology Award, and the National Psychology Awards for Excellence in the Media. *American Psychologist, 42,* 327–336.

American Psychological Foundation Awards for 1987. (1988). Gold Medal Awards for Psychological Science, Psychological Professional, and Contribution by a Psychologist in the Public Interest; Distinguished Teaching in Psychology Award, Distinguished Teaching in Developmental Psychology Award, and the National Psychology Awards for Excellence in the Media. *American Psychologist, 43,* 260–266.

American Psychological Foundation Awards for 1988. (1989). Gold Medal Awards for Psychological Science, Psychological Professional, and Contribution by a Psychologist in the Public Interest; Distinguished Teaching in Psychology Award, Distinguished Teaching in Experimental Psychology Award, and the National Psychology Awards for Excellence in the Media. *American Psychologist, 44,* 659–667.

American Psychological Foundation Awards for 1989. (1990). Gold Medal Awards for Life Achievement in Psychological Science; Life Achievement in the Applications of Psychology; Life Contribution by a Psychologist in the Public Interest; and Distinguished Teaching in Psychology Award. *American Psychologist, 45,* 654–660.

Aronson, E. (1991). *The social animal.* New York: Freeman.

Benjamin, L. T., Jr. (1988). *A history of psychology: Original sources and contemporary research.* New York: McGraw Hill.

Benjamin, L. T., Jr. (1991). *Harry Kirke Wolfe: Pioneer in psychology.* Lincoln: University of Nebraska Press.

Benjamin, L. T., Jr., & Lowman, K. D. (Eds.). (1985). *Activities handbook for the teaching of psychology.* Washington, DC: American Psychological Association.

Binder, A. (1963). Confounded interactions, balanced lattices, youden squares and plain F's. [Review of *Statistical principles in experimental design*]. *Contemporary Psychology, 8,* 267–268.

Boring, E. G. (1950). *History of experimental psychology* (2nd ed.). New York: Appleton-Century-Crofts.

Boring, E. G. (1966). Editors introduction: Gustav Theoder Fechner, 1801–1887. In D. H. Howes & E. G. Boring (Eds.), *Elements of psychophysics* (H. E. Adler Trans.). New York: Holt.

Caldwell, E. C. (1985). Dangers of PSI. *Teaching of Psychology, 12,* 9–12.

Cohen, L. H., & Sechrest, L. B. (1976). The APA evaluation of *Teaching of Psychology. Teaching of Psychology, 3,* 130–134.

Cotton, J. W. (1973). Even better than before. [Review of *Statistical principles in experimental design* (2nd ed.)]. *Contemporary Psychology, 18,* 168–196.

Cross, H. A., & Miles, R. C. (1989). Obituary: Delos D. Wickens (1909–1988). *American Psychologist, 44,* 1151–1152.

Daniel, R. S. (1974). Teaching of psychology has already had a long past. *Teaching of Psychology, 1,* 32–34.

Daniel, R. S. (1977). Birth of a journal: The initiation. *IEEE Transaction on Professional Communication*, PC-20, 82–84.

Daniel, R. S. (1983). Obituary: Fred McKinney (1908–1981). *American Psychologist, 38*, 1245–1246.

Daniel, R. S., & Loveland, E. H. (1976). Report on the status of ToP. *Teaching of Psychology, 3*, 129–130.

Gleitman, H. (1986). *Psychology* (2nd ed.). New York: Norton.

Glickman, S. E., & Zucker, I. (1989). Obituary: Frank A. Beach (1911–1988). *American Psychologist, 44*, 1234–1235.

Howard, A., Pion, G. M., Gottfredson, G. D., Flattau, P. E., Oskamp, S., Pfafflin, S. M., Bray, D. W., & Burstein, A. G. (1986). The changing facts of American psychology: A report from the Committee on Employment and Human Resources. *American Psychologist, 41*, 1311–1327.

Keller, F. S. (1974). The history of PSI. In F. S. Keller & J. G. Sherman (Eds.), *The Keller Plan handbook: Essays on a personalized system of instruction* (pp. 6–13). Menlo Park, CA: W. A. Benjamin.

Keller, F. S. (1985). Lightning strikes twice. *Teaching of Psychology, 12*, 4–8.

Keller, F. S., & Schoenfeld, W. N. (1950). *Principles of psychology: A systematic text in the science of behavior.* New York: Appleton-Century-Crofts.

Lindzey, G. & Aronson, E. (1985). *The Handbook of social psychology* (3rd ed.). Hillsdale, NJ: Erlbaum.

Ross, S., & Hicks, L. H. (1991). Obituary: James A. Bayton (1912–1990). *American Psychologist, 46*, 1345.

Shaffer, L. S., & Shields, S. A. (1984). Obituary: Carolyn Wood Sherif (1922–1982). *American Psychologist, 39*, 176–178.

Underwood, B. J. (1966). *Experimental psychology.* New York: Appleton-Century-Crofts.

Underwood, B. J., & Shaughnessy, J. J. (1975). *Experimentation in psychology.* New York: Wiley.

Winer, B. J. (1971). *Statistical principles in experimental design* (2nd ed.). New York: McGraw-Hill.

Zimbardo, P. G. (1992). *Psychology and life* (13th ed.). New York: HarperCollins.

7

WOMEN: THEIR INFLUENCE AND THEIR IMPACT ON THE TEACHING OF PSYCHOLOGY

FLORENCE L. DENMARK AND LINDA C. FERNANDEZ

In researching accounts of the teaching of psychology, we have noticed that women's contributions were largely overlooked and unrecognized. Yet, women have played an integral part in education and training in the discipline since the 1890s.

To understand some of the barriers to educational opportunity confronted by women in the late 19th century, in this chapter we examine the social norms that generally proscribed higher education for women, as well as the influence of Darwin and Spencer on these norms. We then describe the women who were pioneers in the teaching of psychology, some of those who developed assessment instruments so vital to our current courses in testing, and selected contemporary women who have made key contributions in the teaching of psychology. We also examine the influence of the study of the psychology of women on the teaching of psychology.

It is important to note that as we discuss the contributions of women to the teaching of psychology, our concept of teaching includes, yet goes beyond, the classroom. Women have extended their pedagogic influence by authoring books and journal articles, by mentoring students, and by leading in colleges, universities, and psychology's professional organizations. It is beyond the scope of this chapter to cite all of the women who had an impact on the teaching of psychology. For a more detailed account we refer the interested reader to the two volumes of O'Connell and Russo's (1988) *Models of Achievement*, as well as to Scarborough and Furumoto's book (*Untold Lives*) on early American women psychologists (1987).

HISTORICAL BACKGROUND

The founding of Harvard in 1636 established the precedent that the doors of higher education in the United States should be closed to women. At its inception, the founding purpose of Harvard was the education of the clergy, an occupation that at that time excluded women. Women were not admitted to colleges and professional institutions until the third decade of the 19th century. Georgia Female College opened in 1838; Oberlin College graduated three women in 1841; Geneva Medical College graduated Elizabeth Blackwell, the first woman to become a physician in the United States, in 1849.

Women's colleges faced opposition from the prevailing myths of the 19th century. One of the most damaging myths for women was social Darwinism. Social Darwinism was based on the social theories arising after publication of Darwin's *On the Origin of the Species* in 1859. To explain individual variability and variability among different species, Darwin posited theories of natural and sexual selection. Those who possessed favorable variations survived and reproduced, thus passing the favorable traits to their offspring. Darwin also noted that not all variability seemed essential to individual survival. He tried to account for this nonessential individual variability with his theory of sexual selection. In sexual selection, the struggle is not for survival but between men for the possession of women. Darwin's sexual selection theory espoused an associated law of partial inheritance, which stated that the law of equal transmission (transmission of certain characteristics to *both* sexes) was not always equal. Sometimes transmission was only to same-sex offspring. Darwin said that he was not sure *why* the inheritability of some traits appeared to be mediated by the law of equal transmission, while the inheritability of other traits appeared to be mediated by the law of partial inheritance. Darwin believed that traits such as intelligence and reason were acquired through sexual selection and appeared to be meditated by the law of partial inheritance and *same-sex* transmission.

Now here is the point at which Darwin's inference created a myth. Darwin believed that because women did not compete for men, they did not get the same evolutionary opportunity to develop the same intelligence, perseverance, and courage as men. Thus, for one of the most influential thinkers and shapers of the 19th century, this belief regarding natural and sexual selection resulted in the conviction that men, because of their greater evolutionary experience, were superior to women. This is the central myth of social Darwinism.

Spencer based his theories on Darwin's view and posited that traits were acquired over time as a result of their function. For example, because women were the primary child rearers in society, Spencer believed such traits as maternal instinct and ability to nurture would be acquired as a result of their function, namely, daily care of children. He also believed that these acquired traits were fixed in biological structures and that there would be "constitutional modification produced by excess of function" (Spencer, 1864, p. 252). Spencer theorized that women's reproductive systems required more "vital force" than men's reproductive systems, leaving women with less available "vital force" or energy for their individual mental and physical growth than men. Thus, because of the high energy demands of women's reproductive systems, any other energy demands for mental activity or "brain work" would drain women of their "vital force." This drain, especially during adolescence, could lead to reproductive disorders, inability to breast-feed, or even infertility.

WOMEN PIONEERS

It was in this inhospitable climate that the first generation of American women psychologists sought to overcome barriers to women's higher education and teaching careers. Women were not even permitted to attend institutions of higher learning until the 1830s. They also had to overcome societal expectations of a "woman's place" in order to obtain an education and to develop as a professional. Despite this discrimination, women pioneers in psychology were able to contribute to the teaching of psychology. Furomoto and Scarborough (1986) presented data on the careers of the first 22 American women psychologists. They noted that 12 were active in higher education—7 were teachers or administrators at women's colleges, 4 at coeducational universities, and 1 at a normal school. Although all of these early women psychologists advanced through the academic ranks, space limits us to highlighting only a few.

Mary Whiton Calkins

In 1890, Mary Whiton Calkins attempted to overcome the institutional barriers facing women seeking advanced study at Harvard. Charles W. Elliot, Harvard president, believed that by admitting women students, Harvard would be showing signs of institutional decay (Hawkins, 1972).

Although Calkins had the support of Professor Josiah Royce and Professor William James to attend actual Harvard seminars, Harvard president Elliot would only grant Calkins permission to "gratuitously attend" their seminars. She was not permitted to be a matriculated student and not entitled to registration, simply because she was a woman.

In spite of all the barriers, Mary Calkins was able to persist and to explore *The Principles of Psychology* one-on-one with James (1890). In addition, Calkins sought out laboratory training at Clark University, where she arranged to take private lessons in laboratory experiments from Edmund Sanford. Sanford also served as a consultant to Calkins when she set up a psychological laboratory at Wellesley in 1891, where she served as an instructor. James was impressed with the work of Hugo Münsterberg and had been instrumental in bringing him to Harvard to head the psychological laboratory. In 1893, Calkins, seeking to work with Münsterberg, petitioned the Harvard authorities. She cited her laboratory work with Sanford and James, and Münsterberg also wrote on her behalf. Again, she was allowed to be a "guest" but was not permitted to become a registered student, simply because she was a woman. During the time she worked with Münsterberg in the Harvard laboratory, she also continued to fulfill her teaching duties at Wellesley. Deeply impressed with her work, Münsterberg petitioned Harvard again in 1894 requesting that Mary Calkins be admitted as a candidate for the PhD. His request was denied.

In 1895, Calkins was given an informal examination by the Department of Philosophy that was equal to the official examination of the PhD. degree. The Department not only found that Calkins satisfied their usual requirements but also went on to state that she displayed a level of scholarly intelligence that was exceptionally high. William James said in a letter to a Calkin's classmate, "It [Calkins's examination] was much the most brilliant examination for the Ph.D. that we have had at Harvard. It is a pity, in spite of this that she still lacks the degree" (noted in Scarborough & Furumoto, 1987, p. 46).

After having completed her graduate studies, and still without a degree, Calkins went back to Wellesley in 1895 where she was an associate professor of psychology. At Wellesley, she was able to direct the laboratory, to teach, and to publish. By 1898, she was promoted to full professor.

In 1902, Calkins was offered a PhD from Radcliffe College, which offered only undergraduate courses to women. Calkins firmly believed that to offer a Radcliffe PhD to women who had completed all the Harvard doctoral requirements was simply the Harvard way of continuing to discriminate against women by denying them legitimacy for no other reason than the fact that they were women. She declined the Radcliffe PhD.

Calkins stayed at Wellesley until she retired in 1929. Her major contributions to the teaching of psychology were her development of a system of self-psychology and her creation of the paired-associate experimental technique that is still taught in research methodology classes today. Calkins was also the first woman to become president of the American Psychological Association (APA). In spite of all her scholarly achievements, discrimination against women was still the norm, and as late as 1927, the Harvard Corporation refused the request for her PhD, stating they could see no adequate reason for granting her the degree (Furumoto, 1979, 1980).

Christine Ladd-Franklin

Another woman who was not granted the PhD even though she fulfilled all the requirements was Christine Ladd-Franklin. In 1882 she completed all the work for the doctorate at Johns Hopkins, but that university refused to grant her the PhD because of her gender. Ironically, Johns Hopkins presented the degree to Ladd-Franklin in 1926 (when she was nearly eighty years old).

Christine Ladd married Fabian Franklin soon after she completed her studies at Johns Hopkins. Her employment after marriage was limited to a part-time lectureship first at Johns Hopkins and later at Columbia University, a situation not uncommon to married women. However, she remained scientifically active and had an impact on teaching of psychology through her very influential theory of color vision. Her interest in vision began with her article on binocular vision (Ladd-Franklin, 1887). She traveled to Germany to do experimental work in vision with the eminent German psychologist G. E. Müller at his Göttingen laboratory. She also studied with Herman von Helmholtz and one of his followers studying color vision, Arthur Konig. By the end of her year in Europe, Ladd-Franklin developed her own evolutionary-based theory of color vision. She presented her model to the International Congress of Psychology in London and continued to develop her theory over a forty-year period.

Ladd-Franklin was a pioneer in her tireless efforts to create equal access to education for women. In 1921, she chastised the American Academy of Arts and Letters for their discriminatory policy of excluding women. When E. B. Titchner banned women from an all-male group of psychologists called "the Experimentalists" from 1904 to 1929, Ladd-Franklin began to correspond with Titchner regularly, expressing her dismay and conveying her moral outrage at women's exclusion. In 1929, "the Experimentalists" reorganized and elected its first two women members, June Etta Downey and Margaret Floy Washburn.

Lillien Jane Martin

Lillien Jane Martin began her graduate study in psychology at age 44 after the death of her mother freed her from family obligations and enabled her to make a career change. She studied in Germany at the University of

Göttingen, another university that did not award the PhD to women. After returning to the United States and joining the faculty at Stanford University in 1898, Martin rose through the ranks to become the first woman department chair at Stanford University in 1915. Prior to this, in 1913, she was awarded an honorary doctorate from the University of Bonn, a notable distinction. After reaching the mandatory retirement age of 65 in 1916, Martin went on to found the first mental hygiene clinic for "normal" preschoolers, and she later founded the first counseling center for senior citizens. She also contributed to the teaching of counseling psychology.

In addition to coping with institutional discrimination, Martin and Ladd-Franklin also exemplified women whose teaching careers were affected by societal norms. For example, women were expected to care for their sick parents, so Martin was unable to even begin her graduate study until her mother's death. Wives, such as Ladd-Franklin, not only had to cope with antinepotism strictures but also had to place their husbands' careers ahead of their own.

Margaret Floy Washburn

The first American woman to successfully break the institutional barriers to women's academic achievement and receive a PhD in psychology was Margaret Floy Washburn. She would later become the second woman to be elected president of the APA in 1921. After graduating from Vassar, Washburn studied with James McKeen Cattell at Columbia University. Like Calkins, Washburn was only permitted to audit classes. Cattell advised her to apply to Cornell University where she was advanced to candidacy with E. B. Titchener as her advisor. She completed her doctoral work in 2 years and was awarded her PhD in 1894. Washburn began her teaching of psychology at Wells College for Women and also taught two courses at Cornell. These courses were precursors to areas of psychology to which Washburn would later contribute, namely, social psychology and animal psychology. Washburn accepted a position as assistant professor at the University of Cincinnati, where she was the only woman faculty member. Later Washburn was offered a position as associate professor at Vassar; her long and fruitful career there included writing a classic text in comparative psychology, *The Animal Mind* (1909), and establishing Vassar's psychological laboratory. Her students in the senior seminar conducted studies there that she designed and then submitted for publication with the student as coauthor. From this collaborative research, she published more than 70 articles in the *American Journal of Psychology* (Scarborough & Furumoto, 1987). Washburn not only taught courses in psychology, she also taught her students through mentoring, modeling, and fostering students' professional growth.

Leta Stetter Hollingworth

In 1906, Leta Stetter Hollingworth graduated from the University of Nebraska with membership in Phi Beta Kappa. After marrying psychologist Harry Hollingworth and moving to New York, she sought employment as a schoolteacher and found that married women would not be hired. She then began graduate work in psychology at Columbia University under the tutelage of Edward Thorndike. Her doctoral dissertation was titled "Functional Periodicity: An Experimental Study of the Mental and Motor Abilities of Women During Menstruation" (L. Hollingworth, 1914a). Her study found that women did not become disabled during the menstrual cycle nor did their performance vary with different phases of the cycle. One of Hollingworth's contributions to the teaching of psychology was that she refuted menstrual myths with empirical research.

In 1914, through her research, Hollingworth also disproved some of the myths of social Darwinism (1914b). Darwin's variability hypothesis had mistakenly concluded that the higher status of men was based on their greater variability. Hollingworth and Helen Montague studied the birth records of 1,000 male and 1,000 female neonates. When birth weight and length were examined, they found that if variability "favored" any sex, it was the female sex (Montague & Hollingworth, 1914).

Hollingworth argued that social conditions rather than biologically innate differences could more parsimoniously account for seemingly greater male variability. She reasoned that because there was more societal pressure on men to be competitive and to achieve economically, their deficiencies would be noted earlier. Young women's deficiencies would be less likely to be noticed if they remained at home engaged in housework. Women would be more likely to be institutionalized in old age, especially as widows, because they were no longer useful as wives.

Hollingworth also argued that the essence of understanding female achievement was related to the fact that throughout history women bore children and were their caretakers. Hollingworth did not intend this to be an attack on motherhood but rather a more plausible explanation than a lack of "vital force" à la Spencer or a "lack of variability" à la Darwin. Hollingworth's career in academic psychology was unusual for her time because she was married and held a full-time position since 1916 in the Department of Psychology at Columbia University. In spite of her research, she was never able to secure grants to support her work (H. Hollingworth, 1943).

In summary, Hollingworth's myth-refuting empirical evidence contributed to the teaching of psychology by insisting on scientific stringency to teach facts, not androcentric science fiction. Hollingworth contributed to child psychology and education with her innovative work on exceptional children. She coined the term "gifted," and her book on adolescence is still a classic in the field (Benjamin, 1975).

It is beyond the scope of this chapter to name all the women who have contributed to the teaching of psychology. One area that provides an excellent example of women's contributions is the teaching of psychological testing.

WOMEN'S IMPACT ON TEACHING PSYCHOLOGICAL TESTING

After the turn of the century, professional interest in children's welfare also stimulated psychology's interest in mental retardation and mental testing. This was an area open to women. Many female psychologists, frequently affiliated with universities, developed instruments that are still key components of psychological testing, thus influencing the way testing was taught.

Florence Laura Goodenough, who received her PhD in 1924 from Stanford University, developed the well-known and widely used Draw-A-Man Test, a nonverbal intelligence test for children, at Stanford University as part of her dissertation research. She was on the faculty at the University of Minnesota from 1925 until her premature retirement in 1947. She was a leader in test development and construction, and her students remember her as a generous and conscientious teacher (Stevens & Gardner, 1982). She also influenced the teaching of child development by being an innovator in the development of observational methods and by designing a method of episode sampling used in research on children's social behavior (Sicherman & Green, 1980). One of Goodenough's books, *Anger in Young Children* (1931), is still often cited in developmental textbooks, and her *Developmental Psychology* (1934) is a classic textbook in the field.

In 1910, three years after receiving her PhD at the University of Chicago, Grace Maxwell Fernald joined the faculty at Los Angeles State Normal School (later renamed the California State University at Los Angeles). She remained there until 1918 when she received an appointment at the University of California, Los Angeles, where she remained for 30 years until her retirement in 1948. Fernald was known as a pioneer in the child guidance clinic movement and for her work in learning disabilities and educational reform. She was the author of a widely used nonverbal intelligence test.

Maud Merrill James received her AB in 1911 from Oberlin College and then worked at the Minnesota Bureau of Research where she became actively involved in studying intelligence. After moving to California, she established a small psychological clinic for children and served as its director. Maud Merrill James is best known for having coauthored with Lewis Terman the 1937 revision of the Stanford-Binet Intelligence Test, popularly known as the Terman-Merrill. The alternate forms of the 1937 revised Binet are

"L" (for Lewis Terman) and "M" (for Maud Merrill). James was affiliated with Stanford University until her retirement in 1954, where, in addition to her work on intelligence, she helped develop clinical child psychology.

Karen Machover, who received her MA in 1929 from New York University, developed the now widely used psychodiagnostic Draw-A-Person Test and is the often-cited author of *Personality Projection in the Drawing of the Human Figure* (1949). In addition to her private clinical practice, in which she was noted for her work in child therapy, she taught at the New School of Social Research and at the Long Island College of Medicine.

Thelma Gwinn Thurstone earned her PhD in 1927 from the University of Chicago. While they were both graduate students, she and psychologist Louis Leon Thurstone married in 1924. Like other female psychologists who collaborated with their husbands, Thelma Thurstone's contributions were often not fully recognized and appreciated. She is best known for her contributions to the Primary Mental Abilities Battery, which she developed with her husband in 1938. However, she did not receive recognition until she was in her mid-fifties. She was professor of education at the University of North Carolina and was also made director of the Psychometric Laboratory at Chapel Hill after her husband's death in 1955.

SOME CONTEMPORARY WOMEN

In the brief space allotted to us here, it is not possible to name all of the accomplished contemporary women who left a legacy to the teaching of psychology. Therefore, only a few of the major contributors will be highlighted including minority women, women who have been APA presidents, women who have received APA teaching awards, and a few of the women who have contributed to teaching the history of psychology.

Contributions of Minority Women

As women in general faced barriers to educational achievement, minority women in particular had limited access to advanced education (Russo & Denmark, 1987). Before the 1954 *Brown v. Board of Education* Supreme Court decision, Black women and men were educated in segregated schools. Although "separate but equal" was the intent of the law, segregated schools were far from equal in terms of funding from state budgets. Black children often went to elementary schools with unpaved streets and outdoor toilets, although the same conditions could cause a White school to be condemned. It was very difficult for Black women to develop a sense of legitimacy as scholars. For those who did pursue higher education, professional interests such as psychology were always constrained by such practical questions as, for example, "Would a college or university admit a Black female to graduate school or hire a Black female psychologist?"

Hispanic and other minority women, whose native language was not English, first had to overcome the language barrier. For many Hispanic women, obtaining a doctorate was a violation of cultural norms. Minority women often faced the problem of being the only Hispanic or the only Black member in their graduate classes. For these and many other reasons, it was not until 1934 that Ruth Howard (Beckman) became the first Black woman to receive a PhD in psychology.

Mamie Phipps Clark and her husband Kenneth Clark conducted research on self-concept and social identification of young Black children. Mamie Clark graduated from Howard University in 1939 and received her PhD in 1944. In 1946, she and her husband founded the Child Development Center in New York City. From 1939 to 1950, Clark coauthored several articles with her husband that focused on personality development and color preference of Black children. Their research was cited in the Supreme Court case of *Brown v. Board of Education* and served to promote the U.S. Supreme Court decision to desegregate its schools (Clark, 1983).

Although Clark spent most of her time at the Child Development Center, she had a major impact on many students and certainly on the teaching of psychology. Clark's research taught psychologists that their studies could be used as a tool for social change. In addition to changing public policy, Clark's research changed the way psychology was taught because it sensitized psychologists to cultural differences in the perception of a given stimulus. Psychologists could then recognize that different cultural perceptions start in childhood and influence development of self-esteem.

Carolyn Robertson Payton received her MS in clinical psychology in 1948 from the University of Wisconsin. She began her undergraduate teaching career at Livingston College in North Carolina where she taught for 5 years. She later became Dean of Women and psychology instructor at Elizabeth City State Teacher's College in North Carolina, where she stayed until 1956. In 1959, she became an assistant professor at Howard University. She obtained her EdD from Columbia University in 1962. Payton served as director of the Peace Corps from 1977 to 1979 and was the first woman and the first Black American to do so.

At Howard University she directed the University Counseling Service and spearheaded its growth from a small agency to a large multiservice training and counseling center. In 1979, following her Peace Corps service, Payton returned to Howard as Dean of Counseling and Career Development. She is a pioneer in providing special training in psychotherapy with ethnic minority clients and has served as a mentor to many individuals, particularly women and ethnic minorities.

Overall, the contribution of Hispanic, Asian, and Native American women to the teaching of psychology are underrepresented. A notable exception is Martha Bernal (1984). Bernal in 1962 was the first Chicana to earn a PhD in psychology from the University of Indiana. Her first teaching position was as assistant professor at the University of Arizona at Tucson. She became known for her work in the field of behavior modification and for her development of parent training techniques for conduct-disordered children. Bernal is now professor at Arizona State University and an associate of the Hispanic Research Center, where she serves as a role model for many students.

APA Presidents

The seven women who have been APA presidents have all been involved in the teaching of psychology. Mary Calkins at Wellesley College and Margaret Washburn at Vassar College have already been discussed. Since 1970, the additional following five women have held the high office of APA president.

Anne Anastasi, professor and chair of the psychology department at Fordham University, in 1971 became the third woman to be elected president of the APA. She is considered to be a leading authority in differential psychology, statistics, and test construction. Her three textbooks have been translated into several languages and are used internationally in the teaching of psychology. Her first text, *Differential Psychology* (1937), was instrumental in attracting attention to this area of psychology. Anastasi's other textbooks are *Psychological Testing* (1954) and *Fields of Applied Psychology* (1964), which are both considered to be classics in the field.

Leona Elizabeth Tyler was the fourth woman to be elected president of the APA, succeeding Anastasi in 1972. She is also an authority in the area of individual differences. Tyler began her career as a junior high school English and mathematics teacher. Her 13 years in this capacity stimulated her interest in individual differences, motivation, and behavior. She decided to pursue graduate education and obtained her PhD from the University of Minnesota. After completing her doctoral studies, Tyler became an Instructor of psychology at the University of Oregon. Over the next 31 years, she was a professor of psychology and Dean of the Graduate School. She is best known for her career in teaching of psychology and for the classic text she authored, *The Psychology of Human Differences* (1947).

One of the authors of this chapter, Florence L. Denmark, in 1980 became the fifth woman to be elected president of the APA. Denmark has written and edited several books and numerous articles on the psychology of women. Her presidential address (Denmark, 1980) has been referred to as an important validation for women in psychology. She is noted as a pioneer who helped establish the psychology of women as a field in psychology. Well known for her extensive organizational activities and mentoring of students, Denmark began teaching at Queens College; she later became professor of psychology and executive officer of the doctoral program in psychology at City University of New York (CUNY) as well as Thomas Hunter Professor of Psychology at Hunter College, CUNY. She is now Robert Scott Pace Professor and chair of the psychology department at Pace University. For over 30 years she has remained active in teaching psychology, serving as an outstanding role model and mentor for her students. In 1987, Denmark received the first APA Award for Distinguished Contributions to Education and Training in Psychology. Her invited address on receipt of this award has helped engender new thought about psychology courses and curriculum content (Denmark, 1989).

Janet Taylor Spence, professor at the University of Texas, in 1984 became the sixth woman to be elected president of the APA. Known as the developer of the Manifest Anxiety Scale (Taylor, 1953), she also developed the Attitudes Toward Women Scale (Spence & Helmreich, 1972). In addition, she wrote on the psychology of women in her 1978 coauthored book, *Masculinity and Femininity: Their Psychological Dimensions, Correlates and Antecedents.* She published journal articles that examined attitudes toward women and other gender issues. Her studies led to the inception of another self-report instrument, the Personal Attributes Questionnaire (Spence, Helmreich, & Stapp, 1975), which meassures instrumental and expressive personality characteristics that several theorists believe relate to masculinity and femininity.

Janet Spence and her husband, psychologist Kenneth Spence, came to the University of Texas in 1964. At that time, because of antinepotism rules, she could not become a member of the psychology department. Unfortunately, it was only after her husband's death, that she was able to move to the psychology department and begin to advance her academic career. Neverthelesss, or perhaps because of her own experience of having to overcome barriers to achievement, Spence remains an active role model and mentor to students.

In 1977, Bonnie R. Strickland became the seventh woman to be elected president of the APA. She is a professor of psychology at the University of Massachusetts at Amherst and is known as one of the developers of the Nowicki-Strickland Children's Locus of Control Scale (Nowicki & Strickland, 1973). At the University of Massachusetts, Strickland's research interests led her to supervise several dissertations related to health and adaptive behaviors and depression. She has been particularly interested in women and depression and in women's health issues.

Additionally, Strickland became active in the feminist movement as chair of the Equal Opportunity and Affirmative Action Committee of the Division of Clinical Psychology. She helped to create the section on the clinical psychology of women. She continues to be active in the Association of Women in Psychology and in the Feminist Therapy Institute.

Teaching the History of Psychology

It is very important to keep accurate historical records of scientific progress so that students learn facts rather than fables. Women have participated in psychology from its inception, and some women have been important in recording psychology's history. Because of space constraints, we are limited to a brief mention of a few women who have enriched the teaching of the history of psychology—Edna Heidbreder, Mary Henle, and Virginia Staudt Sexton.

Edna Heidbreder served as an associate professor at the University of Minnesota and later joined the faculty at Wellesley as a full professor. Her most important contribution to the history of psychology was her book *Seven Psychologies*, which is considered to be one of the most important books on the history of psychology (Stevens & Gardner, 1982).

Mary Henle has been closely associated with Gestalt psychology and is well respected for her work in the history of psychology and the philosophy of science. From 1954 until her recent retirement, she was a professor at the New School for Social Research. She was also a founder of Cheiron, an international organization devoted to the history of the behavioral sciences.

Virginia Staudt Sexton, Professor Emeritus at Lehman College of CUNY and distinguished Professor Emeritus of psychology at St. John's University in New York, is well known for her work in the history of psychology. She wrote biographies of many female psychologists, such as Karen Horney, Mary Calkins, and Margaret Washburn. She also coauthored five books on the history of psychology. Sexton was one of the earliest historians to cite women's contributions to psychology. More recently, other psychologists, including Laurel Furumoto, Agnes O'Connell, Nancy Russo, and Elizabeth Scarborough, have enhanced women's sense of legitimacy by acknowledging their active role in psychology's history.

Teaching Award Winners

Teaching awards are important in that they reward an individual for achievement and for exemplary contributions to teaching and education. The awards are also a measure of acceptance by and respect of one's colleagues. The APA and the American Psychological Foundation (APF) presented organized psychology's highest teaching and education awards to the following women.

Florence Denmark was the first person and only woman to date to receive an APA Distinguished Contribution to Education and Training Award. This award, presented by the APA's Education and Training Board, recognized Denmark's considerable contributions to the psychology of women and her leadership in seeing that psychology's curriculum reflects cultural diversity.

To date, six women have received the award given by the APF for Distinguished Contributions to Teaching in Psychology. This award recognizes career contributions that extend beyond the local scope in impact. In chronological order, they are Freda Rebelsky in 1970, Bernice L. Neugarten in 1975, Carolyn Wood Sherif in 1982, Ellen P. Reese in 1986, and Eileen Mavis Hetherington in 1987. The 1992 award was also given to a woman, Patricia Marks Greenfield. Rebelsky, a noted developmental psychologist, was cited as a superlative teacher and role model whose "teaching makes science relevant without sacrificing rigor" (American Psychological Foundation, 1971). Neugarten's work on the life cycle expanded our concepts of adult development and aging. Reese was known for her commitment to undergraduate education through the preparation of films, workshops, and laboratory manuals on the analysis of behavior. Hetherington, another developmental psychologist, was cited as a brilliant lecturer and teacher. She was recognized for her work with children of divorce and single-parent families. Carolyn Wood Sherif's teaching award noted her significant contributions to teaching and research on the social psychology of gender.[1]

PSYCHOLOGY OF WOMEN AND THE DISCIPLINE OF PSYCHOLOGY

The APA contains 45 divisions that reflect groupings of psychologists with similar interests. Division 35, the Division of the Psychology of Women of the APA, came to exist as a result of the Association for Women in Psychology's (AWP) protest regarding the APA's discriminatory employment practices in 1969. At that time, women seeking employment (not men) were questioned about their marital status, their child-bearing plans, and their spouse's employment status. An APA task force on the status of women in psychology was formed, which suggested to the APA Council of Representatives that an APA division on women be created. (This task force later became the Committee on Women in Psychology.) The new division was established in 1973. Its goals were to promote research on women and to foster integration of knowledge about women with current psychological knowledge, for the benefit of society at large.

---

[1]Carolyn Wood married psychologist Muzafer Sherif in 1945 and collaborated with him in research for 35 years. Yet, when their studies were cited in psychology textbooks as "Sherif et al.," students often had the erroneous impression that there was only one Sherif. The authors of this chapter conducted an informal study of five social psychology textbooks (Denmark & Fernandez, 1985) and found Muzafer always received several more listings and was listed by his full name, whereas Carolyn was listed as C. W. Sherif and was cited less frequently. Although Carolyn did not collaborate with him in his 1936 study on the process of conformity, she collaborated with Muzafer on every study since 1945 but has barely been mentioned in connection with this research. Having experienced barriers to achievement in psychology, Carolyn Wood Sherif became a supportive force in the development of the psychology of women.

The psychology of women, a field of psychology in which women predominate, has had a significant influence on the teaching of psychology. It was the emergence of the psychology of women that served to remind social scientists that for results of a study to be generalizable, they needed to be based on representative samples. In the past, psychologists studied behavior, but it was not mediated by the variable of female gender. The psychology of women called attention to the minimizing and even exclusion of women's contribution to psychology (Denmark, 1983). Beginning with APA's endorsements of nonsexist language guidelines (Denmark, Russo, Frieze, & Sechzer, 1988), the road has also been cleared for nonracist language guidelines.

To understand the development of the field of the psychology of women is to view the collective contributions of women to the science of psychology and to the teaching of psychology. The psychology of women has changed the classroom atmosphere by the development of pedagogical methods that are based on feminist values, such as facilitating discussion, sharing leadership, and promoting relevant resources to empower students. Psychology of women courses foster the classroom integration of emotional and factual learning, resulting in greater overall congruence between these aspects of knowledge and enhanced self-esteem. Thus, feminist pedagogy that is based on the psychology of women provides an invaluable contribution to the teaching of psychology.

CONCLUSION

In this chapter we have reviewed the contributions women have made to the teaching of psychology. Women had to overcome such barriers as obtaining the doctorate, obtaining a full-time college or university position, and coping with antinepotism rules. In other instances, women's contributions were "acceptable" in a child-related field, namely, testing.

Despite the discrimination women faced, they have influenced the teaching of psychology. They managed to make such notable contributions as setting up laboratories, developing accurate assessment instruments for children, publishing books, formulating theories, and devoting considerable time to students. Seven women, all teachers of psychology, were elected president of the APA. Seven women also received national recognition for their teaching and contributions to psychological education. However, according to Kohout, Wicherski, and Cooney (1992), as of 1989–1990, women constituted only 25% of the full-time faculty in graduate departments of psychology. The percentage of women full-time professors was even smaller, only 14%. And less than 3% of the faculty were ethnic minority women. With the increasing number of women entering psychology and the ensuing change in sex ratios, more and more women will undoubtedly become teachers of psychology and achieve the highest academic rank. Hopefully, a significant number will be ethnic minority women.

Teaching, within and beyond the classroom, is the most important technique for dissemination of scholarship and research findings, and women have clearly played a key role in the teaching of psychology. Unfortunately only a small number of individuals could be cited by name in this chapter. As more women enter psychology, their teaching contributions should increase and continue to have an impact on psychology.

REFERENCES

American Psychological Foundation. (1971). Gold Medal Award and the Distinguished Contributions to Education in Psychology Awards: 1970. *American Psychologist, 26,* 91–95.

Anastasi, A. (1937). *Differential psychology.* New York: Macmillan.

Anastasi, A. (1954). *Psychological testing.* New York: Macmillan.

Anastasi, A. (1964). *Fields of applied psychology.* New York: McGraw-Hill.

Benjamin, L., Jr. (1975). The pioneering work of Leta Hollingworth in the psychology of women. *Nebraska History. 56,* 493–505.

Bernal, M. (1983). The life of a Chicana psychologist. Paper presented at the 91st Annual Convention of the American Psychological Association, Anaheim, CA.

Clark, M. P. (1983). Personal perspectives: Mamie Phipps Clark. In A. O'Connell & N. Russo (Eds.), *Models of achievement: Reflections of eminent women in psychology* (pp. 267–277). New York: Columbia University Press.

Darwin, C. (1859). *On the origin of the species by means of natural selection* (5th ed.). London: John Morray.

Denmark, F. (1980). Psyche: From rocking the cradle to rocking the boat. *American Psychologist, 35,* 1057–1065.

Denmark, F. (1983). Integrating the psychology of women into introductory psychology. In C. J. Schreier & A. Rogers (Eds.), *The G. Stanley Hall Lecture Series* (Vol. 3, pp. 33–75). Washington, DC: American Psychological Association.

Denmark, F. (1989). Back to the future in the education and training of psychologists. *American Psychologist, 44,* 725–730.

Denmark, F., & Fernandez, L. (1985). Integrating information about the psychology of women into social psychology. In F. L. Denmark (Ed.), *Social/ecological psychology and the psychology of women: Selected/revised papers* (Vol. 7, pp. 355–367). Amsterdam: North-Holland.

Denmark, F., Russo, N., Frieze, T., & Sechzer, J. (1988). Guidelines for avoiding sexism in psychological research: A report of the Ad Hoc Committee on Nonsexist Research. *American Psychologist, 43,* 582–585.

Furumoto, L. (1979). Mary Whiton Calkins (1863–1930): Fourteenth president of the American Psychological Association. *Journal of the History of the Behavioral Sciences, 15,* 346–356.

Furumoto, L. (1980). Mary Whiton Calkins (1863–1930). *Psychology of Women Quarterly, 5,* 55–68.

Furumoto, L., & Scarborough, E. (1986). Placing women in the history of psychology: The first American women psychologists. *American Psychologist, 41,* 35–42.

Goodenough, F. (1931). *Anger in young children.* Minneapolis: University of Minnesota Press.

Goodenough, F. (1934). *Developmental psychology.* New York: Appleton-Century-Crofts.

Hawkins, H. (1972). *Between Harvard and America. The educational leadership of Charles W. Elliot.* New York: Oxford University Press.

Heidbreder, E. (1933). *Seven psychologies.* New York: Century.

Hollingworth, H. (1943). *Leta Stetter Hollingworth: A biography.* Lincoln: University of Nebraska Press.

Hollingworth, L. (1914a). Functional periodicity: An experimental study of the mental and motor abilities of women during menstruation. *Teachers College contributions to education* (No. 69). New York: Columbia University Press.

Hollingworth, L. (1914b). Variability as related to sex differences in achievement. *American Journal of Sociology, 19,* 510–520.

James, W. (1890). *The Principles of Psychology* (Vols. 1 & 2). New York: Holt.

Kohout, J., Wicherski, M., & Cooney, M. (1992). *Characteristics of graduate departments of psychology –1989–1990.* Washington, DC: Office of Demographic, Employment, and Educational Research, Education Directorate, American Psychological Association.

Ladd-Franklin, C. (1887). A method for the experimental determination of the horopter. *American Journal of Psychology, 1,* 99–111.

Machover, K. (1949). *Personality projection in the drawing of the human figure.* Springfield, IL: Charles C. Thomas.

Montague, H., & Hollingworth, L. (1914). The comparative variability of the sexes at birth. *American Journal of Sociology, 20,* 335–370.

Nowicki, S., & Strickland, B. (1973). A locus of control for children. *Journal of Consulting and Clinical Psychology. 40,* 148–154.

O'Connell, A., & Russo, N. (Eds.). (1988). *Models of achievement: Reflections of eminent women in psychology* (Vol. 2). Hillsdale, NJ: Erlbaum.

Russo, N., & Denmark, F. (1987). Contributions of women to psychology. *Annual Review of Psychology, 38,* 279–298.

Scarborough, E., & Furumoto, L. (1987). *Untold lives: The first generation of American women psychologists.* New York: Columbia University Press.

Sicherman, B., & Green, C. (1980). In J. Kantrov & H. Walker (Eds.). *Notable American women: The modern period*. Cambridge, MA: Belknap Press.

Spence, J., & Helmreich, R. (1972). Who likes competent women? Competence, sex-role congruence of interest, and subjects attitudes toward women as determinants of interpersonal attraction. *Journal of Applied and Social Psychology, 2*, 197–213.

Spence, J., & Helmreich, R. (1978). *Masculinity and femininity: Their psychological dimensions, correlates and antecedents*. Austin: University of Texas Press.

Spence, J., Helmreich, R., & Stapp, J. (1975). Ratings of self and peers on sex role attributes and their relations to self-esteem and conceptions of masculinity and femininity. *Journal of Personality and Social Psychology, 32*, 29–39.

Spencer, H. (1864). *The principles of biology*. New York: Appleton-Century-Crofts.

Stevens, G., & Gardner, S. (1982). *The women of psychology: Volume I*. Cambridge, MA: Schenkman.

Taylor, J. (1953). A personality scale of manifest anxiety. *Journal of Abnormal and Social Psychology, 48*, 285–290.

Tyler, L. (1947). *The psychology of human differences*. New York: Appleton-Century-Crofts.

Washburn, M. (1909). *The animal mind*. New York: Macmillan.

8

ETHNIC MINORITIES IN THE TEACHING OF PSYCHOLOGY

L. PHILIP GUZMAN, R. STEVEN SCHIAVO, AND
ANTONIO E. PUENTE

Psychology as the study of behavior hinges on the basic premise that the foundation for knowledge is stable. Such stability hinges on a solid methodology, such as good sampling techniques. Unfortunately, psychology has been a science and a profession largely built on majority concepts by individuals of the majority culture.

In this chapter, this issue is examined in light of ever-changing demographic patterns in the United States. Personnel issues are first discussed and curricular issues are later addressed. Potential solutions to the problem of the paucity of ethnic minority students and faculty are considered. It is important to note that such problems were thought to have been solved when concerns were raised in the 1960s and 1970s. In reality, this chapter suggests, the current status of ethnic minorities in the pedagogy of psychology is quite disappointing.

DEMOGRAPHIC SHIFTS

The composition of the American population has been changing dramatically over the past 10 to 15 years. Although this change has been more noticeable in some states (such as California, Texas, and Florida) than in others, the trend is nationwide. In 1980, ethnic minorities made up 20.2% of the U.S. population. The 1990 U.S. Census (United States Department of Commerce News, 1991) reflects the tremendous growth that has been experienced by ethnic minority communities just within the past decade. In 1990, African Americans constituted 12.1% of the population; Hispanics, 9%, Asian Americans, 2.9%; and American Indians, 0.8%. It is interesting to note that the percentage of change in the population from 1980 to 1990 for Whites was 6%, for African Americans, 13.2%; for American Indians, 37.9%; for Hispanics, 53%; and for Asian Americans, 107.8%. Hence, ethnic minority groups are growing more rapidly than Whites. This demographic trend is not new and has been projected and predicted by demographers. Yet with these demographic trends in mind, has psychology positioned itself for the future? Will psychology be a relevant science and profession that will be able to deal with the changing demographic composition of this country? To answer these questions, we must trace the relationship and involvement of psychology with ethnic minorities to determine from its past and a present course of action what psychology's future direction will be.

ETHNIC MINORITIES AND ACADEMIC PSYCHOLOGY

Students

The representation of ethnic minorities within the field of psychology has been a concern for over three decades. However, data collection on the percentage of ethnic minorities in the field has not matched the expressions of concern. Bayton, Roberts, and Williams (1970) stated that it was difficult to obtain estimates of the number of ethnic minority members who were professional psychologists. They estimated that there were 200 African American PhD psychologists in 1970. It was not until after 1970 that surveys began to assess the ethnic minority representation within the field. One of the early attempts was made by Boxley and Wagner (1971), who surveyed clinical training programs and found that 4.5% of the students enrolled in clinical programs were members of an ethnic minority. Two years later, Padilla, Boxley, and Wagner (1973) surveyed 114 clinical training programs. They noted that there was a significant increase in the percentage of 1st-year minority students as compared with advanced students and that this might be a cause for guarded optimism.

Kennedy and Wagner (1979) also found an increase in minority student recruitment from 1970 to 1977. During this period, there was a tremendous growth in the percentage of ethnic minority students enrolled in graduate clinical psychology programs. In 1970, 4.4% of graduate students enrolled in these programs were members of an ethnic minority. By 1972, this percentage had increased to 7.3%, and by 1977, to 13.5%. Ethnic minority enrollment in graduate psychology programs declined and reached a leveling point of 11.4% by 1986 (National Science Foundation, 1988). Pion, Kohout, and Wicherski (1989) also confirmed that by 1988 this percentage had remained stable, with 11.3% of the graduate students being members of an ethnic minority. Zins and Halsell (1986) reported similar findings in the area of school psychology, in which 11.5% of the students were members of an ethnic minority.

Thus, in the early 1970s, there was not only a rise in concern about the representation of ethnic minorities in psychology but also there were active attempts to recruit ethnic minorities into the field. The increase in ethnic minority graduate students was a clear barometer that measured psychology's commitment to ethnic minority representation. Unfortunately, this commitment was not enduring. Although the concerns surrounding ethnic minorities that were ushered in during the late 1960s and early 1970s are still voiced today, the behavioral indicators of this commitment, as measured by ethnic minority student enrollment, leveled off by the late 1970s. This is evident as one reviews the data on ethnic minorities in higher education. Data collected by the U.S. Department of Education, Office of Civil Rights (cited in Kohout & Pion, 1990), indicate that undergraduate enrollment of ethnic minorities in psychology experienced a modest but gradual increase from 17.7% in 1976 to 19.8% in 1986. The percentage of ethnic minorities who graduated with a bachelor of arts (BA) degree had also increased from 11% in 1976 to a high of 15% in 1981. However, from 1981 until 1985, the percentage of ethnic minority psychology students receiving a BA declined to 12.7% (Kohout & Pion, 1990).

At the level of graduate education, as mentioned earlier, ethnic minority student enrollment had experienced an initial increase in the early 1970s but leveled off toward the end of the decade. In 1980, 11.8% of the psychology graduate students were members of an ethnic minority. By 1988, the percentage had remained relatively static at 11.3% (Kohout & Pion, 1990; Pion et al., 1989).

The same trend was evident for psychology doctoral recipients. Kohout and Pion (1990) found that by 1987 the percentage of new psychology doctoral recipients who were members of an ethnic minority had increased from 6.5% in 1977 to 8.5% in 1987; a modest 2% growth in 10 years. Sanchez, Demmler, and Davis (1990) and Howard et al. (1986) also reported an initial and gradual increase in minority representation from 5.2% in 1975 to 8.6% in 1984 and to 9.2% in 1986. However, the authors noted that this rate of increase had stabilized by the middle of the 1980s.

When the total percentage of doctoral psychologists in the field is reviewed, the limited and relatively static progress psychology has made in increasing the representation of ethnic minorities, especially in light of the increasing growth of ethnic minorities in the general population, becomes evidently clear. In an early census of psychological personnel, Stapp, Tucker, and VandenBos (1985) reported that in 1983 4.9% of the doctoral psychologists were members of an ethnic minority (2.2% African American, 1.5% Hispanic, 1% Asian American, and 0.2% American Indian). By 1985, ethnic minorities grew to represent 5.1% of all doctoral psychologists. Howard et al. (1986) and Kohout and Pion (1990) noted that this was the same percentage as 10 years earlier.

Thus, after a careful review of the data on ethnic minority representation over the past three decades, it appears that there was initial progress but it was relatively short lived. Since 1980, progress has been nonexistent. The percentage of ethnic minority graduate students has not changed in over 10 years, even though undergraduate enrollment in psychology programs has been shown to be steadily, although modestly, increasing since 1976. Ethnic minority representation in the field of psychology has been approximately 5% since 1975, regardless of all of the efforts to recruit more ethnic minorities. Recent data from the Educational Testing Service (ETS) suggest that few ethnic minority high school students are planning to pursue psychology as a course of study. For example, of the students who took the Advanced Placement Test in Psychology the first year it was administered, only 4% were African American (ETS, 1992). What impact do these trends have on the teaching of psychology?

Faculty

The preceding data have tremendous impact on the training of psychologists and the teaching of psychology. One immediate implication is the lack of ethnic minority faculty: A paucity of minority students results in a shortage of minority faculty. Early studies (Boxley & Wagner, 1971; Padilla et al., 1973) found that in 1970 there were only 3.2% ethnic minority faculty members and that by 1972 the percentage had increased insignificantly to 3.3%. From 1972 to 1988, there was an increase of approximately 2%. Kohout, Wicherski, and Pion (1991), in their survey of graduate departments of psychology, found that the number of ethnic minority faculty members has shown little change in the past 10 years. Approximately 5% of all psychology faculty are members of an ethnic minority, with African Americans constituting the largest group (3%), followed by Hispanics and Asian Americans (1% each) and American Indians (at less than 1%). It is also interesting to note that ethnic minorities are significantly less likely to be tenured and more likely to be in tenure-track or non-tenure-track positions. In 1980–1981, the percentage of tenured ethnic minority faculty in doctoral departments was 3.1%, with 50.2% of the ethnic minority in faculty positions being tenured, 42.8% in tenure-track positions, and 7% in non-tenure-track positions (Russo, Olmedo, Stapp, & Fulcher, 1981). In 1988–1989, Kohout et al., (1991) found that 4% of the tenured faculty were members of an ethnic minority, with 38% in tenure-track positions and 13% in non-tenure-track positions. Although there was an increase after 9 years in the percentage of tenured ethnic minority faculty, a larger percentage of the ethnic minority faculty were found to be in non-tenure-track positions.

Ethnic minorities are also more likely to be associate or assistant professors than full professors. One possible explanation for this is that ethnic minorities are new professionals and have not accumulated the required time in academia. However, after 10 years, one would expect some change. In 1980, ethnic minorities made up 2% of all full professors, 4% of associate professors, 8% of assistant professors, and 13% of lecturers or instructors (Stapp, 1981). By 1988–1989, only 3% of all full professors, 6% of associate professors, 11% of assistant professors, and 14% of lecturers or instructors were ethnic minorities (Kohout et al., 1991). Such a distribution influences the pedagogy of psychology. However, as Garcia (1980) astutely pointed out, "the concentration of Black faculty members in the junior ranks has several negative consequences. It severely limits the type of support they can provide for students, and it diminishes their overall effectiveness."

Indeed, recently unpublished data by Wicherski & Kohout (in press) suggest that minority faculty are less likely than White faculty to be tenured. White (1992), with the National Science Foundation, reported that White psychologists constituted 95% of college and university slots, with 54% in tenured positions, 14% in tenure-track positions but not tenured, and 9% in non-tenure-track positions. Ethnic minorities fared much worse. Only 38% were tenured, 23% were in tenure-track positions but not tenured, and 8% in non-tenure-track positions.

The consequences for psychology of a lack of ethnic minority faculty affects the profession's capability to train future psychologists to work with ethnic minority populations. Early concerns about the failure to adequately train ethnic minority and nonminority students has been echoed by a number of authors (Dean, 1977; Dean, Parker, & Williams, 1976; Green, 1981; Sue & Sue, 1977).

ETHNIC MINORITY RECRUITMENT AND RETENTION

Rationale for Diversity

The lack of ethnic minority faculty or ethnic minority-oriented course curricula causes a cyclical reaction that has consequences for the relevancy of psychology for society as a whole and for ethnic minorities in particular.

Ethnic minorities today have a broad range of professional options from which to choose. Some make career choices on the basis of economic factors (e.g., to make better money), and others are motivated by interpersonal reasons (e.g., to contribute to the betterment of society and their ethnic group). In the latter instance, without sufficient ethnic minority presence, either in faculty representation or in training curricula, psychology holds little attraction for ethnic minorities. Hence, ethnic minorities may enter other, more viable scientific or helping professions. Jones (1987) pointed out four reasons ethnic minorities are *not* pursuing doctoral studies in psychology. First, there is the concern about the financial support necessary for 4 to 5 years of training. Second, poor undergraduate preparation or training has limited admission into psychology graduate programs. Third, ethnic minorities are not inclined to see psychology as a professional career in the same way they may see law, medicine, teaching, or social work. Finally, ethnic minorities are not mentored or guided at the undergraduate level to pursue graduate training in psychology.

Recruitment of ethnic minorities into psychology historically has been motivated by the federal policy of affirmative action. However, affirmative action has, over the years, taken on a pejorative connotation, symbolizing "less than qualified" (Iijima Hall, 1990). Ethnic minority faculty and students are viewed, by some, as having obtained entry into academia only through "special" consideration. Their qualifications are, therefore, judged as less than the standard or norm. Jones (1990) and Hammond (1990) both advocate that "affirmative diversity" rather than the moral obligatory stance of affirmative action should propel strategies for ethnic minority recruitment. Affirmative diversity is defined, according to Jones (1990, p. 18), "as the affirmation of the fundamental value of human diversity in society, with the belief that enhancing diversity increases rather than diminishes quality." From this perspective, recruitment of ethnic minorities would not be seen as a moral or legal obligation but rather as a strategy that would increase diversity and therefore enhance the appropriateness and quality of psychology education.

Recruitment and Retention Strategies

Recruitment and retention strategies for ethnic minorities in psychology have been addressed for many years. Potter (1974), in her 1972 survey of 69 clinical psychology programs, indicated that 34% of the programs recruited ethnic minorities. Guzman and Messenger (1991) found, in a survey[1] of doctoral psychology programs, that 62% of the 230 responding

---

[1]The survey was sponsored by the Committee on Ethnic Minority Human Resource Development, the Minority Fellowship Program, the Committee on Graduate Education and Training, and the Committee on Accreditation of the APA.

programs had a departmental plan for recruiting ethnic minority students, and 54%, for recruiting ethnic minority faculty. Obviously, there has been an increase in recruitment activities in the past 20 years. Yet, in light of the static rate of ethnic minority involvement in psychology and academia, why have such recruitment efforts not been successful? A possible reason may be the manner in which recruitment is conducted. To understand better the recruitment strategies currently used by psychology programs, Guzman and Messenger (1991), in their survey, assessed which recruitment and retention interventions were found to be successful or not successful. The results reported in Table 1 indicate that most of the strategies for student recruitment worked moderately well. However, developing ethnic minority-oriented financial aid development and establishing ethnic minority admissions committees were the most effective recruitment initiatives, followed by adjusting admission criteria, using minority students, faculty, and alumni to recruit, and providing visible minority role models. Of particular note was the fact that simply having a list of ethnic minority students who had taken the Graduate Record Exams or who had shown early interest in psychology was not perceived as an effective recruitment strategy.

Regarding recruitment of ethnic minority faculty, the findings were not encouraging. There was no particular recruitment intervention that seemed to be significantly effective (see Table 2).

Bernal, Barron, and Leary (1983), in their study of ethnic minority-oriented graduate school application materials, found a modest but significant relationship between ethnic minority information in application packets and the proportion of minority students in the program. Two pieces of information were thought to be important to minority student recruitment—the description of ethnic minority training opportunities and the use of special admission criteria for ethnic minorities.

Kagehiro, Mejia, & Garcia (1985), in their advocacy to promote diversity, list seven short- and three long-term recruitment strategies. The short-term strategies include contacting universities with large ethnic minority undergraduate populations, contacting ethnic associations, having the departmental recruitment committee develop liaisons with other recruitment committees either on campus or with other universities, advertising in ethnic minority publications, using student locator services, using a multiple institution graduate application process, and contacting community agencies employing ethnic minorities in mental health or related occupations. For the long-term strategies, Kagehiro et al. suggest that psychology departments should become involved in career development at the high-school level, foster involvement of ethnic minority graduate students in ethnic minority communities to serve as role models, and, finally, recruit paraprofessional interviewers from survey research organizations that conduct studies with ethnic minority communities.

TABLE 1
Success Rates of Student Recruitment Methods

Method	Never used	Do not know/ no response	Have used	Level of success: No. reporting (of those who have used)					Mean value
				None (1)	Minimal (2)	Moderate (3)	Good (4)	High (5)	
Generic fellowships/scholarships	49	18	163	27	28	57	36	15	2.90
Minority-oriented fellowships/ scholarships	44	8	178	6	13	33	63	63	3.92
Assistantships	34	13	183	13	31	60	54	25	3.26
Special orientation for minority students	154	13	63	3	11	25	14	10	3.27
Minority admissions committee	167	10	53	1	6	13	15	16	3.81
Minority-oriented program/ curriculum	179	14	37	4	8	10	8	7	3.16
Using minority students/faculty/ alumni to recruit	64	7	159	9	23	59	41	27	3.34
Visible minority role models	67	12	151	9	23	49	48	22	3.34
Minority recruiting brochures/ pamphlets	154	13	63	5	11	25	12	10	3.17
GRE student locator service	93	14	123	45	34	35	6	3	2.09
APA MFP "Early List"	73	10	147	52	49	31	11	4	2.09
Adjusted admissions criteria	76	11	143	7	22	50	44	20	3.34
Visits to minority recruitment fairs	123	11	96	22	21	34	16	3	2.55

Source: Guzman & Messenger, 1991. GRE = Graduate Record Exam; APA = American Psychological Association; MFP = Minority Fellowship Program.

TABLE 2
Success Rates of Faculty Recruitment Methods

Method	Never used	Do not know/ no response	Have used	Level of success: No. reporting (of those who have used)					Mean value
				None (1)	Minimal (2)	Moderate (3)	Good (4)	High (5)	
APA Office of Ethnic Minority Affairs/MFP	109	17	104	43	23	29	5	4	2.08
Vita banks	153	23	54	31	13	7	3	0	1.67
Using minority faculty to recruit	94	13	123	29	25	34	20	15	2.73
Using alumni to recruit	121	19	90	28	22	25	11	4	2.34
Using school location to recruit	94	23	113	37	25	27	18	6	2.39
Recruitment of minority adjunct faculty	108	20	102	28	25	27	15	7	2.49
University affirmative action office	60	14	156	55	41	33	17	10	2.27
Advertisements in ethnic minority newsletters	69	11	150	56	33	40	16	5	2.21
Advertisements in APA Monitor	28	15	187	52	39	55	28	13	2.52

Source: Guzman & Messenger, 1991. APA = American Psychological Association; MFP = Minority Fellowship Program.

Despite their importance, retention issues within psychology have not been given as much attention. More focus has been placed on attracting ethnic minorities than on retaining the ones already in the field. However, as has been noted earlier in this chapter, 11% of the students who enter graduate psychology programs are members of an ethnic minority; yet, only 9% actually obtain a doctorate. Guzman and Messenger (1991) found that financial aid, special academic support, and mentorship were effective strategies to retain such students.

Few universities have used strategies to retain ethnic minority faculty. Those that did created special salary incentives and special faculty support programs. Russo et al. (1981) found that ethnic minorities are more likely than Whites to leave academia before a tenure decision has been made. Suinn and Witt (1982) reported that the major obstacles facing ethnic minorities at the time tenure is decided involved spending too much time in minority services, performing insufficient data-based research activity, and authoring too few publications. Wyatt (1982) in her 10-step recommendations to obtain tenure stressed the necessity of performing research and publishing as well as cultivating a political understanding of the university system and developing a support network.

ETHNIC MINORITIES AND THE AMERICAN PSYCHOLOGICAL ASSOCIATION (APA)

Organizational Perspectives

Early involvement with ethnic minority concerns within the APA can be dated back to the 1950s when the APA Council of Representatives established a policy not to hold its convention activities in hotels or educational institutions that discriminated against individuals on the basis of race or religion (Smith, in press). In 1963, the APA established an ad hoc Committee on Equal Opportunity in Psychology (CEOP) after prompting by the Society for the Psychological Study of Social Issues. CEOP explored the problems encountered in training and employment opportunities in psychology as a consequence of race. More specifically, CEOP was to

> (1) address the question of equality of opportunity in employment of Negro [sic] psychologists in professional and academic positions; (2) examine the recruitment and selection of students for training in psychology; and finally, (3) determine steps that may provide training and exchange opportunities for teachers and scholars in Negro [sic] colleges. (APA, 1963, p. 769)

In 1967, CEOP made the following recommendations to the APA Council of Representatives:

(a) The APA should encourage effective measures to acquaint undergraduates in the Negro [sic] colleges with the career possibilities for Negroes [sic] in psychology.

(b) The APA should adopt appropriate measures to increase the participation of Negro [sic] psychologists in the APA.

(c) The Equal Opportunities Committee should obtain existing comparable statistics for non-Negro [sic] psychologists so that comparisons can be made with Negro populations and additional information be obtained with somewhat greater certainty. (APA, 1967, p. 1073)

In addition to accepting the above recommendations, the Council voted to change the status of CEOP from an ad hoc committee to a continuing committee. As part of its charge, CEOP undertook a survey in 1967–1968 to assess the family background, undergraduate and graduate education, occupational history, and present earnings of African American psychologists (Wispe et al., 1969). Nearly half of the 398 African American psychologists responding to the survey stated that race had limited their professional opportunities in psychology. "The inescapable conclusion to be drawn from this study, therefore, is that being a Negro [sic] psychologist may reduce the handicap of being black, but it does not remove it" (Wispe et al., 1969, p. 149). As Edward Johnson noted in his commentary on the Wispe et al. study, African American psychologists would increasingly become agents of social change, catalysts that would interpret "the current black mood" and usher in change (Johnson, 1969).

Major developments in advancing ethnic minority issues within psychology began to escalate and come to the forefront around 1969. The Proceedings of the APA reported that, at the invitation of the APA Board of Directors and Council of Representatives, that Charles L. Thomas, Chairman of the Association of Black Psychologists (ABPsi), presented a Petition of Concerns developed by ABPsi. These concerns addressed three major areas:

The limited number of black psychologists and of black graduate and undergraduate students in psychology, the failure of APA to direct its scientific and professional energies toward the solution of relevant social issues (with special emphasis on racism and poverty), and the lack of appropriate representation in the APA governing structure of black psychologist members. (APA, 1969, p. 27)

The statement of concerns developed by ABPsi sparked the APA to hold a Conference on Recruitment of Black and Other Minority Students and Faculty, at which the Wispe et al. (1969) study was discussed and from which general recommendations were made to improve the status of African Americans and minorities within the APA (Albee, 1969).

In September 1969, at the APA Annual Convention, students from the newly formed Black Students Psychological Association (BSPA) took the podium during George Miller's presidential address asked to present their list of demands to the APA Council of Representatives that was meeting the following day (APA, 1970a; Simpkins & Raphael, 1970; Williams, 1970). The list of five demands focused on recruiting students, recruiting faculty, centralizing information on scholarship funds, providing practical community experiences for African American undergraduate and graduate students, and developing terminal programs at all degree levels that would equip African American students to function in the African American community. As a response to these demands from BSPA, the Council established the APA Commission on Accelerating Black-Participation in Psychology (CABPP; APA, 1970b; Blau,1970). CABPP, consisting of representatives from the APA, BSPA, and ABPsi, met in November 1969 and began to address essential barriers to minority participation in psychology, such as funding, communication, liaison, leadership, identity, and acceptance. Although CABPP was time limited and finished its work in July 1970, one of the concrete outcomes was the establishment of the Office of the Black Students Psychological Association administrated by Ernestine Thomas and housed within APA headquarters. The BSPA Office was funded by the APA for 3 years, from 1970 to 1973 (APA, 1971).

Again in the year 1969, a group of African American psychiatrists met at the National Institute of Mental Health (NIMH) requesting that an organizational unit be developed within NIMH to promote mental health programs for ethnic minorities and that NIMH develop an affirmative action plan. From these concerns, NIMH established in 1971 the Center for Minority Group Mental Health Programs (CMGMHP). Three prominent activities were prompted by the CMGMHP (Cheung, 1991). The first was the establishment of ethnic minority research and development centers that would conduct research relevant to ethnic minority groups. Six Research and Development Centers were established, with each focusing on the mental health needs and problems of a specific ethnic minority (i.e., African Americans, Hispanics, Asian Americans, and American Indians). The second was the funding of coalitions of minority and nonminority professional consumers. Groups such as the Coalition of Spanish Speaking Mental Health Organizations, and the Pacific/Asian Coalition, functioned as intermediaries between NIMH and the mental health community. The third project was APA's Minority Fellowship Program (MFP). The MFP was designed to support ethnic minority graduate students in their pursuit of degrees in psychiatry, psychology, social work, or sociology. The APA, under Dalmas Taylor's leadership, applied and was granted $1 million from CMGMHP to provide financial assistance to ethnic minority students for up to $7,500 per year for 3 years of study (Taylor, 1977). From 1975 to 1991, 727 ethnic minority students have been supported by the APA Minority Fellowship Program.

Another major development for ethnic minorities occurred in 1973 at the Vail Conference on Levels and Patterns of Professional Training. Although the Vail conference did not focus on ethnic minorities per se, it was the first national conference to actively seek representation of ethnic minorities on the conference steering committee. Having ethnic minority representation influenced the conference format, content, and selection of participants. In fact, 1 of the 10 task groups of the conference was designated to examine the problems of professional training for minorities. This task group focused on identification, recruitment, admission, and graduation of ethnic minority students. Final recommendations suggested that all psychology students be trained to function in a pluralistic society and furthermore that

> (a) training experience should occur in a multicultural context both within the university and in field work settings; (b) the content of training must adequately prepare students for their eventual professional roles vis-a-vis a wide diversity of target groups; (c) students must be helped to maintain a balance between acculturation into a professional and scholarly role, on the one hand and retention of their group identity and cultural sensitivity, on the other. (Korman, 1974, p. 448)

The Vail conference was also important in that it recommended the establishment of a Board of Minority Advocacy and an Office of Minority Affairs within the APA that would be responsible for examining policies bearing on ethnic minority concerns. None of these recommendations were implemented until 5 years later in 1978 when the National Conference for Increasing the Roles of Culturally Diverse Peoples in the Profession of Psychology (known as the Dulles conference) was held "to explore specific ways in which these ethnic minority psychologists of color could become more widely involved in a meaningful and effective way in every aspect of the activities of the Association [APA]" (Attneave et al., 1978). Until this time, there was growing dissatisfaction with the APA Committee on Equal Opportunity in Psychology and with the Board of Social and Ethical Responsibility (BSERP) in that both governance groups had broadened their mandate and diluted their attention to ethnic minority concerns. The Dulles conference reiterated the Vail conference recommendations for the establishment of an Office of Minority Affairs and a Board of Minority Affairs. However, the APA Board of Directors and Council of Representatives approved only the Office of Minority Affairs, which became operational in 1979, and established an ad hoc Committee on Minority Affairs rather than a Board. The ad hoc Committee deliberated for three meetings and recommended to the APA Board of Directors the establishment of a board on minority affairs, which then became the Board of Ethnic Minority Affairs (BEMA). In 1980, BEMA was charged with

> (a) Increasing scientific understanding of those aspects of psychology that pertain to culture and ethnicity;

(b) Increasing the quality and quantity of educational and training opportunities for ethnic minority persons in psychology;

(c) Promoting the development of culturally sensitive models for the delivery of psychological services;

(d) Advocating on behalf of ethnic minority psychologists with respect to the formulation of the policies of the Association;

(e) Maintaining satisfactory relations with other groups of ethnic minority psychologists;

(f) Maintaining appropriate communication involving ethnic minority affairs with the Association's membership as well as with ethnic minority psychologists and communities at large;

(g) Maintaining effective liaison with other boards and committees of the Association;

(h) Serving as a clearinghouse for the collection and dissemination of information relevant to or pertaining to ethnic minority psychologists and students. (APA, 1980)

Since 1980, BEMA has focused on a number of issues that have highlighted ethnic minority concerns. BEMA established a number of work groups that reviewed the incorporation of cultural diversity curricula in psychology training programs (Task Force on Minority Education and Training); the representation of ethnic minorities within the APA, state psychological associations, and APA divisions (Task Force on Communication with Minority Constituents); the representation of ethnic minorities within the field of psychology (Committee on Ethnic Minority Human Resources Development); and the development of treatment guidelines in working with ethnic minority clients (Task Force on the Delivery of Services to Ethnic Minority Populations).

There was another event that occurred within the APA that served as a catalyst to encourage educational institutions to recruit and hire ethnic minority faculty and students. In 1979, the APA approved the Criteria for Accreditation of Doctoral Training Programs and Internships in Professional Psychology. One of the evaluative criteria by which all clinical, counseling, and school psychology programs would be measured was cultural and individual diversity. This criterion, known as Criterion II, stated that

as a science and profession, psychology deals with the full range of human variability. It follows that social responsibility and respect for cultural and individual differences are attitudes which must be imparted to students and trainees and be reflected in all phases of the program's operation: faculty recruitment and promotion, student recruitment and evaluation, curriculum, and field training. Social and personal diversity of faculty and students is an essential goal if the trainees are to function optimally within our pluralistic society. Programs must develop knowledge and skills in their students relevant to human diversity such as people with handicapping conditions; of differing ages, gender, ethnic and racial backgrounds, religion, and life-styles; and from differing social and individual backgrounds. (APA, 1986a, B-3)

In 1986, the Society for the Psychological Study of Ethnic Minority Issues (APA Division 45) was established, formally elevating the study of ethnic minority issues as a valued and legitimate discipline within psychology. The goals of Division 45 are to

(a) advance the contribution of psychology as a discipline in the understanding of ethnic minority issues through research, including the development of appropriate research paradigms;
(b) promote the education and training of psychologists in matters of ethnic minority concerns, including the special issues relevant to service delivery with ethnic minority populations;
(c) inform the general public of research, education and training, and service delivery issues, relevant to ethnic minority populations. (APA, 1986b)

Due to the internal reorganization of the APA Central Office in the late 1980s into four directorates (Science, Education, Practice, and Public Interest), with each having a corresponding oversight board, movement was made to sunset BSERP and BEMA, both situated within the Public Interest Directorate. Two summit meetings were held in 1988 and 1989 that resulted in the eventual establishment of the Board for the Advancement of Psychology in the Public Interest in 1990. After 10 years in existence, BEMA was transformed from a board to a committee (Committee on Ethnic Minority Affairs [CEMA]).

In 1991, APA also sponsored the third conference on undergraduate psychology. This conference, titled the APA National Conference on Enhancing the Quality of Undergraduate Education in Psychology but known as the St. Mary's conference (after the location of meeting at St. Mary's College, Maryland), addressed many issues, including ethnic minorities. One task group focused solely on ethnic minority issues, whereas the other task groups were encouraged to consider ethnic minority concerns across undergraduate educational issues. The primary recommendations involved the issue of understanding psychology as a study of variance (see Puente et al., 1992).

Membership Perspectives

With all the organizational and structural changes that have taken place in the APA that address the concerns of ethnic minority representation, it is interesting to note that the ethnic minority membership within the APA has not proportionally increased since the early 1980s. However, data collection on race and ethnicity was not documented within the APA in the early 1970s. Russo et al. (1981) stated that of the 1978–1979 APA membership, 1,384 or 3.1% of the APA members were members of an ethnic minority. In 1983, Stapp et al. (1985) conducted a census of all psychologists, and it was calculated that ethnic minorities constituted 4.9% of the APA membership at the time (2.2% African American, 1.5% Hispanic, 1% Asian, and 0.2% American Indian).

For unknown reasons, APA members have been reluctant to identify their race and ethnicity in survey questionnaires. When the membership was asked about their ethnic and racial background, only one third of the APA members self-identified themselves as members of an ethnic minority on the APA 1985 Directory Survey. The data indicate that in 1985, ethnic minorities made up 2.6% of the APA membership (APA, 1985) which is approximately the same percentage reported by Russo et al. (1981) for the 1978 APA membership. In 1989, ethnic minorities made up 3.4% of the APA membership (APA, 1989).

Ethnic minority participation within the APA governance structure has been of some concern. In 1991, the Office of Ethnic Minority Affairs (OEMA) conducted a survey of all governance members regarding their race and ethnicity. The survey found that of 445 governance positions, ethnic minorities held 53 or 11.9% of the elected or appointed positions in the APA (OEMA, 1991). This is considerably more than their APA membership representation, yet is less than their representation in society.

In summary, although ethnic minorities have made strides in representation and participation in the past 50 years within the APA, they are far from assuming a significant political role within the Association that can dramatically impact its course of operation.

MULTICULTURAL CURRICULAR ISSUES

Current information about the status of education involving ethnic minority students suggests an inconsistent pattern. Data reported earlier in this chapter indicate that the percentage of ethnic minority psychology graduates at any level has not grown since the early 1980s. In contrast, there is some evidence that there has been an increase in the number of institutions offering courses that focus on minority psychology. In addition, since the mid-1980s there has been a substantial increase in resources that are directly relevant to teaching ethnic minority material and diverse students.

Undergraduate Curriculum

Over the past three decades there have been four professionally sponsored conferences and surveys that have investigated the undergraduate curriculum in psychology. The early McKeachie and Milholland report

(1961) did not consider ethnic minorities in psychology. They did note that one contemporary pressure on undergraduate curriculum development was the increasing "heterogeneity" of students, but their use of this term reflects their prediction of broadening student characteristics that are based primarily on diversity of vocational goals and ability levels. In the next decade, the Kulick, Brown, Vestewig, and Wright survey (1973) asked more specific questions about the inclusion of minority issues in the undergraduate curriculum. They inquired about the percentage of the introductory course time that was spent "in analysis of current social problems such as . . . discrimination" (1973, p. 27). They found that such content was minimally addressed in most courses: 84.6% of the 4-year colleges with psychology majors and 67.8% of the 2-year colleges spent 0–10% of the introductory course time on this topic. In addition, the Kulick survey of curriculum offerings during 1968–1969 specifically asked about the presence of courses that were "designed to meet the special needs of [these] racial and ethnic groups: Blacks, Mexican-Americans, Puerto Rican, American Indians" (1973, p. 67). Their survey revealed that 7.4% of the 4-year institutions with psychology majors and 11.0% of the 2-year colleges had such courses.

The next APA undergraduate curriculum survey (Scheirer & Rogers, 1985) also collected data about the inclusion of ethnic minority courses in the curriculum. Unfortunately, this 1984 survey reported such courses as a percentage of all courses offered, whereas the 1969 survey reported the percentage of institutions offering those courses, so that direct comparison over time is not possible. Nevertheless, Schreier and Rogers found that of over 4,000 undergraduate courses, 69 (1.7%) were specialized courses dealing with specific minority groups or with minority issues. If one assumes that institutions only have a single course on minority psychology (and this is a tenuous assumption), then at maximum such courses were available in 37.3% of the 4-year colleges and 12.3% of the two-year colleges. These estimates do indicate a growth in institutions, especially 4-year colleges, that included in their program courses dealing with minority psychology. There is additional evidence supporting this trend. Hicks and Ridley (1979) reported that among a sample of 103 colleges, the number offering at least one course in African American psychology grew from 35.9% in 1972–1973 to 42.2% in 1978–1979. However, they point out that the majority of these courses were offered by departments of African American studies rather than by departments of psychology.

St. Mary's Conference on Undergraduate Psychology

More promising is the emphasis placed on diversity and minority populations in the most recent undergraduate conference. The St. Mary's conference convened approximately 60 teachers of undergraduate psychology, who were organized into seven working groups. One working group was to consider strategies to increase the attraction of minority undergraduates into the field of psychology (Puente et al., 1992). In addition, all other working groups were to consider their specific charge in terms of ethnic minority groups whenever appropriate.

Puente et al. (1992) recognized the changing demographics in U.S. society and the impact that this will have not only on the undergraduate population but also on the field of psychology. They stressed that multiple strategies will be needed to attract increased numbers of minorities into both the service and the science components of professional psychology. They cautioned that recruitment into the field must begin early—for example, in high schools—and more broadly—for example, in community colleges. They provided suggestions for developing linkages among these educational levels.

Included among the strategies discussed by Puente et al. (1992) is the recommendation to broaden the content of various courses by including both minority scholarship and material addressing minority psychological issues. Adding courses to the curriculum that are specifically concerned with minority content and issues was also recommended.

Issues of classroom atmosphere and instructional techniques in the face of changing classroom demographics were also addressed. Special attention was paid to creating a sense of community within classes containing diverse students and building on minority perspectives and experiences.

Puente et al. (1992) made the additional point that increased diversity of students may also have an impact on aspects of teaching that occur outside the classroom. In this regard, they indicated that faculty may need to reconsider their assumptions and expectations regarding academic advising and career counseling as undergraduate demographics change.

Since the mid-1980s, there has been an increase in available resources that can be used to implement some of these recommendations. This recent growth is in contrast to the sparse explicit treatment of ethnic minority undergraduate issues in many of the regular psychology journals. For example, although there have been a number of articles in the *American Psychologist* addressing ethnic minority issues in graduate education (e.g., Bernal & Padilla, 1982) and in mental health services (e.g., Sue, 1989), relatively few have looked at undergraduate experiences. A similar picture is seen in *Teaching of Psychology*, the publication most directly oriented to teaching psychology to undergraduates. Since the introduction of this journal in 1974, with some exceptions (e.g., DeFour and Paludi, 1991), there have been few minority contributors and contributions that discuss ethnic minorities and undergraduate education in psychology.

Especially helpful in terms of integrating ethnic minority scholarship and research regarding ethnic minorities throughout the curriculum are several annotated volumes recently published by the APA. Each volume describes available resources with respect to specific minority groups: African-American males (Evans & Whitfield, 1988), African-American females (Hall, Evans, & Selice, 1989), and Hispanics (Olmedo & Walker, 1990). In addition, the volume editors classify the research in terms of relevance to courses typically found in undergraduate programs. Another valuable resource is the volume edited by Bronstein and Quina (1988) that presents suggestions for minority content as well as descriptions of specialized courses addressing minority perspectives.

More attention has also been given recently to teaching techniques and activities for active learning in classes that are composed of diverse students or that deal with material regarding minority groups. These are welcome additions because many of the activities readily available (Benjamin & Lowman, 1981; Benjamin, Daniel, & Brewer, 1985; Makosky, Whittemore, & Rogers, 1987) had not been explicitly designed for these situations. Although some of these latter exercises can be adapted for relevant use to gain a perspective on minority psychology, only a few are directly oriented to minority groups (e.g., Engle & Snellgrove, 1981). A number of contributors to Bronstein and Quina (1988) also suggest course-related activities. Two additional sources (Aronson, 1987; Brislin, 1988) consider dynamics in diverse classrooms; these were both presented at the annual APA G. Stanley Hall Lecture Series, which is oriented toward teachers of introductory psychology. A recent article (DeFour & Paludi, 1991) provides discussion questions and experiential exercises that can be used to explore material related to minority experiences in psychology of women courses.

Quina and Bronstein (1988) pointed out that one concern of teachers in dealing with ethnically diverse students and ethnic-related material is handling student reactions. They provide illustrations of instructors' reports of student hostility, defensive reactions, anger over injustice, and concerns with the course, with other students, and with the instructor. Presumably, most contemporary instructors do not have training in incorporating ethnic issues and in dealing constructively with student reactions and emotional responses. In this regard, they include suggestions for relating student reactions, including personal experiences and perspectives, to relevant theory and research. An excellent example integrating theoretical content with student experiences and reactions in confronting such material is discussed by Tatum (1992).

More personal accounts as well as objective assessments of the impact of integrating minority scholarship on classroom process and teaching objectives are needed. These accounts could help to address teachers' concerns about student reactions, discussion processes, and classroom atmosphere.

Progress can also be seen in the availability of materials that consider minority students' expectations regarding their undergraduate experiences and career paths. McGovern and Hawks (1986) provided a useful model for responding to gender and minority group similarities and differences in curriculum and career interests. Woods's (1988) recent volume on advising psychology majors has several relevant chapters directed toward specific minority groups.

On the other hand, relatively little attention has been paid to ethnic minority students' experiences in research internships and in field practica. Prentice-Dunn and Roberts (1985) reported favorable consequences of summer research internships for African American undergraduates' interest in psychology careers, but their article practically stands alone, and they did not do actual follow ups. Although practical field placements are assumed to strengthen professional interests (Puente et al., 1992), both empirical documentation and case studies regarding this assumption are lacking. Reports are also needed regarding the steps toward and problems encountered in establishing such experiences for ethnic minority students. Such reports should address whether ethnic minority students are more sought after in particular settings or in working with particular populations and whether ethnic minority students encounter particular problems in various settings.

Another question that needs consideration is whether teaching styles or learning styles differ among ethnic minority groups. Tharp (1989) reviewed numerous research studies that pointed out that compatibility between some students' natal cultural patterns and school routines and teacher behavior may impact student achievement and school experiences. The extent to which this issue is salient or relevant to undergraduate education in psychology remains to be seen.

Graduate Curriculum

Unfortunately, similar patterns have occurred in graduate education. However, instead of focusing solely on these limitations, it might be more useful to begin with a rationale for diversity at the graduate level. Ridley (1985) lists five clear imperatives for developing culturally relevant training curricula.

1. *The professional participation imperative* holds that psychology and its institutions should reflect in numerical composition the cultural diversity of society.

2. *The ethical imperative* maintains that treatment of culturally different clients by professionals who lack the specialized expertise or training is unethical.

3. *The cultural-context imperative* holds that all mental health practice and psychotherapy occurs in a cultural context.

4. *The scholarly imperative* affirms that there is a need on the part of the profession to correct the inadequate and in-

correct presentation of ethnic minorities in the psychological literature.

5. *The legal imperative* asserts that treatment of culturally diverse clients by a practitioner without certified cross-cultural credentials would be a violation of the clients' civil rights.

Kagehiro et al. (1985) added another dimension: the inclusion of cultural pluralistic training curricula. The authors argued that generalizability may be sacrificed at different stages in the research process because one has not taken into consideration cultural variables. They suggested that there are two negative outcomes of the resulting limited knowledge base: psychology and society suffer, and reduced professional competency and credibility occur.

One of the first major studies on the incorporation of multicultural curricula in psychology training programs was conducted by Bernal and Padilla (1982), who surveyed 106 clinical psychology programs as to their ability to train psychology students to serve ethnic minority populations. They found that programs were lacking in course work that focused on ethnic minority mental health or sociocultural issues. Out of 76 training programs responding to the survey, only 31 (41%) reported that they offered one or more courses that would contribute to a student's understanding of ethnic minorities or other cultures. Only 15 (20%) of the training programs offered ethnic minority courses or cross-cultural clinical courses. No program, however, required students to complete a culturally oriented course for the completion of a doctorate.

Another survey conducted by Wyatt and Parham (1985) found that only 7 of the 169 internships programs surveyed had seminars in which ethnic minority issues were discussed. Dunston (1983), who conducted a survey of graduate psychology and internship programs, found that 66% of the graduate departments and 64% of the internship programs included ethnic minority content within their curricula or training program. Within psychology departments, 48% of the courses on ethnic minorities were elective.

To obtain the current status on the degree of multicultural training in graduate programs, the APA Office of Ethnic Minority Affairs used data obtained from the *1990 Graduate Study in Psychology and Associated Fields* (APA, 1991) on 570 psychology programs that stated that they offered minority-oriented courses or curricula. The data revealed that 34% of all graduate psychology programs, both master's and doctoral programs, self-reported that they offered some course work on ethnic minority issues. When separated into doctoral and master's programs, 40% of the doctoral and 24% of the master's programs offered minority-oriented courses.

In the area of curricula, it appears that since the early study conducted by Bernal and Padilla (1982) not much has changed. Approximately 60% of graduate training programs do not offer any multicultural course work.

CONCLUSION

This chapter attempted to highlight the role ethnic minorities have played within psychology. In the late 1960s and early 1970s, a time when the United States was in the throes of the civil rights movement, psychology's representatives were made aware of the discrepancy in ethnic minority participation and representation in psychology. Both within the APA and in the general field of psychology, attempts were made to rectify this imbalance. Unfortunately, because of many factors, the drive toward ethnic minority parity reached a plateau in and has remained static since the late 1970s. The ramifications of this are many. A lack of ethnic minority students translates into a lack of such psychologists who can teach, conduct research, or provide culturally relevant services. In turn, the noticeable absence of ethnic minority psychologists in the academic or applied world results in the inability of psychology to relate effectively in a society that is ever changing and becoming more ethnically diverse. If this trend is not rectified, psychology will be seen as irrelevant to the problems of society and, therefore, will be less attractive as a profession to ethnic minorities. We believe that psychology is faltering in the recruitment of ethnic minorities. Recruitment for ethnic minority students or faculty has not increased in over a decade, even with conference after conference extolling the value and virtue of ethnic minority curricula and student representation, even with such financial aid programs as the Minority Fellowship Program, and even with the APA accreditation criterion of cultural and individual diversity by which applied programs are evaluated.

The issue is not that psychology is not doing anything, but rather what *is* being done, how it *is* being done, and who *is* doing it. Psychology must operationalize all the goals it has promulgated since the Vail conference. Rhetoric will no longer suffice. Recommendations should be operationalized and put into action that can be behaviorally measured. Reaching and influencing ethnic minority communities will require different strategies. Ethnic minority psychologists must be supported in educating and developing these initiatives. Finally, there is the issue of who is responsible for such actions. The APA has been the lightning rod for developing and implementing intervention strategies. Many turn to the APA for the solution but blame the organization for the current state of affairs. Although it may be convenient to turn to the APA to resolve many of the issues facing psychology, the APA is relatively ineffectual when it comes to *requiring* individual psychologists to act. Furthermore, the Association is seen as even less influential with departments of psychology, where most of the critical pedagogy occurs. Given support and guidance, psychology departments can have the greatest effect on ethnic minorities. They are the ones that admit students. Furthermore, they are often the conduit for the development of new knowledge. The APA can assist psychology programs that want to become ethnically diverse, but it is the individual universities that must take the initiative to diversify their student body and faculty. In a current study performed by the American Association for the Advancement of Science, Matyas and Malcom (1991) found that in a survey of 276 college and universities, there was no concerted effort to attract or retain women, ethnic minorities, or disabled students in science and engineering, despite the abundant rhetoric to the contrary.

Guzman (1991), in a review of a number of psychology training programs, concluded that there were seven characteristics that earmarked good programs that attracted and retained ethnic minority students and provided multicultural training. He found that programs that had a broad-based commitment to diversity from all segments within the university had better chances of recruiting and retaining ethnic minority students and faculty. Second, in these programs funding was appropriately used to attract and retain ethnic minority candidates. Third, the admissions policy incorporated a larger array of factors than standardized academic scores. Fourth, because of the intensity of recruiting and retaining ethnic minorities, successful programs had established an ombudsman or coordinator position that lessened this burden on faculty, allowing them to teach and conduct research. Fifth, all the programs had exerted efforts in hiring one or two ethnic minority faculty who, in turn, showed the dedication and drive to pursue diversity within the department. Sixth, all such programs had shown sensitivity by providing a social support network using some form of mentoring. Finally, all the successful programs offered multicultural training either in the form of course work or actual multicultural training tracks.

As the future of our society continues to change in the direction of cultural pluralism, psychology must take ownership of this challenge that extends beyond a litany of rhetorical recommendations.

REFERENCES

Albee, G. W. (1969). A Conference on Recruitment of Black and Other Minority Students and Faculty. *American Psychologist*, 24, 720–725.

American Psychological Association. (1963). Proceedings of the Seventy-First Annual Business Meeting of the American Psychological Association, Incorporated. *American Psychologist*, 18, 757–772.

American Psychological Association. (1967) Proceedings of the American Psychological Association, Incorporated, for the year 1967. *American Psychologist*, 22, 1066–1094.

American Psychological Association. (1969). Proceedings of the American Psychological Association, Incorporated, for the year 1968. *American Psychologist, 24,* 19–41.

American Psychological Association. (1970a). Proceedings of the American Psychological Association, Incorporated, for the year 1969. *American Psychologist, 25,* 13–37.

American Psychological Association. (1970b). What has APA done? *American Psychologist, 25,* xxix–xxxii.

American Psychological Association. (1971). Proceedings of the American Psychological Association, Incorporated, for the year 1970. *American Psychologist, 26,* 22–49.

American Psychological Association. (1980). Proceedings of the American Psychological Association, Incorporated, for the year 1979. *American Psychologist, 35,* 501–536.

American Psychological Association. (1985). [Unpublished tables compiled by the APA Office of Demographic, Employment and Educational Research on the basis of the 1985 APA Directory Survey.] Washington, DC: Author.

American Psychological Association. (1986a). *Accreditation handbook.* Washington, DC: Author.

American Psychological Association. (1986b). *Society for the Psychological Study of Ethnic Minority Affairs Bylaws.* Washington, DC: Author.

American Psychological Association. (1989). [Unpublished tables compiled by the APA Office of Demographic, Employment and Educational Research on the basis of the 1989 APA Directory Survey.] Washington, DC: Author.

American Psychological Association. (1991). *Graduate study in psychology and associated fields.* Washington, DC: Author.

Aronson, E. (1987). Teaching students what they think they already know about prejudice and desegregation. In V. P. Makosky (Ed.), G. *Stanley Hall Lecture Series* (Vol. 7; pp. 65–84). Washington, DC: American Psychological Association.

Attneave, C., Bernal, M., Jacobs, L. D., Lopez, R., Olmedo, E., Sue, S., Taylor, D., Tomes, H., Waddell, C., & Jones, J. M. (1978). *Report of the National Conference for Increasing the Role of Culturally Diverse Peoples in the Profession of Psychology.* Unpublished manuscript, Washington, DC.

Bayton, J. A., Roberts, S. O., & Williams, R. K. (1970). Minority groups and careers in psychology. *American Psychologist, 25,* 504–510.

Benjamin, L. T., Jr., Daniel, R. S., & Brewer, C. L. (Eds.). (1985). *Handbook for teaching introductory psychology.* Hillsdale, NJ: Erlbaum.

Benjamin, L. T., Jr., & Lowman, K. D. (Eds). (1981). *Activities handbook for the teaching of psychology* (Vol. 1). Washington, DC: American Psychological Association.

Bernal, M. E., Barron, B. M., & Leary, C. (1983). Use of application materials for recruitment of ethnic minority students in psychology. *Professional Psychology: Research and Practice, 14,* 817–829.

Bernal, M. E., & Padilla, A. M. (1982). Status of minority curricula and training in clinical psychology. *American Psychologist, 37,* 780–787.

Blau, T. H. (1970). APA Commission on Accelerating Black Participation in Psychology. *American Psychologist, 25,* 1103–1104.

Boxley, R., & Wagner, N. N. (1971). Clinical psychology training programs and minority groups: A survey. *Professional Psychology: Research and Practice, 2,* 75–81.

Brislin, R. W. (1988). Increasing awareness of class, ethnicity, culture, and race by expanding on students' own experiences. In I. S. Cohen (Ed.), *G. Stanley Hall Lecture Series* (Vol. 8; pp. 141–180). Washington, DC: American Psychological Association.

Bronstein, P. A., & Quina, K. (Eds.). (1988). *Teaching a psychology of people: Resources for gender and sociocultural awareness.* Washington, DC: American Psychological Association.

Cheung, F. K. (1991, August). *Minority mental health research: A national perspective.* Invited Address at the 99th Annual Convention of the American Psychological Association, San Francisco, CA.

Dean, W. (1977). Training minorities in psychology. *Journal of Non-White Concerns in Personnel and Guidance, 5,* 119–125.

Dean, W., Parker, B., & Williams, B. (1976). Training mental health professionals for the Black community. *Journal of Black Psychology, 3,* 14–19.

DeFour, D. C., & Paludi, M. A. (1991). Integrating scholarship on ethnicity into the psychology of women course. *Teaching of Psychology, 18,* 85–90.

Dunston, P. J. (1983). Culturally sensitive and effective psychologists: A challenge for the 1980s. *Journal of Community Psychology, 11,* 376–382.

Educational Testing Service. (1992). [Demographic information on gender and ethnic/racial groups in the first administration of the Advanced Placement Test in Psychology]. Unpublished raw data.

Engle, T. L., & Snellgrove, L. (1981). Stereotypes. In L. T. Benjamin, Jr., & K. D. Lowman (Eds.), *Activities handbook for the teaching of psychology* (Vol. 1, pp. 147–148). Washington, DC: American Psychological Association.

Evans, B. J., & Whitfield, J. R. (Eds.). (1988). *Black males in the United States: An annotated bibliography from 1967 to 1987.* Washington, DC: American Psychological Association.

Garcia, S. A. (1980). Problematic issues for Blacks in doctoral psychology programs. *Professional Psychology: Research and Practice, 11,* 812–817.

Green, L. (1981). Training psychologists to work with minority clients: A prototypic model with Black clients. *Professional Psychology: Research and Practice, 12,* 732–739.

Guzman, L. P. (1991). Incorporating cultural diversity into psychology training programs. In H. F. Myers, P. Wohlford, L. P. Guzman, & R. J. Echemendia

(Eds.), *Ethnic minority perspectives on clinical training and services in psychology* (pp. 67–70). Washington, DC: American Psychological Association.

Guzman, L. P., & Messenger, L. C. (1991). *Recruitment and retention of ethnic minority students and faculty: A survey of doctoral programs in psychology.* Preliminary unpublished analysis, American Psychological Association, Washington, DC.

Hall, C. C. I., Evans, B. J., & Selice, S. (Eds.). (1989). *Black females in the United States: A bibliography from 1967–1987.* Washington, DC: American Psychological Association.

Hammond, W. R. (1990). The commitment to affirmative diversity through student recruitment and retention. In G. Stricker, E. Davis-Russell, E. Bourtg, E. Duran, W. R. Hammond, J. McHolland, K. Polite,& B. E. Vaughn (Eds.), *Toward ethnic diversification in psychology education and training* (pp. 123–129). Washington, DC: American Psychological Association.

Hicks, L. H., & Ridley, S. E. (1979). Black studies in psychology. *American Psychologist, 34,* 597–602.

Howard, A., Pion, G. M., Gottfredson, G. D., Flattau, P. E., Oskamp, S., Pfafflin, S. M., Bray, D. W., & Burnstein, A. G. (1986). The changing face of American psychology: A report from the Committee on Employment and Human Resources. *American Psychologist, 41,* 1311–1327.

Iijima Hall, C. C. (1990). Qualified minorities are encouraged to apply: The recruitment of ethnic minority and female psychologists. In G. Stricker, E. Davis-Russell, E. Bourg, E. Duran, W. R. Hammond, J. McHolland, K. Polite, & B. E. Vaughn (Eds.), *Toward ethnic diversification in psychology education and training* (pp. 105–111). Washington, DC: American Psychological Association.

Johnson, E. E. (1969). Role of the Negro in American psychology. *American Psychologist, 24,* 757–759.

Jones, J. M. (1987). *Student recruitment and retention: A marketing and program development job for psychology.* Invited address at the National Conference on Graduate Education in Psychology, Salt Lake City, UT.

Jones, J. M. (1990). Invitational address: Who is training our ethnic minority psychologists, and are they doing it right? In G. Stricker, E. Davis-Russell, E. Bourg, E. Duran, W. R. Hammond, J. McHolland, K. Polite, & B. E. Vaughn (Eds.), *Toward ethnic diversification in psychology education and training* (pp. 17–34). Washington, DC: American Psychological Association.

Kagehiro, D. K., Mejia, J. A., & Garcia, J. E. (1985). Value of cultural pluralism to the generalizability of psychological theories: A reexamination. *Professional Psychology: Research and Practice, 16,* 481–494.

Kennedy, C., & Wagner, N. N. (1979). Psychology and affirmative action: 1977. *Professional Psychology: Research and Practice, 10,* 234–243.

Kohout, J., & Pion, G. (1990). Participation of ethnic minorities in psychology: Where do we stand today? In G. Stricker, E. Davis-Russell, E. Bourg, E.Duran, W. R. Hammond, J. McHolland, K. Polite, & B. E. Vaugn (Eds.), *Toward* ethnic diversification in psychology education and training (pp. 153–165). Washington, DC: American Psychological Association.

Kohout, J., Wicherski, M., & Pion, G. (1991). *Characteristics of graduate departments of psychology: 1988–89*. Washington, DC: American Psychological Association.

Korman, M. (1974). National Conference on Levels and Patterns of Professional Training in Psychology. *American Psychologist, 29*, 441–449.

Kulik, J. A., Brown, D. R., Vestewig, R. E., & Wright, J. (1973). *Undergraduate education in psychology*. Washington, DC: American Psychological Association.

Makosky, V. P., Whittemore, L. G., & Rogers, A. M. (1987). *Activities handbook for the teaching of psychology* (Vol .2). Washington, DC: American Psychological Association.

Matyas, M. L., & Malcom, S. (1991). *Investing in human potential: Science and engineering at the crossroads*. Washington, DC: American Association for the Advancement of Science.

McGovern, T. V., & Hawks, B. K. (1986). The varieties of undergraduate experience. *Teaching of Psychology, 13*, 174–180.

McKeachie, W. J., & Milholland, J. E. (1961). *Undergraduate curricula in psychology*. Glenview, IL: Scott, Foresman.

National Science Foundation. (1988). *Women and minorities in science and engineering*. Washington, DC: Author.

Office of Ethnic Minority Affairs. (1991). *Summary of data on ethnic minority representation within the APA governance structure*. Unpublished report, American Psychological Association, Washington, DC.

Olmedo, E. L., & Walker, V. R. (Eds.). (1990). *Hispanics in the United States: Abstracts of psychological and behavioral literature, 1980–1989*. Washington, DC: American Psychological Association.

Padilla, E. R., Boxley, R., & Wagner, N. N. (1973). The desegregation of clinical psychology training. *Professional Psychology: Research and Practice, 4*, 259–264.

Pion, G. M., Kohout, J., & Wicherski, M. (1989). *Characteristics of graduate departments of psychology: 1987–88*. Washington, DC: American Psychological Association.

Potter, N. D. (1974). Recruitment of minority group students and women. *American Psychologist, 29*, 151–152.

Prentice-Dunn, S., & Roberts, M. C. (1985). A summer internship for psychological research: Preparation of minority undergraduates for graduate study. *Teaching of Psychology, 12*, 142–145.

Puente, A. E., in collaboration with Blanch, E., Candland, D., Denmark, F., Laman, C., Lutsky, N., Reid, P., & Schiavo, R. S. (1992). Toward a psychology of variance: Increasing the presence and understanding of ethnic minorities in psychology. In T. McGovern (Ed.), *Handbook for enhancing undergraduate education in psychology*. Manuscript submitted for publication.

Quina, K., & Bronstein, P. A. (1988). Epilogue. In P. A. Bronstein & K. Quina (Eds.), *Teaching a psychology of people: Resources for gender and sociocultural awareness* (pp. 215–220). Washington, DC: American Psychological Association.

Ridley, C. R. (1985). Imperative for ethnic and cultural relevance in psychology training programs. *Professional Psychology: Research and Practice, 16,* 611–622.

Russo, N. F., Olmedo, E. L., Stapp, J., & Fulcher, R. (1981). Women and minorities in psychology. *American Psychologist, 36,* 1315–1363.

Sanchez, A. M., Demmler, J., & Davis, M. (1990). *Toward pluralism in the mental health disciplines: Status of minority student recruitment and retention in the western states.* Boulder, CO: Western Interstate Commission for Higher Education.

Scheirer, C. J., & Rogers, A. M. (1985). *The undergraduate psychology curriculum: 1984.* Washington, DC: American Psychological Association.

Simpkins, G., & Raphael, P. (1970). Black students, APA, and the challenge of change. *American Psychologist, 25,* xxi–xxvi.

Smith, M. B. (in press). The APA and social responsibility. *American Psychologist.*

Stapp, J. (1981). *Summary report of 1980–81 survey of graduate departments of psychology.* Washington, DC: American Psychological Association.

Stapp, J., Tucker, A. M., & VandenBos, G. R. (1985). Census of psychological personnel: 1983. *American Psychologist, 40,* 1317–1351.

Sue, S. (1989). Psychotherapeutic services for ethnic minorities: Two decades of research findings. *American Psychologist, 43,* 301–308.

Sue, D. W., & Sue, D. (1977). Ethnic minorities: Failures and responsibilities of the social sciences. *Journal of Non-White Concerns in Personnel and Guidance, 5,* 99–106.

Suinn, R. M., & Witt, J. C. (1982). Survey on ethnic minority faculty recruitment and retention. *American Psychologist, 37,* 1239–1244.

Tatum, B. D. (1992). Talking about race, learning about racism: The application of racial identity development theory in the classroom. *Harvard Educational Review, 62,* 1–24.

Taylor, D. A. (1977). *Ethnicity and bicultural considerations in psychology: Meeting the needs of ethnic minorities.* Washington, DC: American Psychological Association.

Tharp, R. G. (1989). Psychocultural variables and constants: Effects on teaching and learning in schools. *American Psychologist, 44,* 349–359.

United States Department of Commerce News. (1991). *Census Bureau releases 1990 census count on specific racial groups* (CB91-215). Washington, DC: U.S. Government Printing Office.

White, P. E. (1992). *Women and minorities in science and engineering: An update.* National Science Foundation: Washington, DC.

Wicherski, M. M., & Kohout, J. (in press). *Characteristics of graduate departments of psychology: 1990–91. Report of the annual APA/COGDOP departmental survey.* Washington, DC: American Psychological Association.

Williams, R. L. (1970). Report to the APA Council of Representatives. *American Psychologist, 25*, xxvii–xxviii.

Wispe, L., Ash, P., Awkard, J., Hicks, L. H., Hoffman, M., & Porter, J. (1969). The Negro psychologist in America. *American Psychologist, 24*, 142–150.

Woods, P. J. (1988). *Is psychology for them? A guide to undergraduate advising.* Washington, DC: American Psychological Association.

Wyatt, G. E. (1982). Ethnic minorities and tenure. *American Psychologist, 37*, 1283–1284.

Wyatt, G. E., & Parham, W. D. (1985). The inclusion of culturally sensitive materials in graduate school and training programs. *Psychotherapy: Theory, Research, and Practice, 22*, 461–468.

Zins, J. E., & Halsell, A. (1986). Status of ethnic minority group members in school psychology training programs. *School Psychology Review, 15*, 76–83.

9

"I WAS JUST LUCKY": AN INTERVIEW WITH MODEL TEACHER WILBERT J. MCKEACHIE

JANE S. HALONEN

The editors of *Teaching Psychology in America: A History* agreed that this volume would not be complete unless it included a profile of an exemplary teacher from this century. It will surprise no one that Wilbert J. McKeachie was selected to fill this role. Bill graciously agreed to participate in a 2-hour video interview taped during the fall of 1991 in a studio on the campus of Alverno College. This interview served as the basis for the wide-ranging historical perspective that follows.

Bill has been a teacher of psychology since 1946. Born in Clarkston,

Several colleagues were very generous with their time and talent in the development of the interview questions. Randall Wight offered helpful biographical models and important insights into the interview process from the historian's unique perspective. Tom McGovern enthusiastically assisted with the structure and scope of questions regarding curriculum issues. Marilyn Reedy helped to refine questions exploring McKeachie's religious and spiritual issues. Rhoda Miller encouraged me to overcome my awe of Bill to ask the less comfortable questions. Finally, Austin Doherty originated the idea for the chapter and offered substantial conceptual and logistical support for the completion of the interview.

Michigan, in 1921, he was enamored early in life with both psychology and religion. With support from his family and from scholarships, Bill enrolled in Michigan State Normal College with the intention of becoming a high school teacher. He completed all three of the psychology courses offered in the program, along with a variety of courses in other disciplines. In his final year at Michigan State Normal, Bill met Virginia Mack. They married shortly before Bill began his World War II duty as a radio/communications officer on board a destroyer in the Pacific. At the conclusion of his military service, he resolved to become a psychology graduate student. He embarked on an academic career at the same institution where he received his graduate training—the University of Michigan—and completed his PhD in 1949.

His contributions to the development of the University of Michigan Psychology Department are inspiring. He coordinated the introductory course and began a research program to examine the factors that enhance college-level learning. He collaborated on curriculum development and reform within the Department at undergraduate and graduate levels. From 1961 to 1971, he served as chair of the Department. He carefully declined other offers that would take him away from the Psychology Department. He became the director of University of Michigan's Center for Research on Learning and Teaching and has served as associate director of the National Center for Research to Improve Postsecondary Teaching and Learning. In these roles, he has completed significant teaching–learning research while promoting collaboration across institutions. Just in the past few months he has moved formally out of the classroom and into retirement, although his activity level, speaking commitments, and energy remain unchanged.

His enthusiasm for teaching psychology is evidenced by an impressive array of contributions. He radiates fondness for undergraduates, thousands of whom have directly benefited from his talents as a teacher. He is proud of the substantial number of teaching assistants whose ideas about the profession were shaped under his leadership. He wrote a popular introductory text that is still in use today. He has been an editorial advisor to many journals in psychology and education. He was the first teacher of psychology on video, participating in live broadcasts in 1951.

Bill has also been actively involved in the American Psychological Association (APA) throughout his career, including his service as the Bicentennial President in 1976–1977. He was president of Division 2 early in his teaching career. He has participated in the APA in many other roles, including service on the Board of Directors, the Education and Training Board, the Policy and Planning Board, the Board of Professional Affairs, and the Council of Representatives.

Two of his most recent assignments at the APA are particularly related to teaching. He served as a member of a five-person task force to review the state of the discipline for the Study-In-Depth Project of the Association of American Colleges. He also served as a Steering Committee member and participant at the 1991 National Conference on Enhancing the Quality of Undergraduate Education in Psychology at St. Mary's College of Maryland. He has the distinction of being the only person to have participated in all of the formal curriculum projects undertaken by the APA.

His outstanding contributions to psychology and to higher education have garnered many awards. Two such awards are especially cherished. The American Psychological Foundation honored Bill in 1985 with the Distinguished Teaching in Psychology Award. His citation summarized the high regard in which Bill is held: "As a teacher of psychology and as a teacher of teachers, he has remained first and foremost a superb psychologist." Bill was one of the first two recipients in 1987 of the APA's Education and Training Board Award for Distinguished Career Contributions to Education and Training in Psychology.

Beyond his loyalty to psychology, Bill has assisted in higher education in many other ways, including being the president of the American Association of Higher Education, being involved in various levels of the American Association of University Professors, and participating in other educational societies, including the Social Science Research Council, American Council on Education, American Education Research Association, Special Medical Advisory Group of the Veterans Administration, National Institute of Mental Health Council, and others. He has served as an educational consultant across the country and abroad.

But perhaps the activity for which Bill is perhaps best known and most highly regarded is his ongoing work on *Teaching Tips*, which was first published in 1951. The eighth edition of the text was published in 1986 and the ninth edition is in process. Countless college teachers have suggested that their first few months of college teaching wouldn't have been the same without the help they had gotten from Bill through this publication.

* * * *

Halonen: I mentioned in the introduction that you had an early fascination with psychology. Could you describe these early experiences?

McKeachie: I suppose one was reading a paperback book—I was a voracious reader as a child and adolescent—it was a book called *The Return to Religion* by Henry C. Link, who was a psychologist with the Psychological Corporation. This book essentially said that psychology and religion were compatible. In fact, they reinforced each other. I probably wouldn't agree entirely with the book now because I think religion has to stand on its own. The notion that you can get wealthy or mentally healthy because your religion is right is not the reason to practice religion. But it was a compelling book for me. I can also remember reading an article in a Sunday school paper about what psychologists did, and it looked very interesting to me.

But I probably wouldn't have become a psychologist if I had not had a couple of experiences. One was when I finished college, having majored in mathematics—I would have gone on in mathematics if it hadn't been for the war—I wasn't sure if I was a conscientious objector, and I went for several months up to the upper peninsula as a Methodist minister. One of my friends had suggested that because I was in doubt about whether to become a minister or a conscientious objector or join the Navy—this was 1942—to be able to make up my mind, I took a couple of his churches. So I taught mathematics—all junior high school students at the Trout Lake Schools—and was pastor of the Trout Lake and Helbert Methodist Churches, even though I wasn't a Methodist. But I decided then that you really need to understand people better if you are going to be a good minister, and I thought that psychology might help with that. I think it does, but there might be some question about that.

When my draft board decided that I had become a minister too late, I joined the Navy and was on a destroyer during most of the war. There again I had interesting experiences with diverse groups of individuals. I wrote to my wife that if I survived the war, I'd like to go into graduate school to study psychology.

Halonen: Can you explain why you might have had dire predictions about whether or not you would survive the war?

McKeachie: I didn't have any *dire* predictions. I was in one of the first groups of radar officers to go out, and a lot of people got killed. War is not a pleasant thing. If you have actually participated in it, I don't think you would think it is a good thing to have wars.

Halonen: Was it difficult giving up the ministry to stay in psychology?

McKeachie: No. I enjoyed psychology. I felt like I could contribute more by staying in psychology and writing for ministers. For a number of years I wrote for magazines like *The Pulpit* or *Christian Century* and tried to interpret what I thought was relevant for ministers. I also wrote articles oriented toward helping ministers' wives because they have very difficult roles.

Halonen:	Do you think your parents were influential in your career direction?
McKeachie:	I think I would have been a teacher, regardless of what field I entered. If I had stayed in math, I would have taught mathematics as my brother does. He teaches at General Motors Institute in Flint. If I had stayed in the ministry, I probably would have ended up a seminary professor. My father was a teacher. He taught a one-room country school house—I went to him the first 8 years of my education.
	My mother loved to teach. She taught for a year when she was 18, before she got married. When my Dad's one-room school became overcrowded, she took some of the children. She's always taught children, grandchildren, and neighbor children to play the piano, and she taught women to do various kinds of crafts. A couple weeks ago my mother—who is now 95 and very crippled with Parkinson's disease—was teaching my niece how to tat. My mother has always liked to teach, so I think I had an interest in teaching bred into me.
Halonen:	Could you describe how you ended up at the University of Michigan?
McKeachie:	I didn't know any better. I grew up 40 miles from Ann Arbor. I didn't go to Michigan as an undergraduate because Michigan Normal College was cheaper. This was the Depression—1938—when I started college. So when I decided during the war to go to graduate school in psychology, I just thought I'd go to the one closest to home. I took some tests shortly after I arrived in 1945 to see if psychology was a good career, and the people at the psychological clinic said "yes." It looked like my interests fit the right pattern, but they said that I was probably too good for Michigan. I should go to the University of Chicago.
	I was anxious to be close to my family, my wife's family. She's from Detroit. It didn't seem like a good idea to change. Just after I arrived, Don Marquis arrived and built the Michigan Psychology Department into the top department in the world or perhaps among the top three or four. So I was just lucky. The Department turned out to be very good.
Halonen:	What were your early days at the University of Michigan like?
McKeachie:	I had to take undergraduate courses at the University of Michigan. Michigan Normal had had only two or three courses. There had been no major there. I can remember

after a test in one of my first courses, Individual Differences, we were waiting outside to get into the classroom and one of the students was saying, "I heard a graduate student flunked the first test." It was me! . . . I did end up with an A, finally. It was difficult, but I enjoyed it. It was just so great to be out of the war and at peace. I would have enjoyed *anything* at that time. I really enjoyed the subject matter. The teachers were good, too. They probably weren't world famous.

Halonen: Could you describe a few teachers who were influential on your teaching?

McKeachie: The most significant would be Don Marquis, who built the department. He had been chairman at age 29 of the Psychology Department at Yale, which at the time was the preeminent department of psychology in the country. During the war he had served as head of psychological personnel for the government, so he knew everybody. I think he was considered one of the most brilliant psychologists of his time. He taught a course in analysis of variance. Coming from a mathematics background, I thought it was *beautiful*—it was so appealing to me that you could separate out sources of variance. And I have used analysis of variance a great deal ever since.

Marquis also taught a course in contemporary psychological literature. We read current journal articles. He had a very incisive ability to be critical without tearing things apart. I've been in some discussions with philosophers when it seemed they just demolished everything. He was able to be critical and yet value the contributions of the people who wrote the articles. I thought that was useful.

Halonen: Were there others who stand out to you as being really fine teachers?

McKeachie: John Shepard, who'd been the strong figure in the Department. He was the first PhD in psychology at Michigan in the early 1900s and had stayed on. He was really the power in the Department. He probably actually had a bad effect on the Department because his standards were so high that nothing was ever quite good enough to be published. As a consequence, the Department published very little during the years when he was preeminent. The Department assumed that he would become chairman when Pillsbury, the first chairman, retired. But I think the college wisely chose to go outside the Department to get Marquis.

But Shepard was a very strong person, a very rigorous person. I took Experimental Psychology from him. It was a 4-hour course, two semesters. You could start his examinations at 5 o'clock and write as long as you wanted. Usually they ran for 4 or 5 hours of writing. You wrote and wrote and wrote. You really had to know things. When I went over to the Med School to take psychiatry with the medical students, I knew a lot more about the brain and nervous system than they did. You had a real sense of mastery when you got through Shepard's course. He was very demanding. He had very strong opinions, which I think were fairly valid. In some ways his ideas probably anticipated or paralleled some of the Gestalt notions that things were not just simple connections like a telephone network—the associationists' point of view that was dominant at the time. He went beyond that to talk about integration and the importance of the synergy of things.

Halonen: Did you have any specific education or training for college teaching?

McKeachie: Yes. That was one of the good things Marquis did. After my first year of graduate work—I got a master's even though I hadn't had any undergraduate work before—they asked me to be a teaching fellow in the introductory psychology course. This was when veterans were streaming back. At that time you were released from the service in relation to years of service or the amount of time in combat, and I'd had a lot of combat. I was out in 1945, but the big stream of veterans came in 1946. The Department was swamped with students. They needed multiple sections of courses. Harold Guetzkow, an assistant professor at the time, later a professor at Northwestern University, was our mentor. We met weekly to go over the plans for the week, to go over what would be covered in the discussion sessions, and to argue about how to teach it. We had experimentalists, social psychologists, and clinicians, so we had a variety of opinions about how to teach. Harold was a very good adjudicant. He kept pressing us, "Well, if you disagree about this, do some research. Find out who's right." And that really is what got me started on research in teaching. I think it contributed greatly to my interest in teaching and helped me a great deal with some initial skills in teaching.

Halonen: Why do you suppose models like that haven't been more widespread?

McKeachie: Well, it probably takes two things. I think it took a person like Marquis, who was willing to support it and who would himself meet with us at least once a term and encourage that sort of thing and to support Guetzkow in doing it. And it took someone like Guetzkow who was interested enough to take it seriously and do it. I keep running into department heads who say, "Yes, we realize that we should be doing more of that but we don't have a faculty member who really feels confident to do it or who is interested enough to do it." I think we were fortunate that we had that particular combination.

Halonen: Let me ask you to stand back from your own career and reflect on how you see the methods of teaching of psychology may have changed over time?

McKeachie: I think there have been changes in the content that have followed the field of psychology. John Dashiell from the University of North Carolina did the first treatment of motivation in introductory psych back in the 30s. He wrote a good textbook that I used at one time, and he also served as president of Division 2.

               Floyd Ruch of University of Southern California, also a Division 2 president, was the first to try to think about motivation involved in sequencing course content. Typically intro textbooks started out with scientific method and biological bases. Ruch polled students on what they were interested in and began his sequence with personality, abnormal, adjustment, or other student-centered topics to get them well motivated. That happened to be the book I used when I was an introductory psych student in 1938.

Halonen: Are there other major shifts in content over time?

McKeachie: It's my impression that today we are not as worried about differentiating ourselves from philosophy as we once were. We always used to spend time on the mind–body problem. Even when I started, I don't think we did as much on the traditional questions, such as "What is human nature?" "What is truth?" "What is beauty?" Clearly that is what psychology is all about—perception, motivation, personality. The traditional philosophical questions map into some things that we have developed some empirical knowledge about. Robbie McCloud wrote a book called *Persisting Problems in Psychology* in which he argued that human beings are always worrying about what we are here for. Psychology essentially deals with these questions, which philosophers have reformulated over the years, by whittling down the problems through empirical data.

Psychology has changed a lot in terms of its breadth. We have gotten into a lot of new areas. We didn't have environmental psychology when I was a student. We did have the psychology of art and music, and these areas haven't expanded much. Other new areas—psychology and law, sports psychology, health psychology—these are all new. Of course, we know more in the areas themselves. We know a lot better how the brain works—biopsychology. We always taught the brain and nervous system, but it really didn't have much relevance to anything else we taught. Now I think there are some strong connections.

Halonen: Have you seen substantial changes in the methods of teaching psychology?

McKeachie: I think that labs have changed over time. The original laboratory courses were mostly demonstration. When George Herbert Mead taught physiological psychology here at University of Michigan in the 1880s he set the building on fire by smoking while varnishing a brain for a demonstration. At that time the psychology lab was set up in a hospital. (Until the 1960s, psychology always got leftover space.) Prior to that time, the practice was to burn the hospital down. They were built of wood and, without knowledge about bacteria, they knew people began getting sicker when they went to a hospital. Once Pasteur came along, they no longer had to burn the hospitals down, so psychology was in old hospital space when Dewey and Meade were teaching here. Ironically, Mead set the place on fire anyway.

When I started around World War II, I think the traditional course included a new experiment or demonstration every week. We did the Purkinje effect, Weber's law with lifted weights, nonsense syllables with a memory drum, reaction time, things like that. When I began teaching the course in 1948 or 1949, I continued some of those demonstrations. In the last third of the term, I did have the students devise a problem of their own and collect their own data. I think the use of lab experience as early as the sophomore year has increased over time. We no longer see experimental psychology texts that lay out a week-by-week approach to the field as the texts did when I first started. I think this is a good trend. Although students don't get as broad an exposure to some of the tra-

	ditional things that psychologists have explored, they do get a better sense of what the scientific method is all about.
Halonen:	Has there been much variation in lecture over time?
McKeachie:	Teaching methods have been fairly dominated by the lecture approach. I don't know when discussion sections were started as supports for lecture. Although at the University of Michigan history and political science were taught in large lectures, we tried to have smaller sections in psychology to promote discussion. I think we were a little unusual in that regard. Most places tended to have lecture only. For many years, discussion was taught entirely by teaching assistants in small sections that met four times a week, but we couldn't afford that approach any longer. We have had to go back to the lecture–discussion; fortunately, we have had very good lecturers.

There have always been deviations from the lecture format. Back in the post-World War II period the big emphasis was on Rogerian nondirective psychology and Lewininian group dynamics. There was more emphasis later on how to motivate students through group process.

This approach was less prominent when television came in in the 1950s. There was a belief that we needed to become more efficient in education. So there was a big push, particularly by the Ford Foundation, to get colleges to teach on television. A lot of the large universities— Illinois, Ohio State, Purdue, Minnesota—in the Big 10 have always just done large lectures. They still do. They used television—some effectively and some not so effectively. Purdue did pretty well having Joe Rubenstein do the lecture with well-handled discussion sections.

However, on the whole, the use of television turned out not to be terribly effective. Television has been better suited to subject matters like engineering, where you do need to *see* things more. For psychology, television has been pretty much abandoned except at Minnesota. Maybe some other places still use it. I go to campuses where I see these fancy setups that were put in the 1950s and 60s and are no longer being used.

In the 1960s and 70s, there were two opposing approaches that influenced teaching: behavior-based methods and student-centered methods. The behavior-based approaches included Skinnerian teaching machines and Fred Keller's PSI [personalized system of instruction] method. With Skinner's approach, all the big publishers and electronics companies were going to get rich selling the programs. Then they discovered they didn't need machines. This insight led to programmed learning, which was used to some extent.

I think the thing that really took over was Fred Keller's PSI. It was very popular and effective, certainly more effective for learning than the large lecture. In many cases it was taught with true–false and multiple-choice testing, so the approach addressed very low level kinds of learning.

At that time behaviorism was rampant, so there was a push for behavioral objectives. Back in the 40s, we tried to define objectives in psychology behaviorally and produced about 30 pages of objectives in the intro course worked out by my teaching assistants and me. This became the basis for a later article in the *American Psychologist* in which we discussed the major objectives we had identified. We later filed the full set with the American Documentation Institute. Our approach included attitudinal objectives. The heyday of that sort of effort came in the 1960s. It turned out that the objectives didn't seem to make that much difference and may have turned educators away from examining the higher order thinking skills.

Beginning in the mid-60s after Kennedy's death, we began to see the impact of the student movement—an emphasis on the student as a person, sensitivity training, encounter groups. We began to see teaching designed to help students understand themselves and others. Actually this approach was not too different from what I experienced in the late 40s. That same spirit seemed to come back in the late 60s and early 70s.

Current trends move more toward peer learning—more emphasis on team projects, pairing, and active learning within the class itself.

Halonen: What might have shifted us culturally toward a greater interest in active learning?

McKeachie: I think partially a change in goals. We have always emphasized testing. We developed a test in 1947 for scientific thinking, refining it over the years. When I was president of Division 2, I set up a committee on test development and had everyone in the country send in items for introductory psychology that we thought represented higher levels than simple knowledge on Bloom's taxonomy. We had a meeting in Ann Arbor. We classified all the items and tried them out. We developed four tests that we called the Criteria Tests and published them in the instructor's manual of my intro text. So we have always had some emphasis on thinking. But I think it has been a national—and even international—insight that we need to teach people to think more effectively, with less emphasis on simple rote kinds of learning. I think we have realized that if you are going to teach thinking, people need to practice.

There is also good research to support the value of an active approach. I think some of the studies that Howard Gruber did at Colorado and that Tom Gribb and Neil Webb did at St. Norbert's showed peer group learning was more effective than just sitting in lectures. We had supportive studies even then. But I think gradually more data accumulated. The Johnson brothers at University of Minnesota and Slavin at Maryland studying the elementary schools offer increasing empirical support that peer learning is effective. That doesn't mean that peer methods are always effective, but these approaches have been established as ways to help the student think more and remember better.

Halonen: Can you predict what trends might characterize psychology teaching of the 90s?

McKeachie: My bias, of course, is on learning to learn. So I think we will pay increasing attention to thinking as problem solving but also to thinking as it applies to one's own learning, developing skills and strategies for one's own learning. I also think we will see more emphasis on the interaction between thinking about material and intrinsic motivation.

Halonen: Let's return to your personal experience as a teacher of psychology. What do you remember about the earliest days of your own college teaching?

McKeachie: I can remember when I first began teaching in charge of the course and had to start lecturing—I was scared to death. I think I ran out of material after the first half hour. Then after that, I overprepared. No, actually I overprepared from the beginning. I know Marquis always advised, "Don't try to get across more than three points."

I can remember that first year I was doing the lectures in introductory psychology I had two sections of 500 people—a thousand psychology students. I collected ratings in the middle of the term. One student wrote, "Dr. McKeachie is not a good teacher. He summarizes in the lecture what the important points are so everybody can get it. And usually there are only five or so important points. How can I get ahead of everyone when everyone else understands them?"

Halonen: When you began teaching, did anything surprise you about the life?

McKeachie: I guess to some extent that students really accept you as an authority, *that* expert.

Halonen: Do you suppose all faculty feel a little bit like frauds?

McKeachie: Well, maybe in the beginning.

Halonen: What do you enjoy most about teaching?

McKeachie: Interacting with the students . . . and with the teaching assistants. I've almost always taught courses with teaching assistants, and I enjoy it.

Halonen: You couldn't possibly say how many students you have taught over the years, but do you have some estimate of how many teaching assistants you've taught?

McKeachie: Probably 300. Maybe more. There are some years I had 30, maybe more, but I purposely like to work with 6 or 8 or fewer. It is very hard to give each teaching assistant a strong sense that they have input when you are dealing with such large numbers of assistants.

Halonen: Are there things that you find frustrating or unpleasant about teaching?

McKeachie: I suppose everyone finds it unpleasant when students get low grades and protest too long sometimes. I guess I've worked out techniques for dealing with the things that I find unpleasant. There aren't too many. For instance, in grading papers, if there aren't too many, I really enjoy it. I think it's interesting to see how students think.

Halonen: What do you do for the ones who protest too loud and too long over a judgment that you've made?

McKeachie: One technique is to ask them to write out what they think the truth is. Another is to simply listen and not to argue too much. And ultimately I say, "Sorry. That's the way I see it. Let's see if there are some things you can do that will make me see it differently next time." But usually I try to convert it into a problem-solving situation rather than spend a lot of time arguing about it. I sometimes say, "Assuming that I don't agree with you, what might help to give you a better chance next time?" I try to get them to look to the future with different strategies for the next test or whatever rather than "you say this" and "I say that."

Halonen: Are you ever persuaded by a good argument?

McKeachie: Oh yes. I think that's important. If you never yield, I think you can be perceived as pretty arbitrary. I think you have to be ready to concede, "I think you have a good point there."

Halonen: When you look over the 40 years of teaching you did at University of Michigan, can you identify whether students have changed much over time?

McKeachie: I think the postwar period when we were dealing with all the veterans was an interesting period. A lot of the students were older than I was. I can remember one student went into Marquis and said, "I don't want to be taught by a rosy-cheeked boy." I was more rosy cheeked then. Many of my teaching assistants had been in the Army, had experiences in captivity, so that the diversity of their experiences gave it a richness that was pretty good. There was the McCarthy period during the 50s. It was a very sad period for the country.

Halonen: Did that show up in student performance in any particular way?

McKeachie: No, I don't think so. But it was tough for some of my teaching assistants. One of them spent a couple years in prison because he chose to use the First Amendment rather than the Fifth Amendment when he was questioned by the Committee on Un-American Activities. Even though we had active fights against the Communists in the American Veterans' Committee, which I was a member of, I was always of the opinion that we should let the Communists stay in the organization. A number of liberal organizations expelled Communists. "No," I thought. "Leave them in." I thought everyone has a right to his or her own political beliefs, but we ought to mobilize enough so they don't outvote us. We had Trotskyites on our side. Nonetheless, people who were probably not Communists—certainly who were no great danger—suffered greatly during that period. But we fought to protect them and their rights to keep on teaching as long as they weren't propagandizing in classes. It was particularly bad for those who were picked out by McCarthy and by the Committee on Un-American Activities to be persecuted.

Then there were the 1960s and 70s. . . . In some ways it was interesting. I think the students were very idealistic. I had a good many students who founded the Students for Democratic Society. Tom Hayden was the editor of a newspaper during a time I was on the Board of Control for Publications. Many of them worked for me. I had a big research project underway at that time. Some of them actually went underground later.

There was a lot of idealism; at the same time it was scary. There were certainly some of the more radical groups, but probably a small minority. I think some of the things were generated more by media than by the students, but there were some who really felt that unless you tore down the university, you couldn't get a decent start. There was no hope of reform. Being an ameliorist rather than a revolutionary, I essentially liked to work with those who wanted to make the university better, but was scared of those who wanted to tear it down.

I can remember once—I guess I was president of Faculty Senate—I went to meet with the heads of the student organizations who were proposing some action—I can't even remember what it was. It was likely to be very damaging. I took Kenneth Boulding, an economist, with me. Ken has a speech impediment so that if you don't know him you probably think there is something wrong. But he is one of the most eloquent persons I think I've ever known. He said to the students, "If you do this, you could really destroy the university. It takes a long time to build a great university. It takes a long time to rebuild it if it's destroyed. Do you really want to do that?" And they decided that they didn't. It was a significant moment.

During that time we were studying classroom interaction. It was clear that one of the problems our teaching assistants and senior faculty had—I was chairman of the Department at that time—was student hostility. Dan Katz, one of my most distinguished professors, came and said, "I just can't handle the students anymore. I think I should retire." Other faculty members were very disturbed by their inability to respond to the students' aggressiveness. So after I finished the grant I was working on then, I applied for a grant to study how teachers handle hostility in the classroom, and we started the study. Whereas in the late 60s and early 70s, we were getting lots of hostility, by the time I got the grant, we would only get three or four instances of hostility in the term. We really didn't have a big population of instances of how teachers handled hostility by that time. So things change very rapidly.

Halonen: How do students of the 90s strike you?

McKeachie: The attitude of students in the 90s seems to be oriented more toward the end results. The great thing about students in the 60s is that they didn't care so much about grades. Sometimes they didn't care too much about learning either. A lot of students were serious about learning, and I liked their general ideals. It sometimes makes things more difficult if you don't have a grade as a goad for students.

But it is disturbing that students are so grade oriented and job oriented, materialistic, which I attribute to the state of the economy. It is realistic that when jobs are scarce, people are more concerned about what is needed in order to get a good job. I'm not, in a sense, critical of them, but it does make it more difficult in teaching where you are trying to get students interested in learning for its own sake and they say, "Is this going to be on the test?"

Yet there still is a lot of idealism. We still get a great many students involved in the programs we set up in the late 60s. Dick Mann, whom I brought in from Harvard to handle Introductory Psychology, started Project Outreach, which was a community service activity that went along with our introductory course originally. It is now a separate course. Essentially it was to get students out into schools, handling juvenile delinquents, and so forth, projects to be helpful in the community. We still get large enrollments in that.

In my own courses, I have the students do some kind of service. I really think that students can find altruistic activities rewarding, and you can help strengthen that. I think that is what we should really be doing.

Halonen: I'd like to shift to a different kind of outreach. Could you describe what it was like to teach psychology live on television back in 1951?

McKeachie: It was fun. Television was new. I didn't have a television myself back then. None of my relatives did either. Most of my relatives bought a television in order to see me on television. I helped the sale of televisions in southeastern Michigan at least. It was an exciting thing to be doing something with this new technology. I suppose it's like computers or interactive video today.

We did a program on Sundays—"The University of Michigan Hour." It was on Channel 4, the Detroit news station. They didn't have a regular studio. They set up the studio in what had been their warehouse for newsprint. So we had big rolls of newsprint around the outside of the studio and control room. We didn't have video cameras or kinescopes at the time. We didn't have teleprompters, like President Reagan had. I'd go over the ideas for what I was going to do, and we'd make up notes pretty much like my lecture notes. Someone would stand behind the camera with the cue cards and hold them up for me to check periodically. I was speaking extemporaneously in a sense. I would work through the general format. The difficult thing, having been a lecturer to large groups, where you are watching the students for feedback about how things are going, was that there was no feedback. You were just talking . . . so I would throw in every once in awhile something spontaneous to get a reaction from the people in the studio to see how things were going. It was fun. It was very rewarding. I got a lot of mail. Quite a few people took the course. They sent in answers to questions and read materials that we prepared.

Halonen: You mentioned earlier that those appearances had something to do with your political future.

McKeachie: Absolutely. Most of the psychologists wanted to see how badly I was representing psychology, so I became well known. I was only 30 years old, and next year they elected me president-elect of the Michigan Psychological Association. That concern got me active in the conferences of the state psychological association (I had already gotten somewhat active in the APA's Division of Teaching), but it also got me involved in the whole area of licensing psychologists. One of my jobs actually came up just as I got elected president-elect. The chairman of psychiatry instituted a suit against the psychological clinic for practicing medicine without licenses because they were using psychotherapy. We had to respond to that, so I became chair of a committee to get legislation certifying psychologists to practice, including the practice of psychotherapy. I was heavily involved in that activity. It was a great issue. Psychologists who had never been interested in the state association joined. We had people coming out of the woodwork—some who had somewhat suspicious credentials—who joined, but also the academicians, the experimentalists, *everybody* joined to try to protect psychology. We were really unified. Maybe you need an outside threat like that to get a sense of what is important.

Halonen: When you think about the kinds of courses you like to teach today, what courses would be your favorites?

McKeachie: I've always enjoyed Introductory Psychology because you are getting students—a little less now than when I started because of high school psychology courses—when psychology is fresh and new to them. It is not like teaching history. Maybe they already had history two or three times in high school. Generally it is something that is new, and it's also a great learning experience. When you are teaching Introductory, almost anything that you read is relevant. I get a wide variety of journals, and when I'm teaching Introductory, every journal seems to offer me ideas to bring into class. It's a great thing for one's own education. And I like freshmen. They aren't jaded.

I like teaching the Psychology of Aging or Life Span Development. I hadn't ever taken a course in that when I taught it some years ago. It was a real revelation to me how looking at a developmental point of view changes one's perspective on psychology. You realize how much of what we teach in Personality and Social Psychology is really cohort-related and culturally bound. These are principles, in many cases, that hold for a particular culture in a particular time. You have to keep on adjusting as the culture changes and to take account of cultural changes.

I also like Psychology of Religion—that was one of my original courses to teach. The University was having problems because all the people teaching in our program were agnostic or atheist, so they appointed a group of us who were at least affiliated with conventional religious groups and more sympathetic toward the subject. I taught Psychology of Religion for a number of years, and I hope to get back to it in the next year or the year after. That's a fascinating juxtaposition of some of the fundamental human issues. I think psychology has something to contribute.

Of course, my favorite course now is the one that I started in 1982—Learning to Learn—a course for freshmen, essentially a cognitive, motivational, personality, and social psychology course applied to your own learning. I think that students who take the course—if it works— learn psychology better because they are really trying to use it. They learn study skills better because they understand why they work rather than just learning them as recipes.

Halonen: It seems to me that many really fine faculty have a bias against working with freshmen. Do you have any ideas on why that might be?

McKeachie: I suppose partly it is a prestige matter. There is more prestige in working with advanced graduate students, but

I think it is also because it is difficult often to realize how much you take for granted when you are an expert in a field. Issues, which students find difficult to see, you just see a whole pattern. You don't see the details, which the beginner has to go through in order to understand something. There is often the feeling that you have to be an expert to teach at the college level. Sometimes it is a handicap to be an expert, because you have to learn not to talk as though you are talking to other experts. You've got to build a bridge between what is in your head and in the student's head. That means trying to understand and being able to see where the difficulties are and what kinds of examples will make sense to them and trying to make contact with what is already there.

Halonen: Are there any kinds of learning styles that you have a harder time reaching than others?

McKeachie: I think hostile students. I have relative trouble. I tend to be peace loving, I guess. I tend to do better on that now.

Halonen: What would account for that change?

McKeachie: In the 1960s you had to learn how to handle hostility without getting rattled. In some ways it's frustrating to the students who are aggressive if you don't get angry. It may seem as if you are not really responding. Sometimes I do try to respond with more emotion.

A couple of years ago I was giving a lecture at the University of Illinois in a whole auditorium full of faculty members. They seemed to be responding very well. So I called for questions, and the first respondent got up and said, "Dr. McKeachie, I don't see how you can ethically accept a stipend for this lecture. You didn't say a thing that was meaningful." And he went on at some length about what an empty talk I had given. I thought, "Shades of the 60s . . . back again."

I said, "Well, I'm sorry that you felt that way. I know anytime I give a lecture there are always some students who seem to have benefited from it and others with whom I just don't seem to make contact. I hope that there were some people who felt there was something for them. But I'm sorry that you didn't. I'd be glad to talk to you after to see if there were things we could work out."

So he came up afterwards. He said, "You know, I have made similar speeches like this to—he named Nobel prize winners, famous people. . . . He was taking a degree in linguistics and was always hanging around lectures. He said, "You are the first person who has ever treated me with respect. I appreciated that." Then he corresponded with me. He said he really felt that people in those situations were inhibited from speaking their true feelings—which I think is true—and it was important for someone to set a context that would let people speak more freely to the issues. I pointed out that it is difficult in situations like this with strangers, that there are norms that enable discussion to go forward without a lot of personal hard feelings. So we corresponded, and he seems to feel that I'm not such a bad guy after all. At least I've learned a little bit about hostile students.

Halonen: Actually I think that story sheds a lot of light on the next question I was going to ask. How would students describe your teaching style?

McKeachie: I think informality. I'm trying to think of student ratings I've gotten. Generally they are quite favorable. I think they see me as being concerned about their learning. I think people will forgive a lot if they really feel that you are trying.

Halonen: Are there other aspects of style that are critical for successful teaching?

McKeachie: I think enthusiasm is one, although I don't think there is any one thing that is essential probably. No, concern for learning. . . . Well, maybe not. I remember Clyde Coombs was one of our great teachers. He was one of the founders of the field of mathematical psychology. I don't think he was really too much concerned about student learning, but he was just so wrapped up in what he was teaching. Just full of it. Just bubbling over with it. You couldn't help being impressed with how important this was. He could handle things in a lot different ways.

But other things being equal, I think enthusiasm is certainly one. Yet I have known some very quiet, apparently unenthusiastic teachers who were also respected. I think extensive personal interest in the students—not just that you are concerned about the learning in the classroom—but that you know students individually and care about them individually. That is one of the difficulties of large classes, because students are likely to feel, "Nobody knows me. What difference does it make if I am here?"

Halonen: What do you do in large classes to make that connection with the student?

McKeachie: I pass out seating charts so that I can at least call on people by name, even though I don't learn all names. I at least try to give them a sense that I am interested. I ask them to turn in photos or anything else that will help me identify them. I'm certainly not as good as some people who learn all the names in a huge class. I think that's great. But I try to make up for it by forming pure learning situations where they are known. And in all my courses I very seldom have taught a course in which we haven't had discussion sections. The important thing there is that the teaching assistant is really close to them and interested in what they do.

Halonen: Has your style changed at all over the years?

McKeachie: I think the informality is fairly constant but may have been expressed in different ways. But I think I'm still learning. I think I am a much better teacher in some ways now. I use a lot more interactive or pure learning situations. I get students writing and talking to one another in the lecture much more now. I used to lecture pretty much straight through, with maybe some occasional questions. So that my techniques have changed somewhat.

Halonen: Would you agree that there is great resistance on the part of both faculty and students to being more interactive or student centered?

McKeachie: I think that's true. In many cases we hate to lose control. We don't know what is happening. In some sense, we feel that we are not doing our jobs if the students are talking to one another, and we are not giving them the truth.

And the students feel the same way. I can remember that in one of my early classes I got ratings saying, "We spent a lot of time in discussion. I came here to learn from the professors, *not* to hear what other students were saying." So I think we have to continually point out to students what they are getting out of interactive types of situations and why that is important in the long-term retention of what they are learning.

Even though I say I know more about teaching, I'm less effective than I was when I was a graduate student in many ways. I don't know the culture as well as I did. At that time I was still chaperoning student dances, participating in a lot of the activities of students. Now I don't watch television. I listen to classical music rather than current music. Hence, it is much more difficult for me to make that bridge between their minds and mine. So while I have picked up on one part of teaching, I have lost in the other.

Halonen: Do you think anyone can be a good teacher, or are there some who simply don't have what it takes to be good?

McKeachie: Out of the 300 students I have supervised there were 2 whom I felt would not be effective. I think it was anxiety. They were both very anxious about the classroom. It is normal to be anxious, but somehow I couldn't help them get over it. One of them handled the anxiety by being completely laissez-faire; students just got no sense of structure. And we tried various techniques of providing structure. It never really worked well. I think that person would have been within the range of adequacy, but never really a very good teacher. The other one was also anxious—not laissez-faire. She did try to structure things a good deal. Somehow she came through to the students as unsure. Even though she was trying, they never really felt that she was in control. We tried various things, but we still had ratings at the end of 2 or 3 years that were not good. But otherwise, I think anyone bright enough to get a graduate degree could become a good teacher if he or she was interested in it.

I don't think anybody wants to be a bad teacher. Somehow people manage to assume that teachers do a bad job of teaching because they are tied up in their research or they don't really care about it. I never met a teacher who really wanted to be bad. There were some who didn't aspire to be excellent, but they didn't want to come away feeling that they had done something destructive. Bad teachers tend to be those who have had bad early experiences in teaching. They didn't get off to a good start. They got the sense that students were hostile toward them or bored, and they retreated to trying to avoid, as much as possible, this kind of negative feedback. And so they read from their notes and try not to have discussions and try to keep control of a situation.

Halonen: As though reading from your notes would be a safe harbor from criticism.

McKeachie: You don't see the students' reactions as much.

Halonen: How can faculty recover when they get really bad evaluations? Have you seen damage done by this process?

McKeachie: Oh, I think that's the bad thing. I notice that I always get two or three that are pretty bad, and those are the ones that I think about. It's the big problem I have in training teaching assistants. They notice the bad ones and overlook the fact that the majority of students are quite happy with what they are doing. You have to help them see that everybody, or almost everybody, gets some poor evaluations. And you have to think, "Why is this? Is there some way I can try to reach that student without losing the majority?" You have to put it in perspective that it is the minority, and you want to cut that minority down as far as you can. But that it is just in the nature of things, that some people will automatically form friendships with us and others we won't particularly take a liking to. I think students have the notion that through bad ratings they will get the word to the bad teacher, and then they will really shape up. It just makes the situation that much more uncomfortable for the bad teacher. They are not likely to shape up without individual consultation. I've had some people who have had poor ratings whom I have been able to help, but I think in general you can do a lot more for people who are okay than for people who are really bad. In many cases, you have to give them some mechanical suggestions. If they really want to improve, you can work with them, and they can begin to see that there is some hope and there are things they can try that are different and gradually build up confidence again.

Halonen: One of the terms that came out of the faculty development task force at the St. Mary's conference that I really liked was the concept of "dormant faculty." What can be done to help reenergize a dormant faculty member?

McKeachie: My new department chair, Pat Gurrin, asked me to work with some of our dormant faculty. I think basically this work involves building on their strengths. In fact, when I talked with Pat about what she had in mind, I asked, "What does this person do well or what might they do well? Are there ways we can do something that would use that expertise?" Maybe these are, in ways we haven't thought of before--offering workshops, a new course, a mini-course, or maybe team-teaching with somebody he or she might value--not trying to show the person up, but to work cooperatively with that person. When I was chair, I would suggest that they think of a course or topic they would like to teach and offer a special course or seminar in a topic that was new. They could probably get interested and excited about sharing with other people. Sometimes that helps.

Halonen: What was it you enjoyed about serving in the role as chair of a department?

McKeachie: I have always liked to solve problems. The department grew from 70 faculty members to 200 while I was chair. So I had a new problem every half hour. I'm Calvinist by upbringing. I don't know how much an influence that might be here, but you have to feel that you have accomplished something in a day. And with that many problems coming—perhaps it's the gambler's fallacy—you got a couple of them worked out. I may have missed on 10 others, but at least you get the feeling that there were 2 or 3 things that worked. Sometimes in research it is not so easy to feel that sense of accomplishment. So I like the problem-solving opportunities and the variety of problems to solve that the role brings. The most brilliant faculty member can be so ignorant and naive when it comes to getting things done at the university. There are usually ways of getting things accomplished easily, if you know how the university works. So I got a lot of satisfaction out of that aspect.

The other thing I like is that it really gave me a sense of knowing the field of psychology. I guess I have translated a lot of my evangelistic fervor into fervor for psychology. It is so diverse. It covers so many different areas that, as chair, I really had a sense of knowing what was going on, what the new things were. I hired 130—or more than that—new faculty when I was chairman. And I was trying to read what my own faculty members were producing and keeping up with their work. As I said once at a faculty meeting, "Each of you knows a lot about some area of psychology that I don't know nearly as deeply. But I'd be willing to bet that I know more about all of psychology than anyone else in the department." I just have had to. It was the role, and I really enjoyed it.

Halonen: Can you share any wisdom about your hiring practices?

McKeachie: When I was a department chairman, I always tried to keep files anyplace I went on "who's the best." "Who is the best graduate student you have?" "Who was the best PhD you ever had?" I could probably tell you today where the top students were in the 1960s from the filing system. Ralph Tyler, who was the head of Advanced Study of Behavioral Science in Palo Alto, and I would compare notes on our files. Occasionally he would have someone I missed, and I would have someone he missed. You try to get the very best, at least who some people think is the best.

But, in addition, I have always looked for energy. They always accused me of picking people on their athletic ability . . . because we always had a softball team and a volleyball team and even a football team. We always lost in the finals in football because the Phys Ed Department always had these people who played on professional teams. But we did pretty well in the rest of the graduate-faculty league sports. Athletics were a big part of our departmental traditions, I guess. I think the basic idea is that with a given degree of intelligence, whatever the minimum is for getting a PhD, anything beyond that probably doesn't make nearly as much difference as the amount of energy you put in and how hard you work. Those people who are athletic are probably more likely to have that kind of energy.

It did become a factor in admitting graduate students. We gave some extra credit, for example, to those who had been in the Olympics. People who have had to discipline themselves to the degree that they do have developed work habits that are good. Robert Sommers, one of my teaching assistants and assistant professor at the University of Virginia, was a linebacker at Howard University. He turned out an impressive research project as an undergraduate. He has turned into a very fine psychologist, and I'm confident that he'll be productive.

Halonen: You wrote once that faculty must spend a lot of time on committees because faculty members don't trust how deans work. Could you elaborate on that?

McKeachie: My own experience tells me that once a faculty member becomes an administrator, he is somehow seen as having departed from the cloister. Once when I was Faculty Senate president and I was introducing the person who had just become our provost, I believe I said, "When you move across the street to the administration building, it is as if the head of a nunnery had moved across the street to a house of prostitution." The faculty just assumes that you have gone into a whole different way of looking at things and have lost all the values that you formerly espoused, which is not true at all. One of the things that characterizes faculty members is a strong sense of autonomy, so anyone who is above them is likely to be somewhat resisted.

Halonen: Was there anything you didn't like about being a chair?

McKeachie: I don't know. I don't know if I would do it again. . . . I suppose I would. I don't know if I would do it for 10 years. You build up a lot of credits. You have to be in long enough to keep promises. People are not going to take on jobs that need to be done that are going to conflict with their own careers unless they feel that it is going to make a difference and that you are going to recognize the contribution that they have made. At the same time, you inevitably build up some negatives.

One of my colleagues probably still thinks I am a liar. I can remember he came storming in one day to the Executive Committee, accused me of lying and not following through on promises I'd made about recruiting in one of the areas, and my associate chairman said to me, "He's gone senile!" Certainly from his perspective, he had some objective facts. We hadn't been able to get the people we had intended to get.

Universities at that time had nepotism policies preventing hiring two members of the same family, so that Jackie Gibson couldn't be a professor of psychology because her husband Jim Gibson was a professor. I broke the unwritten nepotism rule at Michigan by a kind of devious method of appointing a wife without salary, claiming, "The rule can't hold for someone who is not being paid a salary." And then after her grant ran out, appointing her with a salary saying, "She's already got the title. The least we can do is pay her for what she has done." So I broke that, but I had two cases where I could see the nepotism rule. Partners got very incensed by what they deemed were slights of their wives, and I think they held that judgment against me for a long time. So you build up both positive and negatives.

Halonen: You've had so many roles in psychology. Let's look at your role as author. Why did you write *Teaching Tips*?

McKeachie: Originally it was just that some of the same problems were occurring repeatedly. I thought, "Why can't I warn teaching assistants about some of them and give them some strategies for dealing with them before they get into trouble?" So it was simply an attempt to save time, not having to present the same things later. An then people began writing after they left. They would go out and be heading up introductory courses and would ask, "Could you send us those mimeographed course notes on teaching tips?"

	Then other people heard about it. I published it myself first through one of the local bookstores.
Halonen:	Has the wisdom in *Teaching Tips* changed over time?
McKeachie:	Each time I revise it, I think this time it won't be so hard. I won't have that much. And then I find that it is a major revision. All in all, I should have had a new edition out maybe a year ago. I always am stacking up things. I have a file to put things in for the next edition. I'll think that I'll just insert a paragraph, and then I decide that I need to rewrite a whole lot. There are other newer things. I want in the next edition to have more on ethics. I want to put in something on teaching thinking, on teaching values. My ideas about motivation have changed a good deal. I haven't really looked to see what systematic changes have occurred, but certainly each time I find I have to rewrite a lot.
Halonen:	Why do you suppose that teaching research seems to be less respected than more traditional discipline-based research?
McKeachie:	I don't think it is as fundamental in terms of implications for other fields. Just as mathematics probably has more respect than psychology, mathematics is used in so many other areas. The basic concepts of cognition or experimental psychology tend to be useful in a number of applications, our concepts are probably not so widely generalizable. We are more likely to use concepts than to develop new theoretical insights that will affect other areas of psychology.
	Nonetheless, I think it is gaining. I think, in general, psychology and education are much more closely linked than they were 30 to 40 years ago. I think education has always had a low status in academia in general. Now I think that is beginning to be overcome to some extent. Almost everyone studying basic psychology recognizes that there are interesting problems related to real learning situations that go beyond rats and mazes or Skinner boxes. People are going back and forth between areas. Jim Greeno, who was a mathematical psychologist of the pure type, early on got interested in learning in schools and has been in the School of Education at Berkeley and now at Stanford. I think he may be an extreme example, but there are a lot of people like him who really bridge the areas.
Halonen:	Are there any trends in teaching research currently that you are especially excited about?

McKeachie:	The growing integration of cognitive and motivational variables. I see that as kind of the wave of the future. They were more distinct, separate areas. Now we see them as highly interrelated.
Halonen:	We in higher education suffered an awful lot of criticism about the quality of the job we were doing in the classroom. What is your opinion about that criticism?
McKeachie:	I think it was very much overblown. Take statistics. Until the last 10 years, intelligence was going up almost every year. Reading scores were going up. The Johnson programs or Great Society programs were really quite successful. They were probably still not what their proponents hoped for, but they were making improvements in education up until the budgets started getting cut. The notion that you can do these things without money is misguided.

We were really very unhappy with President Bush. He asked to be our commencement speaker this year after we had already made plans to have someone else. Then he comes and says, "The Great Society didn't work. We've shown that money will not help education." And I think that is simply untrue. You can't solve the problems without doing something about inner city schools. Certainly there are aspects of education that are not good but the statistics aren't that bad. Right now they are talking about SATs [Scholastic Aptitude Tests] going down.

It is primarily a function of the number of students who take the SAT. We have an increase of 40–42% of students who take the SAT. When you have more students taking it, scores are going to go down. Iowa always does well on SAT scores because only the students who are leaving Iowa to go to the Ivy League schools take the SATs. The others take the ACT [American College Test]. Using those kinds of statistics to bash education, I think, is unfair. Some of the other statistics in education are really a function of the number of students who are taking the test more than any comparison across the board.

Halonen:	Let's return to psychology as a discipline. What appeals to you about psychology as a way of thinking.
McKeachie:	The complexity of it. I think human beings innately like a little more complexity than they have. The nice thing about psychology is that there is always more complexity. You can start with very simple ideas and begin to get the notion that—instead of thinking just in terms of good and evil—I need to think about the motivations that people

have, why they do the things that they do. Psychologists encourage looking for the data. "Let's not just jump to a conclusion without looking at the evidence."

The impressive thing to me on university committees is that people, who are great scholars in their own fields, will simply be quite ready to jump to a conclusion without any data on some educational issue. I can remember a couple of years ago Herb Marsh, who was probably the leading expert on student ratings of faculty, went to a meeting of leading faculty members whom we had working individually on courses related to thinking. They were given $25,000 to work on these courses. The meetings were held to explore how they thought they were doing on encouraging the teaching of thinking. So we are having this year-end get-together, talking about the university in general, and student ratings came up. They began bashing student ratings. "The students don't really know what they are doing." "They are influenced by extraneous things." "People don't really know until later whether the course is valuable or not." All the usual criticisms. And Herb, who is an ebullient person to start with, could hardly stand it. Finally, even though he was a guest, he said, "You realize that there is research on many of these points that you are raising?" One of the professors, quite a distinguished one in fact, said, "We don't need to know about the research. We've had experience in our own classes." And I thought, "Here we are, trying to teach critical thinking and saying that we don't need to be worried about evidence."

I found that on university committees usually we and the lawyers tended to be more likely to get some evidence before coming to a decision than people from other fields. The lawyers differ from us in that they would like to have a black-or-white answer. And we are more likely to come out, "Well, it's complicated. Kind of a shades-of-gray approach." When I chaired a committee on athletic policy, a lawyer said, "Either you ought to be completely amateur or hire a professional team. There is no in-between." This was after we gathered all the data. I think they are a little more inclined toward yes-or-no approach. But both psychologists and lawyers are inclined toward evidence.

Halonen: Do you think there is any liability in the psychological ways of thinking?

McKeachie:	Well, it is difficult for us in public policy. That is where people do have to make yes-or-no decisions. We tend to say, "Well, there are these points. But it is complicated by these factors." We are likely to see the complexity as being so great that it is hard to say, "Do this, recognizing that it may not work." But people would rather have us say, "Yes, this is exactly the thing to do. Don't worry about the negatives."
Halonen:	One of the findings of the Association of American Colleges' Study-in-Depth project was the suggestion that disciplines were perhaps political conveniences whose boundaries were likely to erode over the next decade. Would you agree with that position?
McKeachie:	I've heard that almost ever since I have been in the field. There are good reasons why it would be nice if some of the boundaries *did* erode. I've never been convinced that it would really happen. Even though intellectual interest bridges over job placement, for example, is so much tied in with the current disciplinary structure that anyone who gets into something that is truly interdisciplinary has a harder time getting located. We have a plethora of journals, but the core journals still tend to be in the discipline. I think it is a threat to psychology in that people do tend to form a stronger identity with a smaller group of people who are more specifically in their area. So it may well be that neuroscience and cognitive science may develop separate disciplines, just as we broke away from philosophy.
Halonen:	How do you evaluate that challenge to objectivity in psychology that has been generated by feminist scholarship?
McKeachie:	I think they have a point. I guess I'm a captive of my own bringing up. I'm not a positivist exactly. On the other hand, I do think that, despite the fact that things are value laden, there still are things that are more valid than others, regardless of your point of view. You can still find the kind of evidence—we might disagree about the implications— but we would agree that the evidence is real evidence. It can't get discounted. I suppose I am still an empiricist.
Halonen:	How do you balance your strong commitment to religious life with the more empirically oriented values of psychology?
McKeachie:	It gets more difficult in some ways. Originally, I simply took James's position. William James essentially said that we have values that are separate from factual knowledge. I'm not quite so sure that they are that separate. I've always

seen psychology as essentially value laden. I don't think you can escape values, but I think the values that most psychologists accept are those that are part of our Judeo–Christian heritage. They may not go along with various religious, theological conceptions, but for me the heart of the religion is the value system rather than other theological aspects, so that I haven't seen that much conflict. When I came into psychology I think it was harder to be religious. If we had a priest or young Catholic come in, they very often didn't retain their Catholicism. They would drop out of the priesthood before they got the PhD. And that changed probably 30 years ago. I think it's partly a change in the church. It used to be that kids coming out of Catholic high school did not believe in evolution at all. We still get kids coming out of some of the Bible schools with this belief, but Catholic schools seem to be teaching pretty much the same as other schools. I think the Vatican has also had a big impact. Unfortunately, it seems to be dying away.

Halonen: You have had a very good track record with regard to egalitarian values, for example, promoting the careers of people in psychology who were not White men before it was the politically correct thing to do. Could you talk about why that was such an important value for you so early on?

McKeachie: I don't really know. I guess I was shocked to find that it wasn't for other people. I can remember one of my best friends in graduate school was Jerry Gurrin. His wife is our department chair. I was shocked when we were talking about getting jobs and he said, "Well, I probably couldn't go to Ohio State because they don't hire Jews." And I thought, "My gosh! I can't imagine this. I never thought about it."

One of my first teaching assistants in psychology was Ralph Gibson, a Black. And mostly all the others were women because most of the men were drafted. Martha Colby was one of my first professors, so I didn't realize there was a problem. We never discriminated against Blacks or women at Michigan. Before I became department chair I was the chair of Graduate Studies. I think we didn't do a lot of wholesale recruiting. I did go down to Antioch once. One of my former teaching assistants said, "We have a very good Black student here—Del Jenkins—who ought to go to Michigan." I did go down. I was making a trip to

Miami University, and I stopped by and talked with her about coming to Michigan. And she did. She is a professor at NYU [New York University] now.

I think we were always receptive to women. When I was department chair, Bill Hunt was chair at Northwestern. He had Janet Spence. When she left to go to Iowa he said, "I've got to get another woman. I think it is important to have a woman on the faculty." Well, we had 10 or 15.

I thought we needed to have different models for our women students. Some were unmarried. Helen Peak was a very distinguished psychologist who never married. Some were married with children. Libby Douvan was one. She taught half time for awhile but did a good job of raising children while being a researcher and teacher. This did offer different models for young women, and we tried to work out arrangements.

But I don't know that we thought about it carefully. We thought nondiscrimination was just not discriminating against anyone. It wasn't until the late 1950s that the university actively began recruiting Blacks. Pat Gurrin was probably our leader. She was really a great sport, having us go to the Black colleges and appeal to them to come to Michigan, which we hadn't done before.

And the same way with women. I don't think we discriminated against women, but we didn't make any strong efforts ever until the Women's Movement came along and we got to be more conscious. I never thought we discriminated against women in pay, but once the university got some money to redress things, I got as much money as I could to pay our women more. And in some ways, many of our women had worked out part-time arrangements. In some ways, we weren't counting them as if they were equivalent in years, when we really should have given them more credit toward the total experience than just adding up the factors.

Halonen: Some of my colleagues are concerned about a shift in demographics at the undergraduate level. It is described as the *feminization problem*. Is that shift a concern for you?

McKeachie: Oh, I don't think so. You hope that society's attitudes are changing with regard to the professions that are dominated by women. I think we are making progress on that. I was just reading about that last night. Whereas in Sweden women are paid about 90% of the rate of men, we are at only about 70% here or something like that, so we still have a ways to go.

I think whoever's got the talent. Women have a lot to contribute. In general, I think women tend to be somewhat more nurturant and show greater warmth toward our students. I don't know whether it is genetic or cultural but that is a big advantage in teaching. I'm for it.

Halonen: Let's look a little bit at your involvement in the American Psychological Association. Why have you been as active in the APA as you have?

McKeachie: My involvement in many of these things, I think, is interpersonal. You get to meet people and like them, form friendships. Partly I think it is because I am somewhat conscientious. The thing that amazed me when I got on APA committees was that people would take on tasks and not do them. And I usually did. And if you do something, then people ask you to do something else.

I suppose a desire for status is involved, too. I never expected to be APA president. I had always enjoyed being on committees and so forth. I think there were probably those less honorable motives than the ones that serve the profession, but I do feel strongly about the discipline and think we need a strong organization to serve it.

Halonen: You did serve on all the curriculum initiatives that have been sponsored by the APA. Are these task forces distinctively different in your memory?

McKeachie: I was just an assistant professor at the first one in Cornell in the summer of 1951. It was kind of like a 2-month vacation. Dick Solomon was there and would lead us in an exploration in the glens around Ithaca. I was on the Varna softball team, and we won the championship. But we worked all morning and then wrote individually in the afternoon. The six people involved represented six quite different points of view, so it was quite stimulating. I never realized I was a personalist. I never realized I had such a viewpoint in psychology until I encountered Robbie MacLeod, who was a great human being and a very good psychologist. He was more phenomenological. It just was a revelation to me—seeing how things from his point of view put some things in a different perspective.

And I think we also had some good ideas about curriculum. We came up with the idea of sequencing, which is why Dael Wolfle really brought us together. He thought we were teaching all of our courses at about one level

	beyond the introductory and covering the same thing in the advanced course in order to bring people up to some common base so they could go on to the latter part of the course. I think that was important.
Halonen:	All of the people at that gathering represented larger schools. Do you think that shaped the conclusions you came to?
McKeachie:	I don't think so. Neil Bartlett from down in Hobart and William Smith consulted with us on what curriculum would be practical for schools that had at least three psychology faculty members. I think we were looking more at the discipline. I think one of the things also was that I got a sense of what were the core areas and how they related to one another.
Halonen:	Do you have any impressions from the most recent event— the week that was just spent at St. Mary's College of Maryland?
McKeachie:	I think that it was much broader than any of the previous ones. It addressed a lot of issues besides curriculum.

I think in the 1960 initiative, which John Milholland and I chaired, we had the advantage of more data about what people were doing. We had quite a good survey about what schools were actually doing, how much they had been influenced by the 1951 curriculum. Again, we had most of the summer to get acquainted. We did have small colleges. Bill Ray came from Bethany College and Peat Cole from Oberlin. So it was probably a little more representative of the diversity of psychology departments. That had some advantages over the large numbers of people working intensively for a short time at St. Mary's College of Maryland.

It was a great week. We had a lot of fun. I think people worked hard. I guess that astounded me, because when we started with the notion of a 1-week event, I thought, "How could we possibly accomplish anything in 1 week when it took us the whole summer?" And we had so many more topics than we had tried to deal with before. I was impressed with how much work got done and how much came out in such a brief period of time. It was astounding to me.

Halonen:	Would you have any predictions about what kind of impact this report might have?
McKeachie:	I don't think curricula are easily changed. There are so many local constraints. Was it Clark Kerr who said changing curriculum was "like moving a cemetery"? I think,

nonetheless, that each of the curriculum studies did have impact. There will be people in some places that will study the report very carefully and try to implement the recommendations as well as they can. Other people will study it carefully and will say, "Well, let's not do that" or "This doesn't apply to us." What I hope will happen is that people will think more seriously about the curriculum. I don't care so much about whether they follow our recommendations as long as they really get involved with curriculum thinking and planning. Often, curricula arise in kind of a creep due to interests of new faculty or political considerations, without much thought about what it is we are after and how we can best achieve our goals. I'm willing to trust any psychology department to do a good job, if they really take it seriously. They may come up with something quite different than what we recommended. If they work at it and if it stimulates them to think about it, I think it will be very important.

Halonen: How about impact in the other direction? Do you think APA will respond to the recommendations to them that might come out of this work?

McKeachie: I think Charles Spielberger (APA past-president) currently is supportive of education. Certainly Frank Farley (APA president-elect) will be. I think the same will be true whoever the future presidents are who are coming from private practice and other areas. What has impressed me is that it doesn't matter so much what area you are coming from, when you become president, you become conscious of the need to support various things. Some of the people most supportive of scientific and educational activities have been those coming out of a practice area, because they have wanted to show that they really were complete psychologists, that they weren't just representing one area. I'm always optimistic.

Halonen: Let me return to the more personal side of Bill McKeachie. Along with a very distinctive career, you have managed to have a very successful marriage. I know Ginny has attended almost as many APA conventions as you have. How critical has your relationship with her been to your satisfaction with your career?

McKeachie: Tremendously. I have seen a number of very good psychologists really get hung up because of problems in their marriages. I just have been very lucky, lucky to find her, lucky to get her. She's been very supportive.

I have been a strong proponent of the Women's Movement. I never thought my younger daughter would get married. It was nice that you don't have to get married these days to be a respectable woman. My older daughter was an auto mechanic. My younger daughter is an engineer. Great career choices have opened up for women.

I guess my only fear was that women who chose to be homemakers would be denigrated. I suppose that occurs, but I don't think that Ginny has felt particularly discriminated against.

It has made a big difference in my life. She takes care of balancing the checkbook. I do the income taxes. She does a lot of the tasks in a dual career home that have to be shared. I used to do more cooking and baking and such, but now I bake fruitcakes at Christmas. It is about the only baking I do. She does most of the housework and household tasks. I'm interested in this. In an article that I was reading yesterday, even in dual-career families, the women still do 30 hours of housework a week and the men only do about 18. There is still quite an imbalance in most homes. I have saved a lot of time because she has taken care of so much.

Halonen: Are you at all disappointed because neither of your daughters followed in your career path?

McKeachie: No . . . it's nice, I think. I know a number of families where children have followed. It is nice to see families like the Thorndikes, to see the children following in the footsteps of their parents and grandparents. The Wertheimers—Lisa and Mike.

On the other hand, it's a burden sometimes. I remember Charles Seashore. The Seashore tradition goes back to Carl Seashore at Iowa and Bob Seashore who was a chairman at Northwestern and Harold Seashore at Psychological Corporation and Stan Seashore at Michigan—a great tradition. When he heard his uncle had died, Charles, who was a very light-hearted person, became very depressed. He had the feeling that all the weight of that great tradition was falling on him. So it is tough, being the son or daughter of a famous psychologist.

Halonen: Were you satisfied with the amount of involvement that you had with your girls?

McKeachie: I think so. My younger one was always into athletics, so I kind of enjoyed that. I think I was busy. I probably could have spent more time with them. That is one of the problems when there is only one career. It was a lot easier on me when they had problems. I would go to work and I'd be working, and I wouldn't think about it until I got home at night. Ginny would be at home, hanging around the house, and she'd worry all day long. It is a lot harder on the mother than it is on the father. I don't know how they do it in dual-career families, but I didn't do my fair share of worrying. Although we did worry about the girls sometimes.

Halonen: It is good of you to confess that. . . . I would not be forgiven if I didn't ask you about softball because of the central importance it has in your life. Why is that as powerful a force in your life as it is?

McKeachie: I think it is because I was a teacher's kid. In a one-room country school when your father is the teacher, it is sort of like being a preacher's kid. There is something wrong with you or you are different. I was small. I was the youngest in my class. I started school at five, and we didn't have kindergarten. So I think sports were important to prove that I was a normal human being.

Another way people do this is to become deviant, I suppose. I did go through a period when I was about 10 when I swore a lot. I guess you go through that in an attempt to prove that you don't have to conform just because you are a preacher's kid or a teacher's kid, but I think for me sports were a way to prove that I was a real boy.

Halonen: You don't think that as good as you are at the game that that is just a bit deviant?

McKeachie: I don't know . . . my Dad loved baseball. We couldn't afford to buy mitts because of the Depression, so we switched to softball. At the one-room schoolhouse, as long as the weather was good, we would play every noon and every recess. In the winter time, we would downhill ski. During the games, though, he would catch for both teams and we would choose up sides for new teams every day, so I suppose in a sense he modeled it and got me started early.

Halonen: I think another distinguishing feature in your identity is your aesthetic/musical side. Could you talk a little about that?

McKeachie: It was probably more my mother's influence, although my dad liked to sing. My mother persuaded her father to buy her a piano. She wanted to play the piano. The first money that she earned in teaching school, she invested in getting piano lessons.

And she started me playing early. She has a clipping,

"Five Year Old Plays Recital." I'm sure it was a simple piece. But she would start us on piano every fall, and then about the middle of winter she would get discouraged because I would quit. But I learned enough so that by the time I was 12 I really enjoyed it.

My best friend in high school played clarinet, so I'd play piano and he'd play clarinet. We wrote the school fight song. After we graduated from high school, we got very nostalgic about the high school. So one weekend we got together and said the school ought to have its own song. We were using "Anchors Aweigh." So we composed and wrote one and they still play it.

Halonen: And you have continued to play?

McKeachie: Oh, yes. My wife and I have sung in the church choir for over 40 years. We still enjoy it.

Halonen: You are really a relative novice at retirement. How well do you think you are going to like the retired life?

McKeachie: Well, I think I will like it if they let me keep on working. I think they will. I don't think I will make a lot of changes. The department never lacks for things that need to be done. As long as I'm healthy, I expect to keep on. I would like to teach, but maybe not have as big a responsibility. But I like teaching. I like my research. So far I still have three offices. I did a workshop on Monday for the Center on Teaching and Learning about motivation. So I expect not to change drastically.

Halonen: I suspect your retirement will exceed what most people do for regular work life. . . . If you were magically granted the ability to start over again, do you think your career would go in the same direction?

McKeachie: I can't imagine it being better. Everything worked out better than I had any right to expect. Al Bandura makes a big deal of chance, and I think he's right. I've just been very lucky. In my marriage. In my career. In everything.

Halonen: One last question. Future goals. What do you hope to accomplish in the future?

McKeachie: I never really had any goals. I keep telling my students that you need to set goals and work out the implications for what you are doing.

Halonen: You tell students they need to set goals and you don't do that?

McKeachie: I've really just kind of drifted along and done whatever things just happened. I just hope I can stay healthy and keep on teaching and doing research. I don't plan on making any great contributions. I know there are things I know how to do, things I'd like to be able to do, teach other students to be able to do. I've gone beyond any goals I would have even *thought* of setting. Things just worked out very well for me.

III

CONFERENCES ADVANCING THE TEACHING OF PSYCHOLOGY

INTRODUCTION

CONFERENCES ADVANCING THE TEACHING OF PSYCHOLOGY

JANET R. MATTHEWS

Conferences provide a forum for discussing global issues associated with the teaching of psychology. They may also be designed to consider national or regional issues related to how psychologists are trained or to share methods that might be used by teachers to improve their skills. Part III explores four types of conferences important in the teaching of psychology.

Margaret Lloyd and Charles Brewer summarize the conferences that have focused on the undergraduate teaching of psychology. These meetings include the 1951 Cornell conference, the 1960 Michigan conference, the 1973 Kulik report, the American Psychological Association's Committee on Undergraduate Education proposed conference and surveys, and the 1991 St. Mary's conference. As noted by the authors, these conferences have historically emphasized the curriculum. However, over the years, the focus has shifted from specifying courses that should constitute the major to dealing with broader issues, such as teaching techniques. The 1991 St. Mary's conference covered the widest range of topics related to teaching and is discussed in greater detail than the other conferences.

In her chapter on graduate conferences, Cynthia Belar notes that graduate conferences have had two major purposes: They have been used as a problem-solving mechanism and as a vehicle for introducing changes in graduate education. Several of the national conferences on graduate education centered on specialty training in clinical psychology. The 1959 Miami Beach conference was one of the first to encompass the entire discipline. This broad approach also characterized the Utah conference in 1987. Most of the conferences covered by Belar, however, have addressed mental health specialty training rather than the entire graduate curriculum.

In a separate chapter, Belar summarizes internship and postdoctoral conferences. She emphasizes the relationship of these conferences to others concerning graduate education and training. The importance of integrating academic and applied experiences is a major theme. Internship conferences are more recent than undergraduate and graduate conferences. As newer specialty areas have developed in professional psychology, there has been a need to specify the nature of appropriate internship and postdoctoral training for them. Thus, such conferences have tended to include representatives of both educational institutions and training centers. Although postdoctoral training has a long history, not many conferences have specifically addressed this topic. Belar notes that by 1991 only one such conference had occurred and that a second one was in the planning stages.

In the final chapter of Part III, Stephen Davis and Randolph Smith cover regional teaching and student research conferences. They note that regional teaching conferences and student research conferences have a much different history from the other conferences addressed in this section of the book. They tend to attract participants in one geographic region and to have a highly specific focus. They are generally kept at a low cost so that individuals with limited budgets can attend. The teaching conferences focus on teaching tips and issues rather than on long-range planning. The student research conferences provide a forum for students to present their work and receive feedback. Both types of conferences also stress networking among participants. These conferences are important to the history of the teaching of psychology because of their focus on the methodology of teaching, and they have been viewed as a form of teaching for both faculty and students.

In summary, various conferences have addressed teaching from different perspectives. They have considered issues of national policy on teaching and training, curriculum requirements, and the daily activities of teaching and learning.

10

NATIONAL CONFERENCES ON UNDERGRADUATE PSYCHOLOGY

MARGARET A. LLOYD AND CHARLES L. BREWER

Our aim in this chapter is to chronicle the history and recommendations of national conferences on undergraduate psychology, including the forces that led to them. Hence, we review the conferences themselves, a conference that was planned but never held, and several national surveys on the undergraduate curriculum that were conducted during the 31 years between the 1960 University of Michigan conference and the 1991 St. Mary's College of Maryland conference.

The chapter is organized as follows: (a) historical review of the conferences and their major recommendations, (b) trends in undergraduate curriculum recommendations, and (c) conculsion.

HISTORICAL REVIEW OF CONFERENCES

Cornell Conference

The first conference on undergraduate psychology met for 8 weeks at Cornell University during the summer of 1951. The six participants, who described themselves as a "study group," were Claude E. Buxton (Yale University); Charles N. Cofer (University of Maryland); John W. Gustad (Vanderbilt University); Robert B. MacLeod (Cornell University); Wilbert J. McKeachie (University of Michigan); and Dael Wolfle (Commission on Human Resources and Advanced Training), who served as chair. The conference was funded by the Carnegie Corporation and the Grant Foundation. As the title of the conference report suggests (*Improving Undergraduate Instruction in Psychology*), the impetus for convening the study group was a shared belief that the participants could "prepare a set of recommendations concerning undergraduate instruction in psychology which our colleagues would find useful" (Buxton et al., 1952, p. v).

After lengthy debate, the study group identified four objectives that psychology teachers might have for their courses: (a) intellectual development in the liberal arts tradition; (b) a knowledge of psychology's research findings, major problems, theoretical integrations, and contributions; (c) personal growth and social adjustment; and (d) attitudes such as intellectual curiosity, respect for others, and social responsibility. The group recognized that practicality required most teachers to be modest about how many of these objectives they could achieve.

Although personal growth was included on the comprehensive list of objectives, it was not viewed as a legitimate curricular goal on the grounds that it was not directly pertinent to a liberal arts program in psychology. The study group recommended that the remaining three objectives— knowledge, rigorous habits of thought, and desirable attitudes and values— should all be emphasized in curriculum course planning. In actual teaching, however, the group stressed that the knowledge objective or course content was the most important.

Concerning specific curriculum recommendations, Wolfle's committee endorsed the teaching of psychology as a scientific discipline in the liberal arts tradition and recommended one undergraduate curriculum as a model. After the introductory course, the committee proposed five intermediate or core courses: statistics, motivation, perception, thinking and language, and ability. These courses would be followed by advanced courses in specialized areas, such as social, learning, comparative, and physiological psychology. Experimental methodology would be emphasized in all substantive courses rather than in a separate experimental psychology course, in which method might be separated from content. The committee recommended history and systems and personality as integrative or capstone courses for seniors.

The Wolfle committee recognized that local conditions precluded specifying the exact content of the major for all psychology programs. Emphasizing that the core and advanced courses were not for majors only, the committee also suggested a group of special-interest courses designed specifically for nonmajors (e.g., educational psychology, industrial psychology, and the psychology of religion).

The Wolfle group discussed at length the problems of the introductory course and noted that many teachers believe "that it bores students, that it presents much material that is not integrated into any kind of framework, and that it gives the student a poor impression of psychology as a disciplined inquiry into problems of behavior and experience" (Buxton et al., 1952, p. 14). Attempting to deal with some of these problems, the study group proposed two possible organizations and foci for the introductory course. The group also highlighted some things that other courses should cover.

In keeping with their view that a course in personal adjustment had no place in a liberal-arts-based psychology curriculum, group members excluded it, as well as abnormal psychology, from the course roster. In addition, they rejected applied courses with a vocational slant, preferring that such training come after the bachelor's degree. In a similar vein, they also suggested that students who seek employment after completing a baccalaureate degree might learn vocationally oriented technical skills in special summer institutes.

In a final chapter, they acknowledged, with regret, that there was no research evidence to support any of their recommendations. They urged psychologists to conduct research on curricular issues and offered some suggestions for doing so.

Michigan Conference

In the summer of 1960, a follow-up conference on undergraduate psychology was held at the University of Michigan. This conference was directed by two faculty members at the University of Michigan: Wilbert J. McKeachie, the only carryover from the Cornell conference, and John E. Milholland. Four other individuals served as full-time participants: Lawrence E. Cole (Oberlin College), William Hunt (Northwestern University), Robert Leeper (University of Oregon), and Wilbert Ray (Bethany College). Three additional University of Michigan faculty members served as half-time participants: Robert L. Isaacson, James V. McConnell, and Edward L. Walker. As was true of the participants in the Cornell conference, self-selected individuals came together because of their interest in teaching psychology. Specifically, they were distressed by the lack of prestige accorded to teaching, and undergraduate teaching in particular, in most departments and wanted to do what they could to remedy this situation. The conference, funded by the National Science Foundation, published its report, *Undergraduate Curricula in Psychology*, in 1961 (McKeachie & Milholland, 1961).

Following the recommendation of the Cornell conference to conduct more research on curricular issues, the Michigan group surveyed the 548 colleges that granted at least one bachelor's degree in psychology during 1957–1958 to determine how many psychology departments had adopted the Cornell conference curriculum. Seventy-five percent ($n = 411$) of the 548 departments responded, and 274 of these reported having revised their curricula since the publication of the Wolfle report. Of these 274 departments, 26% indicated that they used the curriculum "as much as possible" or "quite extensively," 43% "used some features," and 31% "made no attempt to use it" (McKeachie & Milholland, 1961, p. 16).

After discussing some pressures on the curriculum from different sources, the Michigan report devoted a chapter to special problems arising from three groups: (a) preprofessional students who were not psychology majors, (b) psychology majors who wished to use their bachelor's degree for vocational employment, and (c) psychology majors who were preparing for graduate study in psychology. This chapter explicitly recognized that undergraduates might need different emphases and that no single set of courses was best for all students.

Reaffirming the stance of the Cornell conference, the Michigan conference endorsed the idea that the psychology curriculum should be rooted in the liberal arts curriculum:

> It would be diverse and flexible and, within the college potential, would offer at the advanced level alternate paths for differing interests. But it would be firmly anchored in the liberal arts, rejecting undergraduate vocational training as a primary goal. (McKeachie & Milholland, 1961, p. 33)

Unlike the Cornell conference, however, the Michigan group could not agree on one ideal curriculum, so it presented three possible curriculum structures: the inverted pyramid model, the hourglass model, and the flexible model. The inverted pyramid curriculum was so-named because it began with a brief elementary course and moved through a selected core of content courses with laboratories to a final capstone course (history and systems). The hourglass curriculum started with full-year courses in introductory, statistics and experimental design, and basic concepts. This broad grounding permitted fewer and more specialized core courses at the intermediate level and called for an intensive overview of psychology at the senior level. The flexible curriculum was based on the assumption that the content of the major should be adaptable to meet students' different abilities and interests. In this model, there were no specific requirements, except for a year-long introductory course. Students, with assistance from their advisers, would select the courses they wanted to take.

Almost until the end of the conference, the Michigan group hoped to agree on one ideal curriculum but failed to do so. Their report concluded the following:

What is ideal, we now believe, depends upon the staff, the students, the total college curriculum, and other factors. Our recommendations are intended merely to illustrate some alternatives as starting points for the individual decisions each psychology department must make for itself. (McKeachie & Milholland, 1961, p. 103)

After reporting on some of the research that had been conducted along the lines recommended by the Cornell conference, the Michigan group reaffirmed the need for more research to clarify issues concerning undergraduate education in psychology.

Kulik Report

Ten years after the Michigan conference, the American Psychological Association's (APA's) Programs and Planning Office received a grant from the National Science Foundation to conduct a study of the undergraduate psychology curriculum. An advisory panel was to analyze the results of the study and make recommendations to the APA on the basis of that analysis. The project was directed by C. Alan Boneau (APA's Programs and Planning Office), Stanford C. Eriksen (director of the Center for Research on Learning and Teaching at the University of Michigan), and Donald R. Brown (University of Michigan) James A. Kulik (University of Michigan) was largely responsible for the operation of the project and wrote the report, *Undergraduate Education in Psychology* (Kulik, 1973), in collaboration with Donald R. Brown, Richard E. Vestewig, and Janet Wright (University of Michigan). Margo Johnson, of the APA's Central Office, also made significant contributions to the project, which spanned 3 years (July 1969 through June 1972).

In contrast to the Cornell and Michigan conferences, whose memberships were small and self-selected, 48 individuals representing a variety of diverse institutions were involved in the Kulik report. Robert Isaacson (University of Florida, formerly at the University of Michigan) chaired the advisory panel.

Following the frenetic decade of the 1960s, study of the undergraduate curriculum took a noticeably different turn when it expressly recognized the impossibility and undesirability of stipulating what the curriculum should be. Not wanting to threaten freedom to "innovate, experiment, and do one's own thing," Kulik's group decided not even to try to specify an ideal curriculum (Kulik, 1973, p. v). Instead, the Kulik report merely summarized a national survey of "schools granting bachelor's degrees with a major in psychology, 2-year schools, and 4-year schools that do not offer a psychology major" (Kulik, 1973, p. 4) and site visits to 17 schools, with emphasis on 10 of them.

The purely descriptive Kulik report highlighted the increasing diversity of undergraduate psychology and related its findings to some of the recommendations from the previous Cornell and Michigan reports, especially the latter.

A Conference That Was Planned but Never Held

During 1980–1981, APA's Committee on Undergraduate Education (CUE) discussed the need for another conference to study the undergraduate psychology curriculum. Members of CUE during this period included James Bell (Howard Community College); Charles L. Brewer (Furman University), chair; Judith Goggin (University of Texas at El Paso); James Korn (Saint Louis University); Merle Meyer (University of Florida); Charles Morris (University of Michigan); Barbara Nodine (Beaver College); and Virginia Senders (Framingham State College; American Psychological Association [APA], 1980, 1981a). By its October 1980 meeting, CUE had developed a preliminary proposal for a conference that was approved, in principle, by the APA's Education and Training Board and the Board of Directors (APA, 1981b).

As conceived by CUE, the conference was a 3-year project. During the first year, literature reviews were to be commissioned that were narrow in scope (experiential learning, career education, etc.). Also, 15 psychologists who were nationally recognized as being knowledgeable and concerned about undergraduate psychology instruction were to be invited to serve on a task force. The task force would meet for 1 month during the summer of the first year to draft recommendations responding to challenges in undergraduate psychology education.

Early in the second year, 20–30 psychology departments were to be invited to discuss the draft recommendations and provide written feedback to the task force. The national conference was to be held in the summer of the second year and would be attended by the project staff, task force members, and a representative from each of the institutions providing feedback on the initial recommendations. (Other interested people could attend at their own expense.) Following the national conference, the task force was to reconvene for 2 weeks to write a final set of recommendations. In the third year, the conference report was to be published and workshops held at state and regional conventions, led by the conference participants. An assessment of the conference's impact was also planned.

Because the project would be extensive and costly, CUE sought outside funding. By January 1981, Charles Morris had prepared and submitted a preliminary grant proposal for the conference, on behalf of CUE, to the Fund for the Improvement of Post-Secondary Education (FIPSE). Unfortunately, the proposal was not funded, thus scuttling CUE's plans. Not until 1987 did CUE look again at the idea of a national undergraduate conference, which, this time, culminated in the 1991 St. Mary's conference.

APA Telephone Survey of Department Chairs

To enhance the likelihood of securing grant funding if another undergraduate conference proposal were developed, CUE decided to gather data to demonstrate the need for such an undertaking (B. Nodine, personal communication, August 18, 1991). Hence, in 1982, CUE conducted telephone interviews of undergraduate department chairs as a means of ascertaining their current concerns. One hundred chairs, selected at random from a mailing list maintained by the APA, were contacted between July 1982 and September 1982 by James Bell (Howard Community College); Janet R. Matthews (Loyola University, formerly at Creighton University); Barbara Nodine (Beaver College), chair; R. Steven Schiavo (Wellesley College); and Jeanne M. Stahl (Morris Brown College; APA, 1982).

Department chairs were asked eight questions that dealt with undergraduate psychology education, the role of the APA and undergraduate psychology, and demographic information. Because of space limitations, we highlight only a few of the important findings (APA, 1983). The following issues were identified by at least 40% of the respondents as problems facing their departments: (a) the undergraduate curriculum (65%; e.g., balancing conflicting demands); (b) faculty members (61%; e.g., coping with too few faculty members); (c) pressures from students toward vocationalism (47%); and (d) budget constraints (43%). Eighty percent of the chairs reported that their departments had completed self-studies, and 44% of the departments had courses that incorporated international content. Regarding ways that the APA could be helpful to undergraduate departments, 40% of the chairs said that the APA could assist in determining the structure and content of the undergraduate curriculum, and 26% wanted the APA to provide more information about bachelor's-level careers and graduate school prospects for psychology majors.

Scheirer and Rogers Report

In March 1983, CUE concluded that it would be useful to develop a database on the undergraduate curriculum and recommended to the Education and Training Board that a national survey on the curriculum be conducted (Scheirer & Rogers, 1985). (Members of CUE at that time were James A. Eison [University of South Florida, formerly at Roane State Community College]; Paul J. Lloyd [Southeast Missouri State University]; Janet R. Matthews [Loyola University, formerly at Creighton University], chair; R. Steven Schiavo [Wellesley College]; and Jeanne M. Stahl [Morris Brown College]). In May 1983, the proposal was approved by the Education and Training Board. A plan to expand the idea of a single survey into a triennial survey of undergraduate education in psychology was proposed by CUE in September 1983 and approved by the Educational and Training Board in

October 1983. The plan stipulated that every third survey would examine the curriculum (Scheirer & Rogers, 1985).

For the first survey, C. James Scheirer, administrative officer of APA's Educational Affairs Office, and Anne M. Rogers, administrative associate, conducted the research and wrote the report, *The Undergraduate Psychology Curriculum: 1984*, published by APA (Scheirer & Rogers, 1985). Purely descriptive, this report summarized information from respondents at 2- and 4-year colleges about educational settings, faculty, students, the introductory course, undergraduate curriculum, requirements for the major, psychology for nonmajors, special features of courses, and independent work. Scheirer and Rogers also compared some of their data with those from the Kulik report.

Association of American Colleges Report

Conference Origins

In the fall of 1988, the Association of American Colleges (AAC) launched a project to study the history and current status of 12 undergraduate majors, including psychology. The project grew out of a chapter titled "Study in Depth" from *Integrity in the College Curriculum* (Association of American Colleges [AAC], 1985). The APA was asked to appoint a study group for psychology and selected the following individuals: Laurel Furumoto (Wellesley College); Diane F. Halpern (California State University, San Bernardino); Gregory A. Kimble (Duke University); Thomas V. McGovern (Arizona State University West, formerly at Virginia Commonwealth University), chair; and Wilbert J. McKeachie (University of Michigan). It is noteworthy that this was the first participation of women in a national study group on psychology, to our knowledge.

Psychologists participating in the AAC project, funded by the Ford Foundation and FIPSE, met twice in plenary sessions with the other disciplinary and interdisciplinary task forces, and twice as a small group. By mid-1989, the psychology group drafted a paper that was presented at the annual meetings of the American Psychological Society (June in Washington, DC) and the APA (August in New Orleans). In addition, the paper was circulated to more than 300 psychology faculty members for comment. In January 1990, papers from the 12 study groups were presented at the annual AAC meeting in San Francisco. The psychology task force held an open forum on its report at the August 1990 Annual Convention of the APA held in Boston. Final reports were published as Volume 2 of *Liberal Learning and the Arts and Sciences Major: Reports from the Fields* (AAC, 1990). The psychology report was also published as "Liberal Education, Study in Depth, and the Arts and Sciences Major—Psychology" in the

June 1991 issue of the *American Psychologist* (McGovern, Furumoto, Halpern, Kimble, & McKeachie, 1991).

Conference Recommendations

In keeping with the overall project charge, the final report of the psychology study group included the following sections: defining the field of study, orienting assumptions, undergraduate psychology students, common goals, measurement and evaluation of major field outcomes, structure of the major, and student learning and self-evaluation.

The study group identified several orienting assumptions that guided their discussions. In summary, these were the following: (a) Psychology is rooted in the liberal arts tradition; (b) differences among institutions, departments, faculty, and students must be considered in curriculum planning and teaching; and (c) student assessment and program evaluation should be conducted on a regular basis, using multiple methods. Notwithstanding the institutional differences issue, the psychology study group identified common objectives or goals for any undergraduate psychology program: knowledge base, thinking skills, language skills, information-gathering and synthesis skills, research methods and statistical skills, interpersonal skills, history of psychology, and ethics and values.

Concerning the structure of the psychology major, the study group presented two curriculum models: the generalist model and three variations on a thematic model. These models were based on the principle that "less is more," or the belief that academic skills are more effectively honed by repeated exposure to less content.

The generalist model was structured as follows: (a) introductory psychology; (b) three methods courses (statistics, research methods, and psychometrics and individual differences); (c) two survey courses in the knowledge base, such as social and physiological psychology; (d) two specialized courses (with laboratories) that are matched to the two survey courses previously taken; (e) one integrated senior project (research or field setting) or seminar (history and systems, advanced general, special topics); (f) interpersonal skills and group process laboratory (students learn to work in groups); and (g) electives. In addition, the study group recommended that, whenever possible, all undergraduate psychology majors should have a volunteer experience, either in conjunction with the senior project or the interpersonal skills and group process laboratory.

The thematic model was essentially similar to the generalist model but stipulated that the two survey courses and the two specialized courses with laboratories should be taken within the thematic area. The report described the content of three thematic models—developmental, biological, and health psychology—and stated that models could also be designed for other areas in the traditional knowledge base.

Consistent with past conference reports, the AAC study group reiterated that good teaching actively involves students in the learning process and is essential for effective psychology education. The study group also noted that psychologists are in a unique position to assess educational outcomes, now a major issue in higher education. In addition, the group discussed factors related to academic achievement, such as student involvement, clear and high expectations, and regular assessment and feedback. Effective departmental advising was also mentioned as being important in promoting student academic achievement.

Interestingly, the report suggested that if there is a canon in psychology, "it is probably in evolving methodologies for the study of behavior, emotion, and cognition" (McGovern et al., 1991, p. 604). The authors concluded on a positive note, predicting that psychology should maintain its status as a popular and effective contributor to liberal learning, in great part because the discipline "has the potential to touch the whole lives of students—their intellectual development, their emotional growth, and their behavioral skills" (McGovern et al., 1991, p. 604).

St. Mary's College of Maryland Conference

Conference Origins

The impetus for what would become the 1991 National Conference on Enhancing the Quality of Undergraduate Education in Psychology was a decision by APA's CUE in March 1987 to reconsider the issue of developing guidelines or models for the undergraduate psychology curriculum. Members of CUE at that time were Margaret A. Lloyd (Georgia Southern University, formerly at Suffolk University); Antonio E. Puente (University of North Carolina at Wilmington), chair; Margaret S. Martin (Medical University of South Carolina at Charleston, formerly at Lander College); Janet R. Matthews (Loyola University, formerly at Creighton University); and Mark E. Ware (Creighton University; APA, 1987).

CUE's interest in this issue was prompted by a resolution introduced by the Massachusetts Psychological Association (MPA), on behalf of its Board of Academic and Scientific Affairs, at the August 1983 Council of Representatives meeting. This resolution requested that CUE review the current status of the undergraduate psychology curriculum and provide undergraduate departments, which were experiencing pressures to respond to vocationalism, with direction in curriculum development. Particularly, the resolution called on CUE to clarify

> (1) the role and purpose of the undergraduate psychology major in relation to traditional liberal arts education (and preparation for graduate school in psychology) and preparation for a bachelor-degree-level job in a psychology-related field, and (2) whether APA should set forth

guidelines for curriculum models in undergraduate psychology (with an accompanying rationale). In addition, if such guidelines are deemed desirable, these should be forthcoming along with a timetable for their development and promulgation. (APA, 1987, p. 101)

At the request of the APA Council of Representatives, CUE formulated the following resolution, approved by the Council in August 1985, in response to the MPA request:

The four-year baccalaureate program in psychology is fundamentally a liberal arts curriculum. Neither vocational nor preprofessional training should be a primary goal of undergraduate education in psychology. This position is consistent with the findings of the 1961 Michigan Conference, chaired by W. J. McKeachie and John E. Milholland, which concluded "that a basically liberal arts curriculum is best for students who plan to go on to professional training, to graduate work in psychology, or directly into a vocation."

The American Psychological Association should not prescribe specific course requirements for the undergraduate major in psychology. Such an action would seriously intrude upon the academic freedom of departments and faculty members. However, it is agreed that APA should continue to monitor undergraduate education in psychology by means of periodic surveys. By this means APA and its Committee on Undergraduate Education can continue to weigh the possibility of developing guidelines or models for the curriculum. (APA, 1987, p. 94)

Margaret Lloyd was asked to prepare a briefing memorandum and proposal on the issue of undergraduate curriculum models for CUE's review at its September 1987 meeting. The proposal, adopted by CUE, recommended seeking approval for a national conference on undergraduate education to address curricular and other issues rather than making recommendations about curriculum models. Members of CUE concluded that the formulation of undergraduate curriculum models was too large a task for CUE and one that needed the broad-based input that a conference could provide. Moreover, it had been 26 years since the last conference (Michigan).

As conceived by CUE, the conference would focus on three critical concerns in undergraduate psychology: the curriculum, teaching, and advising. Margaret Lloyd prepared a draft of the conference proposal to be submitted to the Education and Training Board. Later that fall, the Board approved, in principle, a national conference.

During the spring of 1988, incoming CUE member Thomas McGovern (Arizona State University West, formerly at Virginia Commonwealth University) worked with Margaret Lloyd, who by then had completed her CUE term, and developed a more detailed conference proposal to submit to APA's Education and Training Board. After slight modifications, this proposal was approved by both the Education and Training Board and the APA Board of Directors.

Thomas McGovern also wrote and submitted a grant proposal to FIPSE, on behalf of the APA, to fund the planning (1990–1991), implementation (1991), and dissemination (1991–1992) phases of the national conference. Two external reviewers of the proposal for FIPSE praised the proposal but recommended not to fund it because they felt that the APA should use its own resources to underwrite the conference (T. McGovern, personal communication, November 15, 1991). Subsequently, the APA, through its Board of Directors and the Council of Representatives, committed $10,000 to support conference planning in 1990 and 1991 (APA, 1989).

During 1989, CUE continued to plan the conference. In December 1989, on the basis of APA's Interim Board of Educational Affairs (IBEA) recommendation, the Board of Directors appointed the following individuals to the conference steering committee: Andrew Crider (Williams College); Barbara Nodine (Beaver College); Wilbert McKeachie; Pamela T. Reid (City University of New York Graduate School, formerly at the University of Tennessee at Chattanooga); and Richard M. Suinn (Colorado State University). Ludy T. Benjamin, Jr. (Texas A&M University) was appointed IBEA liaison to the steering committee. CUE members who served as ex officio members of the steering committee were Douglas Bernstein; Jane Halonen (Alverno College); Thomas McGovern, chair; and Carole Wade (APA, 1989). J. Roy Hopkins (St. Mary's College of Maryland) later joined the steering committee as coordinator of arrangements at the conference site. Cynthia Baum, Director of the APA's Education in Psychology Office, and Martha Braswell, staff member in the Education Directorate, also played significant roles in conference planning.

In March 1990, the 10-member steering committee met to develop the basic plan for the conference. Seven core issues were identified as those around which the conference would be planned: curriculum, advising, active learning, recruitment and retention of ethnic minority students, faculty development, program assessment, and faculty networks.

The St. Mary's conference was different from previous conferences in several important respects. First, it was much broader in scope than previous conferences. In addition to the curriculum, six other concerns were also discussed. Second, the selection of conference participants was a more open process than had been true in the past. (Interested individuals submitted application materials and most delegates were selected from these applications.) Third, a large number of individuals attended the St. Mary's conference: 60 participants (49 invited psychologists and 11 steering committee members) and 2 APA staff members. Fourth, there was diversity in gender and ethnicity among the participants, mirroring the increasing diversity among psychologists since the first undergraduate conferences were held in the early 1950s and 1960s. That is, all participants in the first two conferences were White men; by 1990, 2 of the 5 members of the AAC task force were White women. Among the 60 St. Mary's participants, 28 (47%) were women and 11 (18%) were members of ethnic minority groups. A final distinguishing feature of the St. Mary's conference was the participation of 5 faculty members from 2-year colleges, 2 high school psychology teachers, 2 international members (Canada and Puerto Rico), and 1 non-psychologist from the American Association of Higher Education.

Conference Recommendations

Curriculum. The St. Mary's report reaffirmed the importance of maintaining psychology's symbiotic relations with other liberal arts disciplines (Brewer et al., 1992). The report stressed that the general goal of undergraduate education in psychology is to teach students to think as scientists about behavior and experience. It also identified six specific goals of the curriculum that complement this overarching goal: attention to human diversity, breadth and depth of knowledge, methodological competence, practical experience and applications, communication skills, and sensitivity to ethical issues.

The St. Mary's report emphasized that the curriculum should be planned to accomplish all of these goals. It suggested that the psychology major should consist of four groups of courses, representing increasing levels of knowledge and skills, to be taken sequentially. The four groups are the introductory course, methodology courses, content courses, and integrative or capstone experiences.

Ideally, the introductory course should be a prerequisite for all other psychology courses, and it should include a survey of topics and methods that evince the discipline's breadth of concepts, principles, and theories. Even so, certain programs might offer the course with applied focus. Therefore, beginning with the first course the St. Mary's conference recognized the importance of flexibility in meeting students' different needs.

Usually taken in the second or third year of study, methodology courses were viewed as pivotal. They should cover the research approaches represented by experimental, correlational, and case study techniques. The St. Mary's report stressed the importance of firsthand data collection and analysis but recognized that some 2-year schools might lack the facilities to provide this experience. In such cases, students who transferred to 4-year schools as psychology majors would be encouraged to take these courses as soon as possible in their new programs.

Statistics and methodology courses should cover statistics, research design, and psychometric methods, and they should be prerequisites for some of the content courses. The content courses should be structured to ensure that students are exposed to the natural science and social science approaches to the discipline, including basic principles and applications.

The St. Mary's report included suggestions, which were neither prescriptive nor proscriptive, for grouping content courses and requiring students to take a certain number of courses from each group. These suggestions were included to illustrate possible ways of incorporating breadth of coverage while allowing flexibility for accommodating students' different career interests.

Integrative experiences for seniors could include internships, research projects, and capstone courses. The St. Mary's report mentioned examples and indicated that some integrative courses might be combined with an internship or a research project in a senior seminar.

One unique feature of the St. Mary's report was a section dealing with the community-college curriculum. It discussed differences between 2- and 4-year programs as well as problems that arise when students transfer as psychology majors from the former to the latter. Another distinctive feature was the section on interdisciplinary and service courses. Recognizing the value of such courses, the report expressed a concern that they not make excessive demands on a department's resources at the expense of the basic program in psychology.

Emphasizing diversity and flexibility throughout, the curriculum report concluded with recommendations and suggestions that highlighted the conference participants' thinking about the undergraduate curriculum in psychology.

Active learning. The conference report recommended that undergraduate psychology instructors use active learning strategies when appropriate: simulations, demonstrations, discussions, debates, games, problem solving, conducting research, writing, computer use, interactive lectures, internships, and so forth (Mathie et al., 1992). The report also included specific recommendations for actions to be taken, at the national and local levels, to promote the implementation of active learning in psychology classrooms.

The report also discussed the benefits of active learning for students (fostering intrinsic motivation in learning, increasing cognitive demands, and improving interpersonal communication and social skills) and faculty (increased satisfaction with classes, closer monitoring of students' learning, and improved student evaluations). In addition, the report reviewed issues to be considered in implementing active learning strategies as well as problems that can arise in using such approaches and ways to address these problems.

Advising. The conference recommended that advising programs should include the following components: (a) responsivity to the needs of a diverse student population; (b) faculty training; (c) rewards for excellence in advising; and (d) both informational advising (giving students information about curriculum and institutional policies) and developmental advising (helping students to clarify their values, interests, and abilities as related to their life goals; see Ware's chapter on collegiate career advising in this book; Ware et al., 1992). In addition, the report described models of advising delivery systems, advising materials, and adviser training in three areas of advising: academic, postbaccalaureate career opportunities, and postbaccalaureate educational opportunities.

Faculty development.   The conference recommended that faculty development programs be based on the following assumptions: (a) that all three faculty roles—teaching, scholarship, and service—are complementary and all should be rewarded; (b) that faculty development is a lifelong process and faculty members should be committed to their own continuing education; (c) that opportunities for continuing education and incentives for faculty to pursue these opportunities should be supported by the institution; and (d) that the particular talents and interests of individual faculty members should be recognized and developed (Fretz et al., 1992).

In addition, the report described a model for faculty development that could be used either by individuals, departments, universities, or the profession at large. Also described were a number of structures (e.g., committees, centers), methods (e.g., courses, orientation programs), and techniques (e.g., mentoring, teaching circles) that could be used in a variety of settings.

Faculty networks.   The participants recommended a number of ways to enhance communication and collegiality among psychology faculty at all levels of education (high schools to research universities) as a means of diminishing the intellectual and professional isolation increasingly felt by faculty (Weiten et al., 1992). The report described a broad range of networking strategies that could be implemented by national organizations as well individuals: workshops, institutes, teaching conferences, student research conferences, local consortia, academic alliances, faculty exchange programs, teaching programs at national and regional conventions, outreach mail campaigns, and computer bulletin boards.

The report also recommended ways to improve the dissemination of information regarding professional development opportunities and to increase the number and diversity of faculty who might avail themselves of these opportunities.

Minority students.   The participants endorsed the idea that diversity in the student population should provide benefits to the science and practice of psychology as well as to minority populations (Puente et al., 1992). They recommended that psychology curricula should reflect the diversity of human behavior and experience by offering courses that deal with the psychology of women, ethnic minorities, older adulthood, and so forth. Ideally, such material would be integrated throughout the standard content courses of the discipline.

The participants also recommended that psychology departments should regularly evaluate their progress in developing resources, support systems, and faculty awareness of the need for recruitment and retention of ethnic minority students and faculty members.

Outcomes assessment. The participants recommended that psychology departments should develop assessment plans in order to improve teaching and learning and to foster student growth and faculty development (Halpern et al., 1992). Although no single method of assessment was recommended for all departments, any assessment plan should be designed to promote faculty ownership and to reduce the misuse of assessment findings.

More specifically, the report discussed forms of assessment that show the greatest promise for assessing psychological abilities and knowledge, described factors to be addressed in creating an effective assessment plan, and explained how to create an assessment program on an individual campus.

TRENDS IN UNDERGRADUATE CURRICULUM RECOMMENDATIONS

Our discussion of this topic is limited in several ways. For one thing, we do not consider recommendations from surveys, only those from conferences or study groups: the Cornell conference, the Michigan conference, the Association of American Colleges' task force, and the St. Mary's conference. Second, because only the St. Mary's conference devoted any significant attention to issues other than the undergraduate curriculum, our discussion is restricted to trends in national conference recommendations about the curriculum. Our discussion is organized around three themes concerning the psychology major: assumptions, objectives, and structure and content.

Assumptions About the Psychology Major

Several common assumptions underlie reports of all of the national conferences. First, psychology has consistently been viewed as a discipline in the tradition of the liberal arts and sciences. Nonetheless, questions have been raised about whether the definition of liberal education may need rethinking—in the AAC report—and about whether the present liberal arts curricula reflect the liberal arts philosophy (Kulik, 1973). A second prevailing assumption is that research methods and data analysis form the core of the major.

Furthermore, breadth of exposure to the discipline is typically emphasized over depth. One exception is the AAC report's use of the less-is-more principle in designing the major and individual courses. The AAC study group advanced the idea that the critical goal of teaching is to help students develop a conceptual framework that embraces relevant facts and concepts rather than isolated bits of knowledge, and to help them achieve a base for lifelong learning rather than a static, encyclopedic knowledge of the current state of the field. (McGovern et al., 1991, p. 601)

According to the study group, a useful way to achieve this goal is to expose students repeatedly to less content—the less-is-more principle. Hence, the AAC curriculum models emphasize depth over breadth.

A fourth consistent assumption recognizes the importance of considering "contextual" issues in curriculum planning (i.e., size and type of institution, size and orientation of the department, nature of the student body, etc.). Thus, particular models for the major are proposed with the understanding that they will be adapted to meet local conditions.

Objectives for the Psychology Major

There is relative agreement between the Cornell and Michigan conferences concerning specific objectives for the undergraduate psychology major (e.g., knowledge of substantive content; rigorous habits of thought; desirable attitudes, such as intellectual curiosity, respect for others, social responsibility). Objectives suggested by the AAC group and the St. Mary's conference are mostly consistent with earlier recommendations, although they are stated differently. Consider, for example, the following objectives recommended by the AAC task force: knowledge base in the content of psychology, thinking skills, language skills, information-gathering and synthesis skills, research methods and statistical skills, and knowledge of the history of psychology. Also, note these similar objectives from the St. Mary's conference: acquiring a scientific understanding of behavior, being exposed to breadth and depth of content in the discipline, developing methodological competence, and acquiring communication skills.

There are, however, some differences among the various conferences' recommendations. For example, the two most recent conferences explicitly recommended sensitizing students to relevant ethical issues in psychology and to "human diversity" issues. The AAC report recommended accomplishing this goal by teaching critical thinking about these issues as well as relevant interpersonal skills, whereas the St. Mary's conference preferred a cognitive context. Although participants in the two earlier conferences were concerned about such issues, they did not address them directly. Instead, these objectives were included, at least by implication, under their objective of promoting desirable attitudes.

Another difference is the AAC report's recommendation to develop increased self-knowledge, interpersonal awareness and sensitivity, and the ability to work effectively in groups. This suggestion flies in the face of the recommendation of the two earlier reports that such objectives have no place in a liberal arts program in psychology. The reason for this dramatic shift is that there now exists in psychology an empirical base of knowledge to justify the inclusion of such courses (T. McGovern, personal communication, November 25, 1991).

Yet another discrepancy is the recommendation of the St. Mary's conference to provide opportunities for students to apply knowledge and for practical experiences. Although the application of knowledge is emphasized in the AAC report, McGovern et al. (1991) did not list it as an explicit objective.

Structure and Content of the Psychology Major

In the 1950s, participants in the Cornell conference agreed on a single model for the undergraduate psychology major. Some 10 years later, however, the Michigan participants struggled to agree on one model, but they finally settled on suggesting three different models.

During the late 1960s and early 1970s, so many nontraditional courses were being introduced and at such a rapid pace that it was impossible to make any prescriptive statements about the psychology major. Rather, the best that could be done was to conduct a national survey of undergraduate psychology departments and their curricular practices and to publish a summary of the results (Kulik, 1973).

Recommendations of the two latest conferences suggest greater agreement on the nature of the undergraduate psychology major in the 1990s. The AAC recommended two models based on the less is more principle: a more traditional, generalist model and a thematic model with variations. The St. Mary's participants embraced a single model that favors breadth over depth but that allows flexibility to suit the needs of particular programs.

To provide a conceptual framework for the information that follows, we use the one suggested in the AAC report—namely, that most psychology curricula have a beginning, a middle, and an end. To start at the beginning, all of the conferences recommended an introductory course as the first course in the major. There is also agreement that the course should be broad based, surveying methodological approaches and reflecting psychology's diversity. The one variation on this recommendation is found in the thematic model of the AAC report. In this model, students study in depth a specific content area, such as developmental, social, or health psychology. For a major with a developmental theme, in place of the traditional introductory course, students might take a course in life span developmental psychology that covers most of the topics in a traditional introductory course but with a distinctly developmental perspective.

In addition, there is general agreement that the introductory course should focus on content rather than practical applications. The St. Mary's report, however, suggested that a more applied focus might be appropriate for some programs.

The middle of the curriculum typically consists of intermediate-level courses in methodology and the principal content areas. Methodology has consistently been given a central role in the undergraduate major (and, in the St. Mary's conference recommendations, in the minor as well). This emphasis is consistent with the AAC report's statement that if there is a canon in psychology, "it is probably in evolving methodologies for the study of behavior, emotion, and cognition" (McGovern et al., 1991, p. 604).

A noteworthy development concerning methodology in both the AAC and St. Mary's reports is that psychometrics has been added to statistics and research methods as part of the methodology sequence. (The Michigan report advocated giving this topic more salience in the curriculum because of the increasingly important role of testing in American society, but it did not suggest that it be part of the required methodology sequence.)

Concerning recommendations about content courses at the intermediate level, all but the AAC report shared an emphasis on breadth of exposure over depth. Both the Cornell and Michigan conferences recommended a common core of courses, although the Michigan group was more divided on the nature of the common core. That is, the Cornell conference suggested four specific courses— perception, motivation, cognition, and ability—but the Michigan conference left to a department's discretion the decision of what specific courses to include, as long as they provided "sufficiently broad coverage to touch all the major areas of psychology" (McKeachie & Milholland, 1961, p. 91).

As the content areas in psychology have proliferated, specifying the particular courses that should constitute the subject matter core of the discipline has become increasingly difficult. It was, in part, because of this problem that the AAC task force suggested a "depth" model rather than one based on breadth. That is, they argued that the splintering of the discipline has made it impossible to design a curriculum that allows for breadth that is inclusive. Moreover, they took the position that the inclusion of learning goals beyond a knowledge base required that depth be emphasized over breadth (T. McGovern, personal communication, November 25, 1991). The St. Mary's conference, leaning more in the direction of a breadth model, dealt with the problem of diversity within the discipline by recommending that students be required to take courses in both the natural and social science domains of psychology.

Coming now to the end of the psychology major requirements, all conferences recommended an integrative experience for senior majors, although the nature of the experience varies. Inclusion of practical or applied work as an integrative experience for psychology majors is a recent trend. The Cornell and Michigan conferences recommended a traditional course that would help the student "achieve an over-all picture of the field of psychology and . . . of psychology's contributions to understanding behavior and experience" (Buxton et al., 1952, p. 12). Such courses might include history and systems, advanced general psychology, or senior seminar.

Both the AAC and St. Mary's reports discussed two types of integrative experiences: (a) traditional classroom experiences as found in the courses just mentioned and (b) practical experiences, such as a research project or an internship, ideally in the context of a seminar with a senior paper. The first type of experience emphasizes the integration of intellectual concepts, and the second involves putting into practice accumulated knowledge, skills, and ethical sensitivities (McGovern et al., 1991).

CONCLUSION

The earlier conferences advocated that the undergraduate curriculum be rooted in the liberal arts tradition, emphasize breadth over depth of exposure to content areas in the discipline, and include a solid grounding in scientific methodology. They also endorsed the view that a liberal arts curriculum was best for all students, whether they planned to go to graduate or professional school or to seek immediate employment.

By the 1970s, demographic changes in higher education and changes in the discipline itself precluded prescriptive statements about the requirements for the undergraduate major. In the 1980s, with only the benefit of descriptive information provided by the 1973 Kulik report, psychology faculty were increasingly frustrated by a lack of national recommendations to guide them in their struggles with curricular issues in their individual departments.

In the 1990s, diversity issues and further changes in the discipline required attention. The AAC and St. Mary's reports provided similar but different conceptualizations of the undergraduate psychology curriculum that continues to evolve.

REFERENCES

American Psychological Association. (1980). *Agenda book for Committee on Undergraduate Education meeting: March 14–15, 1980*. Washington, DC: Author.

American Psychological Association. (1981a). *Agenda book for Committee on Undergraduate Education meeting: February 27–28, 1981*. Washington, DC: Author.

American Psychological Association. (1981b). *Agenda book for Council of Representatives meeting: January 23–25, 1981*. Washington, DC: Author.

American Psychological Association. (1982). *Agenda book for Committee on Undergraduate Education meeting: February 26–27, 1982*. Washington, DC: Author.

American Psychological Association. (1983). *Results: Phase I survey of undergraduate department chairs.* Washington, DC: Author.

American Psychological Association. (1987). *Agenda book for Committee on Undergraduate Education meeting: March 6–7, 1987.* Washington, DC: Author.

American Psychological Association. (1989). *Agenda book for Board of Directors meeting: December 1–3, 1989.* Washington, DC: Author.

Association of American Colleges. (1985). *Integrity in the college curriculum: A report to the academic community.* Washington, DC: Author.

Association of American Colleges. (1990). *Liberal learning and the arts and sciences major: Volume 2. Reports from the field.* Washington, DC: Author.

Brewer, C. L., in collaboration with Hopkins, R., Kimble, G., Matlin, M., McCann, L., McNeil, O., Nodine, B., Nichols Quinn, V., & Saundra (1992). *Curriculum.* Manuscript submitted for publication.

Buxton, C. E., Cofer, C. N., Gustad, J. W., MacLeod, R. B., McKeachie, W. J., & Wolfle, D. (1952). *Improving undergraduate instruction in psychology.* New York: Macmillan.

Fretz, B., in collaboration with Garibaldi, A., Glidden, L., McKeachie, W., Moritsugu, J., Quina, K., Reich, J., & Sholley, B. (1992). *The compleat scholar: Faculty development for those who teach psychology.* Manuscript submitted for publication.

Halpern, D. F., in collaboration with Appleby, D., Beers, S., Cowan, C., Furedy, J., Halonen, J., Horton, C., Peden, B., & Pittenger, D. (1992). *Targeting outcomes: Covering your assessment needs.* Manuscript submitted for publication.

Kulik, J. (1973). *Undergraduate education in psychology.* Washington, DC: American Psychological Association.

Mathie, V. A., in collaboration with Beins, B., Benjamin, L., Ewing, M., Iijema Hall, C., Henderson, B., McAdam, D., & Smith, R. (1992). *Promoting active learning in psychology courses.* Manuscript submitted for publication.

McGovern, T. V., Furumoto, L., Halpern, D. F., Kimble, G. A., & McKeachie, W. J. (1991). Liberal education, study in depth, and the arts and sciences major—Psychology. *American Psychologist, 46,* 598–605.

McKeachie, W. J., & Milholland, J. E. (1961). *Undergraduate curricula in psychology.* Fair Lawn, NJ: Scott, Foresman.

Puente, A. E., in collaboration with Blanch, E., Candland, D., Denmark, F., Laman, C., Lutsky, N., Reid, P., & Schiavo, S. (1992). *Toward a psychology of variance: Increasing the presence and understanding of ethnic minorities in psychology.* Manuscript submitted for publication.

Scheirer, C. J., & Rogers, A. M. (1985). *The undergraduate psychology curriculum: 1984.* Washington, DC: American Psychological Association.

Ware, M. E., in collaboration with Busch-Rossnagel, N., Crider, A., Gray-Shellberg, L., Hale, K., Lloyd, M., Rivera-Medina, E., & Sgro, J. (1992). *Developing and improving advising: Challenges to prepare students for life.* Manuscript submitted for publication.

Weiten, W., in collaboration with Davis, S., Jegerski, J., Kasschau, R., Mandel, B., & Wade, C. (1992). *From isolation to community: Increasing communication and collegiality among psychology teachers.* Manuscript submitted for publication.

11

EDUCATION AND TRAINING CONFERENCES IN GRADUATE EDUCATION

CYNTHIA BELAR

Using principles of contextualism, Altman (1990) provided an excellent historical perspective on the discipline of psychology. His work carefully detailed the centrifugal and centripetal trends within psychology in the context of social, political, and educational issues of the time. As he noted, centripetal and centrifugal forces are not inherently bad or good, although excessively dominant centripetal or centrifugal forces could lead to either stagnation or disintegration of the discipline. In this chapter, I use his work and that of Matarazzo (1983) as bases for describing the six major national conferences on graduate education sponsored by the American Psychological Association (APA) over the past 100 years. These conferences are presented chronologically.

As noted by Bickman (1990), psychologists have historically used

---

The author has had the opportunity to play a significant role in four of the training conferences described in this chapter and the next, as she was a steering committee member for one, chaired the steering committee for two, and delivered a keynote address at the fourth. But her greatest resources in preparing these chapters were her experiences with Irwin Altman and Joseph Matarazzo, whose knowledge, wisdom, and perspective of the field have enriched her understanding.

national conferences both as a problem-solving mechanism and as a mechanism to introduce change in the nature of graduate education. One could also assert that outcomes of graduate education conferences reflect only the current state of the discipline and that what they actually accomplish is a formalization of current practices in education and training. Although it is difficult to judge the impact of a conference per se, it could be that a conference is more likely to be perceived as successful if it reflects the consensus in the field.

PSYCHOLOGY PRIOR TO 1960

Altman (1990) viewed the period prior to 1900 as being primarily centrifugal in nature. He noted that early psychological scholars had little sense of an academic discipline with common values, methods, and approaches and that they were often identified with other fields of study (e.g., philosophy, biology). Many tended to work in a noninstitutional, independent fashion.

Altman described how centripetal forces began to gather strength in psychology in the late 1800s (e.g., the establishment of the American Psychological Association in 1892) and how these forces were congruent with broad societal trends during the first half of the 20th century. Despite political, military, and economic crises, American society was unified in purpose and the average person had a fundamental faith in the democractic system. The heterogeneity associated with the wave of immigration was unified by the philosophy of integration into the American "melting pot."

Within the discipline of psychology, there was a movement away from introspection and phenomenology toward a logical positivist value system in research methodology. The field was unified by the commitment to quantitative, experimental, laboratory-oriented research methods emphasizing operational definitions, the search for antecedent—consequent relationships, and the discovery of laws of behavior. Psychology departments tended to be small and were not often organized by specialty area. Graduate students were educated broadly and tended to identify with the field as a whole. Qualifying examinations were often departmentwide. Small in number, the relatively new field of psychology was perhaps searching for a critical mass in order to present a unified face to the world.

Of course, there were centrifugal forces as well, most notably those reflecting tensions between academicians and practitioners. According to Matarazzo, the American Association for Applied Psychology (AAAP) was formed in 1938 because of the belief that the APA was not adequately addressing the interests of practitioners. "However, World War II helped APA and AAAP leaders forget their differences and . . . again amalgamate into a single national organization" (Matarazzo, 1987, cited in Altman,

1990, p. 43). Psychologists agreed that they were psychologists first and academics or professionals second. During this period of dominance of centripetal forces, there were three major education and training conferences.

Boulder Conference (Raimy, 1950)

The historic Conference on Training in Clinical Psychology is more commonly referred to as the Boulder conference. Held in Boulder, Colorado, in August 1949, 72 invited delegates met for 2 weeks and forged the framework for the majority of clinical psychology training programs in existence today.

According to Altman (1990), the Boulder conference was the capstone of centripetal forces in American psychology that had gained momentum since the turn of the century. The immediate forces that led to the Boulder conference were service driven in nature. There were numerous veterans returning from World War II who were in need of psychological services, but there were not enough well-trained clinical psychologists and other mental health professionals to meet these needs. The Veterans Administration and the United States Public Health Service requested the APA to identify the universities that provided doctoral-level training in clinical psychology and to develop a set of standards that could be used by other universities that wished to develop programs that would qualify for listing as a clinical psychology training program.

The hallmark of the training model articulated at this conference was that the clinical psychologist must be trained as both a scientist and a professional and that the training model needed to integrate both a university and an internship experience. This model of training subsequently has been referred to as the Boulder model. It was a conclusion reflecting the centripetal forces described earlier.

Boulder model programs were to be structured as a 4-year combination of academic and applied training, followed by a 1-year internship and then the PhD degree. As summarized by Dana and May (1987):

> Graduate education was to include general psychology (systematic, experimental, social psychology), clinical psychology (theory, method, technique), field work (variety of problems and levels of responsibility), and research. Research was emphasized as a basis for understanding human behavior, improving diagnostic techniques, developing treatment methods and ultimately focusing upon prevention or mental hygiene. Twelve areas of clinical core content were proposed: human physiology; personality theory; developmental psychology (biological, social, cultural determinants); social relations (social psychology, sociology, economics, anthropology); psychopathology; personality appraisal, clinical medicine and clinical psychiatry (medical model); psychotherapy and remedial procedures; clinical research methodology;

professional and interprofessional relationships; community resources and organizations; practicum and internship experiences. (p. 8)

Interestingly, although general training in the theory and practice of psychotherapy was to be provided, psychotherapy training was to be largely postdoctoral, but postdoctoral training at that time was not yet widely available. Specialization by client population or professional activity was not recommended, and students were to be continuously exposed to content involving both psychopathology and normal behavior.

Stanford Conference (Strother, 1956, cited in Matarazzo, 1983)

The impetus for the next conference, the Institute on Education and Training for Psychological Contributions to Mental Health, was the recommendation made at the Boulder conference that a conference be held within 5 years to review the educational model proposed by the earlier conference. Delegates met at Stanford University in August 1955 and discussed the success of the model, including its strengths and weaknesses. After 4 days of discussion, delegates reaffirmed the recommendations of the Boulder conference.

Miami Beach Conference (Roe, Gustad, Moore, Ross, & Skodak, 1959, cited in Matarazzo, 1983)

The December 1958 Miami Beach Conference on Graduate Education in Psychology was the first graduate education conference, to my knowledge, to deal with issues relevant to all fields of psychology and not just to a specialty area (e.g., clinical psychology). Delegates from a wide range of academic and applied settings were invited for 8 days of discussion on a broad range of topics, including whether there should be a common core to graduate education in psychology, what the nature of this core should be, the extent to which training in psychology could serve society, and issues related to societal controls and educational standards (e.g., licensing, accreditation). Once again, delegates reaffirmed the scientist–practitioner model of education and training for professional psychology.

PSYCHOLOGY: 1960S AND 1970S

During the 1960s and 1970s, American society experienced massive upheavals and significant centrifugal trends. Traditional authority was challenged, leaders were assassinated, the presidency was tarnished, the nation was divided in its support of international policies, and the traditional family structure underwent significant changes associated with sex role diversification and breakdown of nuclear family units. The "melting pot" concept of American society was replaced by the concept of "pluralism," with emphases on ethnic identity and diversity that have continued to the present day. Graduate programs became more concerned about ensuring diversity among faculty and students, and the curriculum incorporated courses on cultural values and ethnic differences.

The 1960s and early 1970s were also periods of expansion and prosperity for higher education. Enrollments mushroomed, government grants were plentiful, scientific endeavors were valued, and the social sciences became increasingly viewed as resources for solving significant social problems in America. Societal upheavals had campus counterparts in student protests, student participation in academic governance, and nontraditional curricula. University departments became increasingly self-centered, with faculty being reinforced for publications, grants, and national visibility rather than excellence in teaching or participation in university affairs. "Over time, the 'university' became a 'multiversity' with entrepreneurial academic units and individuals proceeding along their own separate paths" (Altman, 1990, p. 51).

Within psychology, departments grew and formed specialty areas with their own students, organizational structures, course requirements, and space. Isolation of subfields was often the result. The availability of research support made it possible for students to be financially supported and educated by a single faculty member throughout their tenure in a program. Clinical psychology pressed for increased recognition as an independent profession, human resources for the delivery of mental health services were lacking, and psychologists appeared to be more clearly articulating a sense of social commitment.

The psychology training conferences of the 1960s and 1970s reflected the sociopolitical unrest, diversification, and special-interest groups of the times. The first anticipated the social turmoil and divisiveness in the field yet reaffirmed traditional values; the second was marked by the zeitgeist to overthrow the "establishment."

Chicago Conference (Hoch, Ross, & Winder, 1966)

The Conference on the Professional Preparation of Clinical Psychologists was held in Chicago in 1965. Many of the debates during this 6-day period were more sociopolitical than academic in nature because delegates focused on how to prepare psychologists to be responsive to human needs in a rapidly changing society. Conference participants clearly opposed training at the master's level for the autonomous practice of clinical psychology, although they did support psychology's participation in the training of other subdoctoral disciplines.

For graduate education in clinical psychology, delegates endorsed the establishment of psychological service settings with close ties to university departments. These centers were to be designed to provide training opportunities for graduate students, to serve significant social needs of the community, and to be a setting for the clinical research of faculty. The endorsement of these settings was also an endorsement of psychology as an independent profession. Presently, virtually every accredited doctoral program in clinical psychology has close ties with a psychological services center, most of which are actually housed within the university's department of psychology.

Along with the support for psychological service settings, the Chicago conference recommended diversification of training opportunities (e.g., more than one professional function, various methods of intervention, diverse populations, community action programs). This recommendation was for diversity within PhD programs and not with respect to other models of training, as has sometimes been suggested. However, the hint of a schism in the field was present, as delegates seriously debated the plan for a program leading to the PsyD degree, which would substitute professional training and experience for the research dissertation in psychology.

In the end, conference participants endorsed the scientist–practitioner model as the paradigm for graduate education and training for clinical psychology. In fact, delegates recommended that "research training be so embedded in the program that research orientation becomes an integral part of the clinical psychologist's mode of professional behavior" (Hoch et al., 1966, p. 48). However, delegates "recognized that other pilot or experimental programs in university psychology departments may be attempted" (Hoch et al., 1966, p. 51) and agreed that the results of these experiments should speak for themselves.

Vail Conference (Korman, 1974)

After the Chicago conference, a number of criticisms and internal conflicts continued to escalate within the field. For example, many psychologists continued to express strong dissatisfaction with training in traditional scientist–practitioner programs, especially with respect to their responsivity to social issues. In 1969, the Black Student Psychological Association presented APA with demands including a plan for recruitment of Black students and faculty into psychology. Portions of the field complained of disenfranchisement because people trained at the master's level were endorsed for full membership in the APA in 1971, only to have that endorsement reversed the following year. The Task Force on the Status of Women in Psychology rendered a report in 1972 that contained substantive proposals concerning curricula, recruitment, and issues of sex discrimination.

Mounting tensions culminated in a call for another national conference. The National Conference on Levels and Patterns of Professional

Training in Psychology was supported by the National Institute of Mental Health (NIMH) and held in Vail, Colorado, for 6 days in July 1973. Many of the delegates to this conference were chosen specifically because they did not represent "the establishment" in psychology; thus, a significant number were women and ethnic minorities. Matarazzo (1983) noted that the meeting was marked by acrimonious debate concerning sociopolitical issues such as the future roles in psychology of women, ethnic and racial minorities, and the less affluent. These were issues reflecting concerns in the greater American society as well.

The Vail conference produced 150 resolutions related to education and training in professional psychology, many of which underscored the need for cultural diversity and social responsivity in graduate education. However, there were two major departures from the conclusions of previous conferences; one difference was related to multilevel training and the other to models of training.

The first departure was the acknowledgment of those with master's degrees as psychologists and as professionals. Master's-level professional programs were encouraged to develop, and multilevel training systems were endorsed. Although programs training at the master's level have continued and subdoctoral psychological service providers continue to be of great interest, American psychologists have subsequently voted that the doctorate is the required level of training for an individual to be considered a psychologist.

The other major departure was the explicit endorsement of PsyD training programs as an appropriate model for graduate education in professional psychology. These programs, with their primary emphasis on the direct delivery of professional services, could be housed in a variety of settings (e.g., departments of education, medical schools, freestanding schools) in addition to traditional university departments of psychology. According to the conference report author (Korman, 1974), the Vail conference did not depreciate the value of the scientist–practitioner model. "It is important to view the Conference's entire work in the light of a continuing ideological commitment to the tradition of empiricism and as a clear affirmation of the fundamental importance of the scientific endeavor" (Korman, 1974, p. 442). However, most would agree that the impact on graduate education in psychology has been to facilitate, for a large number of professional psychologists, the provision of basic education in the discipline of psychology outside of university and research settings by part-time practitioner faculty.

However, the proliferation of freestanding, tuition-dependent professional schools, and the development of "universities without walls" with a do-it-yourself curriculum, reflected the "do-your-own-thing" tenor of the times and might have had little to do with the Vail conference itself.

PSYCHOLOGY AFTER 1980

By the mid-1970s, the boom in higher education was over and resources for higher education were declining. The economy faltered, enrollment decreased, and government funding dwindled. Faculty salaries did not keep pace with economic changes and even the tenure system was threatened. Altman (1990) believed that these financial difficulties contributed to the centrifugal trajectory of higher education that was already underway. Under financial threat, many departments, programs, and research laboratories "pulled the wagons into a circle" and became more insular and adversarial.

In an attempt to salvage the system, universities began to focus on "economic development" using the technical and professional parts of the university (e.g., engineering, business, computer sciences, medicine, law, pharmacy). University administrations increasingly encouraged "technology transfer" and the use of private venture capital. Altman (1990) warned of the possibility that as faculty members become more entrepreneurial, their ties with students, teaching, and the university will be further weakened and the university will become just a convenient base of operation. Altman also noted the opportunities that these "university practices" present for the infusion of new ideas and the development of innovations in education.

Within psychology, centrifugal trends have been especially apparent in the continued development of specialties and the proliferation of tuition-dependent, freestanding professional schools of psychology. According to Matarazzo (1983), it was in response to the hordes of professional psychologists coming from these diverse educational backgrounds that groups such as state licensing boards and the National Register of Health Service Providers in Psychology attempted to set basic formal educational credentials (including lists of required courses) in order to determine whether a candidate had been fully trained as a psychologist. The focus on courses by these credentialing groups differed from the focus of previous psychology training conferences; the latter (as well as APA accreditation criteria) had delineated bodies of knowledge, but not particular course requirements. Graduate education soon chafed under the perceived pressures from outside agencies to provide specific courses in the psychology curriculum, and the split between academic and professional parts of the field widened.

Psychologists who were concerned with the growth of various specialties and standards for professional psychology organized conferences for specific subareas of psychology or memberships of their organizations. I now briefly summarize some of these.

Arden House Conference (Stone, 1983)

The National Working Conference on Education and Training in Health Psychology was held in 1983 at Arden House, New York, in response to the rapid development of the field of health psychology over the prior decade. This growth was partly attributable to scientific advances in the understanding of relations among emotional, cognitive, affective, and behavioral variables and physical health; the spiraling of health-care costs and data concerning medical cost offset of psychological services; and the surgeon general's support for behavioral disease prevention strategies and healthy life-style approaches. Although 42 psychology doctoral programs had been identified that offered educational opportunities in the field (Belar, Wilson, & Hughes, 1982), no standards for such training had yet been established. Delegates to the Arden House conference represented many different subareas of psychology, yet they readily agreed on the following: (a) Health psychology education and training should follow the scientist–practitioner model; (b) core psychology as specified by APA accreditation criteria must be included in the curriculum; (c) health psychology didactic and practicum experiences should be part of the core curriculum (e.g., health policy, models of health and disease); (d) those who wish to provide professional services should complete a 1-year internship and a 2-year postdoctoral fellowship; and (e) program faculty should be multidisciplinary. Subsequently, health psychology has become the most popular area of clinical research in clinical psychology doctoral programs and the second most frequent clinic specialty area (Sayette & Mayne, 1990). In 1991, health psychology was recognized as a specialty area of practice by the American Board of Professional Psychology.

Hilton Head Conference (Tuma, 1985)

In 1985, the Conference on Training Clinical Child Psychologists was held at Hilton Head Island, South Carolina. Conference organizers were concerned about the current status of training programs, the shortage of human resources to provide services to children and families, and the failure of previous conferences to deal with issues specific to training clinical child psychologists. Recommendations were made for the training of all clinical psychologists as well as for those preparing for careers as clinical child psychologists. Delegates asserted the need for a life span developmental approach in the education and training of all clinical psychologists. In addition, one resolution called for a course on developmental bases of normal behavior to be a criterion for APA accreditation of any clinical psychology program. Delegates also recommended that all clinical psychology trainees obtain experiences with normal children and youth in the context of normal settings.

There was consensus at Hilton Head that a formal organized specialty status for clinical child psychology was premature; however, a number of specialty training issues were discussed in detail. Delegates believed that all clinical child psychology training programs should include the following: (a) courses and experiences in life span developmental psychology;

(b) experiences with cultural diversity; (c) a systems approach that included the family, school, and community as foci of study; (d) emphases on the special ethical and legal issues involved in working with children and families; and (e) the integration of principles of prevention into education and training. Delegates to this conference also endorsed the scientist–practitioner model for the training of clinical child psychologists.

National Council of Schools of Professional Psychology Conferences

Over the past decade, the National Council of Schools of Professional Psychology (NCSPP) has hosted several conferences as part of its annual membership meeting. Established in 1977, this organization's membership tripled between 1979 and 1989 from 8 to 25 full member programs. The leadership of this group has been especially concerned with the promotion of quality education and training in the rapidly growing professional schools.

The first NCSPP conference was held in 1981 and called the La Jolla Conference on Quality Control (Callan, Peterson, & Stricker, 1986). The purpose was to exchange information about professional schools, with an emphasis on quality assurance. Member programs completed extensive surveys concerning curricula, faculty, administration, and admission, and a number of papers were presented on topics such as the accreditation process, quality control issues, and organizational dilemmas in the education of professional psychologists.

In 1986, the Mission Bay conference was attended by representatives of 28 NCSPP member schools (Bourg, Bent, McHolland, & Stricker, 1989). This conference was designed to continue the work started at La Jolla and to provide input to the APA-sponsored National Conference on Graduate Education in Psychology, which is described later as the Utah conference. Conference recommendations converged with that of the Utah conference in many areas (e.g., endorsement of basic knowledge areas specified in the APA accreditation criteria, emphasis on cultural diversity). However, a significant divergence in policy was apparent in that the Utah conference resolved that all graduate programs in psychology must be tied to university settings, whereas NCSPP supported the organizational model of freestanding schools of professional psychology.

Subsequent NCSPP annual meetings have focused on ethnic diversification (Stricker et al., 1990), the core curriculum (Peterson et al., 1991), and women's issues in professional psychology (Moses, 1991). Although the NCSPP conferences have made significant contributions in raising and examining issues regarding standards of professional education and training, they cannot be viewed as representative of the field of professional psychology because they reflect the viewpoints of a relatively small number of programs training psychologists for professional practice. For example, another organization—the Council of University Directors of Clinical Psychology—

represents 145 programs that educate and train clinical psychologists. In addition, other professional programs are represented by organizations of school psychology, counseling psychology, and health psychology training directors who are not part of the NCSPP membership.

Internship Conference

In 1987, the Association of Psychology Internship Centers sponsored the National Conference on Internship Training in Psychology held in Gainesville, Florida (Belar, Bieliauskas, Larsen, Mensh, Poey, & Roehlke, 1989). The policy statement that was developed there highlighted the need for an integration of scientific knowledge, skills, and attitudes with professional practice and broad general experience versus narrow specialty training at the predoctoral level. Delegates reaffirmed the internship as an integral part of graduate education in professional psychology. (See Belar's chapter on internships and postdoctoral training conferences [this book] for a fuller discussion of this conference.)

Summary of the Early 1980s

Given the number of conferences concerned with education and training during the 1980s, one might assume that the field of psychology had splintered apart. Indeed, it was true that as psychology matured, organizations other than the APA were beginning to play a role in psychology's future. However, a prominent theme throughout these efforts was the search for guidelines and standards for professional psychology education and training, a search for unity within the field.

Other centrifugal trends in psychology as a field were fostered by the increased recognition of the relevance of psychology to other disciplines. Psychologists developed close relationships with other fields (e.g., medicine, the neurosciences, architecture, law) and some seemed to have stronger allegiances to interdisciplinary groups than to the APA. American psychology also witnessed the increased role of single-issue interest groups in governance, an increase in public- and private-sector opportunities for employment, and a change in student demographics suggesting a "feminization" of the field. It was in the context of these centrifugal trends as well as significant concerns about the future of the field and standards for professional training that the next major national conference in psychology was convened.

Utah Conference (Bickman & Ellis, 1990)

The National Conference on Graduate Education in Psychology, often referred to as the Utah conference, was sponsored by the APA and supported generously by the University of Utah. Held in June 1987, delegates reviewed the state of all graduate education in psychology, its centripetal and centrifugal forces, and made 67 recommendations concerning its future. It had been almost 30 years since a national conference (Miami in 1958) had addressed the entire scope of graduate education in psychology.

As described by Bickman (1990), the conference themes were unity, diversity, quality, and humanity. In the context of significant centrifugal forces within the field, centripetal tendencies dominated the conference despite the diversity represented. For example, delegates agreed that psychology is a unified discipline with a core curriculum and that departments of psychology should develop their core curriculum to represent the breadth of the field. Delegates also agreed that programs that educate psychologists for the provision of services require some central oversight by the discipline, and they affirmed the use of areas of basic knowledge as specified in the APA accreditation criteria in this regard. The Utah conference also supported applied endeavors for traditional academic areas of psychology and actively discouraged faculty attitudes that disparaged applied research or practice in any area of psychology. Students' rights not to be exploited were given explicit attention and reflected the consumerism of the period.

Perhaps the most unifying principle adopted was Resolution 1.3: "It is essential in the graduate education of applied and professional psychologists to include education and training in the *conduct* of scientific research as well as the application of products of psychological research" (Bickman & Ellis, 1990, p. 123). Diversity in educational approaches was accepted, with differing emphases on basic science, applied science, and practice aspects, but training in the conduct of psychological research was seen as being fundamental to all psychology. The specific degree awarded was not the issue. However, the "pure practitioner" model of training that did not include training in the conduct of research was obviously not acceptable for graduate education in psychology.

Another centripetal force was the support for diversity in education with respect to characteristics such as ethnicity, age, race, religion, gender, sexual preference, and cultural issues. The diversity of settings for graduate education was also supported, with the exception of nonuniversity-affiliated professional schools. The delegates' concern about quality in graduate education led to the recommendation that all nonaffiliated professional schools should develop formal substantive ties to universities.

National Institute of Mental Health Conferences

Since the Utah conference, the NIMH has sponsored three conferences on clinical training: (a) Training Psychologists to Work with the Seriously Mentally Ill (Johnson, 1990); (b) Clinical Training in Psychology: Improving Psychological Services for Children and Adolescents With Severe Mental Disorders (Magreb & Wohlford, 1990); and (c) Improving Training and Psychological Services for Ethnic Minorities (Myers, Wohlford, Guzman, & Echemendia, 1991). Each conference focused on the best training models for the preparation of professionals to provide services for a specific population. The most salient recommendation from all three conferences was the need for more psychologists to develop careers in the public-service sector for priority populations, as well as the need for more NIMH training support to graduate departments in this endeavor.

Scientist–Practitioner Conference

In 1990, the Assembly of Scientist-Practitioners and the Department of Clinical and Health Psychology at the University of Florida sponsored the National Conference on the Education and Training of Scientist-Practitioners for Professional Practice (Belar & Perry, 1992). This conference was cosponsored by 20 organizations representing the major education and credentialing groups within psychology; delegates represented the diversity within the discipline as a whole.

Major themes included the assertion of the necessity of the model for the ever-changing discipline of psychology, as delegates believed that it was the interlocking skills in science and practice that were the foundation for generating the knowledge base and applications to practice that psychology required in order to continue to develop and contribute to human welfare. The scientist–practitioner model was endorsed for newly emerging areas of applied psychology as well as the traditional practitioner areas. Delegates also underscored that the scientist–practitioner model does not represent a point on a continuum between programs that emphasize practice and those that emphasize research. Rather, it is the integration of scientific methods with professional practice that is the hallmark of the model.

CONCLUSION

At the end of the APA's first 100 years, the resolutions from the various conferences held within the past decade were being considered by the APA Board of Educational Affairs for implementation. The context of this review has both centrifugal and centripetal tensions, and it is not yet clear which forces will prevail. In the broader society, pluralism and diversity remain major themes. However, the political and social conservatism of the 1980s and early 1990s might be interpreted as a search for unity and stability after the turbulence of the 1960s and 1970s. The 1991 Gulf War seems to have been a definite centripetal force in American life.

Within psychology, various organizations are vying for influence on graduate education and training. As in the past, most of the controversies appear to be related to professional psychology, the focus of the vast majority of graduate education and training conferences within the past 100 years. As the century unfolded, the role of women and ethnic minorities received increasing attention in graduate conference design and participation, and policy recommendations reflected increasing sensitivity to issues of diversity. Unifying themes have been the (a) consistent affirmation of the need for a broad education in the discipline of psychology and (b) fundamental nature of psychological research training in graduate education in professional psychology. Most recently, nearly 98% of 90 responding APA-accredited programs in clinical psychology reported that their program follows the scientist–practitioner model (O'Sullivan & Quevillon, 1992). A commitment to behavioral research continues to be the tie that binds the discipline of psychology.

REFERENCES

Altman, I. (1990). Centripetal and centrifugal trends in psychology. In L. Bickman & H. Ellis (Eds.), *Preparing psychologists for the 21st century: Proceedings of the National Conference on Graduate Education in Psychology* (pp. 39–61). Hillsdale, NJ: Erlbaum.

Belar, C. D., Bieliauskas, L. A., Larsen, K. G., Mensh, I. N., Poey, K., & Roehlke, H. J. (Eds.). (1989). *Proceedings: National Conference on Internship Training in Psychology*. Washington, DC: Association of Psychology Internship Centers.

Belar, C. D., & Perry, N. (1992). The National Conference on Scientist–Practitioner Education and Training for the Professional Practice of Psychology. *American Psychologist, 47*, 71–75.

Belar, C. D., Wilson, E., & Hughes, H. (1982). Health psychology training in doctoral psychology programs. *Health Psychology, 1*, 289–299.

Bickman, L. (1990). Introduction. In L. Bickman & H. Ellis (Eds.), *Preparing psychologists for the 21st century: Proceedings of the National Conference on Graduate Education in Psychology* (pp. 3–16). Hillsdale, NJ: Erlbaum.

Bickman, L., & Ellis, H. (Eds.). (1990). *Preparing psychologists for the 21st century: Proceedings of the National Conference on Graduate Education in Psychology*. Hillsdale, NJ: Erlbaum.

Bourg, E. F., Bent, R. J., McHolland, J., & Stricker, G. (1989). Standards and evaluation in the education and training of professional psychologists. *American Psychologist, 44*, 66–72.

Callan, J. E., Peterson, D. R., & Stricker, G. (Eds.). (1986). *Quality in professional psychology training: A national conference and self-study*. National Council of Schools of Professional Psychology.

Dana, R. H., & May, T. W. (Eds.). (1987). *Internship training in professional psychology*. New York: Hemisphere.

Hoch, E. L., Ross, A. O., & Winder, C. L. (1966). Conference on the professional preparation of clinical psychologists: A summary. *American Psychologist, 21,* 42–51.

Johnson, D. L. (Ed.). (1990). *Service needs of the seriously mentally ill: Training implications for psychology.* Washington, DC: American Psychological Association.

Korman, M. (1974). National Conference on Levels and Patterns of Professional Training in Psychology: The major themes. *American Psychologist, 29,* 441–449.

Magreb, P. R., & Wohlford, P. (Eds.). (1990). *Improving psychological services for children and adolescents with severe mental disorders: Clinical training in psychology.* Washington, DC: American Psychological Association.

Matarazzo, J. D. (1983). Education and training in health psychology: Boulder or bolder. *Health Psychology, 2,* 73–113.

Moses, S. (1991, April). Breaking through the glass ceiling. *APA Monitor,* pp. 36–37.

Myers, H., Wohlford, P., Guzman, L. P., & Echemendia, R. J. (1991). *Improving training and psychological services for ethnic minorities.* Washington, DC: American Psychological Association.

O'Sullivan, J. J., & Quevillon, R. P. (1992). 40 years later: Is the Boulder model still alive? *American Psychologist, 47,* 67–70.

Peterson, R. L., McHolland, J. D., Bent, R. J., Davis-Russell, E., Edwall, G. E., Polite, K., Singer, D. L., & Stricker, G. (Eds.). (1991). *The core curriculum in professional psychology.* Washington, DC: American Psychological Association.

Raimy, V. C. (1950). *Training in clinical psychology.* Englewood Cliffs, NJ: Prentice-Hall.

Sayette, M. A., & Mayne, T. J. (1990). Survey of current clinical and research trends in clinical psychology. *American Psychologist, 45,* 1263–1266.

Stone, G. (Ed.). (1983). National Working Conference on Education and Training in Health Psychology. *Health Psychology, 2*(Suppl. 5), 1–150.

Stricker, G., Davis-Russell, E., Bourg, E., Duran, E., Hammond, W. R., McHolland, J., Polite, K., & Vaughn, B. E. (Eds.). (1990). *Toward diversification in psychology education and training.* Washington, DC: American Psychological Association.

Tuma, J. M. (Ed.). (1985). *Proceedings: Conference on Training Clinical Child Psychologists.* Washington, DC: Division of Clinical Psychology, American Psychological Association.

12

CONFERENCES ON INTERNSHIP AND POSTDOCTORAL TRAINING

CYNTHIA BELAR

The previous chapter focused on the major national conferences related to psychology graduate education and training and described them in the context of Altman's (1990) analysis of centripetal and centrifugal trends in psychology, education, and American society. The historical context was also described in chapter 11. This chapter focuses on conferences devoted to internship and postdoctoral training.

INTERNSHIP CONFERENCES

A major thrust of the blueprint for education and training in clinical psychology developed at the 1949 Boulder conference involved the integration of both the university experience and an internship sequence in the training of clinical psychologists (Raimy, 1950). Prior to that time, few clinical apprenticeships were available, and the responsibility for finding clinical training rested with the student who put together his or her own series of applied experiences. The Boulder model formalized the internship in a manner that has continued to this day without significant controversy.

In 1956 the first public listing of American Psychological Association (APA)-accredited, freestanding, independent internship programs in clinical psychology was published, and by 1960 there were 72 internship programs accredited by the APA. By the 1990–1991 internship year, there were 360 APA-accredited internship programs in professional psychology, and 99 nonaccredited internship programs were listed in the Association of Psychology Postdoctoral and Internship Centers' directory.

As described at Boulder, the internship was to be different from the clerkship in that it would involve more intensive, long-term clinical experience in a multidisciplinary setting; develop a degree of competence at a level comparable to that of junior staff members; develop responsibility for case management through semi-independent functioning; provide for socialization in the values of the field training site; and provide an opportunity to contribute to service (Raimy, 1950, pp. 105–106). At that time, specialization was not recommended at the internship level, and psychotherapy training itself was to be largely postdoctoral.

Soon after the Boulder conference, the APA's Division of Counseling Psychology recommended a predoctoral internship for preparation as a counseling psychologist, and school psychology adopted guidelines for practice that included a 6-month internship (Cutts, 1955). Thus, by the early 1950s, programmatic field training was viewed as an integral component for all graduate education in professional psychology.

Subsequent national graduate education conferences continued to affirm the need for an integrated set of university and applied experiences. At the Stanford conference in 1955, a model for a 4-year academic program followed by a 2-year postdoctoral clinical internship as a prerequisite to becoming a clinical psychologist was proposed but not accepted. This model also failed to get support at the Miami conference in 1958, where the 1-year predoctoral internship was reaffirmed. The Chicago conference in 1965 stressed how the internship should be "coordinated and integrated with the rest of the graduate student's training" (Hoch, Ross, & Winder, 1966, p. 46).

In 1968 a formal organization of internship programs was established. This organization was known as the Association of Psychology Internship Centers (APIC) until the spring of 1991, when it changed its name to the Association of Psychology Postdoctoral and Internship Centers (APPIC), a change that more clearly reflects its membership and areas of interest. The mission of this organization is as follows:

> to achieve and maintain high quality training in professional psychology; . . . to develop standards for predoctoral internship training in professional psychology and postdoctoral training in psychology; to provide a forum . . . to represent the views of training agencies with groups and organizations whose functions and objectives relate . . . ; and to provide students seeking internship or postdoctoral training with

information. (Association of Psychology Postdoctoral and Internship Centers, 1985, *By-laws*, Article II)

Princeton Conference

The first conference with a major focus on internship training was conducted in Princeton, New Jersey, in June 1961. University and internship program directors met with representatives from the APA and the National Institute of Mental Health (NIMH) to discuss (a) the appropriate level of support from the NIMH for internship training, (b) the possibility of funding part-time as well as full-time internships, and (c) what criteria should be applied in determining whether an internship facility was worthy of a training grant. It should be noted that this was a small group of people (12 male psychologists) and thus cannot be viewed as being representative of professional psychology. The focus was primarily on advising the NIMH regarding support for internship training. At that time, internships were often described as "G" for general or "S" for specialized. The former served a wide range of patients and disorders, and the latter tended to focus on a more narrow area of practice (e.g., child guidance clinics). To be awarded support for specialized internship training, the group advised that the agency should be considered a leader in its field and that an important feature of this leadership should include research and publication in the area of specialization.

Vail Conference

The next major psychology training conference was in Vail, Colorado, in 1973 (Korman, 1974). In keeping with the tenor of the times, this conference was marked by sociopolitical debate and the zeitgeist to "overthrow the establishment." Although relatively little was said about internship training per se, the conference opened the door for "universities without walls" and changes in professional training that alarmed many in the field. With the proposed alternative models of training, the integration between the internship and university academic experiences was threatened as well. Quality control in education and training seemed to have been loosened, and an influx of practitioners presented themselves to state boards for licensure as psychologists.

In response to these developments and a growing concern about quality control, state licensing boards, the APA, the National Register of Health Service Providers in Psychology, the APPIC, and other groups concerned with standards in professional education worked throughout the 1970s to develop formal criteria for internship training. The APA's accreditation criteria made it clear that the internship was an integral part of training in professional psychology:

> The internship is an essential component of doctoral training programs in professional psychology. Internships should provide the trainee with the opportunity to take substantial responsibility for carrying out major professional functions in the context of appropriate supervisory support, professional role modeling, and awareness of administrative structures. The internship is taken after completion of relevant didactic and practicum work and precedes the granting of the doctoral degree. (American Psychological Association, 1986, p. 18)

Gainesville Conference (1987)

In addition to increasing concerns regarding standards, the 1970s and 1980s also witnessed the proliferation of new specialty areas of practice (e.g., health psychology, clinical child psychology, clinical neuropsychology). Many of these specialty areas developed their own guidelines for internship training (e.g., INS–Division 40 Task Force, 1987; Stone, 1983; Tuma, 1985). However, there had not yet been a national conference to address broad issues specific to internship training in professional psychology, despite the repeated affirmation of this component as integral to graduate education. In 1985, the Association of Psychology Postdoctoral and Internship Centers decided to sponsor such a conference.

The National Conference on Internship Training in Psychology was held in March 1987 in Gainesville, Florida (Belar et al., 1987). Cosponsored by the Department of Clinical and Health Psychology at the University of Florida, the conference was designed to focus on basic policy issues over a 4-day period rather than deal with the "nuts and bolts" of intern training. Questions to be addressed included what was the purpose of internship training, when in graduate education it should occur, for what careers should it be required, what were the entrance and exit criteria, what was the core content of internship training, what were the necessary structures and processes for an internship program, and what were the important financial and administrative variables.

Nearly one third of the 48 delegates represented university graduate programs in clinical, counseling, or school psychology; nearly two thirds represented internship programs in a variety of different settings. In sharp contrast to the Princeton conference, more than 25% of the delegates were women. The product of the conference was a policy document voted on and accepted by the entire assembly.

In debating the purpose of internship training, delegates decided that it was to include the production of an autonomous professional. Delegates then concluded that a 1-year internship as the capstone of professional training was no longer sufficient and that a 2-year process was required. They believed that the field had grown sufficiently that the 1-year model, developed almost 40 years ago, was now outdated. However, according to Shakow (1973), the model had been seen as inadequate even at its inception: "In all the conferences and reports I have referred to, it was either implicitly or explicitly recognized that a doctoral program with one year of internship was insufficient to turn out a truly competent clinical psychologist" (p. 12). Consistent with this, most states had already adopted regulations that required an additional year of supervised experience prior to licensure as an independent psychologist. Some might say that what the Gainesville conference actually did was confirm the zeitgeist by formalizing the status of the postdoctoral year and asserting the need for organized psychology to develop quality-control mechanisms for this aspect of professional training.

Consistent with previous conferences, delegates also affirmed that 1 year of the internship should be predoctoral; the need for continued integration with the graduate program was often highlighted. The development of internships in newly emerging areas of professional practice was noted, and delegates voted that internships should be required of all psychologists who teach or supervise in the areas of assessment and intervention or who are responsible for human service-delivery systems. Conference participants believed that all interns should be funded and agreed on a core set of experiences for the predoctoral year: (a) a variety of methods of assessment and diagnosis across a variety of problems and diverse populations; (b) a variety of methods of interventions and treatment across a variety of problems and diverse populations; (c) experience with culturally and ethnically diverse populations; (d) research and its practical applications; (e) application of empirical skill and critical thinking to professional practice; (f) professional, legal, and ethical issues; and (g) introduction to supervision and management of psychological services.

In general, delegates were firmly committed to the philosophy that organized psychology should assume the role as the developer of standards for internship and postdoctoral training. Although no standards for the postdoctoral year were developed at this conference, it was noted that it could be general or more specialized and that a future conference should be designed to more fully delineate it. In general, there was a good deal of concern expressed over the hit-or-miss nature of the year of supervised experience that states required; delegates believed it to be without standards or quality-control mechanisms within the field and that exploitation of recent graduates was often the result.

POSTDOCTORAL EDUCATION AND TRAINING CONFERENCES

As of 1991, to my knowledge, there has been only one conference that focused exclusively on postdoctoral training in psychology (the Menninger conference in 1972). However, postdoctoral training has a long and well-accepted history in the field and, as noted earlier, received significant attention at the 1987 Gainesville conference.

Historically, attendees at the Boulder conference stated that postdoctoral training was actually required in order for a psychologist to become proficient in psychotherapy (Raimy, 1950). At the Chicago conference (Hoch et al., 1966), "there was no debating the advisability of postdoctoral education. Indeed, the latter was in effect regarded as an ethical responsibility for those who aspire to the status of 'expert' in selected areas of professional function" (p. 44). Delegates to this conference also clarified the difference between postgraduate education (for respecialization) and postdoctoral training taken to extend existing skills; they supported both forms. Delegates viewed postdoctoral training as a way to gain specialty experience in the areas of psychotherapy, clinical child psychology, research and community mental health practice, as well as other developing areas of practice. Postdoctoral training would permit the psychologist to advance beyond journeyman-level skills attained on receipt of the PhD. Themes of excellence, advanced and specialized skills, and expansion of capabilities marked descriptions of this level of experience. Delegates warned that postdoctoral training should not be viewed as a correction factor for deficiencies in training at the doctoral level. The Chicago conference delegates also stated that "although postdoctoral training is desirable for all clinical specialists, it is deemed essential for those anticipating independent professional practice and also for those who are to teach and supervise in specialty clinical courses" (Hoch et al., 1966, p. 45).

Weiner (1968) identified 46 postdoctoral training programs in clinical psychology in 1966. Twenty years later, the APA Office of Educational Affairs identified 161 postdoctoral programs in psychology, 99 of which were either health service provider oriented or a mixture of training in both professional services and research. These programs accounted for 499 students, nearly one third the size of the exiting internship group for that year (Woodring, 1987).

It was in 1972 that a group of 42 psychologists representing postdoctoral training programs, university departments of psychology, the APA, and the NIMH gathered at the Menninger Clinic to focus exclusively on postdoctoral education (Weiner, 1973). Rather than develop specific policy statements, attendees shared information and raised concerns about current and future postdoctoral education. One prominent concern was whether some postdoctoral programs were functioning more as trade schools, thus perpetuating a false dichotomy between research and clinical work. Conference participants supported socially relevant clinical research as being integral to postdoctoral training and agreed that clinical training at this level should enhance already-existing skills or facilitate the development of specialty skills.

Subsequent to the Menninger conference, criteria for postdoctoral training in specialty areas of practice have been developed. For example, specific recommendations have been made for the practice of health psychology (Stone, 1983), clinical child psychology (Tuma, 1985), and clinical neuropsychology (INS–Division 40 Task Force, 1987). Of note is that each of these practice areas has made a commitment to the scientist–practitioner model of education and training, consistent with the model endorsed by most predoctoral APA-accredited programs. Most recently, the American Board of Professional Psychology has taken a leadership role in forming an interorganizational council to begin the accreditation process for postdoctoral training programs in specialty practice areas.

However, although the 1987 Gainesville conference on internship training made a clear commitment to the need for a formal postdoctoral training year, the specific standards for this year have not yet been determined by a national conference representing the breadth of postdoctoral professional training programs. Such a conference is planned for the fall of 1992 under the sponsorship of the APPIC. Named the National Conference on Postdoctoral Fellowship Training in Professional Psychology, delegates to this conference will be asked to address issues related to entrance and exit criteria for fellows; appropriate program content, structure, and setting characteristics; program evaluation; and promotion of innovation and excellence in training.

It should also be noted that some groups have opposed the year of required postdoctoral training that many of the national conferences have asserted to be necessary for professional practice. For example, the Council of University Directors of Clinical Psychology has objected to an additional required year of professional training and has now undertaken its own study of practice areas in which training directors believe their graduates are prepared to practice without required supervision.

CONFERENCES AFTER THE 1987 GAINESVILLE CONFERENCE

In general, conferences held after the 1987 Gainesville conference have not been designed to focus on either internship or postdoctoral training. The last APA-sponsored graduate conference (the 1987 Utah conference; Bickman & Ellis, 1990) dealt primarily with preinternship academic program issues, but its recommendations were not inconsistent with policies developed at the 1987 Gainesville conference on internships. Indeed, Gainesville conference recommendations gained support from subsequent NIMH-sponsored conferences. For example, the conference on Training Psychologists to Work with the Seriously Mentally Ill recommended that NIMH support specialized training in 2-year internships as described at Gainesville, as well as postdoctoral fellowships (Johnson, 1990). The NIMH conference on training for work with children and adolescents (Magrab & Wohlford, 1990) recommended support for both 1- and 2-year pre- and postdoctoral internships, adopting the Hilton Head conference criteria for training in clinical child psychology (Tuma, 1985).

Internship as an integral component of graduate education for every area of professional practice was reaffirmed by the 1989 National Conference on Education and Training of Scientist-Practitioners for the Professional Practice of Psychology (Belar & Perry, 1992). And although the NCSPP membership conferences have been relatively silent about internships and postdoctoral training, the recent conference devoted to women's issues highlighted the need for more half-time internships to promote flexibility in response to student needs (Moses, 1991).[1]

CONCLUSION

At the end of the APA's first 100 years, it has become increasingly apparent that psychology as a profession is dealing not as much with basic identity as with specialty identity issues. How specialty practice areas will be represented is not yet clear, although it is clear that the APA will be sharing leadership with groups such as the Association of Psychology Post-doctoral and Internship Centers; the Chairs of Graduate Departments of Psychology; the American Board of Professional Psychology; and specialty groups such as the American Board of Clinical Neuropsychology, American Board of Forensic Psychology, and so forth. I predict that accreditation mechanisms will be developed for postdoctoral training and that future training conferences will play a significant role in developing standards by which postdoctoral training can be evaluated.[2] I also think that the question of whether the internship should be pre- or postdoctoral will be revisited and that the 4 + 2 model proposed at the Stanford conference in 1955 will receive increased support.

I believe that contrary to the past 100 years, a major focus in future professional education and training will be at the postdoctoral level and that the press for this will come from two ongoing trends. First, the explosion of knowledge related to practice has been significant. No predoctoral pro-

---

[1]Although the American Psychological Association's accreditation rules had long permitted a 2-year, half-time internship, less than 4% of the 3,025 paid internship slots registered with the Association of Psychology Postdoctoral and Internship Centers were available on a half-time basis (Moses, 1991).

[2]The National Conference on Postdoctoral Fellowship Training in Professional Psychology is now scheduled for October 1992 at the University of Michigan. Sponsored by the Association of Psychology Postdoctoral and Internship Centers and cosponsored by the American Board of Professional Psychology, the American Psychological Association, the Association of State and Provincial Psychology Boards, and the National Register of Health Service Providers in Psychology, the conference is designed to articulate criteria and develop standards for postdoctoral education and training in professional psychology.

gram can train in depth the specialized knowledge and skills required for many practice areas without sacrificing the broad education and training in the discipline viewed as being fundamental to all of psychology. Second, the need for cost-efficient delivery systems in health care and the availability of other disciplines to provide general mental health and human services will result in psychologists being better able to compete in the marketplace if they have specialized knowledge and skills (e.g., clinical neuropsychology, clinical health psychology). As I have noted elsewhere (Belar, 1989, 1990), many employers will not hire psychologists to do psychotherapy when they can hire less expensive personnel to perform the seemingly same function.

I also have significant concerns about future standards for professional education and training. For example, if standards for postdoctoral specialty training programs do not reflect the "leader in the field" concept proposed at Princeton, or the scientist–practitioner model endorsed by many pre-doctoral programs, these programs will not be able to produce a professional psychologist with the unique skills required to successfully compete in the future health-care marketplace.

REFERENCES

Altman, I. (1990). Centripetal and centrifugal trends in psychology. In L. Bickman & H. Ellis (Eds.), *Preparing psychologists for the 21st century: Proceedings of the National Conference on Graduate Education in Psychology* (pp. 39–61). Hillsdale, NJ: Erlbaum.

American Psychological Association. (1986). *Accreditation handbook*. Washington, DC: Author.

Association of Psychology Postdoctoral and Internship Centers. (1985). *By-laws*. Washington, DC: Author.

Belar, C. D. (1989). Opportunities for psychologists in health maintenance organizations: Implications for graduate education and training. *Professional Psychology: Research and Practice, 20,* 390–394.

Belar, C. D. (1990). Continued integration of scientific and practitioner graduate education in psychology. In L. Bickman & H Ellis, (Eds.), *Preparing psychologists for the 21st century: Proceedings of the National Conference on Graduate Education in Psychology* (pp. 77–85). Hillsdale, NJ: Erlbaum.

Belar, C. D., Bieliauskas, L. A., Larsen, K. G., Mensh, I. N., Poey, K., & Roehlke, H. J. (Eds.). (1987). *Proceedings: National Conference on Internship Training in Psychology.* Washington, DC: Association of Psychology Internship Centers.

Belar, C. D., & Perry, N. (1992). The National Conference on Scientist-Practitioner Education and Training for the Professional Practice of Psychology. *American Psychologist, 47,* 71–75.

Bickman, L., & Ellis, H. (Eds.). (1990). *Preparing psychologists for the 21st century:*

Proceedings of the National Conference on Graduate Education in Psychology. Hillsdale, NJ: Erlbaum.

Cutts, N. (Ed.). (1955). *School psychologists at mid-century.* Washington, DC: American Psychological Association.

Hoch, E. L., Ross, A. O., & Winder, C. L. (1966). Conference on the professional preparation of clinical psychologists: A summary. *American Psychologist, 21,* 42–51.

INS–Division 40 Task Force on Education, Accreditation and Credentialing. (1987). Reports of the INS–Division 40 Task Force on Education, Accreditation and Credentialing. *Clinical Neuropsychologist, 1,* 29–34.

Johnson, D. L. (Ed.). (1990). *Service needs of the seriously mentally ill: Training implications for psychology.* Washington, DC: American Psychological Association.

Korman, M. (1974). National conference on levels and patterns of professional training in psychology: The major themes. *American Psychologist, 29,* 441–449.

Magrab, P. R., & Wohlford, P. (Eds). (1990). *Improving psychological services for children and adolescents with severe mental disorders: Clinical training in psychology.* Washington, DC: American Psychological Association.

Moses, S. (1991, April). Breaking through the glass ceiling. *APA Monitor,* pp. 36–37.

Raimy, V. C. (1950). *Training in clinical psychology.* Englewood Cliffs, NJ: Prentice-Hall.

Shakow, D. (1973). History and development of postdoctoral clinical training. In I. B. Weiner (Ed.), *Postdoctoral education in clinical psychology.* Topeka, KS: Menninger Foundation.

Stone, G. (Ed.). (1983). National Working Conference on Education and Training in Health Psychology. *Health Psychology, 2*(Suppl. 5), 1–150.

Tuma, J. M. (Ed.). (1985). *Proceedings: Conference on Training Clinical Child Psychologists.* Washington, DC: Division of Clinical Psychology, American Psychological Association.

Weiner, I. B. (1968). Postdoctoral training in clinical psychology. *American Psychologist, 23,* 374–377.

Weiner, I. B. (Ed.). (1973). *Postdoctoral education in clinical psychology.* Topeka, KS: Menninger Foundation.

Woodring, J. (1987). *Preliminary results from the initial postdoctoral survey.* Washington, DC: American Psychological Association.

13

REGIONAL CONFERENCES FOR TEACHERS AND STUDENTS OF PSYCHOLOGY

STEPHEN F. DAVIS AND RANDOLPH A. SMITH

The past few decades have witnessed significant changes in the countenance of psychology. Specialization appears to be the order of the day; rather than simply referring to oneself as a psychologist, psychologists typically add an area of specialization as a descriptor. Thus, we find animal learning psychologists, community psychologists, cognitive psychologists, clinical neuropsychologists, and so forth.

Psychologists dedicated to the teaching of psychology also actively promote their specialty. Many teachers of psychology maintain an allegiance to Division 2 (Teaching of Psychology) of the American Psychological Association (APA). Division 2 serves an important function at the national level for teachers through publication of its journal, *Teaching of Psychology*, and presentation of sessions on teaching at the annual APA Convention. The National Institute on the Teaching of Psychology, founded in 1979 and cosponsored by the University of Illinois and the University of South Florida, provides an opportunity for teachers from across the country to interact and to acquire new knowledge.

During the past decade, a movement grew to meet the needs of both teachers and students on a regional basis. Shrinking travel budgets and a paucity of sessions relevant to teaching at regional association meetings have facilitated the development of regional conferences. In this chapter, we examine the development of regional teaching conferences, the type of programs typically presented at such conferences, and the benefits derived by conference participants. Recent years also have witnessed the development of numerous state and regional conferences for psychology students. Because student conferences provide important benefits for teaching faculty who participate in them, they constitute a second focus of this chapter.

Although the specific benefits of each type of conference are delineated subsequently, the general importance, popularity, and growth potential of these conferences deserve consideration at this point. Because of their regional nature, these conferences attract participants who otherwise would not attend professional meetings. Teaching faculty from institutions of all sizes and types (2-year through PhD-granting schools) learn from one another; participation is on a basis of equality. This equal participation allows for cross-fertilization and thus strengthens teaching at all levels.

Faculty and students return from such conferences rejuvenated; such enthusiasm frequently permeates one's teaching activities during the ensuing months. Recent trends paint a convincing picture of the popularity of such conferences and strongly indicate that additional annual events of this nature will be established in the future. It is arguable that the establishment and proliferation of such conferences may be remembered as the most significant occurrence for teachers of psychology during the 1980s and 1990s.

REGIONAL TEACHING CONFERENCES

The locations of the extant regional teaching conferences are shown in Figure 1.

The reasons for formation, the dominant conference model, general and special features, and conference benefits are presented in the following sections. This discussion is based largely on responses to a questionnaire sent to the founders and organizers of each conference.

Factors in Founding Regional Teaching Conferences

In his article on faculty development conferences, Palladino (1988) reiterated the problems for teachers, such as professional isolation or lack of information about effective teaching techniques, created by limited funds for faculty development and the lack of organized sessions at regional conventions. These factors, coupled with the success of the Mid-America Undergraduate Psychology Research Conference, led to the development of the Mid-America Conference for Teachers of Psychology in 1984. "The consistent success of

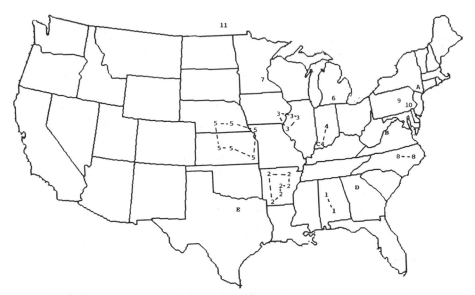

Figure 1: Regional conferences for teachers of psychology as of summer 1991 (indicated by letters) and student psychology conferences as of February 1991 (indicated by numbers). [A = Annual Conference for the Teaching of Psychology, State University of New York, Farmingdale (founded 1986); B = Eastern Conference for the Teaching of Psychology, James Madison University, Harrisonburg, VA (founded 1988); C = Mid-America Conference for Teachers of Psychology, University of Southern Indiana, Evansville, IN (founded 1984); D = Southeastern Conference on the Teaching of Psychology, Kennesaw State College, Marietta, GA (founded 1989); E = Southwestern Conference for the Teaching of Psychology, Texas Wesleyan University, Forth Worth, TX (founded 1991). 1 = Southeastern Undergraduate Psychology Research Conference (founded 1986); 2 = Arkansas Symposium for Psychology Students (founded 1985); 3 = ILLOWA Undergraduate Psychology Conference (founded 1974); 4 = Mid-America Undergraduate Psychology Research Conference (founded 1982); 5 = Great Plains Students' Psychology Convention (founded 1981); 6 = Michigan Undergraduate Psychology Paper Reading Conference (founded 1989); 7 = Minnesota Undergraduate Psychology Conference (founded 1966); 8 = Carolinas Psychology Conference (founded 1976); 9 = Delaware Valley Undergraduate Research Conference (founding date unavailable); 10 = Lehigh Valley Undergraduate Psychology Research Conference (founded 1986); 11 = University of Winnipeg Undergraduate Psychology Research Conference (founded 1982). Multiple listings indicate conference site rotation in a geographic region.]

this annual [undergraduate] conference led us to believe that a conference for teachers of psychology would also be successful" (Palladino, 1988, p. 170). Among the goals for this regional conference for teachers, Palladino listed

1. To provide faculty members with an opportunity to exchange ideas about courses taught at the undergraduate level.

2. To discuss issues such as curriculum and the use of computers in teaching.

3. To provide an opportunity to share ideas for stimulating students' interest in psychology, in introductory courses, advanced courses, and outside the classroom.

4. To assist in the establishment of a network of supportive members. (1988, p. 170)

Although the founders of other regional teaching conferences have echoed one or more of these goals, they also cite another reason for founding their conferences: There was a clear need in their area for a teaching conference. The need for the Mid-America Conference has been clear, and the need for similar teaching conferences was reflected in the testimonies of the teachers who had traveled to Evansville to attend that conference. Limited budgets and limited time precluded many teachers from attending a conference outside of their geographic region; the establishment of a conference that was closer to home appealed to many.

An additional goal of all of the regional teaching conferences is to provide a quality program at the lowest possible cost (Hill & Palladino, 1990). Presently, the cost of attending a regional teaching conference is approximately $100. For this fee, the participant receives meals, refreshments at breaks, and all conference materials. Because regional teaching conferences typically are held on college campuses, it has been possible to keep costs at a minimum. Moreover, it is felt that the campus atmosphere contributes to the collegiality of the conference.

The Dominant Model and Its Development

Without question, the dominant model for regional teaching conferences is the Mid-America Conference for Teachers of Psychology. Since its founding in 1984, the basic format of this conference has remained essentially unchanged. The 2-day sequence of events, as it appeared in 1984 at the inaugural conference, is shown in Figure 2.

The convention organizers feel that this general pattern of keynote addresses, concurrent sessions, and general sessions provides participants with maximum exposure to a variety of topics on the teaching of psychology. One of the important features of the Mid-America Conference that has been imitated by other regional teaching conferences is the strategic use of breaks for refreshments and socialization. These breaks allow participants an opportunity to get to know each other on a more personal basis in an informal setting. Thus, the seeds for the development or expansion of one's professional network are purposely planted. Many individuals take full advantage of this opportunity through the sharing of information, resources, ideas for guest speakers, new techniques and approaches, as well as opportunities for research collaboration.

Who Presents and What Do They Present?

Although the keynote addresses at teaching conferences typically are given by teachers who have achieved some degree of regional or national prominence, concurrent sessions are likely to be conducted by individuals who have attended the conference in the past. This tactic of drawing presenters from the ranks of past attendees reflects the philosophy that this group of individuals best knows the interests and needs of those who attend such conferences. The content of concurrent sessions tends to be rather diverse and changes from year to year (e.g., syllabus construction, gender differences, sports psychology, curriculum review, etc.). On the other hand,

CONFERENCE SCHEDULE

All sessions and meals will take place in the University Conference Center on the campus of Indiana State University Evansville.

OCTOBER 12

11:00-12:00	REGISTRATION
12:00-12:45	LUNCHEON
12:45-1:45	WELCOME—David L. Rice, President, ISUE "USING CURRENT EVENTS IN THE TEACHING OF PSYCHOLOGY" Arno Wittig, Ball State University
1:45-2:00	BREAK
2:00-3:30	CONCURRENT SESSIONS "STUDENT PROBLEMS: CHEATING, HARASSMENT, AND LACK OF MOTIVATION" Joseph Palladino, ISUE Vivian Makosky, St. Lawrence University "CAREER PREPARATION FOR THE UNDERGRADUATE PSYCHOLOGY STUDENT" Charles Brewer, Furman University Stephen Davis, Emporia State University Barbara Jessen, University of Evansville Sandra Singer, ISUE Anne Rogers, American Psychological Association
3:30-3:45	BREAK
3:45-5:15	CONCURRENT SESSIONS "IMPROVING THE WRITING OF TEST ITEMS" James Eison, Roane State Community College "STRESS MANAGEMENT FOR TEACHERS" Paul Lloyd, Southeast Missouri State University
5:15-6:00	COCKTAILS (Cash bar)
6:00-8:00	DINNER "WHAT STUDENTS THINK ABOUT AND DO DURING COLLEGE LECTURES" Howard Pollio, University of Tennessee
8:00-?	CONCURRENT INFORMAL SESSIONS "THE TEACHING OF: a) STATISTICS/EXPERIMENTAL/RESEARCH METHODS" Stephen Davis, Emporia State University b) PERSONALITY/SOCIAL/ABNORMAL" c) HUMAN SEXUALITY" Harve Rawson, Hanover College

OCTOBER 13

8:00-9:00	BREAKFAST
9:00-10:15	ROUNDTABLE ON TEACHING THE INTRODUCTORY COURSE Charles Brewer, Furman University Howard Pollio, University of Tennessee Arno Wittig, Ball State University James Eison, Roane State Community College, Moderator
10:15-10:30	BREAK
10:30-11:45	CONCURRENT SESSIONS "COMPUTERS IN THE TEACHING OF PSYCHOLOGY" Barney Beins, Thomas More College Bert Woodruff, Butler University "THE ONE- OR TWO-PERSON PSYCHOLOGY DEPARTMENT" A roundtable discussion Susannah Woodcock, Brescia College, Moderator "HOW TO BREAK INTO REVIEWING AND PUBLISHING" James Eison, Roane State Community College Joseph Palladino, ISUE
12:00-1:00	PARTICIPANT PAPERS (See section entitled "Submission of Proposals for Participants' Presentations")
1:00-2:00	LUNCH
2:00-3:15	"AND GLADLY LEARN...AND GLADLY TEACH" Charles Brewer, Furman University Participants are encouraged to bring along copies of course syllabi, demonstrations, experiments, etc., for discussion and exchange with colleagues.

Figure 2: Conference schedule, Inaugural Mid-America Conference for Teachers of Psychology, 1984.

there are some recurrent themes for the general sessions. For example, one is likely to find a round-table discussion of teaching introductory psychology on the program. Similarly, a general session featuring live presentations of effective classroom teaching demonstrations has proven to be very popular (Hill, Palladino, & Smith, 1992). This varied program can impact one's teaching in both specific and general ways. For example, among the specific influences are the addition of new exercises, demonstrations, and information to one's repertoire. General influences include the learning of new techniques, approaches, and attitudes relevant to teaching.

Number and Nature of Attendees

In its infancy (i.e., the first 2 years of operation), a regional teaching conference seems to attract approximately 75 to 90 registrants. As the conference becomes more visible as an annual regional event, this number gradually increases until it levels off at approximately 90 to 120 registrants.

An examination of the registration lists of the regional conferences prompts the following general conclusions: (a) more small- and medium-sized institutions are represented; (b) participants typically come from schools having only undergraduate programs; and (c) an appreciable number of individuals from 2-year institutions attend. Moreover, a wide geographical region may be represented. For example, individuals from 14 different states were registered at the 1990 Mid-America Conference. Participants at the 1990 Southeastern Conference came from 13 states, and 14 states were represented at the 1991 Southeastern Conference. More important, the 1990 participants came from 73 different institutions, and the 1991 participants represented 71 institutions. Thus, there is good reason to believe that the information acquired at a conference is disseminated to a very large number of teachers.

Benefits

The following are unsolicited comments that have been made by attendees about recent regional teaching conferences: "These meetings are well planned—well executed—interesting and informative." "This conference always sends me home motivated and consumed with teaching." "The nicest thing I did for my students this year was to attend this conference." "I came. I learned. I had fun. It was most worthwhile." "The evaluation criteria of 'coming home with one good idea' was met in the first hour." Two general themes run through these comments. First, new knowledge about teaching is acquired. This new information may range from a specific activity for a particular class to a new teaching style that can be used in all of a teacher's courses. Second, regional teaching conferences are perceived as having positive motivational effects on the attendees. They leave the conference rejuvenated and ready to meet the challenges of the academic term.

An impressive list of specific benefits for convention attendees was provided by G. William Hill IV, one of the founders of the Southeastern Teaching Conference. The items on Hill's list were

1. Ability to attend a conference of interest at a significantly lower cost compared to national meetings.
2. A quality program featuring practical ideas for teaching.
3. An opportunity to participate in the program as a concurrent session presenter or by presenting a poster.
4. The opportunity to meet with other teachers of psychology who are experiencing the same rewards and difficulties to discuss strategies and experiences. This has contributed to new friendships and networks that benefit faculty members and their students.
5. In some cases almost the entire department attends together.

Therefore, the conference provides an opportunity for departmental team building.

6. Because most of these conferences are held on a campus and sponsored by a particular department, they provide an excellent opportunity to encourage faculty development in the host department by involving faculty in the development, implementation, and staging of the conference. (Hill, personal communication, June 1991)

Future of Regional Teaching Conferences

We can think of no better way to summarize the development, impact, and future of regional teaching conferences than the following statement by Hill:

I believe that the establishment of the regional conferences on the teaching of psychology over the last eight years has provided one of the most significant professional development opportunities in recent history. The overwhelming popularity of the regional conference model is amazing. At the present time, I am aware of four existing regional conferences and one that will occur for the first time this year (1991) in the Southwest. All of these conferences have had consistently strong attendance with many participants returning year after year bringing their colleagues. I am hopeful that we will see the development of additional conferences in regions of the country not served by an existing conference. (Hill, personal communication, June 1991)

These conferences would not be developed or survive if they did not serve their intended purposes—the professional development and rejuvenation of teachers. There is every reason to believe that the popularity and perceived importance of these conferences will continue unabated.

REGIONAL STUDENT PSYCHOLOGY CONFERENCES

Whereas the literature on regional teaching conferences is limited, an array of symposia have been staged and articles published about regional student psychology conferences (Anderson & Rosenfeld, 1983; Furedy & McRae, 1985; Lipton, 1986). For example, a symposium on "The Undergraduate Research Conference in Psychology as an Educational Tool" was chaired by Wilbert A. McKeachie at the 1973 APA Convention in Montreal. One of the papers presented in this symposium, "Undergraduate psychology conferences: Is good research nested under Ph.D.s?" was published by Alan L. Carsrud (1975) in *Teaching of Psychology*. Although some student conferences existed before 1975, this report provides insight into the reasons prompting the proliferation of student conferences in the 1970s, as well as the benefits thought to be derived from such conferences. As

TABLE 1
Annual Listing of Student Psychology Conferences in *Teaching of Psychology*: 1975–1991

Year	No. of conferences listed
1975	10
1976	13[a]
1977	8[a]
1978	11
1979	12
1980	NA
1981	NA
1982	6
1983	12
1984	11
1985	13
1986	16
1987	10
1988	10
1989	13
1990	12
1991	11

Note: NA = not available.
[a]Listings of student paper sessions conducted at regional psychology conferences are not included.

shown later in this chapter, these reasons and benefits appear to remain valid almost two decades later. In addition to the publication of the Carsrud article, 1975 also marked the first year that student psychology conferences were routinely listed in *Teaching of Psychology*.

Factors in Founding Student Psychology Conferences

The listing of student psychology conferences in *Teaching of Psychology* provides an excellent database for their study. Table 1 summarizes the number of conferences that have been listed since 1975. On the basis of these listings, it appears that the earliest conference to be founded was the Annual Psychology Conference held at Mount Holyoke College in South Hadley, Massachusetts. This conference, which was founded in 1948, was listed in 1975, 1976, 1977, and 1986. It is not certain whether this conference is still active.

The regional student psychology conferences listed in the "News Tips From *ToP*" section of the February 1991 issue of *Teaching of Psychology* are indicated by the numerals in Figure 1. In comparison with the regional teaching conferences (indicated by letters in Figure 1), there are a greater number of student conferences. Moreover, several of these student conferences have been in existence significantly longer than the teaching conferences.

Supporting the premise that more undergraduates were conducting more research, Carsrud (1975) saw student psychology conferences as a vehicle by which students could develop a sense of professionalism and competence through the presentation of their research data. Similar sentiments were expressed by Cyril J. Sadowski concerning the founding of the Southeastern Undergraduate Psychology Research Conference in 1986. "The conference was founded to provide an outlet for student work, to promote professional activity, and to give students a chance to meet others in a reasonably safe environment" (Sadowski, personal communication, June 1991). For students, a safe conference environment is characterized by low levels of stress and the presence of a supportive audience.

As seen in the following sketch, serendipity seems to play a role in the founding of student psychology conferences. Regarding the founding of the Carolinas Psychology Conference, Donald Merschon wrote,

> The Carolinas Psychology Conference was originally conceived of as a local seminar to enhance the educational experiences of Meredith College students who had been doing research with Lyn Aubrecht and Jack Huber. It was thus fitting that the initial discussions concerning its format took place in a basement laboratory at Meredith. As the idea was developed, it was broadened to include guests from other schools—as attendees, and as possible presenters. A first letter of inquiry was mailed to colleges and universities in the Southeast in December, 1975. During approximately the same period as these early discussions at Meredith, Slater Newman (North Carolina State University, NCSU) had read a description of undergraduate research conferences and had presented the idea to the Psychology Club. Club members and Ginny Cowgell (their Faculty Advisor) were investigating the possibility of sponsoring such a full-scale conference, when the Meredith plans became known. Rather than establish two competing conferences, NCSU abandoned its consideration of an independent event. Upon hearing of this decision, those involved in the by-then significantly expanded Meredith "seminar" invited NCSU to join in putting on the first Conference. Other local colleges also participated to varying degrees in making the 1976 Conference a success. Following the 1976 Conference, a decision was made to alternate the location of Conference activities between Meredith and NCSU. (Merschon, personal communication, June 1991)

Serendipity also was evident in the founding of the Great Plains Students' Psychology Convention. Students and faculty from Bethany College and Sterling College attended a colloquium presentation at Emporia State University in the fall of 1980. The excellent student interaction that took place following the colloquium address prompted faculty to seek a more formal means by which such student interaction and professional growth could be facilitated. The first Great Plains Convention was held in the spring of 1981. Similarly, a chance conversation between Randolph

Smith and Ralph McKenna at a meeting of the Southwestern Psychological Association led to the founding of the Arkansas Symposium for Psychology Students in 1985.

The Typical Student Psychology Conference

Carsrud, Palladino, Tanke, Aubrecht, and Huber (1984) reported that two common features characterize the format of all student conferences. First, the dominant mode of presentation is the oral paper. Second, a guest speaker is featured at all conferences. These similarities in format persist into the 1990s, and to them we would add the scheduling of a group meal or general social event.

However, as the number of student conferences has grown, conference formats have become more diverse. For example, the number of 2-day conferences has increased. Although some conferences have traditionally featured Friday afternoon and evening activities (e.g., paper sessions, a social event, and a guest speaker), the number of paper submissions has forced others to move to a 2-day (Friday and Saturday) format. Panel discussions and symposia on selected topics are featured at several conferences, and poster sessions are being tried on an experimental basis at two events. Some conferences (e.g., Great Plains) present awards for outstanding papers and posters.

Conferences also differ with regard to whether a registration fee is charged. Currently, three conferences do not charge a fee. At those conferences that have a charge, the fee varies from $3 to $10. Student fees are used to help defray conference costs (e.g., printing, postage, and honoraria). In those instances in which fees are not charged, it is assumed that the conference costs have been absorbed by the sponsoring institutions, individual benefactors, or state or regional associations.

Who Presents and What is Presented?

For most conferences, the answer to this question is rather simple and straightforward. Undergraduate students present the results of research they have conducted. However, in at least two cases, there has been a purposeful straying from the straight and narrow. The Michigan Undergraduate Psychology Paper Reading Conference accepts papers in which the "topics may vary from empirical investigations to historical/theoretical presentations." Thus, not all presentations at this conference are based on research data.

The founding philosophy of providing students with a forum in which they can begin to grow professionally led to the creation of separate research and nonresearch (i.e., literature review or theoretical) categories of submission at the Great Plains Students' Psychology Convention. Moreover, the Great Plains Convention may be unique in its inclusion of these same categories for graduate student participants.

Benefits for Students

Carsrud (1975) delineated the following student benefits derived from participation in a student psychology conference:

1. The student develops "feelings of competence and familiarity with a given research problem" (Carsrud, 1975, p. 112).

2. "These undergraduate meetings give the undergraduate a chance to show his competence to others" (Carsrud, 1975, p. 112).

3. Such meetings serve to instill a feeling of excitement about research in the participants.

4. Such meetings can serve to reinforce students for conducting research.

5. Students can develop their communication skills.

To this list, other convention founders have added the potential to develop or expand one's professional network. The development of a professional network by undergraduates offers several genuine benefits. For example, undergraduates may discover similarities between the program at their institution and those offered at other schools. This knowledge often adds credibility to messages that faculty attempt to deliver in their classes and research collaboration with students. A professional network may include potential graduate school contacts. Students who are included in one's network have the potential to become research collaborators on future projects.

Benefits for Faculty

Although these conferences were developed for students, faculty also may benefit from them. Among the benefits for teachers of psychology who attend student psychology conferences are the following:

1. A decrease in professional isolation of faculty at small schools. A teacher at one school can learn what text, demonstrations, laboratory exercises, and so forth, other teachers are using in common courses.

2. Students are motivated to conduct research after attending such conferences. This motivation facilitates instruction. Students are more enthusiastic about psychology and being part of it. Reports of improved class attendance and increases in the number of questions asked during class sessions are frequent after student conferences.

3. Having students who are interested in research endeavors can spur one's own research pursuits and knowledge of the current literature. If teachers are active researchers and are aware of the current literature, they should be more effective in the classroom.

4. Collaboration on research projects, as well as on teaching-related activities, with faculty at neighboring schools is facilitated.

CONCLUSION

We have seen that the number of regional teaching conferences increased substantially during the 1980s and early 1990s. It is probable that additional conferences will be developed. Because of the lack of teaching conferences in the western half of the United States, such development is predicted to occur in this area of the country.

Substantial numbers of student psychology conferences also are held annually. Like the regional teaching conferences, these student psychology conferences currently tend to be clustered in the eastern half of the United States.

Although the focus of this chapter has been on teaching and student conferences, the importance of these events ultimately resides in their impact on students. In the beginning of the chapter we boldly stated that the development of regional teaching conferences may be remembered as the most significant occurrence for teachers of psychology in the 1980s and 1990s. Having reviewed the development and benefits of these conferences, we would reiterate this contention and offer the following observation. If one assumes that the average attendee at a regional teaching conference teaches four classes, having an average of 25 students per class per academic term, then each convention attendee has the potential to influence *at least* 200 students per academic year (excluding summers). Applying these figures to the attendees at the five extant teaching conferences, it is clear that over 100,000 students will be taught annually by faculty who have attended a regional teaching conference. Acknowledging the fact that the same faculty do not attend both a teaching and a student conference each year, the total number of students who are impacted by teachers who have attended at least one such conference may be considerably higher. The importance and potential impact of these conferences is clear.

REFERENCES

Anderson, D., & Rosenfeld, P. (1983). Letting form follow function: A multi-purpose model for undergraduate psychology conferences. *Teaching of Psychology, 10*, 204–206.

Carsrud, A. L. (1975). Undergraduate psychology conferences: Is good research nested under Ph.D.s? *Teaching of Psychology, 2,* 112–114.

Carsrud, A. L., Palladino, J. J., Tanke, E. D., Aubrecht, L., & Huber, R. J. (1984). Undergraduate psychology research conferences: Goals, policies, and procedures. *Teaching of Psychology, 11,* 141–145.

Furedy, J. J., & McRae, R. C. (1985). Some northerly thoughts on undergraduate psychology research conferences. *Teaching of Psychology, 12,* 220–222.

Hill, G. W., IV, & Palladino, J. J. (1990, September). Teaching conferences offer a lot. *APA Monitor,* p. 24.

Hill, G. W., IV, Palladino, J. J., & Smith, R. A. (1992). Live from across the country: A session of in-class demonstrations for teachers of psychology. *Teaching of Psychology, 19,* 54–55.

Lipton, J. P. (1986). A successful undergraduate psychology conference: Organized through a special course. *Teaching of Psychology, 13,* 111–115.

Palladino, J. J. (1988). A faculty development conference: Psychology as a model. *Journal of Staff, Program, & Organization Development, 6,* 169–174.

IV

ORGANIZED PSYCHOLOGY IN ADVANCING THE TEACHING OF PSYCHOLOGY

INTRODUCTION

ORGANIZED PSYCHOLOGY IN ADVANCING THE TEACHING OF PSYCHOLOGY

JANET R. MATTHEWS

Part IV considers the role various organizations have played in advancing the teaching of psychology in the United States. Many different associations have taken part in the formation of the current approach to teaching psychology. This section provides some history of the role played by the American Psychological Association (APA) since its founding in 1892, the APA's teaching division (Division 2), psychology honor societies (Psi Chi and Psi Beta), and four specialty organizations: Council of Teachers of Undergraduate Psychology (CTUP), Council of Undergraduate Psychology Programs (CUPP), Council of Applied Master's Programs in Psychology (CAMPP), and Council of Graduate Departments of Psychology (COGDOP).

James Goodwin addresses the APA's contributions to the teaching of psychology from its founding in 1892 through its restructuring in 1945. He notes that teaching issues were sometimes raised at APA meetings, but that the APA did little that specifically concerned teaching during those years. This chapter focuses on convention sessions and APA committees that addressed curriculum issues and on reports from APA proceedings that include papers on teaching tips.

Paul Nelson and George Stricker summarize the APA's contributions to teaching from 1946 through 1991. They discuss the early development of specialty divisions within the organization, including one specifically devoted to teaching (Division 2), as well as the recent establishment of the Education Directorate within the APA Central Office structure.

Randall Wight and Stephen Davis provide a history of the APA's Division 2 (Teaching of Psychology). They include a list of its past officers and its membership size from 1951 to the present. They highlight changes in that division over the years and provide suggestions about its future role.

Randolph Smith discusses the role of four groups with specialty interests related to teaching psychology. Two of these groups, CTUP and CUPP, focus on undergraduate education in psychology. CTUP initially limited membership to department chairs but later changed its focus to include all undergraduate faculty. CUPP provides a forum for discussing common training issues among undergraduate department chairs and directors of undergraduate training within graduate departments. CAMPP was formed to address training issues in applied master's programs. This group was originally limited to the Southeastern Psychological Association region but expanded to national membership shortly after its founding. With encouragement from the APA Education and Training Board, COGDOP was formed to provide a forum for considering issues of graduate education and training in psychology. To deal specifically with educational issues and avoid questions of professionalism within the APA, this group was developed as an independent organization.

In the final chapter of Part IV, Ruth Cousins, Carol Tracy, and Peter Giordano describe the founding and development of Psi Chi and Psi Beta, the two national honor societies in psychology. These organizations are considered part of the history of the teaching of psychology because of the integral role they have played in the educational process of future psychologists. Psi Chi was founded in 1929 to honor outstanding psychology students in senior colleges and universities. Psi Beta was founded in 1977 to honor students in 2-year institutions. This chapter chronicles the growth and development of the two organizations and describes their degree of mutual assistance and their interactions with other organizations involved in the teaching of psychology.

In this section, the authors trace the development of a range of associations that influenced academic psychology. Some of these organizations are broader in scope than others, but all have left their mark on the teaching of psychology.

14

THE AMERICAN PSYCHOLOGICAL ASSOCIATION AND THE TEACHING OF PSYCHOLOGY, 1892–1945

C. JAMES GOODWIN

As the title suggests, this chapter attempts to answer the question, "What did the American Psychological Association (APA) contribute to the teaching of psychology in the years before the 1945 reorganization?" Simply put, the answer is "not much." Consider the following report from an APA Committee on the Academic Status of Psychology, which had been formed in 1913 and made several recommendations at the 1914 annual meeting. One was an explicit urging that "at each annual meeting of the Association some topic be chosen which bears on the teaching of psychology" (Ogden, 1915, p. 49). Although this proposal might appear eminently reasonable to a late-20th-century psychologist (especially to a member of Division 2) and encouraging for the historian hoping that the answer to the opening question would be "quite a bit," the sentence immediately after the earlier quoted recommendation showed that the APA was not ready then for a long-term commitment to teaching. It reads as follows: the "resolution was amended to provide [programming related to teaching] *only for the next annual year*" [italics added] (Ogden, 1915, p. 49).

To say this example illustrates the APA's lack of interest in the teaching of psychology at that time probably overstates the case. However, it is fair to say that the APA's involvement with teaching was sporadic at best in the years prior to 1945, and the 1914 resolution is a case in point. There were some noteworthy events, however, and I examine in this chapter the APA's attempts to improve the teaching of psychology in the years between its founding and reorganization. On balance, it will be seen that the APA had other priorities during that time.

APA ACTIVITIES RELATED TO TEACHING

An examination of the APA reports of proceedings reveals three categories of activity at the annual meetings that relate to teaching. First, there are references to papers and discussions on the use of psychological principles to aid education generally and in particular to facilitate the training of teachers. The first mention of teaching to be found in the proceedings is of this type. In a speech at the first annual meeting, Hugo Münsterberg criticized the new experimental psychology for being "too little in touch with the mental sciences, especially philosophy and pedagogics" (Sokal, 1973, p. 283). A more optimistic note was sounded the following year, when George Trumball Ladd, in his presidential address, commented favorably on psychology's ability to contribute to human welfare. As an example, he referred to psychology's "growing capacity to contribute to pedagogics" (Sokal, 1973, p. 287).

This first type of activity, using psychology to aid the process of education, comes under the umbrella of educational psychology. Although obviously an important example of the functional value of psychological principles, it is not directly related to the question of how the APA contributed to the teaching of psychology, and I do not consider it here. Rather, this chapter's focus is on the two other types of contributions made by the APA to the teaching of psychology. First, the APA occasionally sponsored sessions and established committees dealing with questions about the psychology curriculum (e.g., what the first course should be like). Second, the APA reports of proceedings contain a sprinkling of papers that could be classified as "tips on teaching X", with X being some specific topic within a course or a course in itself. Of these two types of reports, those dealing with the curriculum occurred more frequently.

Annual Meetings Prior to 1920

Psychology began to develop a distinct identity in the last two decades of the 19th century, and it is only natural that a discipline trying to define itself would be concerned about what its students should be taught. There are numerous articles in the literature dealing with the curriculum during this time (e.g., Jastrow, 1890; Miner, 1904), and Sanford's (1894) laboratory manual was a milestone in the standardization of laboratory instruction during the 1890s. However, except for a description of the program of studies at the University of Toronto (Cattell, 1895) and an apparently ignored argument by F. C. French (Farrand, 1898) that experimental psychology was too advanced for undergraduates and should be taught only to graduate students, curricular matters received little mention at the annual APA meetings before the turn of the century. Between 1892 and 1920, significant APA events relating to the psychology curriculum were sporadic at best. Some important events did occur, however, indicating at least an occasional recognition of the importance of teaching for the advancement of the new science.

The 1899 Meeting

The first genuine APA session devoted to the teaching of psychology occurred at the 1899 meeting, when a discussion was held on the question of how psychology should be taught (Farrand, 1900). Presentations were made by George S. Fullerton, Joseph Jastrow, H. Austin Aikins, and Charles H. Judd; a general discussion followed. There are several points worth noting. First, the topic was obviously considered to be significant. Three of the four speakers either had been (Fullerton) or would become (Jastrow and Judd) APA presidents. Second, the main concern of all of the speakers was the overall structure of the psychology curriculum. At a time when psychology was struggling for disciplinary and institutional identity, this session went to the heart of the question of how psychology was to be defined. All of the speakers emphasized that the new psychology must be taught as a science.

Fullerton argued that it was important to maintain a balance between the "New Psychology and Old, the psychology of the laboratory and the statistical circular, and that which depends largely upon introspection and reflective analysis" (Farrand, 1900, pp. 128–129). Laboratory work is essential, he continued, and "should be omitted only from stern necessity" because it "awakens in the student's mind a realization of the fact that psychology really is a natural science" (Farrand, 1900, pp. 128–129). Jastrow raised the question of what the first course in psychology ought to be like, a question that has recurred with some regularity throughout the 100-year history of the APA (a symposium on general psychology was held as recently as the 1990 meeting). Psychology, according to Jastrow, was "concerned with a systematic explanation of the student's mental functions, and this functional aspect . . . should dominate the manner of presenting psychology to the student" (Farrand, 1900, p. 130). Jastrow went on to say that the introductory student should be given basic tutoring in the introspective method and should concentrate on learning about fundamental sensory functions. The course should include numerous laboratory demonstrations.

Aikins also discussed the introductory course but gave it even more of a laboratory emphasis than did Jastrow. He made specific reference to the use of Sanford's laboratory manual in the course. Judd talked generally about the necessity of scientific training in psychology as a way of teaching the difference between observation and inference.

The 1905 Meeting

One might think the 1899 session, featuring such eminent psychologists and described in great detail in the proceedings, would be just the first of a continuing series of program sessions concerning the structure of the psychology curriculum. Not so: It took another 6 years for the topic to reappear in the program. At the 1905 meeting, there was a session featuring presentations by Judd and Sanford. Judd spoke mostly on the ways in which different departments could cooperate in order to unify instruction, and he made a special plea (which had no apparent effect) for "the Association to devote more time at its regular meetings to the discussion of methods of instruction and to the discussion of courses in the different phases of psychology" (Davis, 1906, p. 59). Sanford took up the question of the first course again and later published his remarks in *Pedagogical Seminary* (Sanford, 1906). His approach differed considerably from Jastrow's.

Edmund Sanford was known as a devoted teacher (Goodwin, 1987), and his description of the introductory course is a good illustration of how he made student needs a priority. His approach to the first course is an early example of a strategy designed to "turn on" and be "relevant for" the student in general psychology. In Sanford's terms, the course should be designed to answer the question, "What sort of psychological knowledge are these young men or young women most likely to find useful, immediately or remotely, in the actual affairs of life?" (Sanford, 1906, p. 118). Sanford's answer was that the course should teach students some of the basics about how a psychologist tries to think objectively about mental processes, but its emphasis should be on a range of topics that would help the student deal more effectively with other people. These topics would include learning and acquisition, the psychology of truth and error (with subtopics ranging from perceptual illusions to the cognitive distortions of prejudice), emotion, personality and character, the interdependence of mind and body, psychogenesis, and systematic psychology. The minimal coverage of topics such as basic sensory processes, the physiology of the nervous system, psychophysics, and reaction time may seem surprising, especially coming from a well-known experimentalist, but Sanford argued that students should first be taught the things most directly related to their everyday lives. After they have been hooked, he argued, they can be trained more systematically in the laboratory.

Sanford's ideas about the first course apparently led to an extensive discussion; descriptions of the comments of others took up more than 4 pages in the proceedings of the 1905 meeting. The reactions to what Mary Calkins (APA president that year) referred to as Sanford's "invigorating heresy" (Smith, 1906, p. 147) ranged from enthusiastic support for this "ideal course" (Davis, 1906, p. 60) to the more conservative concern that the science of psychology would be best served by giving students a course firmly based in physiology and known laboratory work in topics such as sensation and psychophysics.

One observer of this Judd and Sanford session hoped that there would be a session at the APA meeting in the following year to report on progress in teaching the beginner's course. Once again, however, a session on teaching proved to be an isolated event at an APA meeting. It was another 3 years before the topic of teaching reappeared on the program, this time in the form of the first APA committee on teaching.

The 1909 Meeting: The Seashore Report

Like the 1899 session on teaching, the formation of this first committee in 1908 showed that at least some of the APA leadership recognized the importance of how psychology was being taught. The Committee on Methods of Teaching Psychology was composed of five eminent psychologists: Carl E. Seashore (chairman), James R. Angell, Calkins, Sanford, and Guy M. Whipple, with the latter being the only non-APA president. The committee was charged with gathering information on teaching and preparing a discussion for the 1909 meeting (Pierce, 1909).

Early in its deliberations, the committee decided to focus its efforts on the first course in psychology, and extensive "questionaries" [sic] were sent to colleges and universities in order to evaluate the state of the art in teaching the introductory course. The result of this survey was a 93-page monograph that included a number of recommendations.

Concerning the aims of the course, the committee cautioned the teacher to remember that the course was in psychology, not philosophy. As Seashore (1910) put it in his conclusion to the monograph:

> Strange to say, this is the one exhortation most needed today. While only a few schools lag in the old rut and teach antiquated systems of philosophy in the name of psychology, the common error today is to ramble from the study of mental processes as such into sense physiology, moralizing, loose pedagogy or logical quibble. . . . The primary aim [of the course] is to train the student in the observation and explanation of mental facts. (pp. 81–82)

Concerning ways of teaching this course, instructors were urged to "use methods which develop efficiency in introspection, observation, thinking and action" (Seashore, 1910, p. 85). In particular, instructors were urged to combine lecture with discussion and incorporate demonstrations and experiments or exercises that could be done in class or as homework. "Keep the student doing things, instead of merely listening, reading or seeing them done. . . . Even if he is to be entertained, in the course, let it be most frequently by his own activity" (Seashore, 1910, p. 83).

The committee also recommended that the course be taught in the sophomore year, that it last for the entire year, and that it be taught by senior psychologists. The course

> is perhaps unequalled by other college subjects in its power to influence the life of the student; the introduction to this subject should, therefore, be taught by mature members of the department. Young instructors can handle advanced work better than the elementary. (Seashore, 1910, p. 91)

Also, in a recommendation well ahead of its time, the committee suggested that psychologists in different parts of the country should organize conferences especially designed for teachers of psychology. The long-term effect of this recommendation is not clear, but it appears that Seashore took the recommendation to heart. In March 1910, a conference for teachers of psychology in Iowa was organized and met with the Western Philosophical Association. At the meeting, Seashore was elected president of the group, and the "formal organization of the Conference was perfected" (Notes, 1910, p. 147).

Along with a session on Freud's ideas, popular because of his recent visit to Clark University, the 1909 session on teaching was said to be one of the two most interesting at the annual meeting (Pierce, 1910). The discussion centered on the previously distributed committee report and was led by the five committee members, plus Walter Pillsbury, John Baird, and Howard Warren (three more APA presidents). That psychology still lacked consensus about its subject matter was evident from the discussion that

> showed that the most diverse aims and methods now prevail in different institutions, that everything from physics to metaphysics is taught in the name of psychology with the consequent misfortune that students are confused and the subject too often discredited as a part of an educational curriculum. (Haggerty, 1910, p. 188)

This is not to say the committee's report had minimal effect. Its recommendations were directly quoted on the first page of a well-known introductory text written shortly thereafter by Yerkes (1911), who followed the committee's advice to keep the students active by including at the end of each chapter a simple demonstration exercise. For example, after the chapter on attention, students were given these self-observation instructions:

Listen intently to the ticking of a watch held before the class by the instructor. Note any changes in the clearness of the sounds. Note also the disappearance of the sounds and the nature of the consciousness during the intervals. (Yerkes, 1911, p. 299)

One of the Seashore committee's recommendations was that a standing committee on "class experiments" (like the Yerkes examples) be formed that would report annually on work relating to the teaching of psychology and would "publish from time to time [a listing] of good demonstrations and class experiments . . . and descriptions of demonstrational apparatus (Sanford, 1910, pp. 66–69). This three-person committee was indeed formed in 1910 and chaired by Whipple. Much of the committee's work concerned the cataloging of teaching techniques, demonstrations, class experiments, and so on. It made reports at the annual meetings in 1911, 1913, 1914, and 1916, before being discharged in 1919. These reports appear to be the only published accounts of the demonstrations and class experiments. No other descriptions can be found between 1910 and 1919 in *Pedagogical Seminary, Psychological Review, Psychological Bulletin*, or the *American Journal of Psychology*.

At the 1913 meeting, Walter Bingham, APA secretary and a member of the Whipple committee, arranged an exhibit of "sample outlines, syllabi, examination questions, laboratory directions and other aids to teaching" (Bingham, 1914, p. 31). In the following year, 1914, the usual apparatus exhibited included "the reports on class experiments which have been gathered by the Association's committee" (Ogden, 1915, p. 46). In the immediately subsequent years, however, teaching aids were not specifically mentioned as being part of the apparatus exhibit.

The 1914 and 1915 Meetings

The 1914 meeting also included the first report of the APA's second committee to deal with questions of teaching. As described at the opening of the chapter, the APA formed the Committee on the Academic Status of Psychology in 1913; it made its first formal report (28 pages) at the 1914 meeting. Three resolutions were presented to the membership and passed: one to continue the interim committee as a standing committee of the association; one (as mentioned earlier) to provide a special program on teaching at the next meeting; and a third urging the APA to

adopt the principle that the undergraduate psychological curriculum in any college or university, great or small, should be planned from the standpoint of psychology and in accordance with psychological ideals, rather than to fit the needs and meet the demands of some other branch of learning. (Ogden, 1915, p. 49)

This third resolution suggests that the confusion over the undergraduate psychology curriculum that surfaced in the 1909 session on teaching, and more broadly the concern over the essential structure of the discipline of psychology, still existed in 1914. As Camfield (1973) pointed out, the APA was determined during this time to be a guardian of independent academic status for the field, thereby facilitating the professionalization of psychology in the United States and its separation from disciplines such as philosophy.

The special program delivered in the following year was a discussion of "The Relation of Psychology to Science, Philosophy and Pedagogy in the Academic Curriculum," with papers presented by Raymond Dodge and M. F. Meyer on "Psychology and Science," (illness prevented Dodge from presenting his paper, however), H. N. Gardiner and R. M. Ogden on "Psychology and Philosophy," and C. H. Judd and M. E. Haggerty on "Psychology and Pedagogy" (Ogden, 1916, pp. 51–56). The titles suggest a session much broader than the topic of how to teach psychology; indeed, the discussion centered on the general issue of psychology's independence and its scientific status, in particular whether separate departments of psychology should be the norm. Even the discussion on "Psychology and Pedagogy" did not address the teaching of psychology per se but dealt with what type of psychology course should be given to students in schools of education. The issue apparently sparked some debate because one of the speakers (Judd) contended that

> general psychology is so far removed in its broad statements from the concrete and detailed problems of teaching that the connection has often been hard to trace between psychology as actually taught and practical needs of the teacher. [Also,] the disputes within psychology itself have very largely reduced the value of this science for teachers. [Thus,] psychology in its present form cannot be used as an introductory course for teachers. (Ogden, 1916, p. 54)

Haggerty argued just the opposite, however, and described in detail the psychology curriculum for teachers-in-training at the University of Minnesota.

Like the Committee on Teaching Experiments, the Committee on the Academic Status of Psychology was discharged at the 1919 meeting. In addition to planning the 1915 symposium, this later committee also issued reports on the status of psychology in the normal schools (Ogden, 1916) and on the difference between psychological experiments and mental tests (Ogden, 1917).

Annual Meetings of the 1920s

Some major changes occurred in the APA during the 1920s. After the end of World War I, applied psychology was in ascendancy in American psychology, with one outcome being the creation, in 1924, of the "associate" grade of membership for psychologists, mainly those working in nonacademic settings whose scholarly output was not sufficient for them to be elected to full membership. The shift toward application caused some consternation among the APA leadership, many of whom were academician–scientist types (O'Donnell, 1979). For example, E. G. Boring, acting in his role of APA secretary, wrote in the proceedings for 1922 that

> about 62% of the material presented dealt with applied or clinical psychology or the tests; that only 24% of the papers were in experimental or comparative psychology. . . . It would seem that this distribution represents a shift of interest within the Association. (Boring, 1923, p. 62)

Perhaps this shift of interest and the controversy it provoked helps explain the paucity of material on teaching at the annual meetings of the 1920s. During the decade, the entire contribution of the APA to the teaching of psychology amounted to a handful of papers (two or three at the most) on classroom demonstrations, and two sessions on the introductory course. In the first of these sessions, L. L. Thurstone's argument that "we have entirely failed in our textbooks to deal with socially significant and interesting content" (Boring, 1921, p. 66) was reminiscent of Sanford's 1905 plea for a relevant course. Just as Sanford's proposal was not met with widespread acceptance, Thurstone's "suggestion to introduce the beginning student to some phases of human behavior aside from the simple sensory reactions met with quite violent opposition" (Kantor, 1921, p. 189).

The question of how introductory psychology should be taught arose again at the end of the decade in the form of a roundtable discussion on "The First Course in Psychology," held at the 1928 meeting and chaired by M. F. Meyer. Evidently, the session was not too successful; the discussion was said to be "limited mainly to an account of how different individuals teach the first course, with no progress in the direction of a 'one best way,' if such there can ever be" (Poffenberger, 1929, p. 342). Interest was high, however. Of the 536 psychologists registered for the convention, more than 100 attended the session. The confusion over the structure and content of the first course led to a motion at the business meeting that a committee be formed "to work on the problem of trying to reach an agreement with respect to ideas which should be fulfilled by a first course in psychology" (Fernberger, 1929, p. 127). Whether out of a lack of interest or a sense that the problem was unsolvable (or both), the motion failed to carry and no committee was formed.

Annual Meetings of the 1930s and Early 1940s

One might predict that interest in the teaching of psychology would increase in the years leading up to the 1945 reorganization, especially in light of the fact that one of the divisions in the new structure would be specifically designated for teaching. Once again, however, interest was sporadic and minimal, at least if the reports of proceedings are a reliable indication. There was another inconclusive roundtable discussion on "The Elementary Course in Psychology" in 1939 (Olson, 1939) and roundtables on "Radio in Education" in 1932 (Paterson, 1933a) and "The Subject Matter of the Course on Educational Psychology" in 1936 (Paterson, 1937). The occasional paper describing some teaching technique also continued to occur.

Several ad hoc committees related to teaching were formed in the 1930s. These included committees on (a) teaching psychology in high school and junior college, (b) teaching psychology in schools of education, and (c) standardizing the requirements for the PhD. As part of its work, this latter committee did a study of academic supply and demand between 1929 and 1933 and concluded that graduate students thinking about a career in teaching psychology might want to rethink their decision. For example, although the number of students earning PhDs increased steadily during the 4 years studied, the number of new PhDs being placed in academic settings declined by more than half, from 60 to 22, among the 350 institutions responding to the survey. Furthermore, these schools expected that during the following year there would be a reduction of 39 existing positions then held by those with the PhDs (Paterson, 1933b). That the situation did not improve during the Depression is indicated by an APA committee formed in mid-decade on the "Social Utilization of Unemployed Psychologists" (Paterson, 1936).

One APA committee related to teaching that remained active through most of the decade of the 1930s was the Committee on Motion Pictures and Sound Recording Devices in Instruction of Psychology. The Committee was formed in 1930 and was chaired initially by Walter Miles, an enthusiastic early supporter of the use of film in both research and instruction. In the mid-1920s, for example, he used a 16-mm camera attached to the ceiling to record data for his research with rats on elevated mazes, and in several of his talks during the time he illustrated his results by showing films of typical maze-learning trials (Miles, 1926, July 24).

Instructional films were first shown at the 1933 meeting, followed by a roundtable discussion chaired by Miles (Paterson, 1933a). The Committee organized a second roundtable and gave its first formal report at the 1934 meeting (Paterson, 1934). The report noted the rapid increase in the number of films being made and recommended that the films be reviewed and abstracted in *Psychological Abstracts*, a procedure that was soon adopted (Paterson, 1936). The showing of research and instructional films became a regular feature of the annual meeting.

During 1940–1945, there were no sessions held at the annual meetings that related to teaching. At this time, the APA was concerned with the developing movement for reorganization and with the war. The war led to a cancellation of the general meetings of 1942, 1943, and 1945 (only business meetings were held). A business meeting with a limited program was held in 1944.

CONCLUSION

I opened this chapter by characterizing the APA's contribution to teaching prior to 1945 as minimal. Although some important developments did occur, as documented here, it is not really surprising that Fernberger's (1932, 1943) comprehensive histories of the APA barely mentioned the teaching of psychology. His 1932 article had a brief description of the Seashore committee and the 1914 committee on academic status; his 1943 paper had no reference whatsoever to teaching. Although a Division 2 member in the centennial year might be tempted into a type of presentist history (the importance of active APA involvement in teaching is understood now—why could they not see it then?), the APA's minimal contribution to teaching in its early years is understandable when placed in the context of its early difficulties trying to establish itself. Simply put, although individual psychologists and departments of psychology undoubtedly wrestled with the important questions about teaching psychology, the professional organization of the APA had other priorities in the years preceding the 1945 reorganization. The most important concern, especially in the early years but recurring throughout the period under review here, was the importance of the APA establishing disciplinary identity for psychology and professional status for psychologists (Napoli, 1981).

The reports of proceedings in the APA's first dozen years or so make frequent reference to this identity problem, usually in the form of disagreements about program content at the meetings. In particular, there was much discussion about the place of philosophical papers at the annual meetings, and several attempts were made to separate philosophical papers into separate sections, create a philosophical section, or eliminate philosophical papers entirely (Goodwin, 1985). This latter suggestion was made at the 1896 meeting, when Lightner Witmer proposed that the program contain "only such papers and contributions . . . as are psychological in subject-matter" and that the APA's Council "present . . . a plan for the formation of a [separate] American Philosophical or Metaphysical Association" (Farrand, 1897, p. 109). The eventual outcome was the formation of the American Philosophical Association in 1902. That problems over the distinction between philosophical and psychological studies continued, however, is clear from the 1909 Seashore report and the 1914 discussion of the academic status of psychology.

At the heart of the concern about philosophy was the question of how psychology was to be conceptualized. The desire to define the new discipline as a science was made clear in 1894, when the APA's constitution was adopted. Article I, the "Object" of the APA, would be "the advancement of psychology as a science" (Cattell, 1895, p. 150). With this Bylaw as the cornerstone of the organization, and with sustained effort needed to transform this goal into reality, questions about the teaching of psychology were bound to be secondary.

The attitude that a teaching position was merely the means to provide the opportunity to conduct research was undoubtedly fostered by the goal of making psychology a science and it was an attitude that developed early in the APA's history. One consequence was that the APA's annual meeting provided a means for young scholars to establish themselves as scientists. Perhaps this is one reason why the early sessions that did relate to teaching featured established figures (i.e., former or soon-to-be APA presidents). Their reputations as scholars were already secure.

The controversy over the direction of the APA that occurred after World War I was another manifestation of the identity problem. Teaching again became a secondary concern in the face of the debate between academicians and practitioners over program content, membership requirements, and the threats of fragmentation resulting from the formation of new organizations such as the Association of Consulting Psychologists in 1921 (Hilgard, 1987). Also during this time, the papers became even more clearly differentiated by topic than they had been before. With papers organized into areas such as social, personality, child, and so on, it was difficult to include topics on teaching unless they were special sessions like the occasional roundtable. The Program Committee's report for the 1933 meeting explicitly stated that "topics not logically related to a natural [i.e., disciplinary] grouping of papers for program purposes" had been rejected (Paterson, 1933b, p. 641).

Over the years, the most frequent APA program related to teaching dealt with concerns about the first course in psychology. A long literature review by Wolfle (1942) about the first course described it as "one of the most popular and most frequently scheduled topics for symposia at national and regional meetings" (p. 685). Specific reference was made to the 1909 Seashore report, which Wolfle described as making for "discouraging reading. Now, 30-odd years later, we are still debating many of the same issues and being embarrassed by the same difficulties. Many of the recommendations considered necessary in 1909 are still necessary in 1942" (Wolfle, 1942, p. 686). The recurring presence of this "first course problem" is perhaps an intractable problem, but it is also another indication of concern with disciplinary identity. The student's first encounter with psychology presumably should make it clear how the field is to be defined.

In summary, between 1892 and 1945, with the possible exception of an interest in how the first course was to be taught, enhancing the teaching of psychology was not a priority of the APA, at least as reflected in the program content of the annual meetings. There were indeed sporadic initiatives, committees, roundtables, and special sessions, and even a failed attempt or two (1905 and 1914) to mandate annual programming about teaching. However, these events were irregular and peripheral to the central focus of the APA as it struggled to establish both itself as a professional organization and psychology as a specialized discipline.

REFERENCES

Bingham, W. V. (1914). Proceedings of the twenty-second annual meeting of the American Psychological Association. *Psychological Bulletin, 11,* 29–72.

Boring, E. G. (1921). Proceedings of the twenty-ninth annual meeting of the American Psychological Association. *Psychological Bulletin, 18,* 57–108.

Boring, E. G. (1923). Proceedings of the thirty-first annual meeting of the American Psychological Association. *Psychological Bulletin, 20,* 61–108.

Camfield, T. M. (1973). The professionalization of American psychology. *Journal of the History of the Behavioral Sciences, 9,* 66–75.

Cattell, R. B. (1895). Proceedings of the third annual meeting of the American Psychological Association. *Psychological Review, 2,* 149–172.

Davis, W. H. (1906). Proceedings of the fourteenth annual meeting of the American Psychological Association. *Psychological Bulletin, 3,* 37–75.

Farrand, L. (1897). Proceedings of the fifth annual meeting of the American Psychological Association. *Psychological Review, 4,* 107–141.

Farrand, L. (1898). Proceedings of the sixth annual meeting of the American Psychological Association. *Psychological Review, 5,* 145–171.

Farrand, L. (1900). Proceedings of the eighth annual meeting of the American Psychological Association. *Psychological Review, 7,* 125–158.

Fernberger, S. W. (1929). Proceedings of the thirty-seventh annual meeting of the American Psychological Association. *Psychological Bulletin, 26,* 121–184.

Fernberger, S. W. (1932). The American Psychological Association: A historical summary, 1892–1930. *Psychological Bulletin, 29,* 1–89.

Fernberger, S. W. (1943). The American Psychological Association, 1892–1942. *Psychological Review, 50,* 33–60.

Goodwin, C. J. (1985). On the origins of Tichener's experimentalists. *Journal of the History of the Behavioral Sciences, 21,* 383–389.

Goodwin, C. J. (1987). In Hall's shadow: Edmund Clark Sanford (1859–1924). *Journal of the History of the Behavioral Sciences, 23,* 153–168.

Haggerty, M. E. (1910). The eighteenth annual meeting of the American Psychological Association. *Journal of Philosophy, 7,* 185–191.

Hilgard, E. R. (1987). *Psychology in America: A historical survey.* New York: Harcourt Brace Jovanovich.

Jastrow, J. (1890). Psychology at the University of Wisconsin. *American Journal of Psychology, 3*, 275–276.

Kantor, J. R. (1921). The twenty-ninth annual meeting of the American Psychological Association. *Journal of Philosophy, 18*, 185–192.

Miles, W. R. (1926, July 24). *Letter to H. S. Langfeld.* (Available from the Walter Miles Papers, Archives of the History of American Psychology, University of Akron, OH)

Miner, B. G. (1904). The changing attitudes of American universities toward psychology. *Science, 20*, 299–307.

Napoli, D. S. (1981). *Architects of adjustment: The history of the psychological profession in the United States.* Port Washington, NY: Kennikat Press.

Notes. (1910). *American Journal of Psychology, 7*, 147.

O'Donnell, J. M. (1979). The crisis of experimentalism in the 1920's: E. G. Boring and his uses of history. *American Psychologist, 34*, 289–295.

Ogden, R. M. (1915). Proceedings of the twenty-third annual meeting of the American Psychological Association. *Psychological Bulletin, 12*, 45–81.

Ogden, R. M. (1916). Proceedings of the twenty-fourth annual meeting of the American Psychological Association. *Psychological Bulletin, 13*, 41–100.

Ogden, R. M. (1917). Proceedings of the twenty-fifth annual meeting of the American Psychological Association. *Psychological Bulletin, 14*, 33–80.

Olson, W. C. (1939). Proceedings of the forty-seventh annual meeting of the American Psychological Association, Incorporated. *Psychological Bulletin, 36*, 740–783.

Paterson, D. G. (1933a). The fortieth annual meeting of the American Psychological Association. *American Journal of Psychology, 45*, 174–176.

Paterson, D. G. (1933b). Proceedings of the forth-first annual meeting of the American Psychological Association, Incorporated. *Psychological Bulletin, 30*, 631–741.

Paterson, D. G. (1934). Proceedings of the forty-second annual meeting of the American Psychological Association, Incorporated. *Psychological Bulletin, 31*, 647–754.

Paterson, D. G. (1936). The forty-third annual meeting of the American Psychological Association. *American Journal of Psychology, 48*, 172–174.

Paterson, D. G. (1937). The forty-fourth annual meeting of the American Psychological Association. *American Journal of Psychology, 49*, 140–142.

Pierce, A. H. (1909). Proceedings of the seventeenth annual meeting of the American Psychological Association. *Psychological Bulletin, 6*, 33–44.

Pierce, A. H. (1910). Proceedings of the eighteenth annual meeting of the American Psychological Association. *Psychological Bulletin, 7*, 37–64.

Poffenberger, A. T. (1929). The thirty-seventh annual meeting of the American Psychological Association. *American Journal of Psychology, 41*, 341–343.

Sanford, E. C. (1894). *A course in experimental psychology.* Lexington, MA: Heath.

Sanford, E. C. (1906). A sketch of a beginner's course in psychology. *Pedagogical Seminary, 13*, 118–124.

Sanford, E. C. (1910). The teaching of elementary psychology in colleges and universities with laboratories. *Psychological Monographs, 12*(Whole No. 4), 54–71.

Seashore, C. E. (1910). General report on the teaching of the elementary course in psychology: Recommendations. *Psychological Monographs, 12*(Whole No. 4), 80–91.

Smith, T. L. (1906). The annual meeting of the American Psychological Association. *American Journal of Psychology, 17*, 144–148.

Sokal, M. M. (1973). APA's first publication: Proceedings of the American Psychological Association, 1892–1893. *American Psychologist, 28*, 277–292.

Wolfle, D. (1942). The first course in psychology. *Psychological Bulletin, 39*, 685–712.

Yerkes, R. M. (1911). *Introduction to psychology.* New York: Holt.

15

ADVANCING THE TEACHING OF PSYCHOLOGY: CONTRIBUTIONS OF THE AMERICAN PSYCHOLOGICAL ASSOCIATION, 1946–1992

PAUL D. NELSON AND GEORGE STRICKER

In the preceding chapter on the American Psychological Association (APA) and the teaching of psychology, Goodwin concluded that relatively little attention had been given overall by the APA to advance the teaching of psychology between 1892 and 1945. More attention was given, he asserted, to matters of curriculum content and, apart from academic issues, to matters of professionalism in the field. Certainly, by the end of the period covered in Goodwin's review, the APA was engaged seriously in professional identity issues. One example is the APA Policy and Planning Board's (1947) attention to the question of who is a psychologist. The answer was sought to clarify matters of certification, accreditation, and membership levels in the APA. Those concerns proved to be a harbinger of what was to come in ensuing decades, during which time the field of psychology expanded exponentially as an applied scientific discipline and profession.

It is ironic that relatively little attention seems to have been given by the APA to matters of teaching during a period of time in which a substantial proportion of APA members were affiliated with academic institutions. The earliest members were predominantly affiliated with academic institutions. By midcentury, Clark (1957) reported that half of those awarded their doctorates in 1950 were employed primarily in an academic setting, a reduction from the 64% so employed among those who completed their doctoral programs between 1930 and 1944. By contrast, less than one third are so employed today (Kohout & Wicherski, 1990).

The growth of professional psychology notwithstanding, we believe that the APA has given considerable attention to issues of pedagogy in psychology since 1945. Directly or indirectly, through its Division on the Teaching of Psychology (Division 2), the spawning of national groups of psychology teachers outside of the APA, its initiation of and support for national conferences on education and training in psychology, its public information on careers in psychology, and its monumental growth as a publisher of psychological research and other scholarly writings, the APA has demonstrated a clear commitment to issues of teaching and the needs of teachers since 1945.

A more definitive analysis of those contributions can be found in other chapters in this book. Our focus in this chapter is on the role of the APA governance per se (i.e., APA boards, committees, and task forces) and its Central Office staff in advancing the teaching of psychology during the same period.

Two principal roles exist for membership associations: providing direct, beneficial services to members and, less directly, serving the membership and the discipline as well as the public through policy development and program implementation. It is more in keeping with the latter role that the APA clearly asserted leadership in the immediate post-World War II years to advance the teaching of psychology. It did so partly through reorganization and partly out of concern that, with the increased emphasis on professional issues in education, more general issues of education in psychology would not be overlooked. We now highlight the history of APA governance initiatives on education and training between 1946 and 1992 in support of that contention.

ORGANIZED PSYCHOLOGY REORGANIZES

In the late 1940s, as a consequence of wartime neuropsychiatric casualties and the need for more psychologists trained at the doctoral level, the Veterans Administration and the U.S. Public Health Service turned to the APA for assistance in identifying graduate training centers that would be adequate for preparing clinical psychologists. Sears (1947), reporting for the APA Committee on Graduate and Professional Training, summarized the procedures and criteria by which graduate training facilities were to be evaluated in determining those who were the most capable of preparing clinical psychologists, the origin of accreditation in psychology. Subsequently, the Shakow Committee (APA Committee on Training in Clinical Psychology, 1947, 1949) developed in more depth the initial accreditation criteria and procedures for evaluating clinical psychology training programs.

Needs for clinical training, however, were not the only ones of concern in those years. Indeed, because of the value of psychological principles and methods recognized in civil as well as military defense applications during the war years, there were increasing demands for applied psychologists in general. In fact, one might argue that such demand for and preoccupation with the applications of psychology and for psychologists prepared to work in nonacademic settings, including those concerned with mental health, kindled an equal interest in ensuring that fundamental questions about psychology as an academic and scientific discipline not be neglected.

That certainly became clear by the time of the 1949 Boulder Conference on Graduate Education in Clinical Psychology, in which participants recommended the following:

> The American Psychological Association should have a committee concerned primarily with educational policies, a committee that is not limited to the problems of clinical psychology but . . . [one] with broad powers to examine and review educational philosophy, methods, and standards beyond those serving as the foundation for accreditation in any one field of applied psychology. (Raimy, 1950, p. 178)

These same concerns and aspirations served as the basis for the APA to reorganize its governance at midcentury in the area of education and training. APA Executive Secretary Fillmore Sanford summarized recommendations from the APA Policy and Planning Board, for endorsement by the Board of Directors and subsequent approval by the Council of Representatives, to the effect that there should be a new organizational structure to address more effectively issues pertaining to the training of psychologists. At its meeting in March 1951, the APA Board of Directors resolved to foster "a broadened and integrated concern with the scientific and professional education of psychologists" (Sanford, 1951, p. 1).

In that context, the APA Board of Directors proposed that there should be an Education and Training (E&T) Board, with committees in the areas of undergraduate education, subdoctoral graduate education and training, training in psychology for people in other professions, doctoral education and training, and practicum training, with the latter two having subcommittees for applied specialty areas, such as clinical and industrial. Other committees on education and training existing at that time were discontinued, and their functions were absorbed by the new organizational structure.

The first members of the E&T Board were Edward S. Bordin, Claude

E. Buxton, Stuart W. Cook (Chair), Karl F. Heiser, Carl I. Hovland, E. Lowell Kelly, Lyle H. Lanier, Donald B. Lindsley, David C. McClelland, Bruce V. Moore, Clifford T. Morgan, and Ruth S. Tolman. In addition, for the first time at the APA Central Office, there was a full-time staff officer to work with the E&T Board and a first-year budget of approximately $25,000, of which 60% was to come from a U.S. Public Health Service grant (Sanford, 1951).

Sanford's (1951) memorandum suggested that the new E&T Board should have purview over issues of education and training at all levels and in all areas of learning, not merely those of relevance to professional education and training for clinical or other applied areas of psychology. Indeed, these documents show a sense of urgency among the proponents of an education board that, regardless of how important the new opportunities and challenges in the professionalization of psychology were, it was imperative that organized psychology not lose sight of its responsibilities in addressing more fundamental issues of education (i.e., in psychology as part of a liberal education).

Yet, interestingly enough, explicit reference to teaching per se, or to the advancement of teaching in psychology, was not made in Sanford's (1951) communication or in recommendations to the Council of Representatives from the Board of Directors that were conveyed by his memorandum. Were pedagogical issues implied in discussions about curriculum goals and standards at different levels of education and training? Or, were such matters deemed to be the responsibility of academicians, not of a national membership association, and consequently were not included explicitly among the priorities identified for APA governance attention? Whatever the intent of the new APA governance policy, it became clear at the E&T Board's first meeting, a conference held at the University of Michigan in February 1952, that among the priorities for the APA's educational agenda would be the advancement of teaching, apart from matters of curriculum content or sequence (APA Education and Training Board, 1952).

ADVANCEMENT OF TEACHING

In light of those thoughts and plans, we discuss how the APA governance and staff served to advance the teaching of psychology through policies and programs in education and training. In the sections that follow, we delineate chronologically major themes and types of efforts on the part of the APA governance to advance the teaching of psychology at the precollege, undergraduate, and graduate levels of education and training. For the most part, the events are traced from the advent of the new E&T Board and its committees in the early 1950s. We conclude with a discussion of recent events of the 1990s and what may lie ahead as organized psychology begins its second century.

Precollege-Level Teaching

Interest in attracting youth to the field of psychology prompted the APA in 1946 to have its executive secretary prepare and publish a booklet on careers in psychology (APA Council of Representatives, 1946), a publication for general public distribution that continues to rank among the most frequently requested materials from the APA. Although that publication originally might have been intended more for undergraduate than for high school students and has had more to do with describing the fields of activity in which psychologists are involved than with pedagogical issues, its development reflects a concern by the APA about how the field of psychology is presented to the public, a forethought perhaps to how it is taught.

Still, it was not until the time of the University of Michigan conference (APA Education and Training Board, 1952) that clear evidence existed in support of formal commitment on the APA's part to address the teaching of psychology in secondary schools. That occurred with the authorization by the APA Board of Directors for the formation of the Committee on the Teaching of Psychology in the High Schools, a committee that had not been among the original groups formed with the new E&T Board. This seemed timely because one of the questions posed by Michigan conference participants concerned the educational implications of the rapid increase in the number of high schools that offered courses in psychology.

Relatively little can be gleaned from the APA's records about the high school committee's work in the years immediately following that conference. However, in 1956 the Board of Directors concurred with a recommendation from the E&T Board that concerns about teaching psychology in the high schools be addressed by another new committee of that period: the Committee on Relations with Education (APA Board of Directors, 1956). At about the same time, the Committee on Communications with High School Teachers, under the APA Publications Board, was also at work to publish materials that could be helpful to high school psychology teachers.

Other initiatives in support of high school teachers that developed during the 1960s and continued through the 1970s were APA publications such as the *Ethical Guidelines for High School Psychology Teachers, Guidelines for Specialty Training and Certification of Secondary School Teachers of Psychology,* and *Curriculum Guidelines for the High School Psychology Course.*

In 1970, the APA Council of Representatives adopted a policy intended to advance teaching at the elementary and secondary school levels. Policy goals included (a) the development and continuing revision of psychological curricula for the elementary and secondary school levels in co-operation with other behavioral, biological, and social science disciplines; (b) collaboration with the other behavioral, biological, and social science disciplines in teaching about human behavior; (c) the development of guidelines for the training of teachers; and (d) the establishment of a clearinghouse of information on precollege psychology. Moreover, the policy stated that "APA should take official steps to reaffirm its belief that the role of the teacher is a crucial and significant one in society, such steps to include systematic efforts to support and improve teacher education in general" (McKeachie, 1971, p. 41).

During much of the 1970s, under what by that time was named the Committee on Pre-College Psychology, the E&T Board of APA worked aggressively to achieve the goals set forth by the APA's bold new policy on teacher enhancement in the secondary schools. One such project that was carried out over much of the decade was the Human Behavior Curriculum Project, which was funded by the National Science Foundation and designed to develop curriculum modules focused on different aspects of human behavior. Communication of psychological information to teachers was likewise a theme that received considerable attention by the E&T Board during the 1970s; there were also efforts made to develop liaison networks between secondary school teachers and state psychological associations (APA Education and Training Board, 1975).

Work on high school curriculum issues, teacher guidelines, and communications with high school teachers continued into the 1980s, under what by then was called the Committee on Psychology in the Secondary Schools. In the early years of that decade, efforts were mobilized to develop an advanced placement examination in psychology for high school students, as there is in other fields of science, mathematics, and the humanities. The idea for this development was fostered by the E&T Board, on recommendation by its Committee on Psychology in the Secondary Schools (APA Education and Training Board, 1983). By the mid-1980s, with budgetary constraints that required a cutback in staff and committee work, the E&T Board nonetheless reaffirmed its support for program initiatives focused on the teaching of psychology in the high schools and commended the Committee on Psychology in the Secondary Schools for its successful efforts to effect the Advanced Placement Exam in psychology through the Educational Testing Service (APA Education and Training Board, 1988).

In 1989, under the leadership of Ludy Benjamin, who was serving on the E&T Board, a task force was proposed to develop plans that would facilitate high school teacher development activities and promote honors courses in psychology at the high school level so that students might prepare for the new Advanced Placement Exam. The task force intended to work with the National Science Foundation Teacher Enhancement Program staff and to identify and encourage psychologists who might develop high school teacher workshops, fostering linkages between secondary and postsecondary educational institutions in regions and local communities (APA Education and Training Board, 1989). Since that time, the first series of regional and national workshops for high school teachers was implemented through the APA annual convention and on the campuses of Albion College, Colorado State University, Manhattan College, and Texas A&M University (Janya, 1991).

Related to these initiatives, the APA supports high school psychology teachers through a membership affiliate program and a newsletter providing information of value to classroom teachers. Another activity in which the APA supports high school psychology teachers, consistent with comparable activities of other scientific societies in working with high school students, is its annual participation in the International Science and Engineering Fair (Janya, 1991). That program is intended to encourage science interests among secondary-level students and to promote a better understanding of science among the general public. These are not new developments among APA's projects in support of the teaching of high school psychology but are a continuation of programs that originated in the work of APA committees in years past. An exciting new development occurred in 1992, when the APA Council of Representatives authorized initial planning for the APA to sponsor a national organization of high school psychology teachers (APA Council of Representatives, 1992).[1]

With current estimates that at least 750,000 high school students take a psychology course each year and the existence of more than 10,000 high school psychology teachers (with highly variable educational backgrounds), there is good reason for the APA to have more than a passing interest in how the field is introduced to students in high school and by whom. For most of the public, if there is any formal exposure to the discipline of psychology, it is at the secondary or introductory college course level.

Undergraduate-Level Teaching

What role should psychology play in a liberal arts education? What are the implications for undergraduate teaching? These were the types of questions challenging the Committee on Undergraduate Education in the

---

[1]The APA is among the national leaders of scientific and educational organizations cooperating in efforts to improve the general quality of education in the United States. One of the APA's contributions to this national strategic effort is a working document titled "Learner-Centered Psychological Principles: Guidelines for School Redesign and Reform," a product of the APA Task Force on Psychology in Education, which is chaired by APA Past-President Charles Spielberger (1992). The principles documented and the applications for which they may be useful are intended primarily to enhance general education from preschool through secondary levels. Perhaps psychology teachers may also find them useful regardless of the level of education they teach. After all, the psychology of learning and of teaching is as applicable to those whose subject matter is psychology as it is to other fields or disciplines of study.

early 1950s as a new committee under the E&T Board (APA Education and Training Board, 1952). Among the first initiatives of the newly appointed Committee on Undergraduate Education in the early 1950s was a survey of the responsibilities and conditions of work and scholarship for undergraduate psychology teachers. A few years later, the committee issued a report on undergraduate education (Buxton, 1956). It is clear that teaching and teachers were to be important objects of this committee's work, in addition to curriculum and student issues. Periodic surveys of undergraduate faculties, students, and curricula were carried out over the next 40 years. Although the emphases of the surveys varied, the conditions of teaching undergraduate psychology and the outcomes of such education were always in focus.

The 1970s was an especially active period in moving the APA's agenda on behalf of undergraduate teaching. Developing a newsletter, writing a standing column in the *APA Monitor*, starting the Master Lecture Series by the Committee on Continuing Education, conducting special curriculum projects, and launching a visiting scientist program exemplified the activities initiated during that period to enhance undergraduate teaching. Many of these program activities still exist.

A major contribution of the APA in support of undergraduate psychology teaching was and is the honorary G. Stanley Hall Lecture Series, held at APA's annual conventions since 1980. This lecture series epitomizes the APA's recognition of how important undergraduate teaching is, of how complex the challenge of teaching undergraduate psychology can be, and of how central scholarship is to effective teaching. Established to honor excellence in teaching, in the tradition of G. Stanley Hall, the award recognizes five distinguished psychologists each year, collectively representing the breadth of psychology as a scientific discipline. Benjamin (1981) noted:

> The idea for the lecture series grew out of a meeting of APA's Committee on Undergraduate Education in March, 1979. During a discussion of needs for undergraduate instructors, attention focused on the introductory course as a survey of the diverse areas that constitute the field of psychology. In that course the instructor is faced with the awesome task of covering as many as 20 to 25 topical areas. Adding to the difficulty of that task is the fact that few instructors, if any, can claim familiarity with the current literature in more than a half dozen of those areas. The committee discussed ways that APA might aid the instructor of introductory psychology and settled on a plan for a special lecture series to be presented at the annual meeting of APA. . . . The proposal outlined criteria for the selection of appropriate lecturers. Since the principal goal of the series was to aid teachers of introductory psychology, emphasis was placed on the selection of lecturers who (a) were experts in their particular content area, (b) had a strong interest

in teaching psychology, and (c) had experience in teaching introductory psychology and an understanding of the special problems inherent in teaching a survey course in introductory psychology. . . . As suggested in the original proposal, the lecture program was named the G. Stanley Hall Lecture Series, chiefly to acknowledge Hall's role as founder of the American Psychological Association. Such a designation seemed especially appropriate given Hall's considerable interest in teaching and his diverse interests in psychology, which included perception, child study, mental testing, emotion, hypnosis, prejudice, aging, industrial psychology, and psychoanalysis. (pp. 1–3)

A few years later, Cohen (1988) commented on

a myth, tacitly endorsed on so many college campuses, that says that the highest level courses—the advanced graduate courses in specialized areas—are the ones that are complex and difficult to teach. . . . Indeed, it is the inverse that is true: The lower level courses are the difficult ones to teach, with the introductory course perhaps the most challenging in that respect. (p. 1)

In 1987 the G. Stanley Hall Lecture Series was broadened to respond to the needs of undergraduate teachers in general, not specifically to introductory course teachers.

During the latter part of the 1980s, momentum on undergraduate teaching issues increased in other ways, too. Through the leadership of the E&T Board and the Central Office Staff, the APA participated in an American Association of Colleges (AAC) project concerning the role of the major in undergraduate education. In that project, several distinguished psychology faculty worked with colleagues from other associations, under leadership and at the invitation of the AAC, in an endeavor to address common questions about their disciplines in a liberal education context. In setting the stage for a published report of their work, the authors wrote the following:

We teach psychology in an array of institutional settings. Our students bring to their undergraduate classes different cultural heritages and a range of academic preparation. The [APA] urged us to draw on our collective experiences as classroom teachers, as scholars, and as administrators in framing this report. We listened to the voices of many colleagues. We tried, as William James said, . . . to examine "the roots and the fruits" of teaching psychology. (McGovern, Furumoto, Halpern, Kimble, & McKeachie, 1991, p. 598)

Along the same line of activity, the Committee on Undergraduate Education in 1989 proposed that the APA sponsor a national conference on undergraduate education in psychology, which was to be the first of its kind in several decades (McGovern, 1990). Teaching psychology in a variety of institutional settings was the theme of the conference (McGovern,

1991). Held in June 1991 at Saint Mary's College in Maryland, the conference was timely relative to broader concerns in higher education circles about the foundations of general education (Boyer & Levine, 1981) and practices of scholarship in American higher education, notably at the undergraduate level (Boyer, 1990).

An equally important aspect of this conference on teaching is that it brought together representative teachers from high school, 2-year community colleges, 4-year liberal arts colleges, and undergraduate faculties of universities. This resulted in recommendations for more effective linkages between these levels of education, including the merger of what were formerly separate newsletters to high school and undergraduate teachers into one publication for both titled the *Psychology Teacher Network* (Janya, 1991). Moreover, publications based on the conference proceedings and recommendations should afford faculties and administrators a scholarly basis for many decisions about curricular matters and other teaching practices in different types of undergraduate departments and institutions. Its outcomes reinforce an APA policy statement on undergraduate education, to the effect that

> The four-year baccalaureate program in psychology is fundamentally a liberal arts curriculum. Neither vocational nor pre-professional training should be a primary goal of undergraduate education in psychology. This position is consistent with the findings of the 1961 Michigan Conference, chaired by W. J. McKeachie and John E. Milholland, which concluded that "a basically liberal arts curriculum is best for students who plan to go on to professional training, to graduate work in psychology, or directly into a vocation." The [APA] should not prescribe specific course requirements for the undergraduate major in psychology. Such an action would seriously intrude upon the academic freedom of departments and faculty members. (APA Council of Representatives, 1985, pp. 7–8)

Graduate-Level Teaching

The post-World War II need for clinical psychologists trained at the doctoral level was cited earlier in this chapter. It was in response to that need that the APA Board of Directors, in 1947, authorized the establishment of the Committee on Training in Clinical Psychology, which was charged specifically with implementing what would become the standards and practices of professional program accreditation in psychology. This action signaled the importance of education and training in applied fields of psychology, especially in the direct human service fields of clinical, counseling, and school psychology that became the fields within which accreditation of doctoral programs and predoctoral internships was implemented by the APA.

Applied psychology in those days, however, was not divorced from more general graduate education in psychology. In the year preceding the formation of the Committee on Training in Clinical Psychology, the APA Council of Representatives authorized the formation of the Committee of University Department Chairs, composed of graduate departments that had awarded 10 or more doctoral degrees in psychology between 1934 and 1942 (APA Council of Representatives, 1946). Among other tasks, that committee was to consider plans for the formation of the Independent Association of Graduate Departments of Psychology, or a permanent committee of the APA, an idea that resulted ultimately in the formation of the Council of Graduate Departments of Psychology outside of the APA.

By 1951, the Committee on University Department Chairs had surveyed graduate departments to identify issues of special concern and practices commonly followed, an early form of a graduate department survey that is now conducted annually by the APA through its Office of Demographic, Employment, and Education Research. In these surveys, conditions of teaching and faculty practices are summarized in a way to provide normative information to educational institutions and the public. Therefore, they indirectly serve to advance teachers and undergraduate and graduate teaching.

Another related development of the early 1950s was the formation of the Committee on Psychology in Other Professional Schools, evidence that the value of psychology and psychologists was recognized increasingly, not only in a variety of applied work settings outside of academia but equally in the professional schools of other disciplines (e.g., medicine, business, engineering). What were the needs of teachers in those different settings, and how was psychology taught to students in other professional fields? Mensh (1962) discussed these matters in the context of psychology as a developing profession during the 1950s and 1960s. Although this committee did not survive the period discussed in this chapter, its purpose was prophetic in the sense that psychologists increasingly found employment in academic departments and professional schools related to fields and professions other than psychology. Also increasing in more recent years has been the interest in issues of interprofessional education and practice, a matter that may be more appropriate to postdoctoral than to graduate psychology education.

Throughout the 1960s and 1970s, the E&T Board remained active in discussions and projects related to graduate education, including the promotion of national conferences. In 1981, the APA Council of Representatives formally established the Graduate Committee on Education and Training, which was to report to the E&T Board, a governance group intended to review, evaluate, and recommend policy with regard to all graduate education and training in scientific–academic fields as well as in areas of professional psychology. Supervising the development of an APA publication—*Graduate Study in Psychology*—was among its tasks. That committee's efforts were also effective in early formulations of a proposal for APA sponsorship of a national conference on graduate education and training, the eventual outcome of which was the 1987 Utah conference, discussed by Belar in chapter 11 of this book.

Looking at these organizational developments, one can conclude that the APA governance attended substantially to issues of graduate education and training in the decades following World War II to the present time. Relatively more attention was focused, however, on issues related to graduate education and degree programs, standards of professional education and training, accreditation and credentialing, curriculum content and sequence, and locus or setting of training than to pedagogical issues per se. This seems true for all aspects of graduate education in psychology, not just programs of applied psychology. By contrast, it seems that attention focused on the enhancement of teaching was more clearly directed toward precollege and undergraduate education.

Accreditation and Teaching

Inasmuch as accreditation of professional psychology programs was a major focus of the APA governance in each of those decades and given the potential impact of accreditation on graduate education at the departmental and college levels, in addition to its effect on particular professional programs therein, it seems pertinent to ask the following: How has accreditation enhanced the teaching of graduate psychology? For some, the practices of accreditation seem far removed from the goal of enhancing the teaching of psychology. They might argue, for example, that although faculty qualifications and achievements in scholarly and professional ways are a definite focus of accreditation reviews, the process and quality of teaching has received much less attention than it should have. Others undoubtedly will argue to the contrary. To be sure, advancing the quality of teaching is one of many goals toward which accreditors are expected to strive. That goal is among those specified in the provisions for national recognition of accrediting bodies by the Council on Postsecondary Accreditation (1990).

In the absence of empirical evidence on actual outcomes of the accreditation process related to these matters, it is reasonable to examine the accreditation criteria for evidence of intent to improve the quality of teaching in psychology in professional programs. After all, the criteria by which programs are accredited should refer to standards of quality that are established for programs in professional fields.

In the earliest version of the accreditation criteria, written in the late 1940s, one finds the following guidance to site visitors and committee reviewers: "Courses should be scrutinized for their content, rather than judged by their titles. Equally important is the way the content is handled, that is, the quality of the teaching" (APA Committee on Training in Clinical Psychology, 1947, p. 543). That explicit reference to teaching was followed by numerous illustrations of how an effective teaching process might be characterized.

In the years since those initial accreditation guidelines were developed, some of that prose was lost in the transition to later editions of the accreditation criteria. Yet, there are references to the importance of teaching as a vital part of program quality. The current accreditation criteria, for example, state the following:

> A quality faculty is essential to the development and maintenance of an excellent program . . . . In their research, teaching, and practice, faculty members who are professional psychologists should give evidence of being committed to the application of psychological principles to the problems faced by the practitioner and should be identified as professionally dedicated. (American Psychological Association, 1979, p. 11)

The concept of the faculty member as professional role model and mentor, a vital attribute of the teaching process in graduate and professional education and training, is retained in all later editions of the accreditation criteria (American Psychological Association, 1973, 1979). In an invited address for the 1990 APA Award for Distinguished Contributions to Education and Training in Psychology, Ellis (1992) referred to "mentoring" as one of six important issues for the future of graduate education, as it has been in the past. He concluded that it is important enough to "be part of the APA accreditation process and that timely steps should be taken to integrate this feature in evaluation of graduate training programs" (Ellis, 1992, p. 576).

Although the most attention in the accreditation criteria has been given to the academic setting in which doctoral preparation for the profession takes place, one should not overlook the impact of accreditation on applied service institutions in which the predoctoral internship training takes place. For example, the insistence on evidence that the institution is committed to the purposes and values of professional training is important to the functions of professional psychologists in those settings. Such a standard reinforces the idea that teaching and research go hand in hand with professional services and as such represent activities that are not limited in their value to academic institutions. The extent to which that has occurred as a result of internship program accreditation is debatable, but it is an ideal toward which accreditation strives nonetheless.

Summary

If one were to ask what themes of education and training were the most prevalent within the APA over the years since 1945, one might certainly conclude, as Goodwin did relative to the first 50 years of the APA's life (see the previous chapter), that issues related to the professional practice of psychology prevailed. There is hard evidence that such concerns and interests were present in each decade. Such a conclusion, however, would mask what were comparably significant activities and developments in support of undergraduate and precollege education. Moreover, when one examines the APA activities at all levels of education and training over the past 46 years, apart from the substance of the curriculum, one could conclude that the attention to teaching and teachers is inversely related to the level of education and training.

REORGANIZATION AGAIN, WITH A FOCUS ON TEACHING

Renewed interest in and commitment to teaching seems to occur in organized psychology's history when APA governance leaders, especially those identified with education apart from the profession, become concerned that professional issues are receiving disproportionate attention in the education and training agenda. This contrast effect, as it were, existed in the late 1940s, which resulted in a reorganization and significant increase in activities related to the advancement of teaching in psychology. The same seems to have occurred in the past few years. Indeed, some might say that psychologists have come full circle with regard to education and training in psychology, although they are in a different place in the evolution of their field than they were 45 years ago.

During the past 3 years of reorganizing the APA's governing board for education and training, the Education and Training Board became the Board of Educational Affairs, and a conscious effort was made to strike a reasonable balance in the new board's functions between education and training for professional practice and functions responsive to other issues, including the teaching of psychology. The latter, many argued, had been virtually ignored by the APA (other than through its Division on the Teaching of Psychology), seemingly ironic for a discipline whose roots can be traced to the learning process.

So intense was this concern among those responsible for planning the new APA Education Directorate and its governing board's agenda that, in its July 1989 report to the APA Board of Directors, the Interim Advisory Committee for an Education Directorate proposed the teaching of psychology at all levels as one of the primary functions in need of being addressed by the prospective education directorate and governance.[2] Shar-

---

[2]Members of the Interim Advisory Committee for the Education Directorate were Henry C. Ellis (Chair), Irwin Altman, Ludy T. Benjamin, Jr., Joanne E. Callan, Bernadette Gray-Little, Nadine M. Lambert, Nathan W. Perry, Jr., Tommy T. Stigall, and Ron Fox (Board of Directors liaison).

ing their proposed initiatives to advance the teaching of psychology, the committee wrote the following:

> If psychology is ever to realize its potential in science and human service delivery, the educated public must have an accurate view of the science and practice of psychology. Furthermore, the quality of undergraduate psychology courses must be excellent if the field is to attract students of high caliber to careers in psychology. Thus it is imperative that the Education Directorate of the American Psychological Association have a strong presence in the teaching of psychology at all educational levels. The following functions would address these needs:
>
> a. Develop and arrange for the publication and distribution of teaching aids for instructors of psychology (e.g., activities handbooks, curriculum models, suggested course outlines, lecture ideas);
> b. Foster convention programs relevant to the teaching of psychology;
> c. Assist colleges and universities in the development of conferences, workshops, and institutes on the teaching of psychology;
> d. Assist psychology college faculty in the development of National Science Foundation supported institutes for the improvement of the teaching of psychology in secondary schools;
> e. Work with the Council of Graduate Departments of Psychology, and other relevant bodies, to encourage the development of teacher training for psychology graduate students who might be engaged in teaching functions;
> f. Work with APA's Division 2 (Teaching of Psychology) and other APA groups whose goals are the improvement of the teaching of psychology to assist them in reaching their objectives;
> g. Work with school systems, colleges and universities (and relevant groups) to foster faculty development opportunities that are directed toward improvement of the teaching of psychology;
> h. Work with the Educational Testing Service and secondary school organizations to encourage establishment of Advanced Placement psychology courses in high schools;
> i. Encourage research on teaching, especially as it relates to the teaching of psychology;
> j. Maintain regular contact with the leadership in undergraduate and secondary school psychology teaching (through meetings, standing committees, and newsletters), both as a way to gain new ideas for APA contributions to the field as well as a way to disseminate knowledge of what the Education Directorate has done and is doing;
> k. Assist college and university psychology departments in arranging evaluation of their undergraduate curricula;
> l. Assist college and university psychology departments in the development of service courses, minors, and interdepartmental majors that will allow psychology courses to be taught to a broader range of undergraduate students;

m. Assist colleges, universities, and secondary schools in the development of psychology laboratories (including computers and other equipment) for teaching and student research, by compiling and distributing information on funding sources;

n. Work with the regional and state psychological associations to promote activities related to the improvement of the teaching of psychology at all levels;

o. Foster the development of psychology teaching modules for natural and social science programs at the elementary and secondary school levels. (APA Interim Advisory Committee for an Education Directorate, 1989, pp. 1–2)

This charge is quite a mandate. It is the clearest exposition to date of the APA's role in support of teaching in psychology. It builds on the aspirations and achievements of those who contributed to the advancement of education and training in psychology over the past 50 years, serving as a blueprint for the years ahead, replete with challenge and opportunity. It has the boldness to launch organized psychology into its second century of science and application through excellence in the teaching of education and training.

Thus, we conclude that because of two major APA governance reorganizations of relevance to education and training in psychology, significant attention, however insufficient it might have been, has been given to the teaching of psychology. From what is presently underway with the APA's new Board of Educational Affairs and what may happen in the immediate future in the context of national priorities of education in general and science literacy in particular, one can only speculate that in the remaining years of the 1990s, attention can be expected to increase in education and training.

THE FUTURE

It is interesting to speculate about the direction that APA's education activities will take in the next decade, especially as they pertain to the teaching of psychology. In doing so, it is useful to consider the various levels of education.

The emphasis on secondary school activities is likely to continue and to have its primary emphasis on pedagogy, curricular matters, and faculty development. Two-year college activities may be separated from undergraduate activities as a whole, and the material that is relevant for the secondary school teacher also may prove to be valuable for the instructor in the 2-year college. Undergraduate activities continue to be an important focus, but a distinction may be drawn between pregraduate school curricula and the activities that are available to the majority of students who do not go on to study further. For this general group, the combination of the 4-year college with the secondary school and the community college may prove to be a salutary development. For pregraduate school students, separate activities will be relevant and also require specific attention.

At the graduate school level, questions about the role of the master's degree remain as compelling and unsolved as ever. The same suggestion that was made for undergraduate activities—the separation of general education from pregraduate school activity—may be useful. There is little dispute about the value of the general master's degree, either as an opportunity for general education or as an academic degree preparatory to doctoral study. There is much dispute about the role of the master's degree as a professional degree in preparing the student for a career in psychology. This is an area in which the interests of professional psychologists, who are determined that psychology remain a doctoral-level profession, clash with the interests of the university, which professes academic freedom and does not wish any interference with a program of study.

It has not been our purpose in this chapter to reiterate or resolve that debate, but these issues remain a weighty item on APA's educational agenda for the coming decade. Indeed, the Levels of Education and Training Task Force was formed by the APA Board of Directors in 1992, at the recommendation of the (former) Interim Board of Educational Affairs, to investigate the issues in need of study relative to education, training, credentialing, and employment of people with different types of psychology degrees (APA Board of Educational Affairs, 1991). The outcomes of this APA self-study should have implications for the teaching of psychology.

At the doctoral level, it is safe to assume that the emphases of the past will be maintained. The importance of accreditation and standards remains, and professional considerations will command much attention. At the same time, one might speculate that issues of science education and training scientists in psychology will become more prominent in discussions of doctoral education, much as they were at the 1987 Utah Conference on Graduate Education in Psychology (Bickman & Ellis, 1990).

Finally, increased attention can be expected at the postdoctoral level in the decade ahead: the relationship of that to what has been the predoctoral internship in professional education and training and its significance for specialized practice or other added qualifications beyond the general doctoral education for entry into practice. Part of this will be devoted to continuing education, an area that has a long history of concern within the APA. More attention, however, will be given to formal, organized units or programs of postdoctoral training, with prospects of postdoctoral accreditations as well. It is a footnote in history that at the 1952 conference at the University of Michigan, the first meeting of what was then the new Education and Training Board, participants observed the need to begin thinking about postdoctoral education and training. Since that time, relatively little attention has been given to the postdoctoral level until the past decade, other than through continuing professional education activities.

Although some of these speculations may prove to be wrong and activities may occur that are not yet imagined, there is one prediction that can be made with utmost confidence: The APA will continue to be an active presence in educational affairs and will continue to make the advancement of teaching and learning a priority.

REFERENCES

American Psychological Association. (1973). *Accreditation procedures and criteria.* Washington, DC: Author.

American Psychological Association. (1979). *Criteria for accreditation: Doctoral training programs and internships in professional psychology.* Washington, DC: Author.

APA Board of Directors. (1956). *Minutes of the board meeting, September 1956.* Washington, DC: American Psychological Association.

APA Board of Educational Affairs. (1991). *Minutes of the board meeting, September 1991.* Washington DC: American Psychological Association.

APA Committee on Training in Clinical Psychology. (1947). Recommended graduate training program in clinical psychology. *American Psychologist, 2,* 539–558.

APA Committee on Training in Clinical Psychology. (1949). Doctoral training programs in clinical psychology: 1949. *American Psychologist, 4,* 331–341.

APA Council of Representatives. (1946). *Minutes of the Council meeting, 1946.* Washington, DC: American Psychological Association.

APA Council of Representatives. (1985). *Minutes of the Council meeting, August 1985.* Washington, DC: American Psychological Association.

APA Council of Representatives. (1992). *Minutes of the Council meeting, February 1992.* Washington, DC: American Psychological Association.

APA Education and Training Board. (1952). Educational issues in psychology: A report of the February 1952 Conference of the APA Education and Training Board. *American Psychologist, 7,* 456–460.

APA Education and Training Board. (1975). *Minutes of the E&T Board meeting, May 1975.* Washington, DC: American Psychological Association.

APA Education and Training Board. (1983). *Minutes of the E&T Board meeting, May 1983.* Washington, DC: American Psychological Association.

APA Education and Training Board. (1988). *Minutes of the E&T Board meeting, October 1988.* Washington, DC: American Psychological Association.

APA Education and Training Board. (1989). *Minutes of the E&T Board meeting, November 1989.* Washington, DC: American Psychological Association.

APA Interim Advisory Committee for an Education Directorate. (1989). *Report of the Interim Advisory Committee for an Education Directorate, July 1989.* Washington, DC: American Psychological Association.

APA Policy and Planning Board. (1947). Annual report of the Policy and Planning Board of the American Psychological Association: 1947. *American Psychologist, 2,* 191–198.

APA Task Force on Psychology in Education. (1992). *Learner-centered psychological principles: Guidelines for school redesign and reform.* Washington, DC: American Psychological Association.

Benjamin, L. T., Jr. (1981). Preface. In L. T. Benjamin, Jr. (Ed.), *G. Stanley Hall Lecture Series* (Vol. 1, pp. 1–6). Washington, DC: American Psychological Association.

Bickman, L., & Ellis, H. (Eds.). (1990). *Preparing psychologists for the 21st century: Proceedings of the National Conference on Graduate Education in Psychology.* Hillsdale, NJ: Erlbaum.

Boyer, E. L. (1990). *Scholarship reconsidered: Priorities of the professoriate.* Princeton, NJ: Carnegie Foundation for the Advancement of Teaching.

Boyer, E. L., & Levine, A. (1981). *A Quest for common learning.* Washington, DC: Carnegie Foundation for the Advancement of Teaching.

Buxton, C. E. (1956). Issues in undergraduate education. *American Psychologist, 11,* 84–95.

Clark, K. E. (1957). *America's psychologists: A survey of a growing profession.* Washington, DC: American Psychological Association.

Cohen, I. S. (1988). Preface. In I. S. Cohen (Ed.), *G. Stanley Hall Lecture Series* (Vol. 8, pp. 1–4). Washington, DC: American Psychological Association.

Council on Postsecondary Accreditation. (1990). *COPA handbook.* Washington, DC: Author.

Ellis, H. C. (1992). Graduate education in psychology: Past, present, and future. *American Psychologist, 47,* 570–576.

Janya, M. R. (Ed.). (1991). *The psychology teacher network* (Vol. 1). Washington, DC: American Psychological Association.

Kohout, J., & Wicherski, M. (1990). *Doctorate employment survey: 1989.* Washington, DC: American Psychological Association.

McGovern, T. V. (1990, March). Undergraduate conference set for 1991. *APA Monitor,* p. 32.

McGovern, T. V. (1991, January). APA meeting on education to be held in June. *APA Monitor,* p. 37.

McGovern, T. V., Furumoto, L., Halpern, D. F., Kimble, G. A., & McKeachie, W. J. (1991). Liberal education, study in depth, and the arts and sciences major—Psychology. *American Psychologist, 46,* 598–605.

McKeachie, W. J. (1971). Minutes of the annual meeting of the Council of Representatives, September and October 1970. *American Psychologist, 26,* 22–49.

Mensh, I. N. (1962). Psychology and other professions. In W. B. Webb (Ed.), *The profession of psychology* (pp. 232–252). New York: Holt, Rinehart & Winston.

Raimy, V. C. (Ed.). (1950). *Training in clinical psychology: Proceedings of the Boulder Conference.* Washington, DC: American Psychological Association.

Sanford, F. H. (1951). [Memorandum on recommendations concerning APA organization and procedures for dealing with problems in educating and training psychologists]. (Available from the Executive Office, Governance Records, American Psychological Association, 750 First Street, NE, Washington, DC 20002.)

Sears, R. R. (1947). Clinical psychology facilities: A report from the Committee on Graduate and Professional Training. *American Psychologist, 2,* 199–205.

16

DIVISION IN SEARCH OF SELF: A HISTORY OF APA DIVISION 2, THE DIVISION OF THE TEACHING OF PSYCHOLOGY

RANDALL D. WIGHT AND STEPHEN F. DAVIS

In 1945, the postwar world was shaped at Yalta, the nuclear age began over the skies of Hiroshima, and the American Psychological Association (APA) inaugurated its divisional age with a reorganization plan shaped in the goodwill emerging from the discipline's contribution to World War II. The cornerstone of the reconstituted APA was a divisional structure designed to permit increased attention to the discipline's specialties and special interests (Doll, 1946; D. Wolfle, 1946a). There were 19 original divisions. Of that original number, 18 still exist today. Our intent in this chapter is to tell the story of how one of the original divisions developed a sense of identity: Division 2, the Division on the Teaching of Psychology. This story is somewhat idiosyncratic because we narrate the tale, when possible, through the perspectives of the Division's officers and publications. Never-

We thank Kimberly A. McCarty and Randolph A. Smith for their helpful comments on this chapter.

theless, we believe our narrative reflects teachers' evolving perceptions of their status within the discipline and Division 2's struggle to attain a sense of identity.

PROLOGUE, CONCEPTION, AND EARLY DEVELOPMENT: 1944–1950

The interim between the 20th century's two world wars was a time of dramatic growth for applied psychology (see Napoli, 1981). The emergence of the American Association for Applied Psychology (AAAP) during the 1936 Dartmouth APA meeting symbolized the vitality of that growth. Yet, the discipline did not have a unified voice. When the National Research Council held a meeting in 1940 to discuss a unified wartime role for psychology, the APA, the AAAP, and four other psychological organizations convened (Hilgard, 1987).[1] The war effort provided a unifying influence for the discipline that culminated in a constitutional convention among the various psychological associations of the day that sought to capitalize on wartime goodwill (Anderson, 1943; Recommendations of the Intersociety Constitutional Convention of Psychologists [ICC], 1943; Yerkes, 1943a, 1943b). From this convention arose a plan for structural change within the APA (see Hilgard, 1987).

The ICC (1943) report contained proposed changes in the APA's Bylaws and the unveiling of the divisional structure. The proposed divisions were presented in a survey blank and listed in alphabetical order; psychologists were instructed to place two check marks by their division of primary choice and single check marks by all other divisions they might join. The 16th division on the list was the Division on the Teaching of Psychology. After receiving the completed survey forms, the Joint Constitutional Committee of the APA and AAAP published, without explanation, a revised list of divisions (Anderson, 1944). The second division on the revised list was the Division on the Teaching of Psychology. Doll (1946) observed that the revised list was incorporated, again without published explanation, into the Bylaws the APA adopted during the Association's 1944 Cleveland meeting (see Olson, 1944). The idea of Division 2 and its cohorts emerged in Ohio in September 1944, but it was not until APA's 53rd annual meeting in Evanston, Illinois, in September 1945 that they came into being.

Within a year, Ernest R. Hilgard (1945a) produced an analysis of the survey. In an attempt to assess the opinion of all American psychologists, approximately 6,000 surveys—the same form as in the ICC (1943) report—

---

[1]The other organizations were the Psychometric Society, Section I of the American Association for the Advancement of Science, the Society of Experimental Psychologists, and the Society for the Psychological Study of Social Issues.

were distributed to individuals regardless of their professional association; a total of 3,680 usable ballots were evaluated. Seventy-one respondents chose the Division on the Teaching of Psychology as their primary division without "double-checking" any other division and 41 respondents chose the soon-to-be Division 2 while also double-checking other divisions. The teaching division received 791 single checks (i.e., secondary choice). Thus, the Division 2 prototype received, in some capacity, 903 votes, votes from 25% of the 3,680 respondents (Hilgard, 1945a). The choices receiving the most combined primary and secondary votes were clinical, personnel, and child,[2] selected, respectively, by 53%, 47%, and 44% of the total respondents. Interestingly, an examination of the 71 respondents who checked the teaching division as their primary choice also checked an average of 6 secondary choices, the highest percentage of secondary choices among the divisions. Clearly, teachers had multiple interests.

On occasion, one hears colleagues puzzle over the numbering of APA's divisions. The rearrangement of divisions from alpha order to the Bylaws order that forms the foundational pattern still used today appears also to have been something of a mystery to psychologists active in the APA during the 1945 reorganization. Edgar A. Doll, a member of the committee that sought to guide divisional organization after the Bylaws change, lamented that changes were made without an explicit rationale and remarked that

> the modified hierarchy reflects perhaps the historical evolution of psychology as a movement from scientific-academic background to professional service and applications. But the modified order seems not to reflect either historical evolution or scientific-professional values. (Doll, 1946, p. 339)

Hilgard (personal communication, June 5, 1991) would later recall that the first and second divisions (General and Teaching, respectively) were given their respective numbers during the reordering because they (a) were, in descending order, the least specialized of the divisions and (b) could perhaps serve to include individuals who did not easily fit into more specialized divisions.

Once the Bylaws changes were approved and the divisional structure was in place, the APA turned its attention to organizing the new divisions, a task that fell to the Committee on Divisional Organization. Evidence of the Committee's work appeared in the May 1945 issue of *Psychological Bulletin* (Hilgard, 1945b), in which temporary chairpersons and secretaries were listed for each division. These appointed officers were to formulate a nomination ballot for divisional leadership to be distributed to the APA membership at large in March 1945, to prepare an election ballot to be

---

[2]Later these became, respectively, the Division of Clinical Psychology (Division 12), the Division of Personnel and Guidance Psychologists (Division 17), and the Division of Childhood and Adolescence (Division 7; Doll, 1946).

distributed in June of that same year, and to serve as divisional officers until elected leadership was announced and installed during the September meeting in Evanston, Illinois (Hilgard, 1945b). Division 2's temporary chairman and secretary were, respectively, Herbert S. Langfeld of Princeton and Robert W. Leeper of the University of Oregon. The choice of these individuals was most likely because they were well known and could represent the East and West coasts (E. R. Hilgard, personal communication, June 5, 1991).

In December 1945, the officers of the APA, its Board of Directors, Council of Representatives, and the Division officers met in Columbus, Ohio to permit the Council to conduct business and to assist division officers in developing membership requirements and constructing bylaws (D. Wolfle, 1946a). Going into this meeting, commitment to Division 2 appears somewhat dubious in that its elected president, John F. Dashiell, had resigned to assume the presidency of Division 1 (Marquis, 1946). The APA Board of Directors subsequently appointed Floyd L. Ruch as Division 2 president. (See Table 1 for a list of the Division's officers.) Furthermore, according to APA's Executive Secretary Dael L. Wolfle (1946a), many division officers, who were supposed to be building bylaws, spent their time discussing the continued existence of the very organizations that they had been elected to lead. Wolfle's report stated that the Division 2 leadership was pursuing a merger with the Division of General Psychology. Division 2 emerged from the meeting intact despite what seems less than overwhelming support.

We have been unable to locate a copy of the Division's original Bylaws. A reading of the executive secretary's column in the *American Psychologist* suggests that Division 2 lagged behind other divisions in establishing membership requirements (D. Wolfle, 1947a) and behind the expectations of the APA's leadership in establishing fellowship requirements (D. Wolfle, 1947b, 1948). Membership requirements were clearly in place by 1948 (D. Wolfle, 1948) and were as follows:

> *Fellows*—Being actively engaged in teaching in a recognized institution
> *Associates*—Being actively engaged in teaching in a recognized institution
> *Affiliates*—No [that is, no affiliate status existed]. (D. Wolfle, 1948, p. 140)

Note that at that time, no difference existed between members and fellows in Division 2. Recall that in 1958, the associate category was divided into associates and members. Figure 1 depicts total Division 2 membership from 1948 through 1991.[3] Two hundred two APA members expressed an interest in being charter members of Division 2. To our knowledge, no known

---

[3]We acknowledge our debt and gratitude to Christine Cubby and APA's Membership Office for supplying all of our membership data and to Randy Smith for constructing the graph.

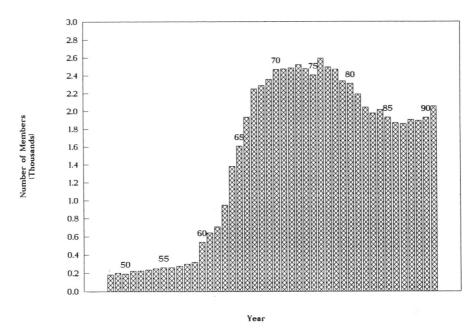

Figure 1: Total Division 2 membership from 1948 to 1991.

membership count exists for 1946. Helen Wolfle (1948) reported that Division 2 had 184 members in 1947 and led all divisions in percentage of members resigning. She implied that the Division's vitality was questionable throughout its early years.

Although the early events of Division 2's history are for the most part unknown, the Division's first full decade began optimistically with the initiation of its original published forum, *Teaching of Psychology Newsletter* (see Daniel, 1974; also see Daniel's chapter in this book on the journal, *Teaching of Psychology*). The newsletter's opening essay was a letter from President Leonard Carmichael (1950) in which he relayed the hope of the Division's Executive Council that Division 2 could become a "more closely knit" organization and work together to address problems related to teaching. Implicit in Carmichael's essay was an issue with which the Division has been repeatedly concerned: Who and what is Division 2?

IDENTITY FORMATION: 1951–1959

In 1951, the United Nations moved to New York, families were furiously digging fallout shelters, and a vigorous examination of identity surfaced with the Division's sixth president, Claude E. Buxton. In his message to the membership, Buxton (1951a) asked whether there was any reason for this Division to continue its existence. Buxton asserted that Division 2 was little more than a "holding corporation" for APA mem-

TABLE 1

Officers and Council Representatives of Division 2, the Division on the Teaching of Psychology of the American Psychological Association, from 1946 to 1992

Year[a]	President	Secretary–treasurer[b]	Council representative[c]
1946	Floyd L. Ruch	Edna Heidbreder	Ruch, Munn, G. Watson
1947	Sidney L. Pressey	Elizabeth Duffy	Ruch, R. M. Elliot, A. R. Gilliland
1948	William A. Hunt	Elizabeth Duffy	Ruch, Buxton
1949	Norman L. Munn	Elizabeth Hurlock	Gilliland, P. R. Farnsworth
1950	Leonard Carmichael	Elizabeth Hurlock	Gilliland, Farnsworth
1951	Claude E. Buxton	Elizabeth Hurlock	Farnsworth, Ray, Buxton
1952	Elizabeth Hurlock	Lillian Portenier	Ray, Buxton
1953	John F. Dashiell[d]	Lillian Portenier	Buxton, Munn
1954	Richard Husband	Lillian Portenier	Munn, Portenier
1955	Wilbert J. McKeachie	Constance Lovell	Munn, Portenier
1956	Frank W. Finger	Constance Lovell	Portenier, McKeachie
1957	Lillian Portenier	Constance Lovell	McKeachie, Harper
1958	Fred McKinney	Robert S. Harper	McKeachie, Harper
1959	Edward J. Shoben	Robert S. Harper	Harper, Leuba, Milholland
1960	Robert S. Harper	T. L. Engle	Leuba, Milholland, Ray, Engle
1961	Robert S. Daniel	T. L. Engle	Leuba, Milholland, Engle, Bartlett
1962	Floyd L. Ruch[e]	T. L. Engle	Bartlett, Engle, McKeachie
1963	Robert B. MacLeod	Robert E. Bills	Bartlett, Engle, McKeachie, Bills
1964	Ralph H. Turner	Robert E. Bills	McKeachie, Bills, Husband, Joyce, Woods
1965	Michael Wertheimer	Robert E. Bills	Bills, Husband, Joyce, Woods, Shoben
1966	Neil Bartlett	Wilbert S. Ray	Husband, Joyce, Woods, Shoben, Ray
1967	John E. Milholland	Wilbert S. Ray	Shoben, Ray, Brown, Ostrander, Turner
1968	Paul J. Woods	Wilbert S. Ray	Ray, Brown, Ostrander, Turner, MacLeod

Year	President	Secretary-Treasurer	Representatives
1969	Wilse B. Webb	Wilbert S. Ray	Ostrander, Turner, MacLeod, Bartlett, Harper
1970	Clarence Leuba	Wilbert S. Ray	MacLeod, Bartlett, Harper, Daniel, Murphy
1971	Donald R. Brown	Wilbert S. Ray	Bartlett, Ray, Daniel, Murphy, Harper
1972	John K. Bare	Lawrence Murphy	Daniel, Murphy, Harper
1973	Wilbert S. Ray	Lawrence Murphy	Harper, Turner
1974	James B. Maas	Lawrence Murphy	Harper, Turner
1975	Edward H. Loveland	Lawrence Murphy	Harper, Murphy
1976	Douglas Candland	Lawrence Murphy	Murphy, Turner
1977	James Deese	Lawrence Murphy	Murphy, Daniel
1978	David Cole	Fay-Tyler Norton	Murphy, Daniel
1979	James V. McConnell	Fay-Tyler Norton	Daniel, Norton
1980	Barbara Nodine	Fay-Tyler Norton	Norton, Harper
1981	Charles L. Brewer	Lucy T. Benjamin	Norton, Harper
1982	Fay-Tyler Norton	Lucy T. Benjamin	Harper, Benjamin
1983	Frank Costin	Lucy T. Benjamin	Benjamin, Nodine
1984	Richard Kasschau	Janet R. Matthews	Nodine, Matthews
1985	Lucy T. Benjamin	Janet R. Matthews	Matthews, J. E. Williams
1986	Marilyn K. Rigby	Janet R. Matthews	Matthews, Williams
1987	James H. Korn	Elizabeth V. Swenson	Williams, Swenson
1988	Janet R. Matthews	Elizabeth V. Swenson	Swenson, McKeachie
1989	Stephen F. Davis	Elizabeth V. Swenson	McKeachie
1990	Patricia Keith-Spiegel	Margaret A. Lloyd	McKeachie, Brewer
1991	Joseph J. Palladino	Margaret A. Lloyd	Brewer
1992	Elizabeth V. Swenson	Margaret A. Lloyd	Brewer, L. Furumoto

Note: We are indebted to Robert S. Daniel for the construction of this table and for graciously permitting us to use it.
aDivision officers begin their term following the annual business meeting in August (formally September). bThis office was secretary alone through 1948. cThe number of council representatives varied as a function of APA seat-assignment procedures. dDashiell was elected to replace Gilliland, who died before taking office. eDivision 2 presidents serve only one term. After taking office in 1962, Floyd Ruch was asked about being elected president a second time. He said he had forgotten about having previously served. Apparently, the nominating committee and the voting membership had also forgotten.

bership in which only a small number of people interested in teaching had shown any interest—a small number fast establishing an in-group of "musical chair" leadership. The Division had failed to articulate its relationship to other organizations that advanced teaching and the relationship between the teacher and his or her chosen area of specialization. Likewise, no definition of purview had emerged: Should the Division focus on the various educational contexts in which teachers of psychology find themselves or on the "status–economic" facets of teaching? Buxton also implied that if Division 2 viewed itself as a seedbed for instruction-centered research, then that conception was misplaced because only a meager cadre of researchers within the Division were pursuing the topic and that group would continue to do so with or without the existence of Division 2. Challenging the membership, Buxton wrote,

> To guide divisional policy, and to satisfy my own curiosity, would you think seriously about the general issue I raise [i.e., whether the division should continue to exist] . . . and write to me . . . indicating your opinions or suggestions? We should get down to the blunt truths, I think, or get on to more satisfying tasks. Which should it be? (Buxton, 1951a, p. 1)

Buxton reported the membership's response in the next newsletter. Opinion ranged from "get rid of Division 2" to "most important Division of APA" (Buxton, 1952b, p. 1). According to Buxton, the membership's responses produced a skewed distribution whose modal response was "don't get rid of it—rather, get it to do what it ought to do" (p. 1). From these responses, Buxton observed that the membership consisted primarily of individuals concerned with conventional liberal arts education and that many individuals with strong teaching interests, particularly graduate-level instructors, were underreprsented (see Buxton, 1951b).

After learning that a sizable portion of the membership believed that Division 2's endeavors could promote satisfaction among the membership, Buxton devised a two-pronged strategy for Division development: membership enhancement and purview definition. The first part of the strategy became evident during the 1952 business meeting in Washington, DC: Buxton proposed a Bylaws change permitting individuals who currently held fellow status in other divisions to become Division 2 fellows without first becoming associates of the Division (Hurlock, 1952). This attempt echoed a question that had haunted the organization since its inception (i.e., how to define the Division's fellows category).

The APA had created the fellows designation from the initial member classification in 1925 when, in response to the need to open the Association to qualified individuals who could not meet the membership requirement of published scientific research, the APA created the associate category that did not include publication as a criterion for membership (Hilgard,

1987). General APA requirements for fellows following reorganization included a doctoral degree based on psychological research, 5 years of professional experience, meeting additional divisional requirements, and receiving divisional nomination (Carmichael, 1952). At the time of Buxton's proposal, Division 2 fellows were required to have taught for 5 years, with 3 of those 5 years at the same institution (Ray, 1952). The Division, although the reason is unclear, was "anxious" for its associates to become fellows (Carmichael, 1952). Buxton's proposal (Hurlock, 1952), which the membership approved by a mail vote, permitted fellows of other divisions to become Division 2 fellows without first becoming Division 2 associates.

The second part of the strategy of Buxton's effort to strengthen the Division was outlined in his presidential address (Buxton, 1952a; also see Buxton, 1951b; Tyson, 1951). In his presentation, Buxton targeted the concerns that had emerged from his informal poll of the membership. He asserted that the Division's creation did not imply a separation of methodology from content, that the Division's interest should not be limited to undergraduate education, and that the Division should dovetail its efforts with the APA's educational efforts. Buxton went on to articulate divisional objectives: (a) communicate research or experience in teaching, (b) facilitate studies of the teaching process and situation, and (c) symbolize the teaching profession itself. Although the third objective materialized as "to work for the good of the teaching profession" (Editor, 1953, p. 5), the Division membership voted to incorporate Buxton's objectives into the organization's Bylaws.

However, the issue of identity was far from solved. A factor-analytic study had suggested that the APA's divisional structure should be simplified to seven divisions: quantitative, theoretical, experimental, personnel, clinical, social, and development (Adkins, 1954). The APA's Policy and Planning Board (Policy and Planning Board of the American Psychological Association, 1954) asserted that the proliferation of special-interest groups seeking divisional status was undermining the intent of the divisional structure. The Board believed that a new reorganization was necessary in order to confine political interests within umbrella divisions.

During the 1954 APA Convention in New York City, Division 2 Past-President Elizabeth Hurlock chaired a discussion titled "The Future of Division 2" (Hurlock, 1954) that centered on the reorganization proposal. The panel was composed of Division President Richard W. Husband; Secretary–Treasurer Lillian G. Portenier; Program Chairman Richard Youtz; and former Presidents Claude E. Buxton, John F. Dashiel, and Norman L. Munn. Husband recalled that "there were nearly as many opinions as persons present" (Husband, 1954, p. 1). Hurlock reported that a "general feeling" (Hurlock, 1954, p. 9) emerged affirming Division 2's usefulness to those who teach in small liberal arts environments. She also reported that when the 42 people present were asked for a show of hands, 18 voted to support the APA's consolidation proposal. On behalf of an ongoing Division 2, President Husband later wrote: "Six states [might] be simpler than 48; but the people of New Hampshire might take a dim view of being merged into a superstate of New England" (Husband, 1954, p. 1). Six months later he added: "We are a unique group—those of us whose first loyalties are directed toward the students in front of us, in preference over a rat, a human subject, a neurotic patient, or an IBM card. I hope we grow and prosper" (Husband, 1955, p. 1).

The most noteworthy event of 1956 within Division 2 was President-Elect Frank W. Finger's establishment of the Policy and Planning Committee (Policy and Planning Committee of Division 2 [PPC], 1957a). Although no specific charge is found in the historical record, apparently the Committee—Edward J. Shoben, Jr. (Chair), Paul Farnsworth, and Richard Youtz—was instructed to examine the role of Division 2 within the APA. Their first report appeared in the May 1957 issue of the newsletter (PPC, 1957a). The report began with the observation that the Division's membership was "plagued . . . with an acute sense of discontent and uneasiness" (p. 2) because of a lack of growth, a dearth of interest in Division 2 among prominent psychologists, and the absence of professional prestige for teachers of psychology. In an attempt to rectify this situation, the Committee offered for discussion seven proposals for Division initiatives: (a) interdivisional committees should be established to examine specific content areas; (b) interdivisional symposia should be planned for the annual APA meeting; (c) interdivisional examination of the instructional aspects of supervision should be inaugurated; (d) membership recruitment efforts should be redoubled and should specifically target "prominent" psychologists; (e) a Bylaws amendment should be introduced requiring fellow status in another division as a prerequisite for fellow status in Division 2; (f) psychology as a component of secondary school curricula should be investigated; and (g) the APA should be lobbied to give greater consideration to teaching interests in any proposed reorganization.

Reporting to the membership during the September 1957 meeting of the APA in New York, Edward J. Shoben, chairman of the PPC, reported that the only overwhelmingly negative response the Committee received to the seven proposals was the requirement of fellow status outside of Division 2 before becoming a fellow of Division 2 (Lovell, 1957). To make Division 2 fellow status contingent on fellow status in other divisions would be tantamount to making Division 2 subordinate to other divisions. Shoben observed that in light of the APA's recent redefinition of *fellow*, the Division would have to establish criteria for outstanding teaching (Lovell, 1957). Fellows were now required to present evidence of an "unusual and outstanding contribution." Within a year, the PPC proposed a Bylaws change defining fellow qualifications as accomplishments in three of five domains: (a) advancement to instructional positions of increased difficulty and responsibility, (b) scholarly contributions, (c) participation in the training of teachers of psychology, (d) contributions to pedagogy and curricula, and (e) organizational participation (PPC, 1958). The general tone of the newsletter's record surrounding this proposed change was that if ratified, these criteria would rectify a long-standing source of embarrassment to the Division. These criteria were entered into the Bylaws by the membership during the 1959 business meeting in Cincinnati, Ohio (Harper, 1959). Also approved by the membership during that business meeting was an aligning of the Bylaws to reflect the APA's redefinition of membership categories: fellow, member, and associate.

As the decade drew to a close, the PPC attempted, using the 1957 APA membership directory, to characterize Division 2's membership (PPC, 1957b). The PPC reported that Division members were equally divided among large and small schools. The specialty interests of members clustered around social, experimental, and clinical–counseling psychology. Twenty-nine percent of the members and 13% of the fellows were associated with no division other than Division 2. Although the majority of the members worked in academia, 20% worked, in some capacity, outside of academia. In 1959, when the APA's Policy and Planning Board proposed to evade the formation of superdivisions (Policy and Planning Board of the American Psychological Association, 1959), the Division evaded the last attempt at organizational absorption. From a beginning as a "holding corporation" for APA membership, Division 2 was beginning to develop a character of its own.

CHARACTER DEVELOPMENT: 1960–1974

As the 1960s dawned, the National Defense Education Act was funneling money into institutes of higher learning, "new" math was infusing the public schools, and Division 2 was finding reasons to be optimistic about its future. Membership was on the rise, the newsletter was acquiring a more polished appearance, and, under the leadership of Wilbert J. McKeachie, the PPC was refining the Division's statement of purpose, which Buxton had sculpted a decade earlier. Specifically, Division 2 evolved from "working for the good of" to "applying the results of research and considered experience to the benefit of" the teaching profession (PPC, 1960, p. 7). Three developments marked the Division's evolution during this period: increased service and assistance to teachers of psychology, marked growth in membership, and conspicuous movement toward exacting standards of scholarship related to the teaching of psychology.

As Division President Robert S. Daniel wrote in 1961, Division 2 "felt a growing pride in [its] service activities" (Daniel, 1961, p. 3), and rightly so. The Division constructed and made available bibliographies of teaching tips, compiled a collection of course syllabi that were individually available at a nominal cost, and took a leading role in the development of educational television. Division 2 also became a clearinghouse for used apparatuses to bolster the equipment cupboards of departments operating on shoe-string budgets, the development of experimental apparatuses on which nonsighted students could learn was facilitated, programs for teachers of psychology in high schools and 2-year colleges were cultivated, and Division 2 successfully lobbied the American Psychological Foundation to establish an annual award to honor outstanding teaching. A reading of the newsletter throughout this period reveals that these tasks were accomplished by a small number of individuals. Often, this group pleaded for greater participation in these projects—*any* project—from among the membership at large.[4]

And the membership was becoming large. Primarily through aggressive membership solicitation and an early decade campaign fueled by the personal efforts and financial support of Floyd L. Ruch (Membership Committee of Division Two, 1964)—the only individual ever twice elected Division president—Division 2 witnessed a 14-year period of unprecedented growth. Figure 1 depicts the surge in membership. By 1965, Division 2's membership outnumbered all other divisions except Divisions 8, 12, and 15[5] (Wertheimer, 1965–1966).

After the APA created the affiliate categories that would evolve into the present-day "international affiliate" and "student affiliate" classifications, Division 2 amended its Bylaws to open its doors to affiliates (Engle, 1961). During the 1962 business meeting, the Policy and Planning Committee recommended that the Bylaws be further amended to permit high school teachers to affiliate with the division (Engle, 1962). The motion carried and a Bylaws alteration was set in motion; in 1963, Division 2 created the "high school affiliate" designation (Engle, 1964). In 1968, when the APA began to make the plight of high school teachers of psychology an associationwide concern, Division 2 again amended its Bylaws, changing the high school affiliate to a more generic affiliate designed to include all interested individuals who were ineligible for APA membership (Ray, 1968). The Division also offered at that time to share the contents of the newsletter with APA's Membership Committee in order to better serve incoming affiliates (Ray, 1968).

Reflected in the evolution of the newsletter is a move within Division 2 to more exacting standards of scholarship. Members of the Division had

---

[4]Krawiec (1970) noted his "unbelievable realization that Division 2 members are far more interested in pursuing either their own specialty, or in doing their 'own thing' rather than to be involved actively with the TEACHING OF PSYCHOLOGY [sic]. To me this pretense of entertaining one set of feelings but acting under the influence of another, explains in part the current dilemma of the academic world" (p. 1).

[5]These divisions correspond to the divisions whose current names are, respectively, Personality and Social Psychology, Clinical Psychology, and Educational Psychology.

desired a journal devoted to the teaching of psychology as early as the 1950s, but some Division members argued that a journal giving teachers an identity apart from their areas of specialization would further lower the Division's already low prestige. The opposition was so vehement that it killed initial efforts to found a journal during the early 1950s.[6] When the Murchison journals were available for purchase, the APA determined that divisions had no business in the journal business (Bills, 1965). Despite these obstacles, a handful of committed editors, epitomized by Robert S. Daniel, crafted the *Teaching of Psychology Newsletter* into an increasingly rigorous publication that culminated in the *Teaching of Psychology's* first issue in 1974 (see Daniel, 1974; also see Daniel's chapter in this book on the journal, *Teaching of Psychology*).

CHARACTER REFINEMENT: 1975–1986

As *Teaching of Psychology* (*ToP*) was making its debut in 1974, London was banning corporal punishment, and B. F. Skinner was publishing *About Behaviorism*. The salient feature of the Division's history during the next several years is a continuing effort to refine and further the advances of preceding years. This effort is best illustrated in the development of *ToP*, attempts to address declining membership (a trend that began in 1974), definition and redefinition of affiliate status within the Division, and the emergence of Division 2's teaching awards.

Teaching of Psychology's emergence and early development owe much to the efforts of one self-effacing man and his family, Robert S. Daniel of the University of Missouri (for a personal history, see Heppner & Reis, 1987). In 1971, when Doug Mitchell resigned as editor of the newsletter, Division leadership asked Daniel to assume the editorship. He conditionally agreed, with that condition being permission to begin changing the newsletter to a journal. Once *ToP* was established, Daniel worked tirelessly producing the cottage publication, with much of the labor being done at home with the help of his daughters and wife, Nola. By 1981, *ToP* was surfacing as one of the discipline's better journals (Buffardi & Nichols, 1981). In an expression of appreciation, Division 2 recognized Daniel's Herculean effort by forever gracing *ToP*'s masthead with "Founding Editor: Robert S. Daniel, 1974–1984" (Benjamin, 1984), an honor to date bestowed only on G. Stanley Hall for the *American Journal of Psychology* and Morton Prince for the *Journal of Abnormal Psychology*. In 1984, *ToP*, acquired a new publisher, Lawrence Erlbaum Associates, and a new editor, Charles L. Brewer (Benjamin, 1983).

---

[6]The McKeachie Papers housed in the University of Akron's Archives of the History of American Psychology reveal the strength of this opposition as McKeachie argued in favor of a journal.

In 1981, Division 2 President Brewer faced the disturbing problem of declining membership, a trend that would continue until 1990 (see Figure 1). Many individuals cited general dissatisfaction with the benefits that the APA offered coupled with rapidly escalating dues as reasons for leaving the APA and thereby dissolving their association with Division 2. During the 1980s, Division 2 membership chairs faced the difficult task of having to recruit enough new members to offset members resigning from the APA. By 1988, the downward trend had been reversed. Techniques such as writing personal letters to all new APA members who expressed an interest in Division 2 and methodically combing the *Directory of the American Psychological Association* for potential Division 2 members appear to have been effective in stemming the agonizing decline in membership during this period. Brewer (personal communication, June 2, 1991; see also, Benjamin, 1982) recalled that the accomplishment for which he was most proud as Division president was the widening of the Division's net of active members.

An aspect of membership over which the Division vacillated during this period was the Division's definition of affiliate status. During the 1976 business meeting in Washington, DC, the Division passed, at the recommendation of the Executive Committee, a Bylaws amendment that widened affiliate status to include all individuals ineligible for APA membership and defined all subscribers to *ToP*, who were not members of the Division, as affiliates of the Division (Murphy, 1976). Four years later, in 1980, the membership was asked to approve by mail ballot the deletion of affiliate status and subscriber-as-affiliate from the bylaws. The Division's membership was told that the Division's affiliate status was no longer needed because the APA Central Office was now performing all of the services once done by the Division (Loveland, 1980). Before another 5 years had passed, the Division was again approving affliate status, first for graduate students and then for high school teachers (Matthews, 1985). As we show, the evolution of this issue was far from complete.

Although exhibiting indecision about its constituency, Division 2 was decidedly decisive about acknowledging exceptional teaching during the 1980s. The Division had discussed establishing teaching awards since the late 1950s. David Cole (Norton, 1980), a former president of the Division, codified the procedure for honoring four categories of teachers: high school, graduate assistant, 2-year college, and 4-year college. The first award ceremony was held in 1980 during the APA meeting in Montreal (Cole, 1980). James H. Korn would later initiate the establishment of an endowment to support the awards (Korn, 1988; Matthews, 1987). One might think that teaching interests were alive and well, but dark clouds were on the APA horizon.

DISCONTENT AND EXPANSION: 1987–1991

In 1987, President Reagan produced the first trillion dollar budget; the Dow rose to a record high in August and then plummeted in October, causing panic on Wall Street; and Division 2's leadership was not sanguine about its relationship with the APA. Reaction to turmoil within the APA and a significant change in privileges among the membership marked the Division's development during this short period.

Details of the strife within the APA that led to founding of the American Psychological Society (APS)—a fascinating story in its own right—does not concern us here. Suffice it to say that during the 1980s, the traditional balance of power within the APA shifted from academics and scientists to practitioners. In an attempt to address concerns of the former group, the APA's Council of Representatives investigated several plans for reorganizing the APA. Yet, Division 2's representatives to the Council reported in 1987 that it was difficult to describe the levels of stress and political manipulation surrounding discussions of reorganization during Council meetings (Matthews & Williams, 1987). This meeting of the Council witnessed the rejection of yet another reorganization plan. During informal, after-hour discussions accompanying the 1987 February meeting, concerned Council members formed the Assembly for Scientific and Applied Psychology (ASAP). In his 1987 presidential message published in *ToP*, Division 2 President Jim Korn (1987; also see Korn, 1988) announced that the Division's Executive Committee was considering eliminating affiliation with the APA as a requirement for Division 2 membership.

According to the Division's representatives to the Council, the mood in the Council's subsequent February meeting—February 1988—was one of "anger, hurt, and frustration" (Matthews & Williams, 1988, p. 168). Animosity came to a head during the 1988 August meeting of the APA when, following the APA membership's rejection of a reorganizing Bylaws change, ASAP voted to form the American Psychological Society, thus ending the attempt to reorganize the APA. Division 2 was not unaffected by the APS's founding that August. For example, teachers of psychology actively recruited new APS members during the Division's Atlanta Teaching Activities Exchange. In addition, while in Atlanta, Division 2, after an acrimonious debate, voted in its annual business meeting to establish a trial affiliation with APS (cf. Swenson, 1988). By October 1988, 12 APA divisions had become affiliated with APS (Staff, 1988).

On the heels of significant changes in the APA's membership, the Division initiated significant changes of its own. The Division instituted no affiliate status when its membership categories were first established in the 1940s but opened its doors to international and student affiliates in 1962; in addition, in 1963, the Division created the high school affiliate. In 1968, the Division converted its various affiliate categories to a generic affiliate status. This membership category was widened in 1976 to include all individuals ineligible for APA membership. In 1980, affiliate status was eliminated from the Division Bylaws; in 1985, the Division changed its mind and began readmitting affiliates. Throughout this evolution, affiliates were never permitted to have voting privileges within the Division. During the 1990 business meeting in Boston, affiliates were given voting privileges. Division 2 members attending the 1991 annual business meeting in San Francisco learned that new affiliates for the year, who did not have to be members of the APA, outnumbered new members associated with the APA 4:1. Division President Joseph J. Palladino speculated that within 3 years, the Division's affiliates would outnumber the Division's APA members (Palladino, 1991). Where this turn in the Division's history will lead is unclear.

Although we have attempted to chronicle the development of Division 2, the Division on the Teaching of Psychology, much of the Division's history still requires disclosure. Stories yet to be told include an accounting of the Division's relationship with the APA, particularly with the Education and Training Board, and with other organizations that advocate and facilitate teaching. A history of the Division's various committees also merits telling, as does an in-depth examination of the Division's fellows. The Division 2 story is the story of a professional organization endeavoring to nourish the art of teaching. Albert Einstein once observed that the teacher's art was to awaken joy in creative expression and knowledge. Perhaps by becoming familiar with the heritage of Division 2's teaching enterprise, one can further kindle exhilaration in the practice of the craft.

REFERENCES

Adkins, D. C. (1954). The simple structure of the American Psychological Association. *American Psychologist, 9,* 175–180.

Anderson, J. E. (1943). Outcomes of the Intersociety Constitutional Convention. *Psychological Bulletin, 40,* 585–588.

Anderson, J. E. (1944). A note on the meeting of the Joint Constitutional Committee of the APA and AAAP. *Psychological Bulletin, 41,* 235–236.

Benjamin, L. T., Jr. (1982). Report of the annual business meeting of Division Two, American Psychological Association, August 26, 1982, Washington, DC. *Teaching of Psychology, 9,* 247–248.

Benjamin, L. T., Jr. (1983). Report of the annual business meeting of Division Two, American Psychological Association, August 28, 1983, Anaheim, California. *Teaching of Psychology, 10,* 243.

Benjamin, L. T., Jr. (1984). Report of the annual business meeting of Division Two, American Psychological Association, August 26, 1984, Toronto, Canada. *Teaching of Psychology, 11,* 256–257.

Bills, R. (1965, February). Annual business meeting. *Teaching of Psychology Newsletter,* p. 2.

Buffardi, L. C., & Nichols, J. A. (1981). Citation impact, acceptance rate, and APA journals. *American Psychologist, 36*, 1453–1456.

Buxton, C. E. (1951a, November). Letter from the president. *Teaching of Psychology Newsletter*, p. 1.

Buxton, C. E. (1951b). Teaching: Have your cake and eat it too? *American Psychologist, 6*, 111–118.

Buxton, C. E. (1952a, November). Brief excerpts from the presidential address: "Unfinished business." *Teaching of Psychology Newsletter*, p. 4.

Buxton, C. E. (1952b, May). Letter from the president. *Teaching of Psychology Newsletter*, p. 1.

Carmichael, L. (1950, November). Letter from the president. *Teaching of Psychology Newsletter*, p. 1.

Carmichael, L. (1952, November). Why not become a Fellow? *Teaching of Psychology Newsletter*, p. 2.

Cole, D. (1980). Teaching award winners, 1980. *Teaching of Psychology, 7*, 135–136.

Daniel, R. S. (1961, December). Presidential message. *Teaching of Psychology Newsletter*, p. 3.

Daniel, R. S. (1974). Teaching of psychology has already had a long past. *Teaching of Psychology, 3*, 32–34.

Doll, E. A. (1946). The divisional structure of the APA. *American Psychologist, 1*, 336–345.

Editor. (1953, May). Revision of the by-laws. *Teaching of Psychology Newsletter*, p. 5.

Engle, T. L. (1961, December). Minutes of the 1961 business meeting. *Teaching of Psychology Newsletter*, pp. 5–7.

Engle, T. L. (1962, December). Minutes of the 1962 business meeting. *Teaching of Psychology Newsletter*, pp. 5–7.

Engle, T. L. (1964, January). Minute of the 1963 business meeting. *Teaching of Psychology Newsletter*, pp. 4–5.

Harper, R. S. (1959, December). Minutes of the business meeting: Division 2, APA. *Teaching of Psychology Newsletter*, pp. 12–13.

Heppner, P. P., & Reis, S. D. (1987). Robert S. Daniel: A man dedicated to teaching. *Teaching of Psychology, 14*, 4–10.

Hilgard, E. R. (1945a). Psychologists' preferences for divisions under the proposed APA By-laws. *Psychological Bulletin, 42*, 20–26.

Hilgard, E. R. (1945b). Temporary chairmen and secretaries for proposed APA divisions. *Psychological Bulletin, 42*, 294–296.

Hilgard, E. R. (1987). *Psychology in America: A historical survey.* San Diego, CA: Harcourt Brace Jovanovich.

Hurlock, E. B. (1952, November). Minutes of the annual meeting of the Division on the Teaching of Psychology, Washington, DC, September 1, 1952. *Teaching of Psychology Newsletter*, pp. 3–4.

Hurlock, E. B. (1954, November). Group discussion: The future of Division 2. *Teaching of Psychology Newsletter*, pp. 8–9.

Husband, R. W. (1954, November). Greetings from the new president. *Teaching of Psychology Newsletter*, p. 1.

Husband, R. W. (1955, May). Message from the retiring president. *Teaching of Psychology Newsletter*, p. 1.

Intersociety Constitutional Convention of Psychologists. (1943). Recommendations of the Intersociety Constitutional Convention of Psychologists. *Psychological Bulletin, 40,* 621–647.

Korn, J. (1987). Greetings from the president. *Teaching of Psychology, 14,* 259–260.

Korn, J. (1988). Greetings from the president. *Teaching of Psychology, 15,* 59.

Krawiec, T. S. (1970, March). Farewell—Almost. *Teaching of Psychology Newsletter,* p. 1.

Loveland, E. H. (1980). Division Two proposed by-laws revision. *Teaching of Psychology, 7,* 128–130.

Lovell, C. (1957, November). Minutes of the annual meeting of the Division of the Teaching of Psychology: New York, September 3, 1957. *Teaching of Psychology Newsletter*, pp. 7–9.

Marquis, D. G. (1946). Proceedings of the special business meeting of the American Psychological Association, Inc., Columbus, Ohio: December 27, 28, 29, 1945. *American Psychologist, 1,* 35–44.

Matthews, J. (1985). Report of the annual business meeting of Division Two: Los Angeles, California. *Teaching of Psychology, 12,* 239–240.

Matthews, J. R. (1987). Annual business meeting: New York City. *Teaching of Psychology, 14,* 260–261.

Matthews, J. R., & Williams, J. E. (1987). Report from February Council of Representatives meeting. *Teaching of Psychology, 14,* 183–184.

Matthews, J. R., & Williams, J. E. (1988). Report from February Council of Representatives meeting. *Teaching of Psychology, 15,* 168–169.

Membership Committee of Division Two. (1964, January). Recruiting to further strengthen Division Two: Membership committee report. *Teaching of Psychology Newsletter*, p. 8.

Murphy, L. E. (1976). Minutes of the annual meeting of Division Two: Washington, DC, September 4, 1974. *Teaching of Psychology, 3,* 197–198.

Napoli, D. S. (1981). *Architects of adjustment: The history of the psychological profession in the United States.* Port Washington, NY: Kennikat Press.

Norton, F.-T. M. (1980). Report of the annual meeting, September 3, 1979. *Teaching of Psychology, 7,* 126–127.

Olson, W. C. (1944). Proceedings of the fifty-second annual meeting of the

American Psychological Association, Inc., Cleveland, Ohio, September 11–12, 1944. *Psychological Bulletin, 41*, 725–793.

Palladino, J. J. (1991). President's message: Reflections and vision. *Teaching of Psychology, 18*, 266–267.

Policy and Planning Board of the American Psychological Association. (1954). Major activities of the Policy and Planning Board during 1953–1954. *American Psychologist, 9*, 749–754.

Policy and Planning Board of the American Psychological Association. (1959). The problem of divisional structure. *American Psychologist, 14*, 489–496.

Policy and Planning Committee of Division Two. (1957a, May). Report of the Policy and Planning Committee. *Teaching of Psychology Newsletter*, pp. 2–4.

Policy and Planning Committee of Division Two. (1957b, November). Who are we? *Teaching of Psychology Newsletter*, pp. 2–6.

Policy and Planning Committee of Division Two. (1958, May). Report of the Policy and Planning Committee. *Teaching of Psychology Newsletter*, p. 2.

Policy and Planning Committee of Division Two. (1960, December). Report of the Policy and Planning Committee. *Teaching of Psychology Newsletter*, pp. 7–9.

Ray, W. S. (1952, November). Urge your colleagues to join Division 2!!! *Teaching of Psychology Newsletter*, p. 2.

Ray, W. S. (1968, November). Minutes of the annual meeting of the Division on the Teaching of Psychology, San Francisco, September 1, 1968. *Teaching of Psychology Newsletter*, pp. 5–6.

Staff. (1988, October). 12 APA divisions affiliate with APS. *APS Newsletter, 1*, p. 4.

Swenson, E. V. (1988). Annual business meeting: Atlanta. *Teaching of Psychology, 15*, 227–228.

Tyson, R. (1951). Dr. Buxton's crusade. *American Psychologist, 6*, 459.

Wertheimer, M. M. (1965–1966, Mid-Winter). Presidential message. *Teaching of Psychology Newsletter*, p. 1.

Wolfle, D. (1946a). Christmas meeting of the APA. *American Psychologist, 1*, 22–25.

Wolfle, D. (1946b). The reorganized American Psychological Association. *American Psychologist, 1*, 3–6.

Wolfle, D. (1947a). It is easy to become a Fellow. *American Psychologist, 2*, 561.

Wolfle, D. (1947b). Requirements for membership in the divisions of the American Psychological Association. *American Psychologist, 2*, 24–26.

Wolfle, D. (1948). Requirements for membership in the divisions of the American Psychological Association. *American Psychologist, 3*, 140–141.

Wolfle, H. (1948). A comparison of the strength and weakness of APA divisions. *American Psychologist, 3,* 378–380.

Yerkes, R. M. (1943a). Preparation for the Intersociety Constitutional Convention of Psychologists. *Psychological Bulletin, 40,* 127–128.

Yerkes, R. M. (1943b). The Intersociety Constitutional Convention of Psychologists. *Psychological Bulletin, 40,* 379.

17

A QUARTET OF COUNCILS
INTERESTED IN THE TEACHING OF
PSYCHOLOGY

RANDOLPH A. SMITH

Two chapters in this section deal with three organizations devoted to the teaching of psychology: Division 2 of the APA, Psi Chi, and Psi Beta. Despite the fact that these organizations endeavor to cover the full range of academic psychology, other groups with specialized interests in teaching have appeared. This chapter deals with four such groups: the Council of Teachers of Undergraduate Psychology (CTUP), the Council of Under-

I am indebted to many people for providing me with information from their files, corresponding with me, or sharing their reminiscences through telephone conversations. These individuals include Robert M. Adams, John K. Bare, Leslie R. Beach, Douglas W. Bloomquist, Douglas K. Candland, Bernardo J. Carducci, David Cole, Al L. Cone, Robert S. Daniel, Stephen F. Davis, David C. Edwards, Henry C. Ellis, Allen Fingeret, Irwin L. Goldstein, Robert S. Harper, Lloyd G. Humphreys, James R. Ison, Edward S. Katkin, Geoffrey Keppel, Gregory A. Kimble, James H. Korn, Margaret A. Lloyd, Joseph D. Matarazzo, Susan H. McFadden, William J. McGill, Wilbert J. McKeachie, Kenneth W. Nikels, Barbara F. Nodine, Sherman Ross, Rick Samples, Sandra W. Scarr, Wilber E. Scoville, Joseph A. Sgro, Michael H. Siegel, Shirley Spragg, Thomas F. Staton, Richard D. Tucker, Ralph H. Turner, Alice Van Krevelen, William S. Verplanck, Randall D. Wight, and John E. Williams. I apologize for any oversight in this listing.

Information for Appendixes A and B was derived from a variety of sources. I was unable to verify all of the entries.

graduate Psychology Programs (CUPP), the Council of Applied Master's Programs in Psychology (CAMPP), and the Council of Graduate Departments of Psychology (COGDOP). All were developed by and for chairs of psychology departments, although CTUP and CAMPP later broadened their scope. CTUP is aimed primarily at undergraduate psychology teachers, CUPP at undergraduate chairs or program directors, CAMPP at master's-level chairs, and COGDOP at graduate chairs. Reflecting a logical progression of focus, the chapter covers these groups in the order listed above. It is not possible to cover the complete history of the groups, so each organization is examined with regard to its founding, purposes, development, and impact on teaching.

COUNCIL OF TEACHERS OF UNDERGRADUATE PSYCHOLOGY

Founding

The need for an organization of undergraduate department chairs was noted at the 1967 American Psychological Association (APA) Convention by both COGDOP and an informal group of department chairs (Nodine, 1973). The Council of Undergraduate Departments (CUD) was founded at the 1968 APA Convention in San Francisco. Robert S. Harper of Knox College was chosen as the first president. (For a complete list of presidents of this organization and its predecessors, see Appendix A.) Within a year, on the basis of objections to the "ruminant connotation" of CUD, the organization was renamed the Council of Undergraduate Psychology Departments (CUPD; Robert S. Harper, personal communication, May 13, 1991).

Purposes

Harper (personal communication, May 13, 1991) remembers that CUD was organized to address various concerns of undergraduate departments, such as curriculum, budget, salaries, equipment, and relations with graduate departments. According to 1970–1971 CUPD President Wilbert S. Ray's description of the organization, "The Council of Undergraduate Psychology Departments is organized to help with the administrative problems of the chairmen of such departments, and including directors of the undergraduate work in large departments which have both graduate and undergraduate programs" (Ray, 1971a, p. 1). Specifically, Ray's CUPD information sheet listed concerns such as funding, dealing with graduate departments to which students are recommended, selecting and training new teachers, and training subdoctoral psychologists. According to Korn

(1973), CUPD was also organized to provide a vehicle for communication among faculty who administer undergraduate programs.

David Cole, 1971–1972 CUPD president, remembers that CUPD leaders realized that many department chairs did not attend APA meetings (personal communication, May 20, 1991). Because of this, CUPD's focus in the early 1970s turned to presenting sessions on various topics for department chairs at the regional association meetings (Nodine, 1973). This focus on the regional meetings continues to be a hallmark of the organization and, in Nodine's opinion (1973), is the "CUPD's most successful venture" (p. 2).

Thus, the rationale for founding CUD/CUPD was to provide a companion organization to COGDOP for undergraduate chairs. Various goals included providing a voice for undergraduate chairs, facilitating communication among them, and providing a forum for workshops and programs designed for interested parties at regional psychology meetings.

Development

A major issue confronting CUPD during its formative years was whether to limit membership to people who were department chairs. According to David Cole (personal communication, May 20, 1991), that limitation was deemed inappropriate and this qualification was removed by 1973 (Korn, 1973). In 1974, the advertising for CUPD contained the information that "anyone concerned with undergraduate education is welcome. It is not restricted to undergraduate psychology departments, for faculty in colleges and universities offering doctoral and masters degrees are welcome, provided they are concerned with undergraduate education" (Candland, 1974, p. 1). This decision to open membership permitted a broader base of support and a greater potential for membership and also led to a change of focus for the organization.

Early compilations of CUPD programs at various regional meetings suggest that this broadened search for members also led to programs designed to appeal to a wider audience than department chairs. In 1971, CUPD sponsored the following sessions: "Selection and Development of New Faculty" (Southern Society for Philosophy and Psychology [SSPP]), "Funding, Developing, and Evaluating the Program for Undergraduate Non-Majors" (Western Psychological Association [WPA]), and Information Exchanges at Eastern Psychological Association (EPA), Midwestern Psychological Association (MPA), Rocky Mountain Psychological Association (RMPA), and Southwestern Psychological Association (SWPA; Ray, 1971b). In 1972, CUPD sponsored "The Future of the BA Degree in Psychology" (California State Psychological Association), "Workshop on Undergraduate Research and Field Experience" (EPA), "Symposium: Graduate Curriculum at the Crossroads" (MPA), and "Graduate Preparation of the College Professor of Psychology" (WPA; Cole, 1972). From these titles it is clear that, while continuing to be involved with concerns of department chairs, CUPD had set its sights on broader horizons. This broadened interest continues to hold true for the organization, as a listing of recent programs included only sessions of general interest and nothing aimed specifically at chairs (Carducci & Gray-Shellberg, 1987).

Because CUPD did not develop a constitution or bylaws, the current organizational structure is rather flexible. In its earliest years, CUPD was headed by a president chosen from a 16-member Executive Committee (Nodine, 1973). Shortly thereafter, the offices of secretary and treasurer were added. In the spring of 1974, the CUPD Executive Committee approved a change to officers of president, vice-president, and secretary–treasurer (Korn, 1974). The Executive Committee was also reduced from 16 to 8 members. The secretary–treasurer position is not mentioned after the 1980 CUPD Minutes (Nocks, 1980).

To help implement the desired regional focus, CUPD began designating individuals whose responsibility was to plan programs for the regional meetings. Two memos to CUPD members from 1978–1979 President Michael H. Siegel (1979a, 1979b) mention regional liaisons and their duty of "organizing programs of interest to undergraduate teachers of psychology at regional meetings" (Siegel, 1979b, p. 2). President Charles L. Brewer referred to these positions as regional coordinators in his report to CUPD members (Brewer, 1980), naming specific individuals to fill these posts for the EPA, MPA, RMPA, Southeastern Psychological Association (SEPA), SWPA, and WPA. Sporadically, there has also been a regional coordinator for SSPP. A coordinator for 2-year colleges was added in 1989. The coordinator positions continue to exist today, with regional coordinators responsible for planning and submitting programs at the regional meetings, planning social activities for members, and recruiting new members in their specific regions. The organization's officers in 1991 consisted of a president and president-elect plus the regional coordinators (Smith, 1991).

At the 1986 CUPD Business Meeting, the members present voted to change the name of the organization to the Council of Teachers of Undergraduate Psychology (CTUP). This change was a way to reflect more accurately the basic focus and membership of the organization (Carducci, 1987). To foster more effective communication among CTUP members, a newsletter, *Significant Difference*, began to be published in October 1989, under the leadership of President-Elect Jane S. Halonen.

Impact

CTUP did not hold to its original focus of being an organization for department chairs long enough to evaluate its impact in that realm. CTUP sponsors more accessible regional events and maintains low lifetime membership fees to provide an economical alternative to attendance at national meetings and APA membership. As an organization devoted to presenting sessions at regional meetings for teachers of psychology, CTUP appears to have been reasonably successful. Reports from regional coordinators appearing in minutes of the annual meeting of CTUP typically mention large and enthusiastic audiences. However, the large audiences and enthusiasm have not translated into a large CTUP membership (see Appendix A for available membership numbers). Thus, if the primary goal is building a large number of CTUP members, the organization has not been overly successful, although the numbers showed a marked increase during the 1980s. On the other hand, if getting information to teachers of psychology who do not belong to or attend APA meetings is the goal, CTUP has done an admirable job.

COUNCIL OF UNDERGRADUATE PSYCHOLOGY PROGRAMS

Founding

At the September 1987 meeting of the APA's Committee on Undergraduate Education (CUE), an organization of undergraduate chairs and directors of psychology programs was proposed (Lloyd, 1988). The members of CUE believed that a group similar to COGDOP but at the undergraduate level would be helpful in promoting undergraduate psychology. Margaret A. Lloyd (Suffolk University) was asked to organize such a group, with help from a director of undergraduate studies at a large university. David A. Santogrossi (Purdue University) was later asked to fill this position. The Council of Chairs and Directors of Undergraduate Psychology Programs (CCDUPP) held an organizational meeting at the APA Convention in Atlanta in 1988 and appointed a 13-person Steering Committee (Lloyd, 1988). Margaret Lloyd was selected to head the group and was succeeded by Norine L. Jalbert (Western Connecticut State University) in 1991. Within the first year, the organization changed its name to the Council of Undergraduate Psychology Programs (CUPP). At the 1989 APA Convention in New Orleans, CUPP organized officially with the adoption of bylaws (Lloyd, 1989). Thus, CUPP was founded with the same audience CUD had targeted 21 years earlier.

Purposes

CUPP seeks to provide a forum for dialogue among undergraduate directors and chairs concerning undergraduate psychology programs, thereby helping to promote undergraduate psychology. CUPP plans to sponsor programs for chairs at national and regional psychological conventions to help develop effective departmental leadership. The organization also wishes to provide a voice for undergraduate psychology programs to regional and national psychological associations, to funding and government agencies, and to other relevant persons and organizations (Lloyd, 1990a).

CUPP undertook specific projects to help achieve its stated purposes (Lloyd, 1990b). A twice-yearly newsletter inaugurated in 1990 is published to update members about important events and issues in undergraduate education, as well as CUPP's activities. An annual membership directory is published to facilitate communication among CUPP members. Also in 1990, a Clearinghouse Service was approved by the Steering Committee. This service is intended to provide CUPP members with a central source of information about topics of interest to chairs and directors of undergraduate programs. Issues to be included are curricula, program assessment, faculty recruiting, and evaluation. David E. Johnson (John Brown University) was appointed Clearinghouse director in 1991 to begin implementing this service. During 1990–1991, a needs assessment survey of CUPP members was conducted. The results of this survey will be used to direct CUPP's subsequent efforts (Lloyd, 1991b).

Development

CUPP's original organizational structure consisted of a Steering Committee of six individuals who chose a chair and a secretary–treasurer (Lloyd, 1990b). Realizing that this Committee was somewhat small and left large regions of the country unrepresented, CUPP leadership added informal regional liaisons in the fall of 1990 (Lloyd, 1991c). This made it possible for CUPP to sponsor panel discussions or presentations at all regional association meetings other than the MPA in 1991. A Bylaws revision in mid-1991 changed the organizational structure to include a chair, past-chair, secretary–treasurer, and six regional coordinators, one for each regional psychology association (Lloyd, 1991a). The duties of CUPP regional coordinators are similar to CTUP regional coordinators in terms of sponsoring programs at regional meetings, sharing information within the region, and recruiting members from the region. At the 1991 CUPP Business Meeting held at the APA Convention in San Francisco, Margaret Lloyd noted that adding regional coordinators would allow CUPP to reach its members and interested parties much more efficiently than sponsoring national meetings alone.

Interest in CUPP has been strong from its beginning. By the time of the first organizational meeting in Atlanta in 1988, 60 people had requested information about the group (Lloyd, 1988). In July of 1990, CUPP had 144 members (Jalbert, 1990) and had grown to approximately 195 in July of 1991 (Jalbert, 1991).

Impact

In 1991, CUPP had been in existence for roughly 2 years. Therefore, it is too soon to assess the impact of the organization. On the basis of the early signs of membership growth and attention, it does appear that there is healthy interest in such a group. Compared with the years when CTUP was aimed primarily at chairs, CUPP has done quite well, attracting as many members in 2 years as CTUP did in over 10 years. It seems likely that this large membership base will provide momentum to keep CUPP a viable organization. Although one of CUPP's original reasons for founding was to provide an undergraduate force analogous to COGDOP, it remains to be seen whether CUPP can have the same type of impact that COGDOP has had.

COUNCIL OF APPLIED MASTER'S PROGRAMS IN PSYCHOLOGY

Founding

For many years there has been controversy revolving around terminal master's programs in applied psychology. Specific concerns have addressed program accreditation and credentialing of graduates. In 1980, COGDOP began discussion of issues relating to applied master's degrees and a Task Force on Master's Issues was formed (Hanson, 1990). Because of some overlap in membership between the Task Force and the Association of Heads of Departments of Psychology of the SEPA, discussion of the master's issue took place within both groups. As it became clear to representatives of master's-level programs that a separate organization was needed, the Council of Applied Master's Programs in Psychology (CAMPP) was formed within SEPA in 1986. Because master's issues were national rather than regional in scope, CAMPP opened its membership within a year and by 1990 counted programs across the country as members, represented by both chairs and training directors (Tucker, 1990). Richard D. Tucker (University of Central Florida) was chosen as chair of CAMPP in 1986 and served in that position until 1990, when Larry A. Alferink (Illinois State University) succeeded him.

Purposes

"The primary purpose of CAMPP is to establish and maintain standards of training and education for masters programs in applied psychology" (CAMPP information brochure, 1990). CAMPP also disseminates information, exchanges ideas, collects data, and formulates policy relating to master's training and education in applied psychology. In addition, CAMPP provides consultation and establishes liaisons with appropriate organizations such as

COGDOP, the APA, the American Psychological Society (APS), and regional and state psychological associations. Finally, CAMPP has taken the lead in developing specific standards for training in applied master's programs and in urging schools to adopt those standards.

Development

To paraphrase an old saying, CAMPP has a short history but the master's issue has a long past. Hanson (1990) suggested that the issue was born in 1947 when the APA developed a policy that identified the doctoral degree as the entry-level qualification for the practice of psychology. Since then the "APA has, as far as official policy is concerned, consistently followed the doctoral emphasis when formulating accreditation and designation procedures for programs, when representing psychology before federal and state legislatures, establishing model licensure bills, and representing psychology before the public" (Hanson, 1990, p. 5).

At the 1987 National Conference on Graduate Education in Psychology held at the University of Utah, the master's issue was recognized and discussed. The following resolution grew out of the discussion:

> At the master's level, it is assumed that students receiving degrees in psychology from programs designed to culminate at the master's level will function under the supervision of licensed doctoral-level psychologists, as the doctoral level is the entry level to the profession for independent, unsupervised practice. There is some sentiment among psychologists that the master's degree should not be offered as a consolation degree for failure at the doctoral level but should stand on its own as a level of proficiency that helps to prepare students for various vocational roles in psychology. Indeed, many feel that standards should be developed for master's degree programs that include a professional emphasis. (National Conference on Graduate Education in Psychology, 1987, p. 1072)

Moses (1990) cited six attempts through the APA hierarchy to develop curriculum guidelines or to hold a national conference to address the master's issue, but none of the attempts ever developed beyond the committee stage. Problems such as these led to the founding of CAMPP. The National Conference on Graduate Education in Psychology did adopt a resolution recognizing that problems of master's issues do exist: "The American Psychological Association, in consultation with COGDOP, should study issues in graduate education at the master's level, especially those issues related to applied training programs. This study should consider the feasibility of a national conference" (National Conference on Graduate Education in Psychology, 1987, p. 1072). COGDOP endorsed the idea of such a national conference at its 1988 meeting and charged CAMPP with planning the conference (Hanson, 1990). After four planning sessions, the National

Conference on Applied Master's Training in Psychology was held June 2–5, 1990, at the University of Oklahoma.

Many of the master's issues have historically revolved around turf battles between doctoral- and master's-level psychologists over licensing and certification. CAMPP, however, has never fought to have master's-level psychologists fully licensed for independent practice. Indeed, Hanson (1990) described CAMPP's model as seeking to define supervised practice in a manner satisfactory to both doctoral-level and master's-level psychologists. CAMPP believes supervision is both necessary and desirable but also wishes that the competencies of master's-level psychologists be recognized.

Perhaps most related to issues of teaching psychology is CAMPP's effort to develop a normative model for applied master's programs. Although Hanson (1990) recognized some advantages to diversity, he concluded that the advantages of a normative model are greater. Among the advantages he listed are representing statistical norms; promoting comparison, clarification, and refinement; distinguishing master's-level training from other levels; and distinguishing applied training from nonapplied. Possibly the most important implication of a normative model is the ability to identify programs that actually fit the applied psychology model. Using a normative model in this manner sounds much like a certification process, something to which CAMPP appears to be committed. CAMPP has two types of membership, full and affiliate, based on whether the program meets the standards of training adopted by CAMPP: "Affiliate Membership is open to any program which endorses the purposes of the Council but which either is in the formative stages of establishing an applied master's program or has a program that does not meet the approved standards of training" (CAMPP information brochure, 1990). An applied master's program must meet the CAMPP's standards for curricula adopted at the 1990 national conference (Curriculum Standards for Applied Master's Programs, 1990) for full membership in CAMPP. These standards are designed to produce students who are broadly trained in psychology rather than solely trained as vocational specialists (Adams, 1990). CAMPP is therefore committed to educating people who can be termed psychologists, in the general rather than in the legal sense, and not technicians, in applied master's programs.

CAMPP has also developed standards of training, adopted in December 1987, for students in clinical/counseling applied master's programs (Standards of Training for Clinical/Counseling Applied Master's Training Programs, 1990). These standards describe the specific training that must be given in assessment, intervention/treatment (including both coursework and clinical or field experience), psychopathology, and research, in addition to meeting the general standards mentioned earlier.

Impact

There is no doubt that CAMPP has become an important group in speaking to, and about, the master's issue. The *Proceedings* of the National Conference held in June 1990 indicate CAMPP's interest in playing a major role in specifying outcomes for applied master's programs, in establishing credentialing requirements and procedures, and in negotiating issues related to the provision of services by master's-level psychologists. It must be noted, however, that CAMPP is not an organization that seeks to speak for all master's-level programs, but only those with an applied emphasis.

Focusing on teaching, CAMPP's influence has probably been somewhat less important than its more general impact. Setting standards for curricula and training in applied master's programs and clinical/counseling programs is probably CAMPP's most important teaching-related contribution. Placing an emphasis on well-rounded preparation, including statistics and research design, is in line with doctoral training in the Boulder model. This emphasis should prove helpful in training master's-level psychologists who will be accepted as legitimate practitioners by the academic community.

COUNCIL OF GRADUATE DEPARTMENTS OF PSYCHOLOGY

Founding

In the early 1960s, Sherman Ross, executive secretary of the APA's Education and Training Board, began convening meetings of department chairs at the Annual APA Conventions. The 1963 and 1964 APA Convention programs (APA, 1963, p. 479; 1964, p. 591) list sessions titled "Informal Meeting of Department Chairmen" sponsored by the APA Education and Training Board and chaired by Lloyd G. Humphreys. At the 1964 APA Convention in Los Angeles, the group formally organized, adopting Bylaws and electing Humphreys chair (Matarazzo, 1989). (For a complete listing of chairs of COGDOP and its predecessors, see Appendix B.) At the 1965 APA Convention in Chicago, the Council of Chairmen of Graduate Departments of Psychology (CCGDOP) held its first formal meeting with Humphreys as chair (APA, 1965, p. 605).

According to Humphreys (personal communication, August 5, 1991), the impetus for moving from an informal group to a formal organization came from an incident in New York. The New York licensing board decided that graduate schools had to have their curricula approved by the board if the schools' graduates were to be licensed in New York. Department chairs were opposed to this move but had no way to present a unified voice. Formal organization provided that opportunity. According to Humphreys, the organized opposition to the New York move was so powerful that the licensing board backed down and left APA in charge of accreditation of graduate programs and their curricula.

Purposes

Humphreys noted that CCGDOP was organized not only to fight the New York licensing board policy but also to provide an opportunity for graduate chairs to discuss issues of interest. He mentioned that new developments in certification, licensing, and affirmative action were early topics discussed by the group. Humphreys was personally interested in forming a group independent of APA because of what he saw as the growing professionalization of the Association. He was a founding member of the Psychonomic Society, which was organized in 1959–1960 in reaction to the perception of the APA's movement in a professional direction (Hilgard, 1987).

The aims of CCGDOP, as revealed in the 1964 Bylaws, were to provide graduate department chairs a chance to discuss problems in training of psychology students and other issues and to provide a vehicle for communication between department chairs and the APA or other relevant organizations. The 1970 Bylaws and the 1982 Bylaws kept these purposes intact, with a 1982 change adding the concept of promoting the development of psychology through those purposes.

Development

CCGDOP played an important role in many aspects of psychology. After the New York crisis mentioned earlier, the group concentrated on its informative purpose. Five discussion sessions were held at the 1967 APA Convention in Washington, DC, on the following topics: "The Place of Psychology on Campus: Relations with Professional Schools, Other Departments, etc."; "Manpower: Selection and Recruitment"; "Graduate and Undergraduate Curricula"; "Departmental Administration: Budgets, Promotions, Expenses"; and "Psychology and Outside Agencies: Granting Agencies, Licensing Boards, etc." (APA, 1967, p. 613). This informative purpose has been one of the organization's strengths through the years. For example, in the early 1970s, a New Chairs Workshop was established to provide information for both new and old chairs. John Williams, a former COGDOP chair, believes that allowing a forum for sharing ideas and solutions has been one of the group's great strengths (personal communication, September 20, 1991).

In the early 1970s, the organization's name was amended to the National Council of Chairmen of Graduate Departments of Psychology (NCCGDOP). (This deduction was made from the fact that the group is referred to as the Council of Chairmen of Graduate Departments of Psychology in its 1970 Bylaws but as the National Council of Chairmen of Graduate Departments of Psychology in the acknowledgment of their assistance in developing the ethical principles for research with participants [APA, 1973].) Gregory A. Kimble was an early chair of the Council, a member of the NCCGDOP's committee on research ethics, and a member of the APA committee that developed the APA's ethical principles. Kimble remembers that a draft of the principles was so strict that research would have been hampered and that NCCGDOP's input helped to develop a manageable set of ethical principles (personal communication, August 1, 1991).

In 1979, under the leadership of Henry Ellis, NCCGDOP began to hold a winter national meeting in addition to the annual meeting at the APA Convention. These meetings were more content-oriented and included the training session for new chairs. The 1979 sessions covered topics such as "Departmental Organization, Budgets, and Policies"; "Faculty Development"; "Tenure and Promotion Policies"; "Graduate Student Recruitment"; "Faculty Salaries"; "Affirmative Action and Minority Issues"; and "Credentialing and Accrediting" (Ellis, 1979). It was at the 1979 meeting in New Orleans that the organization's name was changed to the Council of Graduate Departments of Psychology, with the familiar acronym of COGDOP (Henry C. Ellis, personal communication, September 16, 1991).

According to Ellis, COGDOP's Executive Committee became politically active through lobbying in the mid-1970s (personal communication, September 16, 1991). At the 1981 winter meeting, the COGDOP membership decided to become politically active as a whole with the goal of bringing behavioral sciences to the attention of the legislative system. The 1982 winter meeting was scheduled for Washington, DC, and attendees met with members of Congress, representatives from funding agencies, and Dennis Prager, Deputy Director of Science and Technology from the Office of the President. COGDOP Chair Joseph H. Grosslight termed the meeting "a great success" (Grosslight, 1982, p. 1). He also announced that COGDOP had altered its original plan and decided to meet in Washington the following year rather than 2 years later, to maintain the momentum of the 1982 meeting. COGDOP's active role in the legislative arena continues today, with input on such varied topics as graduate training and animal research and welfare. According to Ellis, COGDOP lobbies for all things that interest and affect departments of psychology.

Another strength of COGDOP is its power to speak on behalf of graduate departments of psychology, particularly with the APA. According to Henry Ellis (personal communication, September 16, 1991), one of the beneficial moves the organization made in its early years was collaborating with the APA on joint projects. Ellis invited representatives from the APA's Educational Affairs Office to the first winter meeting, a tradition that still holds today. The result of this long-standing pattern of interaction is that the APA typically consults with COGDOP when important issues affecting graduate departments arise (John E. Williams, personal communication, September 20, 1991). A prime example of the interaction between COG-DOP and the APA is the publication *Characteristics of Graduate Departments of Psychology: 1988–89* (Kohout, Wicherski, & Pion, 1991). Although this massive survey was conducted by the Office of Demographic, Employment, and Educational Research of the APA's Education Directorate, the support, counsel, and cooperation of COGDOP are acknowledged in the report. Williams noted that this type of survey began as a COGDOP project and evolved into a joint project.

Impact

COGDOP has had a greater overall impact than any of the other three organizations covered in this chapter. In fact, the founders of all three have specifically acknowledged using COGDOP as a model in designing their organizations. COGDOP has been quite successful in generating support for graduate education through influence and legislation. COGDOP's influence with APA is such that COGDOP will have members representing its interests on the APA's new Committee on Accreditation for a 2-year trial period, filling 4 of 21 seats (Moses, 1992).

It must be noted, however, that COGDOP's impact has not been as great in the area of teaching, and its influence on teaching has been primarily indirect. One of COGDOP's goals from the beginning of the organization has been to provide the opportunity for communication among graduate departments of psychology. A good example of such communication is the survey of graduate departments mentioned earlier. Chairs of graduate departments of psychology can refer to this report to determine how their department fares in comparison with others across the country. Providing information about faculty and graduate student characteristics certainly can have important indirect effects on teaching at graduate institutions.

CONCLUSION

The four organizations discussed in this chapter have been important to the development of education in psychology. The common thread that ties these groups together is the idea of providing opportunities for communication among their respective members. In some cases this communication takes the form of specific nuts-and-bolts information that can improve teachers' classroom performance. In other cases, communication is of a more facilitative type—it may not be related to classroom performance per se, but it provides a better context for good teaching. Whether this facilitative communication within the groups involves planning and developing curricula, dealing with faculty development problems, tackling accreditation and training issues, or providing a voice for master's-level psychologists—just to name a few important concerns—providing information about the views and practices of other departments is a valuable service to teachers of psychology. These four councils—CTUP, CUPP, CAMPP, and COGDOP—are to be commended for their efforts in advancing the discipline of psychology and the teaching of that discipline.

REFERENCES

Adams, R. M. (1990). Curriculum issues for applied master's programs in psychology. In R. D. Tucker (Ed.), *Sourcebook for the National Conference on Applied Master's Training in Psychology* (pp. 19–20). Norman: Oklahoma Center for Continuing Education.

American Psychological Association. (1963). Program of the Seventy-First Annual Convention of the American Psychological Association. *American Psychologist*, 18, 337–502.

American Psychological Association. (1964). Program of the Seventy-Second Annual Convention of the American Psychological Association. *American Psychologist*, 19, 445–621.

American Psychological Association. (1965). Program of the Seventy-Third Annual Convention of the American Psychological Association. *American Psychologist*, 20, 465–632.

American Psychological Association. (1967). Program of the Seventy-Fifth Annual Convention of the American Psychological Association. *American Psychologist*, 22, 475–639.

American Psychological Association. (1973). *Ethical principles in the conduct of research with human participants*. Washington, DC: Author.

Brewer, C. L. (1980, September 25). [Memo to CUPD members]. Smith files.[1]

CAMPP information brochure. (1990). Smith files.

Candland, D. K. (1974). [CUPD information sheet]. Smith files.

Carducci, B. J. (1987). [Annual report of CTUP]. Smith files.

Carducci, B. J., & Gray-Shellberg, L. (1987, May). CTUP: Best bargain in town. *APA Monitor*, p. 41.

Cole, D. (Ed.). (1972). [Report of 1972 CUPD symposia]. Smith files.

Curriculum standards for applied master's programs. (1990). In R. H. Lowe (Ed.),

---

[1]All references to Smith files are from the files of Randolph A. Smith, Department of Psychology, Ouachita Baptist University, Arkadelphia, AR 71998-0001.

Proceedings of the National Conference on Applied Master's Training in Psychology (pp. 79–80). Norman: University of Oklahoma Conference Center.

Ellis, H. C. (Ed.). (1979). [Program for NCCGDOP winter meeting]. Smith files.

Grosslight, J. H. (1982, February 26). [Memo to COGDOP members]. Smith files.

Hanson, G. W. (1990). Toward a CAMPP model for master's level training in applied psychology. In R. D. Tucker (Ed.), *Sourcebook for the National Conference on Applied Master's Training in Psychology* (pp. 1–7). Norman: Oklahoma Center for Continuing Education.

Hilgard, E. R. (1987). *Psychology in America: A historical survey.* San Diego, CA: Harcourt Brace Jovanovich.

Jalbert, N. L. (1990, July 31). [CUPP financial report, 1989–1990]. Smith files.

Jalbert, N. L. (1991, August 17). [CUPP financial report, 1990–1991]. Smith files.

Kohout, J., Wicherski, M., & Pion, G. (1991). *Characteristics of graduate departments of psychology: 1988–89.* Washington, DC: American Psychological Association.

Korn, J. H. (1973). *The purpose and structure of the Council of Undergraduate Departments of Psychology.* Unpublished manuscript, St. Louis University, St. Louis, MO.

Korn, J. H. (1974, August 6). [Memo to CUPD members]. Smith files.

Lloyd, M. A. (1988, October 24). [Summary of organizational meeting of CCDUPP]. Smith files.

Lloyd, M. A. (1989, September 29). [Memo to CUPP Steering Committee members]. Smith files.

Lloyd, M. A. (1990a). [CUPP information sheet]. Smith files.

Lloyd, M. A. (1990b, October 5). [Memo to CUPP Steering Committee members]. Smith files.

Lloyd, M. A. (1991a, September 24). [Memo to CUPP members]. Smith files.

Lloyd, M. A. (1991b, February 26). [Memo to CUPP Steering Committee members and Regional Liaisons]. Smith files.

Lloyd, M. A. (1991c, December 20). [Memo to CUPP Steering Committee members, Regional Liaisons, and Newsletter Editor]. Smith files.

Matarazzo, J. D. (1989, February 23). *Some reflections on education accreditation in psychology: Its future.* Address at the meeting of COGDOP, Tucson, AZ. Smith files.

Moses, S. (1990, January). Thorny questions snag master's degrees issue. *APA Monitor,* pp. 32–33.

Moses, S. (1992, April). COGDOP OKs trial for new APA system. *APA Monitor,* p. 40.

National Conference on Graduate Education in Psychology. (1987). Resolutions approved by the National Conference on Graduate Education in Psychology. *American Psychologist, 42,* 1070–1084.

Nocks, E. (1980, September 1). [Minutes of CUPD annual meeting]. Smith files.

Nodine, B. (1973). *A brief history of the Council of Undergraduate Psychology Departments.* Unpublished manuscript, Beaver College, Glenside, PA.

Ray, W. S. (1971a, July). [CUPD information sheet]. Smith files.

Ray, W. S. (Ed.). (1971b, July). [Report of 1971 CUPD regional meetings]. Smith files.

Siegel, M. H. (1979a, July). [Memo to CUPD members]. Smith files.

Siegel, M. H. (1979b, September). [Memo to CUPD members]. Smith files.

Smith, R. A. (1991). [CTUP information sheet]. Smith files.

Standards of training for clinical/counseling applied master's training programs. (1990). In R. D. Tucker (Ed.), *Sourcebook for the National Conference on Applied Master's Training in Psychology* (p. 23). Norman: Oklahoma Center for Continuing Education.

Tucker, R. D. (1990). Introduction. In R. H. Lowe (Ed.), *Proceedings of the National Conference on Applied Master's Training in Psychology* (pp. 3–4). Norman: University of Oklahoma Conference Center.

APPENDIX A

Council of Teachers of Undergraduate Psychology (CTUP) Presidents and Membership Size

Years	President	Affiliation	Size
1968–1969	Robert S. Harper	Knox College	
1969–1970	Edward I. Stevens	Florida Presbyterian College	
1970–1971	Wilbert S. Ray	Bethany College	41
1971–1972	David Cole	Occidental College	
1972–1973	Alice Van Krevelen	Berea College	
1973–1974	James H. Korn	Carnegie-Mellon University	73
1974–1975	Douglas K. Candland	Bucknell University	
1975–1976	Barbara F. Nodine	Beaver College	
1976–1977	Roland C. Lowe	University of Santa Clara	
1977–1978	Douglas W. Bloomquist	Framingham State College	
1978–1979	Michael H. Siegel	State University of New York College at Oneonta	109
1979–1981	Charles L. Brewer	Furman University	168
1981–1983	Robert A. Goodale	Westfield State College	233
1983–1984	Allen L. Fingeret	Rhode Island College	287
1984–1985	Kenneth W. Nikels	Kearney State College	348
1985–1987	Bernardo J. Carducci	Indiana University Southeast	437
1987–1989	Lisa Gray-Shellberg	California State University, Dominguez Hills	494
1989–1991	Randolph A. Smith	Ouachita Baptist University	649
1991–	Jane S. Halonen	Alverno College	

Note: The CTUP was originally named the Council of Undergraduate Departments (CUD) and then renamed the Council of Undergraduate Psychology Departments (CUPD).

APPENDIX B

Chairs of the Council of Graduate Departments of Psychology (COGDOP)

Years	Chair	Affiliation
1964–1967	Lloyd G. Humphreys	University of Illinois
1967–1969	Wilbert J. McKeachie	University of Michigan
1970–1972	William S. Verplanck	University of Tennessee
1973–1975	Gregory A. Kimble	Duke University
1975–1977	Geoffrey Keppel	University of California, Berkeley
1977–1979	Henry C. Ellis	University of New Mexico
1979–1981	Merle E. Meyer	University of Florida
1981–1983	Joseph H. Grosslight	Florida State University
1983–1984	David C. Edwards	Iowa State University
1984–1985	John E. Williams	Wake Forest University
1985–1987	James R. Ison	University of Rochester
1987–1988	Edward S. Katkin	State University of New York at Stony Brook
1988–1990	Sandra W. Scarr	University of Virginia
1990–1992	Irwin L. Goldstein	University of Maryland

Note: The COGDOP was originally named the Council of Chairmen of Graduate Departments of Psychology (CCGDOP) and then renamed the National Council of Chairmen of Graduate Departments of Psychology (NCCGDOP).

18

PSI CHI AND PSI BETA: THE TWO NATIONAL HONOR SOCIETIES IN PSYCHOLOGY

RUTH HUBBARD COUSINS, CAROL TRACY, AND
PETER J. GIORDANO

The purpose of this chapter is to chronicle the history of two support organizations in the teaching of psychology, Psi Chi and Psi Beta. These two honor societies, the former for 4-year schools and the latter for 2-year institutions, seek to advance the science of psychology and to promote the intellectual and professional development of those individuals active in the groups, both students and faculty. For this reason, a history of the teaching of psychology would be incomplete without a discussion of the origin and development of Psi Chi and Psi Beta.

As the reader will discover, the idea for Psi Chi was conceived by two psychology students who felt the need for a scholarly organization to encourage and to reward their interest in the discipline. Since the inception of Psi Chi, and later of Psi Beta, student members, faculty sponsors, and national officers have sought to open the psychological community to students. For some individuals, initiation into Psi Chi or Psi Beta may be "the first tangible evidence that my aspiration to become a psychologist was achievable" (Goodstein, 1986, p. 1).

Psi Chi and Psi Beta have had a lasting impact on the academic and professional development of students. For example, they have both shown strong support for student research. This consistent emphasis mirrors recommendations from the recent American Psychological Association (APA) National Conference on Enhancing the Quality of Undergraduate Education in Psychology held at St. Mary's College of Maryland, June 18–23, 1991. According to the conference curriculum committee, a solid psychology curriculum is one that teaches students to think as scientists (Brewer et al., 1992). This goal may be achieved through specific coursework or, of course, through conducting and presenting independent research. Psi Chi's tradition of encouraging research is important in the history of the teaching of psychology. In addition, Psi Chi and Psi Beta have worked to make psychology conferences accessible to students and to bring students in close contact with eminent psychologists through formal lectures and informal conversation hours.

These developments occurred because of the activity and activism of teachers and students working together. This working relationship was underscored by Frederick H. Lewis, cofounder of Psi Chi, when he wrote, "I am proud of the good health and vigor of Psi Chi, and the increasing role it is assuming in so many campuses in drawing faculty and students together, and in inspiring psychology majors toward excellence in their field" (Lewis, 1969, p. 7).

The chronology presented in this chapter interweaves historical events with how Psi Chi and Psi Beta have been important for teachers and students of psychology. For the sake of brevity and of relevance to the topic of this book, many historical details are omitted. The present history is based largely on information preserved in the Psi Chi and Psi Beta newsletters and in the able histories of the Psi Chi historians. These historians are Frederick H. Lewis, Ruth B. Guilford, Lillian G. Portenier, Thelma Hunt, Michael Wertheimer, and Arthur C. MacKinney. The present chronology is also based on the personal recollections of the first two authors, who both played strategic roles in the history of these societies.

The reader interested in supplementing this chapter with a more comprehensive history will find the necessary material in the Archives of the History of American Psychology, located at the University of Akron in Ohio. The Archives are the official depository for Psi Chi's and Psi Beta's archival materials. Also, Thelma Hunt's (1979) thorough *History of Psi Chi: The National Honor Society in Psychology* provides historical detail for Psi Chi's first 50 years. Her chronology also includes the historical comments of the three Psi Chi historians before her.

A HISTORY OF PSI CHI

The purposes of Psi Chi, the National Honor Society in Psychology, are to encourage, stimulate, and maintain excellence in scholarship and to advance the science of psychology. Psi Chi has two major goals. The first is to recognize academic excellence through induction of members. The second is to provide opportunities for professional growth and creative development through chapter, regional, and national activities. For example, the chapters nourish and stimulate professional growth through programs designed to augment the regular curriculum and to provide practical experience and fellowship through affiliation with chapters. In addition, the national organization offers programs to help achieve the goals of Psi Chi. Among these programs are national and regional conventions held annually in conjunction with the psychological associations; research award competitions; certificates to recognize student research; a quarterly *Psi Chi Newsletter*, which helps to inform and to recognize members' contributions and accomplishments; and a National Office to coordinate the work of the Society.

Psi Chi functions as a federation of chapters located at accredited universities and senior colleges. The chapters are operated by student officers and faculty advisors. They are responsible for inducting members and registering them at the National Office where their membership records are preserved for reference. The chapters nominate and elect the national officers who are psychologists and members of Psi Chi. They serve as a national council to guide and oversee the affairs of the Society.

The programs and teamwork at the chapter, regional, and national levels have added to Psi Chi's prestige and respect in the psychology community. Psi Chi is a member of the Association of College Honor Societies (ACHS) and is an affiliate of the APA and the American Psychological Society (APS). Psi Chi is the oldest surviving national organization of psychology students. There are an impressive number of distinguished psychologists who joined Psi Chi when they were students.

The Beginning

In early 1928, two psychology students, Frederick H. Lewis and Edwin B. Newman, conceived the idea of a national organization for psychology students. They presented their idea to a group of young aspiring psychologists at the University of Kansas. In the spring of 1928, the group voted to establish the Nationalization Committee.

The Nationalization Committee grew through three coordinated meetings. The first meeting was held to assess the views of students from other schools who would be attending the meeting of the Midwestern Psychological Association in May 1928, in Madison, Wisconsin. Among those meeting in Wisconsin were Lewis and Newman of the University of Kansas, Harold Scott of the University of Wisconsin, and T. H. Cutler of Drake University. In the fall of 1928, Newman and Lewis decided to send a letter to every major college and university in the country asking for a response to the following questions: (a) What associations of psychology students were already in existence at the institution? (b) What attempts might have been made in this direction? and (c) What sentiments existed toward establishing a nationwide society? Approximately 100 individuals responded. Roughly a third thought a national society was timely and feasible, a third thought a national society was not needed, and a third was ambivalent. The most enthusiastic response came from June Downey of the University of Wyoming. The least favorable response came from E. G. Boring of Harvard University, who wrote a blistering three-page single-spaced letter deploring the idea, lamenting the "Ph-Disease" and saying that America was already badly overorganized (a copy of this letter may be found in the Archives of the History of American Psychology). Later, Boring became supportive of Psi Chi, delivering Psi Chi's Distinguished Lecture in 1960.

The second meeting was held to develop a plan of organization or to drop completely the idea for a society. As a result of the second meeting, a National Graduate Council for a Psychology Fraternity was established in December 1928, at a meeting held during the APA Annual Convention at Columbia University. All of the respondents to the letter of inquiry, pro and con, were invited to the meeting. Lewis remembered in particular the enthusiastic encouragement of J. P. Porter and Horace English. The results of this second meeting were distributed to the original mailing list, with a request for suggestions.

The third meeting was held at the Midwestern Psychological Association meeting in Urbana, Illinois, on May 10, 1929, where the proposed constitution was presented and adopted by the Council and names were suggested for the organization. Representatives from the Universities of Minnesota, Chicago, Illinois, and Indiana, and from Iowa State College and Wittenberg College attended the Council meeting.

On May 14, 1929, Lewis sent a letter to interested psychology clubs, inviting them to attend the formal organizational meeting to be held September 3, 1929, at Yale University during the Ninth International Congress of Psychology. This was the first International Congress to meet in the United States.

Representatives of 10 psychology departments came to the meeting at Yale University, with the authorization of their respective student groups, to form an association on the basis of the proposed constitution. Points to be settled included the name of the society, qualifications for individual and chapter membership, power of the National Council, provisions for amending the constitution, and the election of officers.

Of the names proposed for the organization, the first choice, Psi Chi, was already in use. After research in the Yale Library by Edwin Newman, Sigma Pi was selected and placed on the Constitution adopted on September 4, 1929. However, it was changed in December, 1929, to Sigma Pi Sigma

TABLE 1
Charter Institutions and Signers of the Original Psi Chi Document

Institution	Signature
University of Chicago	H. A. Swenson
Iowa State College	J. E. Evans
University of Nebraska	J. P. Guilford
University of Southern California	Geo. H. Mount
University of Denver	D. E. Phillips
Wittenberg College	George G. Killinger
State College of Washington	C. I. Erickson
Ohio University	James P. Porter
University of Kansas	F. T. Perkins
Rutgers University	H. E. Starr
University of Arkansas	By proxy
Drake University	By proxy
University of Alabama	By proxy
University of California, Los Angeles	Mary Haven

Note: The document read, "We, tho undersigned, do hereby establish the fraternity Sigma Pi on this fourth day of September, nineteen twenty nine."

when Sigma Pi was found to be the name of a national social fraternity. The name of Sigma Pi Sigma was used for 1 year.

Table 1 presents the 14 institutions and the individuals who signed the original document establishing the Society. The constitution adopted on September 4, 1929, provided that institutions accepting membership by January 1, 1930, should be considered together with the original signers as charter members of the organization. Those additional institutions were the University of Pennsylvania, the University of Wyoming, the University of Washington, the University of Georgia, the University of Montana (Missoula), Washington and Lee University, and Nebraska Wesleyan University. By a special vote of the original 21 chapters, Pennsylvania State College was also accorded charter chapter status, despite being chartered after the deadline.

National officers elected by the first convention were E. B. Newman (Kansas), president; P. E. Martin (Southern California), secretary-treasurer; and M. H. [now F. H.] Lewis (Harvard), historian. The election of four vice presidents, serving the Eastern, Southern, Midwestern, and Western Divisions, was deferred until these divisions could be organized. In this fashion, Psi Chi was born.

First Decade

During Psi Chi's first decade, a number of important developments took place. In the 1929–1930 year, decisions still needed to be made on such matters as insignia, membership cards, terms of office for national officers, a possible ritual, and arrangements for four vice presidents to take office.

At the organization's second convention, held at the APA's Annual Convention in Iowa City, December 1930, the group chose Psi Chi as the Society's new and permanent name. Prior to the meeting, J. P. Guilford discovered that a fraternity at Oregon State College, which had held the name Psi Chi since 1922, had released the name in 1930 when it became a chapter of Theta Kappa Nu. A second important change at that meeting was the selection of Ruth B. Guilford as Psi Chi's second secretary–treasurer. The first *Psi Chi Newsletter*, which was mimeographed, appeared in 1930.

In 1932, the biennial convention of Psi Chi met in conjunction with the APA Annual Convention in Ithaca, New York. A Psi Chi committee was established to study possible revisions of the Psi Chi Constitution. J. P. Porter agreed to develop a plan for cooperative research using the unique nationwide network of Psi Chi chapters. Thus, from the outset, Psi Chi was promoting research activities.

During the 1933 APA Convention in Chicago, a Psi Chi Committee on Cooperative Research was established. The Committee members were J. P. Porter (chair); J. A. Gengerelli of University of California, Los Angeles; G. W. Hartmann of Pennsylvania State College; E. B. Newman of Columbia University; and J. U. Yarborough of Southern Methodist University. Porter suggested that Psi Chi chapters study the relative difficulty of psychology and other college subjects during 1933–1934. Comparative data were obtained from Ohio University and Pennsylvania State College. In December 1934, Porter reported for the Committee. The Pennsylvania State findings indicated that students of education found psychology a "hard" subject, pre-med students found psychology "easy," and engineers found psychology "hard," but not as hard as did students in education.

Several members of Psi Chi suggested that the Society sponsor a new journal to publish research as well as news. A Committee on Publications was appointed with J. P. Guilford as chair. During the September 1934 APA Annual Convention at Columbia University, Guilford reported the results of a Psi Chi survey among the chapters: 11 supported the journal, but 4 of these felt that a connection with Psi Chi would restrict the editor in the material, which could curtail subscriptions. Three were against the journal, and there were several friendly, but definite, warnings of financial failure. The proposal was ultimately rejected. This same proposal for a journal of research was made in the 1960s and the 1970s, but both times the proposals were rejected for the same reasons.

On June 1, 1935, Martin Fritz, then president of Psi Chi, received the news that Ruth Guilford was going to resign. As secretary–treasurer, she had stabilized the work of the organization and left her mark on the Society. The work load of the national secretary–treasurer was such that the Nominating Committee recommended a stipend of $125 a year. The new secretary–treasurer was E. Louise Hoffeditz. As often occurred, Psi Chi did not have a quorum at the APA Annual Convention in Ann Arbor, Michigan, in September 1935, and could not conduct business. However, Hoffeditz was quickly elected by mail. The October 1935 *Psi Chi Newsletter* reported that of the approximately 100 papers on the APA's program that year, 27 of them were read by Psi Chi members.

In September 1935, Psi Chi received a letter from the psychology club of an eastern college suggesting the formation of a new organization for undergraduate students. This club had petitioned the National Council of Psi Chi for a charter and had been turned down because its proposed membership did not meet Psi Chi standards. Applications being received from liberal arts and teachers colleges were not receiving favorable action. With the exception of Wittenberg College, which was a charter chapter, no smaller institution was on the Psi Chi roster. Under the leadership of President Fritz, a discussion began among Psi Chi national officers and chapters as to what areas of the psychology community Psi Chi was designed to serve. The outcome of the discussion was that any school that (a) presented an acceptable major, (b) was taught by recognized faculty, and (c) gave evidence of maintaining a psychological organization of qualified students with a clear prospect of permanence came under favorable consideration. It was not until 1939, however, that the first of the smaller colleges, Beaver College in Glenside, Pennsylvania, and Morningside College in Sioux City, Iowa, were admitted under the policy of broader recognition.

Psi Chi celebrated its 10th anniversary in September 1939 at Stanford University, with 25 delegates in attendance. The Society had chartered 34 chapters. With the resignation of the secretary–treasurer, Louise Hoffeditz, this anniversary closed an important era for Psi Chi.

Second Decade

By the time Psi Chi entered its second decade in 1940, the Society was viewed as the "youth movement" in psychology and suggestions were being made about Psi Chi's usefulness as a national group. The Midwestern Division of Psi Chi formed a Committee on the Problems of Young Psychologists. The Committee surveyed issues related to the professional development of young psychologists. The Committee also studied standards for the training of psychologists, provided information about new fields and new jobs, and proposed a job clearance bureau. A recommendation was prepared for the APA for a national employment service, but World War II was intensifying and Psi Chi began to focus on service to psychology during the war.

Louise Grossnickle followed Hoffeditz, and after 2 years Dorothea Ewers became secretary–treasurer during the trying war years, 1942–1945.

The service of Psi Chi during World War II began with President Stuart Cook's suggestion that chapters participate in national topics pertinent to the war years. "A National Job for Psi Chi" was the title of Cook's introductory article in the January 1941 *Psi Chi Newsletter*. The January 1942 *Newsletter* asked chapters to devote serious thought to the problems of national defense and civilian morale. By 1942 Psi Chi had chartered 41 chapters, 4 of which were inactive. Except for the addition of the Baylor University and the University of Wisconsin chapters in 1942, there were no new chapters added during World War II.

The 1941–1942 national discussion topic prepared by President Cook for Psi Chi chapters was "The Psychologist and National Morale." Psi Chi chapters aided the nation by organizing a campus information office, creating a committee on defense activities, and opening meetings for all students to hear speakers and roundtable discussions on topics such as personality problems in wartime, psychological aspects of participation in military service, German military psychology, and propaganda in wartime. Activities such as these provided valuable opportunities for students of psychology to use their classroom knowledge to understand world problems more fully. Because of the war effort, faculty and students were disappearing from colleges and universities at a rapid pace, yet few Psi Chi chapters found it necessary to suspend operations for the duration of the war.

During 1942 and early 1943, President Cook agreed to stay in office despite his duties in the Army. His call for a national discussion topic for 1942–1943 was looking ahead to peace and was titled, "Psychological Contributions to Winning the Peace." The January 1943 *Psi Chi Newsletter* contained Cook's description of psychological testing in the Army, followed by a memorandum to Psi Chi chapters and a bibliography for the discussion topic of psychologists' contributions to winning the peace. Cook sponsored the same topic for 1943–1944.

Other developments during the war years included the first printed *Psi Chi Newsletter* in October 1943, edited by Ewers. During this same time period, the National Office sent a complete set of *Psi Chi Newsletters* to the Library of Congress. The Library of Congress and the New York City Public Library were now included on the mailing list to ensure easy access to these materials for future historians.

In the summer of 1944, President Cook was suddenly ordered overseas. A. Q. Sartain of Southern Methodist University agreed to serve as acting president. Sartain proposed a national discussion topic for 1944–1945 titled, "Erroneous Beliefs about the Behavior of Men and Animals." As reported in January 1946, this project evoked 1,272 completed papers, the best showing yet in a national effort by the Society.

During the fall of 1945, Florence Goodenough was elected president of Psi Chi. The chapters that had temporarily been inactive began to revive, and the number of Psi Chi chapters increased rapidly following World War

II. In 1946, for the first time, a program of experimental papers was presented by Psi Chi members at the APA Annual Convention held in Philadelphia.

In the fall of 1946, Ewers gave up her job of 4 years as secretary–treasurer, and Katherine M. Maurer became the new secretary–treasurer. President Goodenough retired in 1947 because of illness, and a successor was not found until 1949. Meanwhile Maurer did routine business, but there was no 1948 *Newsletter*. Maurer resigned the office of secretary–treasurer in 1949.

Lillian G. Portenier was elected president in 1949 and Miriam E. Crowley was appointed as secretary–treasurer for a 2-year term. The second Psi Chi historian was Ruth B. Guilford, who started in 1950. At the APA Annual Convention in Denver in September 1949, Psi Chi's cofounder and first president, Edwin B. Newman, was the featured speaker at the 20th anniversary of the Society. Also at the Denver meeting, Frederick H. Lewis resigned his office of historian. By the end of the second decade in 1949, Psi Chi had chartered 69 chapters.

Third Decade

In 1950, Stewart Henderson Britt offered a grant-in-aid through the Britt Foundation, Inc., to any member of Psi Chi who was engaged in research and needed financial assistance to complete the project. The first winner, Walter B. Barbe of Baylor University, received $150 for his study titled, "The Effectiveness of Work in Remedial Reading at the College Level" (*Psi Chi Newsletter*, April, 1951). This award was a significant event in the history of Psi Chi, representing the beginning of a tangible, ongoing commitment to support student research. Such awards demonstrate Psi Chi's sensitivity to student development and achievement. A chronology of past and present Psi Chi research awards is shown in Table 2.

In 1951, Miriam E. Crowley resigned her position as national secretary–treasurer. Her successor, Lucille K. Forer, was absorbed in meeting deadlines for her dissertation research. Therefore, Historian Guilford served again as secretary–treasurer on a temporary basis. The third Psi Chi historian, Lillian G. Portenier, was not appointed until 1954.

The year 1952 marked an important development in the relationship between Psi Chi and the APA. The APA Committee on Student Affairs, under the direction of Lloyd Humphreys, met with Psi Chi officials to consider ways that APA might benefit students of psychology. The APA Council of Representatives passed several motions concerning Psi Chi and the ways in which the two organizations could work together. The executive secretary of the APA was instructed to disseminate information concerning Psi Chi to the chairs of all psychology departments, to provide APA journal subscriptions to Psi Chi members at reduced rates, to print the news of Psi

TABLE 2
Psi Chi Research Awards

Award	Years awarded
Past Awards	
Steuart Henderson Britt Award	1950–1957
Kenneth W. Braly Award	1954–1955
Education, Marketing, and Management Foundation, Inc., Award	1958–1968
J. P. Guilford Award	1967–1968
Psi Chi Research Award for Research Proposal	1969–1971
Psi Chi Graduate Award for Completed Research	1972–1974
Psi Chi Undergraduate Award for Research Proposal	1972–1975
J. P. Guilford Undergraduate Award for Completed Research	1975–1978
Samuel J. Beck Graduate Research Award	1985–1987
Psi Chi/APA Division 21 Undergraduate Research Award	1986–1987
Current Awards	
Psi Chi/J. P. Guilford Undergraduate Research Award	1979–
Psi Chi/Edwin B. Newman Graduate Research Award	1979–
Psi Chi/HarperCollins Research Scholarship	1992–

Chi chapters in the *American Psychologist*, and to provide extra facilities for Psi Chi at the APA Convention in Cleveland in 1953. Thus, in addition to supporting student research, Psi Chi began laying the groundwork that led to Psi Chi's affiliation with the APA in 1958. This development created further opportunities for the professional development of students of psychology. The October 1958 *Psi Chi Newsletter* announced Psi Chi's affiliation with the APA. Affiliation was between the two organizations and did not mean that Psi Chi members necessarily had membership in the APA.

By 1955, the Psi Chi office had moved seven times, and the eighth move was impending when Executive Secretary Lucille Fore announced her resignation at the 1955 Psi Chi meeting in San Francisco. Forer's last duty was to ship the Psi Chi materials to the headquarters in the APA building in Washington, DC, where the new executive secretary, Meredith J. Marks, set up the first Psi Chi National Office in 1956.

At the September 1956 Psi Chi meeting in Chicago, Max Meenes began his first term as president of Psi Chi. During the 1956–1957 year, Wolfgang Kohler of the University of Michigan and Eric Fromm of Michigan State University were inducted as honorary members of Psi Chi.

After 2 years, however, the expense of operating in Washington, DC, had put a strain on the budget. The Society tried unsuccessfully to increase the $5 lifetime membership fee, the organization's means of support. (No dues are charged by the Society.) By the fall of 1958, the financial situation had worsened. Soon after, Executive Secretary Marks resigned.

The 10th executive secretary, Ruth H. Cousins, was appointed and asked to find a resolution to the financial crisis. Cousins agreed to take the job for 1 year. She visualized Psi Chi as a catalyst for students and teachers to strive for excellence. She thought that members might have the incentive to pay necessary increases in fees if Psi Chi changed from a psychology fraternity to an official honor society, with membership in the Association of College Honor Societies (ACHS). However, this idea was rejected because it was feared that the costs of making the transition would be prohibitive. Cousins also believed that students and their faculty advisors would be more inclined to attend Psi Chi conventions if the organization sponsored well-known authors and scientists as speakers to help keep members abreast of current research. This idea found support in the organization.

In 1959, Psi Chi established what is now a tradition of Psi Chi sponsored Distinguished Lectures at the APA conventions. The first lecture was delivered by Leonard Carmichael, who was followed in 1960 by E. G. Boring. Also in 1960, a brief article in the *American Psychologist* discussed some of the activities of Psi Chi (Langhorne & Hoch, 1960).

Fourth Decade

Despite important advances, such as establishing student research awards, affiliating with the APA, and beginning the Distinguished Lecture series, Psi Chi's financial difficulties continued. However, many individuals helped to keep the organization running smoothly, and their efforts ensured adequate communication between the National Office and chapters.

In 1960, Wayne Dennis was elected national president of Psi Chi and, under his leadership, Psi Chi took an important step forward. Cousins had again suggested changing Psi Chi to an honor society. Dennis approved the idea as did the Psi Chi Council. Dennis and Cousins proceeded to seek membership for Psi Chi in the ACHS. Certain changes in the Bylaws of Psi Chi were necessitated. By 1965, the Psi Chi chapters and the Psi Chi National Council had approved the changes and Psi Chi became a member of the ACHS. The name of Psi Chi was officially changed to Psi Chi, the National Honor Society in Psychology, reflecting its new status.

In September 1962, Roger W. Russell was installed as national president of Psi Chi. Russell's international contacts proved important for the Society. The Winter 1963 *Psi Chi Newsletter* published articles by psychology students from Australia, England, France, India, Japan, Pakistan, and Sweden. These articles described the students' viewpoints of psychology at their universities. In addition, Psi Chi chapters sent psychology textbooks abroad and donated money to the APA's Young Psychologist Program to help bring young psychologists from overseas to attend the 17th International Congress of Psychology held in Washington, DC, August 20–26, 1963. Following the International Congress, the international visitors were invited to attend the Psi Chi program held in conjunction with the APA Convention in Philadelphia. Psi Chi's invited speaker was Otto Klineberg, who was president of the International Union of Scientific Psychology. These developments provided American psychology students valuable intellectual exchange with psychology students from other cultures.

In September 1964, Sherman Ross, who had served as Psi Chi's Eastern regional vice president (1956–1963), was elected to the first of three 2-year terms as president of Psi Chi. He emphasized undergraduate psychology students, and it was during his tenure that Psi Chi completed the required changes and achieved membership in the ACHS.

The international boundaries of Psi Chi were extended further when, in the summer of 1964, Executive Secretary Cousins, under the auspices of the International Council of Psychologists, participated in a professional around-the-world tour during which 20 psychologists made a comparative study of psychology throughout the world. A report of the tour by Cousins was published in the Spring 1965 *Psi Chi Newsletter*.

In 1969, the Psi Chi Council proposed to change Ruth Cousins's title from executive secretary to executive director. Chapters approved the title change, which became effective on March 31, 1969. Having initially agreed to serve a 1-year term, Cousins had now been in office for 11 years.

The 40th anniversary of Psi Chi was celebrated at the APA Annual Convention in Washington, DC, August 31–September 4, 1969. The featured speaker was Edwin B. Newman. He discussed "Psychology and Psychologists: Forty Years Later." A message from Frederick H. Lewis was read during the introduction of Newman.

Francis A. Young, a former Western regional vice president of Psi Chi, was president from 1968 to 1970. Reflecting the social upheaval of this time period, Psi Chi experienced its share of unrest. For example, in 1969 Jerome Bruner of Harvard University was to deliver the Psi Chi Invited Address at the annual meeting of the Eastern Psychological Association. However, Bruner, along with others, was held hostage by Harvard University students and could not appear for his lecture. Furthermore, chapters in diverse sections of the United States called on the Psi Chi National Office to send journals to them. Their libraries, and in some cases their psychology departments, had been burned. In another example of the troubled times, a California chapter requested Psi Chi's support on certain political issues. The Psi Chi Council agreed that it would be unwise for the Honor Society to become involved in political issues, but this did not limit the activity of Psi Chi members as private citizens.

During this time, the National Office encouraged Psi Chi members to seek social understanding and to find answers to social problems through conducting empirical research. Scientific skills learned in the classroom could be applied to make constructive contributions to society.

In the course of his presidency, Young focused on serving students more effectively and involving them more in the leadership of Psi Chi. In keeping with the prevailing zeitgeist, he encouraged students to become involved in the issues of their communities and to strive for high standards of scholarship. Young installed Allan Barclay, a former vice president of Psi Chi, as the new president of the Honor Society. Barclay, with the consent of the Council, reappointed the historian, Lillian G. Portenier, and the executive director, Ruth Cousins, for another year.

Fifth Decade

The fifth decade of Psi Chi began in 1970, under the leadership of Barclay. He was elected to two 2-year terms as president and served from 1970 to 1974. In keeping with the previous Council's desire to feature an outstanding speaker at the Psi Chi conventions, B. F. Skinner was invited to speak at the 1971 Annual Convention in Washington, DC, the same year that *Beyond Freedom and Dignity* (Skinner, 1971) was published. The impact of such lectures on the intellectual and professional development of students continues to be positive and enduring.

In keeping with Barclay's emphasis on cooperating with other organizations, Executive Director Cousins accepted an invitation to serve on the Board of Directors of the Washington Society of Association Executives (the first woman to serve, 1973–1976) and was one of the first women invited to join the previously all-male National Press Club in Washington, DC.

Lillian G. Portenier retired as historian of Psi Chi and, in 1973, Thelma Hunt, who was chair of the Psychology Department at George Washington University, was appointed by the Psi Chi Council as the fourth historian. On passage in 1972 of the amendment to change "Honorary Member" to "Distinguished Member," the Psi Chi Council awarded the first Distinguished Membership to William Bevan, vice president and provost of Johns Hopkins University.

President Barclay, the Council, and the chapters successfully brought Psi Chi through a difficult period of social and political unrest. As of June 30, 1974, Psi Chi had registered 5,672 new members, the most in any one year, and added 21 new chapters, bringing the total number of chapters to 361 and the membership to 81,812.

Bruce R. Fretz, a faculty member at the University of Maryland and a former Eastern regional vice president of Psi Chi, was the national president of Psi Chi for two 2-year terms, from 1974 to 1978. During Fretz's presidential term, Psi Chi reached its goal of having one year's operating expense in reserve (1976), reflecting remarkable financial gains since the early years of struggle. Also in 1976, the Psi Chi membership reached the 100,000 mark. President Fretz reorganized Psi Chi's research programs, and in 1976, for the first time, members who presented papers at any of the conventions listed in the convention calendar in the *Psi Chi Newsletter* received a Psi Chi certificate of "Excellence in Research." Later the wording was changed to "Recognition for Research."

In 1976, APA again began charging students a registration fee to attend the Annual Convention. President Fretz convinced the APA to permit Psi Chi members, beginning in 1977, to register for the APA/Psi Chi Convention at whatever rate was applicable for student affiliates of APA. Among the convention speakers sponsored by Fretz were Rollo May (1976), Philip Zimbardo (1977), and B. F. Skinner (1978).

Eastern Regional Vice President Florence L. Denmark was the first Psi Chi president elected to serve under a new 1-year presidential term. She was elected president of Psi Chi in 1978 and reelected in 1979. Denmark was the first person to be president of both Psi Chi and the APA, serving as APA president-elect in 1978–1979 and APA president in 1979–1980. Currently, Psi Chi honors Denmark with an annual national faculty advisor award named in her honor. In Denmark's first presidential message, she urged graduate and undergraduate students to conduct research, to submit their papers to Psi Chi's research competitions, and to submit their findings to psychology journals. Her message demonstrates the continued importance of the role Psi Chi has played in the educational experience of psychology students.

President Denmark also announced a joint Psi Chi/APA Edwin B. Newman Graduate Research Award Competition. Charles D. Spielberger, Psi Chi southeastern regional vice president, was instrumental in helping Denmark to obtain approval from the APA Council of Representatives to cosponsor the graduate research competition. Psi Chi already had an undergraduate award, the J. P. Guilford Undergraduate Research Award. The graduate competition was named in honor of cofounder and first president of Psi Chi, Edwin B. Newman, who also was recording secretary of the APA, 1963–1967.

In 1979, under President Denmark's leadership, Psi Chi celebrated its 50th anniversary, held at the APA/Psi Chi Convention in New York City. Guests at the celebration included the founders of Psi Chi, Frederick H. Lewis and Edwin B. Newman, as well as B. F. Skinner and the golden anniversary speaker, Neal E. Miller. President of the United States, Jimmy Carter, sent a letter congratulating Psi Chi on its 50th anniversary.

Psi Chi's fifth decade closed with Thelma Hunt dedicating her golden anniversary history (Hunt, 1979) to Frederick H. Lewis and Edwin B. Newman. Hunt resigned her post and President Denmark, with the approval of the Council, appointed Michael Wertheimer as historian. Psi Chi chapters had superseded all past years in the number of new members inducted during the golden anniversary year (6,945). A cumulative total of 113,590 members had been registered since the Society was founded in 1929. Thirty-six new chapters were added to the Psi Chi roster, the most ever added in 1 year.

Charles D. Spielberger served as president of Psi Chi from 1980 to 1983. He was the second president of Psi Chi to become president of the APA. He was president of the latter in 1991. Spielberger's presidency was noted for the development and expansion of opportunities for student members to learn about and participate in psychology on an international level. As a member and chair of the APA's Committee on International Relations in Psychology, Spielberger was influential in providing information to assist U.S. psychology students who desired to study or conduct research abroad. In addition, as a member and president of the International Council of Psychologists (ICP), Spielberger worked to establish student affiliate status in the ICP for Psi Chi members. Psi Chi members were also given the opportunity to participate in ICP programs.

Paul J. Lloyd was elected president of Psi Chi in 1983 and was reelected in 1984 and 1985. During his tenure, Lloyd emphasized the activities of local chapters. He believed that the real strength of the Honor Society derived from the activities of the chapters and that they have an important role in shaping the attitudes of students toward the psychological community. Lloyd, with the approval of the Council, appointed Arthur C. MacKinney as historian of Psi Chi. Lloyd also appointed a National Student Committee to help promote Psi Chi and its conventions.

Lloyd was sensitive to the contributions of those who helped to build the foundation of Psi Chi. He and the National Council honored all past national officers of Psi Chi and elected nine psychologists to Distinguished Membership in Psi Chi, the only additions since the honor was first bestowed upon William Bevan in 1972. The new Distinguished Members were B. F. Skinner, Neal E. Miller, M. Brewster Smith, Stuart W. Cook, Otto Klineberg, J. P. Guilford, Ruth B. Guilford, Edwin B. Newman, and Frederick H. Lewis. Their contributions came at critical moments in the history of Psi Chi and helped to determine the future direction of the Society.

Under Lloyd's leadership, the Psi Chi National Council proposed a major revision of the Psi Chi Constitution and Bylaws. The most significant change was the modification of the offices and terms of the national officers. The proposed amendments, approved and instituted in 1985, changed the office of president to a 3-year term to be served as president-elect, president, and past-president. The past-president was to remain on the Council for a year and was responsible for compiling the history for that year. Thus, MacKinney was the last appointed historian of Psi Chi.

During his presidency, Lloyd continued to feature distinguished psychologists and pertinent topics. The 1984 APA/Psi Chi Convention in Toronto included a discussion by B. F. Skinner on current issues in psychology and a Distinguished Lecture by Douglas W. Bray, who developed the first assessment centers. The 1985 Convention in Los Angeles featured

"A Discussion of Twentieth Century Psychology in America" by Ernest R. Hilgard of Stanford University and a student dialogue with Carl R. Rogers. The 1986 Convention in Washington, DC, included the first open meeting cosponsored by Psi Chi and Psi Beta, a student dialogue with Albert Ellis of the Institute for Rational–Emotive Therapy, and conversation hours with D. A. Louw of South Africa and Philip Saigh of the American University of Beirut. The conversation hours allowed students close contact with important psychologists and their ideas.

In addition, Psi Chi continued to offer career-planning programs each year on topics such as preparation for graduate school, careers with a BA in psychology, and nontraditional jobs in psychology. Such programs addressed common and important questions that are asked frequently by students who are making difficult career decisions. Programs such as these are still offered at conventions and are well attended by students. These programs augment information that students obtain through academic advising or through local Psi Chi meetings.

Psi Chi continued during this period to promote student involvement with psychology on an international level, and the development of international Psi Chi chapters was pursued. However, international chapters were not established for two reasons. First, international currency exchange rates were an obstacle. For example, the University of British Columbia in Vancouver, Canada, was the first international group that applied for a charter and was accepted. However, the group indicated that they could not install their chapter because of the unfavorable currency exchange rate. Second, the ACHS told Psi Chi that the problems, benefits, costs, and efforts required to penetrate the international market did not justify the goal of international expansion.

In 1986, under the new system of presidential terms, Virginia Staudt Sexton of St. John's University was elected president, Arthur C. MacKinney of the University Center at Tulsa was elected president-elect, and Paul Lloyd became past-president. The Psi Chi/Florence L. Denmark National Faculty Advisor Award was introduced. Denmark donated her Eastern Psychological Association past-president award money to establish this national recognition for Psi Chi faculty advisors. Stephen F. Davis of Emporia State University, who later became Midwestern regional vice president of Psi Chi, was the first recipient of the award.

The Texas Christian University Chapter suggested that Psi Chi sponsor a national chapter award and the National Council began to discuss the idea. Psi Chi bestowed its highest honor of Distinguished Membership on John A. Popplestone, the founder and director of the Archives of the History of American Psychology and chair of the APA Task Force on Centennial Celebrations. The 1987 APA/Psi Chi Convention was held in New York City and featured a student dialogue with B. F. Skinner and a Distinguished Lecture by Daniel J. Levinson of Yale University.

After several years of consideration, the Council decided to relocate the national office of Psi Chi from the Washington, DC, area to Chattanooga, Tennessee. The APA did not have space for Psi Chi's growth, and the Honor Society would be able to operate more economically in Tennessee with regard to office space and contracted services. In addition, Psi Beta was located in Chattanooga, and the two societies could share office space and develop a more tangible and mutually beneficial relationship.

In 1987, Arthur C. MacKinney became president of Psi Chi, and W. Harold Moon of Augusta College, Georgia, was elected to the office of president-elect. MacKinney, an industrial/organizational psychologist, had served as Psi Chi's historian from 1983 to 1986 and was Midwestern regional vice president from 1986 to 1987. His leadership and organizational skills proved invaluable in the relocation of the National Office, which was effected in November 1987. Under MacKinney's leadership, Psi Chi developed a plan to contact colleges and universities without Psi Chi chapters and to inform them of the benefits of membership in Psi Chi and of having a chapter on campus.

In 1988, Harold Moon became president of Psi Chi, and Lisa Gray-Shellberg of California State University, Dominguez Hills, was elected to the office of president-elect. Psi Chi continued to grow rapidly. For the first time, the Honor Society added over 10,000 new members in 1 year.

President Moon attended the first convention of the newly formed APS in June 1989, and he established Psi Chi's first link to that organization, while continuing to maintain close ties with the APA. Psi Chi celebrated its 60th anniversary at the 1989 APA/Psi Chi Convention in New Orleans.

Lisa Gray-Shellberg, 1989–1990 president of Psi Chi, ushered in a new era for the Honor Society. Michael Wertheimer of the University of Colorado at Boulder was elected to the office of president-elect. Three major events marked the presidency of Gray-Shellberg. First, Ruth Cousins announced her intent to retire in the fall of 1991. Second, with the establishment of the APS it became imperative for Psi Chi to clarify its relationship with the APS, the APA, and other organizations with which Psi Chi had a relationship. Third, the ACHS informed Psi Chi that Psi Chi needed to amend its Constitution and Bylaws regarding organizational affiliations, to bring them into conformity with the ACHS guidelines.

The Council proposed and chapters approved a revision in the Psi Chi Constitution and Bylaws to conform with the guidelines of the ACHS. This entailed eliminating Psi Chi's dependency on any other organization. Therefore, references to the APA in the Constitution and Bylaws had to be removed. However, Psi Chi continued its affiliation with the APA as well as with the APS.

A screening committee was established to find a successor for Executive Director Cousins. In August 1990, at the National Council meeting in Boston, Kay Wilson was selected to succeed Cousins. The Council appointed Wilson to a 1-year position as associate officer of Psi Chi to be served during Cousins's last year, with Wilson's appointment as executive officer to begin when Cousins retired on October 1, 1991.

B. F. Skinner gave his last lecture and received the first APA Award for Outstanding Lifetime Contribution to Psychology at the 1990 APA/Psi Chi Convention in Boston. Skinner died less than a week after the event. In addition, Skinner's daughter, Julie Vargas, was the featured speaker for Psi Chi and Psi Beta at the Convention. President Gray-Shellberg and the Council invited Ruth Cousins to speak on "The Legacy of Psi Chi" at the Convention and brought Frederick H. Lewis to Boston to participate on the program.

Michael Wertheimer was president of Psi Chi for the 1990–1991 year. Wertheimer delivered the first Psi Chi presidential address at the 1991 APA/Psi Chi Annual Convention in San Francisco. The address was given in conjunction with his address as the recipient of the APA's 1990 Award for Distinguished Career Contributions to Education and Training in Psychology.

At the Convention, Psi Chi celebrated the contributions of Executive Director Cousins and her 33 years of dedicated service to the Society and to psychology. Raymond D. Fowler, the executive vice president and chief executive officer of the APA, presented to Cousins the APA's first-ever Honorary Lifetime Full Membership. Psi Chi also honored Frederick H. Lewis by naming the annual Distinguished Lecture the Frederick Howell Lewis Distinguished Lecture. Lewis was invited to present the first Psi Chi address in his honor.

During Wertheimer's presidency, two national awards were announced, both to be presented for the first time in 1992. HarperCollins Publishers announced three undergraduate scholarships for Psi Chi and three for Psi Beta. The scholarship awards are based on essay competitions. The second award is the Psi Chi/Ruth Hubbard Cousins National Chapter Award, which was also presented for the first time in 1992. Also during Wertheimer's tenure, Psi Chi superseded any previous year in the number of new members (14,030), bringing the cumulative membership of the Honor Society to 221,573 as of June 30, 1991. Twenty-eight new chapters were added, bringing the total number of charters granted to 734.

Psi Chi has come a long way from its small but determined beginning in 1929 to its present status as the world's largest psychological organization. Figure 1 shows the steady growth of membership and chapters between 1959 and 1991. In the words of cofounder Frederick H. Lewis,

> From the perspective of one who has enjoyed the privilege of watching the development of Psi Chi from germination to its present notable stature, it is clear that the stated aims of the society are being faithfully met . . . energetically and enthusiastically. One has only to read the chapter reports in today's *Newsletters* to witness the vitality of Psi Chi throughout the nation. For the student, undergraduate or graduate, the

Total Psi Chi Members, 1959–1991

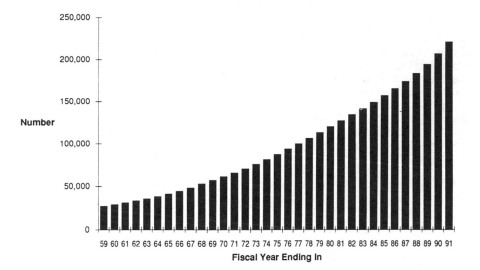

Total Psi Chi Chapters, 1959–1991

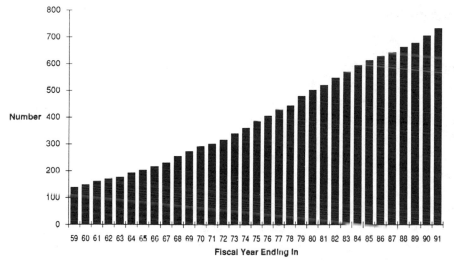

Figure 1: Total Psi Chi members (top panel) and chapters (bottom panel) for 1959–1991.

chapters are generating a sense of professional identify and pride. (Lewis, 1991, p. 10)

A HISTORY OF PSI BETA

Psi Beta's commitment to the development of students and faculty is vigorous. The purpose of Psi Beta, the National Honor Society in Psychology for Community and Junior Colleges, is to promote, stimulate,

TABLE 3
Psi Beta Charter Chapters

Institution	Location
Cerritos College	Norwalk, California
Cottey College	Nevada, Missouri
Des Moines Area Community College	Ankeny, Iowa
Golden West College	Huntington Beach, California
Lincoln Trail College	Robinson, Illinois
McLennan Community College	Waco, Texas
Mountain View College	Dallas, Texas
Piedmont Technical College	Greenwood, South Carolina
Prince George's Community College	Largo, Maryland
St. Phillips College	San Antonio, Texas
South Central Community College	New Haven, Connecticut

encourage, and recognize general scholarship and interest in psychology. Psi Beta strives to promote community service on the individual and chapter levels, to encourage faculty development, and to develop leadership skills in student members.

Another Beginning

Psi Beta was organized in 1977 by Carol Tracy in consultation with her husband, an attorney, and Ruth Cousins, the executive director of Psi Chi. For several years, Psi Chi had received requests from community and junior colleges to obtain charters for Psi Chi chapters. However, the ACHS, of which Psi Chi is a member, would not permit its member honor societies to have chapters at 2-year colleges. Cousins encouraged Tracy, who had worked with Psi Chi and other organizations, to found an honor society in psychology for 2-year colleges.

In 1977, Tracy drafted a Constitution and Bylaws and created a logo. For the logo, Tracy's husband suggested keeping Psi for Psychology and adding Beta, the second letter in the Greek alphabet, since this was the second honor society in psychology. Tracy mailed information about Psi Beta to 2-year colleges, inviting them to become charter members of the Society.

On November 5, 1981, Psi Beta was chartered and incorporated in the state of Tennessee. The charter was signed by Tracy as incorporator. Tables 3 and 4 respectively depict the charter chapters and first members of the National Council. The original Constitution and Bylaws were replaced by the Charter and Bylaws drafted by an attorney in accordance with Tennessee law for not-for-profit corporations. Also in 1981, Tracy began publishing the *Psi Beta Newsletter*, which continues to be published three times a year, in the fall, winter, and spring.

TABLE 4
First Psi Beta National Council

Member	Affiliation
Todd Gaffaney	Cerritos College
Jim Hail	McLennan Community College
Margaret S. Martin	Piedmont Technical College
Sharon Mikeworth	Lincoln Trail College
Irene Osthoff	Cottey College
Ann E. Garrett Robinson	South Central Community College
Alan Schultz	Prince George's Community College
Carol Tracy	Psi Beta

First Decade

In 1982, the Psi Beta National Council elected its first national president, Jim Hail of McLennan Community College in Waco, Texas. Hail worked closely with Tracy, the National Council, and the chapters in finalizing the Bylaws and approving the logo. The Council and chapters adopted official colors of royal blue and gold for Psi Beta. By the end of Hail's 1982–1983 term, 24 chapters had been chartered.

The second national president, Alan Schultz of Prince George's Community College in Largo, Maryland, was elected by the Council to serve during the 1983–1984 year. The first Psi Beta National Council meeting was held by conference call in the fall of 1983. In 1984, Psi Beta divided its chapters into five geographical regions: North Central, Northeastern, Southeastern, South Central, and Western. The first vice presidents to head their regions were elected by the chapters in their respective regions. The Council decided to stagger future elections to provide continuity on the National Council.

In 1984, Psi Beta received its first invitation to participate on a discussion panel at the annual meeting of the EPA. President Schultz was the first Psi Beta officer to represent the organization on a panel at a regional psychological association program. He discussed undergraduate education in psychology at 2-year colleges. Psi Beta had 28 chapters by the end of Schultz's term.

Psi Beta's third national president, Margaret S. Martin of Piedmont Technical College in Greenwood, South Carolina, was elected to three 1-year terms, from 1984–1987. President Martin visited Psi Beta headquarters and discussed plans for Psi Beta with Carol Tracy, who had continued to receive annual appointments as executive director. During Martin's 3 years as president, she emphasized the recruitment of chapters and designed a brochure that was distributed to prospective chapters. Psi Beta published its first *Psi Beta Handbook* for the 1986–1987 year and had honor cords designed in Psi Beta's colors of royal blue and gold.

Martin, as a member of the APA, enhanced Psi Beta's image in the psychology community. The APA's Education and Training Board invited her to serve a 3-year term on the Committee on Undergraduate Education (CUE), and the APA's Educational Affairs Office invited her to serve on the Advisory Board of *Network*, the APA's newsletter for 2-year colleges. Psi Chi invited Psi Beta President Martin and Executive Director Tracy to participate, for the first time, in the 1986 Psi Chi national meeting held in conjunction with the APA Annual Convention in Washington, DC. Psi Beta regional vice presidents had been participating in the regional psychological association conventions of Psi Chi since 1984.

Psi Beta presented its first research award in 1987. Both experimental and archival research papers were eligible. The papers were judged by a Psi Chi chapter, and the award was presented during the APA Convention at the Psi Beta Chapter Information Exchange. The first winner was Cindy Ahlquist, West Valley College, Saratoga, California. By June 1987, there were 50 Psi Beta chapters.

The Psi Beta National Council elected Ann E. Garrett Robinson of South Central Community College in New Haven, Connecticut, as Psi Beta national president for the 1987–1990 years.

In 1987, Psi Beta welcomed the Psi Chi national headquarters to Chattanooga, Tennessee, as mentioned in the Psi Chi history. Psi Beta also participated in a welcoming party for Psi Chi sponsored by the University of Tennessee at Chattanooga, Covenant College, Chattanooga State Technical Community College, Partners for Economic Progress, and friends.

As president, Robinson's first priority was to apply for Psi Beta's affiliation with the APA, which was approved and announced during the APA Convention in Atlanta in August 1988. At this Convention, for the first time, the APA assigned a room and time for Psi Beta to hold a National Council meeting. Also during President Robinson's first term, she sought to recognize the founders of Psi Beta. As a result, the National Council named the Psi Beta Research Paper Award after Ruth Cousins, Psi Chi executive director, who had inspired the founding of Psi Beta. The Council also established the Carol Tracy Community Service Award in honor of Psi Beta's founder and executive director. Diana Benge of the Des Moines Area Community College in Ankeny, Iowa, received the first Community Service Award for helping to establish a women's resource center at the college.

During Robinson's 1988–1989 term, she established contact for Psi Beta with the American Association of Community and Junior Colleges. Psi Beta was invited by the Spanish honor society for 2-year colleges to apply mutually for membership in the ACHS, an organization that had never accepted honor societies from 2-year colleges. The Psi Beta National Council studied and amended the Psi Beta Bylaws to be more compatible with those of the ACHS. Also, Psi Beta changed from a 1-year presidential term to a 3-year term, to be served as president-elect, president, and past-president.

During the 1989 APA Convention in New Orleans, the APA allotted 7.5 hours for Psi Beta's programs and meetings. At this Convention, Sandra L. Ladd, the Western regional vice president, began videotaping historical moments for Psi Beta, including the presentation of the first Honorary Membership in Psi Beta to Ruth Cousins. Sharold Overton of J. Sargeant Reynolds Community College in Richmond, Virginia, who was installed on the National Council, was the first student to serve as a regional vice president. According to Psi Beta's Bylaws, members of the Psi Beta National Council must be members of Psi Beta, therefore permitting faculty sponsors or student members to be elected. Having a student's perspective and enthusiasm on the Council was beneficial to all members, especially for setting goals to encourage more student involvement with faculty sponsors at regional and national meetings. Consistent with the emphasis of Psi Chi, Psi Beta seeks to enhance student educational experience through all possible avenues, both inside and outside of the classroom.

At the 1990 APA Convention in Boston, the first Psi Beta/Virginia Staudt Sexton National Faculty Sponsor Award was presented to an outstanding Psi Beta faculty sponsor. Bernice B. Harshberger of Carteret Community College in Morehead City, North Carolina, was the recipient. The award was established by Virginia Staudt Sexton, a former president of Psi Chi. Psi Beta's first Distinguished Lecturer at an APA Convention was Robert J. Sternberg, professor of psychology at Yale University.

Under the leadership of President Robinson, the Psi Beta National Council voted to apply for affiliation with the APS. Following her 3 years as president, Robinson continued on the Psi Beta Council another year as past-president. She served as historian for the 1991–1992 fiscal year, according to a policy adopted in 1990. Richard E. Miller of Navarro College in Corsicana, Texas, was installed as the 1990–1991 president and Sandra L. Ladd of West Valley College in Saratoga, California, was installed as president-elect. Both Miller and Ladd were recipients of the APA's Division 2 Teaching Excellence Award, with Miller the recipient in 1991 and Ladd in 1990. By June 30, 1990, Psi Beta had chartered 72 chapters.

During President Richard E. Miller's leadership in 1990–1991, the Council concentrated on contacting potential chapters and encouraging participation in regional meetings. Two important events took place at this time. The APS approved Psi Beta's affiliation, and the ACHS voted to permit honor societies from accredited 2-year colleges to become members of the association. Psi Beta applied for membership at the next ACHS Council meeting in 1992.

Psi Beta celebrated its 10th anniversary at the 1991 APA Convention in San Francisco. Past-presidents Jim Hail and Margaret Martin participated in a symposium with Council members on the history of Psi Beta. Philip

Zimbardo, professor of psychology at Stanford University, delivered the Psi Beta Distinguished Lecture at the Convention. The Council awarded its second Honorary Membership to Virginia Staudt Sexton in recognition of her contributions and devotion to Psi Beta. The National Council recognized two charter chapters, McLennan Community College in Waco, Texas, and Piedmont Technical College in Greenwood, South Carolina, for their outstanding activities, unfailing registration of members, and consistent filing of annual reports since their installation. HarperCollins Publishers offered Psi Beta $1,000, beginning in 1992, to be awarded as scholarships to the student authors of three winning essays related to the teaching or learning process. To concentrate on these scholarships, the Council decided to discontinue temporarily the Ruth Cousins Research Paper Award. However, the National Council honored Cousins, retiring executive director of Psi Chi, by naming the Psi Beta Distinguished Lecture Series after her, beginning in 1992. Neal E. Miller, Research Affiliate at Yale University, was the first Ruth Cousins Distinguished Lecturer at the 100th Annual APA Convention. His topic was "The Psychobiography of a Scientist." Richard Miller installed Sandra L. Ladd as Psi Beta national president for the 1991–1992 year, and Dr. Donald B. Irwin of Des Moines Area Community College in Ankeny, Iowa, as president-elect. The second student to serve on the National Council as a regional vice president was installed. Psi Beta had chartered over 80 chapters and registered a cumulative total of almost 4,500 members as it celebrated its 10th anniversary at the Convention.

Second Decade

Psi Beta is now in its second decade, and the Council is excited by the advances that the Society has made during its first decade. The future looks even more promising with Psi Beta and Psi Chi sharing national headquarters and working together for the benefit of honor students in psychology. Psi Beta is an affiliate of both the APA and the APS and has applied for membership in the ACHS.

One goal for the second decade is for National Council members and Psi Beta chapters to participate in the national conventions of the APA and the APS. Another goal is to increase participation in the regional psychological association conventions.

Psi Beta chapter members, faculty sponsors, and the National Council members have dedicated their time and talents to keep Psi Beta active, involved, and expanding. President Ladd and her National Council members are advocating for the inclusion of psychology courses in general education curricula by all 2-year colleges. They also wish to attract and to recognize high ability students at the community college level, by implementing honors programs, by encouraging dialogue between the community college and university systems to establish criteria for transferable general education courses, and by developing a 10-year ethnic mentoring program with the APA Task Force on Minority Recruitment and Retention and the National Institute of Mental Health (Ladd, 1992). During this second decade, Psi Beta hopes to increase greatly its 87 chapters and 5,500 cumulative membership, leave a positive impact on American education, and stimulate more students to excel and to continue their education and careers in psychology.

TWO PROMISING FUTURES

In this chapter, the histories of Psi Chi and Psi Beta, the two national honor societies in psychology, have been presented. Both have shown steady growth since their inception and have demonstrated a consistent commitment to encouraging the intellectual and professional development of psychology students and faculty. The history of these two organizations is an important part of the evolution of the teaching of psychology. Psi Chi and Psi Beta should continue to enrich the educational experience of members for many years to come.

REFERENCES

Brewer, C., in collaboration with Hopkins, R., Kimball, G., Matlin, M., McCann, L., McNeil, O., Nodine, B., Quinn, V. N., & Saundra. (1992). Curriculum. In T. V. McGovern (Ed.), Handbook for enhancing undergraduate education in psychology. Manuscript submitted for publication.

Goodstein, L. D. (1986, Winter). Psi Chi and a career as a psychologist: A personal reminiscence. Psi Chi Newsletter, p. 1.

Hunt, T. (1979). History of Psi Chi: The National Honor Society in Psychology. Chattanooga, TN: Psi Chi National Office.

Ladd, S. L. (1992, Winter). Psi Beta and the promise of diversity. Psi Beta Newsletter, p. 1.

Langhorne, M. C., & Hoch, E. L. (1960). Psychology in the states. American Psychologist, 15, 323–325.

Lewis, F. H. (1969, Fall). Message from the first historian of Psi Chi. Psi Chi Newsletter, p. 7.

Lewis, F. H. (1991, Special Edition). A letter of tribute to Ruth H. Cousins. Psi Chi Newsletter, p. 10.

Skinner, B. F. (1971). Beyond freedom and dignity. New York: Bantam Books.

V

KEY PUBLICATIONS IN THE TEACHING OF PSYCHOLOGY

INTRODUCTION

KEY PUBLICATIONS IN THE TEACHING OF PSYCHOLOGY

CHARLES L. BREWER

The first three chapters in Part V trace the development of important publications in the teaching of psychology: the American Psychological Association's Division 2 (Teaching of Psychology) journal, introductory psychology textbooks, and psychological handbooks. The fourth chapter examines how the teaching of psychology has been depicted in journal articles.

Robert Daniel played a pivotal role in transforming the newsletter of Division 2 into its official journal, *Teaching of Psychology* (*ToP*), which was first published in October 1974. His chapter highlights this arduous but successful transformation, as well as the journal's history since 1974. Daniel served as editor of *ToP* from its inception through 1984, when he was given the honorific title of Founding Editor to recognize his exemplary work. With the style and grace that characterized his editorship, he provides a personal, and sometimes humorous, chronicle that he is uniquely qualified to write.

Surprised to learn that no extensive history of introductory psychology textbooks has been published, Wayne Weiten and Randall Wight set out to fill this lacuna. The first section of their chapter provides a chronological overview of how such textbooks evolved from books on moral philosophy and developed into those that teachers now require their students to read. The second section summarizes an empirical comparison of a representative sample of leading textbooks for each decade from the 1890s through the 1980s. In both sections, the authors discuss aspects of the zeitgeist that produced both stability and change among introductory psychology textbooks during the past 100 years. Their analysis is a valuable contribution for present readers and future historians.

James Pate assumes that the history of psychology is reflected in what students are taught about the discipline. His chapter discusses the history and function of handbooks that have influenced the teaching of psychology during the past 100 years. He discusses handbooks in a variety of substantive areas, including general, experimental, child, and social psychology. His comparative analyses provide valuable insights into the history of psychology. His acumen adds a new dimension to our understanding of how the books we use affect what we teach and how we teach it, as well as how we define our discipline. Pate's appendix lists handbooks not mentioned in his chapter—a valuable source of supplementary information.

Tracing the teaching of psychology through a judicious selection of journal articles, Bernard Beins identifies recurring themes that reflect the social, cultural, political, and educational milieus of successive generations. His chapter focuses on characteristics of students, teachers, pedagogical techniques, and curricula manifested in psychology journals during the past 100 years. His portrayal suggests similarities and differences over time that many experienced teachers will recognize, whether or not they are pleased with what they see. One noteworthy theme revealed by Beins's perceptive analysis is that teaching methods come and go, but the importance of a personal relationship between teachers and students remains constant and paramount.

19

TEACHING OF PSYCHOLOGY, THE JOURNAL

ROBERT S. DANIEL

One of the most important indications of the viability of a professional field is formal, published articles in a topical journal. As a new field emerges, its literature begins to appear in a variety of journals, making access somewhat difficult. Once a topical journal is established, particularly if that journal is owned by a recognized professional association, then there is a clearly defined focal point with which members identify and through which they communicate and achieve greater cohesion. Therefore, the initiation and development of Division 2's journal, *Teaching of Psychology* (*ToP*), is a significant part of the first 100 years of organized psychology in the United States.

GERMINAL PERIOD

The journal was preceded by 59 issues of the *Teaching of Psychology Newsletter*, which was published over a 24-year period, an uncommonly long gestation, even for a journal. The first issue of the newsletter was distributed in November 1950. Although it had no series number, the front-page letter from the president, Leonard Carmichael, clearly indicates that it was indeed the first. This four-page, mimeographed issue also contained a summary of the address of the previous president, Norman Munn. Elizabeth Hurlock, as secretary, reported the minutes from the annual meeting and the financial status of the Division.

It is of special interest that this first issue also reported a letter sent to the American Psychological Association's (APA's) Board of Directors asking that a section in one of the journals be set aside for communications on the teaching of psychology. Later issues revealed that this request was denied, but that small event established that the Division saw the need for widely distributed, printed communication early in its existence.

The newsletter prospered over the years, appearing semiannually (usually in the spring and fall). Although the publication itself does not identify an editor, Elizabeth Hurlock (personal communication, 1974) believed that, as secretary, she produced the first issue. Presumably, a similar arrangement continued through 1957. Table 1 shows the succession of presidents and secretary—treasurers, all of whom produced official Division material that appeared in the newsletter.

In those years of an informal, mimeographed but regular publication of the newsletter, a typical issue contained business of the Division, communications from officers and committee chairs, announcements of APA convention programs (and later summaries of papers and symposia), and news of Division activities. At the 1953 convention, a group discussion was held on the prospects for creating a journal on the teaching of psychology with Howard G. Miller as chairman and panelists Benjamin Burack, John F. Hall, Robert H. Knapp, and Stuart W. Cook. Although considerable enthusiasm was reported, apparently no substantive actions resulted.

Beginning in 1953, the newsletter reported increasing divisional action committees producing information and other services for the teacher. The number of such committees increased annually, and many of them produced effective symposia for convention sessions, as well as reports in the newsletter. Business items of note in the early years included Bylaw changes, upgrading requirements for fellow status, and concern about the future of the Division should APA reorganize. A proposed newsletter for high school teachers of psychology was mentioned in the November 1956 issue, thus anticipating APA's *Periodically* by 13 years. *Periodically* was later renamed the *High School Psychology Teacher*, and in 1991 it was combined with *Network* (for 2-year college teachers) to become *The Psychology Teacher Network*.

EMBRYONIC PERIOD

Wilbert S. Ray became the first appointed editor of the *Teaching of Psychology Newsletter* with the November 1958 issue. Among other format changes, a colored cover with a table of contents improved its appearance. Innovations in content during his term included editorials, a lively letters section, an index to book reviews, and more extensive news coverage. Division presidents, whose membership letter and annual address abstracts were published by Ray, were Fred McKinney and Edward J. Shoben. Robert S. Harper, as secretary–treasurer, made business matters known to the members.

James Joyce was appointed editor beginning with the December 1960 issue. He introduced a new and stylish printed cover; more extensive accounts of convention symposia; and, as supplements to regular issues, two lengthy bibliographies on teaching materials. Other content innovations during his term included a section on teaching problems and solutions, contributed classroom demonstrations, and an American Association for the Advancement of Science address by Richard Evans. The newsletter had also been growing in size over the years and reached 36 pages by June 1963, Joyce's last issue.

During Joyce's term, two Division organization changes influenced the content of the newsletter. Division committees became so numerous (21 in 1961) that they were reorganized into five sections, as recommended by the Policy and Planning Committee chaired by Sumner Hayward. Thereafter, committee and project reports appeared in a more orderly manner. The Division provided affiliate status for high school teachers of psychology beginning in 1962, and a special effort was made to provide suitable materials for that group. Presidents whose material was published by Joyce were Robert S. Harper, Robert S. Daniel, and Floyd L. Ruch. Secretary–Treasurer Thelburn L. Engle made official business reports.

FETAL PERIOD

The first issue under the next editor, Edward Ostrander, was in January 1964. His early issues were similar in format and content to previous ones, except that he introduced contributed articles and the first theme issue in August 1964 on the use of paperback books. In 1965, he expanded the newsletter to three issues per year and upgraded from mimeographing to letterpress printing. Contributed articles became the major content, but the traditional newsletter items continued to appear. One hundred thirty substantive articles on teaching are included in the 30 printed issues published between 1965 and 1974. This set of issues was made available as reprints (APA, Division Two, 1974).

At what point does a developing newsletter become a journal? Ostrander's issues and those that followed were surely as much one as the other in content, if not in name or in reviewing practice. His first issue contained Robert B. MacLeod's influential presidential address, "The Teaching

TABLE 1
Record of Division 2 Officers, Newsletter Editors, and Pages Published

Year[a]	President	Secretary–Treasurer[b]	Editor[c]	Pages
1946	Floyd L. Ruch	Edna Heidbreder		
1947	Sidney L. Pressey	Elizabeth Duffy		
1948	William A. Hunt	Elizabeth Duffy		
1949	Norman L. Munn	Elizabeth B. Hurlock	Elizabeth B. Hurlock	8[d]
1950	Leonard Carmichael	Elizabeth B. Hurlock	Elizabeth B. Hurlock	13
1951	Claude E. Buxton	Elizabeth B. Hurlock	Elizabeth B. Hurlock	13
1952	Elizabeth B. Hurlock	Lillian G. Portenier	Lillian G. Portenier	14
1953	John F. Dashiell[e]	Lillian G. Portenier	Lillian G. Portenier	16
1954	Richard W. Husband	Lillian G. Portenier	Lillian G. Portenier	18
1955	Wilbert J. McKeachie	Constance D. Lovell	Constance D. Lovell	24
1956	Frank W. Finger	Constance D. Lovell	Constance D. Lovell	27
1957	Lillian G. Portenier	Constance D. Lovell	Wilbert S. Ray	30
1958	Fred McKinney	Robert S. Harper	Wilbert S. Ray	40
1959	Edward J. Shoben	Robert S. Harper	Wilbert S. Ray	30
1960	Robert S. Harper	Thelburn L. Engle	James M. Joyce	45
1961	Robert S. Daniel	Thelburn L. Engle	James M. Joyce	56
1962	Floyd L. Ruch[f]	Thelburn L. Engle	James M. Joyce	42
1963	Robert B. MacLeod	Robert E. Bills	Edward R. Ostrander	8
1964	Ralph H. Turner	Robert E. Bills	Edward R. Ostrander	12[g]
1965	Michael Wertheimer	Wilbert S. Ray	Edward R. Ostrander	18
1966	Neil R. Bartlett	Wilbert S. Ray	Theophile S. Krawiec	32
1967	John E. Milholland	Wilbert S. Ray	Theophile S. Krawiec	39
1968	Paul J. Woods	Wilbert S. Ray	Theophile S. Krawiec	47
1969	Wilse B. Webb	Wilbert S. Ray	Theophile S. Krawiec	28
1970	Clarence J. Leuba	Wilbert S. Ray	Douglas A. Michell	

Year				
1971	Donald R. Brown	Wilbert S. Ray	Douglas A. Michell	32
1972	John K. Bare	Lawrence E. Murphy	Robert S. Daniel	45
1973	Wilbert S. Ray	Lawrence E. Murphy	Robert S. Daniel	68
1974	James B. Maas	Lawrence E. Murphy	Robert S. Daniel	132[h]
1975	Edward H. Loveland	Lawrence E. Murphy	Robert S. Daniel	196
1976	Douglas K. Candland	Lawrence E. Murphy	Robert S. Daniel	204
1977	James Deese	Lawrence E. Murphy	Robert S. Daniel	216
1978	David L. Cole	Fay-Tyler Norton	Robert S. Daniel	236
1979	James V. McConnell	Fay-Tyler Norton	Robert S. Daniel	256
1980	Barbara F. Nodine	Fay-Tyler Norton	Robert S. Daniel	260
1981	Charles L. Brewer	Ludy T. Benjamin, Jr.	Robert S. Daniel	256
1982	Fay-Tyler Norton	Ludy T. Benjamin, Jr.	Robert S. Daniel	256
1983	Frank Costin	Ludy T. Benjamin, Jr.	Robert S. Daniel	256
1984	Richard A. Kasschau	Janet R. Matthews	Robert S. Daniel	260
1985	Ludy T. Benjamin, Jr.	Janet R. Matthews	Charles L. Brewer	248
1986	Marilyn K. Rigby	Janet R. Matthews	Charles L. Brewer	240
1987	James H. Korn	Elizabeth V. Swenson	Charles L. Brewer	264
1988	Janet R. Matthews	Elizabeth V. Swenson	Charles L. Brewer	232
1989	Stephen F. Davis	Elizabeth V. Swenson	Charles L. Brewer	264
1990	Patricia Keith-Spiegel	Margaret A. Lloyd	Charles L. Brewer	280
1991	Joseph J. Palladino	Margaret A. Lloyd	Charles L. Brewer	264
1992	Elizabeth V. Swenson	Margaret A. Lloyd	Charles L. Brewer	264[i]

Note: Portions of this table also appear in Wight and Davis's history of Division 2 in this book.

[a]Officers of the division began their term following the annual business meeting in August (formerly September) in the year indicated. Editors of the *Teaching of Psychology Newsletter* generally followed the same schedule, but there was some variation. The journal is on a volume–calendar year schedule. [b]This office was secretary only through 1948. [c]There was no publication until 1950, hence, no editor. [d]The first newsletter was the November 1950 issue. [e]Dashiell was elected to replace Gilliland, who died before taking office. [f]Presidents serve only one term. After taking office in 1952, Floyd Ruch was asked about being elected again, and he said he had "forgotten" about his first term. [g]The first printed newsletter was in February 1965. [h]The newsletter appeared in two issues a year from 1950 through 1962 and in 1964. There were three issues a year in 1963 and from 1965 through 1972, and four issues in 1973. In 1974 there were 32 pages in two issues of the newsletter and 100 pages in two issues of the journal. [i]Number of pages to be published in 1992 is an estimate.

of Psychology and the Psychology We Teach," and the next year he published the widely read "Dithering Devices" address of President Ralph Turner. Both of those papers were reprinted in the *American Psychologist* (MacLeod, 1965; Turner, 1966). Michael Wertheimer's provocative address, "Out of Date Teaching," was also published in the fall 1966 issue. Another theme issue, this one on creativity, appeared in the spring–summer issue of 1966. Secretary–Treasurer Robert E. Bills reported minutes and financial information.

Theophile S. Krawiec was editor from March 1967 through June 1970. He continued with the three-issues-per-year format, introduced a more professional printed format, and provided brief biographical sketches of authors. Contributed articles dominated the periodical, and they were mostly brief, concise, and provocative, but largely informal. Several issues were thematic, a few contained selected reprint articles, and occasionally articles by nonpsychologists appeared. Probably the most significant paper during Krawiec's editorship was Stanford C. Ericksen's "The Science of Teaching—The Art of Learning" in November 1968. Krawiec relinquished the editorship when it became apparent that the content was developing into a journal prematurely. There were two difficulties: the lack of funds to sustain the growth and the time demand on the one-person operation.

Division presidents who wrote for the members through Krawiec's issues were Neil Bartlett, John E. Milholland, Paul J. Woods, and Wilse B. Webb. Wilbert S. Ray served his first term as secretary–treasurer and was reelected to a second term. Bill, as we knew him, was undoubtedly our most colorful officer, as mentioned in the tribute following his death in 1977 (Harper, 1978).

The next editor was Douglas A. Michell, who published six issues (December 1970 to June 1972) during the presidencies of Clarence Leuba and Donald R. Brown. Michell continued previous policies, including many contributed articles. Consideration of expanding the newsletter was included with a ballot on a special assessment, and again by President Leuba in the December 1970 issue. Discussion of a proposed journal by the Policy and Planning Committee of Division 2 in early 1971 was reported in one of those issues. The most notable of several other items on the possibility of a journal was an article in the December 1971 issue by James Korn. He argued convincingly for the need to establish a journal and gave his views on policy and content, most of which eventually materialized.

Meanwhile, three other events reflected the growing interest in a journal. First, at the 1971 APA annual meetings, Division President Leuba held a president's forum on whether there should be a journal on the teaching of psychology. Participants were Michael Wertheimer, Ralph Turner, Margo Johnson, Henry Pennypacker, Barbara Long, and James Korn. That forum was undoubtedly an outcome of the discussion mentioned earlier. Second, in October 1971, the APA Committee on the Undergraduate

Major authorized its chairman, Robert Isaacson, and Donald Brown to form a subcommittee to explore the creation of a journal on teaching. A letter proposing a format was sent to Albert Hastorf, then chairman of the APA Publications and Communications (P&C) Board, and later conversations took place with the P&C Board's next chairman, Arthur W. Melton. Although these efforts evoked no immediate positive action, they probably contributed to the P&C Board's later interest. Third, at about the same time, the APA's Education and Training (E&T) Board had requested the P&C Board to consider a teaching journal. The E&T Board's Wilse B. Webb had effectively brought the matter to the attention of the publication group and interboard communication was continuing into 1972.

The question of why it took so long to get a teaching of psychology journal has been asked by many psychologists. There is no simple answer. One can suppose that the events just recounted had, for the first time, accumulated to a "critical mass" of support. Also, the Division had experienced some dissent at the time of the APA 1945 reorganization and later. Although these problems did not seem to affect the publication program directly, they might have been distracting enough that efforts to create a journal were put aside for more pressing business. In addition, many psychology teachers believe that the APA has never given high priority to their interests. Finally, it should be noted that projects such as the initiation of a journal often depend on having one person who accepts responsibility for guiding the process. That opportunity came to me when I was asked to edit the newsletter, as described in the next section.

PRENATAL PERIOD

When Michell asked to be relieved of the editor's responsibilities, President Brown appointed an Editorial Board and charged it to seek a new editor and to serve as consultants. This group asked me to become editor in the summer of 1972. In consideration of the widespread interest in establishing a journal and a reasonable probability of doing so, I accepted a 2-year appointment. The first issue under that arrangement was December 1972 and the last was April 1974, with three issues in 1972–1973 and four in 1973–1974. During this period, the editor and the Editorial Board worked toward the goal of creating a true journal on two fronts. First, we attempted to make the newsletter itself more like a journal in content and format. Second, we coordinated our plans closely with the APA P&C Board and with its development arm, the Communications Committee.

John K. Bare became president in 1972 and joined the effort by writing in October to the P&C Board an official request for support in establishing a journal. Many details required deliberation, with the most knotty being that (a) the P&C Board considered a year or two as a necessary trial period before initiating an APA journal; (b) the APA Bylaws at that time discouraged, if not prohibited, a division from publishing a journal; and (c) Division 2 had insufficient funds to support a lengthy trial period on its own. Minutes of every meeting of the P&C Board and its Communications Committee in 1972–1973 contain information or action items concerning a journal on teaching. Support and assistance in the venture was given by the new Division officers elected for 1973: Wilbert S. Ray, president, James B. Maas, president-elect, and Lawrence Murphy, secretary–treasurer.

The cooperative plan that evolved was a partnership between the Division and the P&C Board for a period extending through 1975. Financial responsibility was to be shared equally. The Division would have editorial responsibility, and the P&C Board would underwrite and manage subscription promotion, advertising solicitation, and design consultation. Near the end of this trial period, the P&C Board would conduct an evaluation of the journal and make a decision about continuing it as an APA journal. It was further agreed, if that decision were affirmative, the P&C investment would be absorbed as a development cost and the Division would have no liability. If the decision were negative, the Division would have the option of continuing the journal on its own, with a negotiated repayment plan for the start-up funds provided. Other details for the latter contingency were trusted to good-faith negotiation. We began the preparation for publication. (The account of *ToP*'s development up to this point was freely adapted from Daniel, 1974.)

NEONATAL PERIOD

In the first issue of *ToP*, which appeared in October 1974, Division 2 President James B. Maas published a welcoming note that contained these words: "We hope that the new journal will be a strong catalyst in promoting research and development in the area of instruction, and will help us identify a critical mass of psychologists who share a common interest in the teaching of psychology" (Maas, 1974, p. 3). That goal has been an aspiration of the editors, the editorial staff, and the Division throughout *ToP*'s publication history.

From that first issue, we featured a cover design and a typography commissioned from a Washington, DC, designer, Wayne M. Hilburn. In its 48 pages, the first issue contained three general interest articles, four topical articles, a report on *ToP*'s development (Daniel, 1974), three methods papers, two book reviews, one media review, and a news column. There were three pages of paid advertising and two pages of in-house advertisements of APA teaching materials. We had agreed not to charge the APA for appropriate advertisements in exchange for services they provided to us. Volume 1 consisted of only two issues, October and December, and the decision to begin publication in the middle of the year with a short volume was often regretted because a number of library subscribers inquired about "missing issues." From the start, a quarterly was planned but on a schedule of two issues each semester of a typical academic year.

Submissions, subscribers, number of pages, and paid advertising all increased during 1975 (Volume 2). The P&C Board appointed a committee to conduct a formal assessment of *ToP* (as had been done for two previous APA journals) and charged that committee to look into (a) the quality of the journal's content, (b) the need for such a journal, and (c) financial viability. By the end of this period (six issues), the Division was beginning to regret having agreed to the condition that the P&C Board would make a decision on taking *ToP* as an APA journal and the Division could continue it as their own only if the P&C Board's decision was negative. Careful preparation was made for a presentation to the P&C Board in November 1975. The purpose was to request a reconsideration of that decision clause of the agreement: "Although members of the Board were surprised at the change in Division Two's position, they voted to establish a subcommittee to continue discussions and negotiate details with Division Two" (Daniel & Loveland, 1976, p. 129). The Division named its president (Edward H. Loveland) and past-president (James B. Maas) to join the P&C committee (Kenneth E. Clark, Robert Glaser, and Mavis Hetherington) for that task.

Nine articles of agreement were developed by the joint committee and accepted by the full P&C Board in April 1976 and by the Division in September 1976. In essence, *ToP* would continue to be operated as a division journal, the $9,038 advanced by the APA would be repaid without interest, the exchange of services would continue, renegotiations would not be prohibited, and *ToP* would use the *Publication Manual of the American Psychological Association* and would not compete with *Contemporary Psychology* in book reviewing.

During this period, and in the years that followed, certain key people in the APA's Central Office were helpful in getting the infant journal off to a good start. We were indebted to Arthur Melton, Harold Van Cott, Boris Cherney, Russell Nazzaro, Alan Boneau, Anita DeVivo, Elizabeth Reiner, Ed Harner, Bob Hayward, Stephanie Foran, and probably others we never knew about.

Thus, the Division gained full custody and responsibility for the journal while it was still in its infancy. Despite that outcome, the P&C Board's evaluation committee completed its work. This report was published in *ToP* (Cohen & Sechrest, 1976). The committee (chaired by Lee Sechrest) did a thorough and detailed job. They found that authors, subscribers, and "stratified" psychologists at large were overwhelmingly positive in their judgments. The report concluded the following:

> The survey data clearly show that the quality of materials published in

ToP is good, and that the need for the journal exists. . . . We feel that the evaluation was quite extensive and put *Teaching of Psychology* to a rather severe test on which the journal proved itself impressively. (Cohen & Sechrest, 1976, pp. 133–134)

In addition to Lee Sechrest, members of the committee were James Korn, Michael Wertheimer, and Paul Woods. A more detailed account of the background and establishment of *ToP* has been published elsewhere (Daniel, 1977), and some more personal observations appear in Heppner and Reis (1987).

The evaluation report confirmed our original presentation to the P&C Board, in which data were provided that showed that before *ToP*, "seven journals were required to produce 50% of the [teaching] literature [in psychology], 20 journals for 75%, and, in total, 100% of the literature required 115 journals" (Cohen & Sechrest, 1976, p. 133). These data were derived from an analysis of the 717 items in the comprehensive bibliography published by M. Johnson and Daniel (1974). My own unpublished data revealed that those percentages of need required noticeably fewer journals within a year of *ToP*'s first issue. The comprehensive bibliography was continued in the first December issue of *ToP* and has appeared annually since then under a variety of compilers. From the 1990 bibliography, the yield from 2 journals is needed for 50%, 6 for 75%, and 48 for 100%. Thus, *ToP*'s success in collecting teaching articles and narrowing the search base is clearly demonstrated.

CHILDHOOD

From its initiation through Volume 11 (1984), *ToP* was operated on a limited budget. There was no paid professional staff. I had a part-time secretary and used student help at the prevailing hourly rate to prepare issues for mailing. My university department provided space, but supplies and telephone costs were reimbursed from *ToP* funds. As graciously recognized by Charles Brewer (1985) the editor's wife, Nola Daniel, "read every word that has been printed in *ToP*" (p. 3) in assisting the proofing of galleys. A member of the P&C Board commented that *ToP* survived and prospered while being operated as a "cottage industry" for its first 11 years. I made a decision to give up some of my research time for this effort because I felt that getting the journal off the ground was as much of a professional contribution as research would have been.

The editor's first secretary, Dee Thomas (now Dee Hargis), was actually much more than her title would suggest. She was circulation manager, bookkeeper, and assistant editor. *ToP*'s initiation would have been far more difficult had Dee not been there. She left in 1976 to teach high school psychology.

The subscription rate began at $4 per volume for individuals and $10 for institutions. The individual rate applied to Division 2 members and nonmembers alike. A $2 increase in dues, plus a like amount from existing funds, was approved and appropriated at the September 1984 business meeting of Division 2. This plan reduced costs because there was no billing needed for the majority of the subscribers. That individual rate was just 25¢ per copy above the actual cost of printing, which was done at the local University Printing Services. Printing and mailing costs eventually increased to the point that rates were raised to $5 and $10 in 1981 and to $7 and $15 in 1984.

In the first year of publication, 100 contributed manuscripts were received. Yearly input gradually increased to between 130 and 140. From this pool of material, each year we published from 60% to 70%. I preferred to use acceptance rates, rather than rejection rates, and I did not use the APA rejection formula. The acceptance rate was simply the number of manuscripts accepted divided by the number of manuscripts received minus the number withdrawn and pending.

Our circulation started at 3,129 for Volume 1, rose to 3,680 for Volume 4, and then slowly declined to 2,956 for Volume 11. The loss over those 11 volumes was not from institutional or nonmember subscribers but from a decrease in the membership of Division 2 starting in 1977. The total nonmember subscriptions held steady at around 1,200, although the individuals in that category did show a surprising turnover. In 1979, we participated in a study of professional journal subscriber behavior conducted by the Indiana University School of Journalism. The findings were that our turnover in that category was typical and that the most frequent reason by far for dropping a subscription was "I am leaving the field." There is little doubt that the loss of Division 2 members reflected APA resignations, and fewer new APA members from the academic community, as a function of the scientist–practitioner unrest in the parent organization. This problem still exists (Benjamin, 1986; Brewer, 1981; Kasschau, 1985; Korn, 1987, 1988; Rigby, 1987).

These "childhood" years were not without some bumps, scrapes, mishaps, and memorable events. For example, I once phoned a reviewer because he was very late reporting a review of a set of manuscripts, and he declared that he had not received them. Fortunately, there was another set on hand to send him. Six weeks later, my mail included a plastic "body bag" filled with confetti and a note from the Post Office apologizing for the package having been chewed up in a sorting machine somewhere in Pennsylvania. Twice, our mailing of the journal suffered a 1-day delay caused by "unforeseen circumstances." The first was a bomb threat at our local Post Office. The second was caused by a student helper who loaded the entire shipment onto our small elevator (instead of one cartfull at a trip). The elevator's safety system stalled it at midfloor and we could not get engineering help until the next day. The April 1983 issue was printed in the wrong shade of blue because a pressman misread the color chart. Readers might not have noticed because no two issues that year were exactly the same color. Blue printer's ink is tricky and unstable—look at past copies of the *American Psychologist*.

One promotion idea never materialized. *The Industrial Psychologist* (TIP) is a newsletter published by Division 14 of the APA. I wrote a letter to its editor proposing that we arrange a special price to subscribers of both publications so that they could become "*TIP–ToP*" psychologists. I still wonder why he did not reply. We settled for the section heading, "News Tips From *ToP*."

The debt to the APA for start-up costs was fully repaid by 1981 and was celebrated at the Division's annual business meeting. "The highlight of the . . . meeting was the burning of the 'mortgage' (in effigy), noting the final payment to APA for the loan which made it possible for Division Two to develop its journal" (Norton, 1981, p. 247). In fact, it was a festive affair because the members present felt that, finally, after 31 years of trying, the Division really owned a journal.

During its first 11 years, *ToP* published one special issue devoted to a single topic, Undergraduate Psychology Education in the Next Decade (February 1982). This is a good way to make a special contribution to the field, but it does place a burden on the editor. In a quarterly journal, one issue is, of course, one fourth of a year, and that means that the normal flow of papers is delayed by an extra 3 months or more. Less disruption (and less grumbling from authors) results from the plan of allotting a portion of an issue to a special topic. We did this in several issues: Human Sexuality Course (February 1975), Introductory Texts (February 1977), Psychology's Centennial (February 1979), and Teaching Medical Students (February 1984).

A student gave me a cartoon clipped from *Playboy* magazine because it was similar to some "impossible structures" I had used in class for a discussion of perception. This happened while we were preparing the special issue on undergraduate education (February 1982), and I saw a resemblance between the cartoon and models of proposed undergraduate curriculum plans. Therefore, that issue's cover design was constructed. Well ahead of the deadline, I wrote to *Playboy* for reprint permission but did not receive a reply. I then phoned the magazine's office and was connected to a woman in the permissions office. As soon as she understood what I wanted, she immediately gave me oral permission and said that a contract and an invoice for the standard $150 fee would be mailed to me shortly. She then began talking about the upcoming National Collegiate Athletic Association basketball tournament and her favorite team, DePaul, and wondering what would happen if DePaul were to play Missouri. We ended the conversation on a note of friendly rivalry, and I never received the bill for $150.

Decorating the window of *ToP*'s cover was a pleasure on those few occasions when I could take time away from academic and editorial duties. Those windows looked out on graduation events twice (April 1975 and April 1976) and onto a sleeping campus (April 1979). In addition to the special issue, they represented lead articles as bookshelves (February 1977), a classroom demonstration (October 1976), "his and hers" window blinds (February 1975), and a test answer sheet (October 1984). We had psychology centennial reminders on three 1979 covers. The two graduation events were local. The Stephens College photo (April 1975) first appeared in *Life* magazine and was widely reprinted. The university photo (April 1976) was from the files of Missouri's School of Journalism. My artist-daughter, Katy, did the sketches for the February 1977 and April 1979 covers.

A few readers have indicated an interest in doing a content analysis of *ToP*, but none has been completed to my knowledge. Having tried it myself, I can understand why—it is frustrating. As soon as there is a seemingly workable framework, there is an article that does not fit anywhere. The teaching of psychology encompasses a broad range of activities and issues. Nevertheless, my effort resulted in a few generalizations that reveal *ToP*'s emphasis in its formative years. The 44 issues of this period were blocked into six-issue units, resulting in seven equal development steps. Tabulation of the number of the 15 highest yield categories is shown in Table 2.

As can be seen in Table 2, articles on demonstrations and techniques, teacher assessment, and graduate teaching show increasing coverage. Articles on broad methodology decline, probably reflecting the decrease in PSI (personalized system of instruction) research noted by Lamal (1984). The one time-unit increase in articles about curricula reflects the special issue of February 1982, and the history course articles increase may be linked to psychology's centennial. The remaining high-yield categories appear to be flat for the period shown. About 70 other categories were tabulated, and some of those did not appear until the journal had been in publication for a year or more. One of these, the use of computers, has been reported by Beins (1989) to have increased sharply in recent years, and my tabulations are consistent with that trend.

In addition to these patterns of contributed and refereed content, *ToP* carried news items in each issue, media reviews (until 1980), introductory text reviews (nearly every issue), annual bibliographies, frequent reports of Division 2 business, and occasional editorials or policy statements. This content analysis is not suitable as an indication of all that one might find in *ToP* for a particular teacher interest because each article was tabulated

TABLE 2
Incidence of the Most Frequent Topics Appearing in *Teaching of Psychology* From 1974 Through 1984

Topic	Six-issue time block							
	10/74–12/75	2/76–4/77	10/77–12/78	2/79–4/80	10/80–12/81	2/82–4/83	10/83–12/84	Total
Demonstrations and techniques	8	13	13	15	15	21	22	107
Student assessment	5	11	10	14	11	12	9	72
Broad methodology	11	14	10	12	8	8	6	69
Texts and adjuncts	9	17	11	6	9	2	10	64
Teacher assessment	3	6	8	8	6	9	10	50
Introductory course	4	5	11	4	4	8	5	41
Undergraduate research	2	3	7	6	5	3	6	32
Graduate teaching	0	2	5	1	7	5	10	30
Statistics course	3	5	4	4	6	5	3	30
Curriculum problems	2	1	3	5	2	11[a]	1	25
Undergraduate field work	1	2	5	4	2	4	5	23
Child psychology course	3	2	2	8	2	3	3	23
History and systems course	1	0	0	7	7	6	1	22
Teacher training and development	1	0	5	2	5	3	2	18
Student advisement	0	4	2	3	3	2	3	17

[a]Special issue.

in only one category. However, the recent database for content (D. E. Johnson, 1991) is a superb tool for searching by computer.

Psychology teachers were provided with more convenient access to much of ToP's contents with the publication of a handbook of reprinted articles on the introductory course (Benjamin, Daniel, & Brewer, 1985). This was followed by a handbook on advising, career development, and field placement (Ware & Millard, 1986), one on teaching statistics and research methods (Ware & Brewer, 1987), and one on teaching psychology (Hartley & McKeachie, 1990). All royalties from the sale of those four books were paid to Division 2 and used in its mission to improve psychology teaching.

A final observation concerning content should be included in this historical account of ToP's childhood. An article by Buffardi and Nichols (1981) reported an analysis of psychology journals in terms of the citations to them on a per-article-published basis. ToP ranked 30th among the 99 journals studied, above several APA journals. For a journal still in its infancy, that standing was surprising but also gratifying. One could reasonably interpret the finding to indicate that ToP was making an impact and to validate the report of ToP's evaluation committee that "the quality of articles published in ToP is good" (Cohen & Sechrest, 1976, p. 134).

ADOLESCENCE

Having served approximately two normal terms as editor (more, counting the 2 years with the newsletter) and approaching my university retirement, I asked ToP's Editorial Board in 1983 to find a new editor to begin with the February 1985 issue. A search committee was appointed with John Bare as the chairman. After a careful search and examination of credentials, the committee presented three names to the Division's Executive Committee from which they chose Charles L. Brewer of Furman University as the new editor. He was well known as a teacher and was familiar with editorial work. He had been active in Division 2 leadership for many years. It was a good choice.

Shortly after his appointment, Brewer (1984) began negotiations with publishers, organizing an editorial staff, and otherwise setting up shop on his campus. At the 1984 Division business meeting, he announced that the new publisher would be Lawrence Erlbaum Associates. This firm was already publishing psychology journals and was well established. The contractual agreement required some negotiating, including approval by the legal office of the APA, but was completed to the satisfaction of all parties amid a feeling of hearty cooperation and mutual respect. Jack Burton, vice president of the publishing firm, attended the 1984 business meeting to speak about the new arrangement.

The contractual agreement set the new subscription rate at $10 for individuals and $25 for libraries, in an arrangement that protected the publisher against rising production costs but recognized the need to keep the journal attractive to subscribers. All subscription services, advertising, billing, and permission functions were to be handled by Erlbaum. *ToP* was to be copyrighted by Erlbaum, but Division 2 retained ownership. This plan made it possible for Brewer, as editor, to devote full attention to the policy, content, and purpose of the journal. Division 2 members continued to pay the *ToP* subscription with their dues.

As happens with preteens, *ToP* experienced a number of major changes as it was "now approaching adolescence" (Brewer, 1985, p. 3). With Volume 12 there was a new editor, a professional publisher, and a great physical separation of editor, publisher, and printer. Heretofore, all of these functions took place within a two-block area. Working communication now had to be established between Greenville, South Carolina (the editor) and Hillsdale, New Jersey (the publisher), and between Hillsdale and Ann Arbor, Michigan (the printer).

Brewer reported the following in his first issue:

> We have been working for almost a year with Jack Burton and his colleagues at LEA [Lawrence Erlbaum Associates] who are all eager to help us make the transition as smooth as possible, and to maintain the high quality of our journal—an auspicious beginning for what promises to be a worthwhile and pleasant relationship. (Brewer, 1985, p.3)

He retained the original cover design, the content sections, and the criteria for submissions. A new associate editor and new section editors were chosen. By the end of his first year, he had expanded the list of consulting editors to 13 and added 80 reviewers. These lists grew to 26 and 100, respectively, by the end of 1991 and showed improved representation of women and minorities. Thus, participation in the production of *ToP* has broadened significantly since the 1974–1984 era.

In his first annual report to the APA, Brewer stated that "the transition to a new editor and publisher created more problems than we had anticipated; consequently, some issues of the journal were not delivered on time. The delay is decreasing and we should be on schedule [shortly]" (C. L. Brewer, personal communication, July 2, 1991).

The contents of *ToP* in the adolescent years are summarized in Table 3 in the same scheme as was used for Table 2. Eleven topics of the top 15 were common to the two time periods, albeit in a slightly different order. The four new topics in recent years had all appeared earlier, but not as the most frequent. As expected (and reported by Beins, 1989), computers in psychology moved up to second place, reflecting rapid advances in this educational technology (Couch & Stoloff, 1989). Bernard C. Beins became editor of a new section of *ToP*, "Computers in Teaching," which first

TABLE 3

Incidence of the Most Frequent Topics Appearing in *Teaching of Psychology* From 1985 Through 1990

	Six-issue time block				
Topic	2/85–4/86	10/86–12/87	2/88–4/89	10/89–12/90	Total
Demonstrations and techniques	14	8	9	16	47
Use of computers	11	7	4	13	35[a]
Student assessment	7	8	9	3	27
Graduate teaching	4	11	7	2	24
Undergraduate research	7	9	5	1	22
Texts and adjuncts	5	2	10	2	19
Writing in psychology classes	1	1	0	17[b]	19[a]
Broad methodology	5	4	3	4	16
Statistics course	6	4	2	4	16
Introductory course	1	4	6	3	14
Teacher assessment	1	3	4	4	12
History and systems course	3	3	1	4	11
Child psychology course	2	3	4	1	10
Personality course	5	2	2	1	10
Career preparation	1	4	2	2	9[a]

[a]Appeared between 1974 and 1984, but not in the top 15.   [b]Special issue.

appeared in October 1989. More student writing is now being integrated into a wide variety of psychology courses. This trend was recognized by the special issue edited by Barbara F. Nodine and published in February 1990, causing that topic to move up into the top 15. The "Psychologists Teach Writing" issue attracted considerable favorable comment from readers. The third newcomer to the top 15 was career preparation, which, like computers in psychology, was within the top 20 in prior years. The fourth new topic was the personality course, which was represented by only eight papers in 1974 through 1984.

Of equal interest are the four topics that dropped out of the top 15. Curriculum issues showed only three articles and undergraduate field work showed none in 1985–1990 (although there was one in 1991). The curriculum topic had been boosted by the special issue of February 1982. The topics teacher training and advisement were pushed down to 16th and 17th respectively. Of the trends apparent in the 1974–1984 period, the topics demonstrations, teacher assessment, and graduate teaching (which were increasing) showed a slight decline; the downward trend of broad methodology continued; all other topics showed no striking change.

Manuscript submissions increased in this period to an average of 188 per year, and the acceptance rate dropped to 39%. Both of these measures showed low variance over the 6-year span. Acceptance (or rejection) rates were not directly comparable between editors because Brewer changed to the APA formula. Since 1984, rejected papers, if revised and resubmitted, are counted as new submissions, and withdrawn papers are counted as rejected.

Circulation continued to be a disappointment. Losses were caused mainly by the inability of Division 2 to add or retain members. Its membership declined by 22% over the period of ToP's history, whereas total circulation dropped only 6%. During 1985 through 1990, membership showed a peculiar pattern of dropping in even-numbered years and rising in the odd years, perhaps as a function of the APA schedule of dropping members after 2 years of nonpayment of dues or of the Division's biennial membership drives. During those 6 years, the largest circulation was 3,212 in 1989 and the lowest was 2,900 in 1986. Yet, ToP is still a medium-size journal, as professional–scientific journals are usually classified, and has a larger circulation than four of the APA journals.

Under the arrangement with Erlbaum, the Division now has an income from publishing ToP. A portion of profits and all royalties from the four reprint handbooks go to the Division. In the first 6 years of this publication agreement, the Division's treasury has been increased by almost $17,000. As a result, the Division's efforts to recognize and encourage the teaching of psychology have been significantly enhanced.

AND ON INTO ADULTHOOD

Charles Brewer was elected to a second 6-year term in 1989, which will take ToP through Volume 23, well past its majority. Growing pains, adolescent trauma, and other inevitable misfortunes are part of its past. They have left no scars. Indeed, they probably have contributed to its strength of character. Of course, there are problems ahead: Division membership and ToP's circulation; the fission of psychology into the academic–scientist versus the practitioner dichotomy. These problems (and others unforeseen) will be met and resolved. The teaching of psychology will change, as it has in the past, but it will not disappear. ToP, too, will change as it has in its brief history. However, it appears to be well prepared to develop into a permanent and fruitful career. The start of the APA's second century also marks the passage of ToP into adult status. May it have full acceptance and support as it continues to mature professionally. As I have said before, that hope depends on and anticipates continued strong leadership and readership.

REFERENCES

American Psychological Association, Division Two. (1974). *Teaching of Psychology Newsletter*, 1965–1974. *JSAS Catalog of Selected Documents in Psychology*, 4, 107–108. (Ms. No. 734)

Beins, B. C. (1989). A survey of computer use reported in *Teaching of Psychology*, 1974–1988. *Teaching of Psychology, 16,* 143–145.

Benjamin, L. T., Jr. (1986). Message from the president. *Teaching of Psychology, 13,* 49–50.

Benjamin, L. T., Jr., Daniel, R. S., & Brewer, C. L. (Eds.). (1985). *Handbook for teaching introductory psychology.* Hillsdale, NJ: Erlbaum.

Brewer, C. L. (1981). A message from the president. *Teaching of Psychology, 8,* 245.

Brewer, C. L. (1984). Message from the new editor. *Teaching of Psychology, 11,* 132.

Brewer, C. L. (1985). Editorial. *Teaching of Psychology, 12,* 3.

Buffardi, L. C., & Nichols, J. A. (1981). Citation impact, acceptance rate, and APA journals. *American Psychologist, 36,* 1453–1456.

Cohen, L. H., & Sechrest, L. B. (1976). The APA evaluation of *Teaching of Psychology. Teaching of Psychology, 3,* 130–134.

Couch, J. V., & Stoloff, M. L. (1989). A national survey of microcomputer use by academic psychologists. *Teaching of Psychology, 16,* 145–147.

Daniel, R. S. (1974). Teaching of psychology has already had a long past. *Teaching of Psychology, 1,* 32–34.

Daniel, R. S. (1977). Birth of a journal: The initiation. *IEEE Transactions on Professional Communication, PC-20,* 82–84.

Daniel, R. S., & Loveland, E. H. (1976). Report on the status of ToP. *Teaching of Psychology, 3,* 129–130.

Harper, R. S. (1978). In memorial, Wilbert Scott Ray: 1901–1977. *Teaching of Psychology, 5,* 112.

Hartley, J., & McKeachie, W. J. (Eds.). (1990). *Teaching psychology: A handbook.* Hillsdale, NJ: Erlbaum.

Heppner, P. P., & Reis, S. D. (1987). Robert S. Daniel: A man dedicated to teaching. *Teaching of Psychology, 14,* 4–10.

Johnson, D. E. (1991). A *Teaching of Psychology* database: 1974–1990. *Teaching of Psychology, 18,* 49–50.

Johnson, M., & Daniel, R. S. (1974). Comprehensive annotated bibliography on the teaching of psychology at the undergraduate level through 1972. *JSAS Catalog of Selected Documents in Psychology, 4,* 108. (Ms. No. 735)

Kasschau, R. (1985). Message from the president. *Teaching of Psychology, 12,* 56.

Korn, J. (1971, December). A journal on the teaching of psychology. *Teaching of Psychology Newsletter,* pp. 6, 12.

Korn, J. (1987). Greetings from the president. *Teaching of Psychology, 14,* 259–260.

Korn, J. (1988). Greetings from the president. *Teaching of Psychology, 15,* 59.

Lamal, P. A. (1984). Interest in PSI across sixteen years. *Teaching of Psychology, 11,* 237–238.

Maas, J. B. (1974). The challenge of teaching's future. *Teaching of Psychology, 1,* 3.

MacLeod, R. B. (1965). The teaching of psychology and the psychology we teach. *American Psychologist, 20,* 344–352.

Norton, F-T. M. (1981). Report of the annual meeting of Division Two. *Teaching of Psychology, 8,* 246–247.

Rigby, M. K. (1987). Message from the president. *Teaching of Psychology, 14,* 57.

Turner, R. H. (1966). Dithering devices in the classroom: How to succeed in shaking up a campus by really trying. *American Psychologist, 21,* 957–963.

Ware, M. E., & Brewer, C. L. (Eds.). (1987). *Handbook for teaching statistics and research methods.* Hillsdale, NJ: Erlbaum.

Ware, M. E., & Millard, R. J. (Eds.). (1986). *Handbook on student development.* Hillsdale, NJ: Erlbaum.

20

PORTRAITS OF A DISCIPLINE: AN EXAMINATION OF INTRODUCTORY PSYCHOLOGY TEXTBOOKS IN AMERICA

WAYNE WEITEN AND RANDALL D. WIGHT

The time has gone by when any one person could hope to write an adequate textbook of psychology. The science has now so many branches, so many methods, so many fields of application, and such an immense mass of data of observation is now on record, that no one person can hope to have the necessary familiarity with the whole.
—An author of an introductory psychology text

If we compare general psychology textbooks of today with those of from ten to twenty years ago we note an undeniable trend toward amelio-

We are indebted to several people who provided helpful information in responding to our survey discussed in the second half of the chapter, including Solomon Diamond for calling attention to Samuel Johnson and Noah Porter, Ernest R. Hilgard for emphasizing George Trumbull Ladd's importance, John A. Popplestone for underscoring John Dewey's readability, and Wilse B. Webb for noting the contributions of Frederick Rauch and James McCosh.

ration of terminology, simplification of style, and popularization of subject matter.

—A reviewer of an introductory text

When were those remarks made? In the 1980s? The 1960s? Perhaps the 1940s? No, the first quote came from the preface to McDougall's *Outline of Psychology*, published in 1923 (p. vii). The second quote came from a 1937 review of Vaughan's (1936) *General Psychology* (Ewert, 1937, p. 173). These comments, which easily could have come from a contemporary author or reviewer, demonstrate that some aspects of the introductory textbook enterprise have not changed much over the years. Of course, many other facets of introductory textbooks have changed dramatically. Our portrait of 100 years of introductory psychology texts shows that they have been characterized by both stability and change.

In a 1962 review of eight introductory texts, Beardslee, Hildum, O'Dowd, and Schwartz noted that "a history of the Introductory Psychology text does not exist" (p. 123). The situation has not changed in the ensuing 30 years. The scholarly literature on introductory texts remains sparse, and the few articles available typically focus on one text or author. We hope our chapter will help to fill this void in psychology's intellectual history. In the first part of the chapter, we sketch a chronological overview of the field's most influential introductory texts. In the second part, we report on a decade-by-decade comparison of leading introductory books.

In both portions of the chapter, we discuss various forces that shaped the evolution of introductory texts. We believe that these forces fall into four broad categories. First, introductory texts have been influenced by developments in psychology, including research progress, shifting theoretical winds, and the field's expansion into new areas of inquiry. Second, because textbooks are tools for teaching, they have been molded by trends in higher education, including innovations in educational techniques, the emergence of new technologies, and changes in the composition of the student population. Third, because psychology does not evolve in a cultural vacuum, we argue that the field's textbooks have been shaped by events in society at large, including wars, economic fluctuations, and changing values. Fourth, introductory texts are influenced by developments in the publishing industry, including advances in publishing technology, competitive pressures in publishing, and the vagaries of market research. With these thoughts in mind, we begin our chronological overview of psychology's most influential introductory texts.

HOW INTRODUCTORY TEXTS EVOLVED: A CHRONOLOGICAL OVERVIEW

In an often-quoted address, James McKeen Cattell (1929) remarked that there were as many psychologists in America before the 1880s as there were snakes in Ireland after St. Patrick. Nevertheless, American psychology had a rich heritage before the advent of William James's (1890) *Principles of Psychology*. To grasp textbook development during the past 100 years, one must examine that development against the backdrop from which it emerged. Hence, we begin with a brief discussion of how introductory psychology texts came to play a role in American higher education before the 1880s (for a more in-depth analysis, see Evans, 1984; Fay, 1939; Roback, 1964). After this discussion, we describe the major trends shaping introductory texts in a series of six overlapping periods, highlighting the field's leading texts along the way.

Psychology as Moral Philosophy (Before the 1880s)

Textbooks intended to introduce college students to the field of psychology emerged gradually out of work in moral philosophy during the 19th century. Yet, the first American textbook to contain a "sprinkling" (Roback, 1964, p. 35) of what one would recognize as psychology—specifically, Aristotelian accounts of perception, memory, and imagination—was William Brattle's *Compendium Logicae*. The book, a logic text written in Latin, was probably circulated in manuscript form as early as 1696 (Fay, 1939).

In 1754, Samuel Johnson, president of King's College (known today as Columbia University), published the first American philosophy textbook, *Elementa Philosophica*, in which he put a personal spin on the thoughts of Locke and Berkeley. Johnson differentiated natural philosophy, the study of material things, from moral philosophy, the study of spiritual things. He further divided normal philosophy into a speculative component, which included the epistemological operations of humans and, by analogy, deity, and a practical component, which included volition and feeling (Evans, 1984). Johnson's entwining of the mental and the spiritual remained a consistent theme in American academia until the late 1800s.

In the 18th century there was a significant increase in the influence of Scottish thought in American colleges. In 1768, while in Scotland, minister John Witherspoon accepted the presidency of the College of New Jersey (known today as Princeton University). On arriving, Witherspoon found a vibrant growth of idealism, no doubt in part a legacy of Johnson and Jonathan Edwards, and set out to eradicate it. Influenced by the work of Thomas Reid, Witherspoon attempted to realign his institution's conceptual framework with Scottish realism. Witherspoon's son-in-law, Samuel Stanhope Smith, left the family's greatest legacy to psychology with the 1812 publication of his *Lectures on Moral and Political Philosophy* (Fay, 1939). Smith's emphasis on inductive methods; consolidation of psychological faculties under the purview of moral philosophy; and extensive, systematic treatment of psychological topics exemplified America's psychology curriculum during the early 19th century.

Although these authors attempted to collect and systematize psychological information for students, primary source material was the classroom staple of the time. That was about to change, however. The period around the turn of the 19th century was a time of upheaval among students on American campuses. After the French Revolution, deism, materialism, atheism, and general irreverence for conservative values were popular among students as they became more familiar with the Jacobins, Rousseau, Voltaire, and Paine. A conservative backlash emphasizing religious fundamentalism and paternalism began to creep into classroom literature (Evans, 1984). The need for "safe" books opened the door to what Fay (1939) called the "era of American textbooks." Chief among these textbook writers was Thomas Cogswell Upham, a professor of mental and moral philosophy at Bowdoin College.

In the early 19th century, moral philosophy embraced much of what would be recognized today as the social sciences, including psychology, anthropology, sociology, and political science. A course in moral philosophy, often taught by the college president, was targeted at students completing their undergraduate degrees. The course usually had two goals: to present a rational framework depicting harmony between the natural and moral worlds and to prepare students, in light of that harmony, to face the responsibilities of civilization (O'Donnell, 1986). Writing for this course, Upham helped to shape general psychology courses as they would eventually appear (Evans, 1984). Upham published *Elements of Intellectual Philosophy* in 1827 and, 4 years later, enlarged it to two volumes and changed its title to *Elements of Mental Philosophy* (1831). The latter step was taken to reflect his combining of intellectual and sensory topics under one rubric. Despite his intellectual debt to Reid, Upham adopted an eclectic approach that embraced Scottish, English, and Continental thought in a consciously evenhanded style (Evans, 1984; Fay, 1939). According to Roback (1964), Upham provided the best textbook discussion of psychology prior to William James's *Principles of Psychology*.

With an influx of Kantian thought in the 1840s, other noteworthy textbooks appeared, including the first to bear the word *psychology* in its title: Frederick Augustus Rauch's (1840) *Psychology, or a View of the Human Soul Including Anthropology*. The next year a second printing appeared posthumously after the first printing sold out (Fay, 1939). Other influential texts included Samuel S. Schmucker's (1842) *Psychology* and Larens P. Hickok's *Rational Psychology* and *Empirical Psychology*, published in 1848 and 1854, respectively (Fay, 1939; Roback, 1964). According to Roback (1964), the first psychology texts to place bibliographic references either at the end of a chapter or at the end of the book were Francis Wayland's (1854) *Intellectual Philosophy* and Joseph Haven's (1857) *Mental Philosophy*. Mark Hopkins's (1878) *An Outline Study of Man* apparently was the first text to make extensive use of diagrams (Ofiesh, 1959).[1] All of these authors had a theological slant, but they appealed to science for help in articulating the relation between theology and nature. The subject matter of psychology, they thought, provided the appropriate context for addressing these issues.

As the Civil War drew to a close, evolution fueled curricular concerns in America's institutions of higher learning, and moral philosophers found themselves in a dilemma. Moral philosophy had spent decades relating the physical, social, and spiritual domains by an empirical, commonsense account of psychological phenomena. The naturalism in Darwin's (1859) *On the Origin of Species* called into question any necessary relation between the physical and moral worlds. As a case against special creation developed, moral philosophers found themselves in the uncomfortable position of having adopted science as a conceptual ally only to find that science was not loyal to their assumptions. When Darwin's *Descent of Man* appeared in 1871, the days of soul as the cornerstone of psychological reasoning were numbered (O'Donnell, 1986). Although the old guard was reluctant to part with its notion of the soul, the stage was set for a transition to a "new" psychology.

Transition to the "New" Psychology (1880s–1890s)

The 1880s and 1890s witnessed an upheaval in textbook presentations of psychology, which increasingly portrayed the field as a natural science relying on laboratory experimentation to advance knowledge. James McCosh's (1886, 1887) two-volume *Psychology* had been depicted as the old tradition's last gasp in American psychology (Roback, 1964). Shortly after the publication of McCosh's second volume, his student, James Mark Baldwin (1889), broke with tradition and produced the popular *Handbook of Psychology*. Josef Brozek (1984) identified David Jayne Hill's (1888) *Elements of Psychology* as a transitional step between the passing and emerging psychologies. Although not experimental, Hill's book was congruent with new conceptions of the discipline.

Perhaps the first American textbook to use the phrase *new psychology* was John Dewey's highly readable *Psychology*, which appeared in 1887 (see Dewey, 1967). Defining psychology as the science of the facts or phenomena of self, Dewey embraced the emerging psychology in part, but he did not view psychology as an independent discipline. Although Baldwin, Hill, and Dewey contributed, the chief architects of the new psychology as portrayed in textbooks were George Trumbull Ladd and William James. Trained as a theologian, Ladd served 10 years as a Congregationalist minister before assuming responsibility for psychology at Yale in 1881. His move to

---

[1]Hopkins was on the cusp of orthodoxy's thaw (Evans, 1984). One of his stellar students, G. Stanley Hall, remembered Hopkins's openness toward differing viewpoints (Hall, 1923), a rarity among college presidents instilling God's own truth.

Yale University prompted a self-directed absorption of psychological literature. Six years of grueling work led to the publication of Ladd's (1887) *Elements of Physiological Psychology*.[2]

Ladd's text was a massive, encyclopedic summary of research that "advocated experimentation and controlled observation" and made a case for "the relevance of science to the study of mental life" (Mills, 1969, p. 103). Drawing heavily from German monographs that he struggled to translate, Ladd provided the first thorough, English-language overview of the new experimental psychology emerging from Germany, seasoned with his "American interpretation of psychological problems" (Mills, 1969, p. 103). In the first volume of the *American Journal of Psychology*, G. Stanley Hall (1887) wrote a favorable review of Ladd's text, predicting that it would become an indispensable handbook of the new psychology.

Although he emphasized laboratory experimentation, Ladd borrowed liberally from the traditions of moral philosophy. As Mills (1974) noted, "no one tried harder to reconcile the old and the new" (p. 299). Unable to shake his theological training, Ladd defined *mind* as an actual substance. This nod to a "real stuff" conception of soul elicited disappointment in some quarters (e.g., Titchener, 1921). Nevertheless, Ladd's *Elements* became "the standard reference work in English on physiological and experimental psychology" (Henmon, 1912, p. 239), and the text went through 10 printings before it was revised by Ladd and Woodworth in 1911.

In 1888, Ladd forwarded a copy of his book to Harvard University's William James (O'Donnell, 1986), who would soon publish a more secular portrait of psychology that would prove even more notable than Ladd's. In the opening sentence of his lengthy (1,393 pages) two-volume *Principles of Psychology*, James (1890) defined psychology as the science of mental life. Perhaps more to the point, in his preface James elaborated psychology's domain as a natural science of "finite individual minds" whose data include thoughts, feelings, their spatial–temporal parameters, and knowledge of these thoughts and feelings.

Thus began what may be the most influential textbook in the history of modern psychology. Some critics argued that the book was too long, too disorganized, and too saturated with James's personality to function as an effective textbook (e.g., G. S. Hall, 1891). However, these flaws were far outweighed by the book's "richness of descriptive detail" and its "boldness of explanation" that communicated to James's readers "in ways unmatched before or since, the *possibilities* of a scientific psychology" (Evans, 1990b, pp. 11, 28). Thus, *Principles* became standard reading for generations of American students.

---

[2]At the time, the expression *physiological psychology* was used interchangeably with *experimental psychology* to refer to the emerging experimental laboratory science of psychology (Hilgard, 1987). Ladd's text contained extensive discussion of biological topics, but it included many other topics as well, and it was not a physiological psychology text in the modern sense.

Although his text contained extensive citations of experiments, James was not particularly intrigued by laboratory work. He thus wrote a scientific, but not an experimental, psychology text. As Evans (1990b) observed, James, like Wundt, was a transitional figure, spanning the shift from 19th-century philosophical psychology to the new psychology. James helped to lay the foundation for psychology as a natural science. According to Taylor (1990), James intended to fuse German, French, and English laboratory work into a scientific tool to replace the metaphysical approach that previously dominated psychology.

The naturalism in James's (1890) *Principles* probably represented America's first secular psychology (Evans, 1991). However, this secularization had its critics. In particular, Ladd (1892) assailed James's failure to acknowledge the full metaphysical complexities of psychological subject matter and his implicit assertion of an unwarranted metaphysical position (Giorgi, 1990). Ladd praised the book's style but complained that to avoid metaphysics, James had identified psychological explanation too closely with brain states. James's alignment of consciousness with brain function constituted a metaphysical assumption and belied any claim of psychology as a natural science. James (1892a) acknowledged the validity of Ladd's argument but wrote that "I wished by treating Psychology *like* a natural science, to help her become one" (p. 146). James went on to argue that although many metaphysical topics were interesting, psychology would do well to limit its concern to events in time and space.

Their later activities suggest that Ladd and James had different feelings about the experience of writing an introductory text. Ladd, who has been called the "great textbook writer" (Mills, 1974), apparently relished the experience, as he revised his *Elements of Physiological Psychology* (Ladd & Woodworth, 1911) and went on to write four other introductory texts: *Outlines of Physiological Psychology* (1890), *Primer of Psychology* (1894a), *Psychology: Descriptive and Explanatory* (1894b), and *Outlines of Descriptive Psychology* (1898).

By contrast, James endured a sometimes torturous 12-year struggle to complete *Principles.* His delays (the book was originally supposed to be finished in 1880) occasioned a number of rancorous exchanges with his publisher, Henry Holt (Benjamin, 1990). Although Holt prevailed on James to prepare an abridged version of *Principles* titled *Psychology, Briefer Course* (1892b), he never convinced James to revise either book, despite the books' great success. Why? Benjamin (1990) argued "that James found the whole introductory psychology textbook business a little unsavory" (p. 4).[3] Support

---

[3]At the 1990 meeting of the Eastern Psychological Association, Ludy T. Benjamin (1990) presented a delightful, tongue-in-cheek account of William James's disillusionment with the enterprise of textbook writing. The narrative of Benjamin's address is contained in the minutes of that meeting (see Benimoff, 1990).

for this view comes from an 1891 letter concerning *Psychology, Briefer Course*, in which James wrote to Holt:

> By adding some twaddle about the senses, by leaving out all polemics and history, all bibliography and experimental details, all metaphysical subtleties and digressions, all quotations, all humor and pathos, all *interest* in short, and by blackening the tops of all the paragraphs, I think I have produced a tome of pedagogic classic which will enrich both you and me, if not the student's mind. (H. James, 1920, p. 314)

Thus, it appears that James became highly cynical about commercial publishing. Although the writing careers of Ladd and James diverged, both used their introductory texts to articulate influential visions of what psychology should be. Later authors of introductory texts tried to emulate this accomplishment, with varying degrees of success, for several decades.

Dueling Systems: The Era of Theoretical Treatises (1890s–1920s)

As the new science of mental life grew, debate increased about the definition, boundaries, and methods of psychology. Schools of thought and the theoretical systems that they spawned played an increasingly important role. Thus, from the 1890s through the 1920s, authors typically used introductory texts to stake out their theoretical views.

Prominent among these early systematists was Edward Bradford Titchener of Cornell University. Working under the assumption that "the main thing in teaching elementary psychology is to give one's pupils a system, a consistent body of doctrine" (Titchener, 1899, p. viii), he waded into the textbook market with *An Outline of Psychology* (Titchener, 1896, 1897, 1899). Titchener considered the descriptive, nonexperiential, unsystematic, mental function psychology of Dewey, Ladd, and James, although an advance from moral philosophy, to be little more than "muddle" (Evans, 1990a). To Titchener, muddle resulted from mindlessly mixing the perspectives of common sense, science, and technology in one's analysis of phenomena. Titchener intended to establish psychology as an experimental science independent of philosophy.

Titchener (1896) defined psychology as the science of mental processes. He supported other psychological endeavors, with Margaret Floy Washburn's animal psychology being a prime example (Evans, 1990a). However, when Titchener wrote the word *psychology* he meant *his* psychology: introspective, experimental, normal adult psychology. Although he viewed child psychology, psychopathology, and social psychology as legitimate enterprises, these applied topics were not covered in his books, which focused solely on "pure" experimental psychology (i.e., sensation, perception, association, memory, motivation, emotion, and thought).

Titchener's *Outline of Psychology*, modeled after a German text pub-

lished in 1893 by a close colleague from his Leipzig days (Külpe, 1893/
1909), reduced all psychological data to direct sense–experience and sought
to examine these data along the attributes of quality, intensity, duration,
extent, and clarity. This tack left no room for functional or volitional
considerations. The 1899 edition of his *Outline* found Titchener more precisely delineating the lines of argument between the camps of structuralism
and functionalism.

A prolific writer, Titchener (1898, 1910, 1915) eventually wrote three
other introductory texts. Although these were well received, his most influential textbook—perhaps the preeminent text of the early 20th century—was his two-volume *Experimental Psychology* (Titchener, 1901–1905).
To be a true science, psychology needed the controlled observations afforded
by the laboratory. Evans (1990a) maintained that these volumes, referred
to as Titchener's "manuals," were the principal catalyst that moved American psychology from philosophical inquiry toward experimental investigation and that they established the experimental component of the American undergraduate psychology curriculum. After writing the manuals,
Titchener decided that further revision of his *Outline* was futile. In 1910,
he produced an entirely new introductory book titled *A Text-book of Psychology*. Less polemical than its forerunner, this book was written expressly
for classroom use, but it was not an "easy" text (Holt, 1911; Watson, 1911).

The most prominent functionalist introduction to psychology was *Psychology: An Introductory Study of the Structure and Function of Human Consciousness* by James Rowland Angell (1904, 1908) of the University of
Chicago. Angell (1936, p. 21) stated in his autobiography that he cut his
"psychological teeth" on Dewey's *Psychology*, which was published in 1890.
On encountering James's *Principles* and contrasting the two texts, Angell
(1936) related being "breathless and excited as one may imagine feeling
after coming through a great storm, or an earthquake" (p. 22). Angell
adopted *Psychology, Briefer Course* as he began to teach but found James's
style cumbersome—hence, the impetus for writing his own text.

The imprint of functionalism was also seen in other widely used introductory texts of the period, such as Walter B. Pillsbury's (1911) *Essentials
of Psychology*. Although Pillsbury's text was apparently the first to define
psychology as the science of human behavior, his "novel definition" did
not appreciably alter his largely functionalist approach (Cameron, 1911).
The functionalist banner was carried into the introductory texts of the
1920s by Harvey Carr's (1925) *Psychology: A Study of Mental Activity*.

Behavioral approaches to psychology were numerous and growing when
Watson's (1913) influential "manifesto" appeared. Watson did not single-
handedly create behaviorism, but he was its most prominent champion
(O'Donnell, 1986). Watson's (1919) *Psychology from the Standpoint of a
Behaviorist* was a thoroughly behavioral introduction to psychology incor-
porating the terminology of Pavlov and the conceptualizations of Bechterev.

However, two decades after the birth of behaviorism, Pillsbury (1932) credited Max Meyer's (1911) *Fundamental Laws of Human Behavior* with solidifying the behavioral perspective. The behavioral tradition was later carried forward by John Frederick Dashiell's (1928) *Fundamentals of Objective Psychology*.

Structuralism, functionalism, and behaviorism were not the only approaches to psychology that generated expositions in introductory textbooks. In her first text, Mary Whiton Calkins (1901) defined psychology as the science of mental events and conscious self, but her second text (Calkins, 1910) focused squarely on her self psychology (Furumoto, 1991). William McDougall (1912, 1923) mounted a spirited defense of his hormic psychology in his texts. In 1911, Robert Mearns Yerkes's *Introduction to Psychology*, a thinly disguised apology for the comparative method (Wight, 1991), was published. Applied psychology received exposure in Hugo Münsterberg's (1915) introductory text.

Shift Toward Theoretical Eclecticism (1920s–1930s)

The theoretical debates among different schools of thought in psychology gradually became less vitriolic. This trend was reflected in introductory texts, which began to manifest a more eclectic character. As Beardslee et al. (1962) put it, there was a "shift from system orientation to cafeteria orientation" (p. 124). Introductory texts with an explicit theoretical slant never disappeared completely, but by the 1930s most of the leading texts were presenting many conflicting viewpoints, which were ostensibly accorded roughly equal importance.

To some extent this shift was more illusory than real; many authors professed more eclecticism than their textbooks revealed. In a review of a text purporting to be eclectic, Geldard (1936) noted that

> as to the matter of indoctrinating the student, it must be recognized that there is more than one way of setting up a metaphysical bias. . . . Textbook writers therefore, unless they seek a stupid catholicity, must indoctrinate. The device, here as elsewhere, is editorial inclusion and exclusion. (p. 694)

Thus, the overt, openly acknowledged theoretical bias of earlier books was replaced with a more subtle, undisclosed bias cloaked in the disguise of eclecticism. The newer texts were genuinely more eclectic than their predecessors, but the change was a matter of degree.

In 1921, Columbia University's Robert Sessions Woodworth published an introductory book that eventually "outsold all other texts so greatly as to be beyond competition" (Boring, 1950, p. 565). Woodworth's *Psychology: A Study of Mental Life* was one of the first introductory texts to display an eclectic bent. A decade earlier, Woodworth had written most of the 1911 revision of Ladd's classic *Elements of Physiological Psychology* (Mills, 1974). In a sense, then, the mantle of the "great textbook writer" was passed from Ladd to Woodworth.

Using a colloquial writing style, Woodworth (1921, 1929, 1934, 1940; Woodworth & Marquis, 1947) authored a wide-ranging survey that enjoyed enormous popularity from the 1920s through the 1940s. Woodworth asserted that he had no allegiance to a specific school of thought, but his portrait of psychology bore the mark of functionalism. In a review of Woodworth's (1934) third edition, McGeoch (1936, p. 179) noted the following:

> Controversial systematic issues are avoided in this panscholasticism, but there runs through it the constant thread of Woodworthian dynamic psychology, presented without argument and often implicitly. There is a functional system here; it is unnamed and loosely knit, but its outlines are clear. (p. 179)

It is hard to say whether the commercial success of Woodworth's text was attributable to its supposed eclecticism, its interesting and conversational writing, or its lucid portrait of the field. Whatever the case, other authors were soon imitating Woodworth's professed eclecticism.

The importance of Woodworth's text and its various revisions cannot be overestimated. According to Winston (1988, 1990), Woodworth's introductory text—and his more advanced *Experimental Psychology* text (Woodworth, 1938; Woodworth & Schlosberg, 1954)—played a crucial role in reshaping psychology's conceptions of experimentation and causality. The notion that an experiment requires the manipulation of an independent variable while other variables are held constant, and the related notion that causal relations can be revealed only through this experimental method, were not always as widely accepted as they are today. Woodworth did not originate this positivist view; it emerged gradually in psychology during the early 20th century (Danziger, 1979, 1985). However, Woodworth contributed mightily to popularizing this view, which he first articulated in the 1934 edition of his introductory text. Woodworth's texts, which were read by generations of students and professors, exerted considerable influence over the directions taken by psychology during the 1940s, 1950s, and 1960s (Winston, 1988, 1990). Although contemporary psychologists increasingly recognize that causal inferences can be derived from nonexperimental, multivariate methods, introductory textbooks continue to present Woodworth's simpler conception of the connection between experimentation and causality (Winston, 1988).

During the 1930s, the shift toward eclecticism was apparent in many introductory texts besides Woodworth's. For example, the strong behavioral orientation in Dashiell's (1928) *Fundamentals of Objective Psychology* was replaced in 1937 with a more evenhanded treatment and a less parochial title, *Fundamentals of General Psychology*. The emerging eclecticism was not greeted with enthusiasm in all quarters. In a review of Dashiell's 1937 edition, Marquis (1938) complained that "whereas the former edition was frankly and courageously polemical in its behavioristic point of view, the new edition has sacrificed consistency to eclecticism" (p. 96).

The shift toward eclecticism, which undermined the notion that texts should be written with a consistent viewpoint, facilitated the rise of the "team approach" to writing introductory texts. Arguing in their preface that one person could no longer stay well informed about the rapidly expanding science of psychology, Edwin G. Boring, Herbert S. Langfeld, and Harry P. Weld (1935) coauthored the field's first team text, *Psychology: A Factual Textbook*. Boring, Langfeld, and Weld, who were at Harvard University, Princeton University, and Cornell University, respectively, served as editors for a team of 16 specialists who wrote initial drafts for chapters in their areas of expertise.

The team approach was later emulated successfully by Clifford Morgan (1956) and a crew of 14 contributors. The team concept might have reached its zenith in 1969, when 38 psychologists contributed to the first edition of *Psychology Today* (CRM Books, 1969), although one might also cite 1977, which saw the publication of a 9-author text (Weiner et al., 1977) and a 10-author text (Mussen et al., 1977). Contemporary professors often complain that "committee-authored texts" suffer from uneven coverage, conceptual discord, and stylistic inconsistency. However, reviews of the Boring et al. (1935) text suggested that the editors successfully infused the specialists' chapters with a reasonably uniform writing style and conceptual orientation (e.g., Geldard, 1936).

In their preface, Boring et al. (1935) asserted that the "facts of psychology should be presented to the young student of psychology in terms free from the bias of metaphysical presuppositions or of psychological systems" (p. vii). Although they formally embraced the eclectic approach, two of the three editors and many of the contributors had been trained in the Titchenerian tradition, and reviewers noted that the book reflected this bias toward "pure" psychology (e.g., Bentley, 1948; Dimmick, 1940; Geldard, 1936; Hunter, 1935).

Boring, Langfeld, and Weld issued new editions of their successful text in 1939 and 1948. Both editions involved substantial revisions that merited new titles (Bentley, 1948; Webb, 1991). Citing pedagogic reasons, the authors rearranged the order of topics in their second edition, moving social psychology and personality to the front of the book and sensation to the back. In the third edition, the order of topics was shuffled again and the book doubled in size, taking on an encyclopedic character. The Boring et al. text was a demanding, no-nonsense introduction to psychology that generally did not cater to students' interests and preferences (Hunter, 1939). Although Boring et al. remained loyal to this approach through all three editions, many competing books soon became student-oriented, thanks to the success of Ruch's (1937) *Psychology and Life*.

Rise of Student-Oriented Texts (1930s–1940s)

The pragmatism engendered by the Great Depression, the gradual emergence of applied psychology, and the influx of more career-oriented middle-class students into higher education probably set the stage for the rise of student-oriented introductory texts. The first influential text of this genre was *Psychology and Life* by Floyd L. Ruch (1937) of the University of Southern California. The essence of Ruch's (1937) approach is summarized in the preface to his first edition:

> I do not know exactly how many textbooks in elementary psychology have been written in the past thirty-five years. These books were written in loyalty to something. All of them were dedicated to psychology: some to psychology as a science; some to psychology as an exact science; others to the author's system, or to the author's favorite professor's system. I have not seen a textbook of elementary psychology written under a vow of loyalty to the student. . . . I am not condemning these practices. I have at times even praised them. I should merely like to indicate that this textbook in elementary psychology has, rightly or wrongly, been differently conceived. (p. v)

How did Ruch make his book more student oriented than its contemporaries? To accomplish this goal he (a) expanded coverage of topics that students found interesting and compressed coverage of less popular topics; (b) transposed the traditional order of topics by moving the more accessible material to the front; (c) used an "easy personal style" of writing and a "slightly dramatized method of presenting facts" (Buel, 1938, p. 92); (d) introduced a personal adjustment slant that emphasized the application of research and theory to students' everyday lives; and (e) increased the number and prominence of photographs to create an attractive look.

In a review of Ruch's first edition, Buel (1938) enthusiastically concluded that "from the student's point of view, it is probably the most interesting and readable textbook that has been offered in psychology" (p. 92). Some of the features of Ruch's text (e.g., the personal writing style and the rearranged topical organization) had been seen before, but no previous author had put so many student-oriented features together in one book.

Like other introductory texts of the 1930s, Ruch's book was theoretically eclectic, but in other ways it was a radical departure from existing norms. He was the first author to discuss (in his preface) the use of market research to ascertain students' and professors' topical preferences. Breaking with tradition, he completely eliminated coverage of the nervous system.

Unlike his contemporaries, Ruch was not bashful about providing students with practical advice, and he tackled a host of topics that others had been loath to touch, including communism, "crushes," friendship, homosexuality, strikes, marital strife, and study skills.

Ruch's bold experiment drew mixed reactions. Many professors— enough to make the book a great commercial success—responded favorably to the new approach, but many others disliked the notion of catering to students' tastes. In an influential article on the introductory course, Wolfle (1942) argued that

> the mere fact that students find a topic interesting is never justification for including it in the course. . . . Selecting course material to accord with student interest invites the charge that one is "popularizing" the course. By popularizing, the critic usually means cheapening. (p. 695)

In the preface to his second edition, Ruch (1941) acknowledged that the "consensus has been that the writer succeeded rather better in meeting the interests of the students than in developing a uniformly high level of critical scientific thinking" (p. vi). To increase the second edition's scientific rigor without sacrificing student interest, he made a number of concessions to tradition (Buel, 1942). Among other things, he abandoned elaborate photo essays, added two chapters on the brain and nervous system, moved toward a more conventional topical sequence, and bolstered coverage of traditional topics. However, the second edition still emphasized appealing topics, personal adjustment, and friendly writing.

These emphases have been carried through 11 more editions of *Psychology and Life* by Ruch (1948, 1953, 1958, 1963a, 1967a) and his eventual successor, Philip G. Zimbardo of Stanford University (Ruch & Zimbardo, 1971; Zimbardo & Ruch, 1975; Zimbardo, 1979, 1985, 1988, 1992). Zimbardo has maintained Ruch's commitment to engaging writing, intriguing topical coverage, and the application of research and theory to social problems and everyday life while gradually making the book more rigorous and encyclopedic. His revisions have earned high marks from reviewers (e.g., Allen, 1980; Campbell, 1976; Cone, 1976; Heatherington, 1986; Sexton, 1977), and *Psychology and Life* has retained its place among the most widely used introductory books for more than 50 years, a remarkable tribute to Ruch's vision of what an introductory text should be.

Ruch's (1937) first edition sparked a dramatic transformation of introductory psychology texts. Most authors felt compelled to make their texts at least somewhat student oriented. Even the authors of established, traditional texts such as Boring, Langfeld, and Weld (1939) and Woodworth (1940) scrambled to incorporate applied topics to make their books more inviting. The most successful new text of the 1940s, *Psychology: The Fundamentals of Human Adjustment* by Norman L. Munn (1946) of Bowdoin College, also aspired to this goal. Although less student oriented than Ruch,

Munn (1946) encouraged the reader to "look upon this as a book about yourself" (p. xi). Like Ruch, Munn wrote an eclectic book that added coverage of personal adjustment issues and relegated sensation and perception to the back of the book. His widely adopted text went through numerous revisions over a 40-year period that eventually saw a change in title, the addition of collaborators, and movement to a new publisher (Munn, 1951, 1956, 1961, 1966; Munn, Fernald, & Fernald, 1969, 1972; Fernald & Fernald, 1978, 1985). The approach of Ruch and Munn gradually became the dominant model for introductory texts. Even research-oriented texts began to borrow some of their strategies for enticing students' interest.

Advent of Encyclopedic Texts (1950s–1960s)

Subsequent trends in introductory texts were more subtle than the major shift triggered by Ruch. The next discernible trend was a move toward more encyclopedic texts. The 1950s and 1960s were a period of expansion, prosperity, and boundless optimism for higher education. Academicians' contributions to the war effort inspired a new faith in the value of scientific research, which colleges embraced with increased vigor. Psychology departments sought to obtain grants, foster research, win recognition, and enhance their prestige. In this climate, psychological research expanded at a rapid pace. Consequently, the authors of many introductory texts began to compete for respect and adoptions by covering more research on more topics in more detail. As a result, the leading texts increased in words, pages, and references cited.

This metamorphosis was gradual and unannounced. Whereas Ruch had proudly declared his resolve to write a new type of text, no one openly proclaimed a decision to make introductory texts more comprehensive and encyclopedic; it just happened. Thus, it is difficult to pinpoint one book that launched the trend toward encyclopedic texts. However, two prominent texts, first published in the 1950s, clearly contributed: *Introduction to Psychology* by Hilgard (1953, 1957) and *Elements of Psychology* by Krech and Crutchfield (1958).

Ernest R. Hilgard (Stanford University), who was thanked for "many helpful criticisms and suggestions" in the preface to Ruch's (1937, p. ix) first edition, set out to write an eclectic, comprehensive text that would appeal to students and professors. According to Finger (1954), Hilgard tried to achieve these seemingly incompatible goals by covering topics of current interest to psychologists while accommodating students' desires for personal insights. The first edition received largely favorable reviews (e.g., Finger, 1954; Krech, 1954), but feedback from adopters led Hilgard (1957) to tilt the balance of the second edition back toward professors. He added new chapters on physiology, sensation, and statistics and a new feature: separate "critical discussion" sections that addressed controversial theoretical issues in some detail.

Hilgard apparently was the first author to discuss the number and recency of his references in his preface, a practice that many others soon copied. Hilgard's (1957) second edition grew to approximately 300,000 words and more than 900 references (roughly double the number found in a typical 1940s text). In the third edition (Hilgard, 1962), the number of references increased to around 1,500 and reviewers noted that "the sheer quantity of material in this volume is staggering" (Bare & Guthrie, 1963, p. 184). Later editions (Hilgard & Atkinson, 1967; Hilgard, Atkinson, & Atkinson, 1971, 1975; Atkinson, Atkinson, & Hilgard, 1979, 1983; Atkinson, Atkinson, Smith, & Hilgard, 1987; Atkinson, Atkinson, Smith, & Bem, 1990) continued to enjoy a reputation for "scholarly sophistication," "extensive coverage," and "plain language" (Pfeiffer, 1980, p. 119) and the text became "one of the most widely used books in the history of college publishing" (Atkinson et al., 1990, p. v).

The largest and most encyclopedic introductory text published in the 1950s probably was *Elements of Psychology* by David Krech and Richard S. Crutchfield (1958) of the University of California. It had 25 chapters, 736 pages, and roughly 340,000 words. The second edition (Krech, Crutchfield, & Livson, 1969) grew to nearly 900 pages and 50 chapters, and the fourth edition (Krech, Crutchfield, Livson, Wilson, & Parducci, 1982) topped 400,000 words (Weiten, 1988).

Krech and Crutchfield's (1958) first edition contained innovative "boxes" that had a dramatic impact on later books. Their 169 boxes provided relatively detailed discussions of empirical research on specific topics. The idea of highlighting in-depth digressions was not entirely new; Hilgard (1957) had introduced a similar feature a year earlier. However, Krech and Crutchfield's boxes garnered more attention and accolades from reviewers (e.g., Archer, 1959; Bartlett, 1959), and boxes eventually became a staple of introductory texts in the 1970s and 1980s. Boxes are still common, although they have been criticized as disruptive (e.g., Thomas, 1984), and their use appears to be declining.

The trend toward encyclopedic texts was apparent in many other widely used books of the 1950s and 1960s. In 1956, Clifford T. Morgan wrote a hefty 676-page overview of the field that grew to 816 pages in its third edition (Morgan & King, 1966). Gregory A. Kimble (1956) published a more modest 400-page survey of the field, but his second and third editions (Kimble & Garmezy, 1963, 1968) mushroomed to 655 and 756 pages, respectively. The 1960s also brought the publication of lengthy, comprehensive first editions by Kendler (1963), McKeachie and Doyle (1966), and Kagan and Havemann (1968). Already established books also swelled dramatically during this period. For example, Ruch's text grew from 492 pages in 1953 to 758 pages in 1967, and Munn's grew from 497 pages in 1946 to 812 pages in 1961.

Not all influential texts of the 1960s were encyclopedic. For instance, Donald O. Hebb's (1958, 1966) compact text contained 256 pages in the first edition and 353 pages in the second. A throwback to the systematic theoretical treatises of earlier decades, Hebb's *Textbook of Psychology* was widely lauded (Bartlett, 1959; McKenna, 1967) but less widely used.

The emergence of encyclopedic texts eventually stimulated a counterbalancing trend: the publication of abridged versions of lengthy books. Condensed introductory texts had a rich ancestry, as both Ladd (1890) and James (1892b) published brief versions of their classic books, but abridged editions had not been seen for many decades. Munn (1962) and Ruch (1963b) were the first to release condensed editions in the 1960s. Kendler and Kendler (1971), McKeachie and Doyle (1972), and Morgan (1974) eventually followed suit. Even the size of these abridged editions underscored the modern trend toward encyclopedic texts. For instance, Munn's (1962) "brief" edition contained 588 pages and Ruch's (1967b) had 606. Nevertheless, condensed editions clearly filled a need for some professors and became commonplace by the 1980s.

Era of Artwork, Pedagogy, and Homogenization (1970s–1980s)

Eclectic, encyclopedic, student-oriented books continued to prevail during the 1970s and 1980s, but efforts to increase student appeal led to some basic changes. The most prominent changes were the growth of elaborate illustration programs and increased reliance on pedagogical devices.

The late 1960s and early 1970s were a period of turmoil on many college campuses, as students protested against racial discrimination and the Vietnam War. Emboldened by their success in the political arena, students began to demand more self-determination in course selection, more "relevance" in the curriculum, and more influence (through course ratings) on evaluations of their professors. As general education requirements were reduced, many academic departments were forced to compete for enrollments. In response to these pressures, many professors worked to make their courses more appealing for students. One result of this effort was the need for slick, flashy, magazinelike textbooks.

This need was filled in 1969 with the arrival of *Psychology Today* (CRM Books, 1969), a visually stunning text from a publisher that had recently launched a general circulation magazine of the same name. Reasoning that college students would respond to the snazzy graphics that made the magazine a success, CRM modeled its text after its magazine. With the assistance of James V. McConnell, a team of editors and writers attempted to weld the divergent contributions of 38 consultants into a coherent overview of the field (McConnell, 1978). Reviewers characterized the first edition as uneven, unbalanced, and poorly integrated (Brown et al., 1971), but these complaints did not impede the book's acceptance. It was a huge commercial success, selling 186,000 copies the year it was released (Kadushin, 1979).[4]

Psychology Today (CRM Books, 1969, 1972; CRM/Random House, 1975, 1979) was far more heavily illustrated than its competitors, brashly decorative, and four colors throughout. The book's uneven discourse was smoothed out to some extent in later editions (Kasschau & Camp, 1976; Walls, 1980). After the fourth edition, the text was ostensibly taken over by a conventional author team (Bootzin, Loftus, Zajonc, & Hall, 1983; Bootzin, Bower, Zajonc, & Hall, 1986; Bootzin, Bower, Hall, & Crocker, 1991). Although some critics questioned the educational value of its lavish illustration program (e.g., Abma, 1974), *Psychology Today* snared many adoptions, and competing publishers eventually embraced elaborate four-color illustration programs, which became the norm for introductory texts by the mid-1980s.

Innovative graphics were not *Psychology Today*'s only claim to fame; it was higher education's first "managed" text—conceived, designed, and composed by a team of editors and professional writers. Many professors are used as consultants, but the book's contents are closely guided by market research and carefully controlled by the publishing house (Kadushin, 1979). Some of the academic consultants may be listed as authors, but they do not actually write the book and they do not have an author's normal control over its content. Managed texts had long been common in elementary and secondary education, but they were new to higher education.

The managed text created a furor. Professors raised concerns about popularization and plagiarism by professional writers and they bemoaned their loss of control over the content of the discipline's texts (see Fischer & Lazerson, 1977; Kadushin, 1979; McMahon, 1977; P. W. Robinson & Higbee, 1978). Given the success of *Psychology Today*, many academicians feared that managed books would come to dominate the introductory course, but their fears proved unfounded. The weaknesses of the managed text— uneven coverage, lack of an author's "voice," mediocre scholarship, and bland mimicry of other books—gradually became apparent, and later managed texts did not duplicate the success of *Psychology Today* (Kadushin, 1979; McMahon, 1977). The 1980s saw some publishers continue to use the managed text model, but it did not achieve the market dominance that academicians once feared.

In addition to flashy graphics, the 1970s brought increased use of pedagogical aids. This trend was probably attributable to growing concern about the decline of students' academic skills. The 1960s and 1970s were

---

[4]Although sales of this magnitude were not unprecedented, they were remarkably high. Introductory psychology texts that sell more than 40,000 copies in their first year are considered to be commercially successful.

a time of rapid expansion for higher education. The nation's undergraduate population tripled between 1960 and 1980, as community colleges attracted greater numbers. This growth brought more underprepared students into classrooms, along with more "nontraditional" students whose family and work responsibilities strained their commitment to diligent study. As professors increasingly complained about students' mediocre study skills and divided commitments, a new emphasis was placed on pedagogy. Although several learning aids (e.g., chapter summaries, chapter outlines, and glossaries) were used in many popular books by the 1960s, the 1970s brought a host of new pedagogical devices.

The increased emphasis on pedagogy was apparent in many texts, but James V. McConnell's (University of Michigan) *Understanding Human Behavior* in 1974 probably led the way. In the preface to his first edition, McConnell (1974) noted that he "realized that none of the major texts available were actually written in collaboration with the students," so he set out to write a text "for, about, and with considerable help from students themselves" (p. iii). He obtained this assistance by asking his students to critique chapter drafts. They responded with more than 25,000 individual comments, thus providing McConnell with a rich lode of feedback that helped him to assemble an interesting, student-oriented text (Caffrey, 1978; Kasschau, 1974).

McConnell's (1974, 1977, 1980, 1983, 1986, 1989) eclectic, encyclopedic text introduced three innovative pedagogical devices: a page-by-page running glossary, a pronunciation guide for technical terms, and fictional anecdotes to engage interest. McConnell also catered to students' preferences by doing away with the extensive citations and references that had become dense and voluminous in most competing books.

Other introductory texts also tried to "up the ante" for pedagogical aids during the 1970s. For example, Bourne and Ekstrand (1973) used cartoons and boxed-off newspaper clippings on psychological issues to spark students' interest. Several authors began to insert study-guide exercises (fill-in-the-blank, matching, multiple-choice questions, etc.) into the texts themselves (e.g., Coon, 1977; Davidoff, 1976; Vernon, 1974). The 1970s also brought the first use of chapter learning objectives (e.g., Lefton, 1979) and the first book (Coon, 1977) organized around F. P. Robinson's (1970) SQ3R study method. The increased emphasis on pedagogy was reflected in the book reviews of the period, as reviewers in *Contemporary Psychology* started to include charts comparing introductory texts' learning aids (e.g., Brown et al., 1971; Cone, 1976; Kasschau, 1973, 1977). During the 1970s, extensive pedagogical aids were seen mostly in texts designed for the "lower level" of the introductory market, but many of these learning aids began to creep into "upper-level" texts in the 1980s.

This new emphasis on pedagogy also spawned extensive discussions of introductory texts' readability, usually as measured by the formula developed by Flesch (1948, 1951). Although an article comparing popular texts' readability was published as early as 1954 (Ogdon, 1954), the 1970s brought a flurry of such articles (Gillen, 1973, 1975; Gillen, Kendall, & Finch, 1977; Quereshi & Sackett, 1977; Quereshi & Zulli, 1975), and reviewers began reporting Flesch readability (and human interest) estimates (e.g., Abma, 1974; Brown et al., 1971; Cone, 1976; Kasschau, 1973, 1977). The attention devoted to readability measures incited a furor, as many psychologists (Chatman & Goetz, 1985; Croll & Moskaluk, 1977; Griesinger & Klene, 1984; Landrigan & Palladino, 1974) and reading researchers (Bruce, Rubin, & Starr, 1981; Lange, 1982; Maxwell, 1978) raised doubts about the validity and value of Flesch estimates. This criticism presumably contributed to the diminished interest in readability estimates in the 1980s.

Authors' and publishers' commitment to pedagogy also fueled increased competition to provide professors and students with more and more elaborate ancillary packages. During the 1960s, publishers typically furnished adopters with an instructor's manual, test bank, slides, and transparencies. However, in the 1970s and 1980s, publishers started giving away larger instructor's manuals, extra test banks, more slides and transparencies, adopter newsletters, booklets designed to improve students' critical thinking or study skills, computerized test banks and grade books, computerized study guides, computer simulations, reference databases on computer diskettes, audiotapes, films, videotapes, video laser disks, telephone test preparation, educational board games, and replicas of *Time* magazine and the *New York Times* that contained reprints of psychology-related articles. Whether one viewed these ancillaries as valuable teaching and learning tools or superfluous contrivances, they clearly drove up the prices of introductory texts (Griggs & Jackson, 1989; Sommer, Estabrook, & Horobin, 1988).

As competitive pressures led publishers to underwrite expensive graphics and photograph programs, four-color production, elaborate advertising brochures, and a growing plethora of free ancillaries, the investment required to produce an introductory text skyrocketed. As the financial stakes climbed, publishers sought to reduce the risk of a commercially unsuccessful book. Hence, editors turned more and more to market research, surveying professors about their topical priorities, pedagogical preferences, and needs for ancillaries. With their profits squeezed by the acceleration of used-book sales, publishers seemed to become more conservative about deviating from the modal preferences uncovered in their research. The unfortunate result was a growing homogenization of introductory texts (see Farnsworth, 1979; Gould, 1988).[5]

---

[5]The increased consolidation of the textbook publishing industry also might have contributed to this growing homogenization. The 1980s saw a rash of mergers in the industry, which left fewer and fewer independent companies. Many midsize American publishers were absorbed into giant, international conglomerates (Rudman, 1990). Midway through this consolidation, Apple (1985) reported that the 10 largest textbook companies controlled 75% of all sales (the percentage is probably higher today). Some of the newly formed conglomerates found themselves with 10 or more introductory psychology texts, which often shared editors, designers, art programs, and ancillaries.

Concern about the growing similarity of introductory texts was voiced as early as 1962 (Beardslee et al., 1962), but the late 1970s and early 1980s brought complaints (e.g., Fretz, 1979; Jacobs, 1984; Popplestone, 1978; Thomas, 1984). In one review, Thomas (1984) asked why anyone would bother to write yet another introductory text, given that "there appear to be more than an adequate number of texts from which to choose, and the difference between texts often does not exceed the famous jnd (just noticeable difference)" (p. 629). In another review, Jacobs (1984) chided publishers for making their texts too similar, arguing that "there is no compelling reason for all of our introductory books to be spin-offs of one or two popular texts. Trying something different in approach, emphasis, or coverage would enrich the choices available to the instructors and students" (p. 467). Although it is easy to criticize authors and publishers for their reluctance to try something different, they are responding to the realities of the marketplace. Most texts that deviated substantially from the norm in the 1970s and 1980s were commercial failures. For instance, Gazzaniga (1973), Lazarus (1974), Brown and Herrnstein (1975), Malott and Whaley (1976), Levin (1978), Pollio (1981), and Doyle (1987) all wrote refreshingly different texts that did not win enough adoptions to merit a second edition. Thus, teachers share responsibility for the growing homogenization of introductory texts.

Homogeneity is a subjective concept, and it would be an oversimplification to write off the successful texts of recent years as nothing more than clones of one another. Many excellent new texts were published in the 1980s and some of them broke new ground. For example, Henry Gleitman's (1981) "virtuoso explanations of complex ideas" (T. H. Carr, 1982, p. 356) allowed him to take the level of discourse in introductory texts to a new high while returning to traditional topical coverage more reminiscent of the 1940s than the 1980s. One reviewer (Gerow, 1981) asserted that "Gleitman's effort is as close to a truly new and scholarly treatment of general psychology as we have seen in many years" (p. 189). David G. Myers (1986) broke new ground with a superb illustration program that was more didactic than decorative and a witty, elegant writing style that was widely lauded (Griggs, 1990).

The 1980s also saw a reemergence of women as authors of leading introductory texts. After Mary Calkins's (1901, 1910) time, female authors of successful introductory texts were rare and virtually all of them worked with male collaborators. We can only speculate as to why female authors were conspicuous by their absence for so many years. Surely, there were female psychologists who were willing and qualified to write their own texts. Perhaps publishers felt that texts had to have at least one male author to be taken seriously. In any case, the 1980s brought three highly successful new texts written exclusively by women. Camille B. Wortman and Elizabeth F. Loftus (1981) wrote a lean, no-nonsense book that bucked the widespread tendency to load introductory texts with gimmicks and titillating topics; Diane E. Papalia and Sally W. Olds (1985) published a well-written, comprehensive portrait of psychology; and Carole Wade and Carol Tavris (1987) contributed a lively, engaging, concise text that did a superb job of modeling critical thinking for students.

In addition to the aforementioned books, the 1980s brought well-received new texts from Darley, Glucksberg, Kamin, and Kinchla (1981); Rathus (1981); Lahey (1983); Roediger, Rushton, Capaldi, and Paris (1984); Carlson (1984); Santrock (1986); Benjamin, Hopkins, and Nation (1987); and Bernstein, Roy, Wickens, and Srull (1988). Thus, psychology entered the 1990s with an excellent collection of introductory textbooks.

HOW INTRODUCTORY TEXTS EVOLVED: EMPIRICAL COMPARISONS

Despite the dearth of scholarly literature on the history of introductory psychology texts, individuals interested in their evolution have a unique resource available—the books themselves—which, unlike people or events from the past, remain preserved exactly as they were—on library bookshelves. Hence, we set out to identify a representative sample of leading texts from the past 100 years and to analyze how they have changed across the decades. In this section, we report on what we learned from this comparative analysis.

The Sample of Textbooks

Our intent was to scrutinize a handful of the most widely respected introductory texts from each decade between 1890 and 1990 and then make comparisons across decades. We solicited advice from the fellows ($n = 92$) of Division 26 (History of Psychology) of the American Psychological Association and the surviving past-presidents ($n = 30$) of Division 2 (Teaching of Psychology). Both groups responded to the same questionnaire, which asked them to nominate up to three leading texts from each decade. The definition of "leading" was left to the respondents, who were asked to make nominations only for those decades about which they felt knowledgeable.

Our survey was returned by 31 respondents, many of whom invested considerable time and effort to provide a total of 529 nominations. The 25% return rate seems reasonable in light of the substantial work required to complete the survey; also, some of our prospective respondents indicated that they did not feel sufficiently well informed to participate. The mean number of books nominated for each decade was 16.27. Many books were nominated in more than one decade. For example, Woodworth's *Psychology* was nominated from the 1920s through the 1950s. The most frequently nominated book for each decade is identified in Table 1 by a superscript *a*.

After reviewing our data, we decided to select five texts from the 1890s and four texts from each subsequent decade for our comparative analysis. Our selections, listed in Table 1, were strongly guided by the number of nominations the books received. However, for some decades, we had to exercise some judgment in selecting the third or fourth text from several books that received roughly equal support. When two or more editions of a selected book were published in a decade, the specific edition chosen was largely determined by the edition we could find.

Given our small sample size and the discretion we exercised in making some selections, Table 1 should not be viewed as a definitive list of the most successful or widely respected introductory texts from each decade (compiling such a list was not our goal). However, we are confident that the books in Table 1 constitute a reasonably representative sample of the leading texts from each decade. All of the quantitative analyses to be discussed are based on this sample.

Measurement of Text Variables

Our comparative analysis focused on objective features of the texts, in a manner similar to Weiten's (1988) analysis of 43 contemporary introductory texts. The Appendix lists the text variables that we examined and the details of their measurement. We tried to assess a diverse array of variables, including structural parameters (e.g., number of chapters), production qualities (e.g., number of illustrations), pedagogical strategies (e.g., number of learning aids), and substantive matters (e.g., topical coverage). Some of these variables involved easily determined values that could be ascertained exactly (e.g., the number of pages in a book), but most of them involved more complicated estimates based on systematic sampling from each book (e.g., manuscript length in words).

After all assessments of individual books were completed, the data for the books in each decade were averaged. We used these means to assess trends over time. The summary of our findings consists of six sections that focus on trends in topical coverage, topical organization, book size, illustration programs, pedagogical aids, and citations and references.

Topical Coverage

The percentage of coverage devoted to each of the 15 topical areas listed in the Appendix is charted by decade in Table 2. Although Matarazzo (1987) argued that the core subject matter of introductory texts has remained much the same since the late 19th century, our data indicate that topical coverage has changed considerably over the years. In the early

TABLE 1
List of Texts Examined for the Descriptive Analysis Grouped by Decade

1890s	1900s	1910s	1920s	1930s
Ladd (1887)	James (1890)	Calkins (1910)	Woodworth (1921)[a]	Woodworth (1934)
Dewey (1890)	James (1892b)	Titchener (1910)[a]	Pillsbury (1922)	Boring, Langfeld, & Weld (1935)
James (1890)[a]	Titchener (1899)[a]	Ladd & Woodworth (1911)	McDougall (1923)	Dashiell (1937)[a]
James (1892b)	Angell (1908)[a]	Watson (1919)	Carr (1925)	Ruch (1937)
Titchener (1896)				

1940s	1950s	1960s	1970s	1980s
Ruch (1941)	Ruch (1953)[a]	Krech & Crutchfield (1958)	Hilgard, Atkinson, & Atkinson (1975)[a]	Gleitman (1986)[a]
Munn (1946)	Morgan (1956)	Hilgard (1962)[a]	CRM/Random House (1975)	McConnell (1986)
Woodworth & Marquis (1947)	Munn (1956)[a]	Ruch (1963a)	Zimbardo & Ruch (1975)	Myers (1986)
Boring, Langfeld, & Weld (1948)[a]	Hilgard (1957)	Morgan & King (1966)	Bourne & Ekstrand (1976)	Darley, Glucksberg, & Kinchla (1988)

Note. Complete citations for each book can be found in the references.
[a]The most frequently nominated book for each decade (two books tied in some decades).

TABLE 2

Percentages of Topical Allocations Grouped by Decade

Topic	1890s	1900s	1910s	1920s	1930s	1940s	1950s	1960s	1970s	1980s
Introduction/ methods	6	8	11	6	14	7	8	10	9	8
Biological bases	11	6	17	5	7	7	7	7	8	7
Sensation/ perception	21	21	25	15	22	20	13	14	8	10
Aspects of consciousness	3	4	0	1	1	0	0	0	6	4
Learning/ conditioning	6	9	5	9	6	9	7	9	6	5
Memory	4	5	5	9	1	3	5	2	4	5
Language/ thought	16	18	11	15	10	4	6	7	5	7
Intelligence/ testing	0	0	0	3	5	7	7	7	4	6
Motivation/ emotion	16	19	12	16	16	15	11	10	10	9
Developmental psychology	2	0	0	6	4	7	5	7	6	13
Personality	2	3	2	5	7	6	5	6	7	5
Adjustment	0	0	0	0	1	6	5	3	1	2
Psychopathology/ psychotherapy	0	0	1	0	0	0	4	5	15	10
Social psychology	0	0	1	0	3	2	7	8	11	9
Other	13	7	10	10	3	7	9	5	0	0

decades, the dominant subjects were biological bases of behavior, sensation/ perception, language/thought, and motivation/emotion. For example, these four topics accounted for 64% of the coverage in our 1890s sample of books. By contrast, contemporary texts divide their coverage more evenly among more topics. Among the leading topics are several that received little or no coverage in the early books, such as developmental psychology, social psychology, and psychopathology/psychotherapy. In terms of trends over time, the topics basically fall into four groups: (a) those that have declined gradually since the early days, (b) those that have remained relatively stable, (c) those that have attracted increasing attention, and (d) those that have attracted sporadic interest.

Topics that have declined markedly include sensation/perception, language/thought, and motivation/emotion. In the 1980s, these subjects received about half as much coverage as they received in the 1890s. These decreases are probably attributable to contemporary texts dividing their coverage among more areas rather than to declining interest in the older topics. This interpretation is supported by the fact that sensation/perception and motivation/emotion still ranked among the top five most heavily covered topics in the 1980s. Although today's interest in language and thought is often attributed to the so-called cognitive revolution in the 1950s and 1960s, these subjects actually have a long history of ample coverage. However, the focus of this coverage has shifted from attention, imagination, concept formation, and reasoning toward psycholinguistics, problem solving, and decision making.

Topics that have received relatively stable coverage over the past 100 years (albeit with some fluctuation from decade to decade) include history, methods, and introductory material; biological bases of behavior; learning; memory; and personality. The space devoted to each of these areas has generally been between 5% and 9% throughout the past century.

Topics that have attracted increased attention over the years include development, psychological testing/intelligence, psychopathology/psychotherapy, and social psychology. Development emerged as a fairly standard topic in the 1920s, testing in the 1930s, social psychology in the 1950s, and psychopathology/psychotherapy in the 1960s. In our 1980s sample, these topics accounted for 38% of the coverage, compared with less than 3% before the 1920s.

Subjects that have attracted sporadic interest include aspects of consciousness, adjustment, and various topics in the "other" category. James and other early authors discussed the nature of consciousness, but coverage of consciousness dwindled to virtually nothing for the next six decades. The topic surfaced again in the 1970s and 1980s, but the focus shifted from the nature of consciousness to sleep, dreams, and the effects of drugs, hypnosis, and meditation. Coverage of adjustment was begun by Ruch (1937) and Munn (1946) and peaked in the 1940s, when even more traditional texts (e.g., Boring, Langfeld, & Weld, 1948; Woodworth & Marquis, 1947) added chapters on frustration, conflict, defense mechanisms, and maladjustment. In recent years, coverage of adjustment has dwindled and the focus has shifted to stress, coping, and health psychology.

The "other" category was included in our analysis to avoid forcing older topics into a modern organizational scheme. What kinds of topics showed up in this category? There was extensive coverage of will–volition and the mind–body question in early decades. Animal behavior surfaced as an independent topic in the 1920s and again in the 1950s. Finally, a hodgepodge of applied psychology topics received sporadic attention over the years, including the psychology of work, vocational development, and study skills. These topics continue to appear in some contemporary texts, but they were not found in our 1970s and 1980s samples.

Several forces appear to have influenced the reshaping of topical coverage. The most obvious consideration is that psychology has expanded its domain of interest, and textbooks reflect this accretion of topics and the resultant diminution of traditional coverage. For example, in an article on the evolution of introductory texts between 1912 and 1922, Kantor (1922) commented on how the field's expansion led to new chapters on behavior, language, learning, and intelligence. Nearly 50 years later, MacLeod (1971) surveyed the history of psychology teaching and noted that "psychology, without having discarded its classic problems, has been reaching out into a multitude of fields, each of which involves a broadening of its subject matter" (p. 246).

Introductory texts' metamorphosis from theoretical treatises to eclectic research reviews also influenced their topical coverage. The topical coverage of early texts by Ladd, James, Titchener, Angell, Watson, and others reflected the authors' special vision of what psychology should study. However, as texts became more eclectic, the determinants of topical coverage began to change. For instance, Wolfle (1942) noted that "the amount known about each topic was used by Boring, Langfeld, and Weld (1935) as a basis for determining the space allotted to each in their text" (p. 694).

Changes in the student population also appear to have influenced shifts in topical coverage. As Morawski (1990) noted, the authors of early texts envisioned their audience as reflective, upper-class gentlemen seeking knowledge for its own sake. However, as higher education in America expanded its reach, the student population shifted toward middle-class youth who viewed a college education as an opportunity to advance their social standing. During the 1920s and 1930s, students' increasingly pragmatic orientation was documented in numerous studies (Arnold, 1926; Hartmann, 1933; Laird, 1923; Longstaff, 1932; Seward, 1931; Tussing, 1938) that explored students' interests in various psychological topics. These studies consistently showed that students were the most interested in personally practical topics such as personality, mental disorders, social relations, and intelligence and the least interested in classic topics such as physiological psychology, sensation, perception, animal behavior, and the mind–body problem (Wolfle, 1942). Eventually, authors such as Ruch (1937, 1941) and Munn (1946) began to take students' pragmatic interests into account and other authors followed suit.

One can also argue that sociocultural events have influenced the subject matter of introductory texts. For example, in the preface to his second edition, Ruch (1941) acknowledged that the specter of world war was one impetus for his emphasis on social problems. In a similar vein, Buxton (1946) and Finger (1954) discussed how World War II contributed to the increasingly personal and practical orientation of introductory texts and courses. Beginning in the 1970s, introductory texts added coverage of psychoactive drugs, human sexuality, and gender issues. The addition of these topics reflected sociocultural trends in America (i.e., the rise of recreational drug use, changes in sexual mores, and the women's movement).

Topical Organization

Contemporary texts organize topics in a fairly standardized order, as listed under topical allocations in the Appendix. Although there are deviations from this modal organization, the chapter sequence in most modern texts closely approximates the organization depicted in the Appendix. Has this organizational scheme always been the dominant model? Our perusal of leading texts from the past 100 years indicated that the answer is no.

The organizational framework that dominates today moves from molecular, lower order biological processes toward molar, higher order mental and social processes. This approach has been fairly common since the 1890s. However, previous generations of texts exhibited more idiosyncrasies in organization than do modern texts. Calkins (1910), for instance, buried physiology in the back of her book. In his first edition, Ruch (1937) began with topics such as testing, personality, development, and intelligence, and ended with coverage of sensation and perception, learning, and cognition, and omitted physiology altogether.

Moreover, sharp disparities in topical order were often seen in different editions of the same book. For example, the topical sequence in Woodworth's text underwent sweeping reorganizations in its second, third, and fifth editions (Dallenbach, 1933; McGeoch, 1936; Schlosberg, 1948). Dramatically different arrangements were seen in the three editions of Boring, Langfeld, and Weld's text (Bentley, 1948). This diversity led Ruja (1948) to comment that "there is less uniformity in the organization of elementary textbooks than even in their content" (p. 199). All in all, we found considerable variability in organization among the books from each decade, up through the 1960s. In the 1970s, however, topical sequences began to converge, leading Kasschau (1977) to comment on the increasing agreement regarding order of presentation.

What prompted this increasing agreement? One might argue that as the science of psychology "matured," there was a growing consensus about the ideal sequence of topics. We find this hypothesis unlikely in light of widespread comments about the increasing fragmentation of psychology in the 1970s and 1980s (e.g., Altman, 1990). Instead, we suspect that the standardization of topical order is attributable to developments in the world of textbook publishing—specifically, the growing financial risk involved in publishing introductory texts and the resultant reluctance of publishers to deviate from prevailing norms. Thus, the 1970s brought a growing homogenization (a "black hole of sameness," as one of our respondents put it), which was most readily apparent in increasingly similar organization.

Book Size

Many contemporary students and professors voice concern about the great length of today's introductory texts. As already noted, texts have increased in size over the years, but just how much? We looked at three size variables: number of chapters, total pages, and manuscript length (in words). As shown in Table 3, the average number of chapters has remained fairly stable, typically ranging between 18 and 22. However, the average number of pages and average manuscript length have both crept up steadily.

Texts of unwieldy length have been around since the beginning of the century. Indeed, the longest book in our sample, James's *Principles of Psychology*, was published in 1890. The length of this two-volume, 1,393-page book was approximately 516,000 words. James was apologetic about the book's size, noting in his preface that "the work has grown to a length which no one can regret more than the writer himself" (1890, p. v), and he published a condensed version 2 years later.

However, with regard to length, James's epic was clearly a distant outlier for its time. If James's *Principles* is omitted, texts from the 1890s through the 1930s averaged about 516 pages and 166,000 words. In the 1980s, these figures swelled to 764 pages and 376,000 words. The increase in average manuscript length was particularly steep in the 1950s and 1960s, when texts began to take on an encyclopedic character.

The explanation for longer texts seems straightforward. Throughout the century, psychologists have been expanding their domain of inquiry and increasing their production of research. Since 1930, the number of articles summarized annually in *Psychological Abstracts* has increased sixfold. Compared with this explosive growth, doubling the length of introductory texts seems temperate.

TABLE 3
Means for Selected Text Variables Grouped by Decade

Variable	1890s	1900s	1910s	1920s	1930s	1940s	1950s	1960s	1970s	1980s
No. chapters	22.6	23.0	14.5	18.5	19.3	21.5	20.0	21.0	18.3	22.0
Total pages	669	679	529	514	609	640	591	728	670	764
Manuscript length (words)	234,000	232,000	181,000	162,000	186,000	243,000	274,000	354,000	336,000	376,000
No. illustrations	56.8	57.5	77.8	55.3	132.0	175.5	255.0	404.0	459.8	652.0
No. pedagogical aids	0	0	0.25	0.50	0.25	0.75	1.75	2.50	3.75	3.50
No. references	—	—	—	—	—	493	758	1,066	921	1,148
Recency of references	—	—	—	—	—	23%	18%	24%	27%	24%

Illustration Programs

Texts' illustration programs have gradually become more elaborate. The average number of illustrations (figures and photos) in our sample of books increased from 56.8 in the 1890s to 652 in the 1980s (see Table 3). Some of this growth was attributable to the increased size of the texts. To take book size into consideration, we computed the average number of illustrations per 100 pages for each decade. This index has also increased dramatically (10-fold).

Photographs have been used since the turn of the century. Until the 1960s, these photos typically appeared as numbered figures, most of which had an obvious instructional purpose (e.g., depicting a memory drum). Ruch's (1937) text was the first to include unnumbered photos that were largely decorative. Although Ruch's (1941) second edition was less profusely illustrated, use of decorative photos grew gradually during the 1940s and 1950s. Increased reliance on photos was not welcomed in all quarters. For example, in a review of Ruch's (1937) first edition, C. S. Hall (1939) dismissed the photo program as "inconsequential, adding little to the value of the book" (p. 148). Reviewing Hilgard's (1953) first edition, Krech (1954) complained that "recent textbooks have irrelevantly (and irreverently) over-seasoned and over-peppered discussions of psychological concepts with 'text-book cheesecake'—pictures, photographs, and cartoons that add not a whit or a smidgin to such discussions" (p. 562). Despite such negative reactions, decorative photos became a staple of introductory texts by the 1960s. Ironically, both Hall and Krech eventually wrote texts (Krech et al., 1969; Lindzey, Hall, & Thompson, 1975) that included extensive illustration programs.

Color illustrations were introduced into some books in the 1950s (e.g., Hilgard, 1957). These illustrations were typically limited to a few color plates until 1969, when the publication of *Psychology Today* ushered in a new era of slick, sophisticated, four-color textbooks. The movement toward profusely illustrated introductory texts was not unique to psychology. Similar trends were seen in other academic disciplines, such as biology and sociology. Elaborate illustration programs were probably stimulated in large part by advances in printing and production technology, which made it easier to use photos and four-color graphics. Also, publishers' increasing commitment to attractive, interesting, student-oriented texts probably contributed to their willingness to spend large sums of money on extravagant graphics.

Pedagogical Aids

Even rudimentary pedagogical aids, such as chapter summaries, were largely absent from early texts. We checked for the presence of four basic learning aids: summaries, review questions, glossaries, and boldface print for technical terms. The average number of these aids found in our sample of texts, charted by decade in Table 3, increased steadily from the 1940s through the 1970s. Review questions first appeared in Titchener (1898), Calkins (1910), and Woodworth (1921). Chapter summaries showed up first in Munn (1946) and Woodworth and Marquis (1947). Chapter outlines were introduced by Ruch (1953) and Munn (1956). Boldface print for technical vocabulary appeared in a few books in the 1960s (e.g., Sanford, 1965).

These learning aids were fairly common by the 1970s, which witnessed the development of several other pedagogical devices, as many authors tried to make their books "user-friendly." Most reviewers welcomed the increased emphasis on pedagogy, although some learning aids were called "gimmicks" (Hines, 1985, p. 488) and were characterized as "disruptive, condescending, and counterproductive" (Vazquez, 1989, p. 471).

Citations and References

Conventions regarding citations and references have changed considerably since the turn of the century. Between 1890 and 1920, the norm was to use footnotes to cite specific sources, but practices varied. Some books (e.g., Dewey, 1890; James, 1890; Ladd, 1887) provided 500–1,000 such citations, but others (e.g., Titchener, 1896; Watson, 1919) provided none. The practice of supporting specific points with citations declined during the 1920s and 1930s. In most books, footnotes were supplanted by lists of "suggested readings" that were usually placed at the end of each chapter. Books typically contained 200–300 of these recommended resources, which were not clearly linked to text material.

Woodworth (1934) apparently led the movement back to a specific referencing system. Citations in his chapters were numbered consecutively, and the complete references were placed at the end of each chapter. Many other books followed suit in the 1940s, although some continued to provide only lists of suggested readings. By the 1950s, most books adopted a system similar to the American Psychological Association's writing style used today, citing the author and publication year in the text, with full references at the end of the book. Authors in the 1940s and 1950s, however, provided less extensive citations than authors do today. As Table 3 shows, the average number of references found in our sample of books increased dramatically from the 1940s (M = 493) through the 1980s (M = 1,148).

Although much of this growth could be attributed to the increased volume of psychological research, other factors also appear to be at work. Compared with their predecessors, contemporary authors are much more prone to support every assertion, however trivial or noncontroversial, with citations. Why are modern authors so compulsive about referencing? We can only speculate that as research in psychology has burgeoned, many reviewers and teachers have increasingly equated extensive references with excellent scholarship, creating an incentive for authors to compile long lists of references.

To enhance the perception of outstanding scholarship, many contemporary authors tout the recency of their references. To see whether this emphasis on currency was a new phenomenon, we defined "recent" references as those published within 5 years of a book's copyright date and determined the percentage of references that met this criterion for each book in our sample. Table 3 lists the mean percentages of recent references in our sample by decade since the beginning of contemporary referencing (the 1940s). The percentage of recent references has hovered between 18% and 27% and has not increased in recent decades. Moreover, if one considers earlier books that provided suggested reading lists or footnotes, it is apparent that recent citations were common long ago. For instance, 48% of the footnotes in James (1890) and 41% of the suggested readings in Woodworth (1921) referred to sources that were less than 5 years old. Thus, today's emphasis on recent references is nothing new.

In analyzing citation patterns, we also looked at whom the books cited. We ranked the seven most frequently cited theorists and researchers for each book on the basis of the number of index entries for each person. To combine these rankings for each decade, we assigned points for various ranks (7 points for first, 6 for second, 5 for third, etc.) and summed each individual's points. Results of these tabulations are summarized in Table 4, which ranks the seven most frequently cited people for each decade.

These lists reveal that Wundt and Helmholtz were dominant figures in the early decades before giving way to James, who made the top-seven list in more decades (six) than anyone else, including as recently as the 1970s. Freud did not show up among the most heavily cited people until the 1930s, but he has ranked first in citations for the past four decades. Watson (1920s–1940s) and Terman (1930s–1950s) made the top-seven list for three consecutive decades. Others who made the list in several decades include Woodworth, Pavlov, and Skinner. In the past two decades, Freud, Skinner, and Piaget stand out as the most frequently cited individuals. Our results for the 1980s closely resemble those of Knapp (1985), who surveyed a larger sample ($N = 24$) of contemporary texts.

The data in Table 4 suggest that the most frequently cited people in introductory texts tend to be influential theorists rather than prolific researchers. Interestingly, a lag often occurs before a theorist's important work receives heavy coverage in introductory texts. For example, Ebbinghaus, Freud, Adler, Terman, Pavlov, Cannon, Guilford, Skinner, Piaget, Rogers, and Erikson all appear on the most cited list for the first time one to three decades after they began to publish their influential work.

TABLE 4
Most Frequently Cited Theorists and Researchers Grouped by Decade

1890s	1900s	1910s	1920s	1930s
1. Wundt	1. Wundt	1. James	1. James	1. Freud
2. Helmholtz	2. Helmholtz	2. Wundt	2. Watson	2. Galton
3. Exner	3. James	3. Ebbinghaus	3. Helmholtz	2. Helmholtz
3. Martin	4. Bain	4. Helmholtz	4. Woodworth	2. Hull
5. Bain	4. Baldwin	5. Thorndike	5. Köhler	2. James
6. Galton	4. Martin	6. Titchener	5. Stout	2. Watson
6. Kant	7. Hodgson	7. Fechner	7. McDougall	7. Adler
6. Locke	7. Kant	7. Stumpf		7. Pavlov
6. Weber	7. Locke			7. Terman

1940s	1950s	1960s	1970s	1980s
1. Thorndike	1. Freud	1. Freud	1. Freud	1. Freud
2. Terman	2. Terman	2. Cannon	2. Skinner	2. Piaget
3. Woodworth	3. Stevens	3. James	3. Piaget	3. Skinner
4. Watson	4. Woodworth	4. Allport	4. Miller	4. Pavlov
5. Allport	5. Carmichael	4. Miller	5. Bandura	5. Erikson
5. Lewin	5. James	4. Skinner	6. Rogers	6. Rogers
7. Boring	5. Pavlov	7. Guilford	7. James	7. Seligman
			7. Pavlov	

CONCLUSION

Introductory texts are often viewed by academicians with suspicion and scorn. For instance, as Morawski (1992) noted, "at best, such writing is considered 'second-hand' or contrived knowledge. Scientists from all disciplines jest about the deceptions and inaccuracies—made for the sake of clarity, simplicity, or profit—contained in introductory texts" (pp. 161–162). Psychology professors have complained about introductory texts' colloquial language, oversimplification of complex issues, superficial coverage, conceptual and theoretical blandness, and popularization of the field's subject matter almost since the beginning (e.g., Dallenbach, 1922; Ewert, 1937; Hunter, 1939; Rosenberg, 1956).

Authors have made their share of mistakes. In recent years, for example, introductory textbooks have been criticized for misdrawing Pavlov's apparatus (Goodwin, 1991) and Mrs. Cantlie's homunculi diagrams (Griggs, 1988); for misrepresenting the Yerkes–Dodson law (Winton, 1987), Rogers's motivational constructs (Ford & Maas, 1989), and Watson's study of Little Albert (Harris, 1979; Prytula, Oster, & Davis, 1977); for distorting key aspects of sociobiology (Herzog, 1986) and Adlerian theory (Silverman & Corsini, 1984); for confusing the concepts of negative reinforcement and punishment (Morse, 1986); for inaccurately suggesting that researchers have reliably determined the number of neurons in the human brain (Soper & Rosenthal, 1988); for exaggerating the prevalence of multiple personality disorder and the magnitude of the link between stress and illness (Morse, 1986); and for uncritically reporting unsubstantiated claims about hemispheric specialization, extrasensory perception (Hines, 1985), the effects of stress on "executive monkeys" (McGovern, 1978), and the impact of early intervention on underprivileged children's intelligence (Sommer & Sommer, 1983).

However, many of these misconceptions were not unique to introductory texts; they were widely accepted in the field as a whole. Given that introductory texts cover hundreds of issues and thousands of studies, critics are bound to find specific points of contention, especially in their areas of expertise. In preparing this chapter, we read book reviews of more than 400 introductory texts. In these reviews, the vast majority of texts were characterized as accurate, scholarly, and current.

Why, then, are introductory texts the object of derision? In part, this attitude may reflect academicians' distaste for commercial enterprises driven by the profit motive. Another prominent consideration is that modern academia holds teaching and related activities (e.g., writing textbooks) in low esteem compared with basic research. As Tyson-Bernstein (1989) put it, "*real scholars* don't write textbooks" (p. 25). We also suspect that much of the criticism stems from viewing introductory texts as being little more than a series of research reviews. This perspective does not do justice to the complex nature of introductory texts, which must serve many masters. This complexity was perhaps explained best in McConnell's (1978) article, "Confessions of a Textbook Writer." McConnell pointed out that introductory texts must meet the needs of five different constituencies:

> These five different audiences—students, instructors, peers and colleagues, publishers, and one's inner feelings and needs—make very different and often conflicting demands on the writer of an introductory text. Satisfying them all is something of an impossibility. (p. 167)

The difficulties inherent in writing an introductory text have not gone entirely unappreciated. A number of reviewers, such as Matlin (1983) and Greendlinger (1989), have commented on the challenging nature of the task. One of the more insightful analyses came from McGeoch (1936) in a review of Woodworth's (1934) third edition:

> The author of a satisfactory general introduction to psychology is faced with a task of tremendous dimensions. He must present the fundamentals of a subject in which there is still disagreement over what, for the beginning student, the fundamentals are. He must organize the material so that the student is introduced to the field as a single and unified one, but with a minimum of involved and difficult theorizing. If the book is to be used widely, even the implicit theory behind the organization cannot cut too sharply across the theoretical biases of colleagues. He must, withal, take account of recent work in a rapidly moving set of research problems and must write lucidly and interestingly without sacrificing exactness. (p. 178)

In light of these difficulties, it seems shortsighted to evaluate introductory textbooks by the canons of scholarship applied to journal articles.

In general, we believe that psychology's introductory texts have served the discipline well. The influential early books were written by leading theorists and researchers of the time[6] and, as McKeachie (1968) pointed out, they helped to lure many bright, talented people into psychology. These books defined the boundaries of an emerging science of psychology and mobilized students, psychologists, and ideas in ways that transformed the discipline. Today's texts are less ambitious about shaping the field's evolution, but they chronicle psychology's progress effectively. For the most part, contemporary texts provide engaging, balanced, comprehensive, pedagogically sophisticated, accurate portraits of the field. Some critics might argue that the texts have grown too long, too similar, and too gimmicky,

---

[6]It is instructive to examine the list of leading introductory texts found in Table 1. Of the 16 authors listed for the first five decades, 12 were elected president of the American Psychological Association (APA) in an era when this honor was based on scholarly achievement (only 2 of the 17 authors listed for the second five decades served as president of the APA, although the meaning of this comparison is obscured by the increased politicalization of the office).

but on the whole, they do an admirable job of introducing students to the dynamic and exciting discipline of psychology.

REFERENCES

Abma, J. S. (1974). A little old, a little new. *Contemporary Psychology, 19,* 732–736.

Allen C. K. (1980). [Review of *Psychology and Life* (10th ed.)]. *Teaching of Psychology, 7,* 122.

Altman, I. (1990). Centripetal and centrifugal trends in psychology. In L. Bickman & H. Ellis (Eds.), *Preparing psychologists for the 21st century: Proceedings of the National Conference on Graduate Education in Psychology* (pp. 39–64). Hillsdale, NJ: Erlbaum.

Angell, J. R. (1904). *Psychology: An introductory study of the structure and function of human consciousness.* New York: Holt.

Angell, J. R. (1908). *Psychology: An introductory study of the structure and function of human consciousness.* New York: Holt.

Angell, J. R. (1936). James Rowland Angell. In C. Murchison (Ed.), *A history of psychology in autobiography* (Vol. 3, pp. 1–38). Worcester, MA: Clark University Press.

Apple, M. W. (1985). The culture and commerce of the textbook. *Journal of Curriculum Studies, 17,* 147–162.

Archer, E. J. (1959). The book with the boxes. *Contemporary Psychology, 4,* 39–40.

Arnold, H. J. (1926). What parts of elementary psychology are most interesting to students? *Pedagogical Seminary, 33,* 729–735.

Atkinson, R. L., Atkinson, R. C., & Hilgard, E. R. (1979). *Introduction to psychology* (7th ed.). New York: Harcourt Brace Jovanovich.

Atkinson, R. L., Atkinson, R. C., & Hilgard, E. R. (1983). *Introduction to psychology* (8th ed.). New York: Harcourt Brace Jovanovich.

Atkinson, R. L., Atkinson, R. C., Smith, E. E., & Bem, D. J. (1990). *Introduction to psychology* (10th ed.). San Diego, CA: Harcourt Brace Jovanovich.

Atkinson, R. L., Atkinson, R. C., Smith, E. E., & Hilgard, E. R. (1987). *Introduction to psychology* (9th ed.). San Diego, CA: Harcourt Brace Jovanovich.

Baldwin, J. M. (1889). *Handbook of psychology: Vol. 1. Senses and intellect.* New York: Holt.

Bare, J. K., & Guthrie, P. M. (1963). Five elementary texts and one question of identity. *Contemporary Psychology, 8,* 183–185.

Bartlett, N. R. (1959). The bookstore has been trying to reach you on the phone all morning. *Contemporary Psychology, 4,* 65–68.

Beardslee, D. C., Hildum, D. C., O'Dowd, D. D., & Schwartz, S. (1962). Eight introductory texts: Marginal differentiations. *Contemporary Psychology, 7,* 123–126.

Benimoff, M. (1990). Eastern Psychological Association: Report of the sixty-first annual meeting. *American Psychologist, 45,* 1371–1376.

Benjamin, L. T., Jr. (1990, March). *William James's dismay with the introductory psychology textbook market of 1890.* Paper presented at the meeting of the Eastern Psychological Association, Philadelphia, PA.

Benjamin, L. T., Jr., Hopkins, J. R., & Nation, J. R. (1987). *Psychology.* New York: Macmillan.

Bentley, M. (1948). Three Boring-Langfeld-Weld texts. *American Journal of Psychology, 61,* 589–594.

Bernstein, D. A., Roy, E. J., Wickens, C. D., & Srull, T. K. (1988). *Psychology.* Boston: Houghton Mifflin.

Bootzin, R. R., Bower, G. H., Hall, E., & Crocker, J. (1991). *Psychology today: An introduction.* New York: McGraw-Hill.

Bootzin, R. R., Bower, G. H., Zajonc, R. B., & Hall, E. (1986). *Psychology today: An introduction* (6th ed.). New York: Random House.

Bootzin, R. R., Loftus, E. F., Zajonc, R. B., & Hall, E. (1983). *Psychology today: An introduction* (5th ed.). New York: Random House.

Boring E. G. (1950). *A history of experimental psychology.* New York: Appleton-Century-Crofts.

Boring, E. G., Langfeld, H. S., & Weld, H. P. (Eds.). (1935). *Psychology: A factual textbook.* New York: Wiley.

Boring, E. G., Langfeld, H. S., & Weld, H. P. (Eds.). (1939). *Introduction to psychology.* New York: Wiley.

Boring, E. G., Langfeld, H. S., & Weld, H. P. (Eds.). (1948). *Foundations of psychology.* New York: Wiley.

Bourne, L. E., Jr., & Ekstrand, B. R. (1973). *Psychology: Its principles and meanings.* New York: Holt, Rinehart & Winston.

Bourne, L. E., Jr., & Ekstrand, B. R. (1976). *Psychology: Its principles and meanings* (2nd ed.). New York: Holt, Rinehart & Winston.

Brown, L. T., Collins, W. E., Gladstone, R., Jaynes, W. E., McHale, J. L., Miller, T., Ray, D. D., Sandvold, K. D., & Scott, W. C. (1971). Traditional but diverse. *Contemporary Psychology, 16,* 1–5.

Brown, R., & Herrnstein, R. J. (1975). *Psychology.* Boston: Little, Brown.

Brozek, J. (1984). David Jayne Hill: Between the old and the new psychology. In J. Brozek (Ed.), *Explorations in the history of psychology in the United States* (pp. 121–147). Lewisburg, PA: Bucknell University Press.

Bruce, B., Rubin, A., & Starr, K. (1981). *Why readability formulas fail.* Urbana, IL: Center for the Study of Reading.

Buel, J. (1938). [Review of *Psychology and Life*]. *Psychological Bulletin, 35,* 91–94.

Buel, J. (1942). [Review of *Psychology and Life*]. *Psychological Bulletin, 39*, 262–263.

Buxton, C. E. (1946). Planning the introductory psychology course. *American Psychologist, 1*, 303–311.

Caffrey, B. (1978). [Review of *Understanding Human Behavior* (2nd ed.)]. *Teaching of Psychology, 5*, 166–167.

Calkins, M. W. (1901). *An introduction to psychology*. New York: Macmillan.

Calkins, M. W. (1910). *A first book in psychology*. New York: Macmillan.

Cameron, E. H. (1911). Three text-books of psychology. *Psychological Bulletin, 8*, 321–322.

Campbell, D. E. (1976). [Review of *Psychology and Life* (9th ed.)]. *Teaching of Psychology, 3*, 191.

Carlson, N. R. (1984). *Psychology: The science of behavior*. Boston: Allyn & Bacon.

Carr, H. A. (1925). *Psychology: A study of mental activity*. New York: Longmans, Green.

Carr, T. H. (1982). Comparing introductory texts. *Contemporary Psychology, 27*, 354–358.

Cattell, J. M. (1929). Psychology in America. *Science, 70*, 84–95.

Chatman, S. P., & Goetz, E. T. (1985). Improving textbook selection. *Teaching of Psychology, 12*, 150–152.

Cone, A. L. (1976). Six luxury models. *Contemporary Psychology, 21*, 544–548.

Coon, D. (1977). *Introduction to psychology: Exploration and application*. St. Paul, MN: West.

CRM Books. (1969). *Psychology today: An introduction*. Del Mar, CA: Author.

CRM Books. (1972). *Psychology today: An introduction* (2nd ed.). Del Mar, CA: Author.

CRM/Random House. (1975). *Psychology today: An introduction* (3rd ed.). New York: Author.

CRM/Random House. (1979). *Psychology today: An introduction* (4th ed.) New York: Author.

Croll, W., & Moskaluk, S. (1977). Should Flesch counts count? *Teaching of Psychology, 4*, 48–49.

Dallenbach, K. M. (1922). [Review of *Psychology*]. *American Journal of Psychology, 33*, 430–435.

Dallenbach, K. M. (1933). [Review of *Psychology*]. *American Journal of Psychology, 45*, 186–188.

Danziger, K. (1979). The positivist repudiation of Wundt. *Journal of the History of the Behavioral Sciences, 15*, 205–230.

Danziger, K. (1985). The origins of the psychological experiment as a social institution. *American Psychologist, 40*, 133–140.

Darley, J. M., Glucksberg, S., Kamin, L. J., & Kinchla, R. A. (1981). *Psychology*. Englewood Cliffs, NJ: Prentice-Hall.

Darley, J. M., Glucksberg, S., & Kinchla, R. A. (1988). *Psychology* (4th ed.). Englewood Cliffs, NJ: Prentice-Hall.

Darwin, C. (1859). *On the origin of species*. London: Murray.

Darwin, C. (1871). *Descent of man*. London: Murray.

Dashiell, J. F. (1928). *Fundamentals of objective psychology*. Boston: Houghton Mifflin.

Dashiell, J. F. (1937). *Fundamentals of general psychology*. Boston: Houghton Mifflin.

Davidoff, L. L. (1976). *Introduction to psychology*. New York: McGraw-Hill.

Dewey, J. (1890). *Psychology*. New York: Harper.

Dewey, J. (1967). *John Dewey, the early works, 1882–1898, Vol. 2: 1887, Psychology*. Carbondale, IL: Southern Illinois University Press. (Original work published 1887)

Dimmick, F. L. (1940). [Review of *Introduction to Psychology*]. *American Journal of Psychology, 53*, 466–468.

Doyle, C. L. (1987). *Explorations in psychology*. Monterey, CA: Brooks/Cole.

Evans, R. B. (1984). The origins of American academic psychology. In J. Brozek (Ed.), *Explorations in the history of psychology in the United States* (pp. 17–60). Lewisburg, PA: Bucknell University Press.

Evans, R. B. (1990a). The scientific and psychological positions of E. B. Titchener. In R. Leys & R. B. Evans (Eds.), *Defining American psychology: The correspondence between Adolf Meyer and Edward Bradford Titchener* (pp. 1–38). Baltimore, MD: Johns Hopkins University Press.

Evans, R. B. (1990b). William James and his *Principles*. In M. G. Johnson & T. B. Henley (Eds.), *Reflections on* The Principles of Psychology: *William James after a century* (pp. 11–31). Hillsdale, NJ: Erlbaum.

Evans, R. B. (1991). Introduction: The historical context. In F. H. Burkhardt & F. Browers (Eds.), *William James's* Principles of Psychology (pp. xli–xlviii). Cambridge, MA: Harvard University Press.

Ewert, H. (1937). [Review of *General Psychology*]. *Psychological Bulletin, 34*, 173–174.

Farnsworth, D. F. (1979, October 29). College publishing: The need for reassessment. *Publishers Weekly*, pp. 46, 51–52.

Fay, J. W. (1939). *American psychology before William James*. New Brunswick, NJ: Rutgers University Press.

Fernald, L. D., Jr., & Fernald, P. S. (1978). *Introduction to psychology* (4th ed.). Boston: Houghton Mifflin.

Fernald, L. D., Jr., & Fernald, P. S. (1985). *Introduction to psychology* (5th ed.). Dubuque, IA: William C. Brown.

Finger, F. W. (1954). Textbooks and general psychology. *Psychological Bulletin, 51*, 82–90.

Fischer, K. W., & Lazerson, A. (1977). Managing a book versus plagiarizing it. *Teaching of Psychology, 4*, 198–199.

Flesch, R. (1948). A new readability yardstick. *Journal of Applied Psychology, 32*, 221–233.

Flesch, R. (1951). *How to test readability*. New York: Harper.

Ford, J. G., & Maas, S. (1989). On actualizing person-centered theory: A critique of textbook treatments of Rogers's motivational constructs. *Teaching of Psychology, 16*, 30–31.

Fretz, B. R. (1979). Different strokes or reruns? *Contemporary Psychology, 24*, 485–490.

Furumoto, L. (1991). From "paired associates" to a psychology of self: The intellectual odyssey of Mary Whiton Calkins. In G. A. Kimble, M. Wertheimer, & C. L. White (Eds.), *Portraits of pioneers in psychology* (pp. 57–72). Hillsdale, NJ: Erlbaum.

Gazzaniga, M. S. (1973). *Fundamentals of psychology: An introduction*. New York: Academic Press.

Geldard, F. A. (1936). [Review of *Psychology: A Factual Textbook*]. *American Journal of Psychology, 48*, 693–694.

Gerow, J. R. (1981). [Review of *Psychology*]. *Teaching of Psychology, 8*, 189.

Gillen, B. (1973). Readability and human interest scores of thirty-four current introductory psychology texts. *American Psychologist, 28*, 1010–1011.

Gillen, B. (1975). Readability and human interest scores of thirty-two introductory psychology texts: Update and clarification. *Teaching of Psychology, 2*, 175–176.

Gillen, B., Kendall, P. C., & Finch, A. J., Jr. (1977). Reading ease and human interest scores: A comparison of Flesch scores with subjective ratings. *Teaching of Psychology, 4*, 39–41.

Giorgi, A. (1990). The implications of James's plea for psychology as a natural science. In M. G. Johnson & T. B. Henley (Eds.), *Reflections on The Principles of Psychology: William James after a century* (pp. 63–75). Hillsdale, NJ: Erlbaum.

Gleitman, H. (1981). *Psychology*. New York: Norton.

Gleitman, H. (1986). *Psychology* (2nd ed.). New York: Norton.

Goodwin, C. J. (1991). Misportraying Pavlov's apparatus. *American Journal of Psychology, 104*, 135–141.

Gould, S. J. (1988, January). The case of the creeping fox terrier clone. *Natural History*, pp. 19–20, 22, 24.

Greendlinger, V. (1989). A comparative review of three introductory texts. *Contemporary Psychology, 34*, 836–838.

Griesinger, W. S., & Klene, R. R. (1984). Readability of introductory psychology textbooks: Flesch versus student ratings. *Teaching of Psychology, 11*, 90–91.

Griggs, R. A. (1988). Who is Mrs. Cantlie and why are they doing those terrible things to her homunculi? *Teaching of Psychology, 15*, 105–106.

Griggs, R. A. (1990). Introductory psychology texts: Survival of the fittest. *Contemporary Psychology, 35*, 659–662.

Griggs, R. A., & Jackson, S. L. (1989). The introductory psychology textbook market: Perceptions of authors and editors. *Teaching of Psychology, 16*, 61–64.

Hall, C. S. (1939). [Review of *Psychology and Life*]. *American Journal of Psychology, 52*, 148.

Hall, G. S. (1887). [Review of *Elements of Physiological Psychology*]. *American Journal of Psychology, 1*, 159–164.

Hall, G. S. (1891). [Review of *The Principles of Psychology*]. *American Journal of Psychology, 3*, 578–591.

Hall, G. S. (1923). *Life and confessions of a psychologist*. New York: Appleton.

Harris, B. (1979). What ever happened to Little Albert? *American Psychologist, 34*, 151–160.

Hartmann, G. W. (1933). The measurement of the relative interest value of representative items taught in elementary psychology. *Journal of Educational Psychology, 24*, 266–282.

Haven, J. (1857). *Mental philosophy*. Boston: Gould & Lincoln.

Heatherington, L. (1986). A matter of style. *Contemporary Psychology, 31*, 374–375.

Hebb, D. O. (1958). *A textbook of psychology*. Philadelphia, PA: W. B. Saunders.

Hebb, D. O. (1966). *A textbook of psychology* (2nd ed.). Philadelphia, PA: W. B. Saunders.

Henmon, V. A. C. (1912). Physiological and experimental texts. *Psychological Bulletin, 9*, 239–242.

Herzog, H. A., Jr. (1986). The treatment of sociobiology in introductory psychology textbooks. *Teaching of Psychology, 13*, 12–15.

Hickok, L. P. (1848). *Rational psychology*. Auburn, AL: Derby, Miller.

Hickok, L. P. (1854). *Empirical psychology*. New York: Ivison, Blakeman, Taylor.

Hilgard, E. R. (1953). *Introduction to psychology*. New York: Harcourt, Brace.

Hilgard, E. R. (1957). *Introduction to psychology* (2nd ed.). New York: Harcourt, Brace.

Hilgard, E. R. (1962). *Introduction to psychology* (3rd ed.). New York: Harcourt, Brace & World.

Hilgard, E. R. (1987). *Psychology in America: A historical survey*. San Diego, CA: Harcourt Brace Jovanovich.

Hilgard, E. R., & Atkinson, R. C. (1967). *Introduction to psychology* (4th ed.). New York: Harcourt, Brace & World.

Hilgard, E. R., Atkinson, R. C., & Atkinson, R. L. (1971). *Introduction to psychology* (5th ed.). New York: Harcourt, Brace & World.

Hilgard, E. R., Atkinson, R. C., & Atkinson, R. L. (1975). *Introduction to psychology* (6th ed.). New York: Harcourt Brace Jovanovich.

Hill, D. J. (1888). *The elements of psychology.* New York: Sheldon.

Hines, T. M. (1985). Four introductory texts. *Contemporary Psychology, 30,* 487–489.

Holt, E. B. (1911). Titchener's psychology. *Psychological Bulletin, 8,* 25–30.

Hopkins, M. (1878). *An outline study of man.* New York: Scribner's

Hunter, W. S. (1935). [Review of *Psychology: A Factual Textbook*]. *Psychological Bulletin, 32,* 595–599.

Hunter, W. S. (1939). [Review of *Introduction to Psychology*]. *Psychological Bulletin, 36,* 784–786.

Jacobs, B. (1984). Are these books really different? *Contemporary Psychology, 29,* 464–467.

James, H. (Ed.). (1920). *The letters of William James* (Vol. 1). Boston: Atlantic Monthly.

James, W. (1890). *The principles of psychology* (Vols. 1–2). New York: Holt.

James, W. (1892a). A plea for psychology as natural science. *Philosophical Review, 1,* 146–153.

James, W. (1892b). *Psychology, briefer course.* New York: Holt.

Kadushin, C. (1979). The managed text: Prose and qualms. *Change, 11,* 30–35, 64.

Kagan, J., & Havemann, E. (1968). *Psychology: An introduction.* New York: Harcourt, Brace & World.

Kantor, J. R. (1922). The evolution of psychological textbooks since 1912. *Psychological Bulletin, 19,* 429–442.

Kasschau, R. A. (1973). 17 inches of (mixed) pleasure. *Contemporary Psychology, 18,* 617–623.

Kasschau, R. A. (1974). [Review of *Understanding Human Behavior*]. *Teaching of Psychology, 1,* 42–43.

Kasschau, R. A. (1977). 22.1 centimeters of (mixed) pleasure: Psigns of the times. *Contemporary Psychology, 22,* 505–508.

Kasschau, R. A., & Camp, C. J. (1976). [Review of *Psychology Today: An Introduction* (3rd ed.)]. *Teaching of Psychology, 3,* 148–149.

Kendler, H. H. (1963). *Basic psychology.* New York: Appleton-Century-Crofts.

Kendler, H. H., & Kendler, T. S. (1971). *Basic psychology: Brief edition.* New York: Appleton-Century-Crofts.

Kimble, G. A. (1956). *Principles of general psychology.* New York: Ronald Press.

Kimble, G. A., & Garmezy, N. (1963). *Principles of general psychology* (2nd ed.). New York: Ronald Press.

Kimble, G. A., & Garmezy, N. (1968). *Principles of general psychology* (3rd ed.). New York: Ronald Press.

Knapp, T. J. (1985). Who's who in American introductory psychology textbooks: A citation study. *Teaching of Psychology, 12*, 15–17.

Krech, D. (1954). [Review of *Introduction to Psychology*]. *American Journal of Psychology, 67*, 561–565.

Krech, D., & Crutchfield, R. S. (1958). *Elements of psychology*. New York: Knopf.

Krech, D., Crutchfield, R. S., & Livson, N. (1969). *Elements of psychology* (2nd ed.). New York: Knopf.

Krech, D., Crutchfield, R. S., Livson, N., Wilson, W. A., Jr., & Parducci, A. (1982). *Elements of psychology* (4th ed.). New York: Knopf.

Külpe, O. (1909). *Outlines of psychology: Based upon the results of experimental investigation* (3rd ed., E. B. Titchener, Trans.). New York: Macmillan. (Original work published 1893)

Ladd, G. T. (1887). *Elements of physiological psychology*. New York: Scribner's.

Ladd, G. T. (1890). *Outlines of physiological psychology*. New York: Scribner's.

Ladd, G. T. (1892). Psychology as so-called natural science. *Philosophical Review, 1*, 24–53.

Ladd, G. T. (1894a). *Primer of psychology*. New York: Longmans, Green.

Ladd, G. T. (1894b). *Psychology: Descriptive and explanatory*. New York: Scribner's.

Ladd, G. T. (1898). *Outlines of descriptive psychology*. New York: Scribner's.

Ladd, G. T., & Woodworth, R. S. (1911). *Elements of physiological psychology* (2nd ed.). New York: Scribner's.

Lahey, B. B. (1983). *Psychology: An introduction*. Dubuque, IA: William C. Brown.

Laird, D. A. (1923). Reaction of college students to mental hygiene. *Mental Hygiene, 7*, 271–276.

Landrigan, D. T., & Palladino, J. J. (1974). A reply to Gillen. *American Psychologist, 29*, 571–572.

Lange, B. (1982). Readability formulas: Second looks, second thoughts. *Reading Teacher, 35*, 858–861.

Lazarus, R. S. (1974). *The riddle of man: An introduction to psychology*. Englewood Cliffs, NJ: Prentice-Hall.

Lefton, L.A. (1979). *Psychology*. Boston: Allyn & Bacon.

Levin, M. J. (1978). *Psychology: A biological approach*. New York: McGraw-Hill.

Lindzey, G., Hall, C., & Thompson, R. F. (1975). *Psychology*. New York: Worth.

Longstaff, H.P. (1932). Analysis of some factors conditioning learning in general psychology: Parts I and II. *Journal of Applied Psychology, 16*, 9–48, 131–166.

MacLeod, R. B. (1971). The teaching of psychology. *American Psychologist, 26*, 245–249.

Malott, R. W., & Whaley, D. L. (1976). *Psychology*. Kalamazoo, MI: Behaviordelia, and New York: Harper's College Press.

Marquis, D. G. (1938). [Review of *Fundamentals of General Psychology*]. *Psychological Bulletin, 35*, 95–99.

Matarazzo, J. D. (1987). There is only one psychology, no specialties, but many applications. *American Psychologist, 42,* 893–903.

Matlin, M. W. (1983). Introducing psychology. *Contemporary Psychology, 28,* 440–443.

Maxwell, M. (1978). Readability: Have we gone too far? *Journal of Reading, 21,* 525–530.

McConnell, J. V. (1974). *Understanding human behavior.* New York: Holt, Rinehart & Winston.

McConnell, J. V. (1977). *Understanding human behavior* (2nd ed.). New York: Holt, Rinehart & Winston.

McConnell, J. V. (1978). Confessions of a textbook writer. *American Psychologist, 33,* 159–169.

McConnell, J. V. (1980). *Understanding human behavior* (3rd ed.). New York: Holt, Rinehart & Winston.

McConnell, J. V. (1983). *Understanding human behavior* (4th ed.). New York: Holt, Rinehart & Winston.

McConnell, J. V. (1986). *Understanding human behavior* (5th ed.). New York: Holt, Rinehart & Winston.

McConnell, J. V. (1989). *Understanding human behavior* (6th ed.). New York: Holt, Rinehart & Winston.

McCosh, J. (1886). *Psychology: The cognitive powers.* New York: Scribner's.

McCosh, J. (1887). *Psychology: The motive powers.* New York: Scribner's.

McDougall, W. (1912). *Psychology: The study of behavior.* London: Oxford University Press.

McDougall, W. (1923). *Outline of psychology.* London: Methuen.

McGeoch, J. A. (1936). [Review of Psychology]. *American Journal of Psychology, 48,* 178–179.

McGovern, L. P. (1978). The executive monkeys: Fact and fiction in introductory psychology texts. *Teaching of Psychology, 5,* 36–37.

McKeachie, W. J. (1968). Psychology at age 75: The psychology teacher comes into his own. *American Psychologist, 23,* 551–557.

McKeachie, W. J., & Doyle, C. L. (1966). *Psychology.* Reading, MA: Addison-Wesley.

McKeachie, W. J., & Doyle, C. L. (1972). *Psychology: The short course.* Reading, MA: Addison-Wesley.

McKenna, V. V. (1967). Big book; small book: The search for unity and relevance. *Contemporary Psychology, 12,* 58–62.

McMahon, F. B. (1977). The psychology textbook network. *Teaching of Psychology, 4,* 196–198.

Meyer, M. (1911). *The fundamental laws of human behavior.* Boston: Badger.

Mills, E. S. (1969). *George Trumbull Ladd: Pioneer American psychologist*. Cleveland, OH: Case Western Reserve University Press.

Mills, E. S. (1974). George Trumbull Ladd: The great textbook writer. *Journal of the History of the Behavioral Sciences, 10,* 299–303.

Morawski, J. G. (1990, June). *Books in science: Introductory texts and the formations of American psychology.* Paper presented at the meeting of the Cheiron Society, Westfield State College, Westfield, MA.

Morawski, J. G. (1992). There is more to our history of giving: The place of introductory textbooks in American psychology. *American Psychologist, 47,* 161–169.

Morgan, C. T. (1956). *Introduction to psychology.* New York: McGraw-Hill.

Morgan, C. T. (1974). *A brief introduction to psychology.* New York: McGraw-Hill.

Morgan, C. T., & King, R. A. (1966). *Introduction to psychology* (3rd ed.). New York: McGraw-Hill.

Morse, D. L. (1986). Two views of psychology. *Contemporary Psychology, 31,* 984–985.

Munn, N. L. (1946). *Psychology: The fundamentals of human adjustment.* Boston: Houghton Mifflin.

Munn, N. L. (1951). *Psychology: The fundamentals of human adjustment* (2nd ed.). Boston: Houghton Mifflin.

Munn, N. L. (1956). *Psychology: The fundamentals of human adjustment* (3rd ed.). Boston: Houghton Mifflin.

Munn, N. L. (1961). *Psychology: The fundamentals of human adjustment* (4th ed.). Boston: Houghton Mifflin.

Munn, N. L. (1962). *Introduction to psychology* (abridged edition of *Psychology: The fundamentals of human adjustment,* 4th ed.). Boston: Houghton Mifflin.

Munn, N. L. (1966). *Psychology: The fundamentals of human adjustment* (5th ed.). Boston: Houghton Mifflin.

Munn, N. L., Fernald, L. D., Jr., & Fernald, P. S. (1969). *Introduction to psychology* (2nd ed.). New York: Houghton Mifflin.

Munn, N. L., Fernald, L. D., Jr., & Fernald, P. S. (1972). *Introduction to psychology* (3rd ed.). Boston: Houghton Mifflin.

Münsterberg, H. (1915). *Psychology: General and applied.* New York: Appleton.

Mussen, P., Rosenzweig, M. R., Aronson, E., Elkind, D., Feshbach, S., Geiwitz, J., Glickman, S. E., Murdock, B. B., Jr., Wertheimer, M., & Harvey, L. O., Jr. (1977). *Psychology: An introduction.* Lexington, MA: Heath.

Myers, D. G. (1986). *Psychology.* New York: Worth.

O'Donnell, J. M. (1986). *The origins of behaviorism: American psychology, 1870–1920.* New York: New York University Press.

Ofiesh, G. D. (1959). *The history, development, present status and purpose of the first (introductory) course in psychology in American undergraduate education.* Unpublished doctoral dissertation, University of Denver, Denver, CO.

Ogdon, D. P. (1954). Flesch counts of eight current texts for introductory psychology. *American Psychologist, 9,* 143–148.

Papalia, D. E., & Olds, S. W. (1985). *Psychology.* New York: McGraw-Hill.

Pfeiffer, K. (1980). [Review of *Introduction to Psychology* (7th ed.)]. *Teaching of Psychology, 7,* 119.

Pillsbury, W. B. (1911). *Essentials of psychology.* New York: Macmillan.

Pillsbury, W. B. (1922). *The fundamentals of psychology.* New York: Macmillan.

Pillsbury, W. B. (1932). Walter B. Pillsbury. In C. Murchison (Ed.), *A history of psychology in autobiography* (Vol. 2, pp. 265–295). Worcester, MA: Clark University Press.

Pollio, H. R. (1981). *Behavior and existence: An introduction to empirical humanistic psychology.* Monterey, CA: Brooks/Cole.

Popplestone, J. A. (1978). Once more, dear friends. *Contemporary Psychology, 23,* 142–151.

Prytula, R. E., Oster, G. D., & Davis, S. F. (1977). The "rat rabbit" problem: What did John B. Watson really do? *Teaching of Psychology, 4,* 44–46.

Quereshi, M. Y., & Sackett, P. R. (1977). An updated content analysis of introductory psychology textbooks. *Teaching of Psychology, 4,* 25–30.

Quereshi, M. Y., & Zulli, M. R. (1975). A content analysis of introductory psychology textbooks. *Teaching of Psychology, 2,* 60–65.

Rathus, S. A. (1981). *Psychology.* New York: Holt, Rinehart & Winston.

Rauch, F. A. (1840). *Psychology.* New York: Dodd, Mead.

Roback, A. A. (1964). *History of American psychology.* New York: Collier.

Robinson, F. P. (1970). *Effective study.* New York: Harper & Row.

Robinson, P. W., & Higbee, K. L. (1978). Publishing a textbook: Advice from authors and publishers. *Teaching of Psychology, 5,* 175–181.

Roediger, H. L., III, Rushton, J. P., Capaldi, E. D., & Paris, S. G. (1984). *Psychology.* Boston: Little, Brown.

Rosenberg, M. J. (1956). Science? *Contemporary Psychology, 1,* 196–197.

Ruch, F. L. (1937). *Psychology and life.* Glenview, IL: Scott, Foresman.

Ruch, F. L. (1941). *Psychology and life* (2nd ed.). Glenview, IL: Scott, Foresman.

Ruch, F. L. (1948). *Psychology and life* (3rd ed.). Glenview, IL: Scott, Foresman.

Ruch, F. L. (1953). *Psychology and life* (4th ed.). Glenview, IL: Scott, Foresman.

Ruch, F. L. (1958). *Psychology and life* (5th ed.). Glenview, IL: Scott, Foresman.

Ruch, F. L. (1963a). *Psychology and life* (6th ed.). Glenview, IL: Scott, Foresman.

Ruch, F. L. (1963b). *Psychology and life* (brief 6th ed.). Glenview, IL: Scott, Foresman.

Ruch, F. L. (1967a). *Psychology and life* (7th ed.). Glenview, IL: Scott, Foresman.

Ruch, F. L. (1967b). *Psychology and life* (brief 7th ed.). Glenview, IL: Scott, Foresman.

Ruch, F. L., & Zimbardo, P. G. (1971). *Psychology and life* (8th ed.). Glenview, IL: Scott, Foresman.

Rudman, H. C. (1990). Corporate mergers in the publishing industry: Helpful or intrusive? *Educational Researcher, 19*(1), 14–20.

Ruja, H. (1948). The order of topics in general psychology. *American Psychologist, 3,* 199–202.

Sanford, F. H. (1965). *Psychology: A scientific study of man* (2nd ed.). Belmont, CA: Wadsworth.

Santrock, J. W. (1986). *Psychology: The science of mind and behavior.* Dubuque, IA: William C. Brown.

Schlosberg, H. (1948). [Review of *Psychology*]. *Psychological Bulletin, 45,* 89–90.

Schmucker, S. S. (1842). *Psychology.* New York: Harper.

Seward, G. H. (1931). Students' reactions to a first course in psychology. *Journal of Applied Psychology, 15,* 512–524.

Sexton, V. S. (1977). Old and new: There's one for you. *Contemporary Psychology, 22,* 190–192.

Silverman, N. N., & Corsini, R. J. (1984). Is it true what they say about Adler's individual psychology? *Teaching of Psychology, 11,* 188–189.

Smith, S. S. (1812). *Lectures on moral and political philosophy* (Vols. 1–2). Trenton, NJ: Fenton.

Sommer, R., Estabrook, M., & Horobin, K. (1988). Faculty awareness of textbook prices. *Teaching of Psychology, 15,* 17–21.

Sommer, R., & Sommer, B. A. (1983). Mystery in Milwaukee: Early intervention, IQ, and psychology textbooks. *American Psychologist, 38,* 982–985.

Soper, B., & Rosenthal, G. (1988). The number of neurons in the brain: How we report what we do not know. *Teaching of Psychology, 15,* 153–156.

Taylor, E. (1990). New light on the origin of William James's experimental psychology. In M. G. Johnson & T. B. Henley (Eds.), *Reflections on The Principles of Psychology: William James after a century* (pp. 33–61). Hillsdale, NJ: Erlbaum.

Thomas, J. M. (1984). Four introductions to psychology. *Contemporary Psychology, 29,* 629–632.

Titchener, E. B. (1896). *An outline of psychology.* New York: Macmillan.

Titchener, E. B. (1897). *An outline of psychology* (2nd ed.). New York: Macmillan.

Titchener, E. B. (1898). *A primer of psychology.* New York: Macmillan.

Titchener, E. B. (1899). *An outline of psychology* (3rd ed.). New York: Macmillan.

Titchener, E. B. (1901–1905). *Experimental psychology: A manual of laboratory practice* (2 vols. in 4). New York: Macmillan.

Titchener, E. B. (1910). *A text-book of psychology.* New York: Macmillan.

Titchener, E. B. (1915). *A beginner's psychology.* New York: Macmillan.

Titchener, E. B. (1921). George Trumbull Ladd. *American Journal of Psychology*, *32*, 600.

Tussing, L. (1938). What students want from the elementary course in psychology. *Journal of Applied Psychology*, *20*, 633–658.

Tyson-Bernstein, H. (1989). The academy's contribution to textbook impoverishment. *Education Digest*, *54*(6), 25–28.

Upham, T. C. (1827). *Elements of intellectual philosophy*. Portland, OR: Shirley & Hyde.

Upham, T. C. (1831). *Elements of mental philosophy* (Vols. 1–2). Boston: Wells & Lily.

Vaughan, W. F. (1936). *General psychology*. Garden City: NY: Doubleday.

Vazquez, C. A. (1989). Pedagogy versus substance. *Contemporary Psychology*, *34*, 470–473.

Vernon, W. M. (1974). *Introductory psychology: A mastery coursebook with performance objectives*. Chicago: Rand McNally.

Wade, C., & Tavris, C. (1987). *Psychology*. New York: Harper & Row.

Walls, J. W. (1980). [Review of *Psychology Today: An Introduction* (4th ed.)]. *Teaching of Psychology*, *7*, 120–121.

Watson, J. B. (1911). [Review of *A Text-Book of Psychology*]. *American Journal of Psychology*, *22*, 313–316.

Watson, J. B. (1913). Psychology as the behaviorist views it. *Psychological Review*, *20*, 158–177.

Watson, J. B. (1919). *Psychology from the standpoint of a behaviorist*. Philadelphia, PA: Lippincott.

Wayland, F. (1854). *Elements of intellectual philosophy*. Boston: Phillips, Sampson.

Webb, W. B. (1991). History from our textbooks: Boring, Langfeld, and Weld's introductory texts (1935–1948+). *Teaching of Psychology*, *18*, 33–35.

Weiner, B., Runquist, W., Runquist, P. A., Raven, B. H., Meyer, W. J., Leiman, A., Kutscher, C. L., Kleinmuntz, B., & Haber, R. N. (1977). *Discovering psychology*. Chicago: Science Research Associates.

Weiten, W. (1988). Objective features of introductory psychology textbooks as related to professors' impressions. *Teaching of Psychology*, *15*, 10–16.

Wight, R. D. (1991). *Selling a psychobiologist: Yerkes, Münsterberg, academic politics, and an anomalous textbook*. Manuscript submitted for publication.

Winston, A. S. (1988). *Cause* and *experiment* in introductory psychology: An analysis of R. S. Woodworth's textbooks. *Teaching of Psychology*, *15*, 79–83.

Winston, A. S. (1990). Robert Sessions Woodworth and the "Columbia bible": How the psychological experiment was redefined. *American Journal of Psychology*, *103*, 391–401.

Winton, W. M. (1987). Do introductory textbooks present the Yerkes-Dodson law correctly? *American Psychologist*, *42*, 202–203.

Wolfle, D. (1942). The first course in psychology. *Psychological Bulletin, 39,* 685–712.

Woodworth, R. S. (1921). *Psychology: A study of mental life.* New York: Holt.

Woodworth, R. S. (1929). *Psychology* (2nd ed.). New York: Holt.

Woodworth, R. S. (1934). *Psychology* (3rd ed.). New York: Holt.

Woodworth, R. S. (1938). *Experimental psychology.* New York: Holt.

Woodworth, R. S. (1940). *Psychology* (4th ed.). New York: Holt.

Woodworth, R. S., & Marquis, D. G. (1947). *Psychology* (5th ed.). New York: Holt.

Woodworth, R. S., & Schlosberg, H. (1954). *Experimental psychology* (2nd ed.). New York: Holt.

Wortman, C. B., & Loftus, E. F. (1981). *Psychology.* New York: Knopf.

Yerkes, R. M. (1911). *Introduction to psychology.* New York: Holt.

Zimbardo, P. G. (1979). *Psychology and life* (10th ed.). Glenview, IL: Scott, Foresman.

Zimbardo, P. G. (1985). *Psychology and life* (11th ed.). Glenview, IL: Scott, Foresman.

Zimbardo, P. G. (1988). *Psychology and life* (12th ed.). Glenview, IL: Scott, Foresman.

Zimbardo, P. G. (1992). *Psychology and life* (13th ed.). New York: HarperCollins.

Zimbardo, P. G., & Ruch, F. L. (1975). *Psychology and life* (9th ed.). Glenview, IL: Scott, Foresman.

APPENDIX

DESCRIPTION OF TEXT VARIABLES

1. *Topical allocations.* Each book was inspected to determine the number of chapters devoted to each of 15 topical areas. The categorization of chapters was based on their dominant topic. When necessary, chapters were divided in half and assigned to two topical areas. The number of chapters on each topic was divided by the total number of chapters to estimate the proportion of coverage devoted to each topic. Appendixes were included in these analyses only if they were comparable in size to the book's chapters. The topical areas were organized as follows:
   a. Introduction/history/methods,
   b. Biological bases of behavior,
   c. Sensation/perception,
   d. Aspects of consciousness,
   e. Learning/conditioning,
   f. Memory,
   g. Language/thought,
   h. Intelligence/psychological testing,
   i. Motivation/emotion,
   j. Developmental psychology,
   k. Personality,
   l. Adjustment,
   m. Psychopathology/psychotherapy,
   n. Social psychology, and
   o. Other.
2. *Number of chapters.* The number of chapters in each book was recorded.
3. *Total pages.* The total number of pages in each book was recorded, including appendixes, references, glossaries, indexes, and all material that followed the main text (but not front matter).
4. *Manuscript length.* An estimate of the length of the manuscript (excluding front matter, appendixes, references, etc.) in words was made by multiplying the number of words that fit on a full page (based on the page closest to p. 100 that contained nothing but text) by the number of pages of text and then subtracting a portion of this number to allow for illustrations (results were rounded to the nearest 1,000 words). The proportion subtracted was determined individually for each book on the basis of the amount of space devoted to illustrations in a sample chapter (chapter 8 in each book).
5. *Number of illustrations.* The number of figures and photographs in chap-

ters 2, 6, and 10 were counted and averaged. This average was multiplied by the number of chapters to estimate the total number of illustrations in each book. In older books, in which the figures were numbered consecutively across chapters, the last figure was found to determine the number of figures (the number of photographs was still estimated by examining chapters 2, 6, and 10).

6. *Number of pedagogical aids.* Each book was checked for the presence of four pedagogical aids: chapter outlines, chapter summaries, glossaries, and boldface print for technical terms. The total number of these aids incorporated into each book was recorded.

7. *Number of references.* The average number of references found on the first four full pages of the references section was multiplied by the number of pages of references to estimate the total number of references cited. If a book's references were organized by chapter, the estimate of total references was based on the average number of references found in the first four chapters.

8. *Recency of references.* The sample of references used to estimate the total number of references was examined to estimate the percentage of references that were "recent" (published within 5 years of the text's copyright date).

9. *Most frequently cited theorists and researchers.* The index of each book was inspected to determine the number of index entries for various theorists and researchers. The seven people cited most frequently were listed in rank order.

21

PSYCHOLOGICAL HANDBOOKS: HISTORY AND FUNCTION

JAMES L. PATE

The history of psychology usually involves a consideration of great ideas, great events, and great people. Great ideas and great people are undeniably important in the history of any discipline, and Watson and Evans (1991) combined the two approaches in the most recent edition of *The Great Psychologists*, to which the subtitle *A History of Psychological Thought* has been added. Another approach to the history of psychology involves an analysis of textbooks, journals, handbooks, and reviews of various kinds. In part, this approach is based on the assumption that the history of the discipline is reflected in what students are taught. These approaches are not mutually exclusive or even in conflict. Rather, the various approaches are complementary, with each providing information that is not readily available when other approaches are used.

One example of this new approach is Webb's (1991) analysis of the content of three editions of an introductory psychology textbook published

I thank two reviewers and Charles Brewer for comments on this chapter. In addition, I thank D. J. Pate for her critical readings of various versions of this chapter.

Parts of this chapter were presented at the meeting of the Southern Society for Philosophy and Psychology in Atlanta in March 1991.

between 1935 and 1948. He compared the content of those three editions with the content of a composite recent introductory book (a combination of the content of three introductory books published after 1985) and identified three types of changes across 50 years. First, the allocation of space to various topics changed substantially; second, some new topics were introduced; third, old topics were eliminated or incorporated into other major sections of the book. Thus, even introductory textbooks may provide some information about the evolution and history of a discipline.

Boneau (1990a, 1990b) attempted to determine the top 100 concepts in 10 subareas of psychology. He created a ranking by asking textbook authors to indicate the concepts that all psychology majors should be expected to know. For some concepts, there was substantial agreement among the authors; thus, those concepts and the terms referring to them should appear in textbooks and handbooks. A comparison of the top 100 concepts across time and across textbooks would be interesting, but that comparison has not been reported, to my knowledge.

In this chapter, I discuss books that have the word *handbook* in the title and books that have served as handbooks even though that word is not in the title. I begin by presenting some definitions of *handbook* provided by authors or editors of handbooks. The definition may be related to or may refer to the functions of handbooks, which I discuss in the third section of this chapter, but definitions and functions are not identical. I then present an analysis of handbooks in four domains: experimental psychology, child psychology, social psychology, and specialized areas of psychology. Finally, I offer some conclusions on the basis of the previous sections.

DEFINITIONS

Handbooks exist in many disciplines, and certainly there have been important handbooks in psychology. Several definitions of *handbook* can be found in *Webster's New Collegiate Dictionary* (1949). The first definition is "a manual; a guidebook" (p. 374). The second is a bit more interesting— "A betting book of a bookmaker carried in the hand or on the person to evade laws against making books of bets" (*Webster's*, 1949, p. 374). Even though the second definition has more potential for an interesting essay, the first seems more appropriate in the present context.

A guidebook generally provides information about where one should go, how one should get there, and what one should see. In the academic world, one might expect a handbook (a guidebook) to tell one what is important, how information is organized, and how to do research, to teach, or to perform some other activity. A manual has at least some overlap with a guidebook because a manual should tell one how to do something and a guidebook might provide the same information. Thus, I discuss books that provide these types of information, regardless of whether the word *handbook* is part of the title.

Dictionaries are not necessarily helpful when one seeks a definition of a novel word. Miller and Gildea (1987), for example, identified misuses of common terms when children were given only the dictionary definitions. Technical terms are even more troublesome. One may consider what writers or editors of handbooks have stated as the defining attributes of a handbook rather than relying on a dictionary. Eysenck (1961) wrote in the introduction to his *Handbook of Abnormal Psychology* that he would not be much concerned with the meaning of either *psychology* or *handbook*. Many, perhaps most, people have abandoned the attempt to define psychology, but it seems strange that *handbook*, a superficially simple concept, should be difficult to define. Eysenck (1961) offered an operational definition: A "handbook is as a handbook does" (p. xi). His approach is no more satisfactory than the somewhat hackneyed definition of intelligence as "what an intelligence test measures."

The attributes of a handbook may provide more information about the meaning of *handbook* than is provided by a simple dictionary definition. The type of reader for whom the material is written may distinguish handbooks from other publications. For example, some periodicals, such as *Discovery* and *Psychology Today*, are written for intelligent but nonprofessional readers. Or, the *Teaching of Psychology* is a journal for psychologists who are interested in teaching. If one considers the readers for whom handbooks have been written, one finds great variety. Murchison (1933) stated that the *Handbook of Child Psychology* was intended for the "scholar" (p. ix). Murchison (1935) indicated that the *Handbook of Social Psychology* should aid "serious students" (p. ix). Stevens (1951) stated that his *Handbook of Experimental Psychology* was for the "advanced scholar" (p. vii), by which he meant graduate students who would use the book as a text and specialists who would use it as a reference. Graduate students in the 1950s and early 1960s were expected to know (i.e., memorize) large portions of that book. The recent revision of Stevens's handbook (Atkinson, Herrnstein, Lindzey, & Luce, 1988) was intended for scholars and beginning graduate students. Woodworth and Schlosberg (1954) wrote for advanced undergraduates, graduate students, and instructors. Still other handbooks are designed for professional psychologists of various specializations. Thus, handbooks for almost every type of reader imaginable have been published.

Although handbooks are frequently used as textbooks, they certainly are not standard textbooks. In particular, handbooks are not intended for introductory students or naive readers. Typically, the material in a handbook is written by an expert in a narrowly defined area, about which the reader is assumed to be reasonably knowledgeable. A standard textbook, by contrast, is designed to introduce students to concepts or to explicate those concepts in considerable detail. Textbook writers assume that the reader brings only a modicum of information about the domain to the reading of the material. Consequently, much space in a textbook is allocated to defining terms or specifying the relations among terms.

A second attribute that might define a handbook is its content. Unfortunately, content per se cannot be used to define a handbook in psychology because there are handbooks for almost every topic. Consider some of the topics of handbooks. Various types of psychology constitute one class of handbooks. Clinical, counseling, applied, mathematical, and various other forms of psychology are discussed in handbooks.[1] Or, there are handbooks in which different subject groups (e.g., child, adolescent, abnormal, etc.) are discussed. Another major type of handbook is concerned with methodology, which is often taken as the sine qua non of psychology. Boneau (1990a) found that 42 of the top 100 terms that textbook authors thought should be known by all psychology majors were found in the methodology and statistics area. There are handbooks for research in child psychology, adolescent psychology, clinical psychology, human memory, psychological assessment, and most other areas and subareas of psychology. Thus, there are handbooks in which general methods are considered and others in which highly specialized methods are discussed.

In addition, there are handbooks for specialized substantive topics. In part, the proliferation of handbooks might be viewed as having started with Murchison, who thought that his initial book, *The Foundations of Experimental Psychology* (1929), required such extensive revision that several volumes would be necessary to cover all of the essential topics. Rather than Murchison's three handbooks on child, social, and general experimental psychology, handbooks on highly specialized topics such as mental health and aging, learning and cognition, political behavior, psychological literature, eating behavior, sexual abuse of children, the Sixteen Personality Factor Questionnaire, and many others exist today. The increasing specialization seen in handbooks is a reflection of the increasing specialization in psychology and most other disciplines. One can no longer be a general psychologist because the amount of information is simply whelming. Some psychologists resist the trend, but even they cannot hope to master the great variety of topics in modern psychology. Thus, they must rely on experts who present information concisely in handbooks and in other secondary sources.

The scope of a handbook might be its defining characteristic. A handbook differs from an annual review or a review in a journal in that the material in a handbook is usually more extensive. Furthermore, the orga-

---

[1]Some types of psychology for which handbooks have been published include applied, child, clinical, clinical health, correctional, counseling, cross-cultural, developmental, economic, environmental, experimental, family psychology and therapy, forensic, general experimental, industrial, industrial and organizational, mathematical, multivariate experimental, practical, school, social, and work and organizational.

nization of handbooks and reviews is usually different. Generally, a handbook provides information about the current state of knowledge in a particular domain without a limited time frame, whereas the time span for many reviews is for some specified period (e.g., 1 year, one decade).

The attempt to identify defining features of a handbook has not been particularly successful. Smith and Medin (1981) argued that the modern view of concepts—that there are no defining attributes—should be accepted, in which case *handbook* might be defined by giving examples. Assuming that examples may be informative, I consider handbooks in experimental, social, and child psychology (Murchison's three areas) and a set of specialized handbooks. I take a broad perspective and include some books that contain the word *handbook* in the title and some that do not. I do not discuss every book that includes *handbook* in its title, even within the three areas that I consider in detail because the inclusion of that word in the title is no assurance that the book is indeed a handbook. In other cases, I discuss books such as Woodworth's (1938) *Experimental Psychology*, even though the word *handbook* does not appear in the title.

FUNCTIONS

Another important attribute of handbooks is their function. According to many authors, a handbook should provide easy and convenient access to frequently needed information. Thus, if one wants to find facts about a discipline or techniques for performing some activity, one might consult a handbook. It generally is assumed that important facts, and in some cases theories, will be accessible in a handbook.

Handbooks also indicate the organization of the discipline. In earlier times, handbooks included information from an entire discipline. More recently, however, handbooks have become highly specialized, and as indicated previously, there are now handbooks for dozens of subareas of psychology. Furthermore, as shown in detail later, editors have moved topics from one major subarea to another; thus, the microorganization of a field is indicated by the organization of handbooks.

Finally, handbooks provide indirect evidence about important people in the discipline. People who are invited to write chapters in a handbook are usually experts in their research or practice area. Frequently, contributors to a handbook will have become less important or will have died by the time the handbook is revised. Thus, previous authors will be eliminated, and new authors will be included. The only person who wrote a chapter for Stevens's (1951) handbook and its revision (Atkinson et al., 1988) was George Miller, who is one of the more important modern psychologists, as indicated by his having received the 1991 National Medal of Science (Adler, 1991)

For present purposes, I do not devote much space to handbooks of other disciplines even though they may be important in the history of psychology and provide a different perspective on what handbooks are. For example, Johannes Müller's *Handbuch der Physiologie des Menschen* (*Handbook of Human Physiology*) was published between 1833 and 1840 (Boring, 1957) and is mentioned in many books on the history of psychology. The first volume of *Handbuch der Physiologischen Optik* (*Handbook of Physiological Optics*) was published by Helmholtz in 1856, and the last volume was published in 1866 (Boring, 1957). The first edition of *Die Lehre von den Tonempfindungen als Physiologischer Grundlage für die Theorie der Musik* (*Lessons Deriving From Tonal Sensations as the Physiological Basis for Musical Theory*) was published in 1863, and although it does not contain the word *handbook* in the title, Boring (1957) referred to it as a handbook.

Titchener's (1901) *Experimental Psychology: A Manual of Laboratory Practice* might have been the first psychology handbook. In the first volume, Titchener discussed qualitative experiments and described experiments involving sensations arising from most sensory systems, affections, ideation, and other topics, with a description of 37 experiments. In Volume 2, subtitled *Quantitative Experiments* (Titchener, 1905a, 1905b), he discussed the psychophysical methods. In both volumes, Titchener provided specific information about experimental techniques.

A more likely candidate for the title of first handbook is Murchison's (1934) *Handbook of General Experimental Psychology*. However, the first edition of his *Handbook of Child Psychology* had been published in 1931, and a revised edition was published in 1933. In the preface to the child psychology book, Murchison (1931) indicated that his earlier book, *The Foundations of Experimental Psychology* (Murchison, 1929), could not be revised within the limits of a single volume. Convinced that a similar book was needed, he produced three major works: one on child psychology, one on general experimental psychology, and one on social psychology. In the remainder of this chapter, I consider handbooks in those three domains as well as specialized handbooks. I chose the first three types because of their historical precedence and the last because it illustrates a substantial trend in handbooks and in psychology in general.

TYPES OF HANDBOOKS

General and Experimental Handbooks

Although Stevens's (1951) handbook was not, technically speaking, a revision of Murchison's 1929 book, Stevens indicated that, in part, he planned his book because the Murchison volumes were out of print and because there was a need for a "technical survey" (Stevens, 1951, p. vii).

Atkinson et al. (1988) made a similar argument in their revision of Stevens's handbook. However, they claimed that their new version was more a tribute to Stevens than a revision of his previous book. They also considered whether there was a need for a handbook of general experimental psychology, given that there are many specialty handbooks. Obviously, their conclusion was that a need existed. They also considered whether it would be possible to write or edit such a comprehensive volume or set. Again, they concluded that such a task was possible.

If one considers the Murchison (1929), Stevens (1951), and Atkinson et al. (1988) handbooks to be a proper sequence, then their content should be compared. Murchison's handbook was divided into two parts: adjustive processes and receptive processes. Some topics in the adjustive section, which contained 12 chapters, would appear in a current handbook, but others would not. There were chapters on the study of living organisms (Hudson Hoagland), "work of the integrated organism" (Edward S. Robinson), heredity (T. H. Morgan), mechanisms of reaction (Alexander Forbes), and postural mechanisms (J. G. Dusser de Barenne). The largest subsection, which was on learning, contained chapters on maturation (Calvin P. Stone), the conditioned reflex (Clark L. Hull), the nervous mechanisms of learning (Karl S. Lashley), and experimental studies (Walter S. Hunter). In those four chapters, the authors emphasized animal rather than human studies. Philip Bard and Carney Landis each wrote a chapter on emotion. Walter Cannon wrote a chapter on hunger and thirst, which were the only motivational topics in the handbook. These writers were all outstanding experts in their research areas.

The receptive processes section contained three chapters each on vision (L. T. Troland, S. Hecht, and C. H. Graham) and audition (H. Banister, H. Hartridge, and H. Davis), one on chemoreception (W. J. Crozier), and one on the skin sense (J. P. Nafe). Murchison's division was a clear indication of the organization of experimental psychology at that time. Psychologists tended to emphasize sensation and perception, as Titchener had in his earlier books, or to emphasize responses (adjustive processes).

Stevens's (1951) classic discussion of measurement and psychophysics was the first chapter in his book, the remainder of which he divided into six parts. In the physiological section, the authors emphasized basic physiological processes in five chapters, one of which was a discussion of the neuron. For the growth and development section, Roger Sperry, an assistant professor of anatomy at that time, wrote a chapter titled "Mechanisms of Neural Maturation." Genetics, ontogenetic development, and phylogenetic development were allotted a chapter each, and there was a chapter on growth curves. Thus, the increasing importance of genetics and development is indicated by the allocation of five chapters to a topic to which Murchison had allocated only one chapter.

Murchison's (1929) book contained only one chapter on motivation,

TABLE 1
Content of Experimental Psychology Handbooks

Handbook and topic	No. chap. devoted to topic
Murchison (1934)	
Part 1. Adjustive processes	12
Part 2. Receptive processes	8
Stevens (1951)	
Physiological mechanisms	5
Growth and development	5
Motivation	3
Learning and adjustment	7
Sensory processes	11
Human performance	4
Atkinson, Herrnstein, Lindzey, and Luce (1988)	
Volume 1	
Part 1. Perception	9
Part 2. Motivation	5
Volume 2	
Part 1. Learning	4
Part 2. Cognition	9

a topic that Stevens (1951) elevated to a section with three chapters. The topic remained at the section level in Atkinson et al. (1988), which may indicate that motivation is more important now than it was then. These changes in the importance of topics and in the organization of topics within motivation and development reflect changes in psychology per se.

Cognitive psychology, which was not included in Murchison's (1929) handbook, was discussed in one chapter in Stevens's (1951) book. In the Atkinson et al. (1988) volumes, cognitive psychology was divided into chapters on movement control, representation, problem solving, decision making, and attention. Stevens and Atkinson et al. included chapters on speech and language (psycholinguistics) and human learning, both of which are related to cognitive psychology. The change from no chapter in Murchison's book to one chapter in Stevens's book to five chapters in the Atkinson et al. book indicates an exponential growth that is likely to continue. A comparison of the three editions (Murchison, Stevens, and Atkinson et al.) reveals that some major topics were added, some were deleted, some were expanded, and others were condensed or combined (see Table 1). For example, empirical and theoretical approaches were separated in Stevens's handbook but were integrated in the Atkinson et al. volumes. For other topics, the authors renamed the area, with "physiology of learning" (Stevens) being changed to "psychobiology of learning" (Atkinson et al.). This renaming may reflect a change in the basic orientation of researchers in that area. In the case of cognitive psychology, the changes may reflect shifts in the importance of the topic. Thus, a consideration of these three books in one area of psychology indicates some of the ways in which the field has changed in slightly more than 50 years.

Woodworth's (1938) *Experimental Psychology* functioned as a handbook even though the word *handbook* did not appear in its title. Winston (1990) discussed in detail the development and publication of that book, known as the "Columbia bible." Woodworth's book, which has gone through three editions, differed from the other books discussed in that the first edition was written by a single author. For the third edition (Kling & Riggs, 1971), each chapter was written by a different author, so this volume had the appearance as well as the scope of a handbook.

Child Psychology

The 1931 edition of Murchison's *Handbook of Child Psychology* was the first handbook on this topic (Berndt & Zigler, 1985). However, Murchison (1929) had previously included child psychology in his *Foundations of Experimental Psychology*, which he later divided into three books. One of those books was the 1931 edition of the *Handbook of Child Psychology*. The second edition of that book (Murchison, 1933) contained chapters on both prenatal and postnatal development. Another major section was on factors that modify child behavior, in which birth order, sex differences, eidetic imagery, and other topics were considered. Interest in some of these topics diminished, but interest in birth order has reappeared, with Zajonc (1986) in particular having written extensively about that topic. Although research on eidetic imagery has almost vanished, investigations of other forms of imagery have been exceptionally popular. Sex differences recently have been investigated and discussed in many ways. Perhaps the most unusual section in the Murchison volumes concerned special groups, which included the gifted child, the primitive child (a chapter written by Margaret Mead), the "feebleminded" child, and the adolescent child. As pointed out earlier, handbooks devoted to specific subject groups are now numerous.

Carmichael's (1946) *Manual of Child Psychology* can be viewed as a successor to Murchison's (1931) *Handbook of Child Psychology* in the same way that Stevens's (1951) handbook was a successor to Murchison's (1929) book on experimental psychology. A comparison of the content of Carmichael's book with Murchison's (1933) makes clear the increasing emphasis on methodology in child psychology. Carmichael's (1954) second edition contained a chapter on methods and one on measurement. By that time, psychopathology of children was also important enough to be included.

Mussen (1970) edited *Carmichael's Manual of Child Psychology*, which was identified also as the third edition, with Carmichael having served as editor of the first two editions. For the fourth edition, Mussen (1983) changed the title to *Handbook of Child Psychology*, but he made the connection to the earlier editions explicit by including the following subtitle: *Formerly Carmichael's Manual of Child Psychology.*

Social Psychology

In the preface to his *Handbook of Social Psychology*, Murchison (1935) emphasized the need to discover laws that would aid in understanding and ameliorating social problems. There were chapters on organisms as diverse as bacteria and humans, with the latter being divided into groups such as "Negro," "Red Man," "White Man," and "Yellow Man." These terms are not used in current books on social psychology because inappropriate racial implications are no longer acceptable. One might hope that the use of "man" in the generic sense would also be unacceptable, but gender constraints have not been as completely rejected as have racial constraints.

Lindzey (1954) indicated that a new version of the handbook was needed because Murchison's (1935) book was out of print, which was the same justification that Stevens (1951) had used 3 years earlier in his handbook. Lindzey included sections on systematic positions, research methods, and historical background of social psychology in his *Handbook of Social Psychology*.

Young (1957) provided a different perspective and discussed the "dual parentage" of social psychology—psychology and sociology. Although there might have been some rapprochement of psychology and sociology, there are nonetheless some disparities in the dominant viewpoints in those disciplines. In Young's book, for example, there were two sections. The first concerned social interactions and the interaction of the individual with groups and cultures. In the second part, collective behavior was the main topic.

Specialized Handbooks

Although editors and publishers continue to produce general handbooks, the number of specialized handbooks is amazing and appears to be increasing. For example, 12 handbooks were advertised in the 1991 annual convention program of the American Psychological Association, and none of those was about a topic that is a major subarea of psychology. The range of topics is surprising. There were advertisements for handbooks on psychooncology, short-term dynamic psychotherapy, psychodiagnostic testing, and early childhood intervention, among others. For this section, I have chosen handbooks in two specialized domains because, in part, the topics have a long if somewhat cyclical history.

As I discussed elsewhere (Pate, 1987), Fechner is the founder of mathematical psychology (and, in fact, might be the founder of experimental psychology). For many years, psychology was not particularly dependent on mathematics. However, in the late 1950s and early 1960s, mathematical psychology expanded rapidly, with the emphasis being on theoretical developments rather than on statistical techniques or measurement theory. If one takes the founding of modern mathematical psychology to be the publication of Estes's (1950) article on the statistical theory of learning, then it is surprising that the *Handbook of Mathematical Psychology* (Luce, Bush, & Galanter, 1963–1965) was published as early as 1963. However, the decline in mathematical psychology as a major subtopic is almost as dramatic. The claim that mathematical psychology has declined is supported by the fact that the last volume of that handbook was published in 1965, and there has been no revision.

The second specialized area is learning and cognitive psychology. Psychology has a cyclical history in that what is judged to be important in one era may become less important in another. In the early stages of its development, psychology was clearly cognitive, but during the period when American psychology was dominated by behaviorism, cognitive functions disappeared from psychological research. Still later, cognitive psychology reappeared in what some have called a "cognitive revolution" (Baars, 1986; Gardner, 1985) and what others have called a "cognitive renaissance" (Pate, 1989).

The last handbook to be mentioned has a dual title; one reason for that title is that cognitive psychology was in a formative stage of development at the time that the title for the handbook was chosen. Estes, who had been extensively involved in the development of mathematical psychology, served as the editor of the *Handbook of Learning and Cognitive Processes*, which was published during a 3-year period beginning in 1975 (Estes, 1975–1978). Despite the dual title, the editor and the authors clearly emphasized the cognitive approach to psychology. Thus, psychology has returned to its cognitive origins.

CONCLUSION

Many handbooks have appeared in numerous editions, and one index of the rapidity of change in a domain may be the time between successive revisions. Publication dates for handbooks in the three broad areas discussed are shown in Table 2. The variation among times between revisions is substantial. Over roughly the same time period, there have been three editions of the experimental psychology handbook, four editions of the social psychology handbook, and six editions of the handbook of child psychology. The duties of an editor of such books are substantial. The organization of the book must be established, and authors must be recruited. Neither activity is trivial. Submissions must be reviewed, and authors must be convinced to make changes that they may prefer not to make. Thus,

TABLE 2
Dates of Various Editions of Handbooks in Three Areas

Experimental	Child	Social
Murchison (1934)	Murchison (1931)	Murchison (1935)
Stevens (1951)	Murchison (1933)	Lindzey (1954)
Atkinson, Herrnstein, Lindzey,	Carmichael (1946)	Lindzey and Aronson (1968)
and Luce (1988)	Carmichael (1954)	Lindzey and Aronson (1985)
	Mussen (1970)	
	Mussen (1983)	

people may be unwilling to assume responsibilities that are unlikely to produce anything more than intrinsic rewards.

An alternative interpretation is that new editions will be produced when the domain changes so much that the previous edition is no longer useful. In fact, Murchison, in the second edition of the *Handbook of Child Psychology*, indicated that in a mere 2 years the changes had been so great that there was little resemblance between the two editions. The dates in Table 2 indicate that the revision times differed considerably both within and across domains. The shortest lag was 2 years, and the largest lag was 37 years. Furthermore, not all handbooks are revised. The *Handbook of Mathematical Psychology* has not been revised even though the first volume was published 28 years ago. It seems unlikely that it will be revised because mathematical psychology has been absorbed into other areas.

The Appendix contains a lengthy, but by no means exhaustive, list of additional handbooks that I have not mentioned in this chapter. Even a glance at that list indicates that psychology has become highly specialized. Perhaps, as Koch (1981) maintained and as Bevan (1991) reiterated, there is no coherent body of psychological knowledge today. Yet, attempts to unify psychology at some level continue (Staats, 1991). Whether psychology can produce a Newton or an Einstein who can systematize the discipline wholistically remains to be seen. To some extent, handbooks may be viewed as attempts to find a common core of knowledge in the discipline, but psychology may be more a federation than a union. If that interpretation is correct, then the trend toward specialization as reflected in the current plethora of handbooks is likely to continue.

REFERENCES

Adler, T. (1991, December). National Science Medal goes to George Miller. *APA Monitor*, pp. 12–13.

Atkinson, R. C., Herrnstein, R. J., Lindzey, G., & Luce, R. D. (Eds.). (1988). *Stevens' handbook of experimental psychology* (2nd ed). New York: Wiley.

Baars, B. J. (1986). *The cognitive revolution in psychology*. New York: Guilford Press.

Berndt, T. J., & Zigler, E. F. (1985). Developmental psychology. In G. A. Kimble & K. Schlesinger (Eds.), *Topics in the history of psychology* (Vol. 2, pp. 115–150). Hillsdale, NJ: Erlbaum.

Bevan, W. (1991). Contemporary psychology: A tour inside the onion. *American Psychologist, 46,* 475–483.

Boneau, C. A. (1990a). Psychological literacy: A first approximation. *American Psychologist, 41,* 891–900.

Boneau, C. A. (1990b, Fall). Psychological literacy: History and systems. *History of Psychology Newsletter, 22,* pp. 55–57.

Boring, E. G. (1957). *A history of experimental psychology* (2nd ed.). New York: Appleton-Century-Crofts.

Carmichael, L. (Ed.). (1946). *Manual of child psychology.* New York: Wiley.

Carmichael, L. (Ed.). (1954). *Manual of child psychology* (2nd ed.). New York: Wiley.

Estes, W. K. (1950). Toward a statistical theory of learning. *Psychological Review, 57,* 94–107.

Estes, W. K. (Ed.). (1975–1978). *Handbook of learning and cognitive processes.* Hillsdale, NJ: Erlbaum.

Eysenck, H. J. (Ed.). (1961). *Handbook of abnormal psychology: An experimental approach.* New York: Basic Books.

Gardner, H. (1985). *The mind's new science: A history of the cognitive revolution.* New York: Basic Books.

Kling, J. W., & Riggs, L. A. (Eds.). (1971). *Woodworth & Schlosberg's experimental psychology* (3rd ed.). New York: Holt, Rinehart & Winston.

Koch, S. (1981). The nature and limits of psychological knowledge: Lessons of a century qua "science." *American Psychologist, 36,* 257–269.

Lindzey, G. (Ed.). (1954). *Handbook of social psychology.* Reading, MA: Addison-Wesley.

Lindzey, G., & Aronson, E. (Eds.). (1968). *Handbook of social psychology* (2nd ed.). Reading, MA: Addison-Wesley.

Lindzey, G., & Aronson, E. (Eds.). (1985). *Handbook of social psychology* (3rd ed.). New York: Random House.

Luce, R. D., Bush, R. R., & Galanter, E. (Eds.). (1963–1965). *Handbook of mathematical psychology.* New York: Wiley.

Miller, G. A., & Gildea, P. M. (1987). How children learn words. *Scientific American, 257*(3), 94–99.

Murchison, C. (Ed.). (1929). *The foundations of experimental psychology.* Worcester, MA: Clark University Press.

Murchison, C. (Ed.). (1931). *Handbook of child psychology.* Worcester, MA: Clark University Press.

Murchison, C. (Ed.). (1933). *Handbook of child psychology* (2nd ed., rev.). Worcester, MA: Clark University Press.

Murchison, C. (Ed.). (1934). *Handbook of general experimental psychology*. Worcester, MA: Clark University Press.

Murchison, C. (Ed.). (1935). *Handbook of social psychology*. Worcester, MA: Clark University Press.

Mussen, P. H. (Ed.). (1970). *Carmichael's manual of child psychology* (3rd ed.). New York: Wiley.

Mussen, P. H. (Ed.). (1983). *Handbook of child psychology: Formerly Carmichael's manual of child psychology* (4th ed.). New York: Wiley.

Pate, J. L. (1987, March). Fechner as a statistician. In W. G. Bringmann (Chair), *Fechner Memorial Symposium*. Symposium conducted at the meeting of the Southeastern Psychological Association, Atlanta.

Pate, J. L. (1989). Historical problems: A review essay of Baar's *The cognitive revolution in psychology*. *Philosophical Psychology, 2*, 315–324.

Smith, E. E., & Medin, D. L. (1981). *Categories and concepts*. Cambridge, MA: Harvard University Press.

Staats, A. W. (1991). Unified positivism and unification psychology: Fad or a new field. *American Psychologist, 46*, 899–912.

Stevens, S. S. (Ed.). (1951). *Handbook of experimental psychology*. New York: Wiley.

Titchener, E. B. (1901). *Experimental psychology: A manual of laboratory practice. Volume 1: Qualitative experiments: Part 1. Student's manual*. New York: Macmillan.

Titchener, E. B. (1905a). *Experimental psychology: A manual of laboratory practice. Volume 2: Quantitative experiments: Part 1. Student's manual*. New York: Macmillan.

Titchener, E. B. (1905b). *Experimental psychology: A manual of laboratory practice. Volume 2: Quantitative experiments: Part 2. Instructor's manual*. New York: Macmillan.

Watson, R. I., & Evans, R. B. (1991). *The great psychologists: A history of psychological thought* (5th ed.). New York: HarperCollins.

Webb, W. B. (1991). History from our textbooks: Boring, Langfeld, and Weld's introductory texts (1935–1948 +). *Teaching of Psychology, 18*, 33–35.

Webster's New Collegiate Dictionary. (1949). Springfield, MA: Merriam.

Winston, A. S. (1990). Robert Sessions Woodworth and the "Columbia bible": How the psychological experiment was redefined. *American Journal of Psychology, 103*, 391–401.

Woodworth, R. S. (1938). *Experimental psychology*. New York: Holt.

Woodworth, R. S., & Schlosberg, H. (1954). *Experimental psychology* (rev. ed.). New York: Holt.

Young, K. (1957). *Handbook of social psychology* (rev. ed.). London: Routledge & Paul.

Zajonc, R. B. (1986). The decline and rise of scholastic aptitude scores: A prediction derived from the confluence model. *American Psychologist, 41*, 862–867.

APPENDIX

OTHER HANDBOOKS NOT CITED IN THIS CHAPTER

Adelson, J. (1980). (Ed.). *Handbook of adolescent psychology*. New York: Wiley.

Anchor, K. (1991). (Ed.). *The handbook of medical psychotherapy: Cost-effective strategies in mental health*. Göttingen, Federal Republic of Germany: Hogrefe & Huber.

Baum, A., & Singer, J. E. (Eds.). (1982). *Handbook of psychology and health*. Hillsdale, NJ: Erlbaum.

Bellack, A. S., & Hersen, M. (1985). *Handbook of comparative treatments for adult disorders*. New York: Wiley.

Benjamin, L. T., Jr., Daniel, R. S., & Brewer, C. L. (Eds.). (1985). *Handbook for teaching introductory psychology*. Hillsdale, NJ: Erlbaum.

Benjamin, L. T., Jr., & Lowman, K. D. (Eds.). (1988). *Activities handbook for the teaching of psychology* (Vol. 1, rev. ed.). Washington, DC: American Psychological Association.

Bezchlibnyk-Butler, K. Z., & Jeffries, J. J. (Eds.). (1991). *Clinical handbook of psychotropic drugs* (3rd rev. and expanded ed.). Göttingen, Federal Republic of Germany: Hogrefe & Huber.

Birren, J. E., & Schaie, K. W. (Eds.). (1977). *Handbook of the psychology of aging*. New York: Van Nostrand Reinhold.

Birren, J. E., & Schaie, K. W. (Eds.). (1985). *Handbook of the psychology of aging* (2nd ed.). New York: Van Nostrand Reinhold.

Birren, J. E., & Sloane, R. B. (Eds.). (1980). *Handbook of mental health and aging*. Englewood Cliffs, NJ: Prentice-Hall.

Birren, J. E., Sloane, R. B., & Cohen, G. D. (Eds.). (1992). *Handbook of mental health and aging* (2nd ed.). San Diego, CA: Academic Press.

Blechman, E. A., & Brownell, K. D. (1988). *Handbook of behavioral medicine for women*. New York: Pergamon Press.

Brown, S. D., & Lent, R. W. (Eds.). (1984). *Handbook of counseling psychology*. New York: Wiley.

Brownell, K. D., & Foreyt, J. P. (Eds.). (1986–1988). *Handbook of eating disorders: Physiology, psychology, and treatment of obesity, anorexia, and bulimia*. New York: Basic Books.

Camic, P. M., & Brown, F. D. (Eds.). (1989). *Assessing chronic pain: A multidisciplinary clinic handbook*. New York: Springer-Verlag.

Cattell, R. B. (Ed.). (1966). *Handbook of multivariate experimental psychology*. Chicago: Rand McNally.

Cattell, R. B., Eber, H. W., & Tatsuoka, M. M. (1970). *Handbook for the Sixteen*

Personality Factor Questionnaire (16 PF) in clinical, educational, industrial, and research psychology. Champaign, IL: Institute for Personality and Ability Testing.

Ceci, S. J. (Ed.). (1986). *Handbook of cognitive, social, and neuropsychological aspects of learning disabilities*. Hillsdale, NJ: Erlbaum.

Cole, M., & Maltzman, I. (Eds.). (1969). *Handbook of contemporary Soviet psychology*. New York: Basic Books.

Crits-Christoph, P., & Barber, J. (Eds.). (1991). *Handbook of short-term dynamic psychotherapy*. New York: Basic Books.

Dichter, E. (1964). *Handbook of consumer motivations: The psychology of the world of objects*. New York: McGraw-Hill.

DiMascio, A., & Shader, R. I. (Eds.). (1970). *Clinical handbook of psychopharmacology*. Northvale, NJ: Jason Aronson.

Dunnette, M. D. (Ed.). (1976). *Handbook of industrial and organizational psychology*. Chicago: Rand McNally.

Enlow, E. R. (1937). *Statistics in education and psychology: A combined handbook and textbook*. Englewood Cliffs, NJ: Prentice-Hall.

Ewing, C. P. (Ed.). (1985). *Psychology, psychiatry, and the law: A clinical and forensic handbook*. Sarasota, FL: Professional Resource Exchange.

Eysenck, M. W. (1984). *A handbook of cognitive psychology*. Hillsdale, NJ: Erlbaum.

Eysenck, M. W., & Keane, M. T. (1990). *Cognitive psychology: A student's handbook*. Hillsdale, NJ: Erlbaum.

Fine, M. J. (Ed.). (1988). *The second handbook on parent education: Contemporary perspectives*. San Diego, CA: Academic Press.

Franz, S. I. (1912). *Handbook of mental examination methods*. New York: Journal of Nervous and Mental Disease Publishing Co.

Fryer, D. H., & Henry, E. R. (Eds.). (1950). *Handbook of applied psychology*. New York: Rinehart.

Gazzaniga, M. S. (Ed.). (1984). *Handbook of cognitive neuroscience*. New York: Plenum Press.

Gilgen, A. R., & Gilgen, C. K. (Eds.). (1987). *International handbook of psychology*. New York: Greenwood.

Glover, J. A., Ronning, R. R., & Reynolds, C. R. (Eds.). (1989). *Handbook of creativity*. New York: Plenum Press.

Goldstein, G., & Hersen, M. (Eds.). (1990). *Handbook of psychological assessment* (2nd ed.). New York: Pergamon Press.

Greenfield, N. S., & Sternbach, R. A. (Eds.). (1972). *Handbook of psychophysiology*. New York: Holt, Rinehart & Winston.

Groth-Marnat, G. (1984). *Handbook of psychological assessment*. New York: Von Nostrand Reinhold.

Gutkin, T. B., & Reynolds, C. R. (Eds.). (1990). *Handbook of school psychology* (2nd ed.). New York: Wiley.

Hartley, J., & McKeachie, W. J. (1989). *Teaching psychology: A handbook.* Hillsdale, NJ: Erlbaum.

Herman, J. L., Morris, L. L., & Fitz-Gibbon, C. T. (1987). *Evaluator's handbook.* Newbury Park, CA: Sage.

Hersen, M., & Bellack, A. S. (Eds.). (1985). *Handbook of clinical behavior therapy with adults.* New York: Plenum Press.

Hersen, M., Kazdin, A. E., & Bellack, A. S. (Eds.). (1983). *The clinical psychology handbook.* New York: Pergamon Press.

Hersen, M., Kazdin, A. E., & Bellack, A. S. (Eds.). (1988). *The clinical psychology handbook* (2nd ed.). New York: Pergamon Press.

Holland, J. C., & Rowland, J. H. (Eds.). (1989). *Handbook of psychooncology: Psychological care of the patient with cancer.* New York: Oxford University Press.

Iversen, L. L., Iversen, S. D., & Snyder, S. H. (Eds.). (1975). *Handbook of psychopharmacology.* New York: Plenum Press.

Kendall, P. C., & Butcher, J. N. (Eds.). (1982). *Handbook of research methods in clinical psychology.* New York: Wiley.

Knezevic, S., Maximilian, V. A., Murbin, Z., Prohovnik, I., & Wade, J. P. H. (Eds.). (1987). *Handbook of regional cerebral blood flow.* Hillsdale, NJ: Erlbaum.

L'Abate, L. (Ed.). (1985). *The handbook of family psychology and therapy.* Homewood, IL: Dorsey.

Liberman, R. P. (Ed.). (1991). *Handbook of psychiatric rehabilitation.* New York: Pergamon Press.

Lindner, R. M., & Seliger, R. V. (Eds.). (1947). *Handbook of correctional psychology.* New York: Philosophical Library.

Louttit, C. M. (1932). *Handbook of psychological literature.* Bloomington, IN: Principia Press.

Lyerly, S. B. (Ed.). (1973). *Handbook of psychiatric rating scales* (2nd ed.). Rockville, MD: National Institute of Mental Health.

Lyerly, S. B., Abbott, P. S., Birren, J. E., & Schaie, K. W. (Eds.). (1985). *Handbook of the psychology of aging* (2nd ed.). New York: Van Nostrand Reinhold.

Makosky, V. P., Whittemore, L. G., & Rogers, A. M. (Eds.). (1987). *Activities handbook for the teaching of psychology* (Vol. 2). Washington, DC: American Psychological Association.

Makosky, V. P., Sileo, C. C., Whittemore, L. G., Landry, C. P., & Skutley, M. L. (Eds.). (1990). *Activities handbook for the teaching of psychology* (Vol. 3). Washington, DC: American Psychological Association.

Matson, J. L., & Mulick, J. A. (Eds.). (1991). *Handbook of mental retardation* (2nd ed.). New York: Pergamon Press.

Meisels, S. J., & Shonkoff, J. P. (Eds.). (1990). *Handbook of early childhood intervention.* New York: Cambridge University Press.

Miller, D. C. (1991). *Handbook of research design and social measurement* (5th ed.). Newbury Park, CA: Sage.

Millon, T., Green, C., & Meagher, R. (Eds.). (1982). *Handbook of clinical health psychology.* New York: Plenum Press.

Munroe, R. H., Munroe, R. L., & Whiting, B. B. (Eds.). (1981). *Handbook of cross-cultural human development.* New York: Garland.

Mussen, P. H. (Ed.). (1960). *Handbook of research methods in child development.* New York: Wiley.

Neel, A. (1977). *Theories of psychology: A handbook* (rev. and enlarged ed.). Cambridge, MA: Schenkman.

Nesselroade, J. R., & Cattell, R. B. (Eds.). (1988). *Handbook of multivariate experimental psychology* (2nd ed.). New York: Plenum Press.

Reed, J. G., & Baxter, P. M. (1983). *Library use: A handbook for psychology.* Washington, DC: American Psychological Association.

Reynolds, C. R., & Gutkin, T. B. (Eds.). (1982). *Handbook of school psychology.* New York: Wiley.

Shimberg, E. (1979). *Handbook of private practice in psychology.* New York: Brunner/Mazel.

Shumaker, S. A., Schron, E., & Ockene, J. K. (Eds.). (1990). *Handbook of health behavior change.* New York: Springer.

Smith, M. (1944). *Handbook of industrial psychology.* New York: Philosophical Library.

Sternberg, R. S. (Ed.). (1982). *Handbook of human intelligence.* New York: Cambridge University Press.

Stokols, D., & Altman, I. (Eds.). (1987). *Handbook of environmental psychology.* New York: Wiley.

Stone, G. C., Cohen, F., & Adler, N. E. (1979). *Health psychology: A handbook. Theories, applications, and challenges of a psychological approach to the health care system.* San Francisco: Jossey-Bass.

Sweet, J. J., Rozensky, R. H., & Tovian, S. M. (Eds.). (1991). *Handbook of clinical psychology in medical settings.* New York: Plenum Press.

Treffinger, D. J., Davis, J. K., & Ripple, R. E. (Eds.). (1977). *Handbook on teaching educational psychology.* New York: Academic Press.

Tuma, J. M. (Ed.). (1982). *Handbook for the practice of pediatric psychology.* New York: Wiley.

Van Hasselt, V. B., & Hersen, M. (Eds.). (1987). *Handbook of adolescent psychology.* New York: Pergamon Press.

van Raaij, W. F., van Veldhoven, G. M., & Karl-Erik, W. (Eds.). (1988). *Handbook of economic psychology.* Norwell, MA: Kluwer Academic.

Vincent, K. R. (1987). *The full battery codebook: A handbook of psychological test interpretation for clinical, counseling, rehabilitation, and school psychology.* Norwood, NJ: Ablex.

Walker, C. E. (Ed.). (1983). *Handbook of clinical psychology: Theory, research, and practice*. Homewood, IL: Dow Jones–Irwin.

Walker, C. E., & Roberts, M. C. (Eds.). (1983). *Handbook of clinical child psychology*. New York: Wiley.

Ware, M. E., & Brewer, C. L. (Eds.). (1988). *Handbook for teaching statistics and research methods*. Hillsdale, NJ: Erlbaum.

Ware, M. E., & Millard, R. J. (Eds.). (1987). *Handbook on student development: Advising, career development, and field placement*. Hillsdale, NJ: Erlbaum.

Wollman, N. (Ed.). (1985). *Working for peace: A handbook of practical psychology and other tools*. San Luis Obispo, CA: Impact Publishers.

Wolman, B. B. (Ed.). (1965). *Handbook of clinical psychology*. New York: McGraw-Hill.

Wolman, B. B. (Ed.). (1973). *Handbook of general psychology*. Englewood Cliffs, NJ: Prentice-Hall.

Wolman, B. B. (Ed.). (1982). *Handbook of developmental psychology*. Englewood Cliffs, NJ: Prentice-Hall.

Yaremko, R. M., Harari, H., Harrison, R. C., & Lynn, E. (1982). *Reference handbook of research and statistical methods in psychology: For students and professionals*. New York: Harper & Row.

22

CONSTANCY AND CHANGE: TEACHING AS DEPICTED IN PSYCHOLOGY JOURNALS

BERNARD C. BEINS

Since psychology's inception as a formal scientific discipline, psychologists have recognized the difficulties inherent in teaching its principles to students. Psychologists' concerns have sometimes shared a commonality with other disciplines, but other problems are peculiar to psychology. This latter set includes contending with the identity crisis that plagued psychology for so long; the varied misconceptions about human behavior that persist in American culture; and the fact that psychologists use aspects of psychological theory to develop technologies for teaching that same theory, blurring the distinction between theory and application.

In the present discussion, I show that the journals of psychology have dealt with complex issues in teaching, but not from the same viewpoint, not with the same tools, and not from the same theoretical perspective as each previous generation. Despite the similarities in topics, the current literature has evolved into a related but clearly different species. In addition to an enumeration of the problems, there are clear attempts to evaluate the efficacy of proposed solutions and even to assess whether there are singular solutions; in fact, the answers may change depending on the world-view of the students and teachers of any particular generation.

To trace the teaching of psychology through the journal literature, I outline various recurring themes with the hope that, compared with today, the views of previous psychologists will stand out in relief. Consequently, the material discussed here does not exhaust the literature on teaching. For such an approach, readers will benefit from the work of M. Johnson and Daniel (1974) and the annotated bibliographies that have appeared in the December issues of the *Teaching of Psychology* since 1974. D. E. Johnson (1991) has also organized a database covering articles in the *Teaching of Psychology*.

The problems of teaching have never dominated psychology, but there was early recognition that pedagogy merited recognition as a serious part of the development of psychology (e.g., E. C. Sanford, 1906; Wolfe, 1895). The question of the best way to teach psychology has certainly not been put to rest, as evidenced by the continuing appearance of relevant literature.

An important consideration in chronicling the history of teaching is that psychology exists within overlapping social, cultural, political, and educational contexts that shape and perhaps dictate its application. Outside of the colleges and universities, life has never been more complex, the foundation of society has never been more seriously questioned, and the tension and conflict between people and between social, economic, in-dustrial, religious, and racial groups have never been more intense than they are today. As such, publishers claim that the word *psychology* on the title page of a book is a sufficient guarantee for a substantial sale.

Furthermore, within American schools, there are now several trends emerging in higher education, such as lower enrollments in many 4-year institutions, students with a wider range of backgrounds and preparations who are demanding more relevant academic curricula and more vocationally oriented training, and increased pressures for monitoring teaching produc-tivity in a time of budgetary restraint. Such forces help to determine the nature of the student population. In American schools today, wide indi-vidual differences can be found among members of a class in general psy-chology. Important as the differences in intelligence may be, they are overshadowed by much more important differences in maturity, preparation, interests, and religious, social, and cultural backgrounds. It seems that many students have to be taught to read intelligently. Furthermore, despite the difficulties of dealing with undergraduates whose palms sweat at the thought of numbers or who are illiterate regarding them, the trend in psychology is certainly toward more quantification. Similarities among students were more common when a college education was limited to a select few, and doubtless the standardized methods are a relic of those days.

There has been pressure in the classroom to depart from standard lecture formats. Teachers have tried to keep the student doing things instead of merely listening, reading, or seeing them done. Previously, it was assumed that something was being taught by the lecture method that the student could not learn from merely reading the textbook for the course. It is now recognized that there are three common sources of error in teachers' evaluations of the lecture: (a) the warmth they feel over having made things clear; (b) the pleasure in freedom of expression and in hearing themselves; and (c) the failure to note that they have done the thinking so well that the student gladly accepts this ready-made portion without thinking.

From this vantage point, one can begin to view the teaching of psychology in the context of the various forces affecting the discipline. The issues are complex and recurrent, but there is evidence that effective ways have been developed to address pedagogical questions. The preceding paragraphs have encapsulated many of the major problems that face teachers daily. Unfortunately, these are the same problems that all generations of psychology teachers face. In fact, in Paragraphs 5–7 the ideas expressed are nearly direct quotations from teachers of psychology since 1910 (Buxton, 1956; Leuba, 1934; Maas, 1974; Marr, Plath, Wakeley, & Wilkins, 1960; Schoen, 1926; Seashore, 1910; Whipple, 1910). Apart from a few transition sentences and phrases and with the removal of sexist terminology and antiquated phrases, these words were penned by the psychologists who first grappled with the same dilemmas that psychologists face today.

It would be too easy, on reading the journal literature on the teaching of psychology, to argue that little progress has been made: Similar issues appear in succeeding decades, only to lie dormant for a period before springing to life again. A closer reading indicates that the issues are similar but not identical. Contemporary research will undoubtedly cover some of the same ground traversed by earlier psychologists, but much research in the current literature is more theoretically motivated, suggesting that psychologists have established a direction for their work. In this chapter I discuss the manner in which students, teachers, the classroom, and the curriculum have been represented in psychology journals during the past 100 years.

PSYCHOLOGY STUDENTS AND TEACHERS

The Psychology Student

A golden age of learning in which students were firmly committed to their studies and in which faculty members were highly motivated, well trained, and not burdened by administrative concerns is, to borrow from William James, "as mythical an entity as the jack of spades" (cited in Browning, 1965). Comments about students seem virtually indistinguishable across generations; the words are seldom praiseworthy. Students have been disparaged by faculty members who themselves were criticized during their own college years. Statements about students' difficulties with critical reading and writing are legion. McGovern and Hogshead (1990) are probably typical of many psychology teachers when they speak of "our horror at our own students' terrible prose" (p. 5). This perception was apparently no different among psychology faculty members 80 years before, leading Whipple (1910) to note that "many students . . . have almost literally to be taught to read intelligently" (p. 137).

Such claims by psychologists mirror those made even earlier by a renowned chemist. Clarke (1876/1971) asserted that "his students come to him miserably prepared, caring little for what he considers important, and regarding his instruction as so much of an impediment between them and their degrees" (p. 230). Clarke also enunciated sentiments about natural and physical science students that psychologists hear about psychology majors; he asserted that most science courses are "makeshifts" for students who are not bright enough or well enough prepared for study in the classics.

Furthermore, a century ago, the educational community was as distressed over student performance and knowledge as many are today; the so-called Committee of Ten of 1893 suggested a basic body of general knowledge appropriate for that generation's students (Tomlinson, 1987). Similarly, questions of cultural literacy pervade contemporary educational discussions.

The perception of periodic "crises" (usually triggered by factors outside of the educational process) has spurred activity, invariably followed by about 20 years of dormancy regarding the educational system (Deutsch, 1987). The learning environment, notably the teacher, has often borne the brunt of blame for the lack of student achievement. In reality, Tomlinson (1987) pointed out, "it is the students, not the teachers, who learn and, much as the students might like it otherwise, it is they who must perform the work" (p. 16). Students might acquire a large body of knowledge, but that knowledge might not be academic in nature. Tomlinson stressed that learning was not even guaranteed. With certain educational initiatives of the 1960s, anybody who persisted would graduate; "a system of certification had been devised that obviated talent or competence" (Tomlinson, 1987, p. 18).

Eighty years after Clarke's lament, Buxton (1956) bemoaned inadequate student preparation for quantitative courses. Similar problems still exist regarding both the preparation and desire of students for such courses (e.g., Beins, 1985; Dillon, 1982; Hastings, 1982).

The earlier authors aired the problems but suggested no remedies. The trend in the past 20 years has been to suggest ways to ameliorate the situation. Thus, Dillon (1982) developed classroom exercises that encouraged students to overcome their qualms about statistics, and Beins (1985) reported an out-of-class exercise designed to put statistics in a context relevant for the students.

Student skills in writing have also been the subject of intense focus (e.g., Madigan & Brosamer, 1990). Psychology teachers have also worked to develop critical reading skills (Poe, 1990; Price, 1990). McGovern and Hogshead (1990) suggested that helping students to develop reading and writing skills may have an ameliorative effect on teachers, leading them "to think more about our teaching and about how our students learn" (p. 5).

The journal *Teaching of Psychology* has been instrumental in providing ideas and techniques for more effective pedagogy. Previous publications were content to describe teachers' impressions.

The difference in perceptions between what teachers think students need and what the students desire may stem from the different perspectives of faculty and students. Teachers of psychology try to imbue students with their sentiments, using their scientific model as a basis. On the other hand, students seek relevance or preparation for a career in the helping professions or may view the world through different cultural perspectives, including non-Western viewpoints (Desforges, 1982; McGovern & Hawks, 1988; Nakano et al., 1990; Teaching and Research Group of Psychology, 1985).

It might be instructive to identify students' preferences during the past 100 years. R. J. Anderson (1970) found that student interests remained similar from 1951 to 1968. When he ranked broad topics according to relative interest value, the correlation between student perceptions was .915 across the nearly 30-year period, with personality and adjustment issues appearing the most intrinsically interesting, cognition and child development splitting the middle, and physiological psychology having the lowest rating.

R. J. Anderson (1970) suggested that in the 10 years before the initial rankings, students became more oriented toward social issues than toward the laboratory approach to psychology. By the early 1950s, Harper (1952) had already reported that more than 98% of students took their first psychology course either to help them get along better with others or out of simple curiosity. Leuba (1934), Schoen (1926), and others as early as 1904 (Miner, 1904) stressed that students and teachers have different interests. Students have always been fascinated by the applied aspects of psychology. The claim of change in student orientation is suspicious, given that recent reports of student interests (e.g., Quereshi, 1988) could easily have come from virtually any decade in this century (e.g., R. J. Anderson, 1970; Harper, 1952; Leuba, 1934; E. C. Sanford, 1906; Schoen, 1926; Seashore, 1910; Whipple, 1910).

Psychologists have long recognized the importance of teaching applications. E. C. Sanford (1906) hinted at the importance of a teacher's relating psychology to life, and Seashore (1910) and Schoen (1926) reinforced this point. Applications of psychology appeared early in discussions of the nature of psychology, including alliances with sociology and anthropology (Miner, 1904), as well as education (Whipple, 1910) and other areas of business and commerce (Seashore, 1910). By 1910, the first course in psychology was often combined with educational psychology in colleges and normal schools (i.e., postsecondary schools devoted to training teachers).

Regardless of the approach, theoretical or applied, the scientific basis of psychology was a constant that undergirded the teaching enterprise. Anastasi (1947) pointed out that the methods of psychological research are more crucial for some undergraduates than the content. "As for students who are planning to work in an applied field such as industrial, clinical or market research, I would say that experimental psychology is a must whether or not they are majors in psychology" (Anastasi, 1947, p. 61). In her view, relevance is meaningful only within the context of a scientific psychology.

By contrast, Menges and Trumpeter (1972) suggested that "perhaps the students' quest for relevance is an attempt to escape intellectual demands of the theoretical and abstract" (p. 213). Using Osgood's semantic differential and factor analysis to investigate the concept of relevance, they concluded that relevant courses are not synonymous with easy courses and that academic standards do not have to be lowered because difficulty and relevance are independent dimensions of course content.

The notion of the relevance of course work was not defined by those who debated its merits, and its dimensions probably changed with different generations of students. For example, during World War II, Meier (1943) suggested adapting the psychology curriculum to include military psychology, and 30 years later teachers were involved in issues of human sexuality, evidenced by the number of articles in *Teaching of Psychology* related to that topic. Early teachers of psychology seemed to assume that psychology should be applied to various aspects of life. As French (1898) noted, "experimental psychology is a science of the crossroads" (p. 512).

A summarization of student characteristics and interests suggests that the ghosts of previous students linger in academia. As far back as 1876, students of science were maligned as being lazy and uninterested (e.g., Clarke, 1876/1971), ultimately graduating "in complete ignorance both of the methods and aims of science, having learned only a few disconnected facts concerning the great world" about them (Clarke, 1876/1971, p. 235). Common complaints about each generation of students seem to be recycled by each generation of faculty members.

The Psychology Teacher

Even as successive generations of psychology teachers seem to have similar views about students, the psychologists have changed in important ways, most notably in the nature of their preparation. Like the physical and natural sciences, psychology began its academic status in American colleges and universities inauspiciously. As Clarke (1876/1971) reported, science in American schools was accorded low status and often given only lip service as a serious branch of scholarship. According to Clarke, a single professor might have been called on to teach a diverse array of courses, resulting in incompetence in the classroom. Clarke (1876/1971) noted that at a denominational college in Ohio, McCorkle College (no longer in existence), its

> ministerial president is "Professor of Hebrew, Natural, Mental and Moral Science." Surely this gentleman, if his professions are honest, must be the most learned scholar in the world. His "moral science" would, of course, prevent him from undertaking any work which he was incompetent to do. (p. 232)

Clarke (1876/1971) noted that about the only group as inept as the faculty is the board of trustees of most colleges. This jeremiad is not completely ingenuous; he was clearly biased against schools with a religious affiliation, mentioning a conflict between the "injudiciousness of religious people and the requirements of scientific research" (p. 232). In a more dispassionate essay, Newcomb (1874/1971) made a similar point, depicting the inadequacies of the sciences in America 125 years ago; he bemoaned the lack of honor accorded to one with professorial status in the United States. Both authors commented on the great press of work, the low commitment of funding and equipment, and the relative lack of reward for college faculty.

Psychology faced similar problems of identity, status, and funding in higher education. In 1906, prominent psychologists still debated the underlying nature of psychology in its relationship to philosophy as opposed to the natural and physical sciences. Hugo Münsterberg contended that psychology should ally itself with philosophy; this stance is not unexpected, given that he was William James's handpicked successor as a professor of psychology at Harvard University. In opposition, G. Stanley Hall viewed psychology as having its closest allies in biology, physiology, and anthropology. James Rowland Angell pointed out that psychology was just gaining the respect of the sciences but had not lost the respect of philosophers and consequently should not eliminate the sympathies of either (Münsterberg et al., 1906). A few years later, Calkins (1910) declared the identity crisis to be resolved, with psychology "being freed from its entangling alliance with philosophy" (p. 44).

The increasing number of psychology laboratories attested to the cleavage of psychology from philosophy and a trend toward scientific empiricism. Alfred Binet (cited in Miner, 1904) noted that there were 16 psychology laboratories in the United States in the early 1890s, a number that had more than tripled to 54 (including Canada) by 1904. The average value of laboratory apparatuses exceeded $3,900, with a mean annual budget of more than $400. By 1931, the allocation (at least in Ohio) had grown such that the value of apparatuses in psychology laboratories ranged from $1,100 to $3,300 (Reymert & Arnold, 1931).

Within psychology departments, the number of faculty members increased. Columbia University was the largest, with eight full-time and four part-time teachers who offered 20 courses, devoted 10 or more rooms exclusively to psychology, and taught 435 students in the introductory psychology course in a single year. James McKeen Cattell averred that 18 doctorates had been awarded in psychology at Columbia University in 1897, more than in any scientific discipline except chemistry. Diverse approaches to psychology had clearly taken shape 25 years after Wundt's initial monolithic approach. Different institutions specialized in different approaches, with Columbia's being associated with the scientific approach, consistent with Cattell's work there. Other major institutions also reflected their leaders' influences: Harvard University favored a philosophical approach (William James); Princeton University favored biology (James Mark Baldwin); Cornell University favored systematic and historical approaches (Edward Bradford Titchener); and Clark University favored pedagogy (G. Stanley Hall). As psychology separated from philosophy and as the number of psychology graduates increased, fewer college presidents held chairs of philosophy and taught psychology. According to Miner (1904), only nine college presidents still taught psychology, or as Calkins (1910) wrote, "the course is no longer taught by the college president in the intervals of administrative duty, nor as a secondary occupation for the teacher of radically different subjects" (p. 44).

The situation in normal schools was different. Whipple (1910) analyzed the responses of 100 departments that had replied to a questionnaire and found that 78 teachers taught other subjects in addition to psychology; also, most schools had only one psychology teacher for the combined general and educational psychology course that averaged 107 students. (Unfortunately, Whipple asserted, perhaps one half of the students were actually interested in the class.)

Reymert and Arnold (1931) later reported that virtually all psychology teachers in Ohio had formal training in psychology; nearly one half possessed doctorates and another one third had master's degrees. The names of the major professors of these teachers read like a history book: Carr, Cattell, Dewey, Goddard, McDougall, Münsterberg, Pressey, Thorndike, and Woodworth, among others. Research was the province of psychologists at universities and large colleges; the range of career publications was 1 to 84, with small-college teachers at the lower end.

Twenty years later, at small liberal arts colleges, 63% of the psychology departments had at least one member of the American Psychological Association (APA), with about 11% belonging to Division 2 (Miller, 1953). Those psychologists reported little interaction with other psychologists and taught a wide range of courses; "the small college teacher of psychology is like the general practitioner of medicine" (Miller, 1953, p. 477).

Even as psychology prospered and attracted more students, nonpsychologists continued to teach psychology. Cooper, Spragg, Youtz, and Hurlock (1953) reported that among teachers of psychology in junior colleges, a considerable number did not have formal training in the discipline and 27% taught another subject as well. Relatively few belonged to the APA (19%) and fewer to Division 2 (3%).

This historic isolation of psychology teachers at smaller institutions led to consistent pleas for dissemination of ideas about teaching. E. C. Sanford (1910) recommended periodic publication of teaching handbooks, a suggestion brought to fruition some 70 years later in various handbooks, including those published by the APA and by the journal *Teaching of Psychology*. The proliferation of conferences for teachers of psychology and of research conferences for students has also ameliorated the hermetic life of the small college academic (e.g., Carsrud, Palladino, Tanke, Aubrecht, & Huber, 1984). The 1990 volume of *Teaching of Psychology* announced 5 regional or national teaching conferences and undergraduate research conferences from 11 states and 1 Canadian province. Access to others' ideas is also made easier by services such as ComPSYCH, a computer network that lists software for use in psychology (M. Anderson & Hornby, 1989; M. Anderson, Hornby, & Bozak, 1988). The widespread availability of BITNET and INTERNET has facilitated interaction between psychologists who heretofore would have been unaware of one another.

Two final topics to be addressed in this discussion of psychology faculty are "giving psychology away" and teacher training. Expertise alone does not guarantee that one can communicate effectively. Wolfe (1895) noted that, at a minimum, teaching is labor intensive, demanding a close working relationship between teacher and student. More is necessary, however. One has to know the material and be able to impart it effectively. Wolfle (1947) highlighted part of the problem:

> The story is told of one faculty member in a large Midwestern university who lectured to a class for three weeks before discovering that he was using his lecture notes for another course not scheduled for that semester. The students, apparently, were too docile or too accustomed to such confusion to complain. (p. 441)

Slightly more distant from the student, textbook writers have not been regarded highly. Whipple (1910) referred to "the pedagogical blunders of great scientists who know enough psychology to write a book, but not enough to understand the mind of a high school graduate" (p. 11). The situation had changed little with the first textbook review appearing in the new journal, *Contemporary Psychology*. Abelson (1956) reviewed a text by H. H. Remmers on opinion and attitude measurement. Abelson (1956) said that the content was adequate but that with respect to perspective concerning the field, "this book falls short . . . in style, clarity, organization, and precision" (p. 52); the reviewer could not recommend the book for teaching the subject. Matters have not changed dramatically, if current reviews in *Contemporary Psychology* are a good barometer of sentiment toward texts. Reviewers often suggest that textbooks contain the pertinent facts but that authors' presentations are lacking.

The issue of teacher training in psychology seems not to have been addressed until after World War II, at which time psychology was seen as becoming more popular (Buxton, 1949). Psychology has attracted many students for a long time. The psychology major might have shown continual growth before World War II, as demonstrated by Fischer and Hinshaw (1946), who recorded the number and percentage of psychology majors at the University of Illinois during a 20-year period. In 1925, psychology was the 15th most popular major, with 11 students (1.3%), and rose to the 3rd most popular, with 84 majors (13.1%), by 1944. Buxton (1949) queried graduate programs producing large numbers of PhDs about the training of their fledgling teachers. Of 33 inquiries sent, 29 were received. Of the 29, only 5 had a formal course for training teachers. In none of these 5 were graduate students visited in the classroom on a weekly basis and some "infrequently or never" (Buxton, 1949, p. 415).

The environment in psychology departments was right, however, for increased attention to the training of teachers of psychology. By 1950, at least 14 schools were offering formal seminars (Buxton, 1950), including the University of Michigan, which had a multiple-semester training program for selected students (McKeachie, 1951). Webb (1952) reported that 45 of 49 department chairs surveyed believed that a formal teaching internship was either necessary ($n = 14$) or helpful ($n = 31$). These chairs suggested that as many as 40% of their own graduating PhDs would be inadequate teachers; many of their own new faculty members were also seen as being inadequate teachers. The desirability of a program for training teachers, at least at the University of Michigan, is shown by the fact that graduate students went through tryouts to get teaching fellowships (Isaacson & McKeachie, 1959). Nonetheless, pressure against teacher training remained in at least one graduate institution as late as 1975. The dean actively discouraged departments from including teacher training (R. S. Daniel, personal communication, September 23, 1991).

There seems to have been no systematic evaluation of the effectiveness of teacher training, probably because, as Finger (1969) claimed, the definition of good teaching is subjective and fuzzy. One measure of the efficacy of a graduate program is whether a new PhD achieves an academic position. No studies assessed whether a teacher training program confers an advantage, although as Webb (1952) said, department chairs thought that teaching experience was attractive in job candidates. Williams and Richman (1971) reported that department chairs claimed that a "balanced" PhD (i.e., relatively broad background and knowledge about teaching) is a desirable job prospect, but they were cautious as to whether a balanced PhD would be preferred over someone trained in the "standard" fashion.

Formal programs for teaching of psychology have become "invisible" in the sense that graduate students are assumed to get this training. Lumsden, Grosslight, Loveland, and Williams (1988) concluded that "there seems to be a general acceptance of the idea that graduate departments have a responsibility to prepare their students for classroom teaching responsibilities" (p. 9). In fact, academic psychologists have begun to look both forward and backward in the developmental process of teacher training. For example, Cole (1986) suggested students with the greatest potential should be identified when they are still undergraduates and should be encouraged to think about academic careers. McFadden and Perlman (1989) recommended that departments planning to hire new teachers should engage in active steps to define the dimensions relevant to good teaching for the position in question. They noted that "the problem of a good fit between a newly hired candidate and a department dedicated to high-quality teaching is maximized when the processes of departmental self-study and recruitment have been derived from the same model" (p. 198).

The issues of training psychology teachers have spread to high schools (Buckalew & Daly, 1982), to postsecondary schools where nonacademic psychologists teach (Lopater, 1990), and to medical schools (Gabinet, Patterson, & Friedson, 1984; Lemkau, Merkel, McNamara, & Purdy, 1984; Sebastian, Nathan, & Hunter, 1984). Thus, the initial recognition that the demands on teachers are heavy and that psychologists must be willing to invest significant amounts of time to teaching (e.g., Wolfe, 1895) has persisted.

The road to becoming a teacher of psychology has evolved to include significant training for the classroom. Components of formal courses on teaching and other aspects of professional life have expanded to give prospective teachers help in course organization, pedagogical techniques, history of higher education, goals of the liberal arts curriculum, evaluation of students by teachers and of teachers by students, student rights and responsibilities, academic freedom and tenure, and other "hidden" but consequential aspects of a teacher's life (Daniel, 1955; Finger, 1969; Isaacson & McKeachie, 1959; McKeachie, 1969).

The feelings of commitment to teaching as well as the attendant frustrations were captured by Ray (1972), who noted that

> college professors in May of any year ask themselves how they could
> have done so little and done it so poorly. Then they take heart by
> reminding themselves that they can start all over in September and
> that they have three glorious months to plan how to do it the next
> time. (p. 443)

THE CLASSROOM

Lectures, Demonstrations, and Activities

Psychologists have been concerned with effective pedagogical techniques since the formal inception of the discipline. The prime requisite for effective teaching has always been the willingness to devote adequate time to one's students. Wolfe (1895) claimed that psychology laboratories required more attention than chemistry or physics labs and that "if instructors in psychology are unwilling to do this kind of work, we must wait until another species of instructor can be evolved" (p. 385). Since that time, psychologists interested in instruction have both requested and suggested new, varied, and effective teaching techniques. Miner's (1904) comment about psychologists "intensifying instruction" (p. 307) precedes his statement about the merit of research, suggesting that he accorded teaching equal importance with other forms of scholarship.

From the beginning, the lecture has been a staple of the classroom, but the term now has different connotations. Lectures used to involve a one-way transmission of information and were more formal than the lecture of today, which is more likely to involve some discussion. The drawbacks of passive learning have been noted repeatedly (e.g., Johnston & Pennypacker, 1971; Marr et al., 1960; Seashore, 1910), but the lecture has had proponents with reasoned arguments (e.g., Husband, 1949; Keller, 1985; Longstaff, 1932; McKeachie, Lin, Forrin, & Teevan, 1960). Part of the problem is that the lecture format produces learning that does not consistently differ from that of other approaches.

Husband (1949) compared student performance in large lecture courses with small recitation sections and concluded that large lecture classes do not negatively affect students' learning or motivation. He also opined that the lecture approach induces the teacher to work harder and more enthusiastically. Other reports indicated that student experiences with alternate approaches are more positive, perhaps leading to greater appreciation of the content and methods of psychology (e.g., W. G. Johnson, Zlotlow, Berger, & Croft, 1975; Kirschenbaum & Riechmann, 1975). Buxton (1946), however, claimed that the two main advantages of discussion over lecture— increasing student morale and clarifying information—are entirely possible through good lectures. When learning to lecture, in order to maintain student attention, a beginning instructor simply needs to avoid certain behaviors, he said. Specifically, Buxton (1946) noted humorously, "Don't spend your time taking pot-shots at the textbook, organized religion, psychiatry, the Republicans, sociology, the army or other pet peeves" (p. 308). In any case, "the writer knows of no cases in which sophomores have mobbed an instructor during the first three days of his teaching career" (Buxton, 1946, p. 308). These facetious comments are probably not totally out of place considering student responses to any particular classroom format, which some students will like and others will dislike. Eglash (1954) compared lecture formats with discussion formats and found that the morale of the lecture class was higher but that levels of learning were equivalent; McKeachie et al. (1960) found morale higher with discussion groups, but learning did not differ across groups. Furthermore, Eglash reported on the written evaluations by students. These assessments reflected the fact that students vary with respect to their likes and dislikes. With the same lecture class, Eglash (1954) found that two students saw him as "unsocial, withdrawn, impersonal, difficult to know" (p. 262) and as "unusually sensitive to interpersonal relationships" (p. 263). These different comments may reflect student personality characteristics rather than classroom structure per se. Beach (1960) found that, in general, student sociability was associated with the efficacy of classroom format. In a traditional lecture section, more sociable students performed less well than did less sociable students; in a small, interactive class, more sociable students learned more. Comfort with the approach may influence a student's ultimate reaction to the class as a whole.

Perhaps the most compelling reason for augmenting the lecture with other approaches is that the opportunity for a teacher to develop new pedagogical techniques increases the motivation and commitment of the teacher, thereby affecting the students indirectly. A second consideration is that students may learn different things from different formats, not necessarily more or less. For example, Zachry (1985) reported using inquiry teaching in which students mimic researchers in using the scientific process of identifying a problem of interest, developing and testing hypotheses, and drawing conclusions. The effect was greater student involvement and motivation, along with more depth and less breadth of coverage. He noted, however, that the technique is not useful in large classes for reasons that Calkins (1910) pointed out, "perhaps a half or two-thirds will never take part" (p. 49).

A common adjunct to lecturing is the combination of lecture and discussion or discussion alone, although Whipple (1910) cautioned against too much discussion because its chief disadvantage "is the waste of time from the point of view of the exposition of a system of psychology" (p. 24). In counterpoint, Calkins (1910) advocated extensive use of discussions to enhance learning.

Along with lecture and discussion, laboratory techniques (e.g., introspection and observation) were popular early in the century. By the 1920s, however, introspection had fallen on hard times and did not appear in treatments of pedagogy.

Another approach to teaching involved demonstrations, activities, and other aids. Benjamin (1988) and Daniel (1985) documented the history of educational technologies in psychology and other disciplines. E. C. Sanford

(1910) and Whipple (1910) raised cries for useful classroom activities. Walton (1930) responded 20 years later by suggesting such demonstrational apparatuses as a vertical maze to observe animal learning. Andrews (1946) presented an extensive list of demonstrations, including paper-and-pencil types, observational projects to be done outside of the classroom, and suggestions for making slides by drawing on etched glass plates with India ink, at a cost of $6.50 for 25 slides. Film strips and motion pictures were still relative novelties. Andrews emphasized that student participants in classroom demonstrations should never be ridiculed.

If one adopted Andrews's suggestions today, the cost would likely be less than in 1946 with the availability of photocopying and inexpensive transparencies; with films and software given "free" by publishers (i.e., embedded in textbook prices); and with extensive interlibrary loan networks.

Like E. C. Sanford (1910), Andrews (1946) cautioned that activity per so does not lead to learning but noted that well-done classroom activities provide variety in the content and methods of psychology and aid in retention by "associating facts and principles with more vivid experiences" (p. 312).

Half a century later, Keller (1968, 1974) proposed that the role of the teacher be altered dramatically. In his classic "Good-bye, Teacher . . . ," Keller (1968) provided the fundamentals of his personalized system of instruction (PSI) that focused on self-pacing, mastery learning, and the use of proctors to facilitate learning. As Keller recognized, mastery of subject matter comes when the teacher has ceased to be the fountain of knowledge and instead is the engineer of an appropriate learning environment. According to Keller (1974), the adoption of PSI was not immediate, much to his puzzlement. Academic deans were largely unmoved by his process, he said, "though they applauded my enthusiasm" (Keller, 1974, p. 4). Among faculty colleagues, the response differed little initially.

> Somewhat to our surprise, the acceptance or adoption of our plan by other teachers did not automatically occur. In our own Department, for example, only one professor . . . tried it out. A mathematics teacher came and looked, but decided that it meant a lot of work. . . . [T]he faculty . . . response was negative, to put it mildly, and we retired in some confusion to the friendlier atmosphere of students and of proctors. (p. 5)

Nonetheless, the method has found favor among some teachers of psychology, with consistently positive results (e.g., Spatz, 1991). Taveggia (1977) even suggested that the classroom itself may be abandoned in favor of independent work by students. The enthusiasm for PSI has diminished, however, if recent reports are reliable (e.g., Caldwell, 1985; Keller, 1985).

The Technology of Teaching

In a different sense, the technology of teaching has sometimes rendered the classroom obsolete. Fairly early in the history of broadcasting, psychologists used the airwave as a teaching medium. Gaskill (1933) began with the radio broadcasting of two lectures on what would now be termed *sport psychology*; radio listeners slightly outperformed students in the standard classroom. For reasons that are not altogether clear, this approach was not mentioned again until 1968 (Snyder, Greer, & Snyder, 1968). Television, on the other hand, seems a more popular approach, gauged by its continuing use by commercial and public stations (Barden, 1951; Evans, 1955; Husband, 1954; McKeachie, 1952).

The demands of the camera were reported as being different from those of the classroom. The audience looked unfavorably on a teacher who paced back and forth or used typically cautious statements about the tentative nature of scientific conclusions. Husband (1954) suggested that the content should be more oriented toward women because men worked outside the home during the day and "few stations would sacrifice popular, revenue programs in the evening for education" (p. 183). Another demand peculiar to televised courses on commercial stations involved the length of the lecture. Husband's course was broadcast for half an hour three times a week because it was "necessary to sandwich psychology 204 between The Big Payoff and Kate Smith!" (p. 181). The appeal of television has led to its continuous use as a teaching medium; its success in imparting information is clear. Its most frequently mentioned drawback is students' dissatisfaction in not having contact with their classmates.

Probably the most unusual approach to broadcasting was Cutler, McKeachie, and McNeil's (1958) course that was delivered over the telephone. Michigan Bell Telephone Company approached the authors in early 1957 about the possibility; the result was an 8-week introductory psychology course. As may be predicted, there was no difference in knowledge between the phone group and a lecture group, and the ratings for the telephone class were positive.

Benjamin (1988) documented other attempts to improve pedagogy through the development of teaching machines, with the most famous approach being Skinner's (1968) machines for programmed learning. Daniel (1985) also discussed the range of educational technologies, suggesting that in too many cases, teachers used them to avoid teaching. Harkening back to Wolfe (1895), Daniel stressed the student–teacher relationship as being the most crucial element in the teaching environment.

Finally, the computer is the most recent technical innovation in the classroom. Beins (1989) documented its use in teaching psychology. Computers are flexible enough to allow a wide range of uses; they increase the arsenal of available tools but will probably not replace any existing methods.

THE SUBJECT MATTER OF PSYCHOLOGY

The Curriculum

Psychology's place in the curriculum provided fuel for debate through the turn of the century. Its ties to philosophy were unmistakable, but its methods began to rend it away as the "new psychology" replaced the old. As Wolfe (1895) noted, without labs (i.e., the new empirical approach), psychology was simply philosophy. Calkins (1910) declared psychology free of its "entanglement" with philosophy. The chasm between the two was too great at that point for psychology to be anything other than a scientific discipline. Still, psychology was an idea looking for a form. The approach to research, the role of psychology in the undergraduate curriculum, and the content of its courses were all still fairly amorphous early in this century.

Wolfe (1895) suggested that little planning had gone into the curriculum across different departments with respect to laboratory work. Curricular offerings seemed prone to the same problem 50 years later (Henry, 1938; F. H. Sanford & Fleischman, 1950). In fact, the titles of some courses in college and university catalogs were so suspicious that F. H. Sanford and Fleischman (1950) stated that "what actually goes on behind some of the titles may often defy speculation" (p. 34).

Introspection was still a standard research technique and was thought important enough to be covered in the first course of psychology (e.g., E. C. Sanford, 1910; Seashore, 1910). The "mental life" of animals was by no means controversial (Miner, 1904), but the behaviorists were on the horizon and before long would dramatically alter the definition of psychology. The titles of publications soon reflected a behavioral approach (e.g., Longstaff's, 1932, article on the analysis of factors that condition learning in general psychology).

As much as the early psychologists debated the nature and techniques of psychology, they also argued about the placement of psychology courses in a student's academic life. As late as the 1950s, some still debated when students should take their first psychology course. Pressey (1955) reflected on the "extraordinary finding" (p. 344) that sophomores received higher grades in the elementary psychology course than did first-year students. He disagreed with the recommendation that the first psychology course should be taken in the second year. "If the first course were not taken till graduate school, the grade would be still better! Surely not where students do best is the place for a course, but where they need it the most" (Pressey, 1955, p. 344).

Buxton (1956) addressed this issue in more formal terms, posing questions about what students need versus what they want and how a teacher's competence can be best used. Debate about the structure of the curriculum continued. Examining the courses most emphasized in the curriculum, however, suggests that the recommendations concerning appropriate course content made by psychologists such as Calkins (1910), E. C. Sanford (1906, 1910), and Seashore (1910) were adopted and maintained for the next 50 years.

The status of the psychology major was as ambiguous as the structure of the introductory course. One survey presented this picture well (Dungan & Ekas, 1948). The only course recognized as "essential" to undergraduates, according to chairs of graduate departments, was general psychology. Approximately 79% said that experimental psychology was essential. Statistics was the only other psychology course seen as being vital by more than 50% of the respondents. More chairs claimed that a foreign language was of greater importance than abnormal, systematic, social, child, physiological, applied, or educational psychology. A common sentiment was that a broad background was more important than specific psychology courses for students intending to do graduate work.

The emphasis for undergraduates was on experimental methods as much as content. For example, Anastasi (1947) reported that only general psychology, experimental psychology, and statistics (in that order) were typical requirements. For the most part, the experimental course spanned two semesters. Wolfle (1947) noted the disarray in the psychology curriculum and lamented the overlap in content across courses. Of 31 topics, 9 were covered in the introductory course, educational psychology, child psychology, social psychology, and applied psychology; 23 others were covered in 3 of the 5 courses. He provided sarcastic advice on how to write a textbook for those courses: Take any existing book and selectively eliminate two to three chapters, substitute new chapters from another book, and remember to change the word *subjects* to *children* in developmental texts and to *dogs* in learning texts. Finally, he noted, the chapters should be rearranged, but the actual order is unimportant.

At about this time, the core of the psychology major began its evolution toward the contemporary model. Holder, Leavitt, and McKenna (1958) reported that more than 50% of graduate department chairs viewed experimental psychology (95%) and statistics (96%) as being the most important preparatory courses for graduate studies in psychology. Between 50% and 60% agreed on history, testing, social, learning, abnormal, and physiological psychology. The two most widely recommended nonpsychology courses were algebra (80%) and anthropology (79%), although sociology, biology, physiology, English, German, physics, calculus, and philosophy were strongly recommended. The listing had not changed noticeably more than 10 years later, according to Appley (1970). By the late 1950s and early 1960s, psychology as a major had taken its present form, although variations persisted across institutions. Mathie and Brewer (1991) pointed out that contemporary psychologists disagree on the most appropriate structure for the undergraduate curriculum.

The place of psychology within the larger context of the college or university has also been an important topic of discussion. Münsterberg et al. (1906) formalized the debate about psychology's interdisciplinary nature, and Whitehorn and Yerkes (cited in Appley, 1970) speculated about the place of psychology in the ideal university. The uncertain placement of psychology in the curriculum is clear. In some schools, psychology courses satisfied requirements in the social sciences and at other schools in the biological sciences; some schools permitted psychology to fulfill requirements in both of those categories (Daniel, 1962). At the same time, Daniel (1962) asserted that "some time ago, one of my students . . . found faculty members outside of psychology woefully out of date in their notion of what psychologists were doing in research" (p. 6).

In 1991, mathematicians at Ithaca College naively inquired whether psychology students needed quantitative skills for their major. The nature of psychology almost seemed destined to be misunderstood.

Within the discipline, for the past 50 years psychologists have consistently emphasized the social responsibility of psychologists in the application of their discipline (e.g., Harper, 1954; Hunt, 1970; Mann, 1982; McGovern & Hawks, 1988; Remmers, 1944). Harper's (1954) ideas are fairly typical. Four goals included (a) the ability to transfer thought to different situations; (b) learning of factual information regarding human norms; (c) emphasizing the dynamic nature of society; and (d) learning about biology, sociology, adjustment, the scientific approach, correction of psychological fallacies, and the interrelatedness of disciplines dealing with human nature.

Finally, how psychology can help students after graduation has emerged as an important consideration. McGovern and Hawks (1988) suggested that students do not have a good picture of employment and career issues. For example, according to the APA booklet on employment, candidates are better off with well-developed skills rather than knowledge of course content. Undergraduates are more motivated to focus on content and less on skill. Thus, strategic planning to help students prepare for life after graduation should be a faculty function. According to McGovern and Hawks, dealing with curricular issues is difficult without knowing the career orientations of students and the expectations of faculty members. Responsible departments must be sensitive to the diverse needs and expectations of their students. Revising a curriculum without knowledge of need often means that any alteration is done by those who are most stubborn. McGovern and Hawks (1986) cited Rudolph, who asserted that "it is an 'academic truism that changing a curriculum is harder than moving a graveyard'" (p. 177).

Fortunately, it appears that some curricular decisions are based on data. Carducci et al. (1987) queried experts about ideal skills and knowledge for success in the business world. They concluded that students need certain skills typically gained within a liberal arts curriculum (e.g., oral and written communication skills, problem-solving ability, and working knowledge of computers) as well as skills typically associated with psychology departments (e.g., knowledge of tests and measurements, knowledge of research design, ability to interpret statistics, and technical report writing).

Walker, Newcomb, and Hopkins (1987) described an entire psychology curriculum based on empirical information. They polled alumni of the past 20 years; sought input from graduate schools and from business, industry, and social service organizations; and then compared their offerings with those of peer institutions. They concluded that four areas of student development are crucial: knowledge base, methodological skills, communication skills, and independent work. Each of these is developed at four different levels in their course offerings. Improvements that resulted from their curricular changes occurred along five dimensions: (a) There was better use of existing faculty strengths. (b) Development of new courses was enhanced. (c) Advising responsibilities were more focused for faculty members. (d) Faculty members renewed their own professional development in light of curricular changes. (e) Specific goals clarified staffing and facilities needs. This approach to planning the psychology major might have helped to allay Wolfe's (1895) concern about poor planning within psychology departments.

Course Content

E. C. Sanford's (1906) outline of topics for the first course in psychology is remarkably similar to today's introductory course: learning, perception, social psychology, emotion, personality and abnormal psychology, heredity, and the systems of psychology. Nevertheless, notable differences are obvious between psychology then and now. When Calkins (1910) polled 80 schools, receiving 47 replies, she found that about the same number of schools rated physiological psychology as being very important as rated it as being unimportant at the elementary level; the same trend existed for the discussion of practical applications of psychology.

Fields (1949) tried to identify the essential topics for the first course in psychology as it existed at different schools but concluded that "administrative organization, course objectives, texts used, hours of credit given, class size, etc. were so different that comparisons would be useless" (p. 216). Harper (1952) had greater success 3 years later, citing the 14 most popular topics discussed in the course. Motivation received the most attention (20.1%) and systematic psychology the least (0.8%).

Textbooks today are uniform in their topics and ordering of content, reflecting some agreement on the importance of topics. Notably, the importance of neuroscience has grown from its inconsistent emphasis in the past ("Mind Map," 1991).

Numerous other researchers have periodically tried to discover the nature of psychology by identifying its vocabulary. For example, Haggerty (1930) collected 1,600 terms from the indexes of 50 texts and treatises. Twenty of 34 psychology teachers returned the questionnaire indicating the importance of the terms. Fewer than 3% of the terms were checked as being essential by more than 90% of the respondents, although 93% of the terms were seen as being essential by at least one person. Haggerty (1930) concluded that "the total amount of material approved by 25 percent or more of respondents would certainly constitute an intellectually impossible task for most college students within the time allotted to psychology in the training program for teachers" (p. 82).

Jensen (1933) asked 15 psychologists to rate 403 terms on a scale ranging from *leading away from psychology to a different field* (−10) to *maximally useful in psychology* (+10). Most words, Jensen noted, would be familiar to students of psychology then, and most would be now. Both Haggerty (1930) and Jensen (1933) mentioned the mismatch in texts between the perceived importance of a term and the attention it received in the books. Jensen reported that concepts such as *stimulus* and *coefficient of correlation* were seen as being highly important even though they might have been accorded little space in common psychology texts, faring little better than terms such as *automatic response*, which was 399th on the list. Thornton and Thornton (1942) repeated the exercise with 1,246 terms. Thirty-nine of 71 psychologists responded to the request to select approximately 100 important terms from the original list, omitting those to be postponed for later courses, those already well understood by beginning students, and those of little importance for such students.

Thornton and Thornton's (1942) results revealed a vocabulary clearly recognizable by contemporary psychologists, although the relative importance of the terms has changed notably between then and now. For example, the term *independent variable* was ranked 244.5; *experiment* and *hypothesis* were both ranked 138.5. *Mental age* was ranked 1st. The ranks for *IQ* and *chronological age* were 9.5 and 174.5, respectively, which probably reflected student familiarity with the latter term as much as its importance in psychology. The term *cognition* was missing altogether, but *reasoning* was ranked 6.5.

More recently, Boneau (1990) asked authors of textbooks in different subfields of psychology to identify the most important terms in the discipline. *Mental age* was not even included in the top 100 of any of the 10 subfields used. *Age and intelligence* was ranked 45th in the development subfield. Raters thought that the term should be recognized by bachelor's-level psychology students but that it was not important enough that psychology students be able to make knowledgeable statements about it.

Many of the words of psychology have shifted in importance during the past 60 years, which will surprise few who are familiar with the discipline's history. Nonetheless, some terms such as *IQ* have remained important; interestingly, Boneau (1990) included *IQ* in the history and systems category. The term is still important but for different reasons than in 1943.

CONCLUSION

In the past 100 years, approaches to teaching psychology have evolved. The nature of the tutelage has varied, sometimes involving personal contact, sometimes remote interaction. Likewise, the issues of controversy in one generation are resolved and replaced in the next. The need for meaningful student–teacher relationships, however, remains paramount. From Wolfe (1895) to Daniel (1985), the message is clear that technologies gain favor and then disappear, but the need for appropriate guidance by a teacher is constant.

REFERENCES

Abelson, R. P. (1956). Opinion and attitude: Review of *Introduction to Opinion and Attitude Measurement. Contemporary Psychology, 1,* 52–53.

Anastasi, A. (1947). The place of experimental psychology in the undergraduate curriculum. *American Psychologist, 2,* 57–62.

Anderson, M., & Hornby, P. (1989). COMPsych: A description and progress report. *Behavior Research Methods, Instruments, & Computers, 21,* 205–208.

Anderson, M., Hornby, P., & Bozak, D. (1988). COMPsych: A computerized software information system. *Behavior Research Methods, Instruments, & Computers, 20,* 243–245.

Anderson, R. J. (1970). Stability of student interests in general psychology. *American Psychologist, 25,* 630–632.

Andrews, T. G. (1946). Demonstrations for the introductory psychology class. *American Psychologist, 1,* 312–323.

Appley, M. H. (1970). The place of psychology in the university. *American Psychologist, 25,* 387–468.

Barden, J. P. (1951). Instruction by television and home study. *School and Society, 74,* 374–376.

Beach, L. R. (1960). Sociability and academic achievement in various types of learning situations. *Journal of Educational Psychology, 51,* 208–212.

Beins, B. (1985). Teaching the relevance of statistics through consumer-oriented research. *Teaching of Psychology, 12,* 168–169.

Beins, B. C. (1989). A survey of computer use reported in *Teaching of Psychology*: 1974–1988. *Teaching of Psychology, 16,* 143–145.

Benjamin, L. T., Jr. (1988). A history of teaching machines. *American Psychologist, 43,* 703–712.

Boneau, C. A. (1990). Psychological literacy: A first approximation. *American Psychologist, 45,* 891–900.

Browning, D. (Ed.). (1965). *Philosophers of process.* New York: Random House.

Buckalew, L. W., & Daly, J. D. (1982). Problems in preschool psychology. *College Student Journal, 16,* 290–293.

Buxton, C. E. (1946). Planning the introductory psychology course. *American Psychologist, 1,* 303–311.

Buxton, C. E. (1949). The pros and cons of training for college teachers of psychology. *American Psychologist, 4,* 414–417.

Buxton, C. E. (1950). Seminars on college teaching in psychology. *American Psychologist, 5,* 161–162.

Buxton, C. E. (1956). Issues in undergraduate education in psychology. *American Psychologist, 11,* 84–95.

Caldwell, E. C. (1985). Dangers of PSI. *Teaching of Psychology, 12,* 9–12.

Calkins, M. W. (1910). The teaching of elementary psychology in colleges supposed to have no laboratory. *Psychological Monographs, 12*(4, Whole No. 51), 41–53.

Carducci, B. J., Deeds, W. C., Jones, J. W., Moretti, D. M., Reed, J. G., Saal, F. E., & Wheat, J. E. (1987). Preparing undergraduate psychology students for careers in business. *Teaching of Psychology, 14,* 16–20.

Carsrud, A. L., Palladino, J. J., Tanke, E. D., Aubrecht, L., & Huber, R. J. (1984). Undergraduate psychology research conferences: Goals, policies, and procedures. *Teaching of Psychology, 11,* 141–145.

Clarke, F. W. (1971). American colleges versus American science. In J. C. Burnham (Ed.), *Science in America: Historical selections* (pp. 228–239). New York: Holt, Rinehart & Winston. (Original work published 1876)

Cole, D. L. (1986). Attracting the best and the brightest to teach psychology. *Teaching of Psychology, 13,* 107–110.

Cooper, E. M. F., Spragg, S. D. S., Youtz, R. P., & Hurlock, E. B. (1953). The teaching of psychology in the junior and community colleges. *American Psychologist, 8,* 734–739.

Cutler, R. L., McKeachie, W. J., & McNeil, E. B. (1958). Teaching psychology by telephone. *American Psychologist, 13,* 551–552.

Daniel, R. S. (1955). Seminar on professional problems in psychology. *American Psychologist, 10,* 602–605.

Daniel, R. S. (1962, August–September). *What is general about general psychology?* Paper presented at the 70th Annual Convention of the American Psychological Association, St. Louis, MO.

Daniel, R. S. (1985, October). *What have we learned from instructional technology?* Paper presented at the Mid-America Conference for Teachers of Psychology, Evansville, IN.

Desforges, P. (1982). L'enseignement de la psychologie en Algerie [Teaching psychology in Algeria]. *Ethnopsychologie, 37*(3–4), 7–14. (From *Psychological Abstracts*, 1985, *72*, Abstract No. 32051)

Deutsch, M. (1987). Some perspectives on the new "crisis" in American education. In J. A. Sechzer & S. M. Pfafflin (Eds.), *Psychology and educational policy* (pp. 115–124). New York: New York Academy of Sciences.

Dillon, K. M. (1982). Statisticophobia. *Teaching of Psychology, 9*, 117.

Dungan, I. M., & Ekas, G. S. (1948). Essential courses for undergraduates. *American Psychologist, 2*, 450.

Eglash, A. (1954). A group-discussion method of teaching psychology. *Journal of Educational Psychology, 45*, 257–267.

Evans, R. I. (1955). The planning and implementation of a psychology series on a noncommercial educational television station. *American Psychologist, 10*, 602–605.

Fields, P. E. (1949). First report of an attempt to standardize the beginning course in psychology. *American Psychologist, 4*, 215–216.

Finger, F. W. (1969). "Professional problems": Preparation for a career in college teaching. *American Psychologist, 24*, 1044–1049.

Fischer, R. P., & Hinshaw, R. P. (1946). The growth of student interest in psychology. *American Psychologist, 1*, 116–118.

French, F. C. (1898). The place of experimental psychology in the undergraduate curriculum. *Psychological Review, 5*, 510–512.

Gabinet, L., Patterson, M. B., & Friedson, W. (1984). Teaching psychology to medical students on a consultation-liaison psychiatry service. *Teaching of Psychology, 11*, 28–31.

Gaskill, H. V. (1933). Broadcasting versus lecturing in psychology: Preliminary investigation. *Journal of Applied Psychology, 17*, 317–319.

Haggerty, M. E. (1930). Remaking the psychology curriculum. *Journal of Higher Education, 1*, 78–84.

Harper, R. S. (1952). The first course in psychology. *American Psychologist, 7*, 722–727.

Harper, R. S. (1954). The Knox conference on the relation of psychology to general education. *American Psychologist, 9*, 803–804.

Hastings, M. W. (1982). Statistics: Challenge for students and the professor. *Teaching of Psychology, 9*, 221–222.

Henry, E. R. (1938). A survey of courses in psychology offered by undergraduate colleges of liberal arts. *Psychological Bulletin, 35*, 430–435.

Holder, W. B., Leavitt, G. S., & McKenna, F. S. (1958). Undergraduate training for psychologists: Report of the Subcommittee on Curriculum Differences,

Division 2 Committee on the Role of Psychology in Small and Large Institutions. *American Psychologist, 13*, 585–588.

Hunt, W. A. (1970). The place of psychology in the university: Implications for undergraduate education. *American Psychologist, 25*, 450–451.

Husband, R. W. (1949). A statistical comparison of the efficacy of large lecture versus smaller recitation sections upon achievement in general psychology. *American Psychologist, 4*, 216.

Husband, R. W. (1954). Television versus classroom for learning general psychology. *American Psychologist, 9*, 181–183.

Isaacson, R. I., & McKeachie, W. J. (1959). A program for training college teachers of psychology: Mark II. *American Psychologist, 14*, 658–659.

Jensen, M. B. (1933). Relative values of the vocabulary terms of general psychology. *Psychological Review, 40*, 196–208.

Johnson, D. E. (1991). A *Teaching of Psychology* database: 1974–1990. *Teaching of Psychology, 18*, 49–50.

Johnson, M., & Daniel, R. S. (1974). Comprehensive annotated bibliography on the teaching of psychology at the undergraduate level through 1972. *JSAS Catalog of Selected Documents in Psychology, 4*, 108. (Ms. No. 735)

Johnson, W. G., Zlotlow, S., Berger, J. L., & Croft, R. G. F. (1975). A traditional lecture versus a PSI course in personality: Some comparisons. *Teaching of Psychology, 2*, 156–158.

Johnston, J. M., & Pennypacker, H. S. (1971). A behavioral approach to college teaching. *American Psychologist, 26*, 219–244.

Keller, F. S. (1968). "Good-bye, Teacher . . ." *Journal of Applied Behavior Analysis, 1*, 78–89.

Keller, F. S. (1974). Ten years of personalized instruction. *Teaching of Psychology, 1*, 4–9.

Keller, F. S. (1985). Lightning strikes twice. *Teaching of Psychology, 12*, 4–8.

Kirschenbaum, D. S., & Riechmann, S. W. (1975). Learning with gusto in introductory psychology. *Teaching of Psychology, 2*, 72–76.

Lemkau, J. P., Merkel, W. T., McNamara, K. M., & Purdy, R. (1984). Infiltrating the house of God: Teaching psychology to family practice physicians. *Teaching of Psychology, 11*, 19–26.

Leuba, C. (1934). New ways of organization. *Journal of Higher Education, 5*, 136–140.

Longstaff, H. P. (1932). Analysis of some factors conditioning learning in general psychology (Part I). *Journal of Applied Psychology, 16*, 9–48.

Lopater, S. (1990). Postsecondary teacher training in Britain. *Teaching of Psychology, 17*, 193–195.

Lumsden, E. A., Grosslight, J. H., Loveland, E. H., & Williams, J. E. (1988). Preparation of graduate students as classroom teachers and supervisors in applied and research settings. *Teaching of Psychology, 15*, 5–9.

Maas, J. B. (1974). Letter from the president of Division Two. *Teaching of Psychology, 1*, 3.

Madigan, R., & Brosamer, J. (1990). Improving the writing skills of students in introductory psychology. *Teaching of Psychology, 17*, 27–30.

Mann, R. D. (1982). The curriculum and context of psychology. *Teaching of Psychology, 9*, 9–14.

Marr, J. N., Plath, D. W., Wakeley, J. H., & Wilkins, D. M. (1960). The contribution of the lecture to college teaching. *Journal of Educational Psychology, 51*, 277–284.

Mathie, V. A., & Brewer, C. L. (1991, August). *Teaching strategies and curriculum design: Ideas from the national conference.* Paper presented at the 99th Annual Convention of the American Psychological Association, San Francisco.

McFadden, S. H., & Perlman, B. (1989). Faculty recruitment and excellent undergraduate teaching. *Teaching of Psychology, 16*, 195–198.

McGovern, T. V., & Hawks, B. K. (1986). The varieties of undergraduate experience. *Teaching of Psychology, 13*, 174–181.

McGovern, T. V., & Hawks, B. K. (1988). The liberating science and art of undergraduate psychology. *American Psychologist, 43*, 108–114.

McGovern, T. V., & Hogshead, D. L. (1990). Learning about writing, thinking about teaching. *Teaching of Psychology, 17*, 5–10.

McKeachie, W. J. (1951). A program for training teachers of psychology. *American Psychologist, 6*, 119–121.

McKeachie, W. J. (1952). Teaching psychology on television. *American Psychologist, 7*, 503–506.

McKeachie, W. J. (1969). *Teaching tips: A guidebook for the beginning teacher* (6th ed.). Lexington, MA: Heath.

McKeachie, W. J., Lin, Y. G., Forrin, B., & Teevan, R. (1960). Individualized teaching in elementary psychology. *Journal of Educational Psychology, 51*, 285–291.

Meier, N. C. (1943). The introductory course and military psychology. *Psychological Bulletin, 40*, 787–790.

Menges, R. J., & Trumpeter, P. W. (1972). Toward an empirical definition of relevance in undergraduate instruction. *American Psychologist, 27*, 213–217.

Miller, E. O. (1953). Teaching psychology in the small liberal arts college. *American Psychologist, 8*, 475–478.

"Mind map" would guide brain explorers. (1991, July 13). *Science News*, p. 23.

Miner, B. G. (1904). The changing attitude of American universities toward psychology. *Science, 20*, 299–307.

Münsterberg, H., Hall, G. S., Thilly, F., Angell, J. R., Taylor, A. E., & Ostwald, W. (1906). General discussion on the affiliation of psychology with philosophy and with the natural sciences. *Psychological Bulletin, 3*, 48–51.

Nakano, Y., Richey, M. H., Bohs, R. A., Koch, J. E., Mannion, M. E., &

Warbin, R. W. (1990). Undergraduate psychology in Japan and the United States. *Teaching of Psychology, 17*, 152–159.

Newcomb, S. (1971). Exact science in America. In J. C. Burnham (Ed.), *Science in America: Historical selections* (pp. 205–221). New York: Holt, Rinehart & Winston. (Original work published 1874)

Poe, R. E. (1990). A strategy for improving literature reviews in psychology courses. *Teaching of Psychology, 17*, 54–55.

Pressey, S. L. (1955). Teaching in the ivory tower, with rarely a step outside. *Psychological Bulletin, 52*, 343–344.

Price, D. W. W. (1990). A model for reading and writing about primary sources: The case of introductory psychology. *Teaching of Psychology, 17*, 48–53.

Quereshi, M. Y. (1988). Evaluation of an undergraduate psychology program: Occupational and personal benefits. *Teaching of Psychology, 15*, 119–123.

Ray, W. S. (1972). The psychology professor in the liberal arts college. *American Psychologist, 27*, 441–444.

Remmers, H. H. (1944). Psychology—Some unfinished business. *Psychological Bulletin, 41*, 713–724.

Reymert, M. L., & Arnold, H. J. (1931). Survey of conditions and facilities for the teaching of psychology in the state of Ohio. *Psychological Bulletin, 28*, 342–366.

Sanford, E. C. (1906). A sketch of a beginner's course in psychology. *Psychological Bulletin, 3*, 59–60.

Sanford, E. C. (1910). The teaching of elementary psychology in colleges and universities with laboratories. *Psychological Monographs, 12*(4, Whole No. 51), 54–71.

Sanford, F. H., & Fleischman, E. A. (1950). A survey of undergraduate psychology courses in American colleges and universities. *American Psychologist, 5*, 33–37.

Schoen, M. (1926). The elementary course in psychology. *American Journal of Psychology, 37*, 593–599.

Seashore, C. E. (1910). General report on the teaching of the elementary course in psychology: Recommendations. *Psychological Monographs, 12*(4, Whole No. 51), 80–91.

Sebastian, C. S., Nathan, R. G., & Hunter, R. J. (1984). The necessity of teaching psychological principles to medical students in a clinical setting: A pilot study of subsequent patient visits. *Teaching of Psychology, 11*, 26–28.

Skinner, B. F. (1968). *The technology of teaching.* New York: Appleton-Century-Crofts.

Snyder, W. U., Greer, A. M., & Snyder, J. (1968). An experiment with radio instruction in an introductory psychology course. *Journal of Educational Research, 61*, 291–296.

Spatz, C. (1991, August). *Statistics: Success with the Keller plan (personalized system of instruction*). Paper presented at the 99th Annual Convention of the American Psychological Association, San Francisco.

Taveggia, T. C. (1977). Goodbye teacher, goodbye classroom, hello learning: A radical appraisal of teaching–learning linkages at the college level. *Journal of Personalized Instruction, 2*, 119–124.

Teaching and Research Group of Psychology. (1985). The teaching of psychology as a required minor must be strengthened and reformed. *Information on Psychological Sciences, 1*, 46–47. (From *Psychological Abstracts*, 1987, *74*, Abstract No. 20254)

Thornton, G. R., & Thornton, J. S. (1942). Terms that are considered important for beginning students of psychology. *Journal of Educational Psychology, 33*, 39–49.

Tomlinson, T. M. (1987). A nation at risk: Towards excellence for all. In J. A. Sechzer & S. M. Pfafflin (Eds.), *Psychology and educational policy* (pp. 7–27). New York: New York Academy of Sciences.

Walker, W. E., Newcomb, A. F., & Hopkins, W. P. (1987). A model for curriculum evaluation and revision in undergraduate psychology programs. *Teaching of Psychology, 14*, 198–202.

Walton, A. (1930). Demonstrational and experimental devices. *American Journal of Psychology, 1*, 313–323.

Webb, W. B. (1952). The problem of teaching internships. *American Psychologist, 7*, 20–21.

Whipple, G. M. (1910). The teaching of psychology in normal schools. *Psychological Monographs, 12*(4, Whole No. 51), 2–40.

Williams, J. E., & Richman, C. (1971). The graduate preparation of the college professor of psychology. *American Psychologist, 26*, 1000–1009.

Wolfe, H. K. (1895). The new psychology in undergraduate work. *Psychological Review, 2*, 382–387.

Wolfle, D. (1947). The sensible organization of courses in psychology. *American Psychologist, 2*, 437–445.

Zachry, W. H. (1985). How I kicked the lecture habit: Inquiry teaching in psychology. *Teaching of Psychology, 12*, 129–131.

INDEX

in social Darwinism, 172–173, 177

nonsexist language, 514

Genetics

as handbook topic, 511

early research, 104

Germany

development of psychology in, 91–95

early research centers, 92–93

influence in U. S. psychology, 79

Gerontology

first senior counseling center, 176

teaching of, 159

Gestalt psychology, 93, 95, 106, 113

Gleitman, H., 156, 165, 473

Goldstein, K., 95

Goodenough, F. L., 178, 410

Government

Council of Graduate Departments of Psychology and, 396

federal land grants for higher education, 21–22

in Russia, and development of psychology, 109–110

Graduate education

APA advancement of teaching in, 354–356

Arden House Conference (1983) on, 292–293

Boulder Conference (1950) on, 287–288

Chicago Conference (1965) on, 289–290

child psychology, 293–294

Council of Applied Master's Programs in Psychology, 391–394

Council of Graduate Departments of Psychology, 394–397

future of, 361

German model for, 79

health psychology, 292–293

Miami Beach Conference (1958) on, 288

minority issues in curriculum design, 208–210

minority students in, 190–191, 192

National Conference on Graduate Education in Psychology, 294, 295–296

role of conferences in, 286

role of supervisor, 83

social work in, 290

training of teachers for, major figures in, 140–141

Vail conference on, 290–291

Great Britain

development of psychology in, 96–100

student–teacher relationship, 74–76

Gregg, A., 27

Grosslight, J. H., 140, 141

Group processes, 160

Guetzkow, H., 140

Gustad, J. W., 27–28

Hall, G. S., 92–93, 129, 144, 352–353, 458

Halpern, D. F., 30–31

Handbook of Child Psychology, Murchison, 507, 510, 513, 516

Handbook of Experimental Psychology, Stevens, 507, 509, 510–512

Handbook of General Experimental Psychology, Murchison, 510–512

Handbook of Learning and Cognitive Processes, Estes (Ed.), 515

Handbook of Mathematical Psychology, Luce, et al., 515, 516

Handbook of Social Psychology, Aronson, 165

Handbook of Social Psychology, Murchison, 514

Handbooks

cognitive psychology as topic in, 512, 515

defining, 506–509

Experimental Psychology, Woodworth, 513

first in Italian psychology, 106

Methodology, instruction in, 281

Mexico, development of psychology in, 115

Miami Beach Conference (1958), 288, 302

Michael, J. L., 156, 159

Michigan Conference (1960), 265–267

Michotte, A., 110–111

Mid-America Conference for Teachers of Psychology, 312–314

Mid-America Undergraduate Psychology Research Conference, 312

Miles, W., 338

Milholland, J. E., 28–29

Milton, O., 156, 164

Mind-body duality, 89, 101

Minorities. *see also* African Americans
    APA and, 198–204, 210–211, 290
    demographics, U. S., 190–191
    first psychology doctorates, 180
    graduate-level curriculum design, 208–210
    Hispanic Americans, 180–181
    in faculty positions, 192–193, 198
    National Institute of Mental Health conference on service to, 297
    obstacles to, in psychology, 194
    psychology students, 190–191
    recruitment issues, 194–198, 210–211, 290
    retaining, in profession, 198
    St. Mary's conference recommendations, 277–278
    teaching of psychology and, 161
    undergraduate curriculum design, 204–205
    women, in advancement of psychology, 179–180

Morgantown Conference on Graduate Education (1987), 141

Mormon Church, 17–18

Morrill Act (1862), 14, 21–22

Morris, C. G., 29–30

Morris, C. J., 24–25

Morse, Josiah, 16

Moscow Psychological Society, 108

Moscow University, 108–109

Motivation, studies of, 281, 511–512

Müller, G. E., 94

Multicultural studies, 33, 34, 204–210, 211

Munn, N. L., 466–467

Münsterberg, H., 47, 130, 132, 174, 330

Murchison, C., 507, 508, 510–512, 513, 514, 516

Murphy, G., 133, 134, 138, 142

Mussen, P. H., 513

Myers, C. S., 97–98

National Academic Advising Association survey, 40–42

National Conference for Increasing the Roles of Culturally Diverse Peoples in the Profession of Psychology (1978), 201

National Conference on Applied Master's Training, 392

National Conference on Education and Training of Scientist–Practitioners for Professional Practice, 297, 308

National Conference on Enhancing the Quality of Undergraduate Education in Psychology, 33–34, 203, 205–208, 272–278, 279–282, 353–354
    McKeachie on, 252–253

National Conference on Graduate Education in Psychology (Utah, 1987), 294, 295–296, 392

National Conference on Internship Training in Psychology (1987), 295, 304–305

National Conference on Levels and Patterns of Professional Training in Psychology, 290–291

National Conference on Postdoctoral Fellowship Training in Professional Psychology (1992), 307

National Council of Schools of Professional Psychology, conferences of, 294–295

career development materials, 61

careers in teaching and publishing in, 128, 136, 154

classroom technique as topic in, 536–539

critical analysis of, 5

curriculum as topic in, 540–543

early English, 97

early Italian, 105

early Russian, 108

empirical research on undergraduate curricula, 24–26

history of psychology teaching in, 2, 7

minority issues in, 206

of William James, 131–132

on teaching of psychology, 163–164, 369, 525–526, 527, 533

promoting careers in psychology, 349, 354

Psi Chi Newsletter, 409–410

Psychological Review, 95

representation of students in, 527–530

role of, 433, 440

task force/committee reports on undergraduate curricula, 27–31

Teaching of Psychology journal, 529

Teaching Tips, 221

Professional organizations. *See also* American Psychological Association; Psi Beta; Psi Chi

African American psychologists, 199–200

American Association for Applied Psychology, 366

American Association for Counseling and Development, 49

American College Personnel Association, 49

American Personnel and Guidance Association, 49

American Philosophical Association, 339

American Psychological Society, 379

Association for Counselor Education and Guidance and Supervision, 49

Association of American Colleges, 30

Association of Consulting Psychologists, 340

Carnegie Foundation for the Advancement of Teaching, 14

Council of Applied Master's Programs in Psychology, 391–394

Council of Graduate Departments of Psychology, 355, 394–397

Council of Teachers of Undergraduate Psychology, 386–389

Council of Undergraduate Psychology Programs, 389–391

early Russian, 108

for internship training, 302–303

for scientist-practitioners, 297

National Academic Advising Association, 40–42

National Institute on the Teaching of Psychology, 311

National Vocational Guidance Association, 46, 49–50

regional, 311–312

related to teaching, 140, 163–164

role of, 346, 398

role of ethnic diversity in, 193–194

Society of Experimental Psychologists, 141

Protagoras, 86

Psi Beta

founding of, 422

goals of, 421–422

history of, 423–427

role of, 404

Psi Chi, 140

founding of, 403–407

goals of, 404–405

history of, 407–421

role of, 404

Psychological Review, 95

Psychological services center, 289–290

ABOUT THE EDITORS

Antonio E. Puente received his PhD in psychology from the University of Georgia in 1978. He has taught at St. George's University (Grenada, West Indies), University of Madrid, and University of Granada (Spain). He has served as past-president of both the National Academy of Neuropsychology and the North Carolina Psychological Association. He is currently a professor of psychology at the University of North Carolina at Wilmington. In addition to teaching, he maintains a part-time private practice of clinical neuropsychology. He is a fellow of APA's Division of Teaching of Psychology and Division of Clinical Neuropsychology, and he is the recipient of a Fulbright Scholar Award in teaching.

Janet R. Matthews received her PhD in clinical psychology from the University of Mississippi in 1976. Currently, she is a professor of psychology at Loyola University-New Orleans and a consultant and training faculty member at the New Orleans Veterans Administration Medical Center. She also maintains a part-time private practice. Formerly, she was an associate professor of psychology at Creighton University. She is an APA fellow and past president of APA's Division of Teaching of Psychology and of the Southwestern Psychological Association. She is consulting editor of the journal, *Teaching of Psychology*. Her other teaching activities have included serving as southwestern regional coordinator for the Council of Teachers of Undergraduate Psychology and presenting at three of the regional teaching conferences described in this volume.

Charles L. Brewer received his PhD in psychology from the University of Arkansas in 1965. He has taught at the College of Wooster and Elmira College and is now a professor of psychology at Furman University. He is coeditor of handbooks for teachers of introductory psychology and of statistics and research methods. He is editor of the journal, *Teaching of Psychology*. He is fellow of APA Division 1 (General Psychology), 2 (Teaching of Psychology), and 26 (History of Psychology). A past president of Division 2, he is now president of Division 1, president-elect of the Southeastern

Psychological Association, and a member of APA's Council of Representatives and Board of Educational Affairs. He received the American Psychological Foundation's Distinguished Teaching Award in 1989.